TEACHING AND THE CASE METHOD

Instructor's Guide

TEACHING AND THE CASE METHOD

INSTRUCTOR'S GUIDE

Louis B. Barnes

C. Roland Christensen

Abby J. Hansen

HARVARD BUSINESS SCHOOL PRESS
Boston, Massachusetts

The publisher wishes to thank the following for permission to reprint material included in this volume:

Judah Folkman for his "The Fine Line between Persistence and Obstinacy"; Harvard Business School for Donald A. Schon, "The Crisis of Professional Knowledge and the Pursuit of an Epistemology of Practice" and HBS cases, teaching notes, and researcher's perspectives; John Wiley & Sons, Ltd. for Michael O'Hare, "Talk and Chalk: The Blackboard as an Intellectual Tool," *Journal of Policy Analysis and Management* 11, no. 4 (1992). Copyright © 1992 by John Wiley & Sons, Inc. Reprinted by permission of John Wiley & Sons, Inc.; Selma Wassermann for her "How I Taught Myself How to Teach"; James Wilkinson, Director of the Derek Bok Center for Teaching and Learning, for William G. Perry, "Different Worlds in the Same Classroom"; and Jeffrey Zax and Marion B. Gammill, President of the *Harvard Crimson*, for "Hybrids Are Successful Adaptations."

---

8 7 6 5 4 3 2 97 96 95

ISBN 0-87584-565-7

CONTENTS

PREFACE

This *Instructor's Guide* for the Third Edition of *Teaching and the Case Method* has been developed to provide ideas, assistance, and perhaps a bit of inspiration for colleagues who might wish to experiment with starting up a discussion leadership seminar at their own institution. We also hope to provide additional resources for associates who are already involved in similar efforts.

Our debt to the authors of the readings, cases, and teaching notes included in this *Instructor's Guide* is great, and we wish to recognize the special contributions of Ms. Colleen Kaftan and Drs. Marina McCarthy, James Moore, and Lee Warren. Ms. Eileen Heath of the Harvard Business School served with distinction as manager of this project, bringing organization to our customary chaos. We also appreciate the many suggestions we received from our colleagues here at Harvard, as well as from those at other institutions.

This third edition provides all of us with a substantially expanded "case bank," including cases drawn from a wider array of professional schools and liberal arts departments than appeared in the previous two editions. We hope these cases will enrich both the planning and the conducting of your teaching seminar. Graduates of our Developing Discussion Leadership Skills seminars and instructors long familiar with our case bank should not feel unduly upset if they experience disorienting twinges of déjà vu when reading some of our cases and teaching notes. We have reedited some of our "classics" to emphasize the enduring topicality of their underlying issues by eliminating distracting dates and outmoded details, correcting errors, and adjusting some descriptive details to bring them into line with contemporary culture. We have also (we hope) improved some of our teaching notes by incorporating lessons learned from our continuing experience in teaching these cases.

We are pleased that instructors from an ever-widening circle of academic endeavors have been experimenting with these materials, for example in seminars developed for the faculty of training and development departments in private organizations and instructional development centers on college campuses. The work of the Derek Bok Center for Teaching and Learning at our own university has been of great interest, especially its development of programs to assist teaching assistants and teaching fellows in gaining discussion leadership skills. In this connection, we recommend highly the monograph by Dr. Ellen Sarkisian, associate director of that center, entitled *Teaching American Students: A Guide for International Faculty and Teaching Fellows* (available from the Bok Center).

Our *Instructor's Guide* is divided into five sections. Part I, entitled "A Program for Starting Up and Running a Case-Based Teaching Seminar at Your Institution," provides suggestions from getting started to keeping the ball rolling. Part II, "Supplementary Cases," includes B, C, and D cases to be used with seminar materials. (The cases as well as Teaching Notes and Researcher's Perspectives can be ordered from Harvard Business School Publishing, Customer Service Department, Soldiers Field, Boston, MA 02163; phone 617-495-6117 or 1-800-545-7685; fax 617-495-6985. Order numbers appear in the copyright line on the first page of each case.) Part III, "Teaching Notes and Researcher's Perspectives," is presented as an aid for users of our cases bank. Part IV, "Synopses of Additional Cases," lists further resources available from the Harvard Business School Publishing Corporation. Part V, "Readings," provides selections that may be of special interest and use to you in your teaching career.

The first reading is a classic, William A. Perry's "Different Worlds in the Same Classroom: Students, Evolution in Their Vision of Knowledge and Their Expectations of Teachers." The next two essays, Professor Selma Wassermann's "How I Taught Myself How to Teach" and Dr. Jeffrey Zax's "Hybrids Are Successful Adaptations," address the challenges of new instructors. Essays four and five, "Writing Cases: Tips and Pointers" by Professor Jane Linder and "Teaching Notes: Communicating the Teacher's Wisdom" by colleague James E. Austin, contain a great deal of "hands-on" advice on how to write cases and develop teaching notes. Both reflect the context in which they were created: a business school with a mission to help students learn about issues of management and administration, where professors routinely write cases, write teaching notes, and meet with teaching groups. These specific details should not distract the readers' attention from the fundamental issues that both of these essays illuminate. All who write cases—whether for business, liberal arts, or even secondary or elementary schools—can find useful hints in Linder's remarks about timing, interviewing, note-taking, case design, writing, disguise, and release. And all who write teaching notes can profit from Austin's suggestions about the essential elements of such documents and his tips about how to approach them. Essays six and seven discuss seminar group behavior and learning: "Note on Process Observation," by Professors John J. Gabarro and Anne Harlan, and "Foreign Students: Opportunities and Challenges for the Discussion Leader," written by two former seminar participants. The next essay, Professor Michael O'Hare's "Talk and Chalk: The Blackboard as an Intellectual Tool," is delightful. Taking up a mundane topic—blackboards—the author invites us to think creatively about their use and misuse. The final two essays, in the words of our colleague David Garvin, move to a higher philosophic perch: Professor Donald A. Schön's overview of professional education, "The Crisis of Professional Knowledge and the Pursuit of an Epistemology of Practice," and Dr. Judah Folkman's seminal essay, "The Fine Line between Persistence and Obstinacy." Dr. Folkman is the Julia Dyckman Professor of Pediatric Surgery at the Harvard Medical School. His essay should be required reading for all academics.

We appreciate your participation in this adventure in learning about teaching, and we have little doubt that participants in your seminars will find their experiences useful in subsequent classroom practice. We have learned much from our conduct of these workshops; we hope your experience has been, or will be, equally rewarding. Please let us hear your ideas and suggestions for improvement.

TEACHING AND THE CASE METHOD

Instructor's Guide

PART I

A Program for Starting Up and Running a Case-Based Teaching Seminar at Your Institution

Over the years many alumni of our seminars and workshops on discussion leadership skills have asked how to introduce similar programs in their institutions. All settings being unique, we must stress that our program is a prototype, not a blueprint for a prefabricated teaching seminar guaranteed to suit all sites. We offer our suggestions as lessons learned, with the hope of providing encouragement and, perhaps, pointing out a few bogs and quagmires (you can imagine how we have discovered these). Whatever *sui generis* problems or bonuses you may encounter in your own situation, we suspect you will still have to go through a fairly straightforward series of steps to set up, run, and perpetuate a case-based teaching seminar. What follows is our version of how this experience might play out.

We should mention at the outset that while the effort required to start up and run such a seminar is hardly negligible, the rewards we have seen are far reaching and culturally enriching to the institution. When case-based teaching seminars work well, they achieve multiple objectives. Teachers gain improved skills and the satisfaction of doing their jobs better. The often-overlooked enterprise of teaching gains publicity and esteem in the community. And the institution benefits by delivering better teaching to its student population.

We offer the following suggestions for setting up a teaching seminar as guidance, not dogma. Whether you choose to adopt, adapt, expand, or flatly reject our ideas, we hope that they will stimulate you to think about how a case-based discussion seminar might fit your institutional needs.

1. Getting Started

All sound projects begin with some sort of assessment of need. To test the waters for a teaching seminar at your institution, you might want to assemble a group of interested colleagues and hold a few case discussions. This, of course, presupposes identifying such a group. The usual sources are academic development centers, winners of teaching awards, and departments with reputations for interest in delivering high-quality discussion classes.

Once you have identified a pool of candidates for a potential discussion group from these, and other sources that occur to you, we suggest that you offer a sort of "wine tasting." Run a case discussion or two. See how they go over. In our recent experience, a pilot seminar drew a lively, bright, and sympathetic group of faculty, including many senior instructors. Events of this sort often produce a marked elevation of mood in addition to focused and helpful observations about very specific teaching challenges in the setting in question. They also can form the nucleus of an interdisciplinary and diverse (in every sense of the word) community of scholar-teachers.

In our experience, educational institutions always harbor instructors who like to teach and want to do it better. The trick is to find them, get them together, and show them, in a very tangible way, that the institution values their interest in teaching well. Assuming this enterprise goes well, you are ready for the next step.

2. *Selecting the Seminar Format*

On the most practical level, your seminar will have to jibe with the teaching unit at your institution. Do your courses last a quarter, a semester, or some other unit of time? Do you write your *syllabi* in terms of days, weeks, or months? *Teaching and the Case Method* gestated and grew in a setting where the semester runs for about three months, the academic year includes two semesters, and discussion classes last for one and a half hours. We thus planned our seminar to run for twelve to fourteen weeks, with cases being discussed in ninety-minute sessions. During semester-long seminars, which meet weekly, participants have the chance to probe beneath superficial impressions, get to know one another, and develop real *esprit.* Groups coalesce into communities strong and flexible enough to absorb internal tensions and dissensions. And the semester-long format gives the instructor the chance to teach several cases that revolve around the same issue with escalating levels of complexity.

The basic syllabus design of *Teaching and the Case Method* derives from this experience. In semester-long seminars, we begin with start-up issues like the teaching/learning contract and progress to operating problems like balancing the teacher-student relationship, evaluation, and discipline; the impact of gender on classroom behavior; and some of the complexities that cultural, racial, and linguistic diversity can introduce into a discussion classroom.

Our semester-long, weekly meetings—usually fourteen or fifteen of them, held from 3:00 to 5:00 p.m., with the first half hour for informal mingling—give participants a chance to try out ideas in their own classes, report back to the group, and bring up experiences of the moment as topics for discussion.

If the exigencies of your institutional setting dictate a different format—whether it be a weekend-long "retreat" or a four-, six-, or eight-session "mini-seminar"—you will experience other advantages. Efficiency comes immediately to mind, but there are others. Intensive one-and-a-half- to two-day seminars with six to eight cases are relatively easy to schedule, and participants tend to become involved quite rapidly. The improvement in teaching skills that participants often derive from brief but intense seminar experiences can affect a whole institution, and good results generate good publicity.

3. *Seminar Design: Developing a Syllabus*

After you've chosen your seminar format (or had it chosen for you by your institution's scheduling requirements), you will need to consider, in depth, the design of your seminar. Under the eight rubrics of our prototype outline in "Teaching with Cases at the Harvard Business School" (in Part I of *Teaching and the Case Method*), you will find more cases than can reasonably fit into most *syllabi.* Look through the cases, decide which best reflect your institution's current concerns, and make some initial choices.

This new edition of *Teaching and the Case Method* (1994) has a companion, *Education for Judgment* (1991), which includes essays by experienced case method teachers who have been affiliated with our seminars at Harvard University. Some of these essays—on subjects like the essential instructional skills of questioning, listening, and responding; the teaching/learning contract; the ethics of discussion teaching and its fundamental premises and practices—correspond to sections in the prototype seminar program in this edition of *Teaching and the Case Method.* Other essays address specialized topics like discussion pedagogy in technical subjects and the special difficulties and rewards of changing ground, as one highly respected medical lecturer did when he adopted discussion teaching in a course on histology. We do not mean to suggest that the essays in this collection exhaust all of the topics that our cases might conceivably raise for discussion, but we do hope that they can help clarify something of what we had in mind when we designed our seminar materials. Taken as a group, *Teaching and the Case Method,* "Teaching with Cases at the Harvard Business School," and *Education for Judgment* contain ample resources for seminars for a variety of settings and purposes.

We hasten to add that even these complementary texts will not satisfy all instructors' special requirements. Those who teach at (for example) women's colleges, medical schools, graduate schools of management, and executive development programs will face specialized issues as well as the garden-variety challenges (like starting up and running a discussion group) that our materials cover. Although some of our cases address currently topical social issues—sexual harassment, racial and ethnic bias, and special challenges of cultural and linguistic diversity, to name a few—we realize that today's hot topics are tomorrow's dim memories. We encourage you to go beyond our offerings and create cases that embody issues that burn for you.

4. *Materials*

Teaching and the Case Method (including "Teaching with Cases at the Harvard Business School"), *Education for Judgment* (1991), and all source materials, including readings and supplementary cases of interest to instructors in a wide variety of disciplines and settings, may be ordered from Harvard Business School Publishing (617-495-6117).

5. *A Note on Case Design*

Readers will observe that most of our cases are divided into segments, usually labelled (without a great deal of imagination) (A), (B), (C), and so on. This format possesses several advantages. It gives case teachers flexibility in fitting the materials into the time allotted to their discussions. We have found that presenting case events in installments helps sustain students' attention. Nothing sells like suspense. When an (A) case ends in a cliffhanger, students generally want to find out what happened next. Second, the multiple-segment format makes it possible to introduce different perspectives into the discussion. When the (B) case continues an unfolding story, the group gets a long view of a series of interconnected events. The effect is somewhat like watching continuing episodes of an unfolding story, complete with plot twists and reversals of fortune. (Our cases are all based on fact, but, as Byron's Don Juan pointed out, "truth is stranger than fiction.") Some (B) cases present not an extension of the case events, but a different observer's account of them. This type of case segment allows the seminar to consider the core events from different angles, and the effect is somewhat like walking all the way around a statue. (C) cases often introduce yet a different element, personal reflection, by presenting key characters' retrospective analyses of what happened to them and what they, themselves, think it all meant. Of course, seminar groups often find very different lessons in the cases, but retrospective case segments present good opportunities for closure.

One way in which we organize our teaching materials as we develop them is to look for "case breaks" that fit our segmented format. We try to provide material for about an hour's discussion in the (A) segment and divide the rest of the material into pieces brief enough to be distributed, read, and discussed in the last half-hour of the class meeting. This means that our (A) segments tend to be the longest, and to contain most of the core issues that we see in the case events. As a rule, (A) introduces a protagonist and places him or her firmly in a context that includes a teaching challenge or problem and a deadline by which the teacher must make some sort of response. At the end of the (A) segment, as a rule, our protagonists either are or *think* they are in big trouble. Commonly, they face dilemmas, in the literal sense of the word: choices among equally undesirable alternatives. The case characters often have to act quickly, but seminar participants have time to analyze and evaluate the case situations, weigh alternatives, and think about broad principles that seem to emerge from the whole experience.

In institutions where classes last longer than our typical ninety minutes, several case segments may be distributed, or recombined, as the instructor wishes. Sometimes we withhold the portion of the case that presents the protagonist's retrospective view of the events and distribute it as participants leave the classroom. We encourage experimentation and adaptation.

Because all of our cases are based on real dilemmas, most of which caused distress, we try to convey the flavor of the events along with the data, details, and chronologies. This attempt to preserve the human element is the reason, for example, that we often describe case characters physically (disguised, of course, but with essentials intact) and even discuss their family backgrounds. We hope that such details will permit seminar participants to achieve the paradoxical objective of projecting themselves imaginatively into our case characters' skins while simultaneously developing detached, intellectually sound judgments about their situations. (Readings offered with the cases can often provide conceptual frameworks for participants to "try on for size," but even these do not claim to present neat solutions to the intrinsically messy situations the case characters faced.)

In keeping with the mission of writing cases about real people's real problems, we try to use literary techniques that engage readers' emotions and senses as well as their minds. We describe case characters in ways that convey something about the kind of impression they make. For example, if the real character is dark haired and jolly, a disguised description might change or omit the telling detail of hair color but mention the high candle-power of the smile. The intention would be to convey the idea that this teacher generally conveyed the impression of being in a good mood. We try to describe the settings (physical and administrative) within which our case characters work and live, the students with whom they deal. Our goal is to resist a common academic attraction to abstraction. We recognize that teachers and students have bodies, faces, voices, styles of dress, nervous habits, family backgrounds, hobbies, ambitions, pet peeves, dreams, and often a quirk or two. Our purpose in including details of this sort (with due consideration for the feelings and privacy of the people who generously contribute their time and confide their experiences to our case researchers) is to make it possible for seminar groups to feel as if they know these case characters and have, in some degree, shared their experiences.

6. The Make-Up of a Seminar Group

We find twenty-five to thirty-five participants a good size for a discussion group, although good discussions can include as many as sixty and even more. Although it is usually a matter of practicality to include a large proportion from the institution sponsoring the seminar, having a mix of ages, backgrounds, experiences, and, if possible, a contingent of colleagues from other departments or divisions of your own academic institution can greatly enrich the discussions. Including members of other institutions—either as participants or as observers—can also help spread the word about the efficacy (and fun) of discussion teaching and learning. The best advertisement is always word of mouth.

7. Physical Facilities

The physical setting in which a discussion takes place has critical importance. We find the circle or semicircle of seats to be optimal. In discussion teaching, where we encourage the seminar group to become a cohesive learning community, student-to-student communication is essential. Participants must be able to see one another's faces. The traditional lecture hall or classroom with seats bolted down in rigid rows simply doesn't work for this sort of teaching. We have never succeeded in holding a good discussion class in a large lecture hall, but lounges or libraries, where chairs can be moved into U-shapes or circles, can become extremely congenial settings for group dialogue.

8. Laying the Groundwork

Before the seminar begins, we ask participants to write brief, informal autobiographical sheets and submit recent photographs of themselves. Then we collect these materials into a small book for distribution to all participants. While we stress the ideal of community, we recognize that people sometimes forget one another's names or where they teach or what their primary subjects of interest are. By supplying this information, these class books can promote the formation of informal study groups and even, sometimes, of new academic partnerships. By creating and distributing a seminar directory, we also send participants a subtle message: this will not be a collection of strangers. We want you to know who your fellow students are. When the book is complete (it can be rough), we send it out with a syllabus and a letter of welcome.

9. Leading the Seminar

To highlight some very basic points (covered at length in "Teaching with Cases at the Harvard Business School" and *Education for Judgment*), let us simply remind readers of the fundamental importance and subtlety of the teaching/learning contract; the centrality of the skills of questioning, listening, and responding to participants' comments; and the usefulness of having a friendly colleague observe your teaching. In addition, one other point may be helpful to remember at the outset of a case-based teaching seminar: seminar discussions often develop into strongly negative criticisms of case characters (sometimes verging on "teacher bashing"). Should you note this tendency in a seminar you are leading, we suggest that you try to introduce balance, perhaps with good-humored "devil's advocate" questions. "What about the poor teacher? Was he just a villain? Didn't he do *anything* right?" "Do you think most brand-new statistics teachers appreciate the negative potential of reassuring weak students?" We also make it a practice to try to deflect psychoanalytic interpretations of teachers or students, even in dramatic situations, and focus on aspects of pedagogical behavior accessible to the wider community of teachers—those without advanced degrees in psychology. When Lynn Novak surprised her nervous student, George Perkins, with an unexpected request that he go to the chalkboard and try a statistics problem in front of his colleagues, he blew up, dramatically. But we suggest that seminar participants will gain more pedagogical wisdom by concentrating on Lynn's unofficial teaching contract with George, and how she broke it, than by attempting to dissect whatever neuroses her student may or may not have had. Also, as experts have told us, our cases simply do not include sufficient data to support sound psychological assessments.

One way in which we try to suggest the scope of the discussion we would hope to have in class is by including study questions on the seminar *syllabus*.

These questions are intentionally general. Their purpose is to indicate the (hoped-for) direction of the discussion and to note some obvious jumping-off points in the case. We generally ask for analysis, diagnosis, or action in very general terms. We avoid pointing to exquisitely specific details and hope that these will come up in the case discussion. Or we might ask students to look for major decision points and form some rough hypotheses about what different decisions could have been taken and what outcomes these might have produced. The basic point here is that we keep study questions general and use them as gentle suggestions about the broad topics we would hope to cover in the seminar meeting.

10. A Critical Distinction: Teaching Notes versus Teaching Plans

The teaching notes and "researchers' perspectives" in this collection lack a standard format, style, or content because they were written at various times and by various case authors. Even so, like nonidentical twins, they may appear different but have quite a bit in common. They were written to help prospective instructors appraise cases with a very practical purpose in mind: teaching them. All of them provide some kind of rough-cut interpretation. The teaching notes may augment these with "hands-on" suggestions about questions one might pose to stimulate discussion on certain points and answers that a seminar group might produce. Some of the notes (see "The Blank Page," for example), might suggest various ways to use a particularly rich case. In this instance, two major topics (integrating a difficult student into a discussion group and evaluating that student) coexist in one document, and the note addresses this teaching issue. The teaching note on "Trouble in Stat. 1B," by contrast, presents a long list of issues that might emerge under a single "umbrella" issue: "instructional innovation."

The researchers' perspectives in this collection present yet another approach to helping teachers prepare. These tend to stick more closely to the cases as texts to be read and interpreted and give something of a backstage view of what was in the writer's mind during the stages of research, case design, and writing.

All of the teaching materials in this volume share another characteristic: their voice. We are talking to teachers in these pages, but we hope others will overhear. Professional trainers may find our program helpful to adapt to their work in industry and the non-profit sector. Academic administrators interested in faculty development may discover something of value in our materials. And students of teaching may wish to read through our cases and supporting materials with or without the company of a seminar group. Whoever reads these materials, however, should bear in mind that they were written with a practical purpose: to help seminar leaders prepare to run discussions of the cases in *Teaching and the Case Method,* Third Edition.

One highly important aspect of all of our teaching notes is that they cannot do the whole job of helping instructors prepare for class. Teaching notes tend to be written early in the life of a case, sometimes after it has been taught just a few times (sometimes before it has been taught at all). Inevitably, time will have passed between the writing of the note and the instructor's preparation to teach the case. This means that, to some extent, the notes will always be somewhat off the mark. Only a clairvoyant with a perfect track record can foresee what a specific group of participants will make of a case on a particular day. In practice, even the most painstakingly constructed lists of discussion questions can fly out the window when a group gets stuck on details and interpretations that neither the case writer nor the instructor considered critical. Sometimes, this situation arises from social change. For example, in the years before feminist social critiques were widely known, no one noticed that our cases tended to describe women's appearances far more frequently than men's. When this fact was pointed out, we began to rectify this imbalance, but we cannot predict what future groups will see in our materials.

This is one reason that a teaching note can take the instructor only so far toward full preparation. Getting ready to teach a case means having a grasp of current circumstances, and we recommend that teachers bring their teaching plans up to the minute. In a teaching plan, one considers the "right here, right now." What is the prevailing mode of social critique, and who in the class is likely to espouse (and who oppose) it? What is the lead editorial in the student newspaper today? One also considers the needs of the particular seminar group. Who has been talking a lot? Who has been silent? Is there someone who might be hurt by the issues or details of this particular case? If so, what will you, the leader, do to protect that participant? Who would be a good lead speaker?

Our teaching plans take the form of very specific questions that we wish, in the best of all possible worlds, the seminar would cover. In real life, wish lists seldom come true, but that does not render them useless. Sometimes a seminar races through all of our topics and treats them superficially. In such instances, we ask people to revisit and refocus, summarize points previously made, deepen and complicate them. In our experience, no topic is ever exhausted by a single comment, however articulate, and a teaching plan can help an instructor focus on core issues.

We suggest that teaching plans be no longer than a page—two at most—you can glance at while also watching participants' faces, listening to their comments, and thinking about what you are going to do and say next. In a teaching plan, one notes very specific circumstances affecting the impending discussion. What critical issues do you consider basic to this case? We suggest a very short list. What discussion questions (written out word for word) might help the group get at these issues? Are there any key words you want to stress in this case? (Again, remember, you're trying to keep your plan down to a page or two.) Are there some issues that might surface but which you would rather save for other class meetings? These very specific, topical details go into a teaching plan.

Discussion questions differ from study questions in their degree of specificity. "What would *you,* in Janet Macomber's shoes, have replied to Assistant Professor Graham?" "What do you think was going through Bea Benedict's mind when Jack Kesselman said she was stifling the section and they should take a vote?"

11. A Suggested Protocol for Class Preparation

An experienced seminar instructor once put the problem of preparation for discussion poignantly: "How do I plan for a discussion session yet to be born? How do I ready myself for the minute-by-minute job of running the class—to be able to understand, organize, and guide the free-flowing give-and-take of a case class? As soon as I ask the first question, everything is up for grabs. It is a frightening process—traditional approaches just don't seem to work for me. What's the answer?" We empathize with her. Even when one has studied the case and teaching note or researcher's perspective, there are no simple solutions.

We have, however, developed a method of preparing for a discussion class that we find helpful. Obviously, it is but one of many possibilities, and we hasten to note that, while this routine may sound lengthy, it is actually more easily done than said. Our first step is to evaluate the progress that has been made toward fulfilling the teaching objectives of the seminar. We review the substantive material covered to date and the remaining material, which will be introduced in future class meetings. We note the critical issues that have been raised in discussions and try to pinpoint where further examination should be encouraged. What topics remain to be raised, and what upcoming classes offer the best possibilities for exploring them? We keep detailed summary notes of each class (made immediately after the meeting, while key data are fresh). Even in abbreviated, outline form, summary notes can serve at least four useful functions. First, the discipline of writing one's impressions can help an instructor re-examine the class experience while its details are still fresh. Second, the written summary can provide material for a lead into the next class. Third, if an examination is to be given, these notes can help shape it. Fourth, as the instructor teaches the case to different groups and accumulates a "bank" of experiential notes, patterns can begin to emerge that give insights into the case and the ways in which various sorts of groups deal with it.

Next, we begin a preparation in depth of the case that will be discussed in the next session starting, of course, with a reading of the teaching note and/or researcher's perspective. Our objective is to prepare a detailed analysis of the situation, state the conclusions that might be derived from that analysis, and outline a spectrum of action recommendations that might be appropriate to suggest to the case protagonist. Achieving superior command of substantive information and the discipline of performing a rigorous intellectual analysis are basic to any preparation, but discussion leaders find them especially beneficial. Having a command of content enhances the instructor's opportunity to concentrate on understanding and managing the discussion process—which is the only firsthand data that he or she has about the progress of the seminar.

Professor Fritz Roethlisberger captured an important truth about case method learning when he wrote, "For me the important 'facts' existed in the discussion of the case and not in the written case per se. It could be said that they [other instructors] were teaching the written case, whereas I was teaching the discussion of it."[1] Our preference is to try to use both data banks. Once we have given thought to the case as a document to be analyzed, we shift attention to the more complex task of trying to predict and prepare for the process by which students and instructor will discuss the case. Without attempting to draw up a formal statement, we aim to develop an internalized appreciation and command of the complexities that may influence the section dynamic during a specific class. First and foremost, we try to understand each student's academic strengths and weaknesses and read the group's current dynamic. The instructor needs to

---

[1] F. J. Roethlisberger, *The Elusive Phenomena: An Autobiographical Account of My Work in the Fields of Organizational Behavior at the Harvard Business School,* ed. George F. F. Lombard (Boston, Mass.: Division of Research, Graduate School of Business Administration, Harvard University, 1977), 141.

anticipate approximately where in the discussion opportunities are likely to arise to meet the learning needs of individuals and the group. Where are the danger spots? As we develop teaching questions, we try to predict alternative responses the group might make to each, and plan for constructive responses.

More specifically, we work through a simple process review before each class discussion. First we assess the status of the group. Where has it made the most progress, and where the least, toward becoming a true learning community? What is its mood? Are students having fun, or are they glum? What is happening in the overall academic program that might affect our discussion—exams, reports, conferences, vacations, political demonstrations, or controversies? What is the overall university scene?

Second, we review each participant's history and performance. Who might have the most to learn from this particular case? Who might contribute most? If we think the case contains details that might offend some students, how will we handle this? Which quiet students might find this case a useful entry point into the group's give-and-take?

Third, we recognize and try to deal with our own mood. Do we like or dislike this case? Is this a fun section of the course or an academic chore? Are there some sour apples in the group, participants we just plain don't like? Where might our personal biases and prejudices affect our leadership of the discussion? All these considerations, as well as family and personal concerns, influence one's behavior in the classroom. It is helpful to acknowledge and examine the potential impact of such factors on your leadership of the discussion you are preparing.

Fourth, we review the case as a discussion instrument. What are its faults, if any—factual or editorial errors, missing basic data, inadequate description of the situation? Where are the best opportunities to practice needed analytic skills? What will the participants' attitude be toward this case? How well will they prepare? What questions will they bring to the discussion? What issues have high potential for involvement and conflict? How does this case connect with past and future cases?

Fifth, we work up a series of operational guidelines. How active a role do we wish to play as instructor? Should we intervene on numerous occasions or merely enter the discussion when changes in direction or summary statements are needed? What will be the mode of the class? Is it to be a drill in technique or an exploration of questions for reflection? How should class time be divided between diagnosis and action? If there is a chalkboard, how should it be used? What would we hope to have on it at the beginning and end of class? How should the class be paced? Where would we hope for points of high involvement?[2]

Sixth, we think about ways to open and close the class. The opening minutes of a session present the instructor with a series of decisions that, if made appropriately, can do much to promote a productive discussion. Do you ask for volunteers or select one or two lead-off participants? If you select a lead speaker, how do you decide whom to choose? Do you begin with a specific prepared question or just invite a participant to "open up the case"? If you pose the first question, will it be specific and directed or a general request for an appraisal of the situation? What possible responses might the participant make to those questions, and how might you best work with his or her comments? What opening remarks, if any, should you make about the course, the previous class, or expectations for the current discussion?

A similar set of complex decisions confronts the teacher at the end of class. Should you offer a prepared general summary, let one evolve extemporaneously from the discussion, or both? What "mind benders"—fundamental questions—do you want to leave with the group for continuing reflection? What suggestions, if any, do you want to make for the next seminar meeting?

There is no way to predict what will happen in a class, but this preparation regime has proven generally helpful. When one previews the major dimensions of a class systematically—the group dynamic, the participants' needs and goals, the instructor's interests and biases, and the interplay of specific case and general course concepts—it is possible, to some extent, to anticipate the general paths of inquiry a seminar group might want to explore and prepare yourself to seize opportune moments to address important needs, whether of individuals or the group as a whole. At a minimum, such planning helps instructors avoid some errors. At best, it may help them appreciate the power and complexity of a teaching approach that encompasses both content and process.

A still more complicated challenge is to ready oneself for the minute-by-minute leadership of a discussion class. In writing about the development of an analogous skill—playing jazz—David Sudnow offers a valuable perspective: the artist (or teacher) must have a capacity for "the organization of improvised

---

[2] See Laura Nash, "The Rhythms of the Semester: Overall Preparation, Evolving Roles, and Special Classes," in *The Art and Craft of Teaching,* ed. Margaret Morganroth Gullette (Cambridge, Mass.: Harvard-Danforth Center for Teaching and Learning, 1982).

conduct."[3] The discussion instructor must be able to organize and influence the unfolding case discussion instantaneously. Success in this endeavor involves balancing the needs for participants' freedom of inquiry (the encouragement of questioning, willingness to explore the unexpected) with a disciplined direction that ensures the achievement of objectives for the class and the course. Failure opens up the possibility of chaos, as participants with widely diverging agendas bring very different perspectives and objectives to a case problem.

How does one become adept at this minute-by-minute direction of a case discussion? There is no instructional patent medicine, no set of tricks, no neat "how-to" paperback. We all recognize that much of discussion leadership is intuitive: the instantaneous application of past experience to present challenges. Intuition, a sensing that precedes knowing, enables an instructor to understand and respond to the unspoken words and latent feelings of the seminar group. It encourages confidence in the face of awesome complexity.

12. *Some Practical Tips for Running Discussion Classes*

Getting to class early gives the instructor several opportunities: to welcome students graciously and begin to set a comfortable, congenial tone for the seminar; to note who seems more outgoing, and who less; and to get an idea of subgroups that already exist.

Using names during the discussion promotes the formation of a cohesive group. The more participants use one another's names, the quicker the group will jell. Modeling the practice can help. We suggest that you learn and use participants' names and gently intervene to suggest that participants do the same. When a participant makes a comment about another's remark, we often interrupt very briefly to mention the first speaker's name. As a rule, the second speaker picks up the cue, and repeats the previous speaker's name. This simple device does a great deal to promote a basic value, mutual respect, as a classroom norm. To speed the process of using names, it is helpful to display them as visibly as possible. If participants are seated at desks or around a table, try placing large fold-over name cards, with names written both on front and back, in front of them. Such cards can be read from several vantage points.

[3] David Sudnow, *Ways of the Hand* (Cambridge, Mass.: Harvard University Press, 1978).

Discussion leaders also find it useful, particularly early in a class or during one-shot workshops, to sketch a seating plan and keep it visible. Then they try, as gracefully as possible, to say people's names out loud as they invite them to speak or respond to their contributions.

Eye contact is another often overlooked ingredient of discussion leadership. Most people are either right-eyed or left-eyed, just as they are right- or left-handed. This normal asymmetry has practical consequences: we all inadvertently pay less attention to one side of a room. In a discussion class, this means that we risk slighting fully half the class by calling on people seated on one side of the room less frequently than their more fortunately located peers. Consciously ascertaining which eye dominates your field of vision, and compensating for the tendency to ignore the other side, can help you avoid frustrating quite a number of students.

One successful teacher I know begins each new course or workshop by consciously making brief eye contact with each member of the group during her opening remarks. To accomplish this task smoothly, she mentally divides the class into pie wedges and turns her attention first to the faces in the outer left wedge, and then to those in the outer right, proceeding inward until she has filled in all the wedges. This approach has become so habitual that it has lost its original, mechanical feel. Now making eye contact with all of her students is second nature to her.

Body language is also well worth a discussion teacher's attention and contemplation. An all-embracing term that achieved wide popularity in the 1970s and includes all manner of expressive gestures, twitches, blinks, grunts, murmurs (anything that conveys a message without words), body language is unconscious but powerful. When we flinch as a foreign object comes flying at us, we communicate fear. When we grunt softly ("hmmmmph") we are expressing surprise. Similarly, sitting up straight indicates interest; and slumping, boredom or inattention. The discussion leader will do well to attend to some of these physical signals. Without getting paralyzed by self-consciousness or trying to adopt a set of uncomfortable mannerisms, you can begin, in modest ways, to use body language positively. There are subtle ways to encourage a speaker without saying "Right!" during his or her remarks. Sitting forward on one's seat, straightening one's spine in a posture of attention, smiling slightly, or inclining one's ear to the speaker's words can all convey interest and attention.

Body language can also help cue another discussion participant to get ready to pick up the conversational ball. Making eye contact with a listener while another seminar member speaks can accomplish this and help the discussion proceed seamlessly, with as few intrusive stage directions as possible. Hand gestures can convey expansiveness. By extending the hands, palms open, one signals acceptance or resignation. A raised hand can call for "time out." You can urge speed by moving the fingers rapidly (as if saying, "Come on, come on, wrap it up.") Needless to say, one should use only hand gestures that feel natural, but practicing them can expand the repertoire. Although a discussion leader is neither an orchestra conductor nor a baseball umpire, the leader can leaven his or her teaching style with a little judicious staginess, as long as it does not turn into a bid for attention.

In a large classroom, the discussion leader can sit, stand, pace, walk toward a participant, or back away. Remember that, to one seated, a person standing can seem large and threatening. Moving toward a speaker can express interest, but it can also convey hostility or intimidation. Backing off, by contrast, can symbolically bestow intellectual space if one's expression conveys interest in the comments as one moves away.

All of the discussion leaders' motions gain exaggerated impact from the centrality and status of the position of leadership. Even in a course where the participants outrank the leader, the teacher has the position of highest power because he or she calls the shots. Directing a discussion can confer a sort of automatic, if impermanent, promotion. One's gestures thus carry more than customary weight and should be modified according to the impression one hopes to convey.

Voice level also matters. It is advisable to raise the head so that the voice projects. Without shouting, remember that you are trying to address a number of people. If you tend to keep a hand over your mouth when talking (many people do unconsciously) fight this habit when teaching.

Attire can also affect how one functions in a classroom. As our protagonist in "The Day the Heat Went On" discovered with annoyance (she was a woman teacher who got a wolf whistle when she removed her blazer), wardrobe matters. The issue may seem petty, but the exaggerated visibility of discussion leaders magnifies the impression they make. Observing the culture of your institution (tweedy, casual, uniform, business attire, sporty?) and bearing the authority of your position in mind should help you decide how you want to look in the classroom. If the class wears blue jeans, will you choose a severe black suit? If the class wears business attire, will you wear a sweat suit? Teaching attire should reflect the general culture of the institution, but the teacher should feel free to move expressively, knowing that he or she will be watched. It might help to observe yourself in a mirror. Which items of clothing convey the impression you want? Both men and women may benefit from giving attention to this matter.

The catch-all term "mirroring" can be a handy mnemonic to remind teachers that we are all mimics, in the classroom as well as outside. Observation suggests that if the teacher acts nervous, the discussion group usually starts to get edgy too. By the same token, confidence, energy, and good humor are contagious. Mirroring can work subtly, but there is scarcely a human encounter in which one cannot observe it. This is not to suggest that you can remake a discussion group in your own image by modeling values or a particular intellectual approach. The teacher in "I Felt as If My World Had Just Collapsed!" learned with horror that declaring and embodying a passionate ethical conviction did not automatically inculcate similar beliefs in all of her students. She bumped into one limitation of the mirroring phenomenon: looking glasses only reflect appearances. But many teachers have yet to appreciate the existence of mirroring at all.

13. Keeping the Ball Rolling

Once a case-based teaching seminar has successfully gotten moving, the challenge arises to keep up the momentum and, perhaps, establish a continuing program. A long-term effort requires several elements: a flow of participants, instructors, fresh case materials, and administrative support. We have found it helpful to invite colleagues to our discussions. When they like what they see, they spread the good word and also often return as participants. Sometimes they become sources of case material or instructors and case authors for their own courses. When colleagues become friends of the seminar, they suggest other participants and potential "case leads." All of this helps the seminar grow and prosper.

On a practical level, when blessed with guests, we invite them to come early and mingle with seminar participants before the discussion. Then we either introduce them formally or ask the participant who invited them to introduce them. We seat guests out of the circle of participants, to help them resist the temptation to jump into the discussion (which could threaten the group cohesion we consider vital to the seminar process).

We also recommend following up with seminar graduates. We encourage correspondence and generally keeping in touch. We ask them for comments, invite them to suggest further case material, and ask them to propose potential seminar participants.

14. A Final Note: The Many Roles of the Discussion Teacher

Unlike Doctor Seuss's Bartholomew Cubbins, discussion leaders may not have five hundred hats, but sometimes it can feel that way. The multiple roles of a discussion teacher sometimes actually conflict with one another. In acting and reacting to what happens in class, one can switch from gracious host to devil's advocate, supportive parent, coach, conductor, fellow student, fellow teacher, case character (in an explicit role play) and more. The variety of roles the discussion teacher plays can confuse as well as invigorate. In these pages, the terms *discussion leaders*, *instructors*, *educators*, and *teachers* are all used to denote someone who leads a discussion teaching seminar. The linguistic uncertainty of this usage reflects the ambiguity inherent in teaching a teaching seminar whose materials describe teachers. In the give-and-take of case-method instruction, the roles of teacher and student often blur, but never more so than in a teaching seminar.

If you are beginning to experience a slight feeling of vertigo, take comfort in the knowledge that, as an instructor of these materials, you have many advantages on your side. You have access, in this *Instructor's Guide,* to (B), (C), and further segments of the cases, the teaching notes, our suggestions for an effective preparation protocol, and a guide to developing a practical teaching plan. All this should introduce an element of security. One purpose of this volume is to give the instructor additional insights so that he or she can feel confident and enjoy the classroom experience. Trying on a lot of hats can be fun, and the many roles of the discussion leader can bring energy and joy to this sort of teaching.

Discussion leaders often report that they learn more from the participants than they dreamed possible during the hours of lonely preparation. Taking up the challenge of discussion teaching has rejuvenated "burned-out" lecturers, inspired younger instructors to explore and improve their skills, and enriched the teaching lives of many practitioners, both intellectually and emotionally. Like the taste of a vintage Margaux or, for that matter, a well-prepared apple pie, discussion leadership cannot be experienced vicariously. The purpose of this book is to set the table and provide a sample menu. The rest is up to you. *Bon appetit.*

PART II

Supplementary Cases

The French Lesson (B)

After Jack Sothern slipped out of Bert Peters's French class, Bert stewed for a while. Jack's rather dramatic exit and reappearance had been the only snag so far in an enjoyable class. The other students had been visibly, though not deeply, upset by Jack's behavior, and their general edginess had, in turn, unsettled Bert. The whole thing annoyed him; it would take some doing to recapture the good rapport he had created with that group. Some teachers at Bower thought nothing of insulting, reprimanding, and teasing students in class, but Bert consciously eschewed this style of teaching. Such teachers had made him awfully uncomfortable during his student days, and he didn't want to recreate the unpleasantness of their classes.

Bert called Jack at his dorm that evening.

"You really insulted me," Jack said. "I *always* prepare for class. You shouldn't have embarrassed me in front of my friends just because I'm not good at languages." Bert told the student he had only meant to let him off the hook, but he apologized for having insulted him, even inadvertently, and suggested that they have a conference to diagnose Jack's difficulties and, perhaps, arrange for private tutoring. Jack's performance improved a bit, but he remained the least talented student in his class. Bert ended the semester by giving Jack a C+, more for effort than accomplishment. Their relations continued to be strained—Bert noticed that Jack always looked for a way to avoid him when their paths crossed on campus—and Bert felt the class's mood never recovered its initial level of spontaneous buoyancy.

This case was written by Abby Hansen for the Developing Discussion Leadership Skills and the Teaching by the Case Method seminars. Data were furnished by the involved participants. All names and some peripheral facts have been disguised.
(HBS Case No. 9-384-067)

The Day the Heat Went On (B)

Ellen Collins Recalls the Incident

I knew these characters sitting in the top row, and I didn't consider any of them basically hostile, although my instantaneous reaction to the whistle was pure fury. I felt like lashing out, but I immediately rejected the possibility of responding with angry words because it seemed important, somehow, to show that I hadn't been rattled. The idea of calling on a woman student in the hope that she would complain on my behalf occurred to me. That might bolster the women as a group and offer more effective correction than I, as the insulted party, could make.

But I knew that the women in LG VI were demoralized. They were a fairly young group—their average age was 25 (about two years below the average male age)—and they had far less than the typical four years of business or government experience the males had. I had noticed that they acted self-effacing. There was a lot riding on me as their only female teacher. If I called on one of them to defend me, not only would I put her on the spot but she might simply swallow the insult and thereby help create an even worse impression of passivity.

I realized that both I and the women students in that room had much to lose by a wrong response. I don't mean that I deliberated for hours before responding to the whistle. But some form of all these thoughts did rocket through my mind as I stood there. What I did was instinctive. I did not look in the direction of the whistle. Instead I waited for a pause from the speaker, wheeled around to face the part of the room farthest away from where the whistle had originated, and called on a male student. I chose a reliable fellow who I knew would have something pertinent to say, and asked him a direct, simple question relating to something I had just put on the board. While he answered, I collected my thoughts. The class went on with no further jarring incidents.

Ellen Reflects on Long-Term Consequences

Oddly enough, I think there might be some level on which this incident—and my not getting rattled by it—did me some good. I ended up the year with far better teaching evaluations than LG VI gave Charlie Brennan, and he's considered one of the real "old pros" around here. By the way, I think I know who whistled, and I don't think he really meant any harm by it. It was an attempt at humor, quite spontaneous, and flat-footed rather than malicious. The student I'm thinking of happens to be an aver-

---

This case was written by Abby Hansen for the Developing Discussion Leadership Skills and the Teaching by the Case Method seminars. Data were furnished by the involved participants. All names and some peripheral facts have been disguised.
(HBS Case No. 9-384-099)

age guy—average intelligence, average looks—but he has a frankness and naivete that are refreshing at Fleming. He's the sort who would offer daring comments in discussion without calculating every syllable for effect in the interests of his precious course grade. In retrospect, I'm still not certain of what that whistle meant. Perhaps it was a sort of compliment—a recognition that I'd finally joined the club by doing what the men did and teaching without a jacket. I also think this incident could have landed me in real hot water if I'd acted flustered or showed the instantaneous fury that I really did feel. As LG VI's only woman teacher, I was a symbol for all women at Fleming at that moment, and one false step could have crippled my relationship with this group and my credibility as a leader. To me, though, this relatively minor incident is just one of many signs that women live under microscopes at places like Fleming. And—for the record—I still wear a jacket when I teach.

The Introduction (B)

Dianne's introduction of Mike O'Neil had clearly jolted Leslie. As Dianne concluded, Leslie slowly sat back in her seat and crossed her arms.

Leslie Recalls the Last Two Minutes

It was over before I realized it. I was too stunned to interrupt Dianne. My first impulse was to use humor to diffuse the situation. I tried to make light of things by exaggerated sarcasm. "Well," I moaned, "now *there's* a different introduction." I was a bit uncomfortable, however, since the humor seemed to have little effect on the tension in the class. I felt I needed to convey more disapproval. After conspicuously glancing at the clock to convey my concern with time, I then tried to establish eye contact with members of the group. After a short pause, in which I straightened out my papers, I lowered my voice and announced, "See you on Wednesday. You probably all need time to get to the bookstore before the dinner hour." I tried to be deliberate without sounding strained. I hoped that my tone was signaling disapproval of Dianne and Mike to all assembled. Symbolically closing the folders in front of me to emphasize closure, I stood up and went over to the instructor's desk on the raised platform in front of the classroom. I proceeded to file extra syllabi and handouts into my briefcase while nodding and acknowledging students as they somewhat awkwardly left the room.

Students milled about, and connections made in class introductions were slowly pursued. Dianne darted toward me. She began to tell me excitedly that English had been her favorite subject in high school and that she had written a major paper on James Joyce that she wanted to show me during our first conference. Her attempt to ingratiate herself further annoyed me. Her eagerness did not seem at all sincere. Even if all that she had said in her introduction about Mike were true, her lack of discretion irritated me. I was running through several scenarios of what to say to her; instead, I smiled perfunctorily and kept nodding as the other students and Dianne left the room.

After the Students Left

After the class had left, Leslie turned off the lights and took the elevator to her office. Her ensuing discussion with Jo had not resolved much. Leslie stewed for a couple of days before deciding that she was going to ask both Mike and Dianne to meet with her after the next class meeting. Although much was left up in the air that week, she was glad she had initially

---

This case was written by Marina McCarthy in collaboration with C. Roland Christensen for the Developing Discussion Leadership Skills and Teaching by the Case Method seminars. While the case is based on data furnished by participants involved, all names and some peripheral facts have been disguised.
(HBS Case No. 9-386-147)

let the episode drop. To Leslie's surprise, however, Dianne did not come to the next class.

She recalled, "Since I had not anticipated this turn in events, I dismissed speaking with Mike at all. In a way, I felt a sense of relief—as if the problem was over. In my mind, the case had solved itself: Dianne had behaved inappropriately and must have decided to change to another section."

The Introduction (C)

Two Months Later

Two months had passed since that first class. Leslie was pleased with the way her freshman section was progressing. The students seemed happy, and there had been a steady stream of roommates and friends of class members asking to be admitted to Leslie's section second semester. Bringing food had not been an issue at all. Each week two members brought provisions. The weekly conferences were very successful and the class meetings had taken on the ambience of a seminar as hoped. As Leslie had thought, Mike O'Neil proved not to be a difficulty. Interestingly, they developed a quick rapport.

Returning from lunch one late October afternoon, Leslie and Jo grabbed their mail and a cup of coffee before returning to their offices. As Leslie was unlocking her door, she noticed a scrawled note on the floor. Setting her coffee and mail on the filing cabinet inside the door, she read the note. Shaking her head, she murmured, "He's *only* 18 years old!" Then she turned to Jo: "Want an update on my 3 o'clock class? Read this."

> Dear Professor O'Connor,
>
> I appreciate the extension you granted me on this paper. I apologize for not being able to make the 3:00 Wednesday appointment. I was home from Tuesday morning through Wednesday afternoon to participate in the birth of my child by my girlfriend. *She* was born Tuesday afternoon and was named Kathryn Hope O'Neil. Once again, I appreciate your understanding. Thank you.
>
> —Michael O'Neil

Leslie was not surprised by the note. Mike had told her during one of their initial conferences that his girlfriend was pregnant and that they both had decided against marrying. He also admitted to enjoying English class—his most hated subject in high school, where he apparently did not get along with his English teacher.

Upon rereading Mike's note, Leslie noted that "she" had been underlined. She wondered whether Mike meant her to notice with approval that his new child was a girl. "I guess I should congratulate him the next time I see him," Leslie thought. "It's an awkward situation." She looked back on that first class meeting:

I sensed from Michael that even if he was a culprit that first day of class, he has since decided to straighten out. There's a puzzle here that I'll probably never solve. Further, I have no interest in finding out his role that day—it's water under the bridge. He seems to have matured tremendously—in the last several weeks in particular. Perhaps the impending responsibility of a

---

This case was written by Marina McCarthy in collaboration with C. Roland Christensen for the Developing Discussion Leadership Skills and Teaching by the Case Method seminars. While the case is based on data furnished by participants involved, all names and some peripheral facts have been disguised.
(HBS Case No. 9-386-148)

son or daughter began to dawn on him. You know, he seems to have a real need to let a significant adult be aware of his new circumstances. He has an excuse to talk with me since we have scheduled weekly writing conferences of students.

I briefly thought of referring Mike to the counseling or dean of students' offices, but because of previous experiences in which I found them to be of little or no help, I decided to be "Mike's ear."

"Look at the Fish!": Karen Prentiss and Professor Lockwood (B)

Karen Prentiss "felt like giving up—and my husband was the only person to whom I could reveal that kind of weakness. He said, 'What's one grade? You're doing fine in your other courses. I'll support whatever you do, but I know you can handle this course.'" After a "rocky" weekend, Karen decided, "There was no way I was going to back down."

She taught herself to study cases, thinking, *"Look at the fish. Have you seen everything in this fish?"* And she tested each idea she had by "trying it on my study group members or imagining how Lockwood might demolish it." Her grades improved immediately. "We wrote a one-page case analysis every week. I got a check on the second and check plus on all the rest." In class, she "spoke only four or five times, which isn't much for me. But I made sure that my points were concrete and supported with evidence. Lockwood repeated my points and took them to the next person."

Three weeks before the course ended, Karen "was on a team for a videotaped simulation. I played a vice president for sales of a corporation under attack for unethical sales practices. We knew on Tuesday that there would be a mock press conference on Thursday, and that our performances would be discussed in class."

Karen "spent hours thinking about what people might ask and working out very specific answers." On Thursday morning, she "came dressed for my part. Lockwood had us all stand in the center of the room and take questions from the class. I got one question—one that I had prepared for."

Then the simulation team sat down and Lockwood "showed three people's responses." Karen's came last. When it was over, "the class applauded. Lockwood came and stood over me. He put his hand on my desk and asked the class, 'Now, what made that work?' I looked up at him and thought, 'We've come full circle, haven't we?'"

Her final grade in Lockwood's course was an A.

This case was researched, developed, and written by Abby Hansen for the Developing Discussion Leadership Skills and Teaching by the Case Method seminars. It is based on data contributed by the involved participants. All names, places, and some peripheral facts have been disguised.
(HGSE Case No. 12)

Distributed by HBS Publishing Division, Harvard Business School, Boston, MA 02163. Printed in U.S.A.

"Look at the Fish!": Karen Prentiss and Professor Lockwood (C)

Karen Prentiss Reflects on What She Learned from Professor Lockwood

"I learned the crucial role of preparation, especially when you're negotiating with people. And I learned a lot about handling the press—things like how to boil complex thoughts down to one-sentence sound bites. Writing the weekly one-page memos taught me how to formulate a concise analysis of a situation. Not all of this is good—it sacrifices subtlety and feeling. But it does help you deal with people who just want clarity.

"Working under pressure with a study group taught me how important support is to survival. We couldn't have gotten through this course without testing each other's arguments and anticipating ways in which Lockwood might humiliate us in class. There were a few people in the course who didn't join study groups; they had children or time-consuming jobs. They never learned to construct comments to Lockwood's standards. I watched them gradually migrate to the top rows of the class and stop talking.

"I learned how to deal with superiors in a hostile environment—not to present my feelings, but to research and support my ideas. Now, if I have to negotiate with people in authority, I prepare, write things down, and look for evidence to support my views.

"Probably most important, I learned about power, as a female in a male institution. People would say, 'That's a great course. Lockwood's so tough. He's really superior.' I figured out pretty quickly what that meant: he represented the center of power around here, which lies with the older, white, tenured males. Lockwood held virtually all the power in that course. He never gave it up. Sometimes I think about the A he gave me, and I wonder what it cost me. Did I really need to have my idealism and hopefulness crushed in my first semester of graduate school? I wouldn't run a class the way Lockwood did, but I think there's room for his sort of teaching in a university."

This case was developed, researched, and written by Abby Hansen for the Developing Discussion Leadership Skills and Teaching by the Case Method seminars. All data were contributed by involved participants. Names, places, and some peripheral facts have been disguised.
(HGSE Case No. 13)

"How Do You Expect Us to Get This If It Isn't in Your Notes?" (B)

Assistant Professor Mary Ann Demski went on, "Later, I discussed the incident with friends, and we realized that I could have *'thwomped'* Cindy and said, 'Look, your actions are totally inappropriate. Please see me after class.' Or, 'That's your problem. I've told you what to do, now go do it. Don't be lazy.'"

Instead of "thwomping" Cindy, Mary Ann "did exactly what I hadn't wanted to." She "generated five data points, showed the distribution, and showed how the symbols in the equation corresponded to what was going on. When I finished, I looked directly at Cindy and said, 'Is this clear?' She said yes in a very subdued voice."

During the last twenty minutes of her FFT lecture, Mary Ann "could see that I was losing people's attention right and left—heads were lolling; eyes were glazed." Two minutes before the end of class, she turned off the projector and "tried to say something encouraging" to the class:

> "Look, guys, I don't expect you to understand this stuff after one class, or even after reading the materials for the first time. Work with the material. Make up some examples for yourself. Get your hands dirty with it. I know that some of you may be frustrated, like Cindy [she gestured to Cindy], but that's okay. We'll get there."

Then the class was over and the students left quickly. Her teaching assistant, who had been observing Mary Ann's lecture that day, came up to discuss "what had been particularly hard for the students, and what had gone better than last year." While he and Mary Ann were talking, Cindy walked up, "pale and slightly trembling." Cindy said, "Mary Ann, I really didn't appreciate you bringing up my name and mentioning that I was frustrated in front of the whole class. I'm going to be teaching some of these people next semester as their TA."

Mary Ann looked straight at Cindy and said, "I didn't have to tell them that you were frustrated. That was obvious from the way you acted. And *I* didn't appreciate *your* tone. In fact, *I* felt attacked."

Mary Ann shook her head as she remembered Cindy's response: "She didn't apologize. She just said, 'I'm not feeling well; I have a migraine,' and I found myself apologizing to her. 'Cindy, my intention was not to harm you in any way. I understand that you're doing well in this class. The reason I brought up emotion was to let everybody know that it's okay to feel frustrated about not understanding after a class lecture—especially with this material.'"

Cindy left the room and Mary Ann wondered, "What now?"

This case was developed and written by Abby Hansen for the Developing Discussion Leadership Skills seminars. Data were furnished by involved participants. All names and some peripheral facts have been disguised.
(HSPH Case No. 7)

"Trouble in Stat. 1B" (B)

This case was researched and written by Abby Hansen for the Developing Discussion Leadership Skills seminars. The case is based on data contributed by the involved participants; all names, places, and some peripheral facts have been disguised. (HGSE Case No. 14)

Dan Shea's Reply

Dan recalled what happened next.

"I looked at Joan, and she lowered her arm when she realized that I was going to answer her."

"'*Is* it right?' I said. 'I don't know. Marie gave us a formula. I wrote it on the board. Now we have to figure out if it's right. What do you think?'"

Dan frowned, "I wish I'd said, 'Now we have to make it even better,' but I didn't. Joan looked even more upset. Instead of accepting my invitation to work on the formula, she said, with audible emotion, *'That's not fair!'*"

"I looked around the room for someone else to call on, but Joan went on, 'You *have* to tell us if it's right so we'll know whether to put it in our notes.'"

"Her remark astonished me, and my reply may have sounded sarcastic. I said, 'It's not my job to tell you. If I tell you what's right, all you'll learn is how to be in a room with somebody who knows the answer. Nobody will ever hire you to do that. Why would you want me to teach you to do that?'"

Joan didn't answer. But somebody else said, "'Because there's a right and wrong way to do this kind of analysis. We don't see how learning it the wrong way is going to help us know the right way.'"

Dan stopped pacing. He sat down, put his pipe in an ashtray, and continued, "I answered something like, 'There's reason to believe from experience that being told how to do this stuff doesn't equip people to do it. Making what look like guesses and exploring and improving on them is the way people really make mathematical models.'"

"Another student countered, 'There'll be plenty of time to learn to apply this material on the job. Right now we have mid-terms and graded problem sets to turn in.'

"Somebody else chimed in, 'The learning in this class happens in the TAs' review sessions. All you do is mislead us.'"

"About forty students joined in on Joan's side," Dan recalled. "One said, 'We've been subjects in this experiment long enough. It's a failure and we should call a halt to it. Statistics has right and wrong answers. If you don't tell them to us, we can't do anything right.'"

"I said, 'Let's draw a line under this whole conversation. You're taking this course because you'll be in work situations where somebody brings you a messy, real-world problem and you have to get from 'What do these pieces of information tell me' to 'How certain am I?' *with numbers.* That's a skill, like welding."

Dan shook his head, "Those forty students really told me off." He gestured—hands out, parallel, moving in opposite directions. "We were on different tracks. They were talking about 'knowing,' 'right,' and 'wrong,' and I was talking about 'doing' and 'competence.'"

"I had the notion that those forty people were thinking, 'Thank God somebody's finally taking this turkey on,' and 'Why is this teacher so obtuse that he needs us to explain his job to him for twenty minutes?'"

Dan smiled ironically, "The other twenty people in the class remained silent. I had no idea what they were thinking." His smile widened to a grin, "I still wonder why I didn't give them a well-justified punch in the nose for not helping me."

"Trouble in Stat. 1B" (C)

Aftermath

Dan Shea remembered, "In the corridors and around campus, many of the twenty 'abstentions' came up to tell me that they understood and approved of my teaching methods in Stat. 1B. But they also thought that I would probably fail to reform the course.

"At the end of the semester, I got the lowest teaching ratings of my life. On a one to five scale, I may have broken two on the average. I was so injured and angry about the ratings that I didn't read the students' comments. Of course, I didn't feel inclined to take more abuse. But I also thought that I wouldn't respect what students in this environment said—which is different from not respecting the students.

"Later that year there was a petitioned outburst against me to the Dean. The letter was confidential, so I never saw it, but I assume it said I was terrible and was signed by the forty who argued against me in class.

"I want to stress that among those forty people were very smart, inherently capable students—the top group. In retrospect, I have absolutely no sense that I ruined their ability to pass their exams—no feeling that I should have given them tuition refunds and killed myself."

Looking Forward

When the researcher interviewed Dan Shea, he had just accepted a tenured full professorship at a highly prestigious midwestern university. Anticipating his new position, he noted, "I was recruited to teach management, but it turns out that they need me to teach a first-term statistics course to *their* Pre-Career students. I hope I get through it alive!"

This case was researched and written by Abby Hansen for the Developing Discussion Leadership Skills seminars. The case is based on data contributed by the involved participants; all names, places, and some peripheral facts have been disguised. (HGSE Case No. 15)

"Trouble in Stat. 1B" (D)

Dan Shea's Reflections[1]

"The events of this case were a watershed experience for me—epiphanic is the word I often use to describe it. Partly because the students were so uncompromising, I had to think carefully about what their world really looked like to them and why it looked that way, rather than just papering over our differences with a 'negotiated settlement.' Unfortunately, my task was rather complicated and took too long for them to benefit from it, though later students of mine, I think, owe Joan a lot.

"What I realized was that *telling* them stuff was worthless (except in the few cases when someone asked), and that the whole enterprise was a tangled thicket of telling rather than teaching. There was a contract in place—and the students were good at fulfilling it—in which I could tell them stuff and they would *tell* it back to me, in exams, for example. But there seemed no way to get them to *do* anything by telling them. I couldn't *tell* them how the course was supposed to operate, how to be inquisitive and experimental, what the working world was like, how to do mathematical modeling. I couldn't effectively tell them that I was on their side. Nor, for that matter, could Joan **tell** me what I should be doing as a teacher! One learns these things by experience.

"Unfortunately, both their environment and mine were full of signals that communicated a message: what a colleague has called 'I talk, you listen' teaching was the right way to proceed. Fairness also requires me to add this message—that whining and intransigence were useful ways for students to influence the faculty. Everything in their environment—their prior 'math-flavored' course, the problem sets with cookbook tasks, the final examination, what my colleagues seemed to do, the classroom with a blackboard only I could write on, the structure of the textbooks—everything sang one tune.

"It sang the tune in tiny details as well as larger structures: if it's a **final examination**, that must mean statistics is over. But that's just the opposite of what we want; it should be the **beginning** of the students' lives doing analysis on their own! And why do we call them **problem sets** instead of **opportunity sets**? The school's environment sang so loud that I had to reach all the way back to my professional education in architecture, remembering that we had fun in school and still learned to design buildings that didn't fall on people, to find a

This case was researched and written by Abby Hansen for use at the MacDougall Center for Case Development and Teaching Seminar. Names have been disguised. These materials are intended for class discussion rather than to illustrate effective or ineffective administrative practice. The author wishes to thank Carolyn Briggs Style for her technical assistance in this case series.
(HGSE Case No. 16)

[1] This commentary was prepared by Professor Dan Shea some time after the incident described in "Trouble in Stat. 1B" occurred.

context with a different set of signals. What happens in architecture school (and in art school, music school, and on-the-job training of all sorts) is that students are given some fairly demanding task, and then they do it, and then they all talk about what they did. Then they get another, somewhat harder task that raises new issues, and the cycle repeats. We were told some things like where the library was so we could go there when we needed something and which textbook for the structural engineering course had been ordered this year. But practically everything we heard from instructors was either a question ('Why did you give the bedrooms the view of the pond rather than sunlight in the morning?') or an answer to a question one of us posed. What we were told looked like the solution to a problem we knew we had but often turned out to be a new problem to explore.

"I realized finally that my best way to reproduce this atmosphere would be to construct an environment in which the students would realize for themselves some things I knew to be true about mathematical modeling. I also realized that the fundamental responsibility of a teacher is to construct and manage an environment in which the students will figure out what work needs doing and why it's in their interest to do it. When I taught this material the next time, I looked at every potential piece of this environment and asked, 'What would a student think this means?'

"I wound up doing a good imitation of the goddess Kali the many-handed; not much survived this test. But I had little trouble finding devices lying around in the pedagogical storeroom that seemed appropriate. We had a gadget, for example, that would project a computer screen through an overhead projector. It was hard to read, but it enabled me to bring a computer into the classroom and answer questions like, 'What if we left out this variable from the equation?' with 'Well, let's try it and see—but first, what do you expect?'

"I had been letting students grade each other for class participation, counting as much as half the course grade, in management courses for a few years; this seemed to send the right signal about who was supposed to teach whom, especially as the criterion was 'X's contribution to my learning in this course,' not 'X's success at showing me **his** command of the material.' Problem sets could be open-ended and challenging opportunities to make new models in real contexts rather than cookbook exercises testing recall.

"I still haven't got it all right, and I'm not seduced by my teaching evaluations from students, which are stellar lately (probably too high; I suspect I'm not taking enough chances with each year's course design). One more thing I learned was that excellence is a process and not a perfect score. I'm much less afraid of one piece or another of a course failing, just as I hope the students aren't focused on 'making no mistakes' on their problem sets. I've discovered that displaying a willingness to take chances in the expectation of continued progress is recognized by students and reciprocated. Indeed, teaching as though I don't know everything, especially as though I don't know everything about how to teach, is (when I can remember to do it!) the most effective insurance against the mutual infantilization that afflicted Stat. 1B.

"I suppose my principal insight resulting from the case experience is the realization that 'practice what you preach' is a positive rather than a normative proverb. The point is not that you **should** do what you teach; it's that you **will**, willy-nilly, teach what you do. Taking into account my unfulfilled responsibility for the whole course environment, I now believe that Joan and her gang were trying to show me that I was teaching something very different from what I was saying or hoping, and that I had a lot of implementation work to do. And they were right."

The Case of the Dethroned Section Leader (B)

Bea Benedict remembered how she dealt with the "revolution" that Jack Kesselman had instigated, and describes it in her own words.

Bea's Description of the "Revolution"

I stood at the board and said: "Hands up, those who want to have no leader."

Jack and Skip raised their hands. Then four other hands went up. Finally, Elke's and Cliff's did, too. I surveyed the democratic assembly that had just ousted me, put the chalk back on the ledge under the board, and sat down.

"Okay, Section," I said, looking at no one in particular. "Discuss."

Jack began to talk about the passage, mainly in terms of personal likes and dislikes. He used phrases like "I think it's phoney of Richard to say so and so," and "If he were somebody I knew, I wouldn't like him."

The other students didn't seem terribly interested in Jack's personal reactions, nor did he offer any analytical statements for them either to agree with or dispute. Discussion was, therefore, desultory and unfocused. Jack dominated, but a few other people did speak. I said nothing.

After the hour was over, Cliff and Elke remained to talk with me. They were both very embarrassed, and Elke expressed chagrin that Jack would now be running things. They saw him as their new de facto section leader, and they were annoyed to be paying for a college education only to be listening to a fellow undergraduate. I was unprofessional enough to admit my anger at Jack, but I did say that I felt I had been fairly and squarely voted out of authority. Only a new vote could restore our former organization. Elke said she would call for a new vote at the next meeting. I suggested that she leave things alone for a while and see how the discussion took shape when all the students had had a week to prepare.

The next week's discussion was as formless as the first had been. I sat in the seat farthest from the chalkboard—no one sat in the "teacher's seat" I had previously occupied, I noted—and I recall feeling a bit smug at the disarray I witnessed. There was a good deal of vagueness, and some uncomfortable dead silences when no one seemed to know what to say. I thought: maybe I did talk too much as a discussion leader, but at least I gave them substance, and I didn't leave any holes in the discussion.

At the next meeting—the second after the "revolution"—Elke called for a new vote. I left the room while the group voted. They didn't tell me by what

---

This case was written by Abby Hansen for the Developing Discussion Leadership Skills and Teaching by the Case Method seminars. Data were furnished by the involved participants. All names and some peripheral facts have been disguised. (HBS Case No. 9-382-178)

margin, but I was asked to return and lead the group. I confess I had been expecting this, so I had prepared a series of passages for discussion. I really think the students were relieved to have me back. Before getting the new discussion under way, I gave a little informal speech in which I apologized for having monopolized the discussion and asked them to let me know when I talked too much. (Skip took that seriously and actually interrupted me later when I began to lecture instead of discuss—a habit I've always had, and one that my hours of private research had aggravated. Shakespeare was my favorite subject at the time, and I felt like a tightly corked bottle of Elizabethan lore and theories about the plays—always ready to explode and overflow.)

The rest of the semester went on quite satisfactorily. I had feared that Jack might turn sullen and be a problem in the section, but he behaved quite amiably and settled down to participate. I went out of my way to deal with him fairly—his final grade was a B+, and frankly, I treated him more charitably than he deserved in order to avoid any suspicion that I might be retaliating against him. It's probably petty of me, but to this day, I still remember him with dislike.

"A Question of Cookies" (B)

How Allen Hall Responded

Allen mentally "sifted through the implications of Mary Kay's very personal revelation. I could see that my giving out cookies was preventing her from learning in this class. Moreover, I teach about the educator's responsibility to make reasonable accommodations for people with disabilities and had actually *drafted* some regulations on the subject for the Illinois Department of Education. My strong inclination was to make some accommodation for her. I decided to get more information."

Allen said, "How exactly are the cookies a problem?"

"Well, it's hard to watch other people eat them. I want to partake of everything you have to offer the class, so it's painful not to be able to take something that is being given."

"Do you have any idea what we could do here that would make it easier for you?"

"I don't know."

"If I continue to bring cookies, could you sit in the front row with your back to the class while people eat?"

She looked dubious.

"What if I start class on the stroke of 4, give out the cookies immediately, and you arrive a few minutes late?"

"That might be okay."

Allen told the researcher, "We agreed to try it, and she left. Then I started worrying about how to convey the idea, without actually saying so, that I wanted people to stuff those cookies down pronto before Mary Kay came in."

At the Next Class Meeting

Mary Kay arrived at 4:04, with a plastic container of salad. Allen recalled, "Before she came in, I think I must have moved *so* quickly—ripping the bags open, practically throwing cookies at people—that people got the idea that I wanted them to eat fast. Most had finished their cookies before she got there."

For the next few classes, Allen kept hustling the group through the cookie-eating. Mary Kay kept bringing salad, but Allen noticed that she had stopped arriving late. He wondered why.

This case was researched and written by Abby Hansen for the Developing Discussion Leadership Skills and Teaching by the Case Method seminars. The case is based on data contributed by the involved participants; all names, places, and some peripheral facts have been disguised.
(HGSE Case No. 17)

"A Question of Cookies" (C)

This case was researched and written by Abby Hansen for the Developing Discussion Leadership Skills and Teaching by the Case Method seminars. The case is based on data contributed by the involved participants; all names, places, and some peripheral facts have been disguised.
(HGSE Case No. 18)

A Few Weeks Later

Mary Kay continued to arrive on time, with her salad. When Allen ran into her in the library a few weeks later, he said, "Mary Kay! What happened? I've noticed that you're coming to class while people are still eating cookies."

"I felt better after talking with you," she said.

How the Rest of the Semester Went

Allen recalled, "Mary Kay continued to sit by herself in the back row. Her participation still focused on details, and people continued to titter nervously when she asked naive questions, but I really think there were fewer of these. When the class met in informal study groups for the mid-term, I saw Mary Kay at a couple of group meetings in the library. One of these included the woman who had hosted the potluck supper, and I later got the impression that she had adopted Mary Kay in this course. At any rate, Mary Kay found some sort of acceptance. Her written work, although never 'outstanding' or even 'very good,' was certainly in the ballpark."

Allen had a few further meetings with Mary Kay: "She came to my office two or three more times to talk—about job problems, whether she should look for a new job, whether she should perhaps think about law school. I confess I didn't encourage her."

Allen never asked if Mary Kay were seeing a doctor. "She didn't seem desperate. I had no sense of a great unmet need to unburden herself. I assumed she must have already gotten therapy. She seemed to be dealing with it effectively, and she seemed to know how to take care of herself. When she had been afraid to approach me about those cookies, she had gotten the Dean's office to act on her behalf."

A Student's Comment

Allen recalled, "During the summer after the course, I had lunch with Janetta DeForrest. She asked if I wanted to know what the high point of the semester had been for her. Of course I told her that I'd love to know. Janetta said, 'That you never gave up on Mary Kay.'

"Until that moment I hadn't considered my inclusion of Mary Kay in the class discussions as a high point for Janetta or anyone else in the course. On the contrary, I had supposed that most people were annoyed and impatient with Mary Kay—and with me for giving her so much attention."

Allen commented, "When Janetta said that, I got chills. I still do now as I recall it."

George Perkins (B)

Lynn Novak's Reflections on Her Encounter with George Perkins

In my view, there were a number of issues involved in this situation. There are some problems peculiar to being a female instructor in a largely male field, as I was when I taught this Statistics course, but, in retrospect, I think that probably the biggest mistake that I made was to change the "rules of the game" without warning George Perkins. Although I had asked for class participation before, when it had not been forthcoming I had simply proceeded to answer my own question or solve the problem myself. This time I called on George by name.

I now see that as a violation of my implicit "psychological contract" with the class, and it seems understandable that George felt that I wasn't playing fair. He refused to accept my new rules, which I did not realize I had either promulgated or changed. The lesson of this, in retrospect, is that one must clearly understand the explicit rules that one establishes as well as the implicit rules that become accepted by the very nature of one's behavior in the classroom. I was obviously not aware of either and therefore was not sensitive to the fact that I violated those rules by calling on someone who had not volunteered.

Second, I was completely insensitive to the signals that George was sending to me concerning his general insecurity and his apprehension regarding the statistics course in particular. His visits every week were primarily requests for reassurance rather than indications of interest. His selection of a seat very close to the instructor's desk made it easy for him to ask questions regarding the solution of problems without having to get up and walk to the front—in other words, he could obtain all the help he needed (substantively and emotionally) without having to signal to the rest of the class that he needed help. His lack of interaction with the rest of the class and the formal tone of his relation to me should have indicated that he had some problems in his social relationships. However, I consistently misread those signs and therefore blundered into the horrendous situation that I encountered.

Tamara Gilman wrote this case under the supervision of C. Roland Christensen with assistance from Abby Hansen from data supplied by involved participants for the Developing Discussion Leadership Skills seminars. All names and some peripheral facts have been disguised.
(HBS Case No. 9-394-070)

George Perkins (C)

Tamara Gilman wrote this case under the supervision of C. Roland Christensen with assistance from Abby Hansen from data supplied by involved participants for the Developing Discussion Leadership Skills seminars. All names and some peripheral facts have been disguised.

(HBS Case No. 9-394-080)

Lynn Novak Continues Her Reflections

This situation was further compounded by the fact that I was the only female instructor in the course. In retrospect, I recognize that I projected two clear and distinct images in addition to the "neutral" role of instructor.

The first image was that of the helpless "girl" who encountered all those intimidating athletes and who, I'm sure, could not engender respect (and even if I could have, I'm pretty sure they wouldn't have given it). I'm not sure how much of this reaction can be attributed to my own behavior and how much to theirs, but after reflection I am convinced that this is an ever-present problem that a woman instructor faces and a man never does.

My sheer lack of "presence"—in terms of size, voice, and power—was one aspect. And the fact that men students hesitate to attribute competence to a woman, especially in a quantitative course, was another. And the socialization process for women, which emphasizes lack of aggression or assertiveness for women, played a very large part in this situation. For instance, when I realized I was in the middle of a conspiracy that first day, my instinctive reaction was to smile, cajole, and entreat the men to do the work and quit harassing me. That was a typical female-role reaction, and one that I would call totally inappropriate to developing respect and control in a classroom.

Perhaps the image of the woman professional has changed now, but I would guess that if a woman were to walk into a predominantly male classroom even now, she would still have to do much more than her male counterpart to establish the same atmosphere of respect. I know that personally I am now much more aware of my most elementary behavior patterns (i.e., smiling) in order to be certain that I don't unconsciously communicate something that I don't mean to, or project something that a male student body could misinterpret coming from a female instructor.

Second, in the encounter with George, a diametrically different role emerged: that of the maternal comfort-and-security figure. While this role probably continues to emerge in a minority of cases, it indicates the diversity of interpretations and perceptions that can occur and that are significantly different for women. This role is probably less damaging to the classroom situation than the role of cajoler or seeker of approval, but it, too, has the potential to trigger open hostility if the student perceives himself as betrayed (witness George's violent and disruptive behavior). I think that there must be a fine line between being perceived as merely supportive and a security figure, but when these events happened, I did not have any idea of how to establish that line. As a professor, with years of experience, I now find it easier.

Ernie Budding (C)

After delivering his speech of reprimand, Ernie expected to see a distinct improvement in Section I's preparation and participation. The initial results, however, were quite different.

"The Salinas Walnut Company" Case

The next case that was discussed in MM dealt with the Salinas Walnut Company. On that day, several women newly admitted to the next year's MBA program came to visit. Here is Ernie's recollection:

I listened as Cindy Eakens introduced the visitors, and the section applauded as usual. Then a student introduced his fiancée, whom he had previously introduced as his girlfriend. The section made jokes. I went along with the spirit of things and told the newly admitted women, "We always try to waste the first ten minutes of class if humanly possible." Then I gave the usual introductory sort of stuff and went to Mandy Farmer, who'd had some trouble with participation in the second semester, although her first semester work had been excellent. I had included her in a group of students to whom I'd written notes because their second semester participation was off. The notes were merely invitations to come talk to me if there was a particular problem, but I think some students must have seen the notes in people's mailboxes, recognized my handwriting, and figured there must be something gruesome inside. Gossip, I gather, was wild.

Mandy said, "Ernie, I'd rather pass on this one."

Frankly, I was shocked. The Salinas Walnut case *is* a very confusing one—I hadn't liked it myself when I prepared it, and I'd even suggested to the other MM teachers that we drop it in coming years—but I hadn't expected a student simply to refuse to open the case. I had told the section from the first that if they couldn't prepare for a case for some personal or medical reason, all they had to do was tell me beforehand and I wouldn't call on them. That policy had worked well first semester, making "passes" virtually nonexistent, but it obviously wasn't working here.

I said, "Okay," and called on Barry Caslan—a guy who had performed very well. I could tell people were tense.

Barry said, "Ernie, I'm not prepared either. I pass."

The atmosphere in the classroom got even worse. "Okay," I said again, and turned to another student. "Michael?"

I really think Michael would have liked to pass, too, but things were really very uncomfortable by

This case was written by Abby Hansen in collaboration with C. Roland Christensen for the Developing Discussion Leadership Skills seminars. While the case is based on data supplied by participants involved, all names and some peripheral facts have been disguised.
(HBS Case No. 9-381-040)

that time. He started the case, but when I said, "Let's have some analysis," he couldn't do it. Clearly, nobody had understood the case. People were getting more and more tense. Finally, I put the company's options on the board and said, "Now how would you compare these things financially?" People had read the charts in the case, but they hadn't realized that you had to subtract one column of figures from another to do the analysis.

You had to grasp the difference between average cost—the average of all units—and marginal cost—the cost of each additional unit. Absolutely nobody got it, although we had discussed this concept in the Pennsylvania General Steel case, and I thought they'd also done it in Finance. Finally—it was like pulling teeth—I said, "Well, who remembers the Penn Steel case?" They slapped their heads and yelled, "Marginal cost."

"What kind of calculation was that?" I said, and continued to put figures on the board. But the calculations gave them real trouble. It was a pretty awful experience.

Also, I recall being pretty annoyed—saying to myself that after all I said in my speech about not being prepared, should I show them how the numbers go?

That day I tightened the reins and kept them tight. I actually remember forcing some calculations. I took it as a calculation case even though there were a number of important qualitative issues. One certainly could have discussed the case without figures, but given my speech, I was unwilling to accept that approach.

Afterward, a student apologized to the newly admitted women who had visited, saying that the section had had a major paper due in Corporate Strategy that day, and two other big cases as well. Added to this, the complexity of the Salinas Walnut case itself had produced a truly miserable showing. I had become very directive, after having tried quite consciously to hold back, and I had dragged the material out of the students. Even worse, I'm afraid, I didn't conceal my irritation.

A Student's View of the Salinas Walnut Case

Arlene Allen, the educational representative of Section I, also discussed the Salinas Walnut case with the researcher. Here is her account:

I think it's just a poorly written case. It's about cogeneration—energy from crushed walnut shells. I actually know the professor and research associate who wrote it, and they didn't know what they were doing. It's a screwball case. Ernie cold-called a student who passed without excuse, and then another student passed. Ernie was obviously furious. He raced around the classroom as he talked, going at really high speed. The third guy he called on didn't want to start the case either. It was just a bum case. No opening could have been good. But I think the third guy saw how upset Ernie was and realized he'd better go ahead and say something. When Ernie started to write on the board, he was so furious he broke the chalk. The class got really uptight, partly because of his anger, and partly because nobody understood the numbers in the case.

After this episode, I spoke with quite a few members of the section and they were saying, "Ernie's going to kill us." "He's working us too hard." "We're really sick of the cold-calling." Yes, there was a certain amount of sloppiness in our classwork at this point, but that's just life at Bay. People are people. They have to relax sometimes. Ernie didn't relax, though, and he didn't want us to, either. But I have to mention that people still liked him at this point. The problem with our relationship with him was that at first, at the beginning of the year, we just loved being told how things went. By the middle of the second semester, though, we all felt calmer, more confident about casework. We didn't want to be led anymore, but he was still leading. It seemed as if we were all on a forced march. [As the section's elected representative] I decided I'd better go and have a talk with Ernie on behalf of the section, to present their views.

Ernie Recounts the Ed Rep's Visit

Arlene said to me, "Your speech, coupled with the section's poor job on the Salinas Walnut case, has created an enormous amount of tension in the classroom. The section is tired after months of classes, and they're neither willing nor able to prepare each and every case completely."

"Standards have to be maintained," I replied.

"But not everyone has your standards. And not everyone wants to do this sort of analysis."

"I think my standards are high, but not unreasonable."

"It is unreasonable to expect students to be able to lay out every MM case in detail. MM is just one of many courses, and your demands—and your speech—put everyone on edge."

As I listened to her, I realized that removing the section's tensions had to be my first priority. I explained that laying out a case was necessary for every student to do because it meant producing an organized and systematic approach to the whole problem. But I agreed to step back further. I would still ask probing questions, but I would channel the discussion less and relinquish my habit of going through the blocks of analysis in order. I also agreed, as an experiment, to stop the cold calls and take volunteers.

Ernie Describes the Rest of the Semester

It seemed to me that the semester turned out quite well once the section's anxieties had been allayed.

I began the first class (after my talk with the educational representative) with a speech in which I announced a new, relaxed approach, and called for volunteers. There was silence at first, and I was afraid that no one would open the case, but finally, Arlene raised her hand. After her opening, the case went smoothly.

I think the whole course ended very well. The buzzwords didn't disappear, but they were bolstered by explanations. The level of analysis remained high. My student evaluations were almost uniformly good, and the students thought that my change at the end was distinctly for the better. Giving up cold calls seems to have gone all right. I don't know if I lost rigor. Maybe it's a trade-off; how much do you buy by going through a logical structure—A, B, C, D—versus letting it come out A, D, E, C, B? Maybe it's all right as long as all the pieces are there.

But I'm still not certain that stepping back was really justified. Given that I'd begun to get negative feedback for the first time in the second semester, and that I'd noticed a change in the section and observed different successful teaching styles, I was willing to try to be less directive than formerly. But I'm still not sure it's justified educationally, because the subject matter of MM is largely technical though there are important qualitative elements. All this requires careful attention to details, some of which may be overlooked without prodding from the instructor. I also thought—and several students agreed with this—that it was a bit self-serving for them to ask for less direction. They could, frankly, get away with a certain degree of sloppiness.

Ernie Budding (D)

In conversations with the researcher, Ernie Budding reflected on teaching in general, and at Bay in particular. His comments focused on a few central issues: the way an instructor establishes an implicit contract with students; the degree to which it is possible to run a class without intimidation by either the students or the teacher; and the very nature of the Bay MBA program with its enforced grading curve and attendant tensions that lead groups of students to play practical jokes on teachers. The following are extracts from Ernie's statements.

Ernie Describes Contract with Students

For me, the way one establishes a contract with the class is an unresolved issue. Many Bay instructors keep the contract implicit, establishing it subtly, without articulation. For example, I think the pranks my section played on me may have been somewhat restrained.

I made it clear that I'd never treat the students with bad taste and that I expected the same treatment. I tried to keep contracts like that implicit. Similarly, I didn't think I had to say, "Look, I'll prepare for class and so will you." But now I'm not so sure. The students sometimes seemed surprised when I kept my word. Early in the term, for example, I said, "I'll sacrifice quantity in comments for quality any day," and that's exactly how I graded. Some of the students in Section I were gifted orators, but others who clearly thought better did better in my class. Some students said, "Everybody said they'll grade that way, but you're the only one who actually does it." That surprised me.

The matter of the contract—how you establish it, how you observe it—is still an open question.

Intimidation

The issue of intimidation—whether a teacher is intimidated by aggressive students or the other way around—comes up often in discussions of problems that teachers have with their classes. In Ernie Budding's case, his directive teaching style tended to intimidate some students. Here is Ernie's own report:

One very good student of mine told me, "I'm not quite comfortable in your class because I have to think more there than anywhere else." I was frankly delighted about that, but if I had thought his remark contained overtones of intimidation, I would have been upset. Some students did tell me late in the year that I had intimidated them at first. That bothers me, and it's something I'd like very much

---

This case was written by Abby Hansen in collaboration with C. Roland Christensen for the Developing Discussion Leadership Skills seminars. While the case is based on data supplied by participants involved, all names and some peripheral facts have been disguised.
(HBS Case No. 9-381-041)

to change. I still wonder how you let people down easily when they're egregiously wrong. One on one, in private conference, I don't have any trouble because I can point out strengths along with weaknesses. But in the classroom it's harder. Some teachers think you shouldn't correct students' errors because they get out of a case only what they bring to it. I disagree. I think you should at least give signposts. But I may have been too obvious.

One thing some people around here don't seem to realize is that teaching is just another form of human relations—a unique function, with an authority figure interacting with 80 or 90 people at once. I assumed the students would like me because I'm a nice guy, and I also assumed that my very extensive preparation and academic background would preclude any authority problems in the classroom. It simply never occurred to me to be intimidated by my students. For me, a balance of respect is the most desirable situation.

Teaching Style

Much of Ernie's friction with the section in the second semester seemed to stem from his directive teaching style, and his own consideration of that style was far from finished when he discussed this case with the researcher. In Ernie's own words:

On reflection, I still think my approach was basically sound, at least for first semester, when everyone was on edge and students didn't know how to analyze cases. I do have reservations, though, about the way I made the speech or reprimand second semester. I'm afraid it came across as a bit harsh. But how should one deliver a classwide criticism? Is it part of a teacher's job sometimes to be a big bad wolf? Maybe unpleasantness isn't totally bad. The Salinas Walnut case, for example, was one of the starkest teaching moments of the year. Nobody forgot how to do that sort of analysis. It was a miserable experience but it made its point, and they all really learned marginal versus average cost.

Nevertheless, I think I'll do things differently next year. I'll vary my teaching style from class to class, and try to leave students with questions rather than neat summaries. But I don't want to give up cold calls entirely. I think I'll start with them and announce that I'll switch openings sometime in the future. Cold calls do give me the opportunity to match students with cases. Also, I'll not always channel discussions from A to B; I'll let them flow more naturally. I'm going to step back more. After all, the major advantage of the case method is that it can be used as a springboard into the unknown. In the future, I'll exploit the opportunities for more creative discussions when they may arise.

Basically, though, the matter of teaching style doesn't really worry me very much. First semester, in fact, I proceeded alone. Consciously, I didn't even attend teaching meetings, because in the first few I attended someone would invariably say, "This is the way you teach this case." My personal feeling is that you have to go with your own style. I deliberately removed myself from the meetings in order to develop and become comfortable with my own way of behaving in the classroom. I attended meetings only in the second semester, when I had already developed a style of my own. The meetings were looser, too, and I found that I could use what was said within my own framework. Now I can pick and choose from others' styles.

I think part of the reason I don't agonize about style is that I'm just not self-conscious. I may think about a certain technique in advance, but when I go into the classroom, I'm myself. Some teachers whom I know socially become different people when they step in front of a classroom, but I'm always me. I want the students to learn from me, and I don't believe in mystifying them. One teacher told me, "Never tip your hand. Never tell them what's coming next or what's going on. Hide the information." That's ridiculous. I just don't play those games.

In fact, that leads to another problem I have with the case method. Around here you're so firmly told "Hands off" that you don't always recognize when you really should say, "Look, this is the way the numbers go. I'll put them up and then we'll discuss them."

I realize that the section was more comfortable when I just let the discussion drift, but I still wonder if that was rigorous. In the first semester I thought logical build-up was paramount. In the second, I partly changed my view. In the future, I'll vary the two approaches. But one of the best students in Section I did tell me that he thought lower pressure meant lower quality in general.

I do think I erred first semester in equating my understanding of a case with the level of insight that students should take from a discussion. Given the differing amounts of time available for preparation, that's simply unreasonable. Also, in terms of style, I think I may have created an impression that I didn't mean to—of being more calculating than I am. The business of tossing my notes onto the desk and then not looking at them created a stagey impression that I never intended. I don't like the pretense of infallibility. After all, I spent upwards of 20 hours on some of those cases, and I always reviewed right up until the moment I started teaching. That's why I knew the stuff backward and forward. I think that was one source of some of the intimidation some students felt.

Also, I may have overemphasized terseness and made the mistake of trying to squeeze too much information into the class session. I tried to get, say, eight to ten points with no chaff. Maybe I should have allowed four or five points and some chaff. But still, I mentioned to a student once that I'd like to believe that they were in this for the material and because they enjoyed learning. That's what we did when I was in grad school. Here, I'm aware that some percentage of students simply want to have Bay and the initials MBA after their names. That's an unresolved conflict.

Mainly, I'll try to relax without sacrificing rigor, which is still my main concern. But I won't make the mistake of thinking that every tiny detail of a case is crucial. I think I pushed to make some points that probably could have been dispensed with.

Ernie Describes Climate of the School

I think that the forced-screen system—which mandates that a certain percentage of every section must be graded Low Pass in a course—is almost entirely dysfunctional. It creates a pressurized climate that makes the MBA process two very unhealthy years for the students. It seems to use only negative reinforcement, while psychological research has shown that positive reinforcement is far more effective. Nor do I think the grading system is fair. I had to scrape out several Low Passes in my course when those students clearly would have done all right in any other system.

Ernie's View of Pranks

By and large my section's pranks were harmless, I thought, although I have heard of other teachers who have had pretty rough stunts pulled on them. Some stunts, however, were in poorer taste than others, and I did my best to discourage them. In one MM class, for example, we had a case in which an executive had committed suicide. On the day of the case I came in to find a dummy hanging there with "The John J. Jones Memorial Method of Solving Management Problems" written on it. I took it down and said that just wasn't appropriate behavior for this school.

Some other pranks were actually rather charming. On Halloween I heard a rattling behind the chalkboard (which can be raised and lowered electronically). I raised it, and there stood Al Carpenter wearing a Groucho Marx mask. I stared at him for a second and turned back to the class—who had all put on Groucho Marx masks! One student had brought a camera to snap my reaction. The photographs are pretty funny.

The pranks students play are just one indication of the level of tension here. I think I was pretty reasonably treated by my section, but, as I've said, I've heard of other pranks that were a good deal rougher. Those often showed real insensitivity to other people's feelings.

The Offended Colonel (B)

As Ben Cheever scanned the classroom at the Commanding Officers' Senior Executive Institute, he read outrage in only the colonel's expression. But, on the other hand, none of the other participants had leaped to his rescue. It occurred to him to ask the woman her opinion. Her face certainly conveyed no anger to Ben, and he was skeptical of the colonel's accuracy in speaking on her behalf. But Ben realized that she might not want to embarrass her colleague; his predicament might worsen.

Ben considered his colloquial style merely casual and the profanity it often included well within "normal bounds." Never, since he had first begun teaching as a graduate student, had anyone called his language offensive. Part of him was tempted to retort, "Hey, fellow, are you really serious? I learned this language from a Marine!" But he didn't want to insult a workshop participant. Nonetheless, he thought that apologizing might imply intimidation or shame on his part—neither of which he felt. Besides, apologizing might damage his dignity and lessen the group's respect.

The colonel's expression and stance clearly showed that he was expecting the apology he had demanded.

"Look, it would be hypocritical of me to say I'm sorry," Ben told him. "So I won't. This is the way I talk. I'm just being myself, and that's it."

The colonel stiffened. "If that's the case, well, I don't feel I care to stay." He began to make his way out of the row of seats. Another officer, also in uniform, arose and accompanied him from the room. No one else left, nor did anyone say anything.

After their exit, Ben continued the discussion, making no further reference to the exchange. Among those who came to speak with him directly after the session, the woman in question appeared to say that she certainly had not been offended by his language and had, furthermore, enjoyed the case discussion enormously. After the lunch break, several others apologized to Ben for the colonel's hostile remarks and mentioned that he happened to be a "born-again Christian." Ben left the institute feeling that on the whole he'd handled this situation appropriately.

This case was written by Abby Hansen for the Developing Discussion Leadership Skills and Teaching by the Case Method seminars. Data were furnished by the involved participants. All names and some peripheral facts have been disguised. (HBS Case No. 9-383-062)

Distributed by HBS Publishing Division, Harvard Business School, Boston, MA 02163. Printed in U.S.A.

Assistant Professor Graham and Ms. Macomber (B)

"Well, well." Professor Graham's words rang in Janet Macomber's ears.

She slumped back in her chair, feeling like a defendant released from hostile cross-examination. The ordeal was over but the verdict was still out. Janet had been disturbed that the class discussion had followed such a different track than her own analysis. It had taken all the courage she could muster to suggest the class was wrong and assert her own point of view.

Janet listened carefully to Professor Graham's closing remarks. To her dismay, he said nothing to indicate her approach had been right—or wrong. Was it possible that she had been completely off base? Had she made a fool of herself in front of the whole section?

Class was dismissed, and in the minutes before the next class began, Janet was surrounded by her sectionmates. Their comments ranged from good natured teasing to open incredulity:

"You didn't really. . . . How long did it. . . . Hundreds of numbers. . . . Let me see. . . ." The capstone comment came from Peter Anderson, an already popular figure who usually sat with a group of cohorts in the middle of the right-hand bank of seats. "Janet, you really did it this time," he said, laughing. "We [indicating his colleagues] are going to call your achievement THE MACOMBER MEMORIAL MATRIX!"

Janet made a humorous reply, but inwardly she despaired. "Just what I don't need," she thought. "In the second week of school, to be typecast as a number-cruncher! I should be more careful in the future about sticking my neck out when I talk in class." She made a silent resolution: this won't happen again.

This case was written by a member of the Developing Discussion Leadership Skills Seminar under the supervision of C. Roland Christensen. While the case is based on data supplied by participants involved, all names and some peripheral facts have been disguised.
(HBS Case No. 9-379-021)

Assistant Professor Graham and Ms. Macomber (C)

In the fifth week of the term, Professor Graham was going over his student class cards for first-year QAOM, tabulating notes on individual class participation. On the whole, the section's case discussions were shaping up pretty well. Individually and collectively, the class had come a long way in five weeks. Charles grinned: he supposed that, if surveyed, the class would say the same of him.

Halfway through the pile, Charles stopped at Janet Macomber's card. What, he wondered, is going on there?

In the first weeks of the term, Charles had marked Janet down as very promising. She had come to each class prepared and had participated eagerly in the discussions. Her comments had been intelligent, succinct, and to the point. And on that one occasion (Charles remembered with pleasure), Janet had performed an analytic *tour de force,* smashing the case wide open in the last minutes of the class.

Charles now counted the case as a watershed in the section's development. He remembered the first hour and ten minutes of that class as everything a case discussion should not be: floundering, disjointed, indecisive, and entirely irrelevant to the company's problems. Since that day, slowly but with increasing confidence, the section was pulling itself together and becoming (on good days) a working forum.

Janet Macomber's behavior was in abrupt contrast to that of the rest of the class. Charles could not fix exactly when the change had taken place, but Janet had become silent, ceasing to take part voluntarily in case discussions. She had begun arriving late to class (QAOM had been meeting after lunch); she no longer took her characteristic back row seat, but changed her position almost every day—to the point that Charles could not be sure of how many classes she was attending. When Charles had seen her, she had generally seemed sleepy (or bored) and quite evidently had been barely following the discussion. Charles had refrained from calling on Janet unexpectedly on these occasions; he had a strong presupposition she would be unprepared and felt disinclined to embarrass her. Such tacit benevolence ought not continue, however.

"After such an auspicious start," thought Professor Graham, "what can be causing Janet to act this way? And what—if anything—do I do about it?"

This case was written by a member of the Developing Discussion Leadership Skills Seminar under the supervision of C. Roland Christensen. While the case is based on data supplied by participants involved, all names and some peripheral facts have been disguised.
(HBS Case No. 9-379-022)

Distributed by HBS Publishing Division, Harvard Business School, Boston, MA 02163.
Printed in U.S.A.

Bill Jones (B)

Bill Jones looked at Paige Palmer, who was trying to speak, and then at Fred Wilkens. He realized that Paige Palmer had not meant to say what she had. He walked directly to Fred Wilkens and put his hand on his arm and looked straight at him:

> Fred, I know you're hurt and you're probably angry, but she didn't mean to hurt you and she didn't mean to say that. You can't even know how badly she feels right now that she said that. She's probably never felt worse in her life.

Bill turned and looked at Paige, who was flushed and clearly on the verge of tears. Fred turned and looked at her also and simply nodded his head slowly at Bill Jones.

Bill then immediately called on another student to continue class discussion.

This case was written by a member of the Teaching by the Case Method Seminar under the supervision of C. Roland Christensen. While the case is based on data supplied by Bill Jones, all names and some peripheral facts have been disguised. (HBS Case No. 9-378-039)

Bound Feet (B)

"Meryl, this is an extremely important issue, but I don't feel that we're getting at it well this way. If we don't look at a specific passage, or discuss it in its wider historical context, I don't know if we're doing it justice. . . ." Lisa spoke softly but forcefully, hoping to calm the emotions that gripped the classroom. Meryl sighed, rested her head on one hand, and motioned with the other for the group to go ahead.

Mark Stevens, the punk-rock Lutheran minister, gingerly picked up another thread. "Anyway, I was wondering what kind of gods they were, that they got *last* place in the hierarchy."

Somehow the discussion moved on. After a few minutes, almost everyone joined in, most with relief in their voices. By the end of the hour, even Meryl and Ian had taken the same point of view about a question that someone else had raised.

Meryl, Lisa, Ian, Marie-Therese, and several other students stayed for almost half an hour after class discussing oppressive cultures in somewhat calmer tones. Lisa tried to express her conviction that, while the classroom is nothing without emotions, an academic also has a responsibility to develop a firm intellectual grasp of the material—the better to refute it if emotions so require. Meryl, for her part, warned Lisa that she could be coopted in a traditionally male institution, but the group parted on a note of mutual respect.

Meryl also handed in her second written assignment before she left. A cursory first reading that evening showed Lisa that her problems with Meryl were not yet over. The paper—although cogent, creative, and very well written—was really a more articulate repeat of Meryl's outburst in class. Lisa felt that if she assigned a poor grade that reflected the paper's failings, there would be no reconciliation. Meryl would be lost in her anger, never to be brought back to the intellectual work of the class. Yet somehow, Lisa wanted to impress upon Meryl the importance of showing fully she had understood the text, grounding the passion of her feelings on a solid academic foundation. Whatever choice she made, Lisa knew that she would have to face some strong reactions from Meryl.

While thinking about Meryl, Lisa could not help but also think of her own situation. Her last efforts at a thesis proposal had not been received enthusiastically by what she considered to be an overly cautious faculty in the orthodox religion department. They favored a historical or narrowly philogical dissertation when it came to Islamic materials. Lisa disagreed. She was hurt and angry at their apathy for a wider ranging study of the second Islamic caliph, whose name was Omar. In her judgment, Islamic historical and philogical study had not yet illuminated his seminal

---

Colleen Caftan prepared this case under the supervision of Louis B. Barnes and C. Roland Christensen for the Developing Discussion Leadership Skills and Teaching the Case Method seminars. While the case is based on data furnished by participants involved, all names and some perceptual facts have been disguised.
(HBS Case No. 9-491-029)

role as a second founder figure in the religion. Lisa was convinced that a study of the Koran and other religious texts as "literature" would yield patterns and archetypes that could be studied fruitfully from a philosophical or sociological perspective. She had indirectly received some encouragement from two Islamic scholars, one in Israel, the other at the Sorbonne in France. However, there was no such encouragement at home.

Consequently, although Lisa loved her teaching and work with students, she had almost decided that the academic life was not for her. She was considering dropping out of the doctoral program and moving toward another interest by applying to a film school in California. As she said to the case writer, "I'm not sure which is better. Meryl's anger at the system gets expressed outwards. I just turn my anger on myself."

The Puzzling Student (B)

Mark's Response

I had had enough; it had gone on too long: "I'm sorry, Cecelia. I *have* to phone a grade into the Registrar's Office *today*."

There was a brief silence on the other end of the line. Then Cecelia explained that she understood my position; obviously she was worried.

Later that morning I calculated what work she had completed: her mid-term and final exams and her mid-term paper. She received an "F" for participation and an "F" for her final research paper. She ended up with a C−, and I called the grade into the Registrar's Office.

To this day, however, I have neither seen nor heard of Cecelia. I doubt seriously if she is back at Kensington this term. She will always remain an enigma for me.

This case was prepared by Marina McCarthy under the supervision of C. Roland Christensen for the Developing Discussion Leadership Skills and Teaching by the Case Method seminars. While the case is based on data furnished by participants involved, all names and some peripheral facts have been disguised.
(HBS Case No. 9-387-208)

An Earthquake Had Started (B)

Two years later, Brad Park still remembered that day vividly:

> After I said "Ohhh Kayyy," I asked Sam, "Do you think that genocide is a compelling reason to go to war?"
>
> "Yes."
>
> Both Sam and David commented generally on the question of genocide. Their conversations were a little more directed to me than usual, more like speeches than conversation. No one said anything directly to Tracy about her comments. I think they took their cue from me—that I was knocked out by it and so they were too.
>
> After a little while, the class returned to its old form of discussion, although, unusually, Tracy was still silent. At the end of the class, in the last five minutes, we tried to recap the arguments developed during class. I asked the students to do that with questions like, "So what was the first kind of argument for why nations go to war?"
>
> In the course of reviewing the arguments, Tracy blurted out:
>
> "Well, blacks have been persecuted over here for hundreds of years, so why should we go fight because they were persecuting Jews?"
>
> Silence.
>
> I asked, "Well, don't you think those are two different things?"
>
> "No, I do not."
>
> Silence.
>
> "Well, Sam, do you think they are two different things? "
>
> "Yes."
>
> We talked about the ways they were different, and then class ended. I handed out the papers and left.

Brad went on to speculate further about Tracy's behavior:

> I can only surmise a couple of reasons. I think to some black students the lack of attention paid to slavery in particular gnaws at them after a while. I think that many black students feel this. Maybe she was down on the course for that reason, maybe for others. It was clear in our discussions that she was extremely sensitive on issues of race and gender, and that she was very combative on these issues, although in general she wasn't especially combative.
>
> You have to be careful what you say around some students for fear you will be reported either through a letter or by their talking with other students about your horrible remarks. Student evaluations are the only input to professors on the job tu-

---

Lee Warren prepared this case in consultation with C. Roland Christensen and Louis B. Barnes for use in the Discussion Skills Leadership seminars. Data were furnished by involved participants. All names and some peripheral facts have been disguised.
(DBC Case No. 3)

Distributed by HBS Publishing Division, Harvard Business School, Boston, MA 02163. Printed in U.S.A.

tors are doing. They are used for recommendations about teaching ability and affect whether you are chosen to be a Head Teaching Fellow or a resident tutor in a house, among other things.

Tracy was one of those students whom I felt I had to be careful around. I would overhear her talking before class, saying things like, "Did you hear Professor X today? What a racist!!"

The fact is that Tracy scared me. It wasn't just the remarks she made. It was the remarks coupled with my perception of her willingness to make a complaint and her growing disaffection with the course in general. She's a strong-willed person. I felt a growing concern about that combination. I've never felt that way about any other student I've had.

Two years later, Sam Beatty also had clear memories of that day.

I remember thinking after Tracy's first comment, "Oh Wow! She's opened a can of worms!" I wasn't going to touch that one with a ten-foot pole. It was obviously very touchy to her. I thought it was sort of an outrageous remark: there's genocide happening, it doesn't matter what religion. It seemed racist to me, the reverse way.

I looked down at my book. The silence seemed to last a lot longer than it probably did. I was anxious to see if there would be any response. I anticipated that it would blow up between Tracy as a Christian and David as a Jew about the holocaust. But no one said anything to Tracy. Everyone pushed the issue aside. I think this might have been the only time all year that the discussion totally died.

Sam Beatty also remembered thinking that Tracy's final remark was just another of her assertions about the persecution of blacks. He didn't respond to the comment, nor did anyone else, because "we were still stunned by the previous remark. No one would have disagreed that blacks were persecuted, but that didn't seem central to the issue." Sam also had some thoughts on Tracy's role in the tutorial:

Tracy was often out of the mainstream of the discussion, fighting her own battles. On most topics, she came off on an angle. She wasn't a combative person, but she frequently reframed the discussion in terms of black-white issues. People wouldn't disagree with her, but felt she was off the topic. I sometimes felt bad for her. No one saw things her way. With the exception of Tracy we were a homogeneous group in our views. Our discussions were mostly not extreme liberals vs. extreme conservatives. I remember once, near the end of the semester, I agreed with her point of view about low income people. I felt a tie with her on that issue. We both had to overcome hardships to get to Wellhaven. I backed her up against the rest of the class. That surprised others. It made me feel good. I felt it's about time someone stood up for her and I thought, "I hope she now realizes we're not out to get her."

I could predict her response to things by this time in the class. We didn't ignore what she said, but we took it with a grain of salt. We respected her point of view, but usually it was the same. I liked hearing her perspective. I had never heard an argument from the African American point of view—that blacks are continually persecuted, even today, after the Civil Rights movement. It made me sit back and think. It was an awakening for me and increased my understanding of people.

An Earthquake Had Started (C)

During the months following the incident, Brad continued to think about it:

I've thought a lot about that class. If I had to do it all over again, I think I would do exactly what I did—not a sarcastic "OK," but an incredulous "OK." I would have been much more likely to have said something attacking Tracy if she had been Sam rather than Tracy.

I've wondered why the other students didn't speak up. They were looking to me to get the ball rolling. But if one of my other students had said something like that about slavery, I would bet that Tracy would have piped up.

I've talked about this event with others. One knee-jerk response is that you have to argue with an attitude like this then and there. On the other hand, when you do give an awful view the credence of an argument, that can send signals as well.

So I still really have no idea. . . .

As it turned out, and I knew this would probably happen, the worst evaluation I ever got in all the sections I've ever taught was from Tracy. I'm not 100% sure it was her, but you recognize your students' handwriting and tone. When I read her evaluation, it became clear that she blamed me for allowing an open kind of discussion, about the Bakke case, for example, to take place at all.

I think I was lucky that I escaped from that class with only a bad evaluation from Tracy.

I've seen Tracy a couple of times since then, and it's always been very strained. I feel very uncomfortable with her. It's as if I knew a bad secret about her. Last year one time I was doing sectioning for junior tutorials, and was taking names for waiting lists of those who wanted to switch sections. Tracy came up and I thought, 'Oh god, I can't remember her name.' She said, 'Hello, Brad, I'd like to sign up.' I felt awful.

I've kept up with these students. I still see Sam and Mary a lot and write them recommendations. I run into them at lunch; I've even played basketball with Sam. I see William in the Political Science Department, where he is working now. I haven't seen David that much.

I really like the students I've had. I keep up with a lot of them. One guy from the first section wrote a play last year and I went to see it. Teaching is great! After a really good section when everyone leaves excited, it's a great feeling. I like to be liked.

Teaching a lot of times gives you that kind of feedback, if you do a decent job and treat the students as people. It really bugs me when I know someone doesn't like me.

Lee Warren prepared this case in consultation with C. Roland Christensen and Louis B. Barnes for use in the Discussion Skills Leadership seminars.
(DBC Case No. 4)

Sam Beatty remembered Brad's course fondly.

> It was the best I ever took at Wellhaven, because it dealt with practical issues and because the discussion was fun and interesting.
>
> The class was down-to-earth; I got a lot out of it personally. Everybody usually participated. No one dominated—that's what I liked about the class most. No one ever cut off another, no one ever thought their view supreme. This was the only class I was in like that. It was a very good group of people.
>
> Brad was a terrific moderator. Students were leading the discussion, Brad moderating as needed, bringing in a new angle from time to time. From my impression he had an agenda and wanted to cover certain points. As long as the discussion was interesting and getting somewhere, he would let it go. This was not a situation in which the teacher asked a question, a student answered, and the teacher went on to another question. When the discussion veered off track, he'd steer it back with another question.

Bob Lunt (B)

Martha poured herself a cup of coffee and began typing a note to tuck into Bob Lunt's bluebook:

Bob:

If you could have been more receptive to learning from this not-too-strenuous exercise, you might have correctly identified the issues rather than settling for guesswork and a rehashing of ambiguities in management accounting. As it happens, you guessed wrong.

Godard Hospital is a differential cost-accounting problem, not full-cost. [As the dialysis unit volume decreases, some costs and total revenue clearly will be affected—but the implications of this for the unit and hospital can only be gleaned from some hard number-crunching.] The points for Drs. Parker and Leavitt to consider are: 1) how will costs be affected by changes in volume or closure, 2) does revenue at 50% capacity cover or better than cover those costs? If so, the unit can be said to break even and possibly yield a *contribution* to hospital nondifferential costs of fixed expenses. In that case the hospital is better off with the unit than without it unless they have a money-making alternative to replace it with. In that case, one would want to look at the community/medical trade-offs of closing the Dialysis Unit.

The case contained more than adequate data for each of these points to have been pursued in depth using quantitative evidence for defense. I suggested Dr. Parker's perspective because it yields the richest understanding of the case. However, quantitative data can be made to yield any number of interpretations and I deliberately left you at liberty to choose as you saw fit. By not choosing at all, you lost a valuable opportunity to put "number games" to some practical use. The two papers from your classmates attached demonstrate different but equally persuasive thinking on the problem.

The more pressing problem with your paper and your work all semester is attitudinal. As I have repeatedly expressed, quantitative analysis is one part of the accepted form of objective inquiry in the field you're attempting to enter—and a more significant part all the time. Whether your hostility is, as you claim, from a frustration with the "game of numbers" (though you seem to enjoy doing the same with words), from an inner conflict over your choice of careers or resistance to the role of student, I expect you will find that, at most, it will interest only yourself. I suggest you resolve the conflict or consider another field.

Martha

This case was written by Abby Hansen in collaboration with a member of the Developing Discussion Leadership Skills seminars. Data were furnished by involved participants. All names and some peripheral facts have been disguised.
(HBS Case No. 9-382-055)

When she had finished writing the note, she filled in the evaluation form that became part of Lunt's permanent file:

STUDENT EVALUATION

COURSE Fin. Mangmt 220
STUDENT R. Lunt

EXCELLENT ______
SATISFACTORY __X__
LOW PASS ______

INSTRUCTOR'S COMMENTS:[1]

Bob's work has been of dramatically uneven quality in this course starting with satisfactory written analyses and class participation in financial accounting and deteriorating to a marginally unacceptable final exam in management accounting. The cause of this fluctuation seems in no way a failure of intelligence but a blind opposition to the content of management accounting and the idea that quantitative analysis is a part of the accepted form of inquiry in the field he's chosen to enter. Bob's final exam was superficial guesswork, rehashings of the most obvious management accounting generalizations and hostile justifications for his flat denials to think about quantitative data.

As I have expressed to Bob, the most pressing problems with his work all semester has been attitudinal. Whether it stems from, as he claims, a frustration with the "game of numbers," or, as I suspect, an inner conflict over his choice of career fields, or a resistance to the role of student, it is a problem that will potentially interest few employers. I have suggested to Bob that he resolve the conflict or choose another field.

[1] This report is submitted in triplicate: 1 copy for the student, one for the instructor, one for student's permanent file (read by the administrators of the master's program and other professors).

Six months after the completion of F.M. 220, Martha Elliot happened to hear from a Bay administrator that Bob Lunt had been asked to leave the graduate program.

Bob Lunt (C)

The following interpretation is based on Martha Elliot's reflections on the events involving Bob Lunt approximately one year after they occurred. It was written by Ms. Elliot to encourage your reflection on some of the basic issues posed by the Bob Lunt (A) and (B) cases.

The case raises questions about an instructor's fears and anxieties and about her reading of a student's signals. Martha does not realize her power to help or harm Bob Lunt. In the (B) case, one sees her power as a teacher, not only to hurt the student professionally (he is asked to leave the program), but—far more important—to mold him into what she thinks he is. Students whom teachers fail to get to know will often simply act as they perceive they are expected to.

Bob Lunt's signals, though subtle, are clear. Martha feared his background, experience and status, and probably felt relieved that the "number crunchers" usually prevented her from having casual conversations with Bob before class. Nevertheless, he always came early and waited in the hall where he knew she'd pass by. Had she made the effort to talk to him, she might have appreciated his insecurities in *her* world—the world of balance sheets, financial reports, and statistics. Martha, however, let him dangle for an entire semester—defending herself against a threat that never emerged and possibly never existed.

From his distance from other students, gradual withdrawal from class discussions, intensity in the tuition policy case and, finally, his very hostile final exam, one gathers that Bob Lunt may well have been asking for recognition of his past career accomplishments. Returning to the role of student after establishing a career as a college teacher, he may have felt degraded and unrewarded. His promptness, near-perfect attendance, and politeness may have been signals of his respect for Martha. More important, they were overtures. Like most people, Bob wanted to be appreciated.

Bob had more problems in the course than Martha realized, but his difficulties weren't really substantive. If Bob had simply failed to understand specific kinds of numerical operations, Martha would have been able to perform an easily recognizable task and help him. She could have handled such problems efficiently and comfortably. But, unfortunately, his situation involved more subtle difficulties—loss of status, depression, anger, and reluctance to appeal for help. Martha didn't realize his desperation, and she let Bob sink into self-destructive rebellion.

This case was written by Abby Hansen in collaboration with a member of the Developing Discussion Leadership Skills seminars. Data were furnished by involved participants. All names and some peripheral facts have been disguised.
(HBS Case No. 9-382-056)

A second question one might pursue in class discussion: why did Martha miss Lunt's signals? She is young, a new female instructor in a primarily male field (administration). Anticipating a difficult teaching assignment (F. M. 220 is a genuinely difficult course with a terrifying reputation on campus), Martha feels a good deal of empathy and camaraderie with most of her students, those with backgrounds like her own. She mingles easily with them, but seems to hide behind this not-too-difficult rapport in order to retreat from Bob.

One infers she is committed to her teaching career, because she holds extra weekly tutorial sessions and long office hours. We also have indications, however, that she is nervous, concerned about students who might "make trouble" for her. Perhaps she fears that Bob Lunt's long years of teaching will make him silently critical of her fledgling efforts. Perhaps she expects him to show her up in class with his superior powers of expression. (Actually, it is fairly likely that an experienced teacher will feel fellowship with a new teacher. Bob Lunt, remembering his own first teaching assignment, probably felt sympathetic rather than critical or hostile.)

By watching Lunt solely for trouble signals, Martha was, at best, insensitive. At worst, she provoked his outburst on the final exam. By avoiding him and encouraging her "risk-free" students, she alienated him, thus creating his worsening attitude. For his part, Lunt made himself visible and accessible, and then he waited. Martha ignored him. She could have seen his willingness to be approached, affirmed his past achievements, and supported his effort to change careers. Perhaps this would have helped him achieve what she hopes her students will: break old molds and learn new roles. Problems like this one will probably become more prevalent as people return to school for retraining in midcareer and encounter teachers younger and less experienced than they.

Another issue, appropriate to consider: how do you know when you succeed? Students gave Martha compliments and she believed them. Although we know she was concerned about Lunt, her concern seems mainly selfish. She closed her eyes and hoped that rumors about her success were true.

Furthermore, and also important, Martha did not give sufficient attention to another basic issue: how does the instructor evaluate student performance when the course objectives include teaching both judgment and "hard skills"? What does an instructor do when a student has some judgment but says the skills are "uninteresting" and that he or she refuses to "play the game"?

The "what would you do" exam format does create an exercise-like tone. Lunt was saying: "I just don't care about proving to you, Martha Elliot, that I can do this academic exercise!" One wonders: was this a poor exam, or do all exams have an element of artificial gamesmanship? Good exams interest students, who learn and sometimes even enjoy themselves. Too often, however, exams are games played for the sake of a grade or just credits to chalk up. It is disturbing to think that grading comes down to "willingness to play the game." Yet, on what basis could (should) Lunt's exam have been graded?

The Blank Page (B)

Martin Davis threw away two drafts. Then he wrote:

"Learning Style

"Endocrinology appeared to present difficulties for Kenneth. Perhaps the following quotes reflect attitudes of some significance:

"'I can't learn this way, I need to know the rules. I've got to see the forest before I see the trees. You [the instructor] talk in grays, and I need black and white. I just can't get this stuff.'

"Kenneth's learning—and acceptance by the discussion group—may have also been inhibited by a tendency to pursue a point aggressively, then suddenly exclaim that the problem was hopeless and break off. He often asserted how difficult—or impossible—it was to learn endocrinology as it was presented in the course. He appears to have a low tolerance for uncertainty, ambiguity, or frustration.

"Problem-Solving and Critical Thought

"Kenneth appears to need to assimilate new material within a very specific framework with which he is already comfortable—one that begins with major principles, then fills in details. If this is so, he may find it difficult to learn from peers or patients—neither of whom are likely to present information in conformity with his apparent requirements.

"Personal Development and Interpersonal Skills

"My observations may reflect my inability to help with this student's learning needs, rather than some difficulties in his attitude and style. Furthermore, I have observed his performance in only one course and do not know if there is a pattern. I therefore urge that someone with a broader knowledge of Kenneth's record review these remarks—someone in a position to offer help if that is appropriate."

Martin sealed the evaluation form in an envelope and delivered it personally to the course director.

This case was developed, researched, and written by Abby Hansen for the Developing Discussion Leadership Skills seminars. Data were furnished by involved participants. All names and places and some peripheral facts have been disguised. The Harvard School of Public Health gratefully acknowledges the support of a grant from President Derek Bok of Harvard University for the development of teaching cases. (HSPH Case No. 8)

"Herr Faber's New Course" (B)

Walter recalled,

"I was wrong—again. Elaine stormed into my office the next day and said, 'Herr Faber, you can't make me drop 204!' That really pushed my button. I said, 'Really? Not only do I have the right to expel you, I want you to know how sick and tired I am of this lackadaisical performance. What makes you think that someone who contributes nothing and gets nothing from a course deserves credit?'

"She said, 'I deserve credit because I am getting what I want out of this course. I am taking it pass/fail, and you have given me a passing grade on everything I have turned in.' I responded, 'But you've only turned in six out of twelve assignments. Everybody else has done all the work.' She replied, 'I will turn the rest in.' I pointed out, 'Everyone else did them on time.' 'I will do extra,' she said.

Shaking his head, Walter said,

"I couldn't believe it, the same old tune from her again. I had to choke back the tongue-lashing I wanted to give her. She looked at me and said, 'Well, Herr Faber?'"

This case was developed and written by Abby Hansen for the Developing Discussion Leadership Skills seminars. Data were furnished by involved participants. All names and some peripheral facts have been disguised.
(HGSE Case No. 19)

Distributed by HBS Publishing Division, Harvard Business School, Boston, MA 02163. Printed in U.S.A.

"Herr Faber's New Course" (C)

Walter could hardly believe the words that came out of his mouth: "Well, if you do the reading and turn in all the written work . . . ."

He recalled,

"There it was: I had let her steamroll me again. I'm still angry with myself for caving in to her. As I wound up the usual end of semester tasks, I tried to put Elaine Rogers out of my mind. Then one day, right before final grades were due, a pile of written work from her turned up outside my office door. I checked to make sure that she had actually done the assigned number of essays. Her German was terrible, but she had fulfilled at least the letter of our agreement.

"So, I passed her. At the end of my gradebook for German 204 I wrote, 'This has been one of the most difficult and disheartening teaching experiences I can imagine. I should never have let this student into the course.'"

Walter concluded,

"Maybe I couldn't bring myself to throw her out because I'm not good at confrontations in general, and they happen so seldom at Lindhurst that I can't even recognize one when it's brewing. I do think I've gotten tougher since this experience though. Now I stick to the letter of the law. If a student hasn't got the prerequisite number of courses, that's it."

This case was developed and written by Abby Hansen for the Developing Discussion Leadership Skills seminars. Data were furnished by involved participants. All names and some peripheral facts have been disguised.
(HGSE Case No. 20)

Distributed by HBS Publishing Division, Harvard Business School, Boston, MA 02163.
Printed in U.S.A.

The Thin Grey Line (B)

Walt Holland spoke with Bob Spilletti within twenty-four hours of his first meeting with Tina. "I gave him a tough talking-to," he recalled, "and told him he was not tactful—he didn't give people enough space. Bob almost cried." After listening, investigating, and visiting the class in question, Walt concluded that Bob's behavior did not fall into the category of sexual harassment. He met several times with Nancy Dienstag, who agreed that nothing had happened that could be labeled sexual harassment. Walt was concerned, however:

> Bob bestowed inappropriate attention—thinking, perhaps. Does one lynch a person for making someone else feel uncomfortable? Where are the boundaries? This is a very grey area! Both Tina and Sandra felt uncomfortable with some of the readings Bob selected. But does one start to censor avant-garde writers such as D.H. Lawrence and James Joyce?
>
> I believe Bob *and* Tina *and* Sandra—all three. I still do, yet I have a responsibility—an obligation to everyone involved. He didn't pester anyone to have a drink. There were no roving hands.

Walk kept a watchful eye on Bob Spilletti for the rest of that academic year, yet saw no indication of any sexual harassment.

This case was written by Marina McCarthy in collaboration with C. Roland Christensen for the Developing Discussion Leadership Skills and Teaching by the Case Method seminars. While the case is based on data furnished by participants involved, all names and some peripheral facts have been disguised.
(HBS Case No. 9-387-202)

Distributed by HBS Publishing Division, Harvard Business School, Boston, MA 02163. Printed in U.S.A.

The Thin Grey Line (C)

Because of Bob's "general clumsy manner," however, Walt had decided not to renew his contract for the following academic year. Looking back on that decision several years later, he recalled:

> I probably kept him on as long as I did because he was *so* good at responding to student writing. But he was so obtuse. It was not healthy to have him here. I must admit I was disappointed to read in his last course evaluation that five or six students (out of fifteen) complained about his overemphasis on sexual matters. In addition I was concerned that he had invited about a half-dozen of his students at the end of the term (one by one) to the Faculty Club for either a drink or a meal—to reward them for their good work. I got the impression the students felt awkward with this attention. It's fine to invite students out for coffee or something light. But either you include everyone over the course of the term, or you don't do it at all.

Walt found the new issue of *M.W.C. Magazine* in the morning mail. One article was written by a recent alumna who described life as a woman student at MWC. Settled in an overstuffed chair, Walt began to read.

> The alumna painted a nostalgic, generally positive portrait of life at MWC—a very mature piece of writing. I was engaged. Her writing flowed well. Yet I perked up when she began to knock her CS instructor. She denounced both her teacher and the experience in his class. "Sexist," she said. "Inappropriate." I immediately went to our files to see who had been her instructor. My worst suspicion was confirmed: it was Bob Spilletti.
>
> I have replayed my decision many times. I believe I did what was right. But was I too slow to react? Had I kept him on too long? And what should I make of this article? This woman made an accusation, albeit an anonymous one.

This case was written by Marina McCarthy in collaboration with C. Roland Christensen for the Developing Discussion Leadership Skills and Teaching by the Case Method seminars. While the case is based on data furnished by participants involved, all names and some peripheral facts have been disguised.
(HBS Case No. 9-387-203)

A Night School Episode (B)

Sylvia Nevins tried first to minimize the personal aspect of the confrontation by asking the class at large if anyone else had been offended.

Half a dozen women shook their heads, but half a dozen men nodded. Sylvia groaned inwardly: polarization—women against men—was the last thing she wanted in the classroom! She decided, therefore, to change tack by directing attention back to the material. "Frankly," she said, "I find the entire Victorian ideology offensive." This seemed to mollify the man who had objected, and the class resumed its discussion. Afterward, the man disappeared quickly; Sylvia was relieved at not having any opportunity to speak with him privately.

The next class meeting went normally, with Sylvia lecturing for the first hour. But she noticed that the man who had objected the previous week was scowling, and this began to make her feel uncomfortable. During the class break, seeing him sitting alone, Sylvia gathered her courage and walked over to him. Smiling hypocritically, she said: "I'm sorry I missed you after class last time, because I wanted to thank you for your honest, forthright class comments." He looked surprised. "I thought you'd be mad at me for criticizing you in class," he said. "Oh, no," she went on—letting her instinct to placate dominate her instinct to tell him how annoyed she really had been—(in fact, at the time, she had wanted to tell him to shut up or leave)—"I was pleased that you spoke up."

Upon reflection, Sylvia was glad she had trusted the urge to make peace. The man became a more cheerful, friendly, and active member of the class. When he handed in his term paper, she discovered that his views on family life were extremely conservative—ideologically quite far from her own. But she saw no personal animosity in his attitudes.

To Sylvia, the incident held several lessons. Her initial feeling of having been personally attacked had been an overreaction. Her attitude—expressed hypocritically—of welcoming honest comments even when they criticized her in public had been the correct one, the one she *should* have had. Her lack of awareness of the intrinsic sensitivity of some of the material had been unfortunate. And, finally, the success of her "private" class break with the man showed her that classroom dynamics can be greatly improved by informal, out-of-class contacts.

This case was written by Abby Hansen from material submitted by Elaine Tyler May for the Developing Discussion Leadership Skills and the Teaching by the Case Method seminars. Data were furnished by the involved participants. All names and some peripheral facts have been disguised. (HBS Case No. 9-384-086)

Distributed by HBS Publishing Division, Harvard Business School, Boston, MA 02163. Printed in U.S.A.

The Blooper of the Week (B)

At a loss for any more meaningful way to respond as Jen Jacobson clambered awkwardly onto the desk, Nancy O'Donnell rolled her eyes at her colleague Ellen Franklin and tried to look disgusted without directly chastising the students of Section C. None of the other faculty members acted any more visibly, nor did they discuss the matter among themselves after the introduction session. After all, Nancy reflected later, they were invited guests, present by chance at the section's private meeting. For that reason, Nancy felt it would be inappropriate to comment on the incident when her course began the following week. She mentioned the "blooper" in private conversations with Jen Jacobsen twice during Jen's two years at the Heritage, but both times Jen dismissed the subject with comments like "Oh yeah, that. Well, I was embarrassed but it wasn't really such a big deal."

Section C, for its part, developed a reputation as one of the more blatantly sexist first-year sections that year at Heritage.

Colleen Kaftan prepared this case under the supervision of Louis B. Barnes and C. Roland Christensen as the basis for class discussion rather than to illustrate either effective or ineffective handling of an administrative situation.
(HBS Case No. 9-390-144)

Distributed by HBS Publishing Division, Harvard Business School, Boston, MA 02163.
Printed in U.S.A.

Peter Morgan (B)

Peter continued:

I gave Cindy a perfunctory look and said, "Well, fine." It was so frustrating. I don't know whether it showed or not. My tone was matter of fact, perhaps even sardonic. I didn't want to be hostile, but I also didn't want to communicate that I felt any remorse—'cause I didn't. By saying "well, fine," I meant to communicate "okay, you had your say." And then I switched—bang—to the next day's agenda. I didn't want to spend any more time on all this.

Class was over, and a group of people came to the desk. I thought I saw the three women again but they were behind so many people I'm not really sure. People were basically saying, "We don't agree with Cindy." The group was about fifty-fifty male/female. I must say I felt a twinge of vindication.

Marina McCarthy prepared this case under the supervision of C. Roland Christensen for the Developing Discussion Leadership Skills and Teaching by the Case Method seminars. All names and some peripheral details have been disguised. (HBS Case No. 9-389-090)

"Am I Going to Have to Do This by Myself?": Diversity and the Discussion Teacher (B)

This case was researched and written by Abby Hansen for the Developing Discussion Leadership Skills and Teaching by the Case Method seminars. The case is based on data contributed by the involved participants; all names, places, and some peripheral facts have been disguised.
(HGSE Case No. 21)

Distributed by HBS Publishing Division, Harvard Business School, Boston, MA 02163.
Printed in U.S.A.

As the researcher completed this case, she also discussed it with colleagues. A number of wider issues began to emerge. The pedagogical implications of increasing student diversity—diversity of home language, culture, age, preparation, and goals—were but a few. Marian Blanchard faced other difficult challenges in this course, beginning with organization and planning, including preparation and classroom behavior, and extending all the way through to evaluation.

Here are some questions that emerged from our discussions:

To what extent can one mix discussion teaching and lecturing? Are some subjects more or less congenial to this kind of mix?

What are the limits of discussion pedagogy? Is it appropriate for classes with substantial diversity in national, cultural, and linguistic background? How might one assess the degree of diversity in order to plan an effective pedagogy?

What kinds of diversity affect classroom performance and group cohesiveness? Age, preparation, degree requirements, intellectual goals, learning styles, culture, language are but a few. And what are the practical implications of these kinds of diversity?

If some diversity is good for a discussion, but too much diversity becomes an impediment, what rough guidelines might one develop for making a decision about whether or not to employ discussion pedagogy (or how to modify this approach or offer needed extra preparation to students who might benefit from it)? Should there be special pre-class sessions, different kinds of educational contracts (for assignments, participation, and grading), some kind of organized system of student-to-student support? How may an instructor balance his or her responsibilities to all of the various subgroups in a diverse class? While our dialogue with colleagues gave us an increased appreciation for the complexities and rewards of working with diversity, we were left with a bit of unease: Had we overlooked the most important issue?

"When the Cat's Away" (B)

"I opened my next lecture with, 'It was brought to my attention that the last lecturer was unable to finish her remarks because of aggressive questioning and being prevented from responding. Let me make several things clear:

'1. If you wish to speak in class, you raise your hand. To maintain a degree of decorum and order, you must wait to be recognized. I do not guarantee that this will happen immediately, but I promise that you will have a chance to speak.

'2. Questions should be directed to the issue, not the individual.

'3. Discussion is a give and take. When we ask a question, we do not cut off the response.

'4. We treat anyone who comes to speak to us with respect and politeness.

'5. If we have to leave early, we mention it to the lecturer, sit in the back of the class, and make sure that we do not disrupt others.

'I am reiterating these principles in order to stress that they should be in force whether I'm here or not.'

"I didn't look directly at Jay as I spoke. These were general rules of procedure for everyone. After the lecture, a few students came up to me and said, 'I'm glad you said something.'"

This case was developed and written by Abby Hansen for the Developing Discussion Leadership Skills seminars. All data were furnished by involved participants. All names and places and some peripheral facts have been disguised. The School of Public Health gratefully acknowledges a grant from President Bok of Harvard University in support of the case development project.
(HSPH Case No. 9)

"When the Cat's Away" (C)

Greg reflected on what had gone through his mind before he addressed the class as a group, and on the larger implications of the incident:

"I wondered about how to respond to this sort of innuendo. I had gotten my information from Cathy and by stopping people in the hall and bringing the subject up. That was one of the sources of my anger: people hadn't come directly to me. I had nothing but hearsay to go on. I could have chosen to do nothing about it. Or I could have gone to the opposite extreme—called Jay in and berated him. But I didn't want to turn this into a personal issue. And there was a larger point to be made. Jay had interrupted Sylvia repeatedly and impolitely, and no one had stopped him or defended her. I wanted the whole class to know that I was displeased.

"But there were many other issues involved. I'm old-fashioned. When I invite someone to speak in my class, and they do so, I feel that they are like a guest in my house—and guests should be treated with respect. I feel responsible for their being treated properly. It upset me that, in this whole group of adults, no one had asked Jay to be quiet or apologized to Sylvia. They had acted like a bunch of third-graders with a substitute teacher. The cat was away, so the mice played. If I had been there, Jay could have stomped out and I would have still invited Sylvia to finish her lecture. We would have had a class. Here was one of the founders of the world community health movement, with fifty years of experience, and the students didn't get to hear her story. What a lost opportunity! The fact that I wasn't there didn't relieve the students of their obligation to the guest speaker and to each other.

"There was a basic point to be made about behavior in academe: you do not shout someone down if you don't happen to agree with them. Jay had made no attempt to hold an intellectual dialogue. And no student should ever be allowed to destroy a class single-handedly.

"It also bothered me that Jay's behavior had been prejudiced. He was saying, 'No white South African can possibly tell anyone anything about developing countries.' He wasn't reacting to Sylvia, the person, but to what he thought she symbolized: the ruling class, white South Africa, things he didn't like. That's prejudice. And it leads to absurdities like 'only women can teach women, only blacks can teach blacks, only suburbanites can teach suburbanites'—all of which I'm opposed to. What Jay did went against my own belief system.

"I think these events raise many fundamental questions. What responsibility do students have to behave appropriately even when the professor isn't there? What is the proper way to treat a guest? What is the proper way to show respect? How should students discuss and debate issues in a university?"

This case was developed and written by Abby Hansen for the Developing Discussion Leadership Skills seminars. All data were furnished by involved participants. All names and places and some peripheral facts have been disguised. The School of Public Health gratefully acknowledges a grant from President Bok of Harvard University in support of the case development project.
(HSPH Case No. 10)

Bob Thompson (B)

Bob Thompson turned in his chair and sat facing Toby Bona. "I'll do what I can," he said. "Call back in a week and I'll let you know."

Shortly after his conversation with Toby, Bob changed Toby's grade from a B– to a B. The grade-change procedure was simple; he simply signed and filed a change-of-grade form with the registrar. "He didn't really deserve a B, but I guess I'll give him the benefit of the doubt," Bob reasoned.

A week later Toby called, and Bob told him that he had changed his grade to a B. Toby's response was immediate, "You can't do that. That's not enough. I need at least a B+ to graduate. Please, please."

"Toby, I cannot in good conscience give you a B+. You simply did not earn it."

"I must come over and talk with you," Toby replied. Bob reluctantly agreed to see him the next day.

Toby was somewhat more calm at the next meeting, but it was obvious to Bob that he was under a great deal of emotional strain. Toby started the conversation with a pleading request, "Please, please help me. You must. You are my only hope!"

Bob thought of the other students in the course. He had been impressed with the quality of the students at Urban University. They had been very bright, conscientious, and hard-working. He did not feel it would be fair to the other students to give Toby a B+. Toby had probably put less into the course than any of the other students. The only assignment to which he had given much effort was the final paper, and the quality of that paper was somewhat below the class median. When Bob compared Toby's performance to the other students who had received a B+, he felt it would be unjust to change Toby's grade.

Bob again told Toby to ask his other professors for additional help. He also asked Toby whether the review board might make a special exception with him, since his deficiency was only one grade level. Toby said he would pursue these leads, but he had been counting on Bob to change his grade.

A few days later, the registrar of the university called Bob and asked about Toby's final grade.

REGISTRAR: What is Toby's final grade?

BOB: I recently filed a change of grade from a B– to give him a B.

REGISTRAR: You know that Toby will not graduate as it now stands? He also won't get another chance. (Bob replied that he knew that but he could not justify changing Toby's grade again.) I think that you're doing the right thing. This fellow has had more change-of-grade forms than anyone I've ever seen. He's been playing this game ever since

---

This case was written by William Davidson under the supervision of C. Roland Christensen for the Developing Discussion Leadership Skills seminars. While the case is based on data supplied by participants involved, all names and some peripheral facts have been disguised.
(HBS Case No. 9-379-005)

Distributed by HBS Publishing Division, Harvard Business School, Boston, MA 02163. Printed in U.S.A.

he's been here, and I'm tired of it. It was a real mistake to admit him in the first place.

Later in the week, Bob had lunch with the dean of Urban University's Business School. They discussed the possibility of Bob joining the Urban's faculty as an assistant professor the following year. The dean said that everyone had voted positively on Bob's promotion and they would like to have him join the faculty on a full-time basis. On the way back to the dean's office, Bob and the dean stopped to say hello to several faculty members. One of the faculty with whom they talked was a senior professor in the international business area, and Bob would be working closely with him next year. As Bob was preparing to leave, the professor asked him to step into his office a moment.

SENIOR FACULTY MEMBER: How is the Toby Bona situation coming along? Toby had had a lot of problems here, but now that he is so close to completion, we should let him graduate.

BOB: Am I the only person who can help him?

SENIOR FACULTY MEMBER: It seems that way. Toby has been counting on you to change his grade.

With that, the faculty member folded his arms and looked intensely at Bob.

Bob Thompson (C)

Toby called Bob again the next week. He said he was at the end of his rope and couldn't take it any more. He had tried his other professors again and the review board, with no success. "I'm depressed," he said. Bob decided then to allow Toby to make up the first five grading units he had missed in the course. After grading Toby's work on these assignments, he would consider whether the grade could be changed to a B+.

Toby picked up the assignments Tuesday morning and handed them in 48 hours later, as agreed. The assignments were typed and neatly presented. Toby had obviously put a great deal of effort into the presentation. The quality of the work was better than Toby's past efforts. Bob finally decided, well O.K. I'll give him his B+ but I sure am uneasy about this whole business.

Bob then called the registrar and explained the situation to him. The registrar did not comment, but asked Bob to file the change-of-grade form as soon as possible.

This case was written by William Davidson under the supervision of C. Roland Christensen for the Developing Discussion Leadership Skills seminars. While the case is based on data supplied by participants involved, all names and some peripheral facts have been disguised.
(HBS Case No. 9-379-006)

Distributed by HBS Publishing Division, Harvard Business School, Boston, MA 02163.
Printed in U.S.A.

I Felt as If My World Had Just Collapsed! (B)

This case was prepared by Abby Hansen and Joy Renjilian-Burgy in collaboration with C. Roland Christensen for the Developing Discussion Leadership Skills seminars. Although based on data supplied by participants involved, all names and some peripheral facts have been disguised. (HBS No. 9-383-172)

Sue Roper Recalls the Incident

I turned back to Sarah and said the only thing I could think of: "Please take out your minidrama so you can see which one you and Carrie will perform." I was thinking, "Damn it, there's no way I'm going to let Carrie get away with this sort of behavior in my class!" The group was still unnaturally quiet, watching me, aware that I was really upset. Then I turned to Carrie and said, "It doesn't matter if you aren't in the same dorm. You can exchange phone numbers, or get together in the student lounge, or meet in the library, or work in the dining room after dinner. There's absolutely no reason you can't work together."

I didn't wait for an answer, but turned to another student, making a conscious decision not to look at either Carrie or Sarah again for the rest of the class. Somehow I managed to continue pairing students for the minidrama exercise, but I acted wooden because I felt so disturbed. I didn't, in the larger sense, know what to do. This had been an unacceptable display of racism and rejection that had upset me deeply. My heart was pounding and my head had already started aching as I went through the motions of finishing the class. I kept wondering: Should I immediately stop the class to confront the issue that I perceived as racial prejudice? Should I ask Carrie to come see me in my office? Should I ask Sarah? Maybe call the two of them in? Should I inform Cynthia Wilson, one of our black deans? Should I lodge some sort of formal complaint?

I had let the initial remark go by without a direct verbal reaction to its clear undertone of racism, but I felt the issue was terribly important and I was haunted by what long-term action I should take as a person and professor in an epoch and a setting of supposed awareness and sensitivity to social equality.

During the rest of that class I wondered whether I'd done the right thing by not directly confronting Carrie's unacceptable behavior, but I was terrified of not being able to handle the situation and of humiliating both the girls and myself.

When a teacher humiliates a student, it shows the teacher's weakness, not the student's. I also realized that calling further public attention to the incident would only worsen Sarah's hurt. But I knew that something serious had happened, and I felt completely out of control.

I decided to say nothing about the incident to either girl until they had performed their minidrama. It was a matter of integrity to me that they should do this assignment in class. But having had to force the issue so overtly made me feel like a failure because my larger life purpose—creating an open, accepting, interactive atmosphere—had been undermined.

When they did their dialogue in class the next week, I was struck by its innocuousness. They had memorized Sarah's script, which contained lines such as "I've got a blind date tonight; I wonder what he'll be like. What shall I wear?" Both students spoke well and acted pleasant and courteous during the presentation. I gave them each B+ for their work, but I couldn't let the matter rest there. That would have been irresponsible. The underlying issue was too important. I had to take some long-term action to straighten this out. But what?

I Felt as If My World Had Just Collapsed! (C)

This case was prepared by Abby Hansen and Joy Renjilian-Burgy in collaboration with C. Roland Christensen for the Developing Discussion Leadership Skills seminars. Although based on data supplied by participants involved, all names and some peripheral facts have been disguised.
(HBS Case No. 9-383-173)

Sue Roper Recalls Long-Term Outcome of Troubling Events

I always hold individual midterm conferences with each student. I took these interviews with Carrie and Sarah as an opportunity to discuss the incident. The conferences were about one week after they had done the minidrama in class. Carrie acted embarrassed and defensive when I asked her what she had meant by initially refusing to work with Sarah. She completely denied that her remark had been racist. When I suggested that she and Sarah might have become friends through working together, Carrie said that black girls were cliquish at Greenwood. They all ate together, lived near each other in one particular dorm, and played the same loud music. This was exactly the sort of stereotypical comment I remembered hearing over a dozen years before. I later found out that Carrie had initially been assigned a black roommate, but had asked to have her room changed.

With Sarah, the midterm conference went quite differently. She said, rather fatalistically, "I know Carrie didn't want to work with me because I'm black. There's plenty of racism at Greenwood, and this was just another example of it. One teacher here assigns a textbook that describes blacks as inferior. If the teachers are racist, what can you expect of the students?" She said that only her parents' feelings had kept her from leaving the school. They were a working class family, very anxious for her to graduate from a good college and have a career. They were proud of her, and her success meant a lot to them. I told her, "I have an assignment for you: Sit with Carrie again. Make conversation. You've got to make an effort; you can't always expect other people to assume the burden of friendship."

I continued, I admit, to feel distant from Carrie because she had deceived me. I had been honest with the class and told them my feelings about prejudice. But she had given me absolutely no clue to her feelings until—wham!—she openly rejected Sarah. To me that was a betrayal of trust. I still feel that Carrie duped me. And I still feel that I somehow failed the whole group and failed myself. I was self-conscious with them for the whole rest of the semester.

In a very unpleasant way, this incident revealed to me my own ignorance. I had thought I knew the rules and had developed a comprehensive system: how to create a cohesive atmosphere in the classroom, how to communicate with students and get them to communicate with each other. I had also thought my intuition was sharp enough to prevent me from pairing the wrong people, or maybe I mean that my classroom was open enough to allow me the pairing of any two people. But there it was. I had been wrong.

I still ponder the incident. I did mention it to Cynthia Wilson informally, and she shrugged it off as a common experience for blacks. But Sarah thought it was patently racist, and I did, too. Still, Carrie absolutely denied it. Yet I still feel that, after years of lofty idealism, I acted like a coward in front of all fifteen girls and myself. What, I wonder, was I really facing in that classroom? And what will I do the next time I experience racism in my classroom?

Who Should Teach? (C)

Paul Warburton

It was mid-semester, fall term when the researcher met again with Paul.

I decided to go ahead and work with a psychologist at the University Health Services. It's "catch-22" . . . complaining or challenging would only have reinforced Christine and Ellen's point that I was unwilling to take suggestions. I felt I never really had an option. I find it curious that by the spring term I should be "fit to teach." Though my commitment to counseling is not a "put up job," my goal is simply to get my ticket punched so I can student teach.

I'm new at counseling and don't know what to expect. My doubts, however, are stronger than my fears now. I really don't know what the criteria are . . . Is it the number of times I see the counselor? How does one measure progress? One can't bracket everything into time goals.

I guess counseling is not a total loss, but I still find the experience frustrating and upsetting. I do find it interesting to have repeated back to me something I said . . . but didn't initially hear . . . "Did I say that?!" It's also somewhat interesting to hear a neutral party offer perceptions. One thing that I have come to learn, however, is that "silence doesn't mean you have to fill it." Counseling has confirmed for me that bouncing ideas around with friends is very important . . . but that a psychologist is not a substitute for a friend.

I guess I can understand Christine's decision . . . but I don't have to like it. At first I was angry . . . hurt . . . but then I calmed down. I wouldn't want to trade places with her. She's the Director. I find her a dedicated person—not at all vindictive. I know Christine (and for that matter Ellen) were only doing what they thought was best. Further, two against one gives some validity to a problem. In many ways, though, their assumptions and determination about my situation was a quantum leap from reality. It was not that there were no problems, I just don't think it was such a crisis.

At any rate, I feel I am in a powerless position. Despite how much Kensington encourages student-teacher interactions, I feel trapped. My future is in Christine's hands, despite the fact that the Dean of the College has become involved now and will be the ultimate judge of whether or not I student teach next term. I don't think I need help . . . but I'm willing to give the benefit of the doubt. I can't say that it is *not* beneficial to me. But I'm certainly not going to tell Christine she's wrong. I'm fearful for my degree! Further, I am *not* a quitter. I want to student

---

This case was written by Marina McCarthy in collaboration with C. Roland Christensen for the Developing Discussion Leadership Skills and Teaching by the Case Method seminars. While the case is based on data furnished by involved participants, all names and places and some peripheral facts have been disguised.
(HBS Case No. 9-387-141)

teach. I am unconvinced that counseling will help, however.

You know, dealing with a handicap is developmental. One has to reassess it at various stages in your life. Because being short was resolved in junior high doesn't mean that it doesn't have to be resolved again in your twenties. Sometimes I still dream I'll wake up 5′3″.

PART III

Teaching Notes and Researcher's Perspectives

The French Lesson (A) and (B)

TEACHING NOTE

This teaching note has been prepared by Abby Hansen as an aid to instructors in classroom use of the case series "The French Lesson" (A) 9-384-066 and (B) 9-384-067.
(HBS No. 5-384-168)

Distributed by HBS Publishing Division, Harvard Business School, Boston, MA 02163.
Printed in U.S.A.

Special Features

This particular minicase describes a college-level French class in which the teacher, meaning to be kind, quietly asks a hesitant student if he has studied the day's lesson. The gesture backfires to produce intense embarrassment and damaged rapport with the whole class. The strength of this case is the multiplicity of deeper issues that underlie such an apparently simple interchange.

"The French Lesson" will probably inspire a discussion that moves swiftly. It will very likely involve little clarification of case content, and the participants will probably furnish similar experiences and present opinions about the case characters with facility. The discussion should, ideally, also offer many opportunities to reflect on some basic teaching issues, but this desirable turn of events will depend largely on the discussion leader.

Like all minicases, "The French Lesson" should generate a participant-focused discussion. This means that the discussion leader should prepare to use participants' comments to guide the group into complexities that the case implies rather than states. Achieving this will call upon the skills of listening, probing for subtleties, and illuminating the emerging structure of the discussion with periodic summaries.

Mood

The case is relatively light in tone. The teacher insults a student, to be sure, but the insult is unintentional and the damage it inflicts on the student's self-esteem and status, while real, is not catastrophic. Nor is the injury to the whole group's rapport with the teacher irreparable. Other cases in our syllabus take up far more painful issues: racism, sexism, unsettling outbursts in class, for example. "The French Lesson," by contrast, is low-keyed.

Suggested Uses

Because of its accessible material and light tone, this case makes a good ice-breaker. Coming after more dramatic, emotionally draining cases, "The French Lesson" might seem anticlimactic. Its strength is that it can get participants talking without fear of exposing personal weaknesses by over-identifying with a severely troubled case character.

Another reason for using this case early in a workshop or seminar syllabus is that it crystallizes a very basic issue of classroom philosophy: respect. The instructor in this case—Bert Peters—explicitly tries to accord students respect because he thinks this encourages them to learn. Even so, Bert flounders.

This issue should be pointed out, ventilated, and returned to throughout the discussion and the teaching seminar (or workshop) as a whole.

Conflicts, Sensitivities

As we have noted, "The French Lesson" contains no concealed land mines for the unwary discussion leader (although unexpected sensitivities in the members of the group are always possible).

Teaching Objectives

This case focuses on a teacher's well-meant efforts to balance his responsibilities toward a less-talented student and a generally apt, enthusiastic class. It is, basically, a *kindly* case. Since its central issues are responsibility and respect, it presents a splendid opportunity for the discussion leader to act as a classroom model, applying the very principle under discussion: respect. There are many ways to do this. Acknowledging participants by name, speaking with courtesy, consciously maintaining a physical posture that communicates attention when participants speak, and making eye contact with members of the group when they listen as well as speak—all these contribute to creating an atmosphere of respect. It often happens during our seminars that a participant will notice what the discussion leader is doing and call attention to it. If this occurs, so much the better. It should lead to further discussion of ways to demonstrate and convey respect.

The "Blocks" of Analysis

If you happen to find the mnemonic device of breaking a discussion case into analytic "blocks" appealing, this is a good case on which to practice the technique. This writer usually tries to extract approximately six or eight rubrics under which various points may be logically grouped. I then write these, with brief (almost shorthand) references to supporting data in the case, on a single sheet of paper—to be kept constantly in view during the discussion. This device provides a snapshot of the terrain and helps the leader remain oriented as the discussion moves freely. It also helps provide clues for new directions by giving an almost instant reading of which areas have been covered and which have not.

The basic elements of "The French Lesson" are simple and brief enough to be covered during a normal seminar session. One "block" might be case characters. The instructor might, for example, direct attention to Bert Peters and his student, Jack Sothern. What do we know of them? What do our intuitions suggest? What are some implications of their bearing, words, implied attitudes? One should also consider the class as a whole—the way the students and teacher interact: another "block." Furthermore, what is the physical setup of the room? How does Bert Peters move? What are some implications of these details?

And how does Bert use humor? How does his dramatic flair affect the class as a whole? How does it affect Jack?

One should also pay attention to the dialogue, which is brief but suggestive. How do people speak in this case? What do their words imply? What tone do they use? What diction (kinds of words) do they use? All of these details may lead to more general considerations of basic issues. "The French Lesson" presents the discussion leader with a clear opportunity for asking the participants to examine, or at least consider, many constituent elements in the learning environment that often go unremarked in a denser, more complex case.

My own study of this minicase discerns a manageable set of blocks, besides characters and environment: *humor* in the classroom; balancing *responsibility* to a single student with responsibility to the whole class; *rapport; teaching contract;* and the subtleties of expressing *respect.* (All of these are especially relevant to the early days, of course—although they pertain to the whole of teaching as well.)

The elusive but pervasive issue of "chemistry" might also constitute a discussion block. In this writer's estimation the two major characters are disharmonious. Bert is a high-energy teacher whose style reflects his talent and enthusiasm for his subject. Jack is a less-gifted student, especially inept at this particular kind of learning, with a potential for resistance and even disruption in the classroom. The others in the group come across as a unit with a common denominator of relatively high aptitude and a generally congenial acceptance of Bert's teaching style. So, the principal tension occurs first between Bert and Jack, but it then spreads to the class as a whole (tension usually does). The result: a general rise in counterproductive nervousness. The group should devote attention to this situation and try to suggest ways to identify and improve it.

Preparing for the Discussion Opening Speaker; Backstop

Our general practice is to ask *two* participants to open the discussion. This employment of an initial double-call serves several purposes. First, it signals cooperation to the group as a whole, saying, in effect, that this is a seminar in which the long-winded "star performances" that bore and annoy the nonperforming seminar member will be avoided in favor of collaborative efforts. Second, asking two participants to open provides the discussion leader not only with twice as much material to probe, but also with insurance: if the first speaker fails, perhaps the second may present more usable material.

In this case, the protagonist is a young man, the subject is French grammar, and the students are undergraduates in a liberal arts institution. Some participants might find this situation unfamiliar. In the interests of signaling that this seminar will encourage participants to identify with characters in diverse situations, the leader might ask a woman from a discipline other than foreign languages to open the case. This done, it would signal another set of positive values—equality and cooperation—to ask a male to function as backstop. The backstop's task usually is fairly loosely assigned. He or she is asked to "fill out" and comment on the first speaker's remarks, helping the class find direction for further investigation.

Typically, in our seminars, the backstop avoids direct challenge to the first speaker. Even when he or she presents basically contradictory information or opinions, these usually emerge cloaked as agreements. The discussion leader should stress that the first two speakers are opening the territory for exploration. They are not providing an exhaustive analysis.

(At this point, let us hasten to assure any novice teachers that even if the two opening speakers *do* appear to bring up all the points the leader has prepared, this is not cause for despair. The seminar need not end there, some ten minutes after it has begun! On the contrary: the simple mention of a point should not be confused with a thorough discussion of it. It is the discussion leader's task to pose open-ended questions *based on* the points, invite participants to disagree if they feel this is appropriate, and press for further applications.)

Another consideration in the choice of a pair of opening speakers might be their location in the room. Choosing a participant far to one's right might suggest asking another participant seated far to the left to backstop, thus symbolically enclosing the whole group in the arc of attention. In any case, it would be extremely ill-advised to choose participants seated side by side or too near each other. In the first place, if they are seated together they might be friends and particularly averse to contradiction. This could promote a bland opening. In the second case, having two speakers seated very near each other would close the focus of the discussion, eliminating most of the participants from the arena of action.

The question of whether to ask for volunteers is always worth considering. Particularly in the early days of the seminar, when participants and leader are all relative strangers, inviting volunteers to open has the advantage of letting the group know that the leader will not try to impose too much structure on their discussions. The disadvantage is that the seminar will begin with presentations from the more aggressive, attention-hungry members of the group and impose some rejection upon the shyer participants.

The Discussion Questions

Before we begin to consider possible responses to these questions, let us mention that it is generally our practice to make the first calls (pose the first two questions) before presenting a few minutes of introduction and "housekeeping details" (schedule changes, references to secondary readings, written assignment deadlines, and the like). We ask the first speaker to take the time to think about his or her response while the introduction is in progress. Then, after the introduction, we put down our notes, turn in a conversational way to the first speaker, and informally rephrase the first discussion question. The symbolic implication of this gesture is twofold. First, we are trying to convey a feeling of ease along with a moderately colloquial style of speech—no need to grope for elegant expressions and, in the process, get tongue-tied. Second, we are saying, "I've put down my notes; now the time has come to pay attention to *your* reactions, not mine."

The discussion leader should keep in mind that a philosophical assumption underlies these actions: the belief that Bert Peters's desire to accord students respect in the classroom is the most essential element in this case. Not only should the discussion leader try to draw the group's attention to this issue, but he or she should reflect on it personally. It is useful to ask yourself whether you agree with Bert. Do you, too, take pride in "putting students at their ease"? If so, how do you do this? Relaxation is by no means an uncomplicated goal. How much is desirable? How can one encourage the right degree of relaxation? Do relaxed students really perform better? What settings are more relaxing than others? And how can a teacher recognize when relaxation has turned to slackness? (Concomitantly, how can one reintroduce a healthy tension when this occurs?) These open-ended questions—all implied in the primary case material—give "The French Lesson" the potential for stimulating genuinely helpful thought about the whole enterprise of teaching.

Let us now consider the discussion questions, in the order given, with our primary focus being ways in which the discussion leader may capitalize on participants' comments to suggest directions of discussion that will expose as many of the gray areas as possible. Let us stress again that in these cases there is no specific correct conclusion; there are virtually endless subtle ramifications of all points, and these can be "played" in a number of ways. It will always be valuable to ask the group for further implications, or assumptions, or even fantasy scenarios based on analytical points made from the case. All of these exercises will not only help provide depth for the analysis, but also furnish a *healthy* redundancy that may drive some points home for members of the group who are either more leisurely in their pace of thought, or perhaps accustomed to different methods of intellectual analysis than informal group discussion.

Each of our questions might produce a response somewhere on a spectrum that often stretches between two poles—extreme approval of the central case character and extreme disapproval. The discussion leader's task is to devise questions that will nudge the group into providing some intermediate points on this spectrum.

—◆—

After the (A) case has been read, the following questions can be explored:

1. What's going on here?

This should be the question directed to the first speaker. It could produce a simple rehearsal of the facts in the case—devoid of interpretation of the motives and the forces the speaker sees exerting their powers in these events. The question's intended thrust is analytical, but it is meant merely as an opening to an examination of constituent elements. Given a highly wrought, extremely abstract presentation, the discussion leader should make a mental note to ask, later on, the seminar participants to backtrack a bit and turn their attention to describing the event and the people involved. The spectrum of response on these questions, thus, might range from simple repetition of facts to elaborate abstractions. The discussion leader's object would be to try to introduce the missing element—for both are necessary to a complete discussion.

Another answer to "What's going on here?" might address itself to the teacher's personality. One participant might say, "A talented teacher is trying to run an energetic, exciting class despite the dullness of the lesson's content: French grammar." Another participant might read the situation quite differently and say, "A nervous, sharp-tongued prima donna teacher is hogging the limelight and intimidating his students with humor." Neither point is necessarily correct or incorrect. Either—or both—should lead to deeper considerations of the implications of pacing, humor, and the teacher's responsibility to be sensitive to student's reactions to his or her style. Faced with a seemingly opposed set of responses like the above, the discussion leader should not hesitate to ask for further ways to view the situation. If these are not forthcoming, he or she might appropriately introduce a few.

2. What would you advise Bert Peters to do?

Answers to this question will be conditioned by the drift of the discussion. Should Bert apologize? (Perhaps not. If not, why not?) If he ought to apologize, first of all, why? Secondly, how? (Should he apologize in class? Privately? In writing? In a formal or informal setting?) The discussion leader's task in this section of the discussion is to try to get participants to examine the assumptions that underlie each piece of advice. For example, if one suggests that no apology is necessary, is that because a teacher's dignity would be compromised by apologizing to a student? What elements constitute a teacher's dignity, then? If one thinks the apology should be public and involve the rest of the class, what does that imply about one's view of the teacher-student contract?

Almost invariably, seminar participants find it amusing to match their predictions and advice with the actual events that succeeded the decision point of the (A) case. Here, those who recommended apologizing will find themselves vindicated by the reality of the situation, but the "hardliners" may well take exception, asserting that while Jack Sothern *says* he always prepares but lacks language aptitude, he is just taking advantage of his teacher. He actually was *not* prepared, and now he's trying to make Bert feel guilty, in hopes of cadging some preferential treatment.

—◆—

After the (B) case has been read, the following questions can be stressed:

1. Did Bert Peters do the right thing?

Bert decided to treat the issue privately. He made his contact with the student informal—choosing neither to send him a written apology, nor to summon him to his office for a personal conference. What are the ramifications of this course? What would it signal if the teacher had treated this action more formally? What would it signal if he addressed it in front of the other students?

Some participants may note Jack Sothern's whiny tone in the reported phone conversation and point out that the student seems to be taking the opportunity to make retribution for having been insulted. Bert Peters seems to accept the student's statements at face value and take pains to adopt a conciliatory mode of reaction. Is this appropriate? Is the teacher groveling, letting the student get away with too much? What about Jack's assertion that "I'm not good at languages?" Does a student's lack of talent in a specialized field put an increased burden upon the teacher?

2. *How do you explain the effect of the initial incident upon the class as a whole?*

Again, the range of interpretation will probably hinge upon attitudes toward Bert Peters's teaching style. If one is "student-centered," one might say that Bert had been keeping the whole class in a state of nervousness by his movements and jokes, and Jack Sothern's slightly asocial gesture in leaving the class and then returning in a state of obvious upset focused a great deal of the anxiety that the other students were probably feeling but concealing. The opposed point of view is that Jack Sothern's actions were babyish. He spoiled not only his teacher's good mood, but everyone's. Embarrassment—particularly when it is given physical form in a gesture such as leaving the classroom (presumably with a pained facial expression)—is catching. The other students might well have empathized with Jack. He performed poorly in class, so the teacher stood right by his chair and singled him out to question his preparation. What an insult! It is customary in language classes for teachers to stand while the students remain seated (except to walk to the chalkboard occasionally). This physical disparity automatically reinforces the teacher's potential to intimidate. (In this section of the discussion, it will be profitable for the discussion leader to refer to the "blocks" which encompass issues such as rapport, teaching contract, humor, and the separate personalities of Bert and Jack.)

3. *What were some of the ways in which Bert Peters was creating the classroom atmosphere?*

This is a straightforward question that should elicit answers that pay attention not only to the physical arrangement of the room—desk chairs in a "U" that allowed students to see each other, yet focused attention on the teacher as he moved freely around the central space—but also on Bert's use of humor and what little data we have about his gestures (he pretends to eat the chalk, and points to the students—sometimes by surprise—to trigger their participation). In short, Bert is a self-conscious, theatrical sort of teacher, who communicates a desire for the spotlight and a personal preference for laughter and quick pace.

It may well be noted at this point that we have no information about whether Bert ever asked this group how they wanted to proceed, or announced at the outset what sort of pace he expected or what classroom mood he hoped to evoke (another instance of the virtually ubiquitous "one-sided teaching contract"). The question of the value of "spontaneous buoyancy" (Bert's term for his favorite classroom mood) may also occur at this point. What, indeed, is the effect of spontaneity on learning? Is there value in running a slow-paced class? How can a teacher gauge the pace, how alter it, how evaluate its effectiveness?

4. *What were some of the problems facing Bert Peters in the long run?*

Many seminar participants will answer, "Restoring good feeling." This reply will probably find few dissenters. But Bert also faced another decision: What to do about Jack Sothern? Bert had to make an evaluation of the student's problem: Was he untalented, lazy, truculent, or perhaps truly incapable of performing acceptable, college-level work in French? Is it fair to make a genuinely slow student participate in a class populated by talented students? How important is homogeneity in a class? Are the criteria different in language classes?

Another way to approach this question is to wonder whether this might be a good time for Bert Peters to engage in a bit of self-appraisal. Are his jokes intimidating students? Is he moving too fast around that "U"? Is he startling students by abruptly pointing his chalk at them and expecting them to spew good, grammatical French? Should he try to modify his classroom pace according to the students' developing needs? What cues should he look for (besides laughter) to gauge the class's mood?

5. *What underlying issues does this case focus for you?*

It is to be hoped that the seminar group will come up with new and stimulating issues to consider, but the set that this researcher has assembled—respect, humor and its dangers, homogeneity, rapport, the teaching contract—are a reasonable starting point.

Some seminar participants may well have experienced similar incidents in the classroom, either as students or teachers. It would be well to ask the group to give some thought to the underlying issues of this interchange, should they be presented.

Most important for the discussion leader to remember here is the unlikelihood of achieving thoroughness or impressive depth in this part of the discussion. The case is not the sort of emotional "grabber" that is likely to trigger deep, passionate, or profound thought during the discussion period, and the order of the discussion questions happens to place this section last. Final elements on teaching plans tend to be short-changed. The discussion leader's task, thus, is to try to sustain the group's interest with all sorts of cues—verbal and physical—which indicate that this discussion of principles should be pursued after class, either in company or in one's own mind.

The discussion leader would be well advised to wrap the session up with a brief summary of some of the questions the group has posed and finish with a further question to ponder privately: "What have we learned from Bert Peters's mild blunder and what does it mean for each of us in our own teaching?"

The French Lesson (A) and (B)

RESEARCHER'S PERSPECTIVE

This commentary on "The French Lesson" was prepared by Abby Hansen. Its objective is to help instructors in the development of their own teaching plans for this case.
(HBS No. 5-384-068)

Case Informant's Comments

Bert Peters reflected: "This incident still fascinates me in a horrible sort of way because of the shock I felt when my intended kindness to Jack Sothern backfired. I meant well, but nonetheless managed to insult him publicly—which is not something I like to do, although I know some teachers who not only don't mind it but even positively enjoy it. To me, this episode showed that questioning a student's preparation in class creates a no-win situation. You're either saying, 'Aha, caught you unprepared, you lazy bum,' or 'Well, if you *did* prepare, you're so dumb it didn't do you any good!' Neither implication can do anything but embarrass the student in front of his peers."

Bert also perceived a personal loss stemming from the incident: "The class got edgy and stayed that way for a surprisingly long time," he observed. "I paid a price in damaged goodwill, and rapport is worth something, especially in a foreign-language class where people are already guaranteed to be nervous about sounding foolish in public when they make their inevitable mistakes. My strained relations with Jack spilled over and dampened the whole class's enthusiasm, making it necessary for me to work extra hard to restore good relations. The damage was subtle, but real."

Researcher's Comments

We don't see much of Bert Peters in this case, but his teaching style shows energy, confidence, and humor. He also seems to value those qualities and encourage them in his students. In the terms of this teaching seminar, he sets a one-sided contract—making him the sort of high-energy teacher who can deeply intimidate a less-talented student. For those who absorb unfamiliar material more slowly than most of their peers, energetic instructors can be terrifying. Jack Sothern appears to be of this sort. Given Bert's intention to spare his students public embarrassment over their failures, Jack presents a teaching problem: how can Bert include him in the class exercises without sacrificing pace and mood?

Bert sets his fast pace in many ways, verbally and physically. By having the students arrange their desks into a U-shape, he creates an audience for his own theater-in-the-round performances. He moves fairly quickly—one assumes—and carries a piece of chalk to use as a pointer and stage prop, as well as writing implement. Sometimes he proceeds student-by-student in his invitations to participate; sometimes, not. He is, thus, unpredictable, and that is bound to create tension. Bert flings questions at his students almost like a juggler tossing flaming Indian clubs to his partner. He launches each question with a laugh, thus focusing a great deal of heat on the student who must catch it without killing the laughter or breaking the fast pace. Bert's own superior command of material and personal fund of nervous energy set a tone that he finds comfortable. Doubtless many of his students also find it congenial, but Jack Sothern certainly does not.

In the situation as we have outlined it, Bert is using his position (physical and metaphorical) to reinforce his leadership. However benevolently he uses his power in the classroom, he is, nonetheless, inflicting a style on his students—apparently without their consent. Most teachers do the same. When this method works, it goes unnoticed. But here, however, Bert faces a mismatch between student and style. He has only two basic options for improving the situation: change the student or change the style. How can he change the student? He can, perhaps, move him out, transfer him to the jurisdiction of a teacher with a less-threatening style. He can, perhaps, arrange a private contract with Jack and forgo calling on him in class entirely. Perhaps he can change the whole basis of their contract and arrange some sort of private "Independent Study," in which Jack focuses on reading and writing French and relinquishes his efforts to learn to speak the language. (In cases of genuine lack of aptitude, such as learning disabilities or varieties of dyslexia, this might be the only successful course of action.)

Bert Peters's own comments show valuable insight. After reflecting on this incident and its implications, he decided to avoid this sort of confrontation with students in class—even on issues that seem fairly trivial, like one evening's grammar lesson. There seems little question in Bert's mind that he should have spoken to Jack privately. Bert focuses our attention on one of the inescapable facts of teaching: the inequality of power in the classroom that magnifies everything the teacher does, from moving around the room to raising or lowering the voice, to inquiring about a student's preparation. In the classroom, thus, singling a student out—either for praise or blame—causes genuine tension. Praised, a student can begin to worry: What did I do right? How can I repeat this performance? Will this magic rub off? Blamed, a student can be so embarrassed that he or she gives up the desire to improve. The effect on the others in the classroom will also, most likely, be negative. Hearing a fellow student praised, they may feel envious; hearing him blamed, they may feel both empathetically embarrassed and implicitly threatened—wondering when the insult may land on *them*.

Another aspect of classroom dynamics that surfaces in this brief interchange is the ubiquitous phenomenon of emotional contagion. People catch each other's moods and the enclosed atmosphere of the classroom is a hotbed for this sort of infection. In this vignette we see the highly charged, comic energy of a classroom turn into negative tension that spreads from the insulted student to the rest of the class and then to the teacher himself.

Bert Peters's one-sided, implicit teaching contract with this class seems to have included clauses stipulating humor, a fast pace, and talent. Not all of his students, however, were capable of fulfilling these demands, and his contract, unfortunately, made no allowance for these students. Recognition of the situation and some sort of renegotiation would seem to be in order.

The Day the Heat Went On (A) and (B)

TEACHING NOTE

This teaching note has been prepared by Abby Hansen as an aid to instructors in the classroom use of the case series "The Day the Heat Went On" (A) 9-384-098 and (B) 9-384-099. (HBS No. 5-384-278)

Distributed by HBS Publishing Division, Harvard Business School, Boston, MA 02163. Printed in U.S.A.

Special Features

"The Day the Heat Went On" could be considered a "woman's case." The protagonist, Ellen Collins, finds herself heckled in a particularly gender-specific way: when she removes her blazer while teaching in an intolerably stuffy classroom, a loud wolf whistle rings out. This mild impertinence assumes serious overtones only in context. Ellen is one of the very few female instructors at a large, well-known school of business and public management, and she happens to be the only female teacher assigned to this particular group of students for their first-year master's degree program. Furthermore, as we learn in the (B) case, Ellen considers the female students in the class "demoralized," and the prevailing institutional culture unsettling, alien, and basically hostile to women. Since a wolf whistle conveys an intrinsically condescending appreciation for a woman's figure, the "me Tarzan, you Jane" overtones of this interruption to Ellen's finance class could scarcely have escaped the students. Symbolically, the wolf whistle shifts Ellen's identity from "discussion leader" or "finance expert" to "woman on display," and turns a simple action—removing one's jacket on a hot day—into a striptease. The challenge she faces is, thus, more complex and charged with risk (loss of dignity, diminished effectiveness as a leader, personal embarrassment) than might at first appear. It is the discussion leader's task to make sure the seminar considers the broader implications.

To deemphasize the gender issue, the discussion leader can try to stress the "everyman" aspect of this case and treat Ellen Collins as a member of a minority group in the mainstream culture of a large, urban school of management. The wolf whistle may be considered representative of a form of public heckling, and the challenge to Ellen's authority typical of the sort of hazing many new instructors endure from spirited, rather immature, students. Certainly this approach to the case will bear fruit. But the specifics do call for some attention to the problems of young women professors in business and professional schools in general.

Mood

This is a peppy case. The trigger incident is a wolf whistle, and the case informant lively and resilient.

Suggested Uses

"The Day the Heat Went On" deals with events in the last part of the academic year, but the teacher is relatively new to this group of students, due to peculiarities in the academic schedule of her institution. She is, moreover, this group's only female teacher, having inherited the students after they have worked exclusively with male teachers for the better part of the year. Part of her challenge is to establish a working relationship despite this group's habituation to dealing only with men in authority. It is, thus, a "contract" case; the wolf whistle jeopardizes the contract that Ellen would like to establish. The section of the course in which contract issues cluster would seem the natural home for this case, but it could also be positioned in that part of a syllabus that deals with day-to-day classroom procedure (or Operations, as it is termed). How does any teacher respond to an unexpected bit of disrespect in the classroom? Unanticipated impertinences can pop up at any time.

Conflicts, Sensitivities

The discussion leader should beware of polarizing the group on the issue of sexism. One way to work with this potentially sensitive material is to stress the abstract aspects of the case: the underlying challenge to authority that Ellen experiences in her way could have assumed a different form when directed at a male teacher.

Teaching Objectives

Paradoxically, part of the rationale for using "The Day the Heat Went On" directly contradicts the advice of the previous section of this note. This case does have sexist overtones. One salutary effect on discussion might be to allow men in the group to empathize with Ellen Collins's anger at being singled out for unwelcome sexual appreciation. On another level, of course, it should provide a means to air the grievances felt by members of any minority group in a culture with palpable elements of prejudice, condescension, or hostility.

The "Blocks" of Analysis

1. The teacher. Ellen is young, attractive, soft-voiced, competent to handle her teaching role, and ambitious. She is also sensitive to nuances in her classroom, and extremely aware of the symbolic content of students' and teachers' gestures. She understands the unfolding classroom dynamic quite well. This is both an advantage and a handicap, for she not only recognizes a challenge when it occurs, she also knows how much rides on her response.

2. The institution. Fleming Graduate School of Business and Public Management in Toronto seems to be a large school of excellent reputation where advancement as an instructor is extremely desirable. Certainly, Ellen conducts herself as if she would like to be tenured there. The students seem lively, and the curriculum is extremely demanding. Women are a minority at Fleming, but their numbers are significant; there may be just enough of them to constitute an irritating presence.

3. Subject. Ellen Collins is teaching finance—a serious, difficult, and high-status subject in the school of management. She is, in a sense, poaching in a traditionally male preserve, for women in this sort of professional school have traditionally taught the "softer" subjects, like industrial psychology, or business English.

4. The students. The Fleming method is to segment its first-year MBA students into groups of eighty to a hundred students who take all of their courses together. The "Learning Groups" (LGs) meet daily from 8:30 a.m. to 2:30 p.m., and we gather that they spend much of their free time socializing together. This system would tend to encourage strong social identification in the student groups, while positioning the instructors on the outside. Add to this the fact that Ellen is the only female teacher of LG VI, and we can see her vulnerability vis-à-vis the students.

5. The "trigger" event. The wolf whistle can be considered a trivial impertinence, a naive but sincere compliment, or an insult. Whatever point of view emerges most strongly in the discussion, it is advisable to try to elicit the others. In all likelihood the student who whistled meant no harm, but his naivete does not remove the insulting implications of the whistle, especially when addressed to a thoughtful woman teacher who has given time to considering the symbolic overtones of precisely this sort of cultural convention. (All of the above interpretations of the whistle may be valid for different members of the class.)

6. Basic issues. Among the principles that structure this case, the researcher has discerned these: challenge to authority, self-management under stress, response to a potential insult, the instructor's authority (and its tenuousness), and contract.

Preparing for the Discussion

Exhibit 1 lists suggested Study Questions to be handed out to participants for use when preparing the case before class. **Exhibit 2** contains a summary of the Discussion Questions to be used by the seminar leader in preparing for class and in guiding the case discussion when necessary.

Opening Speaker; Backstop

In this case, choosing a man to open has advantages because the material is so heavily slanted in the direction of women. Preferably the man who opens should be able to put himself in Ellen Collins's position. As he responds, listen very carefully for reactions that might suggest differences between the way men and women treat challenges to their authority. For the backstop, a good choice would be a woman, to both balance the opening speaker's recommendations and to signal that despite the presence of sexism as a live issue in this discussion, your group will approach the issues from all sides.

B. The Discussion Questions

The following questions (**Exhibit 2**) can be addressed after the (A) case has been read:

1. [To the opening speaker]: If you were Ellen Collins, what would you do when you heard that wolf whistle?

A male speaker might suggest some vigorous rejoinder to the whistle. One extreme would be to demand to know the identity of the whistler and then ask him to leave. Another would be to turn in the direction of the whistle and briskly say something like "You're out of line, buddy. And this is the last time this sort of thing is going to happen in my class!" Another suggestion for a response is a sarcastic joke: "Well, I guess *your* social life has been uneventful lately!" On the other hand, the first speaker might try to put himself in character, noting that Ellen describes herself as quiet-voiced, not given to large, dominating gestures in the classroom, and generally conciliatory rather than combative. Speaking from Ellen's point of view, one might feel more inclined to stonewall the event, continue the class with minimal fuss, and maintain one's "cool." But she *is* angry.

Another alternative might be to seize the opportunity to make a speech, either on classroom manners (stressing the unacceptability of heckling, catcalls, and whistles in a professional school) or on sexism at Fleming. All of these courses of action should find both their adherents and their detractors. There will probably be a range of responses in the group that includes people who have thought long and hard about the problems of women in society, some who may be bored and discouraged with these issues, and people who have not yet considered these matters in great depth.

As with all cases, the discussion leader should be concerned at first with expansiveness—opening up the discussion to as many points of view as possible. In this instance, the choice is to begin with "action," not necessarily because this case is more operations-oriented than theoretical, but because examining Ellen's options and their consequences will lead naturally to considerations of her position in the closed society of Fleming Graduate School of Administration and Public Management.

2. [To the backstop]: Could you help us appraise Ellen's position? What do you consider to be the critical elements in her situation at Fleming?

At this point, discussion will have to focus on the inescapable gender issue. Ellen is a highly qualified tenure-track assistant professor of finance at a major institution. She is thirty, married, of medium height, with collar-length hair and a soft voice. She does not practice a "tough" style of teaching (as some of her respected male colleagues do), and she is acutely aware that her teaching wardrobe is important. In other words, she is self-conscious, and the focus of this self-consciousness is the fact that she is female—different from the dominant mold of Fleming teachers, who are male. She looks different, sounds different, adopts a different attitude toward students, and has to keep different criteria in mind when she selects her clothing. The "backstop" can hardly fail to mention at least a few of these considerations. Other considerations to expect would include the prestigious, success-oriented school, with its annual graduating class of five hundred master's degree candidates—the great majority of them being men. Another factor is the Fleming method in which the large Learning Groups form strong, sometimes complex, social bonds. Class participation counts heavily in Fleming's grades, so students must learn to assert themselves in discussions with their groups. Teachers who "float" from classroom to classroom to meet the LGs for their classes are almost automatically "odd man out," as the LGs form cohesive social units and gain group identities as the year progresses. This incident occurs in April—seven months after the beginning of the LGs' first year. Seven months are a long time for eighty to a hundred students to spend in each other's company, taught—as the case tells us—exclusively by male instructors. A significant ingredient in Ellen's situation is her conspicuousness as LG VI's only woman teacher.

Alert participants will also notice Ellen's reference to Charlie Brennan, LG VI's tyrannical instructor in industrial psychology. Charlie is a "tough" teacher who, according to Ellen, had "wiped the floor" (symbolically) with all the women students in the class by calling them together for a special meeting in which he treated them with insulting condescension. Unfortunately for Ellen, she teaches the LG immediately after Charlie's class. No wonder she finds the group tense and the women "demoralized."

Certainly germane to Ellen's predicament is the mood in which she usually finds the class: it is flirtatious. The nervous humor that Charlie inspires in his tense students characteristically assumes sexual overtones, and Ellen has to cope with these. Her method for dealing with the moderate suggestiveness of LG VI's jokes had been to permit the group to let off a little steam. Ellen chose to "shrug off" the unwelcome implications in their jokes. Her only reaction to the sexual overtones in some of their humor was to "hope that the jokes would not escalate."

All of these factors, plus the observation that "no one found Charlie Brennan's condescending attitude toward his female students particularly unusual," define the situation in which Ellen finds herself at Fleming with LG VI. These, plus her inexperience (this is her first year at Fleming as a tenure-track instructor), make things difficult for her.

Attention should also be paid to Ellen's description of the general Fleming culture: the "high-level of obscenity in the LGs' humor," and the "assumption . . . that women students couldn't possibly say anything worth hearing." The three "extraordinarily bright women" in Ellen's class, she notes, "seemed to be having as hard a time" as "the less gifted, more intimidated ones." For the bright, assertive women, the problem was social ostracism. Their very intelligence seemed only to have provided their fellow students with a sarcastic label for them, and their best comments in class often inspired bored chuckles. To Ellen, the basic, inescapable fact was that "women—all women—have a very tough time at Fleming." We assume she includes herself in this group.

A discussion participant might draw attention to some of Ellen's central decisions in creating a teaching image: what to wear, and how to move in the classroom. As Ellen herself makes us aware, these are not trivial considerations. Ellen draws the parameters sharply: "Look too frilly, and you come across as an airhead; but if you look too severe, you're a schoolmarm." She also mentions the institutional custom (for men) of beginning class by removing their jackets and rolling up their shirt-sleeves. Given the sexual tension in the air in LG VI's meetings, Ellen felt that following this custom would be completely inappropriate for a woman. She uses the "striptease" analogy to explain why.

Another element in her immediate situation at the end of the (A) case is the unpredictability of the Fleming heating system—quite a familiar problem in most schools. On the first warm day of the year in Canada, the heat went *up,* not down, and the "temperature must have gotten up near 90°." Ellen and the students were all struggling to continue a serious discussion despite increasing physical discomfort and growing mental fuzziness. Everyone must have suffered at least some loss of mental acuity.

All of these factors bear directly on Ellen's situation.

3. *Although a male teacher would have been far less likely to inspire a wolf whistle, do you find some elements in Ellen's predicament that might apply to teachers of both sexes?*

Speakers will probably isolate a few common elements of threat from Ellen's specific challenge: first, she has been unceremoniously interrupted during a class. This violation of conventions would irritate and distract most teachers. Second, she has been symbolically booted from her role as "teacher" or "possessor of superior information and insight" down to a lower level: female creature. This instantaneous loss of status could happen to a man if he felt that an *ad hominem* attack (a prank, insult, or disrespectful personal joke) had occurred in class. If the wolf whistle is taken as just another form of heckling, the challenge to Ellen is not so much sexual as grounded in her right to stand before LG VI at Fleming and act as their leader.

4. *What do you think the whistle implied?*

Responses to this will vary according to how sympathetic the speaker feels toward the whistler. One may take a lenient attitude and call the whistle a good-natured joke, or even treat it as a sincere, if inappropriate, compliment to Ellen's looks. A hard-line feminist would take it as an insult, a symbolic reduction of Ellen to an inferior, available, "sex object"—all the more infuriating because it comes from a member of a group that is, in the nature of the situation, inferior to her. After all, who is the teacher here? Who should set the rules of classroom behavior?

At this point, it would be useful to make sure that attention has been paid to the way Ellen reports reacting to the whistle. She says "anger crashed" over her for a split second. And the verbal content of her anger was this: "What nerve! How childish! What an insult!" We note that Ellen makes no mention of having felt flattered by the whistle.

5. *What should Ellen have done?*

At this point it might be interesting to circle back to the territory we opened with the first question and note whether participants have altered their initial positions. What responses might Ellen have made? They range from tough to lenient, hot to cool. She could have turned on the whistler and demanded that he apologize. Or she could have interrupted the class for a lecture on appropriate manners for MBA students. Or she could have delivered a feminist tirade delineating the unwelcome implications of a wolf whistle. Or she could have made some sort of joke, possibly including sexual overtones of her own, to show that she was not flustered. Or she could have ignored the whistle and continued the class, but made silent plans to deal with the underlying issues at some future date.

As is customary with cliff-hanger questions that precede distribution of the (B) case, the discussion leader should allow the seminar participants time to discuss the pros and cons of a wide range of responses before giving them the (B) case, which contains the description of how Ellen Collins actually did respond to the wolf whistle.

—◆—

After the (B) case has been read:

1. *Ellen considered several options. Would you have included any others?*

She considered turning to the women in the class for help and support—after all, she had been insulted as a woman, and her position as role model for the female students might have dictated recognizing a certain solidarity with them. What might have been the result of this course of action? We know that the women in LG VI were not a distinct social unit—the bright ones had been ostracized by their female as well as male colleagues. We also know that the dominant impression they made on Ellen was one of demoralization. Ellen's decision not to address them in her need was probably correct: they might not have come to her defense. An appeal to them could have seemed like further evidence that women couldn't survive unscarred at Fleming. If a woman teacher crumbles under attack, what can one expect of her students?

2. *What do you think of the response she actually made?*

Ellen decided to keep cool, physically turn away from the whistle (symbolically reject its very existence, momentarily close off the whole area of the room from her realm of attention), and deliberately continue the class. She called upon a male student—one she knew to be competent—and tossed him a "direct and simple question" relating to something *she* had just put on the board. In other words, she acted competently, professionally, and perhaps just a touch condescendingly (a "simple" question could be interpreted that way). Most important: she kept control of the situation. Then she did something that is advisable for all teachers in moments of stress: she used the time while he answered to "collect her thoughts." In other words, she bought time, and she would have calmed down enough by the end of the student's contribution to concentrate on leading the rest of the discussion coherently. Not surprisingly, Ellen mentions, "the class went on with no further jarring incidents."

Most participants will endorse her actions, but there may be some "hardliners" (either feminists or those simply given to bolstering teachers' authority in the face of challenge) who criticize her leniency. These people will maintain that she failed in her responsibility as a teacher when she purposely ignored the impertinence and meted out absolutely no punishment or reprimand (no negative reinforcement for unacceptable behavior). The class could profitably consider this question: What is the best treatment for childishness that verges on insult in class? If a teacher reacts with quiet, cool maturity, may one rely on the heckler's innate sense of propriety and decency to reassert itself and teach the appropriate lesson? May the teacher assume that the student's classmates will gather around after class and lavishly express scorn for such foolishness? In other words, can the lesson about decorum be taught indirectly? Or does it fall squarely on the teacher's shoulders to address the issue in public? What, in short, is the most effective method of teaching the necessary lesson here?

3. *What effect would a pointed—perhaps sarcastic—joke have had?*

Many will assert that a joke, particularly a sexually charged joke, would have been disastrous because it would have symbolically lowered Ellen to the heckler's childish level. Some participants may, however, espouse this sort of rejoinder as palpable proof that the teacher is neither shocked not rattled. But jokes are always dangerous: they frequently evoke embarrassed, rather than appreciative, laughter. A joke in this context would probably have had such an effect. Humor's many implicit complexities provide an inexhaustible topic—one that certainly could surface in this direction. What is the effect when the victim of an insult makes the joke? Are there any humorous ways Ellen could have deflected the condescension of the wolf whistle and turned the situation to the whistler's disadvantage? Would she have lost dignity by engaging in this sort of repartee?

4. *Can we compare the impact of "muddling through" (as Ellen managed to do) with an angry retort and a lecture on classroom manners?*

This topic should have been broached at least indirectly during consideration of the various options Ellen could have taken to respond to the wolf whistle. Many teachers find themselves in a state of hyperacute concentration when they encounter an unexpected challenge or symbolic insult in the classroom. It is surprising how often they report instantaneously considering a wide variety of responses, almost as if a screen were rapidly flashing these alternatives before their eyes. Generally speaking, those who choose the least unsettling response—making *no* direct rebuttal to an insult, and playing for time while their tempers cool—reap the benefits of their instinctive reluctance to create a scene. They generally receive a reward: increased cooperation from the class.

5. *What do you think of Ellen's statement, "Women live under microscopes at places like Fleming"? Is this true of other groups as well as other places? What are some consequences of this situation?*

This question ought to open the discussion to the consideration of other minorities and definitions of "minority." The thrust of thought here should be to call attention to their conspicuousness and self-consciousness, and the inescapable tension that these cause. All "aliens" suffer awkwardness of some sort in a mainstream culture—particularly one like Fleming where the potential stakes of "belonging" are high. Women and other visibly different and underrepresented groups are, presumably, taking their MBA degrees at Fleming because they, like the males of the dominant, traditional business culture, want influential and remunerative positions in the corporate world. But they realize that the folkways of this culture do not come naturally to them, and the culture does not welcome them unequivocally. They have not been bred to its unstated norms, and they know perfectly well that many of its folkways define them as inferior. Note the scorn with which LG VI greeted classroom contributions by women—*even* the extraordinarily bright ones—because, as Ellen observed, women were traditionally ostracized in this culture. The brilliance of a few women made no appreciable dents in this prejudice.

What are the consequences of life in a goldfish bowl? Participants will probably mention Charlie Brennan's irritating influence (notice how he calls attention to the trappings of women's clothing and accessories and thereby heightens their self-consciousness).

The women in the group seem to have reacted, by and large, by losing self-confidence. What does this mean—that they internalized the culture's lack of confidence in them? That they truly doubted their own capacity to contribute and excel? That they labored under extra pressures in an already tense atmosphere and therefore performed all the more poorly? The same generalizations may be ventured about other "standout" groups.

6. *What steps might you advise the administration to take to improve the institutional culture for women?*

This is patently a "take-home" question. It is unlikely that the discussion group will produce a coherent, effective blueprint for social progress in graduate schools of administration and management in the ten or fifteen minutes or less left at the end of a case discusssion. Is it sufficient to bring women (or other minorities) without preparation into a culture that is not only alien but demonstrably (if sometimes subtly) hostile? If not, what sort of preparation? (Support groups, teacher-student conferences, special advising, introductory orientation programs, counseling?) Is it the institution's responsibility to help prepare these people? Or is it the students' problem to survive the unfavorable odds against them and come through their years at Fleming all the tougher? Will the situation improve on its own, without administrative interference, as the numbers of Fleming MBA women in the corporate world increase and improve their status? Should efforts be made to recruit Fleming's women graduates as visitors, counselors, contacts, and unofficial advisers to women students? What might be some potential negative results of creating special support services for women?

This last discussion question, in essence, asks the seminar group to solve a besetting problem of all academic institutions whose dominant culture for many years had been male-oriented. But the issue is indisputably important. Talented, competent, and basically self-confident people like Ellen Collins are now populating these previously closed societies in increasing numbers. The problems these women face—and the problems they pose to the institution—deserve the most serious and immediate considerations if valuable skills and talents are not to be wasted.

EXHIBIT 1 *The Day the Heat Went On*

Study Questions

1. From Ellen Collins's point of view, what is at stake at the end of the (A) case?
2. What immediate course of action would you advise for her?
3. What dynamic do you perceive working in these events? What are some underlying principles? Is this uniquely a "woman's issue"?

EXHIBIT 2 *The Day the Heat Went On*

Discussion Questions

After the (A) case has been read:

1. [To the opening speaker]: If you were Ellen Collins, what would you do when you heard that wolf whistle?
2. [To the backstop]: Could you help us appraise Ellen's position? What do you consider to be the critical elements in her situation at Fleming?
3. Although a male teacher would have been far less likely to inspire a wolf whistle, do you find some elements in Ellen's predicament that might apply to teachers of both sexes?
4. What do you think the whistle implied?
5. What should Ellen have done?

—◆—

After the (B) case has been read:

1. Ellen reports having considered several options. Would you have included others?
2. What do you think of the response she actually made?
3. What effect would a pointed—perhaps sarcastic—joke have had?
4. Can we compare the impact of "muddling through" (as Ellen managed to do) with the alternative that some teachers choose: an angry retort and a lecture on classroom manners?
5. What do you think of Ellen's statement, "Women live under microscopes at places like Fleming"? Is this true of other groups? Other places? What are some consequences of this situation?
6. What steps might you advise the administration to take to improve the institutional culture for women?

The Day the Heat Went On (A) and (B)

RESEARCHER'S PERSPECTIVE

This commentary on "The Day the Heat Went On" was written by Abby Hansen for the Developing Discussion Leadership Skills and the Teaching by the Case Method seminars. Its objective is to help instructors in the development of their own teaching plans for this case.
(HBS No. 5-384-100)

Distributed by HBS Publishing Division, Harvard Business School, Boston, MA 02163. Printed in U.S.A.

This may be regarded either as a "woman's issue" case or as a case in self-management in the face of a moderately insulting form of heckling. Ellen Collins faces several obstacles besides that of her gender: she is young enough to lack the automatic aura of authority that age bestows on teachers; she "inherits" her class extremely late in the semester; and she is different from LG VI's other teachers because besides being female, she is soft-voiced and somewhat more formal in style (she always wears a jacket when teaching). Although in this case the disruption takes the form of a wolf whistle when the teacher sheds her blazer for the first time in the classroom, it might have been some other form of needling—a catcall or other rude noise, perhaps—addressed at a man. Nonetheless, Ellen herself emphasizes the fact that Fleming presents special problems to women—students and faculty members alike. It is not only a male-dominated institution, it has a mission to prepare students for a generally male-dominated field: public administration. It is thus no surprise that the women in the group Ellen is teaching strike her as demoralized. They are reticent in discussions; they avoid making themselves conspicuous; they are silently offended by many of their male colleagues' jokes; and they join in ostracizing the three women in the class who don't happen to conform to the norm—the "outstanding, outspoken" ones.

The general institutional culture seems to sanction the rough-tough style of teaching that Charlie Brennan is espousing (he's considered an "old pro"). Surely his condescending speech to the women of LG VI implies that he thinks little of their ability to grasp the simplest social rules of the professional world into which they aspire to assimilate themselves, and we do not hear of his giving any analogous speeches to the men in LG VI. The final piece of evidence we have for the difficulties women encounter at Fleming (and institutions like it) is the sort of pranks that are considered traditional there. These, we gather, often take on a sexual cast, show poor taste, and present women in a purely physical role. But they are traditional, accepted (by male and female students), and, apparently, destined to continue. For a woman to protest against this sort of humor would mark her as a spoilsport and further isolate her from the dominant culture. This presents a dilemma for both Ellen Collins and her women students: adaptation to the prevailing mode implies accepting it, but accepting it can also imply a tacit certification of one's own inferiority. There's a Catch 22 for women in schools of administration and similar institutions. Ellen must respond to the symbolic insult of the wolf whistle both as a new instructor and as a female leader of a 75% male group. She cannot escape the issue of gender.

But she can underplay it, and this is what she does. Ellen's tactic is to rise above the challenge. She realizes instinctively that revealing her instantaneous fury would be the worst thing she could do. Thus Ellen masks her reaction, focuses attention far from the whistle's point of origin, and continues the class as briskly as possible. She does not relinquish control; she makes the next call, and resists the temptation to choose a woman speaker (which could have inflated this fairly minor irritation into a threatening male-female confrontation). Ellen's calmness achieves a multiple purpose: she keeps the reins in hand, continues the discussion, and—most important—gains time to compose herself and let her anger cool.

Ellen faces a sex-specific version of a common challenge to any young instructor in the second semester at a high-pressure professional school like Fleming: establishing and maintaining authority over a group of students not much younger than oneself who have formed a strong internal social organization while enduring intense academic and social pressure since early September. She handles it successfully by simply continuing to do her job: lead the discussion. April is a crucial month in academics: not close enough to the end of term to signal the imminence of release, but still far enough along for students to feel both fatigued and yet fairly experienced and powerful within the system. An unseasonably warm day at this time of year in a cold climate like Toronto's tends to kindle spring fever, and Ellen seems to have run into a sample of just this sort of thing. It could have been much worse.

Like many young instructors beginning their academic careers, Ellen may also have felt somewhat uncomfortable in her new role of leadership. Permitting one student to flirt (in the interest of relieving the group's tension after a class with Charlie Brennan) might have telegraphed a camaraderie Ellen did not really intend. Ambivalence about having suddenly joined the power structure (holding not only the reins of discussion but the power of the grade over people who are not so very different in age from oneself and possibly even more professionally experienced) is endemic among younger instructors. Ellen, thus, has her own feelings to manage as well as the potential disrespect of her class. The wolf whistle clearly went too far in the direction of reducing the distance between teacher and students. It was tasteless and insulting in implication, if not in intention. It may have been a useful signal to Ellen that the time had come to tighten the reins a bit.

Had Ellen retorted with an impromptu reprimand, she would have risked infantilizing the group and thereby encouraging the same sort of resentment a naughty child feels at being chastised. Further, all the members of LG VI would have felt embarrassed, and some of them might have felt that Ellen, being female, had acted "schoolmarmishly."

Aside from being LG VI's only woman teacher, Ellen has other problems. Her late entry into the academic lives of LG VI is a great stumbling block. The segmentation of the Fleming student body into LGs creates social units that act in a self-protective manner—that is, they band together against instructors. They fear that teachers may try to "wipe the floor" with them—and the Charlie Brennans do so, proving their fears were right. Thus they attempt to support each other and forestall instructors' possible abuse. Sometimes such self-protectiveness escalates into hostility; when an instructor is friendly, it can turn the student body's reaction into either a peculiar sort of group adoration or into contempt (if the teacher shows technical incompetence). When a teacher is genuinely helpful, concerned, competent, fair, and good-humored, a good rapport—and good teaching evaluations—will likely result. We may see Ellen profiting from such a situation here. Teaching directly after Charlie Brennan may be a real blessing for her. If he is the heavy in this case, she is its heroine. Ellen gets the superior teaching evaluations from LG VI—possibly because she is sensitive enough to make the effort to see her students' needs. By serenely ignoring the tasteless wolf whistle, she also shows LG VI evidence of her maturity. She demonstrated self-confidence and a general worthiness to lead them. Grace under pressure is an admirable quality in any leader.

But, issues like grace and leadership aside, the sexual element in this case should not be ignored. Ellen presents Fleming as an institution with antifemale prejudice embedded in its structure, and she furthermore offers this incident as but a minor example of the sort of harassment that women instructors often encounter here. Despite her apparent efforts to steer a middle course and keep a low profile—avoiding the stereotype of the overdressed siren or severe "radical feminist"—Ellen runs into a mild but identifiable form of sexual harassment. She seems very willing to make adjustments to adapt to a male-dominated culture, but she cannot escape symbolic hostility directed specifically at her gender. The "woman's issue" aspect of this case can be played down, but it won't disappear, and it involves far broader concerns than the fairly simple choice of whether or not to wear a jacket while teaching.

The Introduction (A), (B), and (C)

TEACHING NOTE

This teaching note has been prepared by Marina McCarthy as an aid to instructors in classroom use of the case series "The Introduction" (A) 9-386-146, (B) 9-386-147, and (C) 9-386-148.
(HBS No. 5-386-170)

Usage

1) "The Introduction" can be used as a springboard for a discussion on what to do on the first day of class. Seminar participants can examine the manner in which Leslie O'Connor chose to begin her class. They may analyze the choices she made, provide alternatives, or offer versions of how they have begun their own first classes.

2) "The Introduction" can also be viewed as a study in dealing with a problem student.

A related discussion could evolve here, addressing the issue of control in higher education. Some of the seminar participants may feel that control or discipline "is not what it used to be." Participants may see Dianne or Mike as symptomatic of a larger issue.

3) Perhaps less obvious for discussion is the issue of consulting with colleagues about a professional concern or problem. We learn in the (A) case that Leslie is open and frank with Jo Smith, a colleague who notices she is upset. Participants may venture into the pros and cons—risks and benefits—of sharing one's problems or concerns.

Case Summary
The (A) Case

"The Introduction" is about a young but experienced instructor's first class of the academic year—a required freshman English class at Pax Vobiscum College (PVC). Leslie O'Connor, the instructor, has taught at PVC, a large Catholic university, for several years. In addition to teaching at PVC, she is a doctoral student at a nearby university.

Leslie has taught freshman English before. The model that she used with a mixed-class elective/seminar the previous term had proved to be very effective. She decides to adopt it for use with her freshmen in the fall.

After announcing course requirements, handing out syllabi, and so forth, Leslie has the students form a circle, pair up in twos, and interview one another. They are asked to find out about their neighbors so that each student can then introduce the other to the rest of the class. Introductions are proceeding smoothly until the last (twenty-sixth student) introduction. A female student introduces a male student as follows:

> Well . . . Mike is from Westin, Connecticut. He attended Westin Central High School. So far, he likes his roommate. Mike has a red Firebird which he drives too fast. Mike likes to drink, uses cocaine often, has a 21-year-old girlfriend who is . . .

> [pause], oh yes, and he can't wait for this boring class to get over.

Leslie is angry. She returns to her office and recounts "the introduction" to Jo Smith, her colleague from across the hall.

The (B) Case

In (B) we learn what Leslie did with the few remaining minutes of class. She decides to dismiss the group early, hoping that her tone of voice conveys to the group her disapproval of both students involved in the introduction (Dianne Quinn and Mike O'Neil). Leslie then nods and acknowledges students as they leave the room. Dianne attempts to engage Leslie in a conversation about James Joyce after class, but Leslie is perfunctory in her responses and continues to nod and acknowledge the other students as they leave the room. Leslie never notices Mike leave the room; moreover, she never notices his expression or reactions during "the introduction."

After consulting with Jo, Leslie decides that the best resolution would be to ask both Dianne and Mike to see her after the next class meeting. Dianne, however, does not show up in class. Leslie assumes Dianne has transferred to another section and never bothers to pursue talking with Mike. She recalls:

> Since I had not anticipated this turn in events, I dismissed speaking with Mike at all. In a way I felt a sense of relief—as if the problem was over. In my mind the case had solved itself: Dianne had behaved inappropriately, and must have decided to change to another section.

The (C) Case

Two months pass. Leslie feels the class is going very well. She and Mike O'Neil have developed a good rapport. Mike has told Leslie how much he enjoys English class. He is a faithful contributor to class discussions and generally has a very good attitude. Mike also tells Leslie that he and his girlfriend are anticipating the birth of a child. Leslie notes Mike's increasing maturity as the weeks progress. Upon returning from lunch one afternoon, Leslie finds a note under her door from Mike, informing her that a daughter was born several days before. Leslie confers with Jo about the note. She also reflects back to that first day of class and briefly conjectures about the degree of Mike's involvement in the introduction. She then decides "it's water under the bridge."

Questions for Discussion

After the (A) case has been read:

1. What is the teaching situation? Specifically, a) What type of school is PVC? b) What is the physical makeup of the room? c) What is the design of the course?

a) PVC is a traditional Catholic university that became completely coeducational only within the last decade. Originally an urban university for the city's immigrant Catholic population, it later moved to its present suburban Gothic campus. It is currently enjoying an exceptionally healthy admission pool for the fifth straight year, and is expanding its facilities and programs while other institutions of higher learning are experiencing retrenchment.

b) Leslie O'Connor's classroom is a large room, presumably designed for lecturing. It has a raised platform at the front of the room, on which sits a faculty desk. When she initially enters the room, chairs are arranged in rows.

c) Freshman English at PVC is the only small class that entering students experience during their first term. Classes are intentionally small—but the case does not indicate whether this choice is made by the university or the English Department. Leslie O'Connor has taught freshman English before but decides to depart from her customary practices because of her favorable recent experience teaching a mixed-level elective. She drops one class meeting per week, lengthens the second, and adds one-to-one writing conferrences. When members of the group agree to take turns bringing refreshments, Leslie announces she will initiate the tradition and produces a bag of cookies.

2. What do we know about Leslie O'Connor?

Leslie O'Connor is an instructor in a predominantly male department of the university. She is a doctoral student at another institution, though she once had been an undergraduate in the PVC English Department. Her previous success in teaching English is what prompted her old English professor to ask if she would be interested in teaching freshmen at PVC. Leslie is quite friendly with a colleague across the hall from her office.

3. What sequence does Leslie take in opening her class?

a) Distributes her syllabus and discusses course requirements.
b) Informs the group that she is modeling the freshman English class after a mixed-class seminar that she taught the previous term.
c) Substitutes individual student conferences for one class per week. Lengthens the remaining class meetings.
d) Determines first that the class wants to keep the "refreshment tradition," then passes out refreshments (in the spirit of the previous semester's seminar).
e) Asks students to form a circle, pair up and each interview his or her neighbor, then introduce him or her to the rest of the class.

4. How does the class react to Dianne and Mike's "introduction"?

According to Leslie, the students appear uncomfortable. A few gasp, and silence falls. They appear to be avoiding eye contact.

Evaluation

5. What is your evaluation of Leslie's opening? What else might she have done?

6. How well did she carry out her plan?

7. What risks, if any, were involved?

Leslie could have begun by asking for introductions and then discussing the syllabus. Instead, she wanted to deal with administrative issues first. She felt she needed to inform the class that she was canceling one class meeting per week and lengthening a second. Some students might have commitments—other classes, jobs, and so forth—after class. They needed to know about the altered schedule and make arrangements or change sections. Meeting from 3:00 to 4:30 instead of from 3:00 to 4:15 might make a difference to students who worked in the dining hall, for example. Given that the students were "just freshmen," should Leslie have held the announcement for a week?

Each class likes to think of itself as unique. Perhaps Leslie was undiplomatic in giving the impression she was trying to clone a successful class from the previous semester. Conversely, could the freshmen be flattered that Leslie was using an "upperclass" model with them? What were Leslie's assumptions about a required course vis-à-vis an elective?

What is appropriate for one group may not be for another; perhaps passing out refreshments to a group of students fresh out of high school was a mistake. On the other hand, the students seemed eager to talk with their neighbors and introduce each other. The baked goods may have loosened up the tense atmosphere of the first day.

Leslie could have asked students to introduce themselves, but she found that pairing students loosened up introductions. Did the students find the exercise too alien from their experiences—or their expectation of college? Did they welcome the experimentation?

Finally, does one prepare a blueprint for the first day? How much does one allow for flexibility—"adhocracy"? Should Leslie have asked students to write an in-class essay about their backgrounds and saved the introductions until the next meeting? Then she could have handed back their writing samples (an initial connection-building assignment) before the individual conferences began.

8. Why was Leslie angry over "the introduction"?

Leslie may have felt betrayed, embarrassed, offended, or stuck. Participants may add their own descriptions.

9. What risks, if any, did Leslie take in talking with Jo Smith?

It is often difficult to discuss job dilemmas with coworkers. In academia, departmental and academic politics are legitimate concerns of faculty members. What resources do faculty members have to hash out problems and concerns?

Raising this topic, which may seem peripheral to the case, may prompt a fruitful discussion. Some participants may articulate the loneliness of teaching.

Miscellaneous

10. Leslie seems haunted by the "Oh goody!" comment in response to her canceling a class per week. With the benefit of hindsight, was this a signal? What else could she have done?

After the (B) case has been read:

1. What did Leslie do with the remaining few minutes of class?

Leslie was angry and unsure of what to do. "Like a high-speed carousel, options of what to do flashed through my mind," she recalls. With only a few minutes of class remaining, she tried to establish eye contact with members of the class, most of whom, however, were "looking down at their hands." Trying to sound deliberate but not strained, Leslie hoped her tone denoted disapproval of Dianne and Mike. She lowered her voice and announced, "See you on Wednesday. You probably all need time to get to the bookstore before the dinner hour." To further signal closure, Leslie closed the folder in front of her, stood up, and went over to the instructor's desk on the raised platform in front of the classroom. She proceeded to nod to students as they left the room, and was somewhat cool to Dianne, who came up to talk after class.

2. What was Leslie's plan with regard to Dianne and Mike?

Leslie decided the best course of action would be to talk with both students after class the following week.

3. What altered Leslie's plan?

Since Dianne did not show up, Leslie assumed the problem had solved itself: "Dianne had behaved inappropriately and must have decided to change to another section." Leslie then decided to dismiss talking with Mike at all, as if the problem was over.

Evaluation

4. What is your evaluation of the assumptions Leslie made about Mike and Dianne's involvement in "The Introduction" at the beginning of (B)? At the end of (B)?

It appears that Leslie favored Mike over Dianne—less so in the beginning of (B) than at the end. She planned to speak with both students, although she had initially been more angry at Dianne (as bearer of the news) than at Mike (who was silent during the first class).

5. Leslie had an entire week to plan. What alternatives did she have in dealing with Mike and Dianne?

Since she had collected 3x5 index cards with names and phone numbers, Leslie could have telephoned Dianne or Mike. She could have arranged an appointment with either one or both of them before the next class meeting. Instead, she decided to wait.

After the (C) case has been read:

1. Two months have now passed. What has happened with regard to the class? With regard to Mike O'Neil?

The class seems to be moving along smoothly, according to Leslie. Roommates and friends of the students are asking for transfers to the class's second term.

According to Leslie, Mike has been no trouble. On the contrary, he contributes in class and has faithfully attended writing conferences. He apparently has been confiding in Leslie since the beginning of the semester concerning his pregnant girlfriend. He also notes liking Leslie's English class—in contrast to high school, where English was his most disliked subject.

2. What is Leslie's reaction to Mike's note?

Although Leslie knew about Mike and his girlfriend, she still appears to be amazed. She mutters about his "being only 18 years old" and shows the note to her colleague Jo Smith.

3. What is Leslie's assessment of Mike's involvement in "the introduction"?

Leslie's assessment in (A) and (B) is that he is a questionable culprit. At the end of (B), however, and throughout (C), it appears that she feels Mike's involvement is unimportant.

Evaluation

4. Should Leslie ignore the note, congratulate Mike, ask how the mother and daughter are doing, or refer Mike to the counseling department or dean of students' office?

Leslie did not contact the counseling department or the dean of students' office about Mike because her previous experiences led her to conclude that they were of little help. Leslie took on Mike all by herself.

5. Should Leslie have brought up adoption as a possibility? Should she have suggested that Mike get married? That Mike take a term off to support his new family? That he consult his parish priest at home in Connecticut? (Legally, Mike is an adult.) Was Leslie doing all she could just by being an "available ear"? She never mentions the chaplain's office. Could this have been a resource for either her or Mike?

Wrap-up

Seminar participants may want to consider the "now" versus "later" dilemma in dealing with issues in a classroom.

1) By waiting until after class or the following week, one may "lose the moment."

2) "Capturing the moment," however, may be dangerous. What one *thinks* one sees may not be what happened at all.

The tension between (1) and (2) is worthy of discussion. Which is best, considering the case of Leslie O'Connor? Keep in mind that the case says that Leslie was very angry.

Are the issues surrounding "The Introduction" or any other classroom incident really resolved because the *instructor* feels they are? Is there such a thing as a total resolution for everyone? Or does one have to learn to live with uncertainty for oneself *and* for others?

Seminar participants may want to venture at this point into a discussion of when (or if) values fit into the curriculum or a faculty-student relationship. The discussion may be specific to PVC, which is religiously affiliated, or may apply to any university. College students are legally adults. Where does an instructor's responsibility lie in the area of personal life, morals, and values?

"Look at the Fish!": Karen Prentiss and Professor Lockwood (A), (B), and (C)

TEACHING NOTE

This teaching note was developed, researched, and written by Abby Hansen for use with the case series "Look at the Fish!": Karen Prentiss and Professor Lockwood (A) HGSE 1, (B) HGSE 12, and (C) HGSE 13 to help instructors prepare to lead case discussions. It is meant to stimulate discussion, not present a definitive analysis.
(HGSE No. 6)

Distributed by HBS Publishing Division, Harvard Business School, Boston, MA 02163.
Printed in U.S.A.

Seminar leaders may do well to remind participants that "Look at the Fish!" presents a single student's viewpoint. This fact implies imbalance. We do not know how the class seemed to Professor Lockwood. Nor do we know how it seemed to Karen's fellow students. But we do know a good deal about the intensity with which Karen observed, and reacted to, virtually every detail of Professor Lockwood's classroom behavior. If this case alerts instructors to the magnitude of the impact that they can have on students, it will achieve at least one useful purpose.

The case makes it clear that Andrew Lockwood commanded respect at Farwestern Graduate School of Education. But it also makes it clear that Karen's respect for him was tempered with fear. Her ultimate reaction to his teaching style is ambivalent—she learned the course content and many other things, but at a price. Her ambivalent reactions raise some profound questions that all teachers face, implicitly or explicitly. How does one help students prepare for careers in which they will face controversy? Seen through Karen Prentiss's eyes, Andrew Lockwood seems to adhere to the "boot camp" approach; be tough because the real world is even tougher. Karen describes other instructors at the school as taking a different, more nurturing approach. Most teaching seminars will include advocates of both styles (with shades of gray in between), and this case can provide a good jumping-off point into a discussion of style and tone in the classroom.

This note will summarize some major issues that I see in this case. Leaders of teaching seminars will doubtless want to derive their own lists of potential topics from the rich data that Karen Prentiss has given us. But I would be surprised if "power," which Karen mentions explicitly in the (C) case, failed to appear on most of these lists.

Power in the Classroom

Karen Prentiss mentions several lessons that she learned about power, but all of these have a common thread: in the university (the setting in which she would like to make her career), power lies with older, white males. And Karen thinks that such people must be approached with a particular style (terse, factual, unemotional), which Lockwood has taught her to assume—at least as a sort of emotional camouflage. Karen's voyage from initial humiliation and a zero-minus grade to final triumph and an A required abandoning her inclination to speak intuitively and take intellectual and emotional risks in class. It might be useful for a seminar group to take up this issue from several points of view: Did Karen overreact? Might she be overstating the case? If her reaction does seem appropriate, what did she gain (and lose) by adapting to Lockwood's criteria for this class? Did she make a Faustian bargain (as she seems to think) or, perhaps, make the same exchange of innocence for experience that anyone does in the course of becoming more worldly-wise?

Although Karen does not spend much time discussing the asymmetry of power in the discussion class itself, seminar participants may wish to. What does it imply when a teacher sets rules and refuses to accede to students' requests for flexibility? What does it communicate when a teacher calls attention in class to the weakness of students' contributions? Is there a difference between doing this early in the semester (Lockwood does it on the first day) and later? What does it mean when a teacher hands students' first papers back at the beginning of a class session by fanning them out in a prominent location with grades clearly visible?

Cases in which younger instructors experience classroom insurrections make potentially interesting contrasts with this one. It is not uncommon for younger instructors—graduate students or assistant professors, whether male or female—to engender resistance in their students by attempting to dominate discussions. But Andrew Lockwood is a full professor, in his fifties, with an outstanding reputation; the extent of his control over the class surprises Karen. (Note how she catches the tone of his introductory lecture and wonders why the older, mid-career students aren't walking out on him.) It might be interesting to ask some hypothetical questions on this theme—what if a woman had behaved as Lockwood did? What if Lockwood had been in his late twenties? What if Lockwood were a new assistant professor? What if Lockwood hadn't yet published?

The Student

Readers of this case learn quite a bit about Karen Prentiss. What did Professor Lockwood know about Karen's "crazy drive," her eagerness to take on challenges, her resilience, her determination to play and win by his rules? How much of her personality could he have read from her appearance, demeanor, and early classroom performances? What might he have done to learn more about her? What might he have gained, and lost, by making such an attempt?

It might be profitable to discuss the question of whether Professor Lockwood fully exploited Karen's potential as a classroom resource. Given what we, the readers, discover of her ability to adapt, learn, function in a group (her study group), and gain command of the material, did he miss an opportunity by intimidating her so thoroughly that she contributed less in his course than in others? What about the time that his teaching style upset her so deeply that she sat through his class in a funk and could barely keep track of the discussion? What might this mean for *other* students—since Karen was not the only one whom Lockwood criticized in class or graded 0− on the first paper? What might he have gained by granting Karen and the others more power in the leadership of this class?

Teaching Style

I suspect that, more than many cases, this one will engender lively debate about teaching style. Roberta Russell, Karen's Orientation Week adviser, warns her not to take Lockwood's course first semester because he is "one tough cookie." And his behavior in class immediately bears this out. He begins with sarcasm, sets tight rules and invites people who can't accept them to leave, and declines students' requests for flexible deadlines.

But the data do not end there. Karen describes Lockwood's dress as formal (always in a coat and tie, when others wore sweaters). And she found his physical gestures—brisk movements, stiff posture, counting off rules by raising a hand almost in a military gesture—intimidating. His sarcastic opening remarks at the introductory lecture led her to think: "He's putting us down." And the metaphor of height—he *stands* over students when he criticizes them—is repeated implicitly and explicitly in her descriptions and interpretations. By standing and moving up and down the aisles while his students sit, Lockwood physically reinforces the image of hierarchy. He is "superior" (another word she quotes in referring to Lockwood), which implies that the students are inferior.

Notice also how he moves toward Karen (implying menace) when she offers a comment that he considers substandard. And his characteristic gesture of standing over a student's desk and jabbing a finger either at the student or at the student's notes combines superiority and an element of symbolic attack.

I would not expect a discussion group to produce much disagreement on the issue of the effect of Lockwood's style. It would be difficult to interpret his movements, words, and content (a classic "just do what I say" contract) as anything but intimidating. But the question of the value, and costs, of intimidation may very well arise. Even Karen, who seems ambivalent about what she learned from Lockwood, ends (see part C) by saying that she took valuable lessons from his class and can see a place for his sort of teaching in a university.

A seminar group may want to discuss the value of this sort of teaching as preparation for the complexities of real professional life, especially in the field of education, where policymakers in particular are often under fire. Those who design and implement academic policies often find themselves in bitter public battles. Is Lockwood's classroom toughness the best way to prepare students for this? What about the "warm, fuzzy" approach of other colleagues at the Ed School? What helps a student become a more effective practitioner—a nurturing teacher or a tough cookie? Another interesting question: Can one shift style during a semester—start protectively and gradually toughen up, or the reverse?

In many teaching cases, there is a disparity between the styles of teachers and students. This disparity points to a basic question: How qualified is a student to judge the appropriateness of a teacher's behavior, at least until the lessons of the class have had enough time to play out?

Grading

What is the impact of the first evaluations in any course? What signals do they send? (Note what Karen's first grade did to her.) What does it mean to give out low grades without specific comments? What does it mean to give grades out publicly? What does it mean to create one's own internal grading system, divorced from the conventions of the university? (Note that Lockwood used a "0 to check plus" system during the bulk of his course, and only adopted the A through D system of the rest of the institution for final and course grades.)

Students may wish to discuss what Lockwood may have accomplished with his unusual grading system. Some may advance the argument that its very harshness created *esprit de corps* in the class as a defensive measure. Certainly, there is evidence in Karen's words that this occurred in her study group.

Contract

All teachers establish contracts, explicit and implicit, with their students. Lockwood's was probably more explicit than most. (He began the course by laying down the rules in public and out loud.) But what about his implicit contract? How did his demeanor, dress, style of movement, gestures, and expressions contribute to his contract? What did Karen infer? (We have a good deal of evidence on this point. She takes his suggestion to form study groups as a "command" and assumes that he means it in a condescending way—so that students won't waste his time with stupid comments.) She also assumes that part of the contract is that students will pay full attention to Lockwood; in other words, she assumes that he needs to be the focal point of the group (this comes up when he holds a packet of papers, but does not distribute them, and when she mentions that he only left center stage during role-plays, and then that he returned to lead the debriefing discussion).

Students may wish to discuss the pros and cons of the sort of one-sided contract that Lockwood offered his students—"adopt my rules or leave." What allowance does Lockwood make for personal differences in a diverse class that included a wide range of student backgrounds and ages? (We hear of Ed School students, School of Government students, foreign students, students with children in day care, older professionals.) The effect of Lockwood's rigor makes Karen work twice as hard to remedy what she perceives as her deficiencies. Realizing that she has begun with a comparative disadvantage—no idea of how to study with cases or work with a study group—she sacrifices many hours and sleepless nights to this course. And her effort succeeds. We hear little of how the Israeli general fared in this course. Or what the parents of those children in day care did to get through.

Study Groups

Professor Lockwood suggested (commanded) students to form study groups, and they did so immediately, with whoever was sitting nearby. What are some other ways in which study groups might have been formed? Did Karen lose anything by ending up in a study group with other women of similar age? What might Lockwood have achieved by managing this process more closely? What do study groups, in general, accomplish? (Certainly, they foster cooperation over competition. What is the effect of this on the tenor of group discussions, especially in a class where the teacher continues to foster a competitive style?)

Role Playing/Video

This is one of the few cases in our collection in which a student describes the experience of role-plays and videotaping. It might be worthwhile to concentrate on her descriptions and to discuss other ways in which these events might be handled. Role-plays can spring up spontaneously or "be sprung" on the class. Lockwood—at least initially—chooses the latter method. Given that he did surprise students by suddenly announcing a role-play and assigning roles, what might he have done to debrief students when the exercise was over? What is the effect of the way in which he did handle this part of the exercise? We have no data about the way in which the professor selected people to play roles. What are some considerations that he might have used? What might have been advisable for him to know about students in order to make the most productive choices? What are the implications of how he did use the tapes—and how might he have used them differently?

Some Notes on Usage

Given that this case presents a vivid view from the student's perspective of a teacher in action, it might be useful to place it early in a teaching seminar, where its intensity of observation and interpretation can show participants the value of examining their own teaching styles. (There may be an alert and sensitive observer like Karen Prentiss in their next class!)

I would suggest introducing this case with a caveat about its imbalance. Professor Lockwood's observations of Karen and the rest of the class are conspicuously absent. It might be useful to redress this imbalance by introducing some sort of role-playing from Professor Lockwood's point of view.

This case would also fit well in a section on setting the teaching and learning contract. Karen describes how Professor Lockwood presented his expectations, how he reacted to students' requests for amendments to this explicit contract, and how he "behaved" the contract in class (he stuck to his rules). Her observations provide the reader with an unusually complete picture of contract-setting in action.

A final note. The reference to "Look at the Fish!" refers to the reading "Louis Agassiz as a Teacher," found in *Teaching and the Case Method*.

"How Do You Expect Us to Get This If It Isn't in Your Notes?" (A) and (B)

TEACHING NOTE

This note was designed and written by Abby Hansen for use with the case series "How Do You Expect Us to Get This If It Isn't in Your Notes?" (A) HSPH 1 and (B) HSPH 7 to help instructors prepare to lead case discussions. It is meant to stimulate discussion, not present a definitive analysis. The School of Public Health is grateful to President Derek Bok of Harvard University for a grant in support of case development. (HSPH No. 4)

In this teaching note, I will give some general comments on the case and then summarize a few key issues that I perceive in this material. It would be a great mistake to limit the discussion of "How Do You Expect Us to Get This . . ." to math teaching. One principal issue that emerges is the typical confusion that accompanies a shift in pedagogical paradigm—for any teacher. Mary Ann Demski is an academic with an outstanding grasp of her subject. Still in the early stages of evolving from student to professor, she vividly recalls her frustration with the passivity of listening to lectures. As a professor, however, she must function in an institution where this method is still the norm. The conflict implicit in this situation shows in her approach to teaching.

Mary Ann's intrinsic generosity seems to be leading her in two directions: she wants to give her students (1) the gift of active participation *and* (2) the gift of good, clear lectures (during which they can just look and listen while she does all the work). This contradiction seems to suggest that Mary Ann's pedagogical loyalty is divided. She wants to observe faculty norms (note that she is trying to dress more professionally—in tailored slacks rather than jeans—and fine-tuning her work schedule to boost her research productivity). But she is empathetic to her students' feelings (having been in their shoes just two years previously), and the notion that students should understand just "20 percent" of a lecture frustrates her. Her course design, her instructions to students, and her behavior in class all reveal these underlying contradictions.

Like Dan Shea in "Trouble in Stat. 1B," Mary Ann is taking a risk by introducing participatory, discussion-based pedagogy into a lecture-based context where effective teaching doesn't earn promotions. Implicit in her descriptions of the way in which most instructors teach technical subjects at this school (and in her senior colleague's advice to her) is the notion that there is no institutional mandate for pedagogical change.

Thus she and Dan Shea seem to be initiating innovations "from the bottom up." At Farwestern School of Public Health, students spend most of their time in quantitative courses listening to lectures. Mary Ann's mixed style may be catching students off guard. She lectures (this is familiar—all they have to do is listen and *not* expect to "get it" until later). But sometimes she interrupts her own lectures to present a problem for the students to work out cooperatively, right then and there (on these occasions they *do* have to "get it"). Small wonder that confusion results.

There are many universals in this case. Like all teachers, Mary Ann Demski has to find her own style. How does she want to be perceived by her students—

as a friend, a parent, a counselor, a distant authority, a superior, a judge, a comrade? She doesn't know yet. (How many young teachers do?) But clearly she is sensitive to the need to maintain her position of leadership in the classroom—and perhaps is therefore more prone to interpret a challenge as an attack than an older or higher-ranking professor would be.

Cindy Richardson's frustration probably has several sources. It stems partly from the difficult material (Mary Ann realizes this) and partly from Mary Ann's mixed messages about classroom process (Mary Ann does not yet realize this). Just where, when, and how are the students supposed to "get it"? The answers to these questions involve the issues of learning style, pacing, curriculum design, and classroom practice. They are, in short, extremely profound; their roots penetrate the deepest strata of the whole endeavor of teaching.

I would encourage participants in a teaching seminar to consider these underlying issues, rather than to focus on the surface issue—how to introduce the FFT.

Some Key Issues to Consider

1. Usage. This case could fit well in an early class session in a teaching seminar, where role change is under discussion. In this context, it would make a good pair with "The Dethroned Section Leader" (in which another young teacher is, as Mary Ann put it, "making the transition from student to faculty member").

As noted above, it could be compared with "Trouble in Stat. 1B," in which another mathematician sends mixed messages to a group of students by introducing some experimental elements of discussion-teaching into a subject and a context normally characterized by the lecture method.

Planners of teaching seminars might also use this case in a section on operating problems (how to pace a class, or how to respond to a sudden, upsetting challenge) or a section on the teaching and learning contrast.

Several words in the title of this case suggest directions of interpretation that a seminar group might pursue with profit. The case involves "expectations" (different implicit assumptions about what the teacher and students' jobs are), "getting it" (learning), and "the notes" (teaching instruments and their use). It also involves aspects of process (the "how" of teaching and learning—in this instance, a mixed bag).

2. Content vs. Process. The "Fast Fourier Transform" was the centerpiece of Mary Ann's attempted lecture, but this case is about teaching, not math. I would try to direct attention to the deepest level, where this case involves basic assumptions about learning.

Many beginning teachers have yet to sort out their beliefs about learning, or to devise systems that accommodate the potential variety of students' learning styles. Like Mary Ann, they hold on to contradictory beliefs. Mary Ann assumes that the lecturer's job is to dispense information and the students' job is to understand "20 percent" in class and "get" the rest privately. But she herself finds this model frustrating. As a student, she broke the mold and insisted on participating in a lecture class (because she wanted to "think"). As a teacher, she lectures and reassures students that it's "okay" not to understand. But she also wants her students to "think at least once in class." She encourages them to interrupt her lectures and gives them impromptu problems to work out together. These techniques require them to "get" more than 20%, at least for these portions of the class.

Mary Ann's self-contradictory operating rules lit the slow fuse for Cindy's eruption of frustration. (I also acknowledge the possibility that Cindy simply had a migraine that day, and pain made her break the social norms.) Even at Farwestern Graduate School of Public Health—where teaching is a public act, but learning is private—the winds of change are beginning to blow (and they are, not surprisingly, kicking up a little dust).

A seminar instructor would do well to prepare a few questions that direct the group's attention to the way in which Mary Ann set up her classroom process. She invited students to interrupt, and she switched between "giving" them examples and "letting" them talk to each other and work out problems while she stepped out of the process. These are universal aspects of all teaching.

To downplay the mathematical content and emphasize the underlying dynamic, I would suggest that the seminar instructor try to "personalize" the process issues by inviting participants from nontechnical disciplines to present relevant events from their teaching.

3. The Influence of the Past. One of the most fascinating aspects of this case is the way in which Mary Ann reenacts her past educational experience—with a twist. In a sense, her reaction to Cindy's classroom challenge is like a time-delayed, role-reversed replay of the scene in which she interrupted Professor Liu, and he, instead of encouraging and supporting her, called her "stupid"—the very appellation that her college classmates most feared!

It is significant that, in her own student days, Mary Ann (like Cindy) began to feel frustrated with the passivity of attending lectures (like a "stenographer") and eventually found the courage to break the college norms, interrupt a professor, and request an instant explanation (twice, just as Cindy did). In both cases, the student slowed the pace of the class, to the professor's annoyance.

But Mary Ann's interruption of her college professor elicited an unmistakable insult, while Cindy's interruption elicited compliance (however grudging) from Mary Ann, and an attempt at reassurance. Why did Mary Ann violate her own plans and wishes twice—first, by going through an example that she really wanted her students to create for themselves and second, by apologizing to Cindy when she felt that Cindy ought to apologize to her? Was it her youth, her acculturation as an American woman (conditioned to appease rather than confront), her generally warm personal demeanor, her own previous experience of having been "burned" by public humiliation, or something else?

Perhaps the most intriguing aspect of this part of the story is the way in which Mary Ann's attempt to right an old wrong backfired. Instead of recognizing Mary Ann's consideration and sensitivity, Cindy angrily upbraided her for public condescension.

4. Comments on Students' Emotions. Is it ever appropriate to comment on a student's emotional state in class? How can instructors be sure that they are "reading" a student correctly? What effect might the attempt have on the rest of the class? There is always danger in assuming the contents of anyone else's mind or emotions. And the high probability of incorrectly making this judgment call raises one's risk of giving offense and inspiring fear of similar misinterpretation in the other students. The most likely result of an attempt to look into the mind or heart of another person and *announce* what you have seen to the rest of the group will be misinterpretation and hurt feelings on all sides. By Mary Ann's own statement, she meant her reference to Cindy's frustration as a kindness. But Cindy's reaction makes it clear that she found it offensive nonetheless.

5. Loss of Face. There is irony in the double loss of face at the heart of the confrontations in this case. Cindy criticizes Mary Ann for describing her as frustrated in front of students she may be teaching next semester. Her point is that she is a potential authority figure for these students who shouldn't be demeaned in front of them.

The other side of this coin is that Cindy has threatened Mary Ann's authority over this group of students. Mary Ann had good reason to feel "attacked" by Cindy's outburst. In a generally passive, peaceful class (Mary Ann mentions a good, nonadversarial relationship), Cindy's challenge must have communicated overtones of rebellion. It upset the classroom equilibrium and called Mary Ann's leadership and judgment into question.

6. Role-Change. Although the issue of role-change is not paramount in this case, it should not be overlooked. How effective can a 29-year-old woman instructor in slacks (even tailored slacks) be at offering public consolation and reassurance to a graduate student of the same age? There is something parental in Mary Ann's would-be gesture that does not quite suit this particular situation. (What can young teachers do to separate their leadership from the parental style that comes more easily to older instructors? And what can older instructors do to keep their parental impulses in check and maintain professional distance in the teaching situation? Parents and teachers have much in common—nurturing, instructing, encouraging, and helping others grow. But the roles are far from identical.)

7. Conveying Knowledge vs. Helping Others Learn. How can one reconcile the superior position of "expert" instructor with youth and pedagogical inexperience? Mary Ann was young and "green" as a teacher, but her competence at the FFT and other abstruse mathematical operations was light-years beyond that of her students. What role should she have taken to help them learn the material? (I think there's a hint about this in her own reaction to Professor Liu—she knew that she was a visual learner and asked him, accordingly, to teach her the material by drawing a graph. How could she have found out more about her students' learning styles and adapted her presentations accordingly?)

8. Warning Signals. Did the student's written notes to Mary Ann carry a signal that Mary Ann failed to notice? I think so. Any student who reacts at length and in great detail—often with corrections—to a professor's presentations is clearly in dialogue with that professor as a critic. This is not a bad thing, but it is a signal that the student is not a passive participant in a "you give, I take" relationship. It's not surprising that Cindy moved her dialogue from the out-of-class/written arena to the in-class/spoken forum.

Another clue to Cindy's potential to explode was her reputation for having "a passion for detail." Reflecting on these events, Mary Ann described Cindy—albeit in piecemeal fashion—as "thorough," extremely concerned with "understanding" things, very wrapped up in details, and the "chair" of the department's student committee. To me, these characteristics show that Cindy was not the sort of person to understand "20 percent" of her lectures day after day after day without taking some fairly vigorous action to correct this uncomfortable situation.

9. Power in the Classroom. This case contains the almost ubiquitous element of power struggle in the classroom. Cindy's challenge was milder than some, but the implicit content of her remark, "How do you expect us to get this . . . ?" conveys some message about Mary Ann's competence as a teacher. In a sense, she is saying, "You've failed us. You've misled us. You're asking us to get something you haven't given. You're wrong!"

10. Textbooks vs. Lectures. If a lecturer's job is to explain the material while students "get" about 20 percent, what does a lecture accomplish that written notes and a textbook cannot?

11. Handling Outbursts. In facing an outburst of this sort, what should any teacher do? Certainly the teacher has to react, but how? Mary Ann wanted to defuse the situation in general and Cindy in particular. How well did she accomplish her purpose? This issue might be an appropriate springboard for a series of hypothetical action questions that could lead to deeper issues. What else could she have done in response to Cindy? (Mary Ann mentions "thwomping" as one option. What would have been the consequences of a public reprimand?) How well did she address the concerns of the class as a whole? Should she have involved the rest of the group more directly? How? What did Mary Ann have to gain in this situation, and what to lose? As a rule, classroom outbursts have a ripple effect that does not cease when the class hour is over. No matter how well an instructor deals with such an outburst, there will usually be a residue of upset feelings—classwide—that persists for several weeks. What might Mary Ann have done outside of class to deal with this emotional overflow?

And, perhaps most important, what might she have learned from these events?

"Trouble in Stat. 1B" (A), (B), (C), and (D)

TEACHING NOTE

This teaching note was developed, researched, and written by Abby Hansen for use with the case series "Trouble in Stat.1B" (A) HGSE 2, (B) HGSE 14, (C) HGSE 15, and (D) HGSE 16 to help instructors prepare to lead case discussions. It is meant to stimulate discussion, not present a definitive analysis. (HGSE No. 7).

Aims and Methods of this Note

I intend this note as a hybrid (part interpretation, part instructional suggestions) for instructors to use as a point of departure for their own reflections on Dan Shea's misadventure with his class. The remarkable range of issues in this case makes it difficult to anticipate which topics a particular seminar group will select. I shall present an overview of eight fundamental issues—issues that I consider critical for discussion teaching:

- The teaching/learning contract;
- The value of a learning community;
- Partnership with students;
- Power and ownership of the classroom process;
- Grading;
- Getting help;
- Innovation in an institutional context; and
- The tension between knowledge and skill (a problem familiar to instructors in professional schools, but important in all teaching).

But before taking up each of these topics in some detail, I have two caveats.

Two Teaching Challenges

The technical dialogue—"sigma sub beta," "standard deviation," and values of "n"—in this case may distract attention from its pedagogical issues in two ways: it may intimidate those for whom math means misery or it may fascinate the statistically inclined (What *were* the flaws in Marie's equation; How could Joan have improved them?). It would be a pity for participants to get "hung up" on the math in this case because "Trouble in Stat. 1B" contains profound implications for all teaching. An instructor writes a few symbols on the board, and the class explodes into a passionate argument about pedagogy. What does it mean when a student stops the class ("Wait a minute!") and demands that a discussion teacher abandon his methodology and "give" the answer? What does it symbolize when the instructor writes something on the board? More than chalk scratches on slate, to be sure! This is one of the richest cases I have encountered.

To maximize the likelihood that a seminar group will begin to appreciate the range and depth of the pedagogical issues in this case, I would suggest that discussion leaders encourage participants who get stuck in the regression analysis to refocus their attention (for purposes of the present discussion, at least) and look for teaching issues with broad applicability.

Second, I would discourage facile criticism of Dan

Shea. Yes, he failed to pay sufficient attention to the dangers of introducing discussion teaching into one subsection of a lecture course. Yes, he "grafted on" extra work without extra reward. And, yes, he ran the class on his own assumptions about mission and purpose and discovered how sharply these differed from those held by two-thirds of the class. But the clarity with which these insights emerge from the case springs in great measure from our distance from these events. What would we have done in Dan's place?

"Trouble in Stat. 1B" portrays a gifted teacher tripping over his own virtues. Dan's energy, dedication, social purpose, and willingness to take risks conspire to undo him in this particular situation. But why did twenty members of this class stay aloof from the classroom protest? Probably because they were both enjoying and learning from the Problems of the Day, discussions, and Dan's high-energy teaching style. A distinguished sociologist who read this case commented, "I would love to have taken Stat. 1B with Dan Shea!"

Some Fundamental Pedagogical Issues

1. Contract

It is no coincidence that this case contains imagery of railroad trains and tracks. The student who waves her hand, palm out, as if trying to flag down a locomotive is trying to halt a speeding teaching process to which she does not subscribe. Like parallel railroad tracks, Dan's assumptions and goals and the class's seem to have no point of contact. The body language Dan uses to illustrate the distance between his intentions for the class and those of the forty protesters also conveys this image: he holds his hands out and moves them like trains on different tracks with different destinations.

It is telling that Dan remembers his students generically ("the forty," "the twenty abstentions"), not specifically. Even the names of two high-profile participants—the women he dubs "Marie" and "Joan"—elude his recollection. Neither their looks nor their personalities come back to him. Perhaps this fact suggests that Dan put more energy into "the numbers" (designing problem sets, waiting for specific configurations to write on the board) than the people. If so, he could not have had a very effective, bilateral teaching/learning contract with the group.

All teachers have contracts with their students, and all contracts include both explicit and implicit agreements. Explicit agreements are usually written in the syllabus: implicit agreements often condition classroom culture and remain unspoken, almost subliminal. Modes of behavior are usually set by the implicit contract. (Abusive language will not be tolerated. Humor is welcome; sarcasm is not. Honest puzzlement will be treated as an asset to group learning.) Contracts are unspoken sets of norms that govern everyone's expectations about a class. In teaching, they are vastly strengthened when students help set their terms. Given what we know of Dan (his directive teaching style, his inability to remember his students by name and appearance), what kind of contract was he likely to have set with this group? (I would guess that it was one-sided, more a matter of "thou shalt" than "what shall we?") The weakness of one-sided contracts is that they rarely inspire real commitment or feelings of trust all around.

What Dan discovered in this incident is that he had erred in assuming that all of these students subscribed to his intention to help them develop independent, mature competence with regression analysis. Instead of making sure that their assumptions jibed with his, Dan went ahead and taught the group as if they had all worked out the details together. Is there any evidence in the case that preliminary discussion about goals and means took place? (I don't see any.) How might Dan Shea have held such a discussion? How might he have "pitched" his innovative teaching plans to this group to obtain their cooperation? He might have started by asking them "where they were": what was their work experience, what did they anticipate their future jobs would be, how did they expect to use regression analysis in the coming years? Then he might have delineated "where he was": how his experience made him envision their future responsibilities. Dan mentions that he considered teaching statistics to future Fairchild GSPP master's degree holders a chance to "improve government by indirect means." It might have improved his rapport with this group and gotten them all pulling in the same direction, if he had discussed this assumption, asked for their "input," and explored what he meant by "improve."

As I read the case, I find no hints that Dan consciously set a teaching/learning contract in any form but the syllabus. How might this group of students have felt at being handed a list of responsibilities that included extra, ungraded work? How might it have struck them that they—unlike members of other teachers' sections—were supposed to come to class prepared? (Compare Frank Preston's description of typical Pre-Career math preparation: none. These students had been conditioned to expect to read the assignments *after* class.) How might it have struck them that they would be expected to work with regression analysis in class when their fellow students just sat back and listened to their instructor?

Frank Preston's brief description of the semester from the students' point of view shows many disparities with Dan's. Dan looked for energetic participation—hard thinking in class. But the students wanted to play a more passive role: to be taught.

How might things have been different? How might Dan have come to know these students well enough to weave their points of view into his course design and teaching style? On a very basic level, he could have learned and used their names in class. He could have looked up (or simply asked) details of their backgrounds and plans for the future. Perhaps more, and more personal, conversation—in class and out—might have revealed the distance between them and made it possible for Dan (with his engineering skills) to design and construct a bridge.

Mutual respect is vital to a functional teaching/learning contract. Clearly, the students respected Dan. Note that Joan turns to him for "truth" when he writes the incorrect formula on the board. And Dan says that he respected the students' intellectual ability. But he also recounts two episodes that appalled him sufficiently to make him undertake an unpopular teaching assignment and—even more significantly—attempt to "reform" Stat. 1B. After seeing two classrooms full of master's degree students fail to apply what they had supposedly learned, Dan had probably developed a healthy disrespect for *something* in the system—if not the students' abilities, then the means by which those abilities had been groomed.

Is it possible that what prevented two-thirds of this class from granting Dan its loyalty (loyal students neither attack the teacher in class nor sign formal letters of complaint to the Dean) was some perception of this duality in his attitude toward them? How might a more explicit understanding—with more open discussion of assumptions, goals, and methods—have prevented this situation from developing or, once it had emerged, from worsening?

2. Community

When a group of people has common goals, standards of behavior, trust in one another, and mutual loyalty, community exists. And community is a fundamental requisite for the sort of group problem-solving Dan is trying to implement in Stat. 1B. What evidence do we have that this group has become a community? Except perhaps for the shared attitude and purpose that the forty attackers demonstrated?

There is evidence to suggest that the twenty "abstentions" understood what, why, and how Dan was teaching. But they were a subculture in this class, and they seem to have felt disenfranchised. Note that they did not speak up in his defense or, one gathers, write a letter to counter their fellow students' protest to the Dean. It seems that, instead of one learning group, the Stat. 1B students formed two distinct subgroups—the majority who wished they were taking a traditional lecture/problem set course, and the rest, who "sided with" Dan Shea, but felt out of the mainstream, like their instructor.

The class seems to have divided naturally into these two subgroups. Could Dan have helped them overcome their differences and become a single learning community? People who don't know one another's names, habits, and humors will certainly have difficulty in such an endeavor.

What might Dan have done to promote the formation of a community? (He might have modeled the use of people's names, supported the formation of study groups, integrated group projects into the grading scheme, made sure to refer students' comments to *other students* for reactions in class, etc.)

3. Partnership

The issue of the teachers' and students' "jobs" (roles) comes up explicitly in this case—both in Dan's opening musings and in the incident itself, when he thinks the protesters must be feeling frustrated at having to explain his job to him for twenty minutes. In discussion teaching, instructor and students have many jobs. But fundamentally they are partners in a collective quest that begins wherever the students are and ends at the highest point of enlightenment they can reach by the end of the course. And partners share power (although not always equally). When instructors share power—allow students to help determine the pace, level, and direction of discussion—they are working in partnership.

In this case, Dan seems to grant virtually no power to the students. He dictates the terms of the assignment, sets the pace of discussion, controls the flow of information (he wants "something with an equals sign and letter n in it—an equation to write on the board"), and waits impatiently (he comes across as brisk—a fast thinker and talker). When he gets what he wants, he rewards the student with a smile and words of approval: "Good formula!" What are some other possible responses he might have made? (In other words, what did he communicate by praising the equation instead of her willing cooperation, partial success, or the progress she had made on behalf of the class?) The wariness with which most of the students view him becomes all too apparent at this point. Marie is floundering. Does Dan seem to notice? (Maybe she hasn't done the reading. Maybe Dan knows but doesn't care, because he really does trust the students' intuition. Maybe the other students don't know this and just see him as grilling Marie.)

The final straw is when Dan writes Marie's "wrong" equation on the board. The correct equation appeared in the students' textbooks. Perhaps Joan had rechecked her textbook in class—when she interrupted, "Wait a minute! *Is that right?*" What would the effect have been if Dan had invited Marie to the board to write her developing equation?

Even greater proof of the distance between Dan and the class emerges in the (B) case when Dan reacts to Joan's frustrated question. Instead of saying, "No, it's not right, but it's close, so let's explore it and see what we can come up with," or something else straightforward, he says, "I don't know," because a senior colleague has told him that discussion teachers (like magicians) never tell. This reply must have frustrated Joan and her comrades all the more. Not know? Of *course* Dan knew. It seems likely that this willing withholding of information increased the lack of trust between him and "the forty."

One looks in vain for any clues to suggest partnership between Dan and this crop of Stat. 1B students. Whatever kinship the twenty "abstentions" may have felt with Dan (enjoyment of his teaching style, similar goals for and assumptions about the class), they had not formed bonds strong enough to make them leap to his defense. Perhaps his very competence, combined with high energy and a one-sided teaching/learning contract, had created such a distinct imbalance of power that they failed to perceive that he had any vulnerability at all.

4. Ownership—Whose Class Is This?

It doesn't seem necessary to dwell on this point. The students' perspective makes it clear that the Fairchild Pre-Career Master's students took their courses and instructors with a grain of salt. Their purpose was to get through the program and collect a piece of paper that would ratchet them up the career ladder. Frank Preston says, "Most people were just interested in getting what they could use." But what would they "use" it for? To pass yet another examination? This group saw the math courses as opportunities to hear the material clearly explained step by step, so that they could memorize it, apply it to problems of familiar design, and pass tests. That's what they had always done, with tangible results.

But Dan doesn't seem to see it that way. To him, the class is part laboratory and part training ground, *his* opportunity to "improve government" by preparing policymakers to solve real world problems creatively with regression analysis, among other conceptual tools. Dan feels free to impose his vision on the group of people assigned to his class. Why not?

If Dan's students had been free to elect his Stat. 1B section—if it had been presented to them as an opportunity to flex their mental muscles with regression analysis by means of challenging, open-ended problems and group discussion—then perhaps Dan and the students might have developed a contract of shared ownership. The whole group might have learned from Dan's teaching method and enjoyed the process. But that's not what happened.

To this researcher, if the students in a class aren't participating willingly, the teacher (however energetic) isn't teaching with full effectiveness. In a fundamental sense, the students "own" the class. At times, they manifest their power in negative ways: by withholding cooperation, by protesting. At times, they show it by contributing enough energy to educate the teacher beyond his or her fondest expectations. It is a truism that teachers also learn, but only when they acknowledge that the goal of teaching is to serve the students, to give them their opportunity to learn.

5. Grading

Dan makes his attempt to reform Stat. 1B within a pre-existing grading system that seems to present at least two different kinds of problems. First, we learn that 60 percent of the graders are TAs who had taken the course the previous year (before Dan introduced problem-based discussion teaching). This puts distance between Dan and the TAs and creates yet another opportunity for cultural dissonance. We may assume that these TAs, like the students, have enjoyed academic success under the "old dispensation" of lecture/problem set/exams. Second, Dan has created a new format—open-ended, "messy" discussion problems—but not integrated it into the reward system. His probable intention—to innovate without creating undue stress for the already overworked students—backfires in this culture where students work for grades.

Stat. 1B seems like a half-finished course design. Dan has delineated his purpose (to train students to apply mathematical modeling to the "real world"), his premise ("messy, real world" problems and group discussions will accomplish this end), and his means (the Problems of the Day). But without reward, he hasn't completed the picture. His students know that they can get points off for mistakes on conventional problem sets (which they still hand in to the TAs), but they get no extra points for creative problem-solving or stimulating contributions to class discussion.

6. Getting Help

Dan seems to be flying solo. Instead of holding some form of meeting with either the forty protesters or the twenty abstentions, he guesses what's on their minds (the protesters are thinking that he's a "turkey" who doesn't know his "job"; the silent twenty probably like his teaching, but are too intimidated by the majority to say anything). His only source of direct information from the twenty "abstentions" is chance meetings in the hall. Nor does he report going to a colleague for help in understanding or improving this painful situation, although there are indications that he had friends and supporters on the faculty, including experienced and enthusiastic case method instructors.

What questions might he have asked the students? Other faculty? Given their advice, what could he have done to modify the course at this point? How might he have enlisted a sympathetic faculty member's help perhaps as a friendly observer?

7. Institutional Context

Fairchild GSPP seems to be a grade-driven school with a dual personality: two levels of Master's programs, two kinds of courses (case-based management courses and lecture-style quantitative courses), and no explicit means of integrating these elements. Like the "left" and "right" brain in one current conceptual model, the two sides of the curriculum function in different styles. The right-brained courses are taught by the case discussion method. These courses include traditionally "soft" disciplines (those involving skill, subjective reasoning, and value judgments). The other, left-brained courses tend to be scientific and objective material not for value judgments but rather for "absolute truth." Dan attempts to blur this distinction (which corresponds roughly to the traditional definitions of "academic" v. "professional" school) because his experience and that of respected colleagues tell him that the distinction is not only false, but potentially damaging to students' later performance.

But the Fairchild culture hasn't caught up with Dan's reasoning. Thus far, the students have been given every indication that statistics will be taught in the traditional manner. Before Dan started stirring things up in Stat. 1B, the course was constructed of step-by-step lectures, conventional problem sets with clear answers, and exams that were more of the same kind of problem. Dan trespassed over every one of these unwritten boundaries. Perhaps the remarkable thing here is that more of his students *didn't* rebel.

The problem doesn't seem to be whether Dan was correct in his assessment of what the students *really* needed (or what society needed them to learn), or whether his method might have worked. Dan got into trouble because he was attempting to implement an experiment-in-progress without weaving it into the existing context or obtaining his students' informed consent. How might he have better integrated his innovative course design into the existing *milieu*? Surely a new grading policy and persistent attention to the creation and maintenance of a two-sided teaching/learning contract with the students would have helped.

8. Teaching Knowledge and Teaching Skill

All teachers, and all learners, must find the means to resolve the fundamental dichotomy between the concepts of "pure" and "applied" knowledge. As Donald Schön makes clear in *The Reflective Practitioner,*[1] even in the most rarefied intellectual disciplines, the boundary between thinking and doing is far from distinct. Although the issue is complicated, I would suggest as a working hypothesis that thinking and problem-solving are both activities; things we *do.* Certainly, there is a difference of emphasis between, say, a course called "Principles of Econometrics" and one called "How to Buy and Sell: Making a Fortune in Real Estate." One stresses knowledge; the other, skill. But I would argue that these exist on the same continuum.

Joan's furious challenge to Dan Shea directs our attention to the end of the continuum that we call "knowledge." "Is that right?" she demands—seeking to *know.* Dan replies, "What do you think?" hoping that she will work with the incorrect formula and tease out its misleading implications by putting it into practice. His answer directs Joan to work in the area of *skill.*

The symbolic act of writing a formula on the board both triggers the confrontation that brings all these assumptions out into the open and helps us, as readers and students of this case, to focus on the complexity of this issue. To Dan, writing symbols on the board is just a routine part of problem-solving. To the students—conditioned by the culture of the institution and their own preparation for getting there—a teacher's act of writing a formula on the board means, "Here is the truth: write it down, memorize it, and get it right or you'll lose points on the quiz."

Dan and Joan seem to be speaking two different languages—or, at least, two mutually unintelligible dialects of the same language. Their noncommunica-

[1] D. A. Schön, *The Reflective Practitioner: How Professionals Think in Action* (New York: Basic Books, 1983).

tion goes to the heart of very basic teaching questions: What *is* Dan's job—to impart knowledge, model skill, create a structure of assignments that force students to apply their increasing knowledge with increasing skill? And what is Joan's job—to copy concepts from the board and learn them, to learn *how to* figure them out for herself, to strike some sort of balance? Does the choice of one mode of teaching or learning imply abandoning the other?

Student and teacher seem to hold clashing assumptions about roles, goals, and teaching techniques. Joan wants to memorize the meaning of concepts like "standard deviation." Dan thinks her job is to absorb these concepts in a way that goes deeper than memorization. He bases his opinions on his own experience, his reading, and many conversations with colleagues whom he respects. Joan bases hers on the experience of having taken a number of math courses in college, worked for a few years, scored high on the GREQ, gotten into Fairchild GSPP, and passed Stat. 1A.

This disparity of perception tinges every academic discipline to some extent, but it becomes particularly evident in graduate professional schools, like Fairchild's GSPP. It is, I think, artificial and potentially counterproductive to separate the teaching of knowledge from the teaching of skill (rather like attempting to teach each half of the brain separately). In the realm of learning, knowledge and skill are one.

Some Tentative Conclusions

In Stat. 1B, Dan Shea made a daring foray into the "no man's land" between two academic cultures. The dangers of his adventure became obvious when his classroom exploded into protest and several students later lodged a formal complaint with the Dean. What basic lesson may one draw from Dan's misfortune? Perhaps he might have prevented this particular blowup with some specific actions: setting a two-sided teaching/learning contract with the group, taking care to listen to the students, address their concerns, deal with their preconceptions, and pay more attention to helping the group develop mutual trust. Finally, Dan might have avoided some unpleasantness by seeking help from members of the class and colleagues and asking them, in a spirit of friendship, to observe and comment on his teaching and the students' reactions.

A Note on Usage

Instructors who plan to use this case in multisession teaching seminars may want to devote some time to thinking about where to place it in the syllabus. Two potential ways to exploit the richness of "Trouble in Stat. 1B" suggest themselves: as a seminar "opener," this case can raise a remarkably broad range of fundamental teaching issues for the group to explore in other guises as the course goes on. Paired with other cases on instructors shifting from knowledge-based to skill-based teaching (like "The Dethroned Section Leader," for example), this can help students begin to recognize issues that they will meet time and again, in cases and in their own teaching practices.

Instructors who use this rich case at the beginning of seminar, however, run the risk of sacrificing its depth to an inevitably broad, but superficial overview. The details of Dan Shea's interaction with his material, his institution, and—most important—his students will repay close attention by suggesting ever more sophisticated implications. To avoid this potential sacrifice, instructors might consider positioning "Trouble in Stat. 1B" as a "wrap-up." In this situation, the challenge will be to give ample time and consideration to the many profundities that may arise when a now-experienced group tackles a case of this depth. At the end of a seminar, participants will most likely have developed their powers of perception and ability to the point where they create long and valuable chains of argument. One way to give the group time and intellectual space to forge these chains would be to discuss the case during a first session, and then distribute the Instructor's Perspective—Dan Shea's extremely sophisticated, provocative reflections on the implications of these events—as the basis for a second discussion.

However an instructor chooses to use this case, some consideration of time planning will probably come in handy. This case contains so many suggestive details, and so many universal teaching challenges, that a group may well "run away" with it and make the instructor feel like a straggler at a marathon race. Attention to the potential blocks of argument will help keep the instructor oriented and ensure that the group attains some coverage of issues.

See Donald Schön's remarks on the thorny issues of professional versus academic teaching in "The Crisis of Professional Knowledge and the Pursuit of an Epistemology of Practice," found in Section V.

The Case of the Dethroned Section Leader (A) and (B)

TEACHING NOTE

This teaching note has been prepared by Abby Hansen as an aid to instructors in classroom use of the case series "The Case of the Dethroned Section Leader" (A) 9-382-177 and (B) 9-382-178.
(HBS No. 5-384-240)

Distributed by HBS Publishing Division, Harvard Business School, Boston, MA 02163. Printed in U.S.A.

Special Features

This case portrays a young instructor (twenty-six, still a graduate student) in a college Shakespeare course who faces a small classroom revolt against her leadership. The struggle that lurks beneath the surface of much classroom interaction appears with unusual clarity in this case, but many other perennial problems of teaching are also embedded in its events. For example, Bea Benedict operates without a workable teaching contract: she fails to listen carefully and respond constructively to her students; she tries to control the class rather than direct or guide discussion; and she reacts hastily and self-defensively to Jack Kesselman's "attack." Finally, the question of evaluation—Who has the right to criticize whom?—is also important in this case. In short, most of the issues our teaching seminars probe can be extracted for preliminary consideration from this brief history of Bea Benedict's adventures with her Shakespeare section.

Mood

A contentious case, "The Case of the Dethroned Section Leader" portrays a public confrontation and its attendant embarrassments. The material incorporates a good deal of classroom dialogue, and can stimulate spirited role playing. (Almost every teacher can identify with the protagonist's dislike of the fractious student.)

Suggested Uses

This case has special appeal as an opener for a seminar or workshop because it provides glimpses of many teaching issues we normally consider during the whole course of a semester. These include: 1) setting and maintaining a teaching contract, 2) creating a free, open climate for discussion, 3) the critical skills of posing questions and responding to students' contributions, 4) classroom management—especially self-management, 5) the important difference between directing and controlling the discussion process, and 6) evaluation. Let us go through these briefly.

1) Student-teacher contract. In this case we see Bea Benedict leading her students according to an unstated, probably unconscious unilateral contract—the kind many teachers set without much thought about reciprocal rights and responsibilities, unaware that they have latitude in designing a syllabus, making up assignments, and selecting a format for opening the discussion sessions. Bea seems unaware of the breadth of her options in determining what the section will do and how it will do it—much less of the students' options.

2) Classroom climate. The climate Bea creates with her dominating style and rigid assignments seems chilly. It could hardly be expected to promote the kind of spirited, engaged discussion that Bea herself probably wanted.

3) Question and response. Bea's style of speech, which is quoted in the case, betrays the classic tendency of the inexperienced teacher to overwhelm the students (at the risk of arousing hostility and boredom). Bea's verbal responses seem hasty and ill-considered, and they show no attempt to engage the students with each other. Her reply to Jack Kesselman's complaint, for example, seems almost self-destructive (Did she really have to preside over her own impeachment?).

4) Classroom- and self-management. Faced with a revolt, Bea veers between schoolmarmish authoritarianism and self-defensive whining—neither of which seems likely to engender respect and cooperation in the students.

5) Direction versus control. Directing a section resembles moderating a panel discussion. The discussion leader gives the students' comments shape by rephrasing them, poses questions that suggest directions in which the analysis might profitably move, and offers new ideas for the students to consider. Direction is not dictatorial. Control, on the other hand, connotes rigidity. The teacher who tries to control a discussion risks turning the students into parrots. Bea transmits confusing messages in this area. She looks casual: she wears slacks; she sips coffee during the discussion; she meets the students on their home ground, within earshot of a frisbee game. But she also stands while they sit, uses a rather conservative style of opening, and gives such long introductions to her questions that she practically answers them herself.

6) Evaluation. Although most colleges and universities routinely ask students to evaluate their teachers, the balance of power in this respect is still tipped toward the teacher, who has the customary role of providing feedback, not only in class (by praising or criticizing students' contributions as they are offered) but also in the concrete form of grades. Jack Kesselman breaks this convention publicly; this accounts for much of Bea Benedict's feeling of having been attacked.

The purpose of this rehash of Bea's foibles is not to excoriate her. On the contrary; Bea's errors are due mainly to her inexperience and lack of guidance. (Her senior professor seems to have offered no advice about teaching.) Given that Bea wishes to improve her effectiveness as a teacher—that she really wants to help her students learn—she must shift her focus from herself and how she handles the material to her students and how she can nudge, guide, charm (but not push or drag) them to a more sophisticated grasp of Shakespeare, according to their lights. Like all discussion teachers, Bea must create some stimulating, open-ended questions and think carefully about how to phrase them in order to get her students to talk more than she does in class. These are far more difficult tasks than simply showing off one's erudition, but they are necessary for success.

It should be apparent by now that "The Case of the Dethroned Section Leader" is a fertile case. Although relatively brief, it contains the seeds of a variety of important teaching issues.

One of the most salient of these is *contract*—the agreement that sets the form the teacher-student relationship will take. This is a common concern in the early stages of all courses, and the maintenance of the relationship continues to be important, for it will change over time. This case shows a radical disruption in contract; many other teaching situations change, but with less drama. Whenever the issue of contract is à propos, this case is relevant. One very basic question it raises—*how* to exercise power in the classroom—is always of interest, for students' attitudes toward their classwork and teachers often approach rebellion or belligerence.

Still, a young woman teaching Shakespeare in a liberal arts college is the focus of this particular case. Some seminar participants in very different disciplines or at more advanced stages of their careers may feel little fellowship with Bea Benedict. The discussion leader should try to steer these people past the specifics to general considerations of classroom dynamics as swiftly as possible.

Conflicts, Sensitivities

The most potentially sensitive point in this case is the inescapable fact that Bea Benedict is female, and Jack Kesselman—who questions her leadership—is male. In discussion, some participants have interpreted his protest as simple sexism, and the discussion leader should be prepared for this. One way to prevent the seminar discussion from focusing only on this observation would be to give this point of view some "air time," but then ask participants to brainstorm a bit. (What if a male teacher had behaved precisely as Bea did? Would Jack have reacted differently? What elements in Bea's style might have triggered his protest?) Calling attention to the rigid way she seems to conduct class—contrasted with the casualness of the setting and her attire—should help broaden the focus. Bea's confusing signals have nothing to do with her gender.

Teaching Objectives

This case offers a fine opportunity to explore such important topics as *how* one helps students grapple with primary materials without cramming one's own interpretations down their throats. What are genuinely stimulating questions? The crucial pair of skills—question and response—may also be approached through this case: Bea Benedict makes some blunders in both areas, and Jack Kesselman, in his blunt way, points them out. This case gives seminar participants a chance to think about whether they have committed similar errors, and, if so, how to avoid them in the future.

The "Blocks" of Analysis

As always, every comment in the discussion may be associated with some major category of interpretation that relates to the past, present, future, or theoretical aspects of the events. The "past" includes what Bea and the students did before the decision point in the (A) case. The "present" includes the clearest possible assessment one can make of her situation at the end of (A). (Was Bea really attacked? Had she been insulted? Did she have to step down as leader?) The "future" category includes prediction and prescription. The situation has to change for better or worse. How should it change? What should Bea do? The theoretical issues include the basic principles that operate in this set of events. In this case, power, question and response, and contract should certainly come under discussion.

Study Questions 2 and 3 (see Exhibit 1) refer to Bea's constraints, as opposed to factors she could control. Each of these could constitute a "block."

1. Constraints. Bea has to teach, as part of her graduate fellowship. She does not run the whole course, and she finds Professor Glendower's lectures "superficial." This leads her to supplement his material in her sections. (She also has to do her own graduate work while teaching. This double focus usually produces stress.)

2. Choices. She chooses to dress casually and wear her long hair loose. She chooses to teach after dinner in a residence hall in a formal conference room and bring her coffee mug. She chooses to assign oral reports and set the rules for their delivery. She chooses to read and excerpt criticism for her students but discourages them from reading it themselves. She also chooses to begin the section by writing key terms and dates on the blackboard, suggesting that these should organize the evening's discussion.

3. Power. This issue is deeply embedded in these proceedings. Who has the right to direct the class? Who has the right to say who shall speak, to whom, and when? Who has the right to evaluate? How? All these issues surface when Jack criticizes Bea in class.

4. Character. Consider Bea Benedict's personality and background. Still a student playing the role of teacher, she does not seem comfortable exercising power over other—albeit younger—students. Also, she is competitive and—one gathers from her reasons for attending graduate school—primarily interested in studying literature, rather than in teaching students. And Jack comes across as a rebel, or at least in a rebellious phase.

5. Environment. This includes the physical setup, the course, psychological atmosphere, time of day—any factors that surround and condition the classroom dynamic.

6. Classroom dialogue. There are infinite numbers of ways to pose questions and infinite numbers of ways to respond to students' answers and suggestions. Tone of voice, physical gesture and posture, and choice of language have subtle but enormously powerful effects.

7. Methodology. One basic challenge of discussion teaching is that the teacher learns the material and wants to help the students learn it too. But this cannot be accomplished by a simple transfer of knowledge from brain to brain. Most teachers choose the profession because they have been successful and happy as students. But effective teaching requires the exercise of different skills. Some teachers never learn this, and their students suffer (causing them, in turn, the frustration of feeling less outstanding as teachers than they have been as students).

Preparing for the Discussion

Exhibit 1 lists suggested Study Questions, to be handed out to participants for use when preparing the case before class. **Exhibit 2** contains a summary of the Discussion Questions, to be used by the seminar leader in preparing for class and in guiding the case discussion when necessary.

Opening Speaker, Backstop

This case features a woman teacher and a male antagonist. The discussion leader's choice of opening speaker and backstop will depend upon the immediate goal for the opening mood of the discussion. Do you want to begin with an emotional "high" and generate some involvement at the risk of detachment? This will leave cool analysis for a later point in the discussion. If so, pick an assertive woman to speak for Bea Benedict's point of view and an equally assertive man (possibly even a contentious one, if you have such a participant on tap) to speak for Jack Kesselman. On the other hand, asking a man to speak for Bea and a woman to speak for Jack could have the opposite effect: it would signal empathy as the opening mood. In fact, there is no reason the discussion leader should not state this choice of opening mood quite openly, saying, for example, "Poor Bea! Mary, as a woman teacher yourself, perhaps you can help us sympathize with her." "Sam, would you play devil's advocate and step into Jack Kesselman's shoes for a moment to provide us with some reactions he might have been having to Bea's teaching style?" Choosing opening speakers from disciplines quite divergent from Bea's would be a way to signal that identification with Bea's predicament need not be rooted in a similar background. (All our teaching cases are meant to raise issues that puzzle most teachers at some point in their careers.)

The Discussion Questions

I would suggest running a discussion of this case with primary attention to general concerns that emerge from the whole range of events in **Exhibit 2**. I have supplied an equal number of questions on (A) and (B). But the operational issues seem less crucial than the more general, basic questions we have noted.

After the (A) case has been read, the following questions may be introduced:

1. [To the opening speaker]: What's going on here? What do you make of Bea's remark that she "felt attacked"?

There may be divergence of opinion on this point, depending on how people feel about authority. Jack behaved in a manner that some might find insulting simply because it is insubordinate: He "slouched," looked away from Bea, and then blatantly ignored her instructions to report. Instead of analyzing the assigned passage from *Richard II,* which Bea had just exhaustively introduced, he launched into a criticism of her teaching style and included the bombshell-statement that instead of listening to her introduction he had timed it and, furthermore, found her presentation "pretty boring." It was at this point that Bea felt attacked.

Most teachers would probably feel the same. But what, in particular, insulted her is worth considering: Was it Jack's criticism of her lecture style? Or was it his rejection of her right to tell him what to do in class? It may be worth probing a bit to expose this. What is damaged besides Bea's ego?

One may also assume that preparing the minilecture must have cost Bea both time and effort: she had grounds for feeling both insulted and unappreciated. Most teachers will empathize with her defensiveness. But there may be differences of opinion over how she should have responded to Jack. Hardliners will probably say she should have tossed the upstart out of the classroom. Others, taking a more lenient stance, might defend Jack's right to protest. After all, his education (and those of his fellow students) is at stake here—not Bea Benedict's right to show off. Some may excuse Bea's handling of his criticism. She actually gave him permission to defy her because she was caught off guard, felt hurt, and, possibly, felt guilty and embarrassed at having taken up so much class time with her minilecture. Still, her reaction was ill-considered and her querulous rhetorical question ("Don't you think I've got anything to teach you?") was unfortunate.

The opening speaker will probably side with either Bea or Jack, and the discussion leader should find an opportunity to elicit support for whichever point of view the opening speaker has not espoused. This could be done with a pointed ("*Why* do you say such and such?") question or some role playing. To expand the focus this early in the discussion would signal a certain welcome amplitude. This case will support a variety of interpretations. (It is this researcher's feeling that a reasonable degree of ambiguity in a case produces the most useful discussions.) The leader should try to keep shifting ground and probing for shades of opinion and different ways to view the events and characters and their implications. The advantage of case analysis over real life is that one can view and review case events. They "stay put" better than episodes in one's own experience, and permit one to profit from many vantage points.

2. [To the backstop]: How might things have looked to Jack?

Some participants have suggested Jack's protest was just a cover for lack of preparation. He simply hadn't done his homework. Another point of view is that he was actually telling the truth. He had both read and thought about the assigned passage. (Bea's assignments seem to be brief and compact; he *could* have done his assignment right before class.) But Jack is described as a performer and "political activist," familiar with the rhetoric of formal, public protest. Had he, quite sincerely, felt that he and his fellow students were being ill-served by an egotistical discussion leader's attempts to exhibit her erudition at their expense, public protest would have suggested itself as an appropriate means to improve the situation. This might have been a matter of conscience for Jack.

Bea describes him as "something of an operator"—a manipulator of the system. Perhaps he did affect the rhetoric of ethical protest to camouflage his own laziness. But we must remember that we have *only* Bea's descriptions in this case, and she admits that her feelings for Jack after this episode coalesced into solid dislike.

3. How about the others in the class?

Bea gives us other descriptions: Elke Gunnarson is a sporty, socially conventional sort of person, it seems. Her boyfriend, Cliff, appears to be a male version of Elke. They might be expected to occupy the middle ground of a political struggle. One certainly would not anticipate their marching to the cry of "Revolution!" from Jack. The other student Bea recalled in any detail was Skip Townsend, a Californian who, unlike Elke and Cliff, might either promote a rebellion or, at least, be amused by any sort of anarchism that might crop up in a formal situation. Anyone who writes "beachcomber" under "Professional Plans" on a student information card shows both a sense of humor and a tendency not to take authority too seriously.

There is, thus, a balance of personalities in this little group: two conservatives, two radicals. The others seem to have impressed Bea so little that—at a distance of a few years—she was unable to furnish any information on which to evaluate them.

One can imagine the class reacting along a political spectrum, with the conservatives groaning inwardly at Jack's familiar line, and the radicals thinking something like "Right on!"

But primary attention should be paid to the disruption that Jack's ploy (whatever its intent) created in the normal operation of the section. If one believes that the business of a Shakespeare section is Shakespeare, Jack was destructively diverting attention from the task at hand—an offense much more serious than any "boring" lectures from Bea. If, on the other hand, one believes that education cannot be pigeonholed by subject, and that there are many things to learn in a classroom and many ways to learn them, Jack may be furnishing a more educational episode than the students could have experienced if the class had proceeded more normally.

Some seminar participants may offer their own recollections of the time at which this case occurred. They were a time of protest, frequent political demonstrations—some fairly good-humored, some literally deadly—and widespread, highly publicized civil disobedience. As a student, Bea must have taken this atmosphere for granted and felt comfortable working within it. One gathers, from her extremely controlled and orderly structuring of the class, that she was probably not a radical herself. Certainly, she was no anarchist. But the popularity of public protests in her milieu may have, at the very least, created some guilt for her regarding autocracy in the classroom. Perhaps the students looked at her—long hair, running shoes, and blue jeans—and saw a potential comrade. As we have noted before, Bea's appearance could have misled them: she behaved like a teacher, but looked like a student. All of these factors may have combined to unsettle the students in her Shakespeare section.

4. How did Bea get into this fix?

At this point, the discussion leader's task will be to try to direct attention to those factors in Bea's environment that we have mentioned in the "blocks" under *Constraints* and *Choices*. There were some aspects of her environment that she simply had to accept: her students, the class size, primary texts, Glendower's lectures. On balance, though, it seems that she also had quite a broad area of choice. Did she unwittingly stack the deck against herself? The discussion leader might point out some items to consider. ("What about the room in which she was teaching?" "Could she have changed it? To what?" "What about the meeting time?" "Do *you* encourage students to eat and drink in your discussion classes?" "How about those frisbee players right outside their window?" "What do you think about her opening gambit—putting terms on the board?")

The object is not to pillory Bea for gross foolishness in setting up this section, but rather to show the extremely significant effect of such small choices as whether or not to "condition" a discussion with key terms (or let them emerge in progress), whether to permit or encourage eating and drinking, whether or not to run a discussion around a conference table, whether or not to try to discuss Shakespeare in competition with frisbee players' shouts. There are many other aspects to this question: one way Bea "got into this fix" was by accepting a fellowship at Fairchild

University that entailed teaching. Is she ready to teach? Is she interested in teaching? Has she given enough consideration to how her students learn? After the discussion has dwelt on some of these extremely basic considerations, one should move into the "action" area (which, as I have noted, I find essentially less important in this case than in many others, even though the threat of deposition makes it dramatic).

5. What should she do?

One would hope for brief, trenchant suggestions here. Bea hasn't many options: like anyone handed an ultimatum, she can take it or leave it. What she should do, thus, boils down to a choice of whether to accept the ultimatum or not—complicated by a not-so-simple (because partially unconscious) choice of style. Much will be implied by the manner in which she responds. She could react personally, saying, "You have really insulted me, Jack; your manners are atrocious!" She could cling to her official role and lecture him: "This is inappropriate behavior, Jack. I think we should go on with our discussion as planned. Please either present your report or leave and allow us to continue." Or, she could capitulate gracefully, and with some retention of authority—say, by taking a vote herself, standing at the board in the "teacher's place." She could also capitulate ungraciously, by stalking out. An unpleasant refusal to give in might have sounded something like, "Okay, Jack. You want to run things? Let's see *you* come up here and give a coherent and interesting fifteen-minute minilecture on *Richard II!*"

Participants almost invariably enjoy role playing and supplying dialogue for the "prediction" sections of discussions, and this case can provide material for lively contributions. It might be advisable for the discussion leader to end this section of the seminar meeting on an upbeat, high-energy note, with suggestions for Bea and guesses about the outcome of this dramatic confrontation.

—◆—

After the (B) case has been read:

1. What is your appraisal of how Bea responded to Jack's challenge?

Varieties of response to this question will probably align themselves along the same axes as response to the first question on the (A) case. How one feels about Bea's permissive response will correlate with one's feelings about a teacher's proper role. Bea acted instinctively—as one often does in teaching, where crises develop too fast for much planning. She combined a democratic acceptance of the students' right to vote (some participants may scream at her pusillanimity) with a tacit refusal to relinquish her intrinsic right to lead. She "stood at the board" and gave a deceptively tough-sounding order: "Hands up, those who want to have no leader." In fact, she leapt to a self-destructive conclusion. There were many middle courses between her previous controlling style and her leaderlessness, but she ignored them. Ironically, she may be seen to have engineered her own downfall. Some participants may detect in her action an essential ambivalence about power: Bea Benedict invites her own deposition in terms of crisp command! The discussion leader should solicit reactions, and try to respond to them by directing participants' attention to the precise details of the (B) case. Bea Benedict stood at the board and viewed the vote against her. Jack and Skip—the radical and anarchist (in gross oversimplification)—raised their hands. That left the two conservatives and the rest of the students, whom Bea couldn't even remember without her gradebook. We'll never know why Elke and Cliff chose to vote with Jack and Skip; perhaps they also found Bea boring. Perhaps they were environmentally attuned to protest. Perhaps they found the novelty intriguing. Perhaps they were influenced by Jack's forceful personality. But they did raise their hands, so (again, some seminar members might scream "pusillanimity") Elke and Cliff joined the majority. The dynamic here is worth discussing. We have a very small section with a clear conflict and three general groups—left, right, and middle. What happens in this situation is probably a microcosm of many far larger events. A squeaky wheel makes noise, attracts attention, rattles authority, and manages—by energy, or novelty, or perhaps even intrinsic rightness—to effect a revolution.

At any rate, the group's vote against Bea was unanimous. From the point of view of her self-respect as leader of this group, this is the nadir of the situation. She has just been unconditionally rejected. The discussion leader should try to direct attention to the *manner* in which Bea accepts this defeat. She describes a clear sequence of actions in terms that reveal a certain bitterness. She "surveyed the democratic assembly that had just ousted" her (feeling just like a deposed political leader, apparently), "put the chalk back on the ledge" (relinquished the scepter), and "sat down" (symbolically stepped down from power to join the group on its level—no lower). She could have left the room.

"What is the impact of Bea's watching the vote?" might be a useful question to ask. "What do you think you might have felt as you watched her put down that piece of chalk and take a seat?"

An important question here is "What do you think the impact of her 'abdication speech' might have been?" Bea reports saying three words: "Okay, Section—discuss!" She's still giving orders. At this point, all we know is that Bea has allowed herself (even helped, some might say) to be voted out of authority. Her previous contract—to lead the group in discussion of Professor Glendower's Shakespeare lectures—is completely void. But no contract has taken its place. In a sense, Bea has no right to her parting shot. No one has said *what* the class is going to do now. The new direction must emerge from the section itself. It can't come from Bea.

If the seminar has polarized around reactions to Jack Kesselman and what he stands for in this case, reaction about what *did* happen next will also be vehement. Jack "began to talk about the passage" (people who think he was totally unprepared may be surprised at this), but he spoke "mainly in terms of personal likes and dislikes" (another hint that, maybe, he *hadn't* prepared after all). Was he reading it for the first time right there? Was that why he gave only superficial reactions?

But there is a serious issue embedded in the rest of Bea's report of the sort of comments Jack was making. He spoke of his personal reactions to a literary character, without historical context, and without reference to published scholarship. He spoke naively but, we gather, honestly. Bea, the graduate student, would have done it differently. "What's wrong with Jack's 'report'"? one might ask. Participants should spend some time on the issue of the teaching potential of naive comments as a teaching tool. Is there value in simple "gut reaction" commentary like Jack's? Many teachers (privately, at least) think not. The discussion leader should ask participants to try to suggest ways to use naive remarks to get the students in the class to examine the primary data. In literature, one would ask what descriptions, kinds of diction, images, bits of dialogue (or whatever) might be making Jack feel he "doesn't like *Richard II* very much." Jack's reaction seems genuine; it could lead to extremely important observations—observations that the rest of the class could furnish, building from Jack's simple contribution.

Bea's task is to use her sophisticated appreciation of the material to focus the students' attention on details to which they are (perhaps unconsciously) reacting. All teachers of introductory courses should bear in mind that they were once as innocent and ignorant of their special subjects as *their* students are now. This seems obvious; but in practice, most teachers—particularly the more experienced ones—often forget this truism. Contempt for one's average students (be it unconscious, veiled, or even denied) is widespread and debilitating in the teaching profession.

2. *What about the aftermath of her abdication? What factors do you see at work here?*

This section of the discussion provides the leader with an opportunity to strike theoretical bedrock. What happened was "the other students didn't seem terribly interested in Jack's personal reactions." Why? Are we looking at some clue to the essence of an interesting, involving discussion—a hint at the difference between one person's purely private reaction to a subject (be it literature, art, music, history, or politics—anything with human content) and a *useful* classroom approach from which many students can profit? How can someone like Bea present students with the fruits of years of advanced study without stifling their emotional involvement?

The problem with Jack's reactions to *Richard II* as *material for educational discussion* is that they are too personal to sustain the other students' interest for long—we all know that sinking feeling when a fellow student's report or class commentary threatens to drag on and on, leaving us with fixed expressions, pretending to pay attention. This is the signal of a class in limbo. No good teacher will allow such a situation to persist for long. The reason that undiluted personal testimony fails is that emotion is ultimately not truly communicable. It is very difficult to share another's pain, pleasure, or boredom; but we *can* communicate ideas. It is the teacher's task to balance emotion with thought. For effective learning, you can't have one without the other. Students' unpracticed and unconsidered attempts to lead class discussions almost always err by excluding one element. But pure emotional effusion will alienate the other students just as certainly as dry intellectualism (unless it is full of true genius) will end by boring them.

The question for us is "Can Jack's personal reactions constitute a useful report? If so, how?" The answers will lie in attention to problems of pacing, artful questions, referring one student's insight to another student for criticism (rather than responding oneself, as the teacher), and the *judicious* introduction of critical and historical material. All this is the "meat and potatoes" of discussion teaching.

Bea goes on to describe the whole aftermath. After a "desultory and unfocused" attempt at discussion, the hour ended. Bea "said nothing" during this period. But afterward Cliff and Elke stayed to talk to her. Both were "very embarrassed." Why? At their treachery, because they both voted to oust her? At Jack's impoliteness? At the damage to Bea's self-esteem?

A good question to ask the section at this point is "What do you think of Cliff and Elke's perception that Jack has become their new section leader?" Many participants will agree: There seems to be two strong personalities in this case—Bea and Jack—whose revolt could be boiled down to a good, old-fashioned personality conflict.

The discussion leader should focus attention on several remarks Bea makes in the (B) case. She mentions that she confided her anger at Jack to Elke and Cliff, but combined this with her opinion that she "had been fairly and squarely voted out of authority." The issue of authority seems to surface over and over in this case. What do your seminar participants make of it? What authority did Bea have at the beginning of the case that she relinquished? Of what authority did the vote deprive her? Was she forced to take that vote? What else might she have done? What did she lose (or gain) by the vote?

Bea also makes a revealing remark about her approach to discussing the section's behavior with Elke and Cliff. She calls herself (with the advantage of hindsight) "unprofessional." Is she? What is professionalism in a situation like this? Has she acted unprofessionally in other ways? What ways? When? How?

It might be useful to point out that Elke proposed to call a new vote at the very next meeting, and Bea rejected the suggestion. Is Bea being manipulative? If so, why? What is her ultimate aim? (What would yours be in her situation?)

The (B) case describes (in compressed, summary form) events that took weeks to develop. Bea mentions that the seminar limped along with no one actually leading it. In the realm of symbolism, someone in the seminar is likely to point out that Bea sat "in the seat farthest from the chalkboard" and "no one sat in the teacher's seat." What is the significance of these details of position? (The discussion leader might call attention to them if they do not emerge by themselves from participants' comments.) The manipulation of classroom space is always significant.

It may also be noted that the second vote, unlike the first, was held in Bea's absence. Having haunted her section for two weeks (one wonders about the effect of her silent presence in that room), Bea seems to have retreated a bit. At least she let her students vote a second time away from her gaze, without taking the opportunity to make mental notes of her partisans and enemies.

The section of the discussion dealing with the "factors at work" during the aftermath is likely to touch on a number of points without exhausting any. There is, in fact, a great deal suggested in these encapsulized events. Bea remained in the room, but refused to participate as a student. It is likely that her presence had a dampening effect on the students' discussions. Did she help create the disorganized confusion she criticizes?

Once Bea was voted back, she found the students relieved to have her back. One might ask whether they were relieved to have her leading them again, or simply relieved to end the embarrassing arrangement whereby she watched their "formless," self-conscious discussions. (One cannot imagine an assertive person like Bea sitting expressionless during a discussion of which she basically disapproves!)

It is probably not surprising that Bea felt that the semester went "quite satisfactorily" after the students voted her back into power. The discussion leader might probe for some reasons for this. Was Bea simply pleased to feel vindicated, ratified, and appreciated? Wouldn't anyone enjoy a vote of confidence? Or did the situation really improve, once Bea had learned, from personal embarrassment, how brittle a teacher's authority can be? Did Bea endeavor to involve her students more? Write fewer directives on the board? Spend less time disguising lectures as questions and try to ask more genuinely stimulating questions?

3. *What were the critical turning points of Bea's situation?*

The crucial turning points in this case begin with Jack's initial refusal to present a report and his unsolicited public criticism of Bea (in the (A) case). How might Bea have reacted, instead of allowing him to provoke her into taking the all-or-nothing vote that ousted her from power? (This may already have been covered in the discussion of the (A) case, but one could summarize remarks from that portion of the discussion.) The second "turning point" was Bea's private discussion with Elke and Cliff—two social leaders in communication with the rest of the students. Elke, a student-government type, is probably as competent as Bea to take the situation in hand, and she seems to have pegged Jack Kesselman as a heckler anxious to overturn the applecart partly for the thrill of it and partly to flex his muscles. She probably could have done Bea's "dirty work" quite efficiently. Should Bea have allowed Elke to take a vote at the very next class meeting? Should she have tried to get more information about the other students from Elke and Cliff? If so, what kind? What is appropriate information, and what isn't?

The next turning point is, of course, the vote that restored Bea to power. The class should take up the question of *contract* here. How should Bea run the section now? What should she have learned from Jack's insurrection? What elements of her teaching style should she modify? In essence, what was she doing wrong at first?

4. How does power operate in discussion teaching?

This is one of the most basic, far-reaching, and important questions—not only in this case, but in the whole seminar. The class will certainly not exhaust it in the space of ten or so minutes of discussion. The discussion leader should ask the class to consider both the (A) and (B) cases. What specific details in the (A) case tell us how Bea exercised power? (Power, for discussion purposes, may be simply defined as the ability to make other people do what you say.) What factors in Bea's situation gave her this ability? The issue of evaluation is pertinent here. Seminar participants will probably mention that she had the absolute power to grade her students. She had the power to make class assignments, to tell the students when to present oral reports, and, presumably, written papers. She had some power to decide where the class will meet, and she could say whether the students would bring food and drink to class, who would speak, when they would speak, to whom they would speak, when and what they would or would not read. (They were required to read certain passages of the play for their reports; they were discouraged from reading criticism.) Such details will probably emerge fairly easily in class.

The more difficult aspects to plumb will be the students' power. What could they do to Bea? In this case, Jack Kesselman affords us a particularly blatant example: he criticizes openly, grabbing the power of evaluation out of her hands. All students evaluate teachers, both inwardly and in informal gripe sessions with their friends, but it is very rare for students to break the conventions and criticize teachers in class. A student can also refuse, tacitly or overtly, to be taught. If this happens, the teacher's function has, in effect, been nullified. The teacher-student relationship is reciprocal. It requires trust and acceptance on both sides. The teacher must trust the student to be making an effort to learn; the student must trust the teacher to be guiding his or her developing perceptions in useful directions. Either side can break this relationship—a point many teachers forget. The teacher-student relationship always has contractual elements, and all contracts require cooperation.

The symbols of power—position in the classroom, right to write on the board—are also prominent in this case. So is the issue of dress (costume, if you will): What is Bea signaling by dressing like a student and bringing her coffee mug to class? Does she seem to be aware of the symbolic overtones of her choices? The seminar should discuss these issues—not to praise or criticize Bea, but rather to make each other more alert to the many subtle details of the teaching situation that the teacher can control. Unconsidered choices may send unintentional messages.

Other issues of power in the classroom have to do with information: Why did Bea read criticism, but suggest that her students should not? Why did Bea write historical and critical catchwords on the board, rather than give research assignments to her students and ask *them* to write on the board? Why did Bea ask such long-winded questions? How much time should a teacher spend talking? Who should ask the questions? Who should talk to whom? (There is no student-to-student dialogue in Bea's class before the "revolution"; afterward, it exists with no moderator.)

All these are meant to be provocative questions—certainly not answerable in ten or fifteen minutes' worth of discussion time at the end of the seminar. But they are central, and should be returned to again and again.

EXHIBIT 1 *The Case of the Dethroned Section Leader*

Study Questions

1. Bea Benedict "felt attacked" by Jack Kesselman's protest. How would you describe and evaluate her situation at the end of the (A) case? (Think not only of her point of view, but also of Jack's and that of the rest of the class.)
2. Under what constraints was Bea working?
3. What elements in her situation *could* she control?
4. Evaluate her choices in setting up the teaching situation.
5. What would you advise Bea to do at the end of the (A) case? Why? What is at stake, and what can she gain?

EXHIBIT 2 *The Case of the Dethroned Section Leader*

Discussion Questions

After the (A) case has been read:

1. What's going on here? What do you make of Bea's remark that she "felt attacked"?
2. How might things have looked to Jack?
3. How about the others in the class?
4. How did Bea get into this fix?
5. What should she do?

After the (B) case has been read:

1. What is your appraisal of how Bea responded to Jack's challenge?
2. What about the aftermath of her abdication? What factors do you see at work here?
3. What were the critical turning points of Bea's situation?
4. How does power operate in discussion teaching?

The Case of the Dethroned Section Leader (A) and (B)

RESEARCHER'S PERSPECTIVE

This commentary on the "Case of the Dethroned Section Leader" was prepared by Abby Hansen. Its objective is to help instructors in the development of their own teaching plans for this case.
(HBS No. 5-382-179)

In the view of the case researcher, the Bea Benedict case depicts a power struggle that she herself engendered. By her own (unexamined) attitude toward the students, Bea almost guaranteed some sort of resistance. The particular time of this case happened to be propitious to open rebellion, but her behavior would have triggered truculence in the section under any circumstances. This commentary will suggest some points in the case that lend themselves to this view.

The Instructor

Note Bea's background: She is an honors graduate of the same institution in which she is now teaching. Unmarried, and back at her own former school, Bea is probably feeling herself something of a *revenant*. Not quite a faculty member, but no longer her own former undergraduate self, she hasn't yet adopted a completely new adult identity. She lives with students, dresses like a student, and—at least part time—*is* a student. Furthermore, Bea's statement of her purpose for being back at Fairchild University ("I felt ready for a good, nourishing drink of great literature") doesn't mention teaching at all. We can only infer that teaching is secondary to studying among her reasons for having returned. It seems reasonable that we should examine Bea's teaching style for evidence of competitiveness: outtalking the students, refusing to relinquish authority to them, reluctance to grant them class time to find their own tentative analyses of the material. Bea is so impressed with her own increasingly sophisticated appreciation of Shakespeare's plays that she tends to force her interpretations on her students, hoping thereby to accomplish their instant elevation to her own state of comprehension while simultaneously impressing them with her brilliance and preparation. Inexperienced teachers frequently fall into this trap, partly from a desire to demonstrate their legitimacy as leaders, partly from the habits of long years of competition with peers in the classroom, and partly from simply not having directed their attention to what they actually want to accomplish in the classroom—namely, helping their students learn how to come to grips with the material.

The Setting

Bea has chosen a difficult teaching situation. Not only is she on the students' territory, she is teaching at a particularly relaxed time—right after dinner, and in an atmosphere full of distractions (e.g., within earshot of the frisbee games). If she wished to teach a Falstaff House section, she might have taken some time and trouble to find a more secluded room in which she would not have had to sit facing her students around an excessively large conference table. One of the "common rooms" (similar to a living room) with arm chairs, sofas, and coffee tables) would have lent itself to creating an informal discussion circle. Bea also might have tried to have the section meet *before* dinner, as most students tend to think of the evening as a social time, or at least a time when *they* may use the hours as they please, not as a section leader dictates.

The Course

Teaching a discussion section of a large lecture course involves specific constraints. The discussion leader must work within a framework not of his or her own design. Bea felt it necessary to work against the grain—presenting supplementary material in a way implicitly disparaging to Professor Glendower's course organization and presentation. Her approach may have raised some resentment from undergraduates who liked Glendower (a popular raconteur) and found Bea's fact-laden, intense graduate-studentlike style pedantic.

The Students

Here Bea shows her greatest weakness. She has analyzed literature, not people. She describes the students rather baldly, giving little information about their personalities and styles of learning. This implies that she gave little, if any, attention to the primary problem of discussion teaching: finding how to present the material *to this particular group*. The discussion teacher should take the opportunity to find out as much personal information about each student as possible, within the bounds of propriety. Bea's student-information cards were a step in the right direction, but she seems to have failed to read students' attitudes from their behavior. She ought to have spotted Jack as a potential threat to her authority, if maintaining authority was one of her primary concerns (as it seems to have been). Bea's descriptions of the four students she remembered show Jack to be rebellious, Skip to be a potential accomplice to him, and Elke and Cliff to be conventional middle-of-the-roaders, capable of allying themselves either with authority or rebellion.

Bea's Style

The distinguishing characteristic here is dominance. Note the way Bea asks Jack her initial question: she all but answers it herself, launching into a capsule analysis of her own, and even interrupting herself to underline a previous lesson to the class (her reference to the importance of middle acts of Shakespeare's five-act structure).

Bea's desire to control everything in the classroom is further shown by her habit of standing at the board to write catchwords that she hopes will organize the hour. No discussion so programmed is truly free. One gets no sense that Bea intended the students to have any real control over the content or direction of their own discussion. Her classes seem to have been lectures in disguise.

Given Bea's apparent need to control the class, direct its discussions almost as if she were writing scripts, and thereby demonstrate her intellect and authority in the classroom, it is not surprising that she perceived Jack's (admittedly impolitely phrased) resistance to her teaching style as an "attack." She takes it quite personally (reflecting on how much she dislikes him) because her teaching style has placed enormous emphasis on power. Her ego must have been bruised indeed by Jack's statement that she had been "boring" as a teacher.

The Lesson of the Rebellion

Possibly the most salient lesson is that a discussion teacher should carefully attune his or her approach to the constituency in question. Students should have a say in how they are going to be taught. Bea might have actually devoted some class time to questions of format, asked the students to generate some recommendations for topics they'd like to discuss, and offered some critical readings for them to present to each other in the form of reports or discussion questions.

Bea's experience shows a pendulum swing from too much structure in the classroom to none at all. Neither is optimal for students' learning, but, as the (B) case implies, no structure is probably the less desirable alternative of the two. The best alternative, however, is a middle path. Bea had the fruits of superior skills and several years' worth of study to offer her students. She simply failed to learn from the group how she might make her offerings both palatable and accessible to their inexperience.

It is not surprising that, instead of a truly leaderless section, Bea's group simply exchanged their assigned teacher for an informal leader: Jack. Jack had a somewhat exhibitionistic element to his personality: he was a performer and, at this point in his life, manipulator of authority in the system in which he found himself. The classroom struggle between him and Bea included an element of pure competition. She liked the limelight, and so did he. Given that Bea possessed the natural advantage of superior preparation and expertise, it is not surprising that after a period of floundering the students voted Bea back into authority. Jack didn't devote any more time than Bea had to finding out what his fellow students wanted from the discussion process. The lesson of rebellion is, all too often, that one tyrant simply replaces another.

Apparently Bea *did* modify her style to allow for more freedom for the students. One gathers this from Bea's remark that Skip later in the semester actually took her up on her invitation to interrupt her when she slipped into lecturing instead of leading a discussion. This shows that Bea learned by her experience.

Underlying Issues

Authority. Simply by virtue of position, any teacher enters a class with authority. By standing to teach seated students, or otherwise taking stances that reinforce the idea of superiority over the group, the teacher is simply gilding the lily and acting defensively. Defensiveness, in turn, tends to engender a certain edginess in students that can turn to sullenness or even open rebellion, as in this case. When this happens, issues of power in the classroom come to the fore and the teacher can only lose face, either by forcing the issue and remaining, uncomfortably, in control, or—like Bea—being (albeit temporarily) dethroned.

Operationally, the teacher should guard against (1) cutting off students' comments, (2) answering his or her own questions in lengthy introductions before students have a chance to speak, and (3) signaling (by boardwork or otherwise) a rigid agenda for a supposedly free discussion. Informal meetings with students early in the semester might provide the teacher with clues to the group's social organization and help the teacher identify, for example, the group's natural leaders, "troublemakers," and middle-of-the roaders. Finally, the teacher would profit by bearing in mind, quite explicitly, that the best technique for leading a discussion is asking provocative, open-ended questions that will trigger the students' creative responses to the material. The object of the exercise is getting students to learn. Simply demonstrating one's own intense interest in, and mastery of, a subject will not accomplish this end.

Role change. Bea demonstrates the confusion of role that is a common trait of inexperienced teachers, particularly those who have not yet (or only recently) completed their own studies. She behaves too much like a student in the classroom, answering her own questions, competing with her students, and depriving them of a chance to participate fully. This failure to appreciate her true role—that of teacher, not fellow-student—shortchanges her students, who look to her to help them learn Shakespeare, rather than flaunt her own knowledge. Many of Jack's criticisms of Bea underscore these failures of hers.

Contract. Bea seems to have given no thought to the expectations that her competitive behavior, studentlike dress (jeans, track shoes, very casual hair style), and the setting (directly beside the students' recreational area) imply, namely, that the members of the section will treat her like a fellow student. In a sense, she has brought herself from a position of potential authority down to their level by behaving like one of them. Thus, her attempts to exert power over the students have confused and annoyed them. To unbend further from her position of equality would mean lowering herself to a status inferior to theirs, and this is what does happen when Jack "dethrones" her. A new contract is forged, under the terms of which Bea may not even participate in the section she has been hired to lead. She should have given some attention to the sort of behavior she wanted to elicit from her students, and then worked out strategies to help gain her ends.

"A Question of Cookies" (A), (B), and (C)

TEACHING NOTE

This teaching note was developed, researched, and written by Abby Hansen for use with the case series "A Question of Cookies" (A) HGSE 3, (B) HGSE 17, and (C) HGSE 18 to help instructors prepare to lead case discussions. It is meant to stimulate discussion, not present a definitive analysis.
(HGSE No. 8)

Distributed by HBS Publishing Division, Harvard Business School, Boston, MA 02163.
Printed in U.S.A.

Usage

In this writer's opinion, "A Question of Cookies" possesses qualities that make it particularly appropriate to use early in a teaching seminar. The action issues in this case are both accessible and complex. They aren't difficult to spot, but the closer you look at them, the richer they appear.

Allen Hall, the teacher in this case, seems to be doing everything right. He runs extra sessions to help students become familiar with difficult new material; he holds long office hours; he takes the time to get to know his students outside of class (by attending some of their social functions); he announces publicly that he encourages cooperation rather than competition. How many teachers do as much for their students? Allen's stellar teaching evaluations suggest that most of his students understand the lengths to which he goes to help them. He takes practical steps to implement his wish to come across as a competent, helpful, teacher. Yet even this paragon of good intentions and intelligent policies runs into trouble because of something he does—the seemingly simple act of giving out cookies triggers a complaint that ends up in the Dean's office.

At the end of the (A) case, Allen Hall must decide what to do about the dissatisfied student's very specific complaint. She has no quarrel with how he teaches, how he assigns material, how the other students react to her. She objects to sitting in a room while other people eat cookies, and Allen quickly comes to take her objection as valid, serious, and full of implications for classroom policy. He focuses on what to do: stop giving out cookies, tell the rest of the class that one of their number suffers from an eating disorder, accommodate the majority by continuing to give out cookies and make some sort of private deal with Mary Kay? Seminar participants may tease out other possibilities. In fact, one might graph multiple options and their potential implications as a many-branched decision tree. A discussion leader might want to ask questions designed to highlight the implications of various courses of action. How might each policy affect Mary Kay? What signals might it send to others in the class? Would it send different signals to different participants? What are the potential risks and benefits to the various courses of action? What can Allen gain or lose in each instance? Even students unfamiliar with case method learning (and therefore with detecting the complexities under the surface of apparently simple actions) can isolate specific actions and begin to discuss them.

Another argument for placing this case early in a teaching seminar is its imagery. Who can read the word "cookies" in a syllabus without having some sort of reaction? For many people, this reaction will be positive. (I, for one, often find the adage "life's short—eat dessert first" running through my mind when I think of this case.) And there is a homey quality to much of its imagery—bags of cookies, a plastic container of salad, a potluck supper—that makes this case attractive. There are few things more universal, basic, or visceral, than food. For most seminar participants, cookies mean childhood parties, comfort, and good cheer. For others (like Mary Kay), cookies may mean something different.

Complexities

Accessible as it is, this case contains much more than just an agreeable teacher and a visceral central image. As it clearly demonstrates, any teaching situation can explode. And the implications of the explosion will touch the most fundamental assumptions of any teacher. Whose rights predominate in the arena of discussion: the teacher's, those of the majority, those of students with unusual sensitivities or needs? To what extent should a teacher accommodate those unusual, or even unique, requirements? How much should a teacher know about a student's private life? Where is the border between private and public?

Some Teaching Possibilities

One way to help a discussion group begin to explore the complex implications of the case details is to construct a string of "what ifs," or hypothetical action questions. It is a truism that changing any element in a situation changes the whole situation. The answer to each "what if" question implies a unique set of underlying assumptions and, indeed, a whole philosophy of teaching. Discussion leaders will, no doubt, want to develop their own "what if's" for this case, but here are a few that occur to me: What if Allen Hall had dismissed Mary Kay as a crank? What if he had tried to verify her story? What if he had capitulated completely and stopped giving out cookies? What if she had complained about something other than cookies—like her perception of his politics or his treatment of her contributions to the discussion, for example? What if he had held a class discussion about whether to stop serving cookies? What if Allen Hall hadn't been a civil rights lawyer? What if he had already been tenured? What if he had sought help in dealing with this baffling situation?

Particularly because this case leads to a discussion of actions, the instructor may devise a teaching plan that incorporates some role-play. Students might take the point of view of Allen Hall, Mary Kay Compton, Janetta DeForrest, the woman who ran the potluck supper, law students, or Ed. School students. What do these "players" in the case have to gain or lose? What do they want? How do they view one another and Allen? How might their views—especially of Mary Kay—come to change?

Students might also take the point of view of hypothetical advisers. What would they have counselled Allen to do if they were his friend and colleague?

Case Segments

The (A) case is designed to trigger a discussion lasting about an hour, with the (B) and (C) cases being distributed in class and discussed for about fifteen minutes apiece. Needless to say, there are many other ways one might "play" these segments, but this note will assume this distribution of time.

The (A) case focuses primarily on actions and leads Allen Hall—a teacher with good reason to expect nothing but success in the classroom—to the brink of a cliff. If seminar participants have come to class prepared to discuss this segment, the discussion could embroider at length on the "what ifs" and focus on specific moments of the case. It might be helpful to ask seminar participants to look at Allen's conversational style—the specific questions he asks. What assumptions seem to underlie them? Do the participants share these? And what do we know about Allen's educational contract with this group? To what extent did he share power? How might he have set a different contract (and what would the effect of his actions have been in the context of a different contract)? What might Mary Kay's peculiar classroom contributions have meant? How might he have approached her to try to find out "what made her tick" as a student in this course? *Should* he have approached her? And, if so, how? After an hour's discussion anchored in the plentiful details of action and speech in this segment, the discussion leader might wish to lead the class to the prediction that the case sets up. At the end of the (A) case, Allen is wondering how to handle this situation. Students might want to predict what he actually did and how it turned out. The obvious teaching question is something like, "What do you think Allen Hall did?" or "What should Allen Hall do?" (These have different implications.)

The (B) case is designed to be distributed and read in class. It describes what Allen actually did and the results of his action. It also contains the puzzling information that Mary Kay almost immediately broke the contract that she and Allen had forged: he continued to "throw" the cookies at the class on the dot of

4:00 p.m. and encourage everyone with his hurried body language to eat the cookies "pronto." But Mary Kay made these accommodations unnecessary by arriving on time and simply eating salad while others were still eating cookies. Seminar participants might wonder (as Allen no doubt did) why she had made such a fuss in the first place. Allen's role was not to diagnose or treat Mary Kay for an eating disorder; it was to deal with her as a student in his course. The issue under consideration is not, "What does it mean when a symptom is alleviated by an authority figure's simply paying attention to a patient," but something more like, "How did Allen's inclusion of Mary Kay in a policy decision about serving cookies in class change the way she functioned in this learning group?"

The (B) case ends with Allen marveling at the swiftness with which Mary Kay found the courage to come to class while others were still eating cookies. Instructors will probably wish to invite the discussion group to speculate about the same question. I suggest that they try to avoid plumbing the wellsprings of Mary Kay's motivation and concentrate instead on Allen's actions in making his "deal" with her. What was the process? How did their new contract play out in class?

The (C) case is a denouement: it tells what happened during the rest of the semester from Allen's point of view. Mary Kay stayed with the course, did the assignments, continued to contribute to class discussions, and even made a social adjustment (Allen says that she was "adopted" into a study group). Allen reports that he continued to work to incorporate her comments into the mainstream of the discussion, but that perhaps he worked a bit less hard than previously. The seminar might want to discuss what sort of progress this represented. What might have happened if Allen had changed the way in which he responded to her comments in class? What were some other responses he might have made? Nonetheless, for Allen, the class ended rather successfully, with the *piece de resistance* (dessert, if you will) coming in the form of the compliment he received from a very high-status student, Janetta DeForrest.

The last vivid word in this highly charged case is another one with visceral overtones: "chills." Allen reports an intense physical reaction to Janetta's comment that "you never gave up on Mary Kay." I read his remark to mean that he took Janetta's comment as a profound compliment: the "sage" of the class had noted, with approval, his hard work to bring an outsider in the fold.

But Allen's decision to pay attention to Mary Kay—give her "air time" in class—exacted a price. According to his description, her comments were usually off the mark; they distracted other students (often making them laugh or squirm), and diluted the quality of the discussion, if only momentarily. Allen mentions his fear that the other students in the course, including Janetta, had felt impatient and annoyed—annoyed with Mary Kay for making unrelated comments, and annoyed with him for not cutting her off and devoting more time and attention to better contributions.

The instructor might want to call for a range of reactions to the implications of this point. Should Allen have "played to" the better students in the class? Where was his primary responsibility? How well did he seem to balance the one against the many? What should he have done? How good an indicator of quality is the reaction of a group of students in a class? How damaging is a poor contributor to the quality of the overall discussion?

Finally, what are some other potential meanings of Allen's phrase, "I got chills." What might students in the discussion mean if they used that phrase—relief, lingering doubt about whether they had short-changed the rest of the class in order to pay attention to its weakest member, some worry about whether they had really helped Mary Kay reach her highest potential with this material? The discussion could broaden from Allen Hall to Anyteacher. How does it feel to be on display, available for the observation and evaluation of dozens of students at any given time? What do they notice about you, the teacher? What do you want them to notice? To what extent—and how—can teachers affect what students notice?

It might be useful to play devil's advocate in the brief time that the class will have to discuss the (C) case. A range of opinions will probably emerge. *Did* Allen give up on Mary Kay in some sense (and if so, when)? What does "giving up" mean? What might he have done, other than rephrase her questions in class, to help her learn legal analysis and argument? What might he have done, other than speak to her in his office hours, to help her become socially and intellectually integrated with the class as a whole? The point of this part of the discussion is certainly not to criticize Allen Hall. On the contrary, he seems to have behaved as one would expect a liberal, sensitive, benevolent, teacher with legal training and fantastic teaching evaluations to.

But Allen did not have the benefit of distance from these events. He lived them. What might he have done differently? ("Nothing" is one possible answer. So is "everything," and all points between.) And how might things have turned out if he had behaved differently?

It would not be surprising if members of a discussion group left the classroom still chewing on the implications of the details of "A Question of Cookies." It is a high-calorie case.

Summary: Some Basic Issues

1. The "chills." What are the implications for teachers of being "noticed" by students?
2. Getting help. Could Allen have turned to colleagues, other students in the group? If so, how, and when?
3. How can a teacher balance responsibility to a single student and to the group?
4. The complexity of weaving "off the wall" comments into the thread of discussion. Who benefits, who loses? How should it be done?
5. The teaching/learning contract. Could Allen have involved the whole group in the decision about the cookies? What sort of contract did he have with this group? How did he set it? Should a teacher have separate contracts with separate students or subgroups? If so, under what circumstances?
6. Alliance with students. What is the nature of his alliance with Mary Kay? He seems to see little academic potential in her. What are the implications of how he (and the others in the class) respond to her comments in class? What are some other ways in which he might have responded to her comments?
7. What are some appropriate ways for a teacher to do "rescue work" with students in trouble?
8. Self-management, self-perception. Did Allen overreact?
9. Self-protection. How can one balance a reasonable concern for one's own reputation with concern for a student?
10. Students' reactions. What might the other students in the group have been noticing? Might things look different to law students, education students, women?
11. Timing. This issue comes up in the first month of the course, when the teacher is still setting the academic contract with the group. What does it do to a working relationship when someone raises a strong objection?
12. Power-sharing. Note Allen's dialogue with Mary Kay in his office. He includes her in the decision about what to do—but not with complete equality. How might other teachers respond in this situation? What are the implications of different kinds of reactions?

George Perkins (A), (B), and (C)

TEACHING NOTE

This teaching note was prepared by James Moore as an aid to instructors in the classroom use of the case series "George Perkins" (A) 9-394-069, (B) 9-394-070, and (C) 9-394-080. It was revised by Abby Hansen.
(HBS No. 5-394-071)

Special Features

Although all cases—being "slices of life"—have the potential to raise multiple issues, this particular one was designed primarily to highlight the critical issue of the teacher-student "learning contract." I have defined this contract elsewhere as "a matrix of reciprocal agreements that determine the ground rules of behavior for instructor and students," and noted that it includes unstated as well as explicit elements.[1] The explicit elements comprise statements, often written in a syllabus, about grading policies, attendance and participation requirements, reading and writing assignments, and the like. The implicit aspects of the contract, by contrast, can almost defy detection. They have to do with behavior, attitudes, and tone—what can and cannot be said and done in class, how people will treat one another, what kinds of jokes will be accepted, what the pacing will be, the level of trust, and other elusive but extraordinarily powerful aspects of relationship that give it flavor and uniqueness. One hallmark of a healthy contract is evolution. A teacher who starts out behaving like a parent will probably become more collegial by degrees, as students gain competence and confidence. Although the explicit contract may stand more or less unaltered, throughout a whole course, the implicit contract will almost always change. C. R. Christensen has observed that an *un*changing contract may be a sign that something is wrong. Students can and should develop over time, and so should teachers. Learning is a process of change. Neither the students nor the teacher are exactly the same people at the end of a course as they were at its inception. One of the many problems with Lynn Novak's teaching contract with George Perkins is that it changed so abruptly: instead of warning George that she was going to call on him to demonstrate his competence in front of the class, Lynn simply asked him to do a calculation (and in less than encouraging words). Given that all of her previous dealings with him had been protective in the extreme, one can understand that he felt betrayed and humiliated. At the time, however, Lynn did not realize that she had developed any sort of behavioral contract with George, and her lack of awareness prevented her from managing the contract in a positive, helpful way.

The basic purpose of this case is to make it possible for Lynn's future colleagues to avoid similar problems with their teaching/learning contracts, primarily by

[1] See Hansen, "Establishing a Teaching/Learning Contract," Christensen, Garvin, and Sweet, eds. *Education for Judgment.* Harvard Business School Press, 1991.

realizing that such things exist, and that they can be consciously evaluated and changed, when necessary.

An important feature of the case text is that it includes interviews with almost everyone who is centrally involved *except* George Perkins. It should be emphasized, if the participants do not pick this up on their own, that we see him only through Lynn's eyes. Thus the information we have about him is not only limited but filtered through her perceptions and memory. Although George is a dramatic presence in the case, its focus is not on him, but on Lynn Novak, and how she handled him and her other students in her first teaching assignment.

A Major Issue: Teaching/Learning Contract

In the (B) segment of this case, Lynn Novak calls attention to a central issue in this story: the teaching/learning contract, to which she alludes as "the rules of the game." The contract evolves over the course of the semester, is negotiated both overtly and unconsciously between instructor and students, and profoundly shapes the experience for all concerned. In our outline, "George Perkins" is usually followed by "Ernie Budding," which addresses contract in a business school class where the teacher loses touch with the class over time because the students are changing and he does not recognize this. By contrast, "George Perkins" explores how a learning contract, primarily between a teacher and a student, develops without either one explicitly realizing it, and causes trouble when violated. In (B), Lynn Novak notes that she changed the rules of the game "without warning George Perkins." The lack of warning in itself constituted a kind of breach of contract. "George Perkins" gives student-readers a chance to appreciate the degree to which such contracts are commonly negotiated and established outside the awareness of both parties. And it points up the dangers of remaining unaware of such contracts.

In this case, she did realize that she had a contract, but not until well after the fact. By contrast, in the "Ernie Budding" case, the instructor did make a conscious choice during the course to change the teaching/learning contract as his goals for the section changed. It might be useful to ask the discussion group how Lynn might have changed her contract, and when, if someone had alerted her to its existence and structure.

Other Themes

Other important themes that emerge from "George Perkins" are (1) the problems of any abrupt shift in practice—even in an apparently minor way; (2) the problems of changing one's identity from student to teacher; (3) some ways in which the instructor can begin to read the often subtle signals given by a section and by individual students about their hopes and fears, their strengths and weaknesses; and (4) some of the difficulties that young female instructors have in leading groups that consist primarily of male students.

Seminar participants may also raise the issue of Lynn's preparation for this teaching assignment. They may conclude that Lynn Novak's problems stem primarily from her lack of adequate preparation for either the substantive content or the process aspects of her teaching role. Participants may describe their own understanding of adequate preparation, and point out how Lynn Novak's falls short.

Another theme is the instructor's self-management. In particular, Lynn Novak's attitude toward her students—assuming that they labored under high math anxiety and required reassurance—may have blinded her to their real needs and strengths. Participants may note that Lynn's assumptions about the students seem more appropriate to her situation than to theirs. This raises the issue of how instructors can become aware of and manage their anxieties, and, more generally, how they can stay aware of and manage their attitudes toward the students.

Participants may mention the instructor's need to read cues given by students and the section as a whole—to discover who they are, what they are experiencing during the discussions, and what their attitudes and intentions are toward the instructor and the learning process in the class. Lynn Novak has time to observe and interact with George and the rest of the section members, and the questions raised by George's behavior are much more involved than simply determining the momentary motives of a student. Lynn must assess George's potential to master the course material and to handle the social demands of speaking in class.

How can such judgments be skillfully made? Participants may want to discuss what data are available to instructors seeking insight into a section and individual students. They may also want to explore what sorts of inferences are necessary and appropriate to teaching. In addition, they may want to discuss how the instructor can use outside-of-class sources to supplement observations and to check hypotheses (e.g., one can sometimes discreetly speak to a member of the class to gain further information; one can speak directly to the student or students in question, and so forth).

The case also raises issues about getting help with

one's teaching. Lynn Novak might have sought more help, both while preparing for teaching and during their actual teaching time. Students may wish to discuss her choice of mentor. Is her somewhat cynical office mate a good choice? What are his advantages and drawbacks for Lynn? Instructors need to learn when and how to ask for help—from other colleagues, their superiors, and the students themselves—and how to manage the process of being helped.

Participants sometimes point out that issues of control, including self-management and self-control, are central to responding effectively to all classroom surprises. How the instructor follows up on an incident can be as important or even more important than how he or she responds immediately. Follow-up is particularly important as a way of reestablishing rapport and a learning contract with the section.

Two discussion themes inherent in the case data are difficult to handle productively at this stage in the life of the seminar. Some guidance from the instructor will probably be needed to prevent the discussion from dwelling on these themes to the detriment of other issues raised by the case.

The first such issue is the tendency to label George Perkins with a psychological "diagnosis"—something for which we have no professional competence, and for which the case does not provide enough information.

A second problematic theme is that of sexism and gender-based conflict. The case presents data, in Lynn's own words, about her difficulties in dealing with men in her teaching life. All of the problems in the case involve men—the incident with the jocks, her office mate's interruption of her student conference, and the situation with George Perkins. Lynn's own analysis, in the (C) case, suggests that she considered sexism and gender-based conflict central to her difficulties in communicating with, and managing, male students. Thus this case can open a discussion about the role of sexual stereotyping and gender-based conflict in teaching. This is an important theme, and we encourage discussion of it later in the semester, when this case may be cited in the context of others that focus on this issue more directly.

We try to downplay this issue in the "George Perkins" case for several reasons. Sexism is a powerful and attractive theme—one that can easily overwhelm a discussion and polarize a group that has not yet formed a good working relationship. It can also distract attention from central issues, like contract and preparation, which we believe need to be covered early in the seminar. Later units of our curriculum are built on the assumption that the group will have covered issues of contract and preparation early in the seminar and developed a healthy set of interrelationships that can sustain potentially volatile exchanges about sexism, with good humor. Our approach to this problem is to try to get the discussion centered on the matter of contracts before the question of sexism is raised. Then when the issue is introduced, it can be seen as one of a variety of problems that can interfere with the establishment of a productive learning contract. One way to encourage the early development of the contract theme is to pick lead speakers who are more likely to focus on contract than gender-based issues. (In practice this means that we tend to open this particular case discussion by calling on two men.) In addition, using our license as instructors, we amplify comments and build bridges between comments in a way that encourages a central focus on the issue of establishing learning contracts. The intention is not to exclude considerations of gender, but rather to hold them to one side and begin with a topic of importance to all teachers, male and female, for *no* instructor can lead a group effectively without setting (and maintaining) a workable teaching and learning contract.

Case Summary
The Institutional Context

The case takes place in an undergraduate statistics course at a large university that does not feature a great deal of discussion teaching. Most of the students in this statistics course are not quantitatively oriented, and are taking the course only to fulfill the requirements of their majors. It has large lectures (during which many students read the college paper or sleep) and section meetings in which problem sets are worked in an uncomfortable basement "boiler room" setting. Because these problem sets provide direct preparation for the examination questions, students attend section meetings regularly.

The Instructor

A young woman barely older than her students, Lynn Novak is inexperienced as a teacher and not very familiar with the quantitative material in the course. She finds both the process and substantive content of the course difficult to manage. She has taken this teaching position (with some surprise at not receiving a research position) because it is a requirement of her financial aid package.

The Section

The section consists of 24 sophomore students, including 20 women, mostly majoring in human ecology, and 4 men. One of these, George Perkins, stands out from the beginning because of his atypically neat and unstylish dress, his isolation from the other students, and his anxiety about the course, as expressed in weekly visits to Lynn during her office hours. Unlike others in the section, George is majoring in industrial relations.

The Teacher-Student Relationship

Lynn seems automatically to aim at a warm, emotionally supportive style of teaching. She states her belief that most of the students are suffering from various degrees of math anxiety, and that the way to help them is to be "as cheerful and supportive as possible."

Lynn does not try to challenge her students intellectually during the section meetings. When she demonstrates a problem, she asks for a volunteer to work the example, and if none is forthcoming she herself does the calculation on the board. (In so doing, she unconsciously sets a contract with the group: she does not make "cold calls," and the students do not expect her to.) She provides many hours of individual conference time each week, and devotes a great deal of her time during section meetings to individual coaching.

The Incident

The focal incident of this case occurs in the middle of the term. Lynn begins a lab meeting by summarizing the major points covered by Professor Fitzsimmons that week in lecture, and then presents what she perceives as a simple problem. As usual, she asks, "Can anyone get us started on solving this?" When no one volunteers, she does something minor (or so she thinks) but unprecedented: she calls upon a student who has not volunteered. But she does not call upon one of the stronger students. She calls upon one of her most anxious students, one who has specifically told her of his lack of confidence in his ability to do the work: George Perkins. "Well, George," she says, "why don't you give it a try?" Her words, while casual, do not express confidence: she doesn't say, "do it for us," or "show us your calculation and we'll work with it," or anything that either invites him to fail without penalty or expresses an expectation that he will do the job right. She says, "give it a try," and thereby includes the possibility of failure.

Suggested Study Questions

Study questions can be handed out with the case, for use in preparing for class. The following may be helpful in preparing students for a discussion that will focus on the basic issue of the behavioral contract:

1. How did Lynn Novak end up in this situation?
2. What are the most important factors that contributed to her predicament? When did her problem begin?
3. What are the unique problems confronting a new instructor?
4. What should Lynn Novak do now?

Suggested Discussion Questions

The instructor must decide how focused or directive the discussion questions should be. In teaching "George Perkins," for example, the instructor can try to focus the attention of participants on the learning contract issue by using a set of questions that raise this issue and help ensure that it is thoroughly explored. One could give an advance reading assignment about learning contracts, and begin the discussion by asking, "What sort of contract has Lynn set with her section?"

Alternatively, the instructor can use a more open approach, which might be helpful, for at least two reasons. First, we want to find out what sorts of interests participants have, and what sorts of analyses the section as a whole tends to support. Second, open discussions give the participants a better sense of discovery. Participants (and the instructor!) tend to find these sorts of discussions much more exciting and engaging. Instructors still shape these discussions by encouraging the development of certain participant responses, while letting others drop.

Open-Focused Discussion Questions

1. Can you help your seminar group understand Lynn Novak's situation? What do you see as the one or two critical factors contributing to her current problem?
   Or (somewhat more provocatively): How did Lynn Novak get into such a mess? (She obviously had the best of intentions; she worked hard; and she tried to improve her work and be helpful to the students.)
2. *When* did the problem begin? What decisions or actions did Lynn take before the day of the blowup that may have contributed to George Perkins's outburst?
   Or (more provocatively): What was her first mistake?

3. We suggest that one or both of the following questions be used:
   a) Why didn't Lynn Novak see this problem developing?
   b) Why did she have such a difficult time in her first semester?
4. What is your appraisal of George Perkins's "speech"?
   a) What do we know about George? Of what significance could these observations have been to Lynn Novak?
   b) Why did George Perkins feel wronged? Why the intensity of his attack?
5. What can Lynn do now? In the class? After the class?

Topic-Focused Discussion Questions

1. What was Lynn Novak's contract with her section?
2. Did Lynn Novak have a special contract with George Perkins? If so, what was it? How did she set it? How could she have known she was setting it?
3. What do we know about Lynn Novak's behavior on the day of the outburst? How might her actions have contributed to the outburst?

Some Notes on a Potential Process Plan

Using the open-focused discussion questions, our typical overall plan involves directing the discussion toward diagnosis, holding the action recommendations until the end (or omitting them entirely).

We typically start the diagnostic discussion by asking, "What are one or two key factors that contributed to the present problem?" This question gives the participants great latitude in choosing issues to bring into the discussion, while encouraging each one to identify the items he or she believes to be most salient.

As more and more factors are introduced into the discussion, it is useful to turn the section's attention to the temporal dimension of the case by asking, "When did Lynn's trouble begin?" This question helps the participants to begin putting the various factors into a sequential order and to see how some factors build on the others to amplify the problems. In addition, participants begin to appreciate how early Lynn Novak, and others in a similar spot, could begin to get help and/or make preparations that would minimize later difficulties.

As the discussion continues, the participants get a sense of the sequential development of the problem. Then we begin to ask them to generalize from Lynn's experience and examine the wider issues raised by the case. This shift can be encouraged by asking, "What questions does this case raise for you about teaching, and about your own teaching experience?" These themes include the need to establish a good learning contract between instructor and students, and the importance of preparation for teaching, instructor self-management, and knowing when and how to get help. Raising these wider issues also helps participants realize that Lynn's problems are not unique, and enables them to relate the case discussion to their own teaching experience. Only at the close of the class do we ask participants to suggest what Lynn Novak might *do*.

The (B) case gives the reader Lynn Novak's reflections on her troubling experiences with George Perkins. The passage of time has permitted her to see the difficulties that changing the "rules of the game" caused, and particularly to see how unsettling this change must have seemed to George "without warning. She also sees subtleties of which, as a first-time teaching assistant, she was completely unaware: she now appreciates the additional pressure she put on George by using his name, and understands the danger to any teacher of establishing a behavioral contract with a student or a group, and now knowing what that contract is. Students can hypothesize, not only about Lynn's contract with George and the other students, but about how that contract might have been different, given small changes in her behavior. At what points in the case did she inadvertently encourage dependency? How might she have prodded him to take more responsibility for his own learning, while still providing reassurance and support? How might she have gotten a clearer view of the implications and effects of her own automatic actions?

The (C) part of this case presents more of Lynn's later reflections, but focuses on a different topic: the implications of her gender in this particular context. Since part of Lynn's "psychological contract" with the class, in her view, involved her automatic adoption of what she considered to be a maternal role, considerations of gender roles and the details and implication of her contract with George and the other students will probably blend together. If the group devotes much time to this segment of the case, it will probably be useful to note that Lynn is remembering events that happened years ago, and to note how women's roles, expectations, and customary behavior have changed in professional and educational situations. (Note, for example, the tone of Lynn's mother's advice in this case. Would it be different today? Would the proportions of male to female students be the same today in similar classes? Would women and men students behave differently?)

We hold both the (B) and (C) portions until late in the class hour, or hand one or both for students to take home. If they are used in class, we might ask, "How does Lynn see this situation?" "Do you agree?" "Why do you think she places her emphasis where she does?" "Where else might one place it?"

Finally, participants usually point out that Lynn's reflections do not tell us how she responded to George Perkins's outburst, or what happened to their relationship after the incident. She does, however, present a fairly thorough diagnosis of the situation, and her reflections underscore our emphasis, at this phase of the seminar, on diagnosis rather than action recommendations.

Suggested Reading

Abby J. Hansen, "Establishing a Teaching/Learning Contract," Christensen, Garvin, and Sweet, eds. *Education for Judgment.* Harvard Business School Press, 1991.

Ernie Budding (A), (B), (C), and (D)

TEACHING NOTE

This teaching note was prepared by James Moore as an aid to instructors in the classroom use of the case series "Ernie Budding" (A) 9-381-038, (B) 9-381-039, (C) 9-381-040, and (D) 9-381-041.

(HBS No. 5-384-092)

Introduction

"Ernie Budding" focuses on the first case-teaching experience of a young man who has just completed his Ph.D. and is now an instructor.

In discussing "Ernie Budding," we explore the different sorts of contracts an instructor can make with a section, and the ways in which contracts can be negotiated and renegotiated.

The first three segments of "Ernie Budding"—(A), (B), and (C)—deal with the situation in a section as it develops during an academic year. As detailed below, we generally teach this as a "prediction case." That is, we hand out (A) and (B) in advance, and then discuss them in class—asking participants to predict the results of Ernie's actions in (B). After they have made their predictions, (C) is handed out.

The (D) case, presenting Ernie's reflections as he looks back on the year of teaching, is sometimes handed out at the end of class for the participants to read at their leisure. It can also be used in a subsequent discussion centering on instructional philosophy. For such a discussion we often pair it with "Class on World Hunger (B)," which contains similarly philosophical reflections by another case method instructor.

In summary, the case emphasizes the degree to which section needs and teacher learning goals may change over time, and how an instructor can respond to a changing situation by intentionally renegotiating the learning contract. In addition, it points up several important aspects of changing a contract, including:

1. the difficulty of realizing when a contract is not working and needs to be modified;
2. the complexities of actually negotiating a change (in particular, when the instructor tries to alter the contract unilaterally); and
3. the importance of the instructor's willingness to depart from a personally preferred style of teaching and learning, in order to respond to the needs of the section.

Special Features of the Case

"Ernie Budding" is a long case. We find it helpful to warn participants in advance that they should allow more time than usual to prepare for the discussion. More important, the discussion itself must be moved along quickly to ensure that at least (A), (B), and (C) are discussed.

Despite its length, our experience is that this case series stimulates relatively focused discussion centered on Ernie's teaching style and learning contract.

This centripetal tendency seems largely due to the way "Ernie Budding" is written. By and large, the information presented pertains directly to the core issue, and there is very little material to stimulate an alternative focus.

This series examines closely the interaction between instructor and students. With direct data about the interactions, participants can more concretely understand the facts of the situation. We find it valuable to call the participants' attention to the details of Ernie's classroom question and response style. This sets the stage for a later section of the seminar which focuses on questions, responses and examines brief interactions between instructor and students.

Because the (A) and (B) cases consist primarily of direct quotations from Ernie about his experience with the section, they amount to a representation of Ernie's perceptual world as he tries to deal with his teaching task. As readers of the case, the seminar participants have virtually the same information as Ernie. More precisely, the (A) and (B) cases give them the information to which Ernie is paying attention, plus the snippet of classroom interaction. A central point of the case discussion, as we encourage it, is the discovery that Ernie does not have enough information to assess his section's progress and mood, nor is he asking the most relevant questions of the data he does have. It can be useful to call seminar participants' attention to the restricted viewpoint of the (A) and (B) cases. This lead can encourage them to explore what other information they might want to have if they were in Ernie's shoes. Such a line of thinking can lead to a discussion of how instructors can get information about the mood and learning progress of their sections, and how students are interpreting their interactions with the section and experiencing the teacher-student learning contract as it evolves.

Notes for the Discussion Questions

1. *As a friend and colleague of Ernie Budding, could you please help our seminar group understand the situation confronting Ernie Budding at the end of the (A) case?*
   a) *What do you see as the one or two critical factors contributing to his current situation?*
   b) *Given these elements of the situation, what is the problem?*

Usage Note

This broad question sets the stage for the rest of the session. We encourage participants to work back and forth between identifying relevant situational factors and trying to articulate the central problem.

Analysis

Participants typically point to the following features of Ernie's situation:

a) Ernie is using a very directive teaching style: he leads the class with a very short leash through his own tightly ordered analysis of each case.
b) Because he relies so much on leading questions, organized in a logical sequence, students who want to contribute to the discussion must guess his line of reasoning and anticipate its unfolding. Their thinking must become closely attuned to his, and they are given little room to develop their own independent lines of thought.
c) Ernie's personal epistemology centers on his understanding of "rigor," which to him means precise, comprehensive, ordered analysis of situations. Ernie believes his own ability to be rigorous was sharpened by submitting himself to a quantitative program during graduate school—a program which ran counter to his inclinations. He seeks to impart this same quality of rigor to his students, and he appears to be doing so by enforcing a disciplined teaching process which may run counter to their inclinations.
d) The instructional situation changes over the course of the year. The students' instructional needs, abilities, and, most important, their desire for structure appear to be changing. They seem to be seeking a more open, less directive contract, which would allow them to do more synthetic thinking. Further, they are learning to function as a group (as shown by the pranks and triaging), and thus are capable not only of coordinated learning, but also of coordinated resistance and rebellion.

   The course subject matter is changing, too, moving from material designed to elicit relatively mechanical applications of concepts and techniques to material that calls for high-level strategic thinking. This sort of thinking is better pursued and displayed in a more open discussion format than that used by Ernie.
e) Ernie is attempting to maintain a unilaterally imposed teacher-student learning contract with the section. Though he seems to be aware of other teaching styles, he apparently does not realize there are other, more negotiated ways to establish a learning contract.

f) Section members, at first, like Ernie's approach but as time passes they became restive and are no longer willing to acknowledge its legitimacy and submit to it. Instead, they are rebelling against Ernie's contract, both passively and actively.
g) Ernie is not aware of the situation. Ernie senses some resistance to his teaching style, but he does not see that this may keep him from accomplishing his teaching objectives. Further, he does not seem to realize that he needs to change the unilateral way in which the contract is being maintained. Viewing the section's behavior as a sign of laziness and a shirking of rigor, he does not consider interpreting these signals as attempts to renegotiate the contract, or as signs that the contract is inappropriate to the present situation.
h) Ernie believes that the section is "slipping" and that externally imposed sanctions may be needed to reinforce discipline and encourage high performance.

The discussion of critical features can be developed by employing the optional probes listed in *Exhibit 2.* By asking participants to compare Ernie's understanding of the situation with that of a typical class member, and with their own, the instructor can help them recognize key factors in the breakdown of communication about the learning contract. They fairly quickly realize that Ernie defines the problem as "slipping" or slacking off, while they probably define it in other ways, and that there is no direct explicit communication between them that would permit the negotiation of a mutually agreeable contract. This line of discussion should help participants identify the breakdown of the learning contract as Ernie's fundamental problem.

Participants tend to feel the central problem is a breakdown in *something* in the teacher-student relationship. Some will call it "respect"; others will talk about an implicit contract. Our response is often to ask the participants to articulate what they mean by "the elusive term 'respect.'"

In so doing, they will often describe several aspects of a successful learning contract. In addition, they may express different views about how learning contracts should be established and maintained, and what kinds of contracts are desirable. These different approaches can be discussed, with the instructor encouraging participants to clarify the distinctions (as well as similarities) between the different approaches, and to explore the strengths and weaknesses of these alternatives.

In our judgment the central problem illustrated in the case is that Ernie is trying to retain an unchanging and unilaterally imposed contract with a section whose instructional needs and desires have changed. The problem persists because Ernie is unaware of it, since he misreads the signals from the section. He appears to believe that the section's pranks, nonperformance, and use of buzzwords are signs of resistance to an appropriate and appropriately negotiated contract. He might better read these as signals that the contract is not being voluntarily maintained by both parties, and needs to be examined and perhaps renegotiated.

The longer he tries to maintain the unchanging contract unilaterally, the more the section resorts to active and passive resistance. Thus the section's performance and compliance with Ernie's directives continues to decline.

2. *Why didn't Ernie see the need for a change in his contract with the section?*

Usage Note

This question is used to turn the seminar's attention away from the central problem and toward the reasons for Ernie's failure to recognize it. Participants typically identify a variety of features about his background, training, and personality that may underlie his particular teaching style. The key generalization we encourage the participants to discover is that a new instructor's teaching approach is often based primarily on his or her background, personal style, and values—and may have little or nothing to do with the present teaching situation. One of our aims in teaching this case is to heighten participants' sensitivity to their actual situations as they develop their approach to teaching.

Analysis

Some of the factors in Ernie's experience that participants identify as important contributors to his present teaching style are:

a) He has little experience with the substantive content of the course. Thus he tries to control the discussion and keep it within limits within which he knows he can be competent.
b) Ernie apparently has not been exposed to case method teaching. Given this lack of experience with effective alternative approaches, he may be justifiably reluctant to vary his style.
c) Perhaps because this is his first term as an instructor, he appears not to have considered the development of the students and the

section in his teaching plan. Thus he was not attuned to the possibility that students' development might call for a change in instructional style.

d) Perhaps because he is new to the substantive material of the course, he does not seem to realize that the shift in pedagogical aims in the second term has implications for teaching style. The early segment is designed to show students a variety of tools of analysis, and familiarize them with the concrete conditions and the common terms of the world of manufacturing management. The second half is designed to let the students build on this foundation and move into strategic thinking. In our opinion such thinking is best expressed when students are relatively free to structure their approach to the material and their actual presentations during the class discussion, and are given an opportunity to understand and critique each other's approaches, thus learning by making comparisons.

e) Ernie tends to see the problems presented by the cases as solvable by one or at most a range of ordered solutions. Hence the "conceptual blocks" he uses in teaching and also, perhaps, his failure to see the value of letting the students discuss and compare their approaches to the MM problems. In our judgment, Ernie is too confident that there is one best solution to each case. This seeming lack of appreciation for the complexities of actual situations may be the result of his own highly analytical training, his limited academic experience with manufacturing management issues, and his lack of any actual experience dealing with manufacturing problems on the shop floor.

f) It appears that Ernie attributes his own academic development, and thus by implication his current success, largely to the externally imposed discipline he experienced in his graduate program at Carnegie Mellon. He tries to give the students the pedagogical gift he himself received: "rigor." He interprets the students' signals as a slacking off from the demands of rigor and decides, for their own good, to intercede to force them to submit again. Thus he is unable to see the students' behavior as a sign that an appropriate and pedagogically helpful change in the learning contract is needed.

g) Participants may note Ernie's taste for highly demanding individual sports. This proclivity, combined with his academic rather than manufacturing background, may indicate a lack of experience working with groups. Thus he may not have developed his sensitivity to group process. As a result it may simply not occur to him to stay alert to group signals, and to question his first interpretations, considering alternative explanations and paths of action.

3. How would you describe Ernie's teaching style?

Usage Note

It may not be necessary to ask this question directly during the discussion—particularly if the group has quickly picked up and explored the issue of learning contracts. However, this question and the two that follow are helpful in focusing the seminar discussion on how a learning contract is expressed in and maintained by a teaching style, and how a teaching style is embodied in a particular way of using question and response.

To move the discussion toward question and response, we often urge participants to describe the nature of Ernie's teaching style in detail. We ask them to draw upon the data in the case—for example, the snippet of class interaction presented in the (A) case.

Analysis

Our own assessment is that Ernie's style is highly directive. Its dominant feature is that the students must learn to predict Ernie's train of thought, and supply facts at the appropriate times to support the unfolding of Ernie's argument. The classroom dialogue included in the (A) case makes it clear that Ernie's queries, while leading, do not lead precisely enough so that students can always anticipate what he is looking for. This, we suspect, makes the game both risky and mildly exciting, and allows some students to shine by showing themselves particularly adept at anticipating Ernie's line of thought.

Ernie's teaching style is part of his overall learning contract with the section; it is unilaterally set by Ernie (to the best of his ability) and places him in a dominant, directing role, with primary responsibility for analyzing the case and presenting the result.

4. What are the advantages and disadvantages of this approach—in terms of student learning?

Usage Note

This question is used to turn attention from Ernie's style itself to its impact on the students.

Analysis

In our opinion, the central advantages of Ernie's approach are:

a) By learning to understand and anticipate Ernie's thinking, the students learn a language and basic techniques of approaching manufacturing management problems.

b) The directive, leading style of teaching provides a clear and relatively risk-free role for the students, particularly after they have mastered the basic concepts in the field. Thus the students probably at first feel quite relieved to slide into this directive contract. It probably helps alleviate their anxiety at being new MBA candidates who are not yet confident of their ability to analyze and discuss cases.

The disadvantages are that the students are prevented from practicing their own integrative, imaginative, and synthetic thinking. They do not get an opportunity to present and discuss with others their appraisals of complex and ambiguous situations, to make plausible diagnoses of situations, and to present plans for action that they have created and to which they feel committed.

5. Why does Ernie Budding use this instructional style?

Usage Note

This question brings the participants back to exploring Ernie Budding and what he brings to this teaching situation. Probable responses to this question parallel those listed earlier under Question 2. The purpose of this question, once again, is to highlight the ways in which instructors can overlook important aspects of their teaching-learning situation by being too much influenced by their own preferred styles of teaching, their own intellectual talents and traditions, and their desire to avoid chaos and lead a tightly controlled classroom.

—◆—

Following a discussion of these five questions, we suggest that attention turn to the (B) case and Question 6.

6. How effective do you think Ernie's speech was? What, if anything, does he do now—or has he dealt with the problem?

Usage Note

This question builds participants' involvement in the discussion, since they are asked to take the personal risk of committing themselves to an action recommendation.

We offer two suggestions for fielding responses to this question. First, the discussion leader may want to press participants to identify the diagnostic assumptions behind their judgments of whether Ernie's reprimand will be effective. This ties the discussion of intervention back to the earlier discussion of the key factors and the central problem in the situation. Second, if participants believe that Ernie's reprimand will not be effective, they should be asked how they would respond. This encourages the seminar members to consider the range of alternative actions available to instructors faced with problems like Ernie's.

Analysis

We might appraise Ernie's reprimand as follows: if the assumptions that underlie his analysis are correct, then the reprimand may be effective. Ernie appears to assume that the students tacitly agree that they are in class to submit to externally directed rigor, and that they believe Ernie's sort of rigor is appropriate to their learning goals. Further, Ernie appears to assume that the students feel he has a legitimate right to set the learning contract unilaterally. If these assumptions are not correct, Ernie's reprimand is unlikely to evoke a new commitment to high-quality work. Instead, the result is likely to be either resentful submission or continued rebellion and/or passive resistance.

In our judgment Ernie's assumptions do not fit reality. As an alternative to the reprimand, it would be helpful for him to try to discuss the educational process within the section directly with at least some of the students. Perhaps it would be most appropriate to talk with the educational representative, but he could also speak to any section member he has come to know and trust. Unfortunately, he does not seem to have built relationships with the students that would allow him to make ongoing tests of the suitability of the contract. Thus, he has little established access to them now.

At this point in the discussion, participants may become somewhat polarized, with one faction wanting to give all the power to the students, while others support Ernie's reprimand. It may be useful to raise this dispute to the general level by asking, "What ways are there to negotiate a contract while at the same time maintaining one's power and legitimate authority?"

7. What is his contract with the section now?

Usage Note

This question brings participant attention back to the learning contract. By implicitly assuming that

Ernie's reprimand will change the contract, it emphasizes the evolutionary nature of such tacit agreements.

Analysis

In our judgment, an assessment of the contract would require more in the way of student comments, and/or reports of the relationship between Ernie and the section in the following class. (Both kinds of data are included in the (C) case.) If Ernie's intervention is effective, he will have expanded his directive role to include a parenting, disciplinarian aspect.

8. How do you know when to change a contract? How do you change it?

Usage Note

This is the fundamental question of the discussion, in that it encourages participants to move from Ernie's case to their own experience and begin to articulate some general guidelines for maintaining a productive learning contract.

Analysis

In our opinion, the keys to knowing when to change a contract are first to stay in communication with the section members, and second to try to anticipate changes in the learning situation that might render the learning contract obsolete.

To stay in communication, instructors must try to develop informal channels of communication with the students (e.g., meeting with a few students for a beer after class and/or talking informally with them after the class and during breaks). In addition, they must learn to read the covert behavioral signals the section sends. For example, Ernie's students' pranks were partly a signal which he failed to read.

Changes in the learning situation can often be anticipated. Curricula and course content are modified, and individuals and groups develop over time, particularly with effective teaching. These developments often require changes in teaching style, and thus in the learning contract.

If there is time, the (C) case can be handed out to let participants know what actually happened. We normally suggest that the participants read only the first two sections of the (C) case during discussion time (through "A Student's View of the Salinas Walnut Case"). The following questions can then be used to guide discussion.

Alternatively, the (C) case can be given to participants at the end of the discussion period, to be read at their leisure. The questions can then simply be mentioned as the (C) case is passed out, in order to stimulate further thinking.

9. Why didn't the reprimand work? And why did the discussion of Salinas Walnut go so poorly?

Usage Note

This question calls the participants back to the consideration of their basic diagnoses of the situation. Most will modify their earlier positions to some extent on the basis of the new data.

Analysis

In our judgment, the reprimand did not work because Ernie's assumptions about the students were not correct. The students were not willing to submit to his discipline: they did not find it helpful to their development. Thus, he could not get them to accept the legitimacy of his unilateral control, or the superordinate goal of attaining rigor.

We believe the students' lack of preparation for the Salinas Walnut case discussion may have been a form of resistance. Their explanation—that no one in the class realized that a particular sort of calculation would "solve" this particularly difficult case—is not plausible. After all, this is by all accounts a very bright group of students who have a history of high performance and intensive preparation. And they had already been introduced to the type of calculation required.

10. What does Ernie do now?

Usage Note

This question turns the seminar's attention to action. It lets participants explore their own ideas before they are influenced by reading about what Ernie actually did.

Analysis

Ernie needs to open up some channels of communication with the section members. Now that his plan has failed, and he has some sense that his assumptions about the section are incorrect, he must develop some way to find out what is really going on. Thus he might, for example, talk with the educational representative to ask her perspective on the problems of the section. Or if he has developed some rapport with individual students, he could perhaps talk with them.

Second, he might discuss the situation with another faculty member. The ideal person would perhaps be a trusted colleague who will not be judgmental, but who can help Ernie rethink the situation.

Third, he must develop a new hypothesis about

what is happening in the section, and about how to relate to the section as its instructor. He may have to reconsider his teaching style and manner of leading the discussions, and do some new thinking about learning contracts.

Fourth, Ernie must consider how to renegotiate a new contract. How is he going to open up the negotiation? Should he do it with the entire class, or with the representative? How can he conduct a truly bilateral negotiation? (Just giving in to the section would represent another form of unilateral contracting—this time student-directed.) And how should he deal with what has already gone on? How should he respond to it? Should he acknowledge the problems of the past, or should he simply try to correct them and go on, without comment?

—◆—

After participants have read the entire (C) case, one can ask:

11. What do you think of Ernie's response to Arlene's visit?

Usage Note

This question directs attention to how the negotiation was actually carried out, and invites participants to consider in detail the process of negotiation.

Analysis

In our judgment Ernie's response was effective. He articulates his perspective to Arlene, but he also listens to hers. And he decides to try a compromise. The negotiation is carried off in two stages. First, by listening to Arlene seriously, as well as presenting his own views candidly and clearly, Ernie takes the first steps toward renegotiation. Second, while he definitely maintains his prerogatives as instructor, he states his willingness to experiment with changing his teaching style. During the next section meeting, the contract negotiation is carried forth on the behavioral level. Ernie begins by "announcing" his new approach, which may seem a unilateral approach. But his announcement is really simply an opening offer. When Arlene volunteers to speak, and the class as a whole joins in the discussion, they signal at least tentative agreement to the new contract.

12. Teaching this section raised a number of questions for Ernie Budding about the nature of effective teaching. What questions does reading about it raise for you? Have any of you had similar experiences?

A variety of questions are raised by this case. Perhaps the most important are:

a) How can you read a section and know when a contract needs changing?
b) How can you change a contract and/or renegotiate one?

EXHIBIT 1 *Ernie Budding*

Study Questions

The (A) case:

1. What is your appraisal of the situation confronting Ernie Budding as of the end of the (A) case? How does Ernie see the situation? How might a member of the class explain the section's behavior?

The (B) case:

1. What is your evaluation of Ernie's speech?
2. How do you interpret the class's reaction to his comments? Would you, as Ernie Budding, take further action before the next class?

EXHIBIT 2 *Ernie Budding*

Open-Focused Discussion Questions

1. As a friend and colleague of Ernie Budding, could you please help our seminar group understand the situation confronting Ernie Budding at the end of the (A) case?
   a) What do you see as the one or two critical factors contributing to his current situation?
   [or]
   What features of the situation are important to note in sizing up this situation?
   (Optional probe): How does Ernie see the situation? How do the section members see the situation? How do you see the situation?
   (Optional probe): What is Ernie's teaching style? What are the pluses and minuses of such a style? [These questions can be introduced here, or saved for use as outlined below in Questions 3 and 4.]
   b) Given these elements of the situation, what is the problem?
   [or, somewhat more provocatively]
   How did this good section turn bad?
2. Why didn't Ernie see the need for a change in his contract with the section?
3. How would you describe Ernie's teaching style?
4. What are the advantages and disadvantages of this approach—in terms of student learning?
5. Why does Ernie Budding use this instructional style?

Following the above discussion, we suggest that attention turn to the (B) case, with:

6. How effective do you think Ernie's speech was? What, if anything, does he do now—or has he dealt with the problem?
7. What is his contract with the section now?
8. How do you know when to change a contract? How do you change it?

If there is time and if the seminar participants want to know what actually happened, the (C) case can be handed out. We normally suggest that the participants read only the first two sections of the (C) case during discussion time. These contain the discussion of the Salinas Walnut Company, and "A Student's View of the Salinas Walnut Case." After participants have read this much, Questions 9 through 12 can be used to guide discussion.

Alternatively, the (C) case can be given to participants at the end of the discussion period, to be read at their leisure. The questions can then simply be mentioned as the (C) case is passed out, in order to stimulate further thinking.

9. Why didn't the reprimand work? And why did the discussion of Salinas Walnut go so poorly?
10. What does Ernie do now?

After the entire (C) case has been read:

11. What do you think of Ernie's response to Arlene's visit?
12. Teaching this section raised a number of questions for Ernie Budding about the nature of effective teaching. What questions does it raise for you? Have any of you had similar experiences?

The Offended Colonel (A) and (B)

TEACHING NOTE

This teaching note has been prepared by Abby Hansen as an aid to instructors in classroom use of the case series *"The Offended Colonel" (A) 9-383-061 and (B) 9-383-062.*
(HBS No. 5-384-203)

Special Features

The salient event in this case involves a teacher's difficulty with a cultural issue: linguistic propriety. Ben Cheever, a visiting professor of economics and management, leading a model case method discussion at a military policy institute, tries simultaneously to enliven a lackluster discussion and prevent a "premature conclusion" by greeting a participant's comment with a familiar, but still off-color, expletive ("Bullshit!" to be precise). This so offends a colonel in the group that he later demands a public apology from Ben, not only on his own behalf but also to the "ladies present." This element in the colonel's protest is jarring because there is actually only one woman in the group, and he could not possibly have seen her reaction to Ben's language.

Mood

This case makes for a good icebreaker because it is short and lively. Participants often find Ben's exclamation amusing and quote it repeatedly. (The discussion leader who finds this language disquieting or inappropriate to a teaching seminar should decide in advance how to handle this probable aspect of the discussion.)

Suggested Use

In teaching this case, most of your class time should be assigned to the (A) segment. Recommendations for action and comparison of these with what Ben actually did are less valuable here than thorough and insightful considerations of the subtle implications inherent in the situation itself. This researcher, accordingly, would schedule two-thirds or more of the discussion time for the (A) case and the rest for the (B) case.

Conflicts, Sensitivities

The central event of this case is potentially offensive (it certainly offended the colonel) because it involves a breach of etiquette (although a minor one) by a respected professor in a formal setting. The discussion leader will have to use discretion in assigning this material. Are some of the people in this particular group so straitlaced that the material—and the implications that will probably be explored in discussion—might so offend them that they will withdraw from participation and possibly disrupt the group? Discussing this case might trigger a replay of its problems in the teaching seminar itself. This would *not* necessarily be a bad thing. Many participants will agree that Ben Cheever won his confrontation with the colonel. Nonetheless, the discussion leader should be aware of these possibilities.

Second, the final paragraph of the (B) case mentions that several members of Ben's discussion group accompany their apology to him with the information that the colonel was a "born-again Christian." The discussion leader should also prepare to handle vehement reactions (pro or con) to this detail.

Teaching Objectives

A fundamental issue behind this case is the establishment of rapport—an essential ingredient for discussion teaching. Ben Cheever unwittingly offends a member of a discussion group. When challenged about his language, Ben is intransigent. He refuses either to apologize or change his style. Doing either, he implies, would be hypocritical. This, in the researcher's opinion, is an overstatement born of conflict. No teacher as experienced and canny as Ben appears to be is likely to be blind to the fact that there are many styles of communication, and teachers—more than most people—have several of these styles at their command. Teachers do not speak or move the same way in casual conversation as in teaching—particularly when they appear before large groups in auditorium-like settings. There is far too obvious an analogy to stage performance implicit in these occasions—and the teacher, like Ben, who self-consciously plays devil's advocate to stimulate a more interesting discussion cannot be blind to the dramatic overtones of what he is doing. Ben's choice of dress, style, and diction seems highly conscious. The issue is whether it was wise. As often happens in a teaching seminar, the discussion leader may be scrutinized for his or her handling of the same problem: establishing rapport. How can one strike the right note with this particular group to produce trust, friendliness, and openness in order to have genuine discussion? Sensitivity to the participants' professional position, experience, personal styles, and motives for joining the seminar—combined with an awareness that the discussion leader has options in approaching these people—might spare the leader some of Ben Cheever's discomfort.

The central issue here is how to use the options of behavior, language, dress, and classroom setup to help establish the right atmosphere for useful discussion. No discussion leader can afford to sacrifice all of the creative tension that goes with the formality of the teaching situation. Nor should the leader abdicate his or her responsibility to keep order and give direction to the proceedings. But teaching seminars are often conducted by and for one's peers, if not superiors. One dreads seeming pompous in their presence. Casualness is an attractive antidote to this danger, but extreme laxity can lead to chaos. The problem is, and always will be, how to find the happy medium. This case should produce a discussion in which the multiplicity of possible teaching styles becomes apparent. There is no single way to teach. Ideally, a teacher should behave differently (within reason) with every new group of students.

The "Blocks" of Analysis

The researcher has discerned several general rubrics into which discussion of this case might fall:

1. Methodology. Ben Cheever comes to the Commanding Officers' Senior Executive Institute as an apostle for an alien methodology: the case method. There he meets military officers whose educational experience, both as students and teachers, has probably included only lectures, with a few supplementary small-group discussions. The question arises: How well can one introduce an unfamiliar educational approach like the case method, which requires time for a group to learn to work creatively for full effectiveness, in two days' time?

2. Culture clash. The obvious civilian/military disparity deserves attention. In the military world, rank and hierarchy prevail. Academics, by contrast (certainly at the senior levels where Ben Cheever operates), generally regard themselves as a loose confederation of peers. In their research, and often in their teaching, professors tend to think of themselves as extremely independent. Ben is trying to encourage military personnel to set aside their professional constraints temporarily for the sake of his educational demonstration. The enterprise involves obvious difficulties.

3. Expectations. Ben seems to have limited enthusiasm for the whole workshop. What, then, can one expect of his audience? Many of them have come under orders, and this workshop is going to take two days of their normally free time. We see obstacles to full, enthusiastic participation on both sides.

4. Environment. The room seems to be a conventional auditorium where participants can see Ben, but not each other. This setup is appropriate for lectures, not discussions.

5. Characters. Ben Cheever seems competent, experienced, and perhaps a bit jaded by his twenty years of teaching. The military personnel seem self-protective. Their reluctance to move into case method discussion in the presence of fellow officers (whose interconnecting webs of obligation this case does not detail) is understandable. The colonel comes across as a "crank," alienated from his colleagues. It is noteworthy that only one other participant leaves the room with him. In the (B) case, some participants actually apologize to Ben for the colonel's hostility. In this section, one would hope to encourage participants to pay attention to the case's descriptions. How, exactly, do people dress, speak, move? The colonel, for example, is in uniform, as are several others in the group. The rest wear rather conservative civilian clothing. Ben seems to be more casually dressed than most of the participants. What signals are being sent?

6. Communication. Dress, stance, tone of speech, actual words—all comprise a complex phenomenon called communication. The colonel implies much by his stance (rising to speak when others have stayed seated), dress (having chosen to come in uniform), and tone. He speaks with obvious hostility, using a rhetorical question—"Don't you think you ought to apologize?"—as if he were speaking to a naughty child. This is condescending. The sum total is an impression of self-righteousness. One would not expect such a man to be a beloved member of this group. Language is the all-important crux of this case. No discussion of "The Offended Colonel" would be complete without some attention paid to the professor's expletive. Was he wrong? Did he unwittingly break the conventions of leading a case method discussion? What is the effect of vulgarity in an otherwise fairly formal situation? How does such a break in tone affect the participants? What do we see happening in this case? Although people possess varying degrees of sensitivity to subtleties of language, virtually all of us both notice and adapt to linguistic conventions in the groups with which we come in contact. It doesn't take most college freshmen long to call the "American Civilization" course "Am. Civ.," or refer to the local soda shop, whatever its real name, as "The Spot." These familiar abbreviations and nicknames set members of a group off from nonmembers. To use them is to belong. The same phenomenon operates within any group. What is Ben communicating to this particular group of people by being the first to introduce mild vulgarity into their discussion?

7. Challenge to authority. Ben reacts rather defensively to the colonel's demand for an apology. What is Ben defending? And does his defense succeed? How seriously should any case discussion leader treat such an unexpected personal criticism? What is at stake for Ben? If he does apologize, is he damaging his credibility, losing respect?

8. Rapport. Ben, like any other case method teacher, has to establish some sort of rapport with the group. In fact, unlike other teachers, the case method teacher also has to try to encourage the group to establish its own rapport. The trust should not be extended merely from student to teacher, but also from student to student. It would seem fundamental to this enterprise that the discussion leader size up the particular group, sense its specific quirks and sore spots, and endeavor—at least in the early phases of their association—to be, if not ingratiating, at least not irritating.

Unlike lecturing, where simple competence and cogency (combined with a little showmanship) may carry the day, case method teaching is greatly enhanced by amicability. It helps if the participants like the teacher, and vice versa.

9. Characters' attitudes. This is a sensitive, elusive, and important topic that warrants exploration. Ben "sensed from the outset" that he would have trouble "getting the workshop moving in the right direction." When the discussion started, it shaped up as "particularly lackluster." What is the relationship between the discussion leader's expectations and the group's performance? What could Ben have done, first of all, to prevent the group from becoming "wary, tentative, and unsure of how to proceed," and second (given that the group was hesitant and relatively uncooperative), what could he have done to improve the situation?

10. Symbolism. Under this rubric, the researcher would include style of dress, physical movement and stance, and tone of voice. What should one make of Ben's apparently deliberate choice of casual clothing, a "breezy, informal approach" to the discussion, and a humorous style? What was he trying to accomplish? Did his tactic backfire? If so, why? What should he have done differently?

Preparing for the Discussion

Exhibit 1 lists suggested Study Questions, to be handed out to participants for use when preparing the case before class. **Exhibit 2** contains a summary of the Discussion Questions, to be used by the seminar leader in preparing for class and in guiding the case discussion when necessary.

If participants have considered the study questions in **Exhibit 1**, they should have paid some attention to the unpromising details of Ben's situation. He seems unenthusiastic about the whole enterprise, having come to "get his ticket punched." And he is an alien. Despite his extensive military experience, he comes to this workshop as an apostle from the civilian world of academics. He dresses far more casually than most of the participants, and the commanding officer of the institute has given him a daunting buildup. It is challenging, to say the least, to be introduced as "the best." Furthermore, he is introducing and demonstrating a new methodology to people who are not only unfamiliar with the case method, but also largely uncommitted to teaching as a profession. Last, Ben is taking up time that these people normally devote to leisure.

Under these circumstances, it is not surprising that Ben found the ensuing discussion lackluster. His choice of a moderately shocking slang word to enliven the proceedings seems to have accomplished his purpose: it caused enough of a rupture to shake people and loosen them up a bit. Like most unexpected uses of mild profanity in rather formal situations, it got a laugh. But what was going on under the surface? Were others in the group beside the colonel upset that this expert from the world of scholarship chose not to behave professorially? Perhaps the slang is a symptom of Ben's real frustration, and the colonel's reaction a sort of lightning rod for other people's (milder but real) dissatisfaction.

Opening Speaker; Backstop

This case involves an "alien" (a civilian academic demonstrating case method teaching at a military institute) and a born-again Christian with a particular aversion to profanity and obscenity, however familiar or mild, who tries to speak for the group's moral standards. If the teaching seminar includes participants who might conceivably fall into either category, diplomacy would suggest that one avoid singling them out to speak for either of the principal characters. (On the other hand, if the group is obviously good-natured and uses labels with reliable affection and acceptance, it would seem reasonable to take advantage of the existing group dynamics and ask the obvious people for their comments.)

The arrogance of the colonel's unsolicited protest on behalf of the "ladies present" does not usually escape the attention of women in the seminar. It might be advisable, thus, to ask a woman to open the discussion of the colonel's remarks, but by all means, men should also be encouraged to provide interpretations. The sheer lack of observation involved in referring to a single woman in the plural highlights the peculiarity of the colonel's protest. He seems far more out of step with the group than does Ben.

If there are any current or former military officers in the group, the discussion leader will have to decide whether or not to stress the unique setting of this case by choosing someone with military experience to begin the discussion. Certainly the cultural clash inherent in the material could be highlighted by having a military officer appraise the situation from the audience's point of view and describe how Ben Cheever's teaching style might have struck the staff of the institute. One way to downplay the military setting without completely ignoring it would be to ask someone with military experience to "backstop" the opening comments.

The Discussion Questions

To get the seminar started, the following questions (**Exhibit 2**) can be addressed after the (A) case has been read:

1. ***[To the opening speaker]: Please outline the situation for us. Let's review the what, when, where, and who, to get our discussion started.***

This question ought to focus attention on the groundwork for any discussion. Neglect for the specifics can only produce vagueness. In this case, there are many significant details to consider. As part of the *what*, one should note that Ben is attempting to introduce case method discussion in two days of demonstrations and discussions. How feasible is this? Discussion teaching requires the evolution of group trust and cooperation. What can one expect from the very first case discussion of a concentrated workshop? The *when* might bring up an explanation for the rather understandable lack of enthusiasm on the part of the participants (many of them there because their superiors volunteered them). These people have not come out of curiosity, and certainly not out of dedication to teaching. The *where* points to the environment, both metaphorically, as an organizational system, and also in purely physical terms. The room seems unsuitable for discussion teaching because it is apparently an auditorium, set up for lectures rather than conversations. Auditoriums focus undue attention on the discussion leader and guarantee that the participants will suffer difficulty in seeing and hearing each other. Culturally, the *where* also involves the web of command and obedience that constitutes a military organization. Surely this setting must condition the expectations and social behavior of its personnel.

Other details to consider include the fact that it is Friday morning (normally free time for the staff), Ben's unacknowledged status as an outsider (visiting

Washington, D.C., from a home base in New England), and the impact of the commanding general's "warm and humorous speech" that mentions Ben's military experience and the fact that Ben had once been his boss. The general's parting comment—according to Ben's report—that "he considered case method teaching something they ought to know a bit about and that we [Ben and his university's faculty] were the best" must have had an effect on the audience. What was it?

Some participants will add these factors up and assess Ben's situation as perilous: the general's introduction has placed him on a pedestal—rather an exposed perch for a discussion leader with a potentially hostile group to lead—and, in this case, simply an exacerbation to Ben's status as an outsider. Others may see the general's buildup as beneficial to Ben; these people will find Ben's subsequent difficulties with the group as surprising as Ben did. The discussion leader's task will be to explore both points of view and try to get participants who naturally gravitate to one or the other attitude to see each other's lines of reasoning. One would hope that this opening section of the discussion would produce enough varying reference to specific details to provide material for a substantive discussion. The case is both brief and rich enough in circumstantial facts to allow the discussion leader to encourage frequent specific references to the case.

2. *[To the backstop]: Would you please help us begin to evaluate Ben Cheever's actual "offense"? What do you think provoked the colonel to protest?*

The backstop's personality will condition his or her response to Ben's remark. Some will find it harmless; some, annoying; some, juvenile; some, perhaps, offensive. Whatever one thinks, however, Ben's exclamation is the dramatic core of this case. It usually causes amusement, and members of the seminar often quote it repeatedly. If the discussion leader wishes to prevent this (based on an appraisal of the group, or on his or her own sensitivities), it would be advisable to preface the initial question with a friendly, good-humored request: "Please, spare us Ben's predicament; you don't have to quote him here!" Most members of our seminars consider Ben's language run-of-the-mill, but recommend using such expressions cautiously. This case shows how they can damage rapport. If discussion were to remain on the stylistic level of Ben's remark, the result would probably lack intellectual content: the vocabulary of profanity is quite limited. Another possible reason for preventing overzealous repetition of Ben's exclamation is the potential for insulting seminar members who share the colonel's sensitivity, if not his whole outlook. They could be extremely useful to the discussion. The articulate presentation of a conservative point of view—without the colonel's self-righteousness—would be a great contribution to the elucidation of this case. After all, the colonel had a point: why shouldn't a visiting professor leading a model case method discussion observe the normal proprieties of classroom conduct? Vulgarisms, however common in everyday experience, are still substandard as public speech. When a professor uses this sort of language, a conservative member of the group may well feel offended and suspect him either of contempt or unusual insensitivity. Ben could have spoken differently. (Most of us do not use the same vocabulary when we, let's say, wrestle with recalcitrant income tax forms in private as when we address convocations of our colleagues.)

Profanity has its uses. It makes an effective emotional safety valve by substituting name-calling for physical attack. But why should Ben Cheever bring this language into the classroom? Perhaps the colonel is not too far from the mark in sensing a touch of contempt, however inadvertently expressed.

Another question that the backstop might raise is the extent of Ben's responsibility to the whole group. Even granting that most of the officers found his exclamation unremarkable, did Ben have the right to risk insulting even one of their members? This line of reasoning points out why it might be advisable for the discussion leader to plan in advance how he or she will handle Ben's actual exclamation.

3. *What about the colonel's actual demand? Could we take a look at his words and begin to think about some of the implications behind them?*

The matter of precisely what provoked the colonel to protest involves an adjustment of focus. Rather than concentrate exclusively on Ben's exclamation, the discussion should widen at this point. The backstop may not provide this broadened perspective. If not, the leader should ask questions that direct the group's attention back to the case for circumstantial details. The timing of the colonel's objection, for example, seems significant. He waited through the whole discussion. Then, when Ben opened the question period and called on him, he stood up (unlike the other members who had all remained seated) and delivered an extremely hostile rhetorical question. His wording—"Do you always use profanity when you teach? Or is it that you just feel you have to talk down to us servicemen?"—is not a question. It's an accusation.

Furthermore, some seminar participants may detect in it a certain contempt for Ben. The colonel's tone is schoolmarmish. His words have the same ring as, "Young man, don't you think you ought to take that chewing gum out of your mouth and sit up straight?" Questions like this are thinly veiled commands.

The second part of the colonel's protest includes the reference to "ladies present," which usually provokes women in the teaching seminar to accuse him of arrogance. It is also possible to defend the colonel and define his intent as chivalrous. If these two viewpoints emerge, confrontation may be avoided by keeping this section of the discussion as analytical as possible. Prompt the group to deal with the colonel's words, not so much in terms of their emotional responses to them but as evidence for interpretation. (In practice, this case does not tend to produce acrimony in the seminar, but the discussion leader should be alert to possible flashpoints, and this is one.) A way to divert attention from the male/female issue here is to ask if anyone *else* in the group Ben was leading might have been offended by Ben's exclamation. Was only the colonel just a crank, or might he have had a silent constituency? (Whoever made the comment that provoked Ben to respond with "Bullshit!" had reason to feel insulted.) It is relatively rare in case method teaching for the leader to jump in so directly. One usually tries to get participants to expose each other's fallacies. In a sense, Ben violated the conventions with his comments.

Some questions the discussion leader might use to probe for thorough discussion of this section of the colonel's remarks would include asking the seminar to think about the layout of the classroom. Could the colonel have known if the woman was offended? Do we have any indication that she expressed dismay by some remark, a gasp, a shift in posture? (No.) What are the implications, then, of his speaking up for her? Further probing in this area might go beyond the specific incident to some theorizing about the whole enterprise of case method teaching. Success requires participants to speak as openly, sincerely, and alertly as possible because open discussion is the primary tool in this educational method. To hold back or disguise one's reactions is to cheat oneself and, in a sense, deform the whole process. Given this responsibility to be honest, which falls on every participant, the colonel's decision to speak for another participant (with neither permission nor encouragement from her) is a violation of the basic contract. He doesn't know what she is thinking and therefore cannot present her viewpoint. Furthermore, the implication of his statement is that she is incapable of speaking for herself. This implies contempt.

4. What should Ben do? What are his risks and potential gains in this situation?

If the foregoing discussion has exposed a broad range of the subtleties that can be drawn from this case, this question should elicit a similar variety of suggestions. Upon first reading, one might think Ben had two simple choices: apologize or not. To apologize would be to admit a breach of etiquette. To refuse would be to stand his ground and defend his right to self-expression in the face of protest by a stuffed shirt.

Some participants will doubtless counsel apology, and there are many reasonable arguments for this course of action. A dignified admission of error can enhance a leader's authority. Not every capitulation is a defeat. On the other hand, others may suggest that—since only the colonel protested, and, in fact, Ben's remark brought a laugh and picked up the tempo of discussion—the colonel should be treated as the wet blanket he is. Another possible response to this question is to look for compromises. Ben could make a personal apology for having—even unintentionally—offended a discussion participant. Then in the next breath, he might suggest that he is, however, glad to see that no one *else* seemed offended.

Experienced teachers may point out that most instructors facing sizable groups (and, therefore, occupying the spotlight) instinctively see all challenges as threats. Ben might be expected to react self-protectively.

What is at stake? Possibly his credibility as leader, the group's respect for him, and the whole workshop. In a sense, like every teacher, he may have felt—in that split second that he had to consider how to react to a direct, unexpected criticism of his competence—that his fundamental right to be standing before this group had been attacked: an overreaction, perhaps, but not an unimaginable one. Others may downplay this whole aspect of confrontation. The colonel is a crank. Military personnel hear (and use) language far saltier than Ben's remark every day of their lives. Ben should shrug this off and get on with the task at hand. A canny participant may note that the colonel's remarks have a great deal to do with the matter at hand. Ben is leading the last segment of the discussion which is an analysis of the case discussion these people have just held.

In the course of their discussion, Ben used a deliberate technique—a modified form of role playing, with a distinct change in verbal tone—to jostle the group out of a rut. This was a pedagogical tactic, and its success or failure could provide material for this section of the workshop.

It often happens that hindsight reveals a shining

opportunity in the most seemingly devastating threats. Ben could, perhaps, have turned the colonel's peevish complaint to pedagogical advantage by saying something like, "Wonderful question, Colonel! Could we discuss this? What do you other participants think of the technique I used there? What was its purpose? What kind of tactic was it? Did it succeed?"

But few teachers think *that* quickly on their feet. The purpose of this section of the discussion is to gain insight into how Ben might have felt when faced with the colonel's unexpected, hostile question, how the colonel might have felt as he delivered his challenge, and what some of his reasons might have been.

It will be valuable to discuss the overtones of the several responses available to Ben, if only because they illuminate some of the complexities inherent in teaching by discussion. The particular response the group recommends for Ben is less important than an open-minded consideration of the many possibilities.

—◆—

After the (B) case has been read:

1. *What do you think of the way Ben responded to the colonel's challenge?*

Proponents of apology will doubtless express their disappointment or annoyance with Ben. They may, perhaps, begin to like him less in the character of intransigent leader than they did as beleaguered colleague. Certainly, Ben reacted defensively. Both his critics and defenders will probably notice the self-protective tone in his description of the way he felt and what he said. Ben scanned the classroom first—a good, sensitive move. After all, he had just been accused of inappropriate behavior *in the name of the whole group.* Trying to gauge people's reactions from their expressions would be the obvious corroborative gesture.

The faces in the room did not look angry, and Ben chose to stand his ground, rejecting a sarcastic, teasing retort he could have made. He seems to have decided that, rather than strike at the colonel, he would simply explain himself.

The discussion leader would do well at this point either to quote Ben's words or ask participants to do so. "Look!" Ben says, "It would be hypocritical of me to say 'I'm sorry.' So I won't. This is the way I talk. I'm just being myself, and that's that." There is much here to analyze. From this point on, the discussion should keep referring to Ben's words.

The same attention to tone that is recommended in analyzing the colonel's remarks ought to be paid to Ben's reply. What is the impact of that introductory *"Look!"*? It usually prefaces an argument. Perhaps it says something like, "You fool! I'm going to point out something that's obvious to me even if you haven't noticed it." (Would you believe someone who asserted his or her good spirits by saying, *"Look,* I'm not angry!"?) Having the dialogue read aloud will greatly help analysis here. Some discussion participants will focus attention on the word *hypocritical*—a label Ben (specifically) rejects. Apparently he values honesty above diplomacy. The discussion leader might probe this point. What *is* honesty in teaching? How much of one's true self is it appropriate to reveal? Where is the boundary between leadership and manipulation, courtesy and hypocrisy? (These issues should come up again and again in this discussion.)

After Ben's reply to the colonel has been examined, consider the colonel's reaction. Again, the discussion leader should direct attention to the details. The colonel "stiffened" before his exit line: "If that's the case, well, I don't feel I care to stay." What does this stiffness convey? (Some will note the extremely personal tone—the colonel repeats the word "I" twice, and refers to his emotions: he doesn't *"feel"* that he *"cares"* to stay.) But in truth, even as he stiffens, the colonel has given ground. Instead of defending public morals, he is now leaving because *he* feels uncomfortable.

Ben has reacted with instinctive (and understandable) defensiveness. Interestingly enough, his slight shifting of ground—from arguing about the word he used to defending his whole personal style—has made the colonel shift accordingly. The confrontation has narrowed to a private test of wills, and the colonel backs down—not by ceding a point, but physically, by leaving the arena. The colonel probably considers his exit a moral statement, a gesture of protest. But he also seems to be something of a spoilsport. The fact that only one other officer follows him suggests that they are "odd men out" in this group.

2. *Briefly contemplating the following reply—"Hey fellow, are you really serious? I learned this language from a Marine!"—how might it have worked?*

The effect of this reply is quite sarcastic. It would be antagonistic to call the colonel "fellow," and unpleasantly ironic to ask if he is really serious (he is). There may be several points of view on this: participants who, like Ben, express themselves with frequent punctuations of profanity (and there are many, many such people in all walks of life, from the manual trades to academe!) may find this reply basically good-humored. Others might find it provocative, even unfair. The colonel seems to have had little sympathy from the group. Playing on this apparent alienation by teasing him might have seemed almost cruel and thus lost Ben some of the sympathy that the group had probably felt at seeing him attacked for a remark that, in fact, only brought a laugh.

3. What effect do you think the colonel's exit had?

There is likely to be little disagreement on this point. The colonel and his colleague have isolated themselves. Moreover, they have cut off the dialogue by removing themselves from the arena of discussion. They are the ones who refuse to exchange viewpoints. It seems fairly obvious that this permits Ben not only to retain his leadership, but also to gain enhanced esteem for having survived a confrontation that threatened his authority. He and the colonel were eyeball to eyeball, and the colonel not only blinked, but ran away.

The discussion continued after the colonel's exit. The discussion leader might ask participants what they make of the fact that people came up to speak to Ben after the session. Most experienced discussion teachers consider it a good sign if participants seek to prolong the momentum of the class. Certainly, seeking the discussion leader out is no signal of rejection. Among those who approached Ben was the only woman in the room who came to assure him that she had not been offended. This fact provides an opportunity for the seminar to consider why she remained silent when the colonel took it upon himself to speak for her. Ben mentions having looked directly at her to read her reaction, but she seems to have wished to remain silent in public. The point of this question would not be to guess the woman's real reason for not rescuing Ben, but rather to emphasize the undesirability of putting discussion participants on the spot. Whatever her reasons for silence, Ben, as discussion leader, behaved responsibly in respecting her right to keep quiet.

As it turned out, instead of Ben apologizing, he ended up receiving informal apologies from some of the participants. The tables were completely turned.

4. Do you agree with Ben's assessment of his handling of the situation?

Here, the discussion leader might cite Ben's own words, that on the whole "he'd handled this situation appropriately." What does "appropriately" mean? What were his goals? What was at stake? Did winning this confrontation constitute success? Are there *other* ways in which we might define "appropriateness"?

5. What larger issues does this case pose for you?

The purpose of this last section should be to pose open-ended questions on a higher theoretical level than much of the preceding discussion. Some salient issues that most people will extract from the case are rapport, respect, and challenges to authority. But the most telling one—at least for this researcher—is the elusive, fascinating human problem of communication. The nuances of the various interchanges in this case are extremely complex, and it is likely that no two seminar groups will assess them the same way. Diction (choice of words), tone of voice, and physical posture in communication all carry enormous impact; teachers who ignore them do so at their own peril.

In teaching this case, you will want to encourage participants to consider what messages they wish to convey by such details as dress and diction. Leaving aside the questions of *appropriateness,* was Ben wise in seeming *more* casual and slangier than the discussion group he was leading through a case method demonstration? What is the difference between projecting calmness and a feeling of ease and unintentionally conveying disrespect? At the very least, all teachers should be aware of the complexity of communication.

EXHIBIT 1 *The Offended Colonel (A)*

Study Questions

1. How would you have appraised Ben Cheever's chances for success at the opening of this teaching demonstration? On what details do you base this appraisal?
2. What do you think of Ben's use of slang to prevent the group from reaching a "premature conclusion"?
3. Why did the colonel's demand for an apology catch Ben by surprise?
4. What issues does the colonel's challenge raise for you?
5. How would you have advised Ben to respond to the colonel's demand?

EXHIBIT 2 *The Offended Colonel (A) and (B)*

Discussion Questions

After the (A) case has been read:

1. [To the opening speaker]: Please outline the situation for us. Let's review the what, when, where, and who, to get our discussion started.
2. [To the backstop]: Would you please help us begin to evaluate Ben Cheever's actual "offense"? What do you think provoked the colonel to protest?
3. What about the colonel's actual demand? Could we take a look at his words and begin to think about some of the implications behind them?
4. What should Ben do? What are his risks and potential gains in this situation?

⸻◆⸻

After the (B) case has been read:

1. What do you think of the way Ben responded to the colonel's challenge?
2. Briefly contemplating the following reply—"Hey, fellow, are you really serious? I learned this language from a Marine!"—how might it have worked?
3. What effect do you think the colonel's exit had?
4. Do you agree with Ben's assessment of his handling of this situation?
5. What larger issues does this case pose for you?

The Offended Colonel (A) and (B)

RESEARCHER'S PERSPECTIVE

This commentary on "The Offended Colonel" was written by Abby Hansen. Its objective is to help instructors in the development of their own teaching plans for this case. (HBS No. 5-383-183)

Ben Cheever faces several obstacles to a successful demonstration of the case method. He is a civilian, albeit one with a military background and a personal friendship with the commanding general. Furthermore, the pedagogical method he is trying to demonstrate differs radically from most military procedures. In a group of "85% colonels, lieutenant colonels, and some majors," Ben is facing a large number of people who are more used to giving orders than reaching a free consensus of ideas with peers. Furthermore, Ben and his colleagues, despite their military experiences, have come to this institute as civilians. They are academics, representatives of a distant professional school of management. In this character they have traveled from their university to the military institute for two days. Perhaps Ben's expectations for the very first case method discussion under these circumstances are overly optimistic. Unfortunately for him, he seems to have drawn the short straw: it is his task to follow the commanding general's fulsome praise with an impressive demonstration of case method teaching. The task of creating the initial rapport with this stiff and basically unpromising audience has fallen to Ben, and the issue of the scope of method teaching is well worth considering. But Ben has agreed to participate, and he has many problems to overcome.

The classroom in which Ben finds himself seems to be of the familiar auditorium design. He stands facing an audience of seated participants in a configuration likely to remind most of them of all their years of conventional schooling, beginning with first grade. In such settings the discussion leader—regardless of age or experience—wears an invisible sign saying "adult," while the participants wear corresponding signs that read "children." Especially when some of the participants are older than the discussion leader, these roles can chafe and produce resentment. In this case, it is possible that the "offended colonel" expressed a hostility that others in the class also felt. Unlike the others, however, he attached his hostility specifically to Ben's rather commonplace, mildly scatological exclamation.

Whatever the source of the colonel's irritation, Ben might have taken his objection more seriously—not as a signal to eliminate profanity, necessarily, but as a tip that he had made some fundamental errors in establishing rapport with this group. Rapport is perhaps the most essential ingredient to success in case method teaching. A lecturer can succeed through superior control of the material, but a discussion leader's material is, in a sense, the participant's. It is the leader's complex task to elicit pieces of analysis from the class, and then, with fine tact, structure the emerging discussion without overtly controlling the proceedings. The case method teacher does not quiz students. It is not his province to ascertain whether they can solve quadratic equations. Rather he is a guide who leads the whole group—himself included—on a voyage of discovery through a complicated problem grounded in the messy circumstances of real life. Most students need some time to realize this.

There are no pat answers in case discussion because cases are true events—disguised, but presented with as much complexity as the actual problems possessed when they perplexed the original case characters. Discussion participants must learn to take public risks in the name of exploration. Newcomers to the case method usually begin by assuming that their status depends on producing unassailable correct answers. Ben has to combat this assumption in inimical surroundings. His real challenge—if his discussion is to demonstrate the case method at its best (as the commanding general promised)—is to produce enough enthusiasm and trust in this group to permit its members to advance hypotheses and constructively disagree with each other. He must enable them to give and take criticism in a spirit of cooperation.

A military organization, hierarchical by nature, provides unpromising soil for the swift cultivation of such free-wheeling equality. Furthermore, the members of this group exhibit their fair share of the common human tendency to reduce tension by avoiding open conflict. They shy away from disagreeing with each other. Ben describes the result of this as a "lackluster" discussion in which the participants are "wary," "tentative," and "unsure." He also pinpoints several other obstacles to success. The lack of committed teachers is one. His own lack of commitment to the institute is another. But possibly the worst is the scheduling of the workshop. Ben is trying to start the workshop on Friday morning—a time the faculty usually has free. Ben is inadvertently competing with the participants' daydreams of what they'd rather be doing than sitting in a classroom looking at him.

Ben knows he has to create rapport by getting these people to relax, but his tactic—adopting casual dress and language—backfires and produces open resentment from the colonel. Perhaps the image that Ben presented with his sporty clothes, slangy speech, and jokes disturbed a significant proportion of his audience. Certainly their style of dress—conservative civilian clothes and some uniforms—communicates a measure of stiffness.

Ben's demeanor indicates just the opposite, yet he comes to these people stamped with the prestigious label "professor" and certified by their commanding general. He may be sending crossed signals to an audience that would prefer to cede him formal authority. Similarly, his title implies intellectual accomplishment, but his choice of vocabulary and use of humor to warm up the group may also have baffled many of their expectations. "I expected a professor," some might have been thinking, "but this guy is telling jokes." Ben might have done better to dress conservatively—suit and tie—and signal relaxation by shedding his tie. Similarly, he might have spoken somewhat formally at first, and then relaxed, introduced some humor, and ventured into a few slangy expressions when he could sense the group relaxing along with him.

Ben seems to dislike hypocrisy. Challenged by the colonel, he replies: "This is the way I talk. This is me, and that's it." He isn't the sort of man to apologize for form's sake, but nonetheless he is willing to do some playacting. He plays devil's advocate when he drops that coarse, familiar exclamation that so infuriates the colonel. But it seems significant that Ben's remark comes in response to a comment with which he actively disagrees. Given his morning of frustration with this group, isn't it possible that his reaction was heartfelt, spontaneous, and very much in his own voice? At any rate, its slangy tone produced a laugh from the group in general. In the classroom, profanity and vulgarity, used unexpectedly and with good humor, usually do provoke laughter—possibly because they break decorum. They are mildly shocking, and if they carry no threat, their very inappropriateness will seem funny. Ruptures in the normal scheme of things usually do amuse: think of people's first reaction when somebody trips and sprawls on the sidewalk. But this sort of laughter carries a nervous edge, and a case method teacher will have to manage this nervousness.

The colonel is in uniform. Perhaps this shows a particular desire for formality in him. Perhaps he wishes to stay hidden behind his institutional identity. He seems to have felt some personal threat or challenge behind Ben's breach of decorum. One wonders: Could Ben have noticed this colonel and read some warning in his reactions throughout the discussion? Was the colonel showing a mounting anger? Could Ben somehow have headed off his interruption and avoided being insulted?

The outburst itself is instructive to examine. It attempts to call attention to Ben's differentness—making the group "us servicemen" and Ben the alien interloper. But, since Ben's language did not, in fact, deeply insult most of the members of the group, the colonel's challenge boomeranged and ended by isolating the colonel and one follower. It is they, not Ben, who leave the room. The colonel has abrogated an implicit contract of free discussion by simply assuming the right to speak for the whole group. It is he who has insulted them.

More specifically, he has insulted the only woman in the room. Alluding incorrectly to "ladies" when there was just one female—and further alluding to her assumed outrage at Ben's language when in fact the colonel, sitting a few rows behind her, had no way of gauging her reaction—the colonel has implied that this poor female couldn't possibly be expected to speak for herself. This presents a complication of the challenge to Ben: what is his responsibility to this woman? Should he ask her to comment for herself? Should he apologize to her? Should he ask the colonel to apologize for daring to speak for her without consultation? Or should he resist the temptation to get out of the heat and avoid putting the woman into the spotlight?

In the heat of the moment—surprised, annoyed, and generally frustrated by a less than stellar discussion—Ben seems to have reacted only to the colonel's challenge to his authority. He treats the colonel's demands like a showdown, and he wins the confrontation. But perhaps Ben has lost an opportunity to examine the tactics by which he attempted to set a contract with this group of strangers.

Many of the thorniest issues in this case cluster around the elusive matter of the desirable social tone to set in the classroom. Certainly, different groups will elicit different styles of discourse. What's appropriate for a military institute will probably not be appropriate for a group of Gestalt psychotherapists. But the question of the proper sort of language to use remains somewhat universal. Profanity and vulgarity are current coin in many subcultures—the armed services and many university graduate departments, for example—but the classroom (particularly when a formal teaching demonstration is taking place) should be the setting for intellectual communication of the highest order. The content of many of our slang expressions is at best embarrassing and at worst downright sickening or sadistic. These associations are unavoidable on some level of consciousness, no matter how familiar the terms or how dead the metaphors. To use scatological or obscene or racially insulting language is to arouse emotional overtones in the participants' minds—overtones that lead in directions that can have nothing to do with the intellectual work of the class. Not that emotion is inimical to learning—on the contrary. But the emotion of the classroom should be focused on the issues under discussion. Locker room language instantly makes women feel conspicuous because women's bodies are the focus of so much of its lexicon. The same is true of all racial slurs and stereotypical slang remarks. These tend to focus unwelcome attention upon any members of the group under discussion who happen to be participants. Even if these people take the remarks in stride with good humor, they have nonetheless been singled out for distracting attention. Furthermore, most obscenities greatly impoverish one's range of verbal nuance. It takes a brilliant speaker, a trained and talented actor, to use obscenity with elegance in the service of real communication. And surely communication is the most basic goal of classroom dialogue.

In teaching this case, the discussion leader might wish to enter a plea for diplomacy. It isn't necessarily a virtue to insist on one's right to speak the same way all the time. It is the teacher's duty to gauge the audience and adapt accordingly. After all, no one speaks the same way all the time. There are many kinds of discourse—baby talk, pillow talk, locker-room banter, social chitchat, prayer, howls of anger. Classroom language should be adjusted to the occasion and should always be in the interest of establishing the best sort of rapport with the group that one has agreed to lead through the voyage of discovery that is case method discussion at its finest.

Assistant Professor Graham and Ms. Macomber (A), (B), and (C)

TEACHING NOTE

This teaching note was prepared by James Moore as an aid to instructors in the classroom use of the case series "Assistant Professor Graham and Ms. Macomber" (A) 9-379-020, (B) 9-379-021, and (C) 9-379-022.
(HBS No. 5-384-095)

Distributed by HBS Publishing Division, Harvard Business School, Boston, MA 02163.
Printed in U.S.A.

"Assistant Professor Graham and Ms. Macomber" deals with a classroom interchange between Charles Graham, an instructor in his second year of case teaching, and Janet Macomber, a first-year, first-semester MBA candidate. The incident described involves Ms. Macomber's presentation of her analysis of a case problem, Professor Graham's response, and the reactions of Janet and the other students to the exchange.

"Graham and Macomber" is an extremely popular case. We believe that at least part of its appeal stems from the universal importance of a skillful question-and-response style. This seminar is based on the premise that the essential artistry in case discussion leadership rests on the use of questions and the development of responses to students' comments. The present case, which describes a dramatic cross-examination of a student, raises participants' awareness of (1) the power of questions in shaping students' classroom experience, (2) the different sorts of questions one can use, and (3) the likely effects of particular types of questioning. "Graham and Macomber" describes a situation in which the professor is unaware of the impact of his questions. As a result, his intervention does not help his students learn, and it actually damages one person's self-esteem and willingness to participate in class discussions.

"Graham and Macomber" is presented in three brief segments. Generally seminar participants are asked to read and consider the (A) case before the class discussion. The (B) and (C) cases are handed out in class.

The (A) and (B) cases deal with the interchange between Professor Graham and Ms. Macomber—first from his point of view, then from hers. The (C) case presents the thoughts of Professor Graham as he reviews his records on student participation some three weeks later, puzzled by Janet Macomber's marked drop in performance since the early class sessions.

Case Summary
The Institutional Context

At New Dominion, the first-year class of MBAs is divided into approximately 10 sections, each containing 80 students. Each section is assigned an amphitheater-shaped classroom, in which the students assemble daily at 8:30 a.m. for the first of three classes; each class lasts 80 minutes. The instructors move from one section's classroom to another's during the day.

Section members work together throughout the day during the entire first year. Personal interaction between students is very high, and intense social dynamics of one sort or another can develop within a section. At the beginning of the year—the time of "Graham and Macomber"—students are often highly concerned about the image and reputation they are establishing within the section.

The Course

Quantitative Analysis and Operations Management (QAOM) is a technically oriented course in which students learn quantitative methods of analyzing problems in the design and organization of manufacturing processes.

The Instructor

Charles Graham is an assistant professor in his second year at New Dominion. Little information is given in the case about his background, age, or appearance.

The Section

The section consists of first-year MBA students. Since the course has barely begun, it can be assumed that section members do not yet fully understand what is expected of them in classes, nor have they yet gotten to know the strengths, weaknesses, and personalities of their peers.

Janet Macomber is an atypical student in several respects: she is younger than most students (the median age of New Dominion's MBA candidates is 27); she is female in a largely male-dominated school and content area; and she has strong quantitative skills developed at California Institute of Technology.

The (B) case, which focuses on Janet's experience of the incident, introduces a second student—Peter Anderson, "an already popular figure who usually sat with a group of cohorts in the middle of the right-hand bank of seats."

The Teacher-Student Relationship

"Graham and Macomber" focuses on a relatively short span of time—i.e., during a 10-minute classroom incident.

During the previous 70 minutes of the class, students have been discussing a management problem presented in the case. Charles's thoughts are described as he listens to the final few minutes. In his judgment the discussion does not reveal an adequate analysis of the case. He concludes that the discussion has "gone nowhere" and that "he would have to exercise the basic dictatorial prerogative of any instructor; he would have to tell them how wrong they were." "One more comment," he thought, "and then they are in for it." These statements suggest his impatience and irritation with the discussion, and his readiness to treat the students as wayward subjects in need of correction.

The (A) text gives very little information about the students' orientation toward the course and/or toward Charles. It is probably safe to assume that they are still "feeling out" the school, the course, the instructor, and their peers. Thus it is a time of uncertainty about one's role, one's competence, and the rules of the game. Students are trying to read signals from peers and instructors in order to determine unspoken rules of conduct.

The Incident

The (A) case describes the incident from Charles Graham's standpoint, detailing the crucial interaction between instructor and student. The text includes quotations from both participants, and observations that Charles could have made. The case problem given to the class is how to layout (design) a factory, a question for which, of course, there is not a single, neat "answer—there are always multiple "good ways."

The focal incident of "Graham and Macomber" is an exchange between Charles Graham and Janet Macomber—a student who, in the closing minutes of the session, finally offers the analysis of the case that Charles had been expecting. Through a series of pointed questions, he forces her to describe the steps through which she proceeded to "crack the case," but studiously refrains from indicating his agreement. When she has finished, his only comment is an ambiguous "Well, well!"

The (B) case describes the same incident from Janet Macomber's point of view. She experiences her recitation as a terrible ordeal. Without any feedback from the instructor, she wonders whether she has gone off on completely the wrong track. After class ends, the other students cluster around her desk and tease her. Clearly, they do not realize that her point was correct, nor that Professor Graham was impressed by her insight. Peter Anderson, the popular figure in the class, ridicules her loudly and christens her analysis "The Macomber Memorial Matrix." Janet feels crushed and resolves not to expose herself to further ridicule by sticking her neck out in discussions.

The (C) case takes place three weeks later, as Professor Graham reviews the participation records of the students. He is puzzled by Janet's performance, which has slipped markedly. She no longer volunteers comments in class, she often seems unprepared, and she shifts seats so often that he is not sure whether she is attending all sessions of the class. She often looks sleepy or bored. He wonders why her behavior has changed and what, if anything, he should do about it.

A Suggested Process Plan for the Case

Our overall goal is to help participants see how the instructor's questions and responses shape the experience of students in the classroom. We hope to raise awareness of the effect of such factors as the selection and timing of questions, and especially the manner in which a question is phrased.

Participants in the seminar are asked to read the (A) case, reflect on what Charles does in the interchange and how he sees it, and then predict how Janet and the other students might experience it. The (B) case allows participants to check their judgments against an account of what actually happened. In discussion we encourage an exploration of why this result occurred, and what it suggests about the nature of students and sections, and about the effect of an instructor's style of questioning.

We feel it is important that the section spend a good deal of time examining in detail the interchange between Charles and Janet. If an opportunity for this discussion arises while the (A) case is being considered, we may prolong that discussion and spend relatively less time on the (B) case. In some sessions, however, the (A) case is discussed without going into detail about the interchange. We are then likely to move ahead to the (B) case and seek a later opening to direct the section's attention back to Charles's interrogation.

In working with the (A) case, we focus on Charles's definition of his situation, and on what he did, and *why* he may have done it. Participants are encouraged to scrutinize the elements of his interactional style, for we feel that such details are often crucial to a teacher's success. We also underscore the link between a teacher's instructional philosophy and his or her operating style in the classroom.

We then move to a discussion of the probable effect of Charles's actions on Janet Macomber and on other members of the section, using clues provided in the (A) text. Often the discussion becomes quite spirited at this point, with some participants condemning Charles's approach out of hand, while others argue that his approach may be constructive, even if abrasive.

The (B) case can be a real eye-opener for the latter group. We encourage a careful exploration of the new data on the immediate results of Charles's actions. Participants typically concentrate on both Janet's experience and the section group dynamics revealed by Peter's comments about the "Macomber Memorial Matrix." As the seminar discussion develops, we call attention to the (A) case's detailed account of Charles's questioning and response, asking what elements in his comments contributed most to the final effect. We find that doubling back in this way to reconsider the (A) material helps participants appreciate the significance of details and the critical role played by an instructor's style of questioning and response.

The (C) case raises the broader question of how an instructor can understand the students' experience of his or her actions. We acknowledge the difficulties involved in accurately reading the effect of one's questions and responses, and typically conclude the session with a discussion of how instructors can overcome these problems. Because we use this case to stimulate a detailed consideration of questioning and responding, there is often little class time to discuss the (C) case. In such instances we hand it out to be read at home.

Notes for Discussion Questions

The first five questions are related to the (A) case.

1. How do you think this situation appears to Professor Charles Graham? How does he see the situation facing him, here in the second week of classes? What might he see as the problem? What might he focus on as the two or three key features of the situation?

We open with this broad question because we want to encourage participants to present their own analyses of the case without being unduly influenced by our directives. However, there are several issues that we feel should be raised early in the discussion. If they do not arise spontaneously, we use special probes to elicit them, as indicated below.

a) As a teacher of this section, what does Charles see as the critical challenge facing him?

Usage Note

This probe focuses attention on the problem as Charles himself defines it. Since the problem, as he defines it, is one that participants have probably encountered in their own teaching, this approach helps them develop some empathy for him.

Analysis

Charles appears to believe the problem is related to the content of the course. As he puts it, the class has "entirely missed the point of the case." Time is running out, and it seems improbable that any student will make the discovery that would "crack the case."

Further, Charles is concerned about setting a bad precedent early in the first term. He seems to believe that if he does not confront the class with the deficiencies of their analyses, he will be tacitly encouraging mediocrity. As he states it, "I could not conscientiously allow 80 apprentice managers to leave class thinking that the last hour passed for an adequate case analysis."

The assumptions that underlie Charles's understanding of his situation are worth examining. First, he appears to assume that there is a single answer that solves the case, and that once discovered it will provide a key for understanding the situation and making sensible recommendations for action. And he apparently sees case discussions as a time for collective thrashing about in search of this answer, followed by an examination of its implications for action.

In the first weeks of a course like QAOM, which draws on specialized quantitative methods of analysis, students may well fail to discover the key points of a case independently. Unfortunately, Charles has apparently developed no way to point students toward a critical solution. He sees no alternative to the unpleasant task of making a speech to the class in the closing minutes of the session—to give them the "answer."

b) What is Charles's concept of the section leader's role?

Usage Note

This question directs participants' attention to Charles's operating philosophy of case method teaching.

Analysis

Charles sees a case discussion as a search for an answer that solves a case. This answer appears to be *his* answer and not necessarily that of the class. An alternative view would see the case discussion as a disciplined process of exchanging and testing ideas.

Charles seems to feel the instructor's role is to inform the section when it has gotten the answer and indicate whether their search process was adequate. Charles does not seem to feel it is appropriate for him to guide or even actively facilitate the search.

Further, he seems to assume that *the class* has failed if it does not come up with *his answer.* He does not acknowledge that the instructor has some responsibility to help the students attain overall learning goals. Irritated by their "failure," he feels an impulse to chastise the section. Thus "One more comment," he thought, "then they are in for it."

2. How well, in your judgment, did Charles handle the questioning and response with Janet Macomber?

This question provides the first of several opportunities to encourage the section to examine in detail the elements of Charles's interaction with Janet. We now shift the discussion into the critical area of the skilled use of questions and responses. We hope to sharpen participants' awareness of the various ways an instructor can intervene in a discussion, and the different effects created by different kinds of question-and-response techniques. Finally, we hope that participants will begin to develop their own "contingency theories" to guide them in the use of questions and responses.

The following probes can be used to direct the discussion further when necessary.

a) What was Charles's approach?

Usage Note

By asking participants to consider Charles's "approach," the question provides a framework within which his use of questions and responses can be examined. A careful dissection of his comments is vital to sensitize participants to the impact of their own comments as instructors.

Analysis

A crucial feature of Charles's approach is his sudden, unannounced shift from a laissez-faire posture to a highly controlling style of managing the discussion. This transition is made somewhat ambiguously, for his first comment to Janet ("And just what is your analysis?") is a broad question of the type often used at the beginning of a case discussion. Such a question suggests that students should lay out their thoughts in their own way, showing their initiative and creativity in organizing a useful approach to the case problems. But Charles follows up this opening with a series of questions that tightly control the dialogue and thus force Janet to present her analysis in a manner that he chooses.

The ensuing interchange resembles a courtroom cross-examination. Like an advocate moving in on a hostile witness, Charles asks, "*And* what *exactly* did you have?" "*And* what did you find from this matrix?" "*And* what did you conclude based on this observation?" He uses short, logically linked questions that walk his subject through an argument he himself lays out. This style of questioning strips Janet of her initiative and autonomy, and makes her merely a supporting actor in his presentation. Further, Charles uses what might be termed "hook words"—beginning sentences with "and" and lacing his queries with "exactly" and "just." These words evoke the image of a prosecutor moving in for the kill, and implicitly place Janet in the position of a guilty defendant.

In the middle of his cross-examination, Charles asks a personal question, "And how long did that take you?" which prompts snickers from the side of the room, and leaves Janet nonplussed. In our opinion this question is problematic on two levels. First, it can be construed to imply that her approach involved a foolish investment of time—thus discouraging student explorations that require substantial effort. Second, by focusing on Janet's process of working, rather than her results, Charles's question shows a lack of respect for her ability to work independently. He has treated her as a subordinate whose efforts must be closely supervised, rather than one capable of autonomy.

It is also significant that Charles does not indicate his displeasure with the previous performance of the section or his satisfaction with Janet's work. At several points in Janet's comments, he chooses not to show his approval. The first is when she clarifies the company's problem (i.e., how to move work-in-process through the plant) and observes that the class's recommendations miss the point. The second is when she points out the significance of multiplying the two exhibits together. And finally, Charles in his summary avoids any signal that would clarify either the significance of Janet's comments or his reason for taking time—at this late point in the period—to allow her to lay out a new analysis.

Charles's careful avoidance of praise raises an important question: When (and how) should a discussion leader use praise? If excessive, praise can establish a teacher-student contract built around "pleasing the teacher" rather than openly exploring the issues of the case. Yet praise can be useful in motivating students and providing feedback about the value of their work. In general, we tend to use praise sparingly, and to address it either to the section as a whole or to specific comments that are helpful to the class's work.

Finally, by commenting "Let me understand"—rather than "Let us understand"—Charles signals that the dialogue is being conducted primarily for his benefit (and perhaps for Janet's). He misses an opportunity to suggest that the other students have something to gain from her comments.

b(Why do you think he chose that approach?

Usage Note

This question helps participants see that Charles's intervention style was not simply the result of a random error, but reflected a conscious decision on his part.

Analysis

The case text tells us that Charles wanted the class to understand the import of Janet's analysis, but gives little indication of the thought process that led him to the intervention style he chose. However, we can speculate that he was concerned primarily with getting her complex analysis out fast (only a few minutes remained in the class period) and thus wanted to speed up and prestructure her remarks so they would be as clear and as concise as possible. He may have thought that a crisp, rapid-fire cross-examination would accomplish this most effectively.

Just before the exchange with Janet, Charles was gearing up to exercise the instructor's "basic dictatorial prerogative." He seems frustrated at the direction the discussion has taken. His reaction seems to be to abandon his earlier noninterventionistic style in favor of *dictatorial* control. Many instructors must wrestle with the urge to exercise excessive control over discussion. Often this desire stems from simple impatience, and a desire to help the students discover as many key insights as possible. Instructors sometimes forget the long years it took *them* to master the field, and hope to bring their students "up to speed" unrealistically quickly. The desire to overcontrol a discussion can also reflect insecurity about one's grasp of the material being discussed, and/or one's ability to manage a more free-flowing exchange.

Some members of our seminar have commented that Charles's tone is angry, ironic, and attacking. Some participants have suggested that this tone may be a reflection of his frustration at the preceding discussion, directed toward Janet. Case data indicate that Charles feels it is the students' responsibility to get the answer, and that praising them for success amounts to pampering them. Thus he shows no reaction to Janet's remarks. Unfortunately Chris seems to have left him still stewing in his anger toward the rest of the class. The case text reports that "he only wanted the class—each and every one of the other seventy-nine—to realize the import of Janet Macomber's words." Charles seems to believe that the anger he expresses through the tedious interchange with Janet will be felt by the section as a criticism of their earlier work. Unfortunately, the students appear to assume that his irritation is with Janet, and not with them.

c) What was the impact of his approach on Janet? What signals was Janet sending that might have helped him anticipate and monitor his impact?

Usage Note

This crucial question shifts attention from Charles's intervention to its impact on Janet. Participants now are asked to identify the clues or signals that might have enabled Charles to anticipate the effect of his questioning.

This question asks participants to assess Charles's impact without having any more data than he did—no easy task. It is useful to press participants to commit themselves as to what they think is the likely impact of Charles's comments. The (B) case will then allow them to test their speculations against Janet's actual experience.

Analysis

In our opinion, Graham's approach was intimidating and left Janet feeling vulnerable to ridicule from her new classmates and confused about the value of her contribution. She had signaled her timidity and difficulty in asserting her viewpoint by sitting in the back of the room, by speaking in a quiet voice, and by pausing and restarting apologetically when interrupted by the shout of "Louder, please!" from across the room. Nevertheless, Graham responds initially with the sarcastic and domineering "And just what is your analysis, Ms. Macomber?" Charles's responses give Janet no sense of the value of her contribution. Thus she feels she has been ridiculed by the instructor and branded as a "number cruncher" at best, and perhaps also as an overachiever.

d) What background information would help him choose a more effective approach to Janet?

Usage Note

The appropriate use of background information is one aspect of the broader issue of understanding and managing the dynamics of a section of students.

Analysis

Charles knows that Janet is younger than many others in the section, that she has little work experience, and that her academic background is technical and quantitatively oriented. This information might alert him to the possibility that she would feel intimidated by the rough-and-tumble case discussions in which many participants draw on their personal backrounds in business and industry to inform their comments.

3. At the end of the interchange, Charles says, "Well, well!" What do you think of this response? What will be the effect of this response? How else might he have responded?

Usage Note

This question raises the broader issue of how to use feedback to enhance individual and section learning. When should instructors refrain from assessing the value of a contribution? When should they give feedback on the process of discussion? When should they comment judgmentally on the content of student contributions?

Analysis

Charles's response to Janet is intentionally vague, giving no information as to the value of her comments. As a result, both Janet and the section are left confused as to how to evaluate her insights—insights which call into question the entire previous discussion.

Understandably partial to their own ideas, the other students are likely to dismiss Janet's comment as irrelevant, particularly in view of the evident lack of respect shown by Charles's adversarial questioning. Thus his failure to support (or reject) her challenge to the section discussion probably leaves her feeling vulnerable in her relationship with the other section members.

Instead of neutrality, Charles could have acknowledged the importance of Janet's insights and expressed gratitude for her willingness to risk bucking the tide of the discussion. Such a response would give the class and Janet clear feedback—reducing their confusion, giving them a sense of direction in their work, and accomplishing Charles's original goal of letting them realize the inadequacy of the earlier discussion. In addition, it would encourage other students in the future to risk bringing up analyses that run counter to the consensus of the group. The multiplying of viewpoints which is so important to case method teaching depends on the willingness of group members to take such risks.

4. What is your evaluation of his summary? Was it appropriate to this class session?

Usage Note

This question directs attention to another important instructional tool—the end-of-class summary—and it encourages participants to consider how summaries can be used (and misused) in influencing the learning of students.

Analysis

Charles's summary simply relates the case to the course plan, and he carefully avoids "passing judgment on Janet's analysis or on the preceding case discussion." Thus it compounds the problem of inadequate feedback.

Summaries are among the most potent teaching tools available to a case discussion leader. They provide valuable opportunities to reinforce important points and to comment on the section's developing ability to function as a forum for the exploration and testing of ideas. To the extent that Charles's section had missed the point of the case under discussion (and we are not sure his views on this point are reliable), he could have helped them by suggesting some directions for further exploration of the case material. In our own practice we sometimes feel that a section has missed considering an important aspect of a case problem. In such situations we often conclude our summary with a short provocative question that signals the importance of this dimension and reinforces the class's sense of the complexity and richness of the issues raised by the case. Charles could have concluded the session by calling attention to the critical problem faced by the company and the potential value of the quantitative data contained in the case text.

5. Should Charles have dropped by the group around Janet's desk?

Usage Note

This question raises awareness of another tool available to the case discussion leader: the informal, after-class chat with students. Many discussion leaders cultivate such opportunities to speak with students, since these encounters may provide clues to otherwise hidden section dynamics and may allow the instructor to reinforce student learning and give less formal feedback on student participation.

Analysis

In our judgment Charles would have been wise to drop by Janet's desk in order to get a feel for what was going on. He realizes that something important is happening, but apparently assumes that the students are congratulating her and/or seeking to learn from her approach. Had he stopped by her desk he could have checked out his assumptions rather quickly, and then made whatever intervention seemed appropriate.

—◆—

At this point in the discussion, we suggest that the (B) case be handed out, read quickly by the participants, and discussed, using the following approach:

6. What is the situation from Janet Macomber's point of view?

Usage Note

With the data of the (B) case, it is possible to compare Janet Macomber's experience with that of Charles.

Analysis

Janet seems to be a conscientious student who finds herself in the difficult position of holding views very different from those of the rest of the section. In the closing minutes of class, she marshals "all the courage she could muster" and presents her analysis. She points out that "the class's recommendations simply do not answer the company's problem. . . ."

In bringing forward an analysis contrary to the consensus, she takes several risks. First, she effectively takes on the entire class—by contradicting their work. Second, if she is right, she risks being stereotyped as a teacher's pet. Third, by presenting a highly quantitative analysis, she risks being stereotyped as a "number-cruncher." Fourth, if her analysis is wrong, she risks making a fool of herself in front of the class.

Charles's adversarial cross-examination adds to what she calls her "ordeal." When it is over she feels "like a defendant released from hostile cross-examination." Charles puts her under pressure, effectively ridicules her in front of the class, and then gives her no feedback. ("The ordeal was over but the verdict was still out.")

She does get feedback from her peers, ranging from "good-natured teasing to open incredulity" at the highly mathematical approach she had taken. One of the most popular members of the section caps off the session by saying, "We are going to call your achievement The Macomber Memorial Matrix!" Thus she feels she has made a fool of herself and added little to the case discussion. In the absence of any signal from Charles, neither she nor the other students have any information to contradict this verdict.

7. What was Peter Anderson signaling?

Usage Note

This question directs attention to another element of section dynamics: peer relationships and peer pressure. A student is always managing two sets of relationships, and two sets of self-images—one with instructors, the other with peers. Both are of vital importance to the student. Clearly an important part of Janet's experience is the indirect result of Charles's comments as they influence the section's view of her and the section's relationship to her.

Analysis

Peter Anderson appears to us to be summing up the sentiment of the group, and in effect announcing one of two possible verdicts: 1) that Janet has made a fool of herself by presenting an analysis that seemed to the rest of the students to be ridiculously off target, or 2) that she has shown up the section and thus become a "rate breaker" violating section norms.

In our experience, students who attain early popularity often do so because they have a highly developed ability to read the attitudes and values of the group, and to act as a standard bearer for it. Thus it is likely that Peter is signaling and in some ways crystalizing the sentiment of the group through his comment about "The Macomber Memorial Matrix."

8. What might Janet have done afterward? Why didn't she speak to Charles?

Usage Note

Teaching is a two-way interaction, and students as well as instructors have choices and responsibilities. This question directs attention to the ways students can influence their relationship with the instructor, and the ways instructors can make it harder or easier for students to approach them directly.

Analysis

Both Janet and Charles would be better off if she had spoken to him after class. At a minimum, she could have gotten Charles's assessment of her contribution. This would have relieved her confusion and, while not altering her relationship with other students, could have encouraged her to continue participating actively in the class. Ideally, she might have been able to tell Charles about her feelings during and after the interrogation, and/or the reactions of her classmates. A sensitive, supportive response from Charles would have done much to help her regain confidence and self-esteem. In addition, Janet's comments could perhaps have helped Charles improve his teaching style and even take specific corrective action in the section.

Unfortunately, it seems unlikely that someone in Janet's situation would choose to speak with Charles. To do so would be emotionally, and perhaps academically, risky for the student—particularly in the first weeks of a new and highly competitive graduate program. To take such a risk usually requires that the student feel some trust for the instructor.

9. What was it, precisely, about Charles's comments that created the devastating impact?

Usage Note

If participants have not already discussed the details of Charles's question-and-response style, this question provides an opportunity to direct attention to that crucial issue. Since participants now have developed an understanding of Charles's impact upon Janet Macomber, the discussion can focus on Charles's techniques as such rather than their effects. We find it is crucial in guiding discussion of this question to push the seminar to examine Charles's use of questions and response in word-for-word detail.

Analysis

Several aspects of Charles's approach are particularly important: the sudden, unexplained shift from a noninterventionistic approach to a highly controlling one; his adversarial stance toward Janet, including the use of short, logically linked questions and provocative "hook words"; the personalization of the interrogation by asking about her process of working out her analysis; and the studied avoidance of a clear signal to Janet or the class about the value of their contributions.

10. How does an instructor encourage student risk taking?

Usage Note

This question asks the seminar members to generalize about the case, focusing on risk taking and the ways in which a safe climate for participation can be created in class. The key idea here is that the instructor who wants to get students to take risks in discussion must also assume the responsibility of protecting students who have taken a venturesome position.

Analysis

There are a variety of ways in which an instructor can create a climate that encourages students to explore ideas, challenge the status quo and conventional wisdom, and take initiative in creating new approaches to the problems presented in the cases. From the opening of classes, the instructor can seek to establish a learning contract in which student risk taking is valued and protected by the instructor.

By their behavior, and by what they demand from

the students, instructors can establish mutual respect as a basic operating rule of their classes. Such respect helps to ensure that students will not be ridiculed for their contributions—and that indeed students will feel valued when they participate in discussions.

The instructor should try to recognize when a student has taken a particularly risky stand, and to respond in a supportive way. It is helpful for the instructor to take a respectful but not patronizing stance toward a comment that seems to be made with much difficulty. Peer support can be built by asking other students who agree to build upon the contribution. Finally, we try always to keep in mind that student comments really are the stuff from which discussion classes are built. We will sometimes thank a student, on behalf of the section, for making a particularly risky—but often also valuable—contribution to our learning.

—◆—

At this time the (C) case can be handed out, read, and discussed. We suggest the following discussion questions:

11. What is Charles's diagnosis at the end of the fifth week? How is he likely to handle this situation?

Usage Note

The (C) case shifts the focus from the encounter itself to its longer-term effects. This question asks seminar participants to examine Charles's ability to diagnose the problem at this point, when he has had an opportunity to read signals sent over a period of several section meetings.

Analysis

In the first weeks of the term Janet came to class obviously well prepared, and participated eagerly in discussions. Charles notes that her comments "had been intelligent, succinct and to the point . . . and that on one occasion [the time of the incident] . . . Janet had performed an analytic tour de force, smashing the case wide open." Now Janet is silent, no longer participates voluntarily, arrives late, and changes her seat position every day.

Charles thinks Janet "seemed sleepy—or bored," and "quite evidently had been barely following the discussion." He has "a strong presupposition" that she is unprepared.

As Charles reflects on the situation, he does not question his reading of Janet but rather his handling of what seems to him a clear-cut problem. He notes he has refrained from calling on her so as not to embarrass her. He chastises himself mildly, noting "such benevolence ought not to continue."

Though the text does not indicate what he is likely to do, his comments suggest that he feels a need to take corrective, and perhaps somewhat punitive, action. It seems likely that he will make it a point to call on Janet in class, perhaps with a sense of applying discipline, and challenging her to prove her preparation for discussion. If so, it is likely she will be further intimidated by him.

Alternatively, he may decide to speak with her in his office. The two of them might then finally be able to communicate their respective experiences of the incident, and to reopen communications. If so, there is a possibility of reestablishing mutual respect, trust, and thus a workable learning contract.

12. What else might someone in Charles's shoes do in this situation? What would be an effective way to handle this situation?

Usage Note

Asking participants to put themselves in Charles's place tends to increase involvement and helps them realize the variety of options open to someone in this situation. It also helps them develop their ability to respond creatively and inventively to challenging teaching situations.

Analysis

Participants are likely to come up with many valuable suggestions. The common theme will probably be the need to open communication between instructor and student, whether by calling Janet in for a conversation or by talking with her less formally after or before class.

The point of such a conversation must be to ask her what the problem is, from her point of view. Charles persists in assuming he knows her experience of the class and his interventions. He does not. Instructors need to find ways of checking what students' experiences actually are. Often the simplest approach is to ask the student directly but tactfully, and with respect for the difficulty he or she may experience in responding.

13. Faced with the situation as he sees it, what questions might he have asked himself?

Usage Note

This question invites participants to consider how instructors can challenge their own complacency and recognize that their perceptions of reality may not be entirely accurate.

Analysis

Clearly, Charles should have asked himself, "Why is Janet acting this way? What is her experience of the section?" More generally, we find it important to keep asking these questions about our own students—and to note particularly the little details that seem surprising and perplexing. Such details (like the shift in Janet's participation) are often clues to realities of which we have been unaware.

In some ways a more important question is, "Why do we, as instructors, so often take for granted the accuracy of our 'reading' of teaching situations? How might we teach ourselves to question our interpretations more often?" We have found that the simple pressures of time, and the absence of ready opportunities to talk candidly with students about their learning, inevitably create a tendency to take quick readings and rely too heavily on them. There seems to be no easy solution to this problem. In many situations, the most helpful approach may be to arrange frequent, informal meetings with small groups of students and deliberately cultivate their willingness to give us their candid views.

14. Charles believes his class is going well. Do you agree? Why or why not?

Usage Note

This question raises a broad issue to which we return again and again in the seminar: How do you know when your class is going well?

Analysis

The case text gives very little data on the progress of the entire section. Nevertheless, we doubt that the class is going as well as Charles may believe. First, we wonder about his concept of an ideal class session. He characterizes the session in which the incident with Janet occurred as "everything a case discussion should not be: floundering, disjointed, indecisive, and entirely irrelevant to the company's problems." But sometimes floundering is an indication of real work being done. We, as instructors, may want things to flow logically—but for students, "floundering" can be a groping exploration of difficult questions and issues that is immensely valuable. Students often feel such discussions are very productive and useful.

Second, just as Charles imagines he can understand Janet without difficulty and without testing his attributions, we suspect he may believe he can read the section's progress with the same ease. As he reflects on their accomplishments, there is little evidence of self-critical questioning of his assessment. He thinks to himself, "Individually and collectively, the class had come a long way in five weeks." Charles grins: he supposes, if surveyed, "the class would say the same thing of him." But would they? There is no evidence that he has carried out such a survey—formally or informally.

EXHIBIT 1 *Assistant Professor Graham and Ms. Macomber (A)*

Study Questions

1. What is your diagnosis of the situation confronting Professor Charles Graham as of the end of class?
2. Should Professor Graham stop by the group gathered around Janet at the end of class?

EXHIBIT 2 *Assistant Professor Graham and Ms. Macomber*

Discussion Questions

The first five questions are directed to the (A) case.

1. How do you think this situation appears to Professor Charles Graham? How do you think he sees the situation facing him, here in the second week of classes, in the discussion session described in the case? What might he see as the problem? What might he focus on as the two or three key features of the situation?
   a) As a teacher of this section, what does Charles see as the critical challenge facing him?
   b) What is Charles's concept of the section leader's role?
2. How well, in your judgment, did Charles handle the questioning and response with Janet Macomber?
   a) What was Charles's approach?
   b) Why do you think he chose that approach?
   c) What was the impact of Charles's approach on Janet? What signals was Janet sending that might have helped him anticipate and monitor his impact was making?
   d) What background information might have helped him choose a more effective approach to Janet as an individual?
3. At the end of the interchange, Charles says, "Well, well!" What do you think of this response? What may be the effect of this response? How else might he have responded?
4. What is your evaluation of his summary? Was it appropriate to this class session?
5. Should he have dropped by the group around Janet's desk?

At this point in the discussion, the (B) case is handed out to be read quickly by the participants and discussed, using the following approach:

6. What is the situation from Janet Macomber's point of view?
7. What was Peter Anderson signaling?
8. What might Janet have done afterward? Why didn't she speak to Charles?
9. What was it, precisely, about Charles's comments that created the devastating impact?
10. More generally, how does an instructor encourage student risk taking?

At this time the (C) case can be handed out, read, and discussed, using the following discussion questions:

11. What is Professor Graham's diagnosis at the end of the fifth week? How is he likely to handle this situation?
12. What else might someone in Charles's shoes do in this situation? What would be an effective way to handle this situation?
13. Faced with the situation as he sees it, what questions might he have asked himself?
14. Charles believes his class is going well. Do you agree? Why or why not?

Bill Jones (A) and (B)

TEACHING NOTE

Introduction

"Bill Jones" describes an instructor facing what he sees as a potential racial incident in his class. It draws attention to the critical role of listening in the classroom.

In our seminar, this case generally follows "Assistant Professor Graham and Ms. Macomber," which emphasizes ways of using questions. "Bill Jones," in contrast, focuses on the unpredictable dimension of case discussions, and the need for sensitive listening and quick creative thinking to turn apparent crises into opportunities for teaching and learning.

Case Summary

"Bill Jones" is divided into two parts. Before class, students read and prepare an analysis of the (A) case which describes the incident and gives background information. After discussion, the (B) case, describing Bill Jones's response to the incident, is handed out in class, read, and discussed.

The Institutional Context

The case takes place in an MBA course at Metropolitan Business School. Metropolitan is a pseudonym for a large, highly selective business school with a two-year, case-based curriculum. The incident occurs in an elective course that is part of the second-year curriculum.

The Course

The incident occurs in a labor relations conflict resolution course that is being taught for the first time. Bill has 90 students in his section. Students apparently find the case material very stimulating, and Bill's class has had exciting discussions.

The Instructor

Bill Jones is an energetic young associate professor—a former college football quarterback and Phi Beta Kappa member—who brings to class a booming voice, a great deal of enthusiasm, and a quick wit. He was hired directly out of graduate school—with no postgraduate work experience—to teach on Metropolitan's Production and Operations Management faculty. Bill has six years' case teaching experience at Metropolitan, including four in his department's first-year MBA course and two in a course he had designed himself on management of nonprofit organizations.

This teaching note was prepared by James Moore as an aid to instructors in the classroom use of the case series "Bill Jones" (A) 9-378-038 and (B) 9-378-039.
(HBS No. 5-384-093)

The Section

Though courses in production and operations management at Metropolitan had traditionally been a male domain, Bill's section includes 12 women.

Several students are introduced in the case text, among them the following:

Dave Young, who Bill thinks represents "a somewhat radical point of view about labor policy," is 27 years old, has a B.A. in economics from the University of Wisconsin, and has worked with Cesar Chavez's United Farmworkers Union and with the California State Department of Labor as assistant to the secretary.

Paige Palmer is a recent graduate of a well-known eastern women's college where she majored in art history. She came directly to Metropolitan where she has done well academically, though her in-class comments are viewed as naive by some of her more experienced classmates.

Fred Wilkens is a Stanford engineering graduate with bachelor's and master's degrees; he worked for Hewlett-Packard for two years before coming to Metropolitan. Fred is the only black student in the section. Initially, he does not participate in class discussions, and acknowledges to Bill that his priorities lie elsewhere. Bill asks him to contribute to discussions anyway and Fred begins to do so.

Jim Casey has worked four years with General Motors. The text provides little more on his background, but does note that Jim is somewhat conservative politically, and is appreciated by his classmates as a bright, articulate person who often draws on his General Motors experience to contribute interesting insights and anecdotes.

The Teacher-Student Relationship

There is little information in the text about Bill's style of discussion leadership. It appears, however, that he follows a laissez-faire approach, allowing students great freedom in their responses to his questions. In addition, he appears to enjoy conflict in the classroom, and perhaps elicits it by calling on participants with predictably opposed views.

The Incident

The incident takes place during discussion of a case about a General Motors experiment with the use of worker teams to assemble automobiles. Opening comments in Bill's class address the issue of estimating the cost of assembling cars by the team method. Jim Casey, the former GM employee, suggests that the experimental team is not representative of other workers, and probably is made up of "rate busters"—that is, employees who are willing to work harder and faster than average.

Bill Jones does not reply to this comment, but calls on Paige Palmer, who is sitting next to Fred Wilkens. Paige says, "Well, I disagree with Jim; I don't think the workers could be 'rate busters' because three of them are black, and. . . ."

From the case: "At that moment, the entire class gasped. Fred Wilkens shot back in his seat so that his chair seat banged loudly; his fingers tensely gripped the desk. Paige did not finish her sentence; an icy silence prevailed in the room. Fred . . . slowly gathered his papers . . . and . . . turned . . . as if to leave the classroom." The (A) case ends without indicating Bill's response.

In the (B) case, we learn that Bill assumes Paige has made a racist comment, and that she is now ashamed of her error. Bill responds by walking over to Fred, putting his hand on Fred's arm and apologizing for Paige. Fred nods his head back at Bill, as if to signal agreement and acceptance. Bill then turns back to the class as a whole and continues the case discussion, without referring directly to the incident again.

A Suggested Process Plan for the Case Overview

Our overall aim is to help the participants become more conscious of the complexity of listening and responding to students during a case discussion. The art of case method teaching lies largely in the skillful use of questions, listening, and responses. In "Assistant Professor Graham and Ms. Macomber," we emphasized the use of questions. In the present case, we move into the domain of listening and response—a much more complex topic.

A key dimension of discussion leadership is listening. Experienced discussion leaders listen for the content, logic, and consistency of a statement. They listen to the relationship between the present comment and those that have preceded it, looking for emerging themes that could provide ways to connect various insights. And they listen with an ear to the future, seeking opportunities to move the discussion toward potentially profitable areas. Good discussion leaders also try to attend to the needs of the individual student—challenging at some times, protecting, supporting, and encouraging at others—looking for ways to help the individual student have an important learning experience.

Given effective listening, the range of potential responses is enormous. One can say nothing; this will be interpreted as a comment of sorts. One can write on the board. One can restate, paraphrase, highlight, and/or comment on some aspect of the student's statement. The student can be questioned or simply encouraged to say more. One can ask other students to comment, either on the matter at hand or on the statement just made. One can move the discussion down the path it has been following, or one can redirect it. All this may be done in words, but can also be done with simple gestures.

To help seminar participants sharpen their abilities in these areas, we concentrate the case discussion on how Bill listens to and interprets Paige's comment, the nature and impact of his response, and the range of alternatives he might have used.

We begin discussion of the (A) case by asking what the problem is. There are a number of good responses to this question, and we encourage participants to explore different ways of conceiving the problems in Bill's situation. The most obvious problem is the potential racial incident. A more important problem, some participants may suggest, is that Paige does not finish her comment. Although the class may have felt she was making a racist remark, no one really knows what Paige might say if she finished. We feel this point is crucial, and we do all we can to encourage the seminar to mull over the class's lack of listening, and the various ways Paige's comment might be completed. In addition, some participants believe Bill's teaching style is a central problem and has contributed to the development of a crisis.

We then move to discussion of what Bill Jones should do. A wide range of alternatives are usually suggested, which helps expand participants' sense of possibilities. We press each person to make a commitment to a particular course of action, perhaps personalizing our question by asking, "Imagine you are now caught in this situation. What are you going to do?" This approach helps participants feel the urgency of the situation and appreciate the difficulty of choosing effective responses to complex, fast-developing situations.

We usually spend about half the class session on the (A) case, dividing this time about equally between diagnosis and consideration of action. However, our allocation of time depends, in part, on when the seminar picks up the point that Paige has not finished her comment. If the implications of this observation are not discussed in response to the (A) case, we move ahead more quickly to (B) and raise the issue during that phase of the discussion. After the (B) case has been handed out and read, we first ask what Bill did, and why. In discussing this question, participants build a detailed understanding of Bill's response with particular attention to his presumptions, the rapidity with which he moved in, and the controlling nature of his interventions. They also distinguish between his conscious thoughts about Paige's motives and the situation facing him and the possible unconscious reasons for his actions. For example, many participants feel that his actions may have emerged more from a felt need to control the situation than from a considered pedagogical strategy.

Next we examine the consequences of Bill's intervention, particularly for Paige, who we feel is potentially the most misunderstood and vulnerable participant in the case. This shift in focus underlines the influence of instructor listening—or lack of it—on students' experience, and emphasizes the potential for harm in prematurely conceived and insensitive responses. Finally, we ask participants once again to consider how they might have handled the situation, thus linking the previous analysis back to action, and emphasizing once again that effective teachers must be able not only to analyze their situations, but to act with commitment.

Notes for the Discussion Questions

1. What is the problem here? What went wrong?

Usage Note

Participants' responses to this broad diagnostic question are likely to identify levels of problems—some obvious, some more subtle. We try to help them see connections between their comments, thus highlighting the main problems presented in Bill Jones's class.

Analysis

Perhaps the most obvious problem, and the one that is usually identified first, is that a racist incident *may* be about to occur in the classroom. In fact, however, Paige has not finished her statement. The class's interpretation of her meaning and her motives is based on only the first part of an incomplete sentence. It is clear that her statement dealt with race but nothing more is known.

When discussing this point, we have sometimes asked participants to suggest some possible endings to the sentence. For example, the case text indicates that younger workers are less productive on average than older workers, and that the plant's black workers were almost all less than 40 years old. Thus, Paige might have intended to say, "I don't think the workers could be 'rate busters' because three of them are black, and thus probably young. And we know that the young workers tend to be more dissatisfied with their work and less productive." While this may not be a very strong argument, it is not necessarily a racist one either.

A central concern in teaching this case is the importance of letting students be heard, and of listening closely to their statements before taking action in response. Thus, the fact that Paige has not finished her statement is crucial. After that observation has been made by several participants, we often ask participants to explore it further—perhaps by brainstorming alternative endings to the sentence or by considering how Bill Jones might have made it possible for Paige to finish. However, we usually do not underscore the point the first time it is raised—particularly if this occurs in the first two or three comments—for to do so can signal to the section that "this is the point of the case" and discourage the development of other important insights. In addition, the fact that one or two students have grasped a point does not mean that most students share the insight. In our experience, the class as a whole is best able to learn if the instructor waits until several students have raised the point before underlining and encouraging its development.

A less obvious but very important problem is Bill's style of managing the day's discussion. The case text provides no evidence that Bill uses questions or responses to shape and control the discussion. Rather, it appears that he calls on one student after another, following the drift of the discussion and exercising control primarily by choosing who would speak next.

Selective calling on students is a useful way of shaping a discussion. Some students open discussions well; others are masters at summary. Some students raise the emotional heat and involvement of discussions; others cool them down. Some are more practical, while others shine at theoretical analysis. An instructor can pick students when their strengths are needed by the class. And by contrast, an instructor will sometimes help students develop breadth by asking them to contribute in ways that are uncharacteristic for them individually. However, if an instructor limits him- or herself to this mode of discussion leadership, a great deal of control is given up. If Bill has been operating in this way, it may have contributed to the volatility of the situation by allowing a relatively free-wheeling discussion to develop.

Moreover, Bill's choices of student participants do not seem to be based on a very detailed analysis of the needs of the class or of individuals. Rather, his choices appear to be based primarily on predictions of conflict. On the day of the incident, Bill "anticipated a lively discussion particularly between Jim Casey, who . . . was fairly conservative, and Dave Young." Bill's comments throughout the case suggest that he equates success with exciting discussions that include clamorous student participation and open conflict.

Experienced teachers in our seminar sometimes wonder aloud whether Bill is succumbing to one of the temptations of case teaching: the creation of drama for its own sake. Case materials are usually designed to be emotionally as well as intellectually stimulating. Add to this the intrinsic excitement of conflict, particularly for the more aggressive students, and you have a mixture that makes it relatively easy for a case teacher to create dramatic classes upon demand. Some students love them, and so do many instructors.

However, our experience has been that too much drama leads to game-playing. The more aggressive students adopt stock roles—the class radical, the class conservative, the feminist, the antifeminist—and create predictably polar analyses of each case. The lead players and the rest of the class soon learn to avoid the more tedious, confusing, complex, tentative thinking that leads to less predictable but often more profound insights. In a section that is "playing games," careful listening declines because it is unnecessary. As long as most persons play their parts, the discussion remains shallow and easy to follow.

From painful experience with our own indulgence in classroom theater, we have discovered that it can create problems for individual students as well as for the class as a whole. The instructor becomes a director, calling up each part when he or she feels it is dramatically appropriate. Unfortunately, the same players tend to lead in discussion after discussion, and become typecast in their roles. Their original purpose in taking the class—to grow and change and broaden their repertoire of analysis and action—is too easily forgotten. By the same token, less aggressive participants are relegated to the audience. As spectators, they soon become bored by the predictability of the show.

2. What should Bill do now? Why?

Usage Note

This question asks the seminar to consider action. We do not push for any particular choice, but rather press the participants to clarify what they think needs to be done, how it should be accomplished, and in what order steps should be taken. We are particularly interested in having them set priorities and define a plan for the first moments following Paige's comment.

Analysis

In our judgment, the top priority is enabling Paige Palmer to finish speaking. At the same time, it is important to get Fred Wilkens to stay in his seat, at least until she is finished. Both aims could perhaps be accomplished by quickly gesturing to Fred—catching his eye and motioning for him to pause just for a moment—and asking Paige gently to "please go on."

We believe both students will probably comply with these kindly signaled requests. Although emotions are running high, the instructor derives considerable social power from his or her formal role, and a stronger intervention might be overwhelming. Fred is described as basically a shy person, slightly built and studious—seemingly not the type to challenge the instructor's authority at such a moment. Paige has a more direct reason to continue, for it is the only way she can make her point and perhaps redeem herself with the other section members.

Once Paige has finished, new decisions must be made. In our opinion, it is unlikely her comment will prove to be racist. But if it is, one way to handle the situation is for Bill to ask her to examine the assumptions her statement is based upon, thus exposing to scrutiny the unfounded inferences that underlie such stereotyping. Racism is a way of thinking, and it can be discussed and analyzed profitably in the classroom—as long as the students' (and instructors') emotional reactions can be contained.

We would not suggest simply throwing the ball to another student, as Bill is apparently in the habit of doing. With a section already primed to create dramatic conflicts, such a move could lead to truly damaging personal attacks on Paige. After an analytical exchange with Paige, Bill might involve the rest of the section by asking a student to comment on his or her reactions to Paige's statement. The choice of respondent would be very important here. We suggest a student who is basically kind, and tends to be able to see various viewpoints and bridge them. Such a person might be able to verbalize some of the feelings of the class, thus making them discussable, without attacking Paige and/or provoking more emotional reactions in the section. We would not call on either Dave or Fred initially. Fred is particularly vulnerable—being the only black in the room—and might feel very much put on the spot. Dave's aggressive manner and emotional intensity make it unlikely that he could contribute constructively to the early moments of such a discussion. Fred, and perhaps Dave, could be brought into the discussion at a later point.

We believe it is much more likely that Paige's comment will not be objectionable. Bill then faces other choices. He can continue the case discussion by ignoring the potential incident. Or he can focus the section's attention on its own reactions to her comment. To some extent, his decision must be based on his estimate of the section's readiness to become self-reflective, as well as his own ability to lead such a discussion profitably. We feel, however, that something very important may have been revealed by the reaction to Paige's comment, and it requires some action by Bill, either immediately or in the near future.

The section's response is symptomatic of two possible problems. First, its members may not be listening attentively to each other's statements; they may have gotten into the habit of quickly forming a general impression of a comment and reacting immediately on that basis. If such poor listening is widespread, it can devastate case discussions. It needs to be corrected. Second, Bill and the section members may not be able to discuss racial issues effectively. This possible inability to discuss a truly controversial issue also suggests that the section may have been playing games, and that the "open conflict" Bill noted has been mock conflict.

More important, the inability to discuss issues involving race is a serious weakness at both the section and individual levels for people who are studying labor relations. Race and racism are important factors that must be dealt with in modern labor relations. Future managers, especially those going into either production management or labor relations, need to learn to discuss such matters routinely and rationally.

If Bill seizes the opportunity, the class's reaction provides a wonderful chance to make discussable the importance of listening closely.

Bill might start such a discussion in a variety of ways, either just after Paige finishes or after a short period of case discussion had allowed students to calm down and gain some perspective on the incident. Bill might say, "One thing I noticed a few minutes ago, and I think provides us with an important opportunity for learning, was the strong response of various class members to Paige's mention of the race of the workers in this case. Can anyone see how our reactions might relate to problems that are important in labor relations?"

This statement strongly reaffirms the central aim of the course—to learn about how conflict resolution emerges in a negotiating situation and puts a discussion of the class's reactions clearly in the context of that aim. Further, it asks students to make an analytical connection between their reaction and these aims, thus encouraging initial replies that are more intellectual than emotional. Such an approach helps students develop some reflective distance from their own reactions, and makes volatile issues more manageable.

Questions inviting a more personal exploration can follow later if that seems desirable. For example, Bill could ask, "What was your reaction, [student's name], and what did you learn from that?"

The following questions are used after the (B) case has been read by participants:

3. What did Bill do? Why?

Usage Note

This question asks the seminar to examine the sequence of Bill's assumptions and actions. We usually teach the case by asking for a detailed, sequenced, play-by-play recapitulation. We want the participants to take this particular response apart to see how it is constructed.

Analysis

Bill assumes that he knows Paige's and Fred's thoughts and feelings without being told. He takes very strong action to keep Fred in his seat, and he speaks for Paige to Fred, making an apology. Then he resumes the case discussion, apparently without further direct reference to the incident.

Key points include the following:

a) Bill acts quickly, while Paige is still trying to speak.

b) He makes quick and damaging attributions about Paige's comment and her intentions—that she had made a racist comment (when in fact, she had not finished her sentence) and that the comment was made accidentally: "He *realized* that Paige Palmer had not meant to say what she had." That is, Bill immediately assumes he knows her thoughts. He does not wonder what she was going to say or what she meant and he does not ask her for a clarification or even allow her to finish her sentence.

c) He walks directly toward Fred—a very dominant move for a discussion leader to make, particularly an ex-football player facing a shy, slightly built student. He puts his hand on Fred's arm—an even more dominant gesture. In most case classrooms, instructors never touch students at all. And Bill completes this sequence by looking directly at Fred—also an intimidating action in this context.

d) Rather than asking Fred how he feels, Bill assumes he can read Fred's mind: "Fred, I *know* you're hurt and you're probably angry . . . you *can't even know* how badly she feels. . . ."

e) Speaking for Paige, Bill makes what amounts to an admission of guilt and an apology: ". . . she didn't mean to hurt you and she didn't mean to say that. She's probably never felt worse in her life."

f) Looking over at Paige (seated next to Fred), Bill sees that she is flushed and apparently on the verge of tears. Bill chooses not to respond to her directly.

g) Fred also looks at Paige and nods his head slowly at Bill—perhaps to signal agreement (the case is ambiguous on this point).

h) Bill does not reply, but instead immediately calls on another student to continue class discussion. Bill appears to assume that the incident is now closed, not only for Paige and Fred, but for the rest of the class members. The case text gives no indication that he considers the reactions of the other class members or thinks of checking with them directly to find out how they are thinking and feeling about the situation. Bill apparently resumes the discussion by signaling another student to carry on. There is no information in the text to suggest that Bill poses a specific question, or gives much thought to the best way to direct the discussion in the minutes after the incident.

Why does Bill act as he does? His reaction seems to be to manage the crisis by controlling the participants and suppressing potential conflict. He perceives a potential problem, quickly sizes up the nature of the problem, and takes forceful action—an effective strategy for a football quarterback, but probably not for a discussion leader.

Like the section itself, Bill has perhaps not yet developed a capacity to discuss controversial issues—or at least the issue of race—comfortably. His own discomfort appears to drive him to act as he does. Yet he enjoyed earlier dramatic class sessions with their periods of open conflict—perhaps he, too, has become comfortable with mock conflict, rather than with authentic discussions of difficult and personally relevant concerns.

4. What are the implications of his particular response to this situation? What result is it likely to have?

Usage Note

Seminar groups vary in their responses. Some have reached an early consensus that Bill's approach was inappropriate; this question then evokes a kind of "working session" on alternative approaches. In other instances, a sizable group of participants may insist that Bill's action was warranted. In our opinion, this perspective deserves to be heard, but it is important to examine explicitly the assumptions on which it is founded (e.g., that such issues are too explosive for the class to handle; that this intervention "protected" Paige).

Analysis

Bill's response has several damaging implications. First, it signals to the section that questions of race cannot be discussed in class. This is a particular problem in a class on labor relations, since racial problems constitute one of the fundamental problems of the field.

Second, his intervention implies that Paige was making a racially objectionable comment, and that she is guilty primarily of a "slip" by making the comment in public. This stereotypes Paige in the worst possible light. His reading of her has special weight because he is not just a student in the class, but is the professor in charge—the expert, and the official judge of student contributions.

Though we have little data about the effect of the incident on Paige, we can make some plausible guesses. The immediate pain and frustration of being so forcibly misunderstood could be tremendous, and might lead her to decide to contribute much more cautiously in future discussions. In addition, she probably feels humiliated and angry at having been labeled a racist in front of Fred and the other members of the class. Already handicapped by a reputation for naivete, she will have still greater difficulty in the future in trying to overcome the effect of this negative stereotyping.

Third, some students will probably realize—either immediately or later—that Paige was at best interrupted and more likely misunderstood and prevented from making a correction. They will interpret Bill's intervention as a sign that he cannot be relied on to help them should they be misunderstood by the class. This, in turn, may discourage some students from making controversial comments in class.

Fourth, members of the class are reinforced in their tendency to jump to conclusions when listening to other students. Bill misses an important opportunity to show them the importance of listening carefully. Learning to listen more effectively would increase students' ability to profit from future case discussions—not to mention from conversations and discussions throughout their lives. In a labor relations course, such a lesson is particularly relevant.

There are many other ways in which this situation might have been handled, and each time this case is discussed, participants suggest insightful new ways to approach it. In general, we believe that the incident can, with skill and luck, be turned into a valuable learning experience for the entire class.

EXHIBIT 1 *Bill Jones*

Study Questions

The (A) case:

1. What is your diagnosis of the situation at the end of the case? What went wrong?
2. What response should Bill make? To whom?

EXHIBIT 2 *Bill Jones*

Discussion Questions

After the (A) case has been read:

1. What is the problem here? What went wrong?
2. What should Bill do now? Why?

After the (B) case has been discussed:

3. What did Bill do? Why?
4. What are the implications of his particular response to this situation? What result is it likely to have?

Bound Feet (A) and (B)

TEACHING NOTE

Introduction

"Bound Feet" poses a major dilemma for any teacher who takes pride in *caring about,* as well as teaching, individual students. We use this case for discussions of teacher response to difficult student-in-classroom comments. "Bound Feet" begins with aspects of the teaching-learning contract, and moves on to issues of questioning, listening, and particularly teacher responses in an emotionally loaded situation. Where does a teacher draw the line with regard to his or her own personal involvement? And with whom? Are there limits and backlashes when a teacher shows concern for students over and above the intellectual concerns of the subject matter?

Lisa Wheelwright was a popular section teacher who worked hard at relating herself and her subject matter to her mixed section of 16 graduate and undergraduate students. Ten weeks into the semester, Lisa's hand-picked section seems to have gone well. Lisa knew her students individually, spent time outside of class with them, gave them her home phone number, and told them to call at any hour of the day or night if they needed help. She relied upon their good judgment not to abuse the privilege. One is immediately led to ask if this is a wise way to set up the learning contract, and if it is, what are the possible risks?

Lisa Wheelwright

Lisa Wheelwright was a 27-year-old fourth year doctoral student in the Religion Department at Heritage University. She had led discussion sections in the department's Scriptures and Classics course each year since she had arrived on campus. The course was organized around the "Great Books" of religious thought and was among the department's most popular offerings. Lisa had received "distinction" teaching certificates twice and "was considered particularly creative" in finding ways to relate current thinking with historical religious views. She was a woman of mixed Native American–European background with wide-ranging interests. Her doctoral work was focused upon Islamic studies, but the (B) case informs us that she was also interested in film making and had potential dissertation help from academic experts in both Israel and France. Her own sense of religious ideology apparently came less from fixed beliefs or background than from "a fascination with the worlds people create and the meanings they assign to life."

Truth, for Lisa, thus came from a variety of people's different perceptions, and not from any single dogma. For her, it was important to learn *both* the intellectual and emotional meanings of a topic area. Lisa tried to

Louis B. Barnes prepared this teaching note as an aid to instructors in classroom use of the case series "Bound Feet" (A) 9-491-028 and (B) 9-491-029.
(HBS No. 5-394-158)

walk that delicate line by encouraging intellectual topic discussions and also student (and her own) emotional involvement in those topics. She seemed to do well at it. The case adds that:

> Most students appreciated Lisa's insistence on drawing out their emotional reactions as well as their intellectual responses to the course material.

By valuing emotional impressions as well as intellectual ideas, Lisa created demands upon both herself and her students. Seeking a balance between the two, Lisa was temporarily overwhelmed when Meryl Dorsey, an outspoken 34-year-old graduate student, attacked the concept of the male chauvinist family assumptions found in a reading assignment on Confucianism. Lisa and the other students were at a loss as to how to deal with Meryl's outburst. It was a traumatic moment in class.

On the other hand, a reader can wonder if this kind of emotionalism is any worse than overly dull intellectualism at the other extreme. The problem becomes evident during the "Bound Feet" case which raises a number of other questions. For example, whose feet are really bound in this case in addition to those Chinese women of long ago? Meryl seems to be one. Lisa is also having problems putting her own intellectual and emotional life together around an acceptable thesis topic. Are their feet metaphorically bound by narrow-minded course contents and faculty members? Or by their needs to do things their own way? Is departmental tradition as binding as Lisa has been led to believe? Is too much energy going into Lisa's teaching and her students' learning? Indeed, Lisa wondered if her consuming commitment to classroom teaching had slowed down her dissertation progress, and there is some evidence that it had, as suggested in the (B) case.

At a more general level, when is emotionalism useful in the classroom, and when is it not? What if Meryl's outburst had come from a male student around the same or a different cause? And ultimately, what are the major differences between Meryl and Lisa anyway? In some ways they resemble each other in that each feels that she has come up against a rejecting, unresponsive system. They just deal with their perceptions differently.

A Possible Class Teaching Plan

Again, we typically ask two participants at the beginning of class to begin the case discussion. An open ended general question is one good way to begin. One possible question:

> In a few minutes, would each of you talk about the particular issues that interest you in the "Bound Feet" case?

Alternatively, an instructor might also find it interesting in this case to take an initial sounding on a more personal level by posing another question to the entire class. This question would ask participants to initially approach the case in ways that make either an emotional or an intellectual reply appropriate. Thus:

> Could we get a sampling of thoughts on this question? With whom do you most closely identify in the "Bound Feet" case in terms of your own interests and background? Lisa? Meryl? One or more of the other students? The course professor? The Religion Department? Why?

If your class contains both men and women students, some of them may identify initially with Meryl as rebels with justifiable causes. Others will identify with Lisa—a person who cares about individual student concerns in an often uncaring system. Still others may identify with other students who feel that they have to put up with domineering colleagues like Meryl. It may help to get those spokespersons identified early in the class so that you can return to them later as resource persons.

You can then go back to calling on the two beginning discussants who may well take sides on Lisa's actions as a teacher. Some people will argue that Lisa is too caring and too naive. Others will contend that she exemplifies many of their own values. They point out that Lisa's teaching has gone very well in the past and that Meryl's tantrum is a cry for help and the kind of wild card behavior that Lisa needs to rationally deal with in slow motion, not by overreacting in class. Further discussion may also bring up questions of teacher control and how important this is to different people in the class. Is the class getting away from Lisa? If so, is it her own fault for not creating appropriate boundaries? What are those boundaries anyway?

There will almost inevitably be different opinions on the balance issue of intellectual vs. emotional learning. To what extent does an instructor encourage—or want to encourage—one without the other in a higher education classroom? Some participants will say that it should depend upon subject matter, course level, faculty agenda, class size, or the topic at hand. Others will assert that you never want one without the other. One issue worth discussing is what Lisa has done explicitly to create the learning contract as it exists. Has she indeed set the stage for the kind of emotional dynamics we find in the particular incident described in the case? How would each of us do this differently? Or wouldn't we?

In addition to participants trying to tease out some causes of the incident, it is useful to discuss Lisa's handling of Meryl's tirade. Lisa deliberately tried to remain analytically cool, going almost to the other extreme of Meryl's emotionalism. She focused upon the textual issues and depersonalized the attack by trying to "control herself" and willed "herself to stay calm and not appear defensive," avoided "jerky movements," and "forced herself to keep leaning forward (while) nodding at Meryl." But meanwhile, Lisa was thinking:

> . . . oh my God, I've got to stop her. I've got to get the class back. I don't want to subject the other students to this (and) . . . I've got to help her. I've got to bring her back. If I can't get through to her now, I will lose her trust, her participation, her vote of solidarity forever. And if I don't do it right, I may lose some of the other students too.

That is a great burden for the young instructor to take upon her own shoulders. It is worth pondering these fears and judging the extent to which they seem reasonable to participants. Some will point out that Lisa is demanding too much of herself and needs to trust other class members and the discussion dynamics more. Others will be annoyed by Meryl's behavior and suggest that she is living a charade. They may argue that her anger in class is only surface anger covering up other problems—e.g., a recent breakup with a man, rebelling against her own father, an impending career change, her own denial of aging, and her needs to be an authority as one of the older members of the class.

But what about Lisa's responses to Meryl's anger? Lisa chooses *not* to respond to Meryl's emotion, even though she publicly declared that she wanted emotional reactions to be part of the learning process. Instead Lisa made four relatively rational comments. Each dealt more with the historical text and meaning than with Meryl. Only the last one directly contradicts Meryl's assertions. It's worth asking participants if they would respond to Meryl in a similar intellectual fashion. Or is Lisa missing an opportunity to explore the powerful emotional issue of women's status in most or all religious movements? Lisa's actual responses to Meryl are:

1. "Well now, wait a minute. You're getting at a very interesting problem here. I mean the status of women in the Confucian society."
2. "Not included at all?"
3. "But Meryl, do you find that in the text at all?"
4. "Meryl, are you sure that Confucianism required foot binding? I mean, did you know that Confucianism began in the 6th century BCE, and that foot binding only began around the 12th century CE under the Sung dynasty?"

Several other questions emerge from the "Bound Feet" case and are worth raising, though one's responses may well vary from situation to situation. For example:

- How does an instructor know when an "attack" is intended as a (sometimes thinly veiled) personal attack? How does he/she deal with such an assault? In the classroom? Outside of it? By questioning? Responding to the person at the personal level? At a total class level?
- How does one *not* appear to be defensive? (Sometimes our nonverbal signals give us away, even when we try to appear rational.)
- When does a teacher abandon the class plan in the face of forces and emotions beyond, though sometimes related to, that plan?
- What is your own position with regard to such out-of-class practices as:
  - Office hour appointments?
  - Home phone numbers and out-of-class availability?
  - The blurring of other traditional boundaries between teacher and students?

The (B) Case

We tend to hand out the one and one-half page (B) case about a half hour before the end of class. There are several new issues and questions that appear in it. The case begins with another more forceful statement by Lisa:

> Meryl, this is an extremely important issue, but I don't feel that we're getting at it well this way. If we don't look at a specific passage, or discuss it in its wider historical context, I don't know if we're doing it justice. . . .

Meryl acquiesces, rests her head upon one hand, and motions with the other hand for the group to go ahead. It does, and Meryl's tantrum disappears during the rest of the class hour. But why? Was her anger simply a tempest in a teapot? Was Meryl indeed simply playing the angry feminist role for a new audience? Was Lisa's authority over, or respect from, Meryl that complete?

In addition, there are several other specific questions for discussion:

- How should Lisa deal with Meryl's latest paper, a "cogent, creative, and very well written" repeat of Meryl's outburst in class? From Lisa's point of view, Meryl had not done the assignment. Lisa felt that if she assigned Meryl a poor grade "Meryl would be lost in her anger, never to be brought back to the intellectual work of the class." Would she really be lost in her anger? Should Meryl be asked to rewrite the paper (which is what Lisa actually did)? Or would that be too much of a compromise on Lisa's part?
- One more subtle question to raise at this point is, how does Lisa's own situation resemble Meryl's? And even if the situations are similar in that both have come up against inflexible institutions, what do you think of the two women's very different responses? Meryl strikes out in anger, but in safe territory, and then retreats. Lisa says that "I just turn my anger on myself" and contemplates withdrawal. Neither one has yet figured out how to directly confront the awesome powers that be. Should they?
- As a friend or advisor to Lisa Wheelwright, how would you respond to her request for guidance?

Postscript

Lisa did not withdraw from the doctoral program, but in some discouragement, she did go to Israel for the year. There she continued to get encouragement for her ideas. She returned to Heritage the following year, now determined to finish her dissertation. During that year, she taught another section of the Scriptures and Classics course and applied for a fellowship which would permit her to work at the Sorbonne with the French educator who had previously been so supportive of her ideas. Lisa did get the fellowship, returned a year later and completed her dissertation, but now with considerable support within her own department. She then found a teaching position in a highly respected university known for its excellence in teaching. At the same time, she still wanted "someday" to take courses on film making.

Class on World Hunger (A) and (B)

TEACHING NOTE

Students in the "Class on World Hunger" confront their instructor with an in-class prank. Central questions are: How can an instructor maintain authority without stifling students' initiative and voluntary contributions in the classroom? And when the instructor's authority is challenged by student behavior (for example, by tardiness or pranks), how might he or she respond to that situation?

The (B) case describes the instructor's philosophy of case education and how it has been shaped by his experiences. We sometimes ask participants to contrast it with "Ernie Budding (D)," another reflective piece. This discussion can be particularly useful in helping seminar members review, integrate, and elaborate upon their own evolving thoughts about case teaching.

"Class on World Hunger" is a richly detailed case which provides a rare opportunity to enter into the experience of a talented newcomer to the case method and to share his insights. We find it helpful to warn participants to allow plenty of preparation time, as the case text is relatively long and "Ernie Budding (D)" may also be used in this seminar session.

A Suggested Process Plan for the Case

We want the seminar group to consider closely how Clarkson responded to the prank. We especially want participants to appreciate that Clarkson made an active, considered response; he faced up to the situation constructively. In addition, we want them to appreciate that pranks seldom "just happen." Though the food fight could probably not have been predicted, several identifiable factors might have alerted the instructor that the section was ripe for a prank.

We ordinarily hand out and discuss both the (A) and (B) cases at the same time. In a 90-minute session, we typically begin by asking the seminar members to examine the case, gradually focusing more and more closely on Clarkson's series of actions. We generally spend about 30 minutes on this tack. Question 1 asks participants to give a comprehensive interpretation of the case, centering their remarks on an evaluation of Clarkson's response to the prank. Question 2 directs the seminar to a closer analysis of Clarkson's response. Together, these two questions require participants to integrate analysis, action planning, and generalization in their comments.

During the final 30 minutes of the session we raise the level of generality. Our questions direct participants to consider the role of the instructor in case teaching. They are asked to compare and contrast their own approaches with those of Bob Clarkson. In some instances, we also ask seminar members to con-

This teaching note was written by James Moore as an aid to instructors in the classroom use of the case series "Class on World Hunger" (A) 9-381-042 and (B) 9-381-043.
(HBS No. 5-384-046)

trast Clarkson's philosophy with that of Ernie Budding. The resulting dialogue usually provides participants with a valued opportunity to consider their own educational philosophy in light of both "Class on World Hunger" and their wider experience.

Notes for Discussion Questions

These notes parallel the suggested discussion questions presented in Exhibit 2. We briefly indicate the pedagogical intent and use of each question and provide our best attempt at a reasoned response. These analytical responses are intended primarily to sensitize the instructor to key issues when preparing for the discussion. They represent our current thinking on the questions raised by the case, not definitive solutions.

The following questions refer primarily to the (A) case:

1. *How well, in your opinion, did Bob Clarkson handle the problem? What is the worst thing he could have done?*

Usage Note

By asking seminar members to evaluate Clarkson's action, this question accomplishes several things. First, it focuses attention on the fact that he was not simply passive but made an intentional response to the prank. Moreover, by asking participants to speculate as to the worst thing he could have done, it helps them appreciate the range of possible actions and/or unplanned reactions. In addition, this question asks seminar members to examine the impact of Clarkson's responses. Third, it requires them to take an evaluative stand, making a comparison between their own approaches and Clarkson's.

Analysis

Seminar members vary in their evaluations of Clarkson's intervention, although most see his actions in a favorable light. (After all, it is clear from the case that the situation turned out well.) Clarkson has rolled with the prank itself, maintaining rapport with the section and playing along with the comedy by exaggerating his own perplexity. Then he invited section members who were not involved in (or particularly supportive of) the prank to join him in reestablishing the class as a serious discussion session. Once these members began to speak, Clarkson supported case-related contributions by calling on only those students likely to make good contributions, and by using his end-of-class summary to reward those who were most helpful.

It seems likely that the prank was primarily an expression of the section's need, at that point in the semester, to let off steam. If so, Clarkson's action was probably effective in allowing the release of tension. Had he tried to suppress their actions, he could easily have created more tension, and thus further trouble later in the session and term.

The prank was perhaps also an initiation rite for Clarkson—simultaneously an expression of students' affection for him and an attempt to get him to loosen up and become socially more "one of them." In this case, Clarkson appears to have succeeded in demonstrating that he can take a joke and even contribute to the fun. Although he may feel that his role as instructor makes it inappropriate for him to socialize with students, he has shown that he is not simply standoffish. In contrast, it might have been disastrous to become angry and lecture them about the prank. This would have been a rejection of the implicit offer of friendship in the prank, and would have established Clarkson as manifestly not "one of them"—possibly creating a seriously alienated student-teacher relationship.

On the other hand, Clarkson did not let the prank usurp his overall agenda for the day, for he clearly did not want to send the message that class could be sacrificed whenever the section felt more like playing. Moreover, to cancel the session would not have been fair to the students who had prepared for class and wanted to have a discussion, both as an opportunity to raise their grades and as the substantive basis for the rest of the course. Even the pranksters probably did not want the class canceled. Cancellation might make many of them feel guilty about the impact on their sectionmates (who might very well be angry with the disrupters), awkward about having created more of a stir than was intended, and upset—in retrospect—at missing out on a case discussion that played a crucial role in the course.

Clarkson chose an effective means of bringing the section back to its academic priorities. In essence he allowed the students to do most of the work of reestablishing order. He called on those who seemed to want to make a serious contribution, and worked with them to create a case discussion in which the others joined.

In our experience this response is very often the best way for an instructor to recover from challenges to his or her authority—whether the challenges are basically friendly, as in Clarkson's situation, or more hostile. When some members of a group attack or undermine the leader, there are almost always others who, if given an opportunity, will come to his or her aid. Because this support is normally freely given, the best way to mobilize it is often simply to make an opportunity for students to express it. Clarkson did this by simply asking, "Can anyone suggest where we can go from here?" and then calling on students who he thought would support a reestablishment of the conventional norms of the classroom, including his own authority.

2. *What precisely did he do? What specific aspects of his response do you believe were most helpful? Why?*

Usage Note

This question moves the seminar to a more detailed consideration of Bob Clarkson's response, and helps illuminate the specific series of actions Bob took—each of which contributed to its effectiveness.

Analysis

Clarkson retreats behind his desk to assess the situation. This was his first effective move, for it gave him time to determine whether the prank was orchestrated (he concluded it was), to experience his initial reactions (shock and surprise, fear about how the incident would look to outsiders, and repugnance at the moral symbolism), and to consider his options and decide how to respond (suppress his anger and magnify his shock, while maintaining rapport with the students).

When he came out from behind the desk, Clarkson appeared stunned—taking an honest response, exaggerating it, and thus making it comic. This got a laugh, and created rapport with the section. The friendly laughter also reassured Clarkson that the section was not hostile. Appearing stunned and perplexed also bought more time, for this role did not require him to direct the events.

Clarkson then played into the joke even more by asking, "Is it safe to come out now?" and getting another laugh. At this point he noted that it felt like a fraternity setting—and indeed this sense may have reflected accurately that he had passed his initiation and moved into a new level of emotional acceptance by the section.

The initiation accomplished, Clarkson still had to decide where to go next. He chose to share his uncertainty—an approach that might seem risky to instructors who equate leadership with a constant facade of assurance. However, Clarkson appears to have made the admission with a certain humorous quality, even conveying a sense that he shared the section's enjoyment of his own discomfiture. Instead of seeming defensive, he was able to retain his authority while deepening his rapport with the section by being honest with them.

Clarkson then looked around carefully, observing individuals. This had the effect of creating even more rapport and contact between instructor and students. Moreover, he noticed that the section was not monolithic in support of the prank, and that several students looked quite concerned. Reaching out to these individuals, he asked, "Can someone suggest where we should go from here?" This appeal mobilized their support, and hands shot up.

Finally, Clarkson was very careful in choosing students to call on. Had he recognized one of the jokers—for example, Jack Law or Amanda Brown—the disruption might have continued. But Clarkson picked Elliott Farmer, a student who appeared prepared and motivated to do well.

Elliott performed beautifully, which helped immensely. By laying out the case in detail, and giving a very clear first analysis, Elliott made it possible for students who were not prepared at least to understand the core of the case. Later in the class they even contributed. Moreover, by taking fifteen minutes, Elliott gave both the class and Clarkson time to settle down. Even if Elliott had not done so well, however, Clarkson could probably have made the discussion work. All he needed was a few serious contributions—not necessarily brilliant—to set the tone for effective discussion.

After Elliott finished, Clarkson continued to lead the discussion. He was careful not to call on Jack Law—and presumably others who were involved in the prank—until they seemed ready to make serious contributions. At the close of the class Clarkson suppressed an urge to comment on the incident. Instead he complimented Elliott and two others on their contributions, thus reinforcing the classroom norms.

Overall, Clarkson managed to go along with the prank and be seen as a "good guy" who can take a joke—while remaining steadfast in communicating the importance of the central task of the section: case analysis and discussion.

3. *Could Bob Clarkson have anticipated this incident? If so, how and when? Could he have prepared for it? How?*

Usage Note

This query shifts attention from Clarkson to the section, asking participants to consider the factors that made the section ripe for a prank, and to identify observations that Clarkson might have interpreted as signs of this condition. Further, it encourages participants to consider what can be done with such information before a prank actually occurs.

Analysis

It seems unlikely that Bob Clarkson could have predicted the specific incident. A more experienced instructor, however, might have sensed a risk that the section would come up with something along these lines. Pressure had been high on the section, and no end was in sight. Students had recently learned to enjoy playing together in organized ways—for example, in baseball and the class play—and a prank is another expression of this capability. The highly successful (and highly humorous) class play had just been presented; now, on a pleasant Friday afternoon, many students are in a spirited and frivolous mood. Finally, Clarkson—who is about the same age as many of the students—has spurned several of their invitations for more informal contact. The students may be looking for a way to break through his formal manner and test his ability to "come down to their level." These factors, which are likely to be raised at this point in the discussion, are examined in more detail later.

Clarkson might have paid attention to two sorts of signals. First, the section had been trying to involve him in its social life. These overtures may be seen as friendly attempts to rewrite the instructor-student learning contract. While Clarkson may feel he is most effective when he maintains a relatively formal relationship with the section, he should probably respond to these student initiatives for change by attending carefully to the contract issues at this time. It might have been helpful to discuss the situation informally with students, to get a better sense of their perceptions of the contract, and the nature and strength of their interest in changing it. Clarkson might thus have become better able to decide what contract he wanted to work toward, and how to go about getting it.

Second, in the days before the prank, Clarkson might have noticed the frivolous mood of some students and their increasing capacity for enjoyment of organized play. Had he attended to the signals offered by Amanda (and probably others), he might have modified his teaching plan; to capitalize on students' desire to work together, for example, he might have asked small groups to prepare for joint in-class presentations. Or he might have put their desire for group games to work in the classroom by asking two groups of students to argue against each other on some point, and then asking the remaining students to vote on which group was more convincing.

Before class began, Ian tried to warn Clarkson of the impending prank. Had he probed Ian's oblique statement a bit farther, he might have learned of the prank. Even so, Clarkson would have had only moments to prepare, and there are limits to what he could do. His best bet might have been simply to go along with the plan, feigning ignorance—but with the advantage of having a few moments to consider possible responses and to brace for the shock.

4. ***Why are pranks such a recurring phenomenon, especially in professional schools?***

Usage Note

This question leads the seminar to begin actively generalizing from the case, if it is not already doing so.

Analysis

Prank-prone schools and organizations often put members under a great deal of pressure to work hard and perform on demand, and the students look for release. Pranks are exciting, diverting, and great releasers of tension. In addition, the infantilizing effect of highly structured educational programs can be quite irritating to people who are used to more autonomy. Pranks may reflect both students' hostility to their condition of formal powerlessness and their desire to demonstrate their own informal sources of power and autonomy.

Finally, students often chafe at the rigidity with which they are cast in a student role, while others, who may be their own age or younger, are cast as instructors. Student pranks serve to remind instructors that they are human and not gods—and give everyone a few precious moments to experience each other out of role. An instructor who responds to the prank favorably demonstrates that he or she is a "regular person." The experience then can lead to a much deeper bond between instructor and students. In many cases the experience is tantamount to initiating the instructor as an honorary member of the section tribe.

The following questions refer to the (B) case:

5. ***What do you think of Bob Clarkson's philosophy of education? What do you see as the instructor's primary role in a case discussion?***

6. ***In the earlier case, Ernie Budding argues for an interventionistic style of discussion leadership which seems to contrast with Bob Clarkson's "discussion pastures" approach. How would you characterize your own position, vis-à-vis theirs?***

Usage Note

These questions require participants to articulate the educational philosophies of Bob Clarkson and Ernie Budding, to evaluate them, and to compare them with their own ways of thinking about teaching.

All participants are encouraged to read "Ernie Budding (D)" in preparation for class. However, it is optimistic to assume that all participants will do so. Therefore, we often ask two or three participants to prepare for the day by rereading "Ernie Budding (D)." Seeding the section's memory in this way helps ensure a good discussion.

We have combined our analytical notes for Questions 5 and 6.

Analysis

The contrast between Ernie Budding's and Bob Clarkson's educational philosophies may be best summed up in their respective metaphors of teaching. Ernie speaks of "conceptual blocks" of material to be covered in each discussion. He specifies for himself not only the overall content to be taught in his course, but the subordinate topics to be covered in each class period. He organizes these in a logical sequence, creating building blocks of content. He prepares for class very much as one might for a lecture.

In his first year of teaching, Ernie uses sequences of rather closed-ended questions to get the section to consider the major points in his blocks. He asks students to supply key case facts and insights at a relatively low level of generality. After the experiences described in the "Ernie Budding (A), (B), and (C)" cases, Ernie opens up his questioning, and allows more student-initiated discussion. Rather than leading the students through the blocks in a predetermined sequence, Ernie now allows them to raise issues in any order that makes sense within the context of the day's discussion. Even in the (D) case, however, Ernie still sees his course as a series of topics that students must master. The cases are vehicles for bringing these topics to the attention of the students, and for giving them practice in applying key concepts to real situations. Under his ground rules, student excitement comes primarily from the progressive mastery of powerful concepts.

Clarkson, by contrast, uses the metaphor of "discussion pastures" and sees the instructor as a shepherd "policing the fences"—moving his "grazing students" to a new area whenever a particular pasture becomes overworked. The cases provide the "fodder" which students digest to produce insights. These insights may be very much like Ernie Budding's "conceptual blocks." In Bob Clarkson's class, however, generalizations are more likely to be introduced by the students, and may well differ from the concepts Clarkson would have drawn out of the same cases. Clarkson does exercise some leadership in guiding students toward particular ideas. But he appears to put more emphasis on the richness and complexity of the cases, and on student generation of insights, than does Ernie Budding.

We believe a course should be supported by an overall conceptual scheme. Moreover, the instructor should consider the most effective order in which to present key concepts. Cases, readings, and other materials should be carefully chosen to introduce and allow the students to explore these concepts. In this sense Ernie Budding is on the right track.

However, we also think it is important that students learn to appreciate the complexity of situations, and to recognize that any situation is richer and more mysterious than the concepts that may be used to explain it. Moreover, history makes it clear that, in any field of knowledge, today's useful concepts will eventually be superseded by others. Thus we must help the students to use our concepts as starting points, rather than as conclusions. To this end, we believe, it is essential that students learn to produce, value, and use their own insights.

Thus we see the discussion class as a workshop in which students can get involved in the raw materials of cases and, under our increasingly light-handed guidance, learn to create usable, action-relevant insights. In this sense, we lean toward Clarkson's approach of grazing in "discussion pastures." We have found, however, that it is also important to incorporate elements of Ernie Budding's teaching style. An instructor must understand the conceptual structure of his or her subject and at times may need to focus student attention on key concepts—teaching, in the conventional sense, a point.

However, too much teaching of this kind can encourage students to put too much confidence in the particular models presented—to their future detriment. More important, it can prevent them from testing out and developing their own capacities for understanding and insight. Thus we believe that the most appropriate role for the instructor is often to manage the discussion process—to "police the fences," as Clarkson puts it.

Clarkson's and Budding's views differ in other interesting ways. Ernie stresses the importance of "rigor"—and what he seems to mean by the term is that students should learn to pay attention to and account for the facts in the case. That is, as their education progresses, their views should become increasingly grounded in the particulars of situations. This seems to us an important goal. Clarkson's primary concern, in contrast, seems to be creating enthusiasm about the course questions. He describes the ideal instructor as being "tinder for discovery." He tries to create rapport with the students, presumably so that they can experience together the excitement of solving the conundrums presented in the cases—and, by extension, in the professional world.

Both rigor and enthusiasm are needed for a successful case learning experience. Without enthusiasm, the student's rigor will be hollow and pointless. Without rigor, enthusiasm may simply generate a lot of half-baked ideas. However, we would define rigor somewhat more broadly than Ernie does. Rigorous work by students involves developing a logical and plausible understanding of business situations that is based on the facts of the situations and is chosen after an examination of alternative interpretations. Moreover, the understanding they adopt must be considered in light of their implications for action. Commitment to a perspective involves not only accepting a particular view of a situation, but also deciding on a course of action. And finally, the students should attempt to "feel into" these actions, to get a sense of whether they could really live with the decision.

Good teaching, then, combines rigor and enthusiasm. Perhaps significantly, the "Class on World Hunger (B)" case concludes with Clarkson wondering, "How do you uphold the standards of your school and the intellectual enterprise without becoming obnoxiously authoritarian so that you destroy or interrupt a delicate rapport?" It may be that Clarkson sensed a conflict between standards and rapport because he took too narrow a view of rigor, without reference to what the students need and value. In our view rigor is not something an instructor insists upon because it upholds some abstract standards, but rather a means of helping students generate better, more usable ideas. This goal is one that students understand and appreciate, and can become enthusiastic about.

At the outset of their teaching careers, Ernie Budding and Bob Clarkson have radically different views of the instructor-student learning contract, but they move closer together after two years' experience. Ernie originally tries hard to maintain a consistent and relatively explicit contract with the students. Sticking with his contract—particularly the formal aspects—seems to be a matter of pride. For example, he promises students that his grades will be based on the quality of class comments rather than the quantity, and takes some satisfaction in the students' shock when he carries through consistently. Ernie also gets into difficulty because he does not notice when his contract no longer fits the students' evolving situation. At the end of the "Ernie Budding" case sequence, he recognizes the need to modify contracts to match the students' needs.

Bob Clarkson, in contrast, starts his teaching career feeling insecure about his ability to maintain authority. He deliberately introduces uncertainty in his behavior, and thus in his contract, with the students as a means of strengthening his control. After some experience with the effects of this strategy, he comes to feel students are better served by more consistency in their instructor.

Interestingly, both instructors seem to be developing a more situationally based understanding of their teaching. Clarkson describes the importance of rapport. Though for him this seems to be largely a matter of enthusiasm and emotional closeness, good rapport inevitably gives him a more detailed understanding of his section's learning process at any given moment. It is likely to enable him to adjust his contract with them more sensitively. Budding explicitly recognizes the need to become more attuned to his section, so as to be able to shift his contract as the students grow and change.

EXHIBIT 1 *Class on World Hunger*

Study Questions

For student use when reading the (A) case:

1. How did Bob Clarkson handle the food fight? What is the worst thing he might have done? Why did his response work out well from both his point of view and from the point of view of many of the members of the class?

—◆—

For student use when reading the (B) case:

1. Why are pranks a recurring phenomenon in many educational and organizational settings? Can their occurrence be predicted by an instructor? What dangers and opportunities do they present to you, as a section instructor?
2. What do you see as the critical elements in Bob Clarkson's teaching philosophy? In what key dimensions, if any, did it differ from Ernie Budding's? Your own?

EXHIBIT 2 *Class on World Hunger*

Discussion Questions

The following questions refer primarily to the (A) case:

1. How well, in your opinion, did Bob Clarkson handle the problem? What is the worst thing he could have done?
2. What precisely did he do? What particular aspects of his response do you believe were most helpful? Why?
3. Could Bob Clarkson have anticipated this incident? If so, how and when? Could he have prepared for it? How?
4. Why are pranks a recurring phenomenon especially in professional schools?

—◆—

The following questions refer to the (B) case:

5. What do you think of Bob Clarkson's philosophy of education? What do you see as the instructor's primary role in a case discussion?
6. In the earlier case, Ernie Budding argues for an interventionistic style of discussion leadership which seems to contrast with Bob Clarkson's "discussion pastures" approach. How would you characterize your own position, vis-à-vis theirs?

That Discussion Just Fell Apart

TEACHING NOTE

Introduction

We've all been there! When discussions die, the most natural tendency, of course, is to ask, "What did I do?" The second tendency is to ask, "What did they not do?" and then get angry at something. Discussions fall apart for a variety of reasons—some never get off the ground, others bog down in midstream and die an anguished death, or we as teachers somehow suffer an acute foot (or words) in mouth problem that kills all further conversation. In "That Discussion Just Fell Apart," Frank Taylor joins the rest of us who have lived through, but never fully understood, the prolonged agony of such sessions.

In this case, it is hard to put blame on an incompetent teacher or a section of students with poor discussion habits. Frank Taylor was apparently a strong candidate for tenure, had carefully prepared his teaching plans, had a reputation for high standards, enjoyed a strong and cooperative section of students, and didn't seem to have had this problem very often. He had a good idea of the section subgroups, recognized individual strengths and weaknesses in his students, and carefully considered who he would call on first.

However, there were three warning flags at the beginning of the discussion. One was the case itself, Addison Meats, which had apparently gone poorly for Frank the previous year. We don't know how other Corporate Strategic Planning instructors taught it in the past, but Addison Meats may have been one of those cases that almost no one could teach well. Under those conditions, almost any instructor would have been pleased to have a Neil Hafner burst into the classroom full of enthusiasm for the case and the issues it raises. Unfortunately, the presumed advantage turned out to be more swamp than springboard for Frank Taylor. Neil Hafner helped more to push the case into the ground than to lift it into the air.

The second warning sign was Neil Hafner's appearance in class with his senior honors thesis, *Economic Analysis of the Meat Processing Industry.* Like a warrior trying to refight old battles, Neil seemed determined to live in the thesis past, not the classroom present. From an academic family, a keeper of copious class notes, and with "inklings of high quality" in his class work, Neil might have provided a good set of initial case comments if it hadn't been for his determination to relive early triumphs as a thesis writer on the meat industry. Like all too many professors with old lecture notes, Neil launched into an apparent rerun of his thesis—and eventually lost the class, even if Frank hadn't.

The third warning flag showed up in the early moments of Neil Hafner's behavior, too late to undo the

Louis B. Barnes prepared this teaching note as an aid to instructors in classroom use of the case series "That Discussion Just Fell Apart" No. 9-383-039.
(HBS No. 5-394-159)

first call, but not too late for Frank Taylor to begin thinking how he would handle this runaway train to nowhere. Neil's initial enthusiasm for the case was surprising in light of his earlier "tentative and diffident" behavior in class. The student who frequently apologized for the relevance and quality of his good in-class comments now seemed ready to take over the spotlight. That concern was intensified when Neil turned to his section mates with a smoothing wave of his hand and said, "Okay—sit back. I've got this in hand." There was a subdued moan and an undercurrent of "Oh, no . . ."

From then on, it almost appeared to be out of Frank Taylor's control. Possibly it was.

The Teaching Issues

The early warning signals Frank Taylor *recognized but did not act on* may be present in most cases when discussions fall apart. The early warning topic is worth some exploration, and one way to start is to draw a sample of experiences from class participants. Assuming that almost all of us have had surprisingly dull classes at one time or another—classes that can then turn mean-spirited—it is interesting to explore the question of early warning flags that participants experience. What kinds of signals have they seen? What do they do when they see them, and when do we assume that the die is cast beyond our control? Frank Taylor seemed to draw this fatalistic conclusion several times during Neil Hafner's prolonged introduction.

> I was beginning to wonder: How can I suppress this fellow? Should I suppress him when I've never seen him so enthusiastic?

And:

> Neil's disquisition must have lasted a minimum of twenty minutes: it seemed like an eternity. When he finally stopped, the discussion began.

Should Frank have been more blunt in closing down Neil's lengthy discourse? Did kindness end up being cruelty for everyone else in this class? Neil's reputation is probably indelibly established, and not necessarily in ways that he would have chosen. Should Frank Taylor have acted sooner and chosen another speaker to open up the discussion? Given Neil's enthusiasm to participate, that might have been only a temporary stopgap, as Frank discovered later when Neil burst into the discussion uninvited.

Another general teaching issue in this case involves just what do *we* do when a discussion is on its way downhill? After all, the discussion methods teacher is at the mercy of the students he or she calls on to move the discussion forward. The question of what participants do in their own classes is another possible opener, to be raised before getting into the details of this case, but it *can* be raised in reference to this case—something like this:

> This doesn't seem to be a very exciting case on the surface of it. There are no great crisis events or immediate choices that need to be made. How would you keep the discussion from dying during the next minutes? Where would you start and what would you do?

A major issue for discussion in this case is not just the demise of the discussion, but the handling of verbose or irritating students along the way. Neil Hafner fell into the first category, and Gary, "one of the more contentious section members," fell into the second. Some participants will be highly critical of Frank Taylor for not putting a tighter rein on Neil. At the very least, it might have been worth a conversation with Neil afterwards, for he may have seriously tarnished his section reputation on this day. Neil also preempted and prevented inclusion of another discussion topic later in the class by stage whispering some postdate information into the dialogue. And finally, he used data to make another point that could not have been made using only case data. No wonder Taylor was annoyed.

Another discussion track was closed off by Gary's flippant rejection of Elliot's numbers and Neil's presentation. As Gary said:

> I don't know where in the world you got those numbers, Elliot. They're cockeyed—totally off the wall—and won't help us one bit. And furthermore, Neil's last argument just didn't make any sense at all.

But Gary wasn't helping either. Frank Taylor states that he didn't see any hands raised at this point, but he apparently didn't choose to call Gary's bluff either. The one block of students that Frank may have failed to utilize well were those whom he called the "contentious group whose members not only argued, but usually presented their points unpleasantly." Gary certainly fit that description, but it might have been an occasion for lively discussion if Frank had asked Gary to give more specific comments and then had gotten a rebuttal from Elliot or counterchallenges from other students. Sometimes it is the contentious students who breathe life into an otherwise dormant class.

The issue here is, How does the instructor jumpstart the discussion again once it is on its way downhill?

Challenging Gary or closing off Neil earlier might have provided two such opportunities. It might be useful to ask the participants if they see any others. There are several possibilities.

- The point where Frank noticed "a good bit of paper rustling and faces were registering boredom" might have been a place where Frank could have called "time out" and asked for comments on what Neil had presented thus far.
- Frank might have taken the same step toward someone else when he noticed that several hands were up. Rather than interrupting Neil *and then asking him to go on with an action plan,* Frank might have asked another student that question. Neil had already gone on too long.
- Frank mentions that he "had spent an extraordinary amount of time in preparing this case and knew it cold, its strengths, and imperfections." He also notes that he had divided his teaching plan into four blocks or modules of attention. It appears, however, that Neil's introduction threw Frank's teaching plan out the window. At some point, did Frank ever try to catch up, or revise his plan? There's no evidence that he did so.
- "Worse, the section simply didn't seem to be listening," notes Frank after the discussion began to bog down. But why? This was the group that Frank described as "displaying a quality he valued highly: the students listened to each other." What had pulled them off track on this particular day? Possibly Neil's boring beginnings had made them tune out for the day. Frank responded by asking questions that were increasingly pointed and directive, but these may have been punishment enough. Given his diagnosis of uncharacteristic section deafness, Frank might have come in more strongly at another level and wondered aloud what people were hearing others say.
- Frank sensed an air of growing hostility as the discussion went on and contributions became too vague and too general. As the clock crept toward the 9:50 closing time, Frank had the option of ending the discussion as he did with hopes "that tomorrow's discussion would be better," or he might have stopped the discussion ten minutes early and asked why it had gone so poorly—at least in his judgment. That may sound like a high-risk strategy, but it seems clear that the discussion was not going to be salvaged in the last few minutes. A better prelude for tomorrow might involve getting today's problems cleared up today.

A Teaching Plan

As noted above, our inclination would be to begin this class by tapping into the similar experiences of class participants—almost all of whom will have had these same difficulties in their own classrooms. How have they faced such events, and how did they deal with them? The bridge from their own episodes to Frank Taylor's will probably be a short one. We would then tend to examine the theme of early warning signals, as the discussion moved from their own experiences to those of Frank Taylor and his students in Section A.

Then the question of what else Frank might have done comes up. What might he have done at several places mentioned earlier in this note? How might he have taken these different steps? Finally, what, if anything, might Frank have done *after* the class was over? It might be a fitting time for Frank to get some indications from students on what bogged the class down during the Addison Meats case. Our speculations in this note, and during the discussion class, might be on target, but there are all kinds of other reasons that discussions die. The section may have had a day of hard assignments; they may have had a tough exam in another course, or be studying for one; there might have been a mid-term slump on its way; or they may have attended an earlier class where things had gone badly. In general, instructors sometimes take too narrow a look at the causes of a poor class. It is worth trying to explore the wider context of student life as well.

Finally, a teaching plan for this case might prompt the instructor at some point to ask what had, or had not, turned this class into or away from a discussion that did or did not fall apart. What could participants learn from this discussion as well as from each other about other classes and other students?

We're Just Wasting Our Time

TEACHING NOTE

"We're Just Wasting Our Time" is a case that concerns a nearly universal problem in teaching: how to deal with apathy and students' failure to prepare for class. In addition, it highlights the difficulty of accurately "reading" a section so as to stay in touch with its process of learning and development.

Some Thoughts on Study and Discussion Questions

Typically we prepare at least two sets of questions for use with each case. The first consists of study questions (see **Exhibit 1**); these can be handed out with the case for participants' use in preparing for class. The second set is a series of discussion questions (see **Exhibit 2**), to be used by the seminar leader in preparing for the case discussion and in guiding the case discussion when appropriate. For all discussion questions, but not for study questions, we have provided detailed usage and analytical notes.

A Suggested Process Plan for the Case

In discussing this case, we emphasize ways to deal with classroom apathy and lack of preparation. We ordinarily combine a standard case discussion (developing diagnoses, action plans, and conclusions/generalizations) with a working session on how to increase classroom involvement and student preparation.

In the working session, we first raise the issues, then ask participants to think about the underlying causes of these problems and to suggest ways to deal with them. The working-session approach is particularly valuable because apathy and lack of preparation are among the most perplexing and complex difficulties instructors face. Moreover, most participants have directly experienced these difficulties and have already given them serious thought.

Our first question, "From your experience as a student, why don't students prepare?" and our third question, "What questions does this case raise for you?" encourage seminar members to define the issues presented by the case. Typically, a cluster of concerns will be raised, all related to the general topics on involvement and student preparation. Opening the session with these concerns stimulates participants to generalize from the case and consider their own experiences, thus setting the stage for the later working session.

The effect of these opening questions is also to make the case itself somewhat less central than it is in most discussions. Instead of being an all-important, perplexing mystery, this case is made subordinate to

---

James Moore prepared this teaching note as an aid to instructors in the classroom use of the case "We're Just Wasting Our Time" No. 9-378-035.
(HBS No. 5-384-048)

Distributed by HBS Publishing Division, Harvard Business School, Boston, MA 02163.
Printed in U.S.A.

the complexity of the participants' own experiences with similar problems.

After this initial foray into generalization, we use Questions 2, 4, 5, and 6 to move the seminar's attention to the case situation. Our overall plan is first to examine the facts of the situation, and then to highlight the professor's understanding of it. We then move to a consideration of the section's perspective, building up to a discussion of why its understanding of the situation is so different from Rowe's.

We hope in this discussion not only to emphasize the complexity of the situation facing Rowe, but also to suggest that most instances of sustained apathy and lack of preparation involve a mesh of intertwined factors that are difficult to understand. We underscore the risks of jumping to conclusions, as well as the need to create ways to "listen in" on the learning process of one's sections.

Questions 7 and 8 move the seminar to an examination of Rowe's actions, and thus set the stage for a discussion of both tactics appropriate to his particular situation and more general approaches to dealing with apathy and lack of participation. The seminar often moves into what we have called the working-session mode at this point. Questions 9 and 10 then encourage a broad discussion of means for creating involvement at the section level.

Notes for Discussion Questions

We have briefly indicated the pedagogical intent and use of the suggested discussion question in **Exhibit 2**. These notes are provided to aid the instructor in preparing for class and are intended to sensitize him or her to key issues in the case. The responses represent our current thinking on the questions raised by the case—not a definitive solution.

1. From you own experience as a student, what are some of the reasons that people don't prepare for class sessions?

Usage Note

This opening question asks participants to probe their own experiences, thus identifying more deeply with the students in the case and perhaps becoming more appreciative of the complex variety of reasons that may lie behind lack of preparation and/or apathy.

Analysis

There are many, many possible reasons for lack of preparation. Individual students have a variety of commitments competing for their attention. A student under pressure from other quarters may decide to risk not preparing for a particular class on a given day. Personal problems may also interfere. Individuals may find the class work overwhelmingly difficult, and give up in frustration. Students may become angry or discouraged with the professor, with what is going on in the course, and/or with their school experience—and some may express their frustration by consciously or unconsciously withdrawing commitment and preparing less.

When an entire class ceases to prepare, the causes most likely lie in the experiences they share—often within the particular class, and sometimes within their overall school program. Possible explanations of apathy are still myriad, however. For example, the course material may be discouragingly difficult, and the students may not be able to find ways to communicate their problem and get adequate help. The process of the class sessions may also be discouraging. Some instructors are unduly severe with students, often without being aware of it. Students may react by resisting participating in class. Other instructors are themselves apathetic, withdrawn, and uninterested in the daily dynamics of the classes—and students soon realize this and find it hard to stay engaged.

Moreover, what goes on in any given classroom plays only a small part in the students' overall experiences. Students must cope with the demands of several separate courses while also dealing with the human dynamics of their overall educational program group and the school or university as a whole.

2. Summarize, as a friend of Rowe: how and why did Rowe get into trouble?

Usage Note

This question provides four levels of direction to participants. First, it asks them to examine the factors that led up to the incident on December 1, thus beginning the discussion with analysis rather than action planning, and suggesting a temporal perspective (by asking how he got into trouble rather than what the trouble is).

Second, by implying that Rowe, rather than the section, is "in trouble," the question invites the seminar to look for aspects of Rowe's behavior that could have contributed to the problems with the section. Third, it asks participants to take the role of a friend of Rowe, thus encouraging collegiality and identification with his plight. Fourth, it asks participants to summarize their answers and be succinct. This last directive is not always used, but is an option to consider if the particular seminar group tends toward wordiness and lack of focus.

Analysis

In the opinion of most seminar participants, Rowe got into trouble primarily by not taking Section III's problem more seriously earlier, when he still had time to try to discover its nature and to respond more gradually and perhaps less dramatically.

Though colleagues had alerted Rowe to a potential problem in Section III, his only response was a one-way communication of his expectations. There is no evidence that he tried to speak with section members, including the educational representative, about the reports of difficulty. Nor did he take any measure to increase preparation over the firs few weeks—for example, asking students to work in groups and present panel reports, or assigning students specific preparation tasks in advance.

3. *What questions does the case pose for you?*

Usage Note

This very broad query encourages generalization and typically brings a number of issues out on the table for consideration. By following it with probes about what specific items in the case stimulated these questions, one can encourage the seminar to consider the complex set of factors that contributed to apathy in Section III.

Analysis

This case raises a variety of issues, including but not limited to the following: How can one encourage preparation for class? How can one create involvement during discussions? When an entire section is "going downhill," how can it be turned around? How can an instructor read and respond to conditions in the section that he or she has not created—for example, problems apparently caused by other instructors? How can one help a collection of individual students become a learning community?

4. *What were the significant factors that contributed to this situation?*

Usage Note

This question is similar in effect to Question 3 but promotes less generalization. It encourages an understanding of the many intertwined factors that may have contributed to the problems of the section.

Analysis

Participants usually identify a wide variety of factors that apparently contributed to Section III's apathy and lack of preparation. One issue is the relationship that has evolved between the section and its instructors (other than Doug Rowe). The group's early energy, which might have been harnessed to productive purposes, was apparently killed by the faculty coordinator who verbally chastised the section and followed up by punishing a student for a poor contribution. The section's feeling of powerlessness was then apparently reinforced by Professor Richard Hagey's style of teaching, which the section members experienced as manipulative. Finally, Professors Roger Williams, Irv Kincaid, and Francis Gress added to the problem in that none was able to create rapport and excitement in his classes—rather, these instructors taught over students' heads or missed them completely, thus making the section even more discouraged.

Doug Rowe began his course in a way that ran counter to the expectations of the students, did not meet their needs, and was more or less unilaterally imposed. The students, according to Jim Catterson, expected and felt they needed a conceptual overview of Rowe's course. Their anxiety at not getting one was probably magnified by the course's reputation for difficulty—a reputation reinforced by Rowe's early remarks. Rowe seemed unaware of the section's anxiety and did not respond to it in a way that the students perceived as helpful. He laid out what he expected of students, pointing out the need to be prepared. He did not ask what they expected of him, either informally out of class or in the classroom. This relatively one-way mode of communication did little to mitigate the alienation that had been developing in their other courses.

During the following weeks, Rowe seems to have been preoccupied with the progress in the other sections and not to have worked consciously enough to build a good relationship with Section III. Thus, a bad situation deteriorated further.

Splitting a long and probably difficult case around the Thanksgiving vacation probably added to the apathy. Students have enough trouble recalling case facts and discussion points from one class to another. After six days, the problem is much worse. Further, many of the students had been absent just before the vacation, and thus were probably lost in the (D) case discussion, which built on work in the previous sessions.

Rowe's handling of the class on December 1 did not include any special response to either the previous absenteeism or the long break. For example, he could have begun with a review of the earlier case segments, or asked students who had actively participated in those discussions to provide such a briefing for the section. Instead, he seems to have called upon students without considering how well prepared they might be. The result in retrospect probably was predictable: many ill-prepared contributions. At this, Doug Rowe became angry. Turning to the class, he asked a relatively simple question and, getting unsatisfactory responses, went down a row asking the same question to each person in the series. The students, already turned off and feeling hostile toward the school and their instructors, may have experienced this action as punitive and insulting—and showed their consequent resentment and anger by not cooperating.

5. Why was Rowe so angry? What is going on for him? What was his perception of the situation?

Usage Note

The question shifts the focus from the development of the situation to Rowe's perceptions and motivations. Our hope is first to help the seminar understand how complex a problem apathy can be, and then to examine the difficulty that even experienced instructors—like Rowe—may have in reading such situations accurately. Concurrently, this question moves consideration from the background of the crisis to the current situation.

Analysis

Rowe seems to see the problem as a lack of effort on the part of the students. Not knowing what has happened in their relationships with other instructors, and not sensing his own contributions, Rowe cannot find an explanation for their apathy and lack of participation. This is frustrating, especially for an experienced "teacher's teacher" like Rowe. Many people in such a situation would wonder whether the section were just being perverse, lazy, or "bad." If Rowe sees things in this light, he may feel let down by the section, and may think that students are challenging his authority and competence. Either conclusion could be insulting and angering for a dedicated teacher.

More than other PCS instructors, Rowe has strong personal reasons for wanting the section to perform well. He takes pride in his work on the content and presentation of the course. Further, as the course head, with responsibility to supervise other instructors, he could find it embarrassing if his section did poorly.

6. Jim Catterson, the student section's leader, says that it took Rowe a month to become fully aware of the section's problems. Why didn't Rowe, a sensitive and seasoned professor, read his section better?

Usage Note

This question continues the line initiated in Question 4, encouraging participants to appreciate the factors that kept Rowe from understanding his section—factors like those which participants may encounter in their own teaching.

Analysis

Rowe's wider responsibilities as course head apparently distracted him from his own section. The apathy in Section III, although recognized as a problem from the first, perhaps did not, on balance, seem serious enough to warrant extensive attention—until the December 1 incident.

Rowe's problem was complicated by the fact that the section was responding not only to his actions, but to the present and past actions of five other instructors. Though Rowe was keeping abreast of developments in other sections of *his course,* he was not attending to Section III's experiences in *their* other courses. Rowe could probably have learned about such circumstances through candid discussions with the students such as the educational representative, as well as by discussing the section's progress in detail with the other instructors. Because Rowe did not cultivate the sorts of relationships that would promote such candid communication, he remained unaware of important factors on his own in-class situation.

The next two questions move the discussion to a consideration of action:

7. What are the pros and cons of Doug Rowe's action—chastising the section and walking out?

Usage Note

This question shifts the focus from analysis to a consideration of action alternatives, while encouraging participants to take a broad, evaluative approach to the case.

Analysis

Many participants believe Rowe's response may shake up the section and turn it around. Such an outcome is possible if Rowe's assertion that he has never seen a class so poorly prepared is successful in mobilizing the section's collective self-esteem. Students' liking and respect for Rowe will also be an important ingredient, perhaps motivating them to work hard so that he will be willing to continue teaching them. Finally, the section members may make an effort to avoid the schoolwide scandal that might be associated with an instructor's refusal to teach them.

Rowe's action could backfire, however. If enough section members do not like his teaching, they might welcome his departure and resist his further leadership in either subtle or overt ways. Rowe would then face a very difficult situation. It is unlikely that he could carry through his threat to quit teaching the section, and thus he would be left with his bluff called and a section that felt rejected and rejecting.

In addition, seminar participants often point out that Rowe's denunciation of the class's poor preparation misses the true nature of their situation. It may shake them up, forcing them to realize that even if they have valid reasons for not liking the way they are being taught, they must continue to prepare for class. But it does nothing to address their underlying concern that their instructors cannot understand and relate to them, and continue to impose unilateral teacher-student contracts. Thus, though this intervention may force compliance from the section, it is unlikely to produce, in itself, a renewal of the personal engagement that is central to effective learning.

8. What is the situation as a result of his speech and walking out? What are his alternatives for following up?

Usage Note

This question asks participants to consider the important issue of monitoring and following up on interventions. Whatever one believes about Rowe's action, it is important to consider what to do next.

Analysis

The case text tells very little about students' reaction to Rowe's intervention, except that they became very angry. It is not clear what sorts of collective and individual conclusions they came to, or how these were expressed in their actions following the incident.

Participants in the seminar usually suggest a broad range of options for follow-up; which one is best would depend on the section's response to Rowe's intervention and on his preferred style of leadership. To begin with, most participants suggest that he should try to learn more about the section, perhaps talking with the educational representative (who the test suggests is sympathetic to Rowe's aims), or with other students with whom he can develop some rapport.

If the intervention seems to have shaken students out of the lethargy, Rowe can continue the next class without changing his basic approach, hoping that the class will be better prepared and more involved. The disadvantage of this strategy is that it does nothing to help the section members with their substantive problems with the course material. Moreover, leaving a major, four-part case poorly analyzed may put them at a further disadvantage.

To address students' substantive needs, Rowe could ask the students to reconsider the International Trading Company case in the next class. He could go further and analyze the case himself for the section. To show the level of discussion expected, he could provide tips on preparation, as well as review the course outline and goals, in order to help the students become oriented to the central aims of the course. These interventions would begin to respond to the students' learning needs and might be well received, since the ultimate underlying goal of most students is to learn the course content.

Such an approach, however, would still represent a unilaterally imposed contract. Even though it responds to some of the students' needs, they may still feel angry and alienated. If Rowe's intelligence gathering suggests that such feelings are running high, he might call a meeting, perhaps outside of class time, to discuss the overall situation in Section III and to work collaboratively toward a better learning process. Though this session could prove very difficult to manage, it would restore a two-way contracting process. Alternatively, if Rowe is not confident that his group leadership skills would ensure a happy outcome in such a session, he could meet informally with small groups of students from the section, listening to their views, creating rapport, and signaling that he intends to stay in closer touch with them and respond more sensitively to the needs of the section.

The last two questions help us shift now to generalization.

9. What questions does this case raise for you?

Usage Note

This broad question encourages generalization while allowing the seminar members virtually complete freedom to follow whatever lines of discussion they find important. The same question was asked earlier as Question 3, and it can be interesting to compare participants' original responses with those made after the discussion. This slant can be emphasized by asking participants, "Now that we have discussed the case, what new questions does it raise for you?"

Analysis

This question allows seminar members to bring in a wide range of concerns. In addition to the questions typically mentioned at the beginning of the discussion (see the analysis of Question 2), participants sometimes wonder how instructors can set up channels of communication to their students and other instructors, and how instructors can remain sensitive to the subtle signals of the classes when they are under a variety of other pressures. Usually, seminar members return to the difficult questions of how to encourage students to prepare well for class and how to create involvement with course material. Finally, they often focus on the instructor's role in creating an involved community of students (i.e., the section as a whole) rather than simply engaging individual students.

10. What, in general, can an instructor do to counter apathy and poor preparation when these problems first appear?

Usage Note

Following the very broad discussion of Question 9, we now return to the specifics of responding to apathy and lack of preparation. This question can be a springboard for turning the seminar into a brief session in which participants can share insights and techniques for handling these two recurring problems.

Analysis

One of the least helpful approaches to an apathetic class, many experienced instructors suggest, is to discuss the situation directly with the students as a problem of poor preparation. This labels the situation in a way that gives students only two options: either they can continue as they are, thus doing something now defined as "bad," or they can "shape up" and comply with the instructor's standards. At best, the students are likely to feel that they are succumbing to pressure, rather than becoming genuinely engaged in learning. Further, any special teaching techniques that the instructor uses after raising the problem explicitly will be readily identified as "ways to manipulate the section into participating more." Section members may not recognize that, while the instructor has some effect, it is their genuine response to those interventions that makes the difference. Their involvement is real, and they can be proud of it. Students will find it more difficult to achieve this recognition if the section has been explicitly labeled a problem group.

Seminar members usually offer a wealth of suggestions for creating involvement. Most of these techniques work best when used subtly, so that students are more aware of their own improving performance than of the instructor's interventions.

Instructors can use their questioning style to increase involvement in the classroom, in ways that have been described in earlier teaching notes. For example, one can ask students for increased personal commitments to their arguments by personalizing discussion questions (e.g., "Jane, what would you do if you were Doug Rowe?"). One can create excitement and potential conflict by beginning discussion with action planning rather than analysis. By the way that the instructor bridges comments and summarizes discussion, he or she can highlight conflict and differences of opinion, thus sharpening the dialogue between groups of participants.

Competition within the classroom can be heightened even more by creating formal, though temporary, competing groups. For example, the instructor can assign one role to the left half of the class, and another to the right, and pose questions to each side. Students sitting in the middle can then be asked which group did better and why.

Section performance can be improved by inviting guests to be present, and announcing their visits in advance. It is especially useful to invite guests whom students see as having some potential impact on their futures. For example, one can mention in passing that "the dean of the graduate program is interested in Monday's case and will be sitting in with us." To avoid looking bad before such guests, students are likely to invest a good deal of extra effort in these sessions.

If the students seem to be frustrated with the difficulty of the materials, a variety of approaches may be helpful. At the beginning of class each day, the instructor can summarize the previous session's case in order to create a better sense of continuity and to give students a map of where they have been. This practice can be continued for several weeks.

In addition, one can create success experiences by addressing discussion questions to individuals with relevant strengths. For example, a student who is a good lead-off person should be used in that role. Another student who is clearly effective in summarizing might be asked to provide integration and direction when it seems appropriate. And the instructor can provide opportunities for students with background in particular areas to share their experience through their comments in class.

One can also make the section more attentive to its own process, and offer instructive guidance, by providing fast and frequent—but unobtrusive—process feedback. This approach is often most effective when used to signal something done well. For example, "Our discussion of the case so far has been most productive, because we have been able to highlight . . . and get a clearer understanding of the issues of. . . . "

In addition, it is often possible to insert into the course schedule a substitute case that is known to be both exciting and relatively easy for students to analyze. When the section does a truly excellent job on a case, students know it; often their morale rises and they become enthusiastic to tackle bigger challenges.

The instructor can approach particular students in advance and ask them to be the opening speakers in class, thus giving them an opportunity to prepare carefully. Students can be assigned such roles as much as a week in advance. To provide further structure, the instructor might ask each of several students to take a different position, or to describe the case from a particular point of view. The class can then be asked questions about these presentations.

These techniques can be used with small groups as well as individuals. Several students can be asked to work together and report to the class as a panel. (Groups can be self-selected or chosen by the instructor.) Other students can then question the panel members about their remarks.

One can also make it a regular practice to meet outside of class with subgroups of section members—discussing the forthcoming case and/or other aspects of the course material. Held shortly before a class session, such a meeting provides a warm-up for the following discussion. In addition to stimulating the students and signaling concern about their learning, these informal sessions allow the instructor to learn more about how the students are doing and how they are experiencing the course. These meetings can be regularly scheduled, perhaps over breakfast or lunch before class. In another case, "Class on World Hunger," the instructor made excellent use of such sessions. Students participated on a voluntary, rotating basis.

EXHIBIT 1 *We're Just Wasting Our Time*

Study Questions

(For distribution with case)

1. What is your diagnosis of the situation? Of Rowe's action?
2. What should Professor Rowe do now?
3. As a section instructor, how do you evaluate the overall section's progress toward becoming a learning group? How do you evaluate *section* performance?
4. What are the key techniques for tracking the performance of individual students in a section? What constitutes a positive contribution? What constitutes grounds for a poorer evaluation?

EXHIBIT 2 *We're Just Wasting Our Time*

Discussion Questions

(For use by seminar leader)

5. From your own experience as a student, what are some of the reasons that students don't prepare for class sessions?
6. Summarize, as a friend of Rowe's: How and why did Rowe get into trouble?

The following questions can be used to deepen the diagnostic discussion:

7. What questions does the case pose for you?
8. What are the significant factors that contribute to this situation?
9. Why was Rowe so angry? What is going on for him? What was his perception of the situation?
10. Jim Catterson, the student section's leader, says that it took Rowe a month to become fully aware of the section's problems. Why didn't Rowe, a sensitive and seasoned professor, read his section better?

The next two questions move the discussion to a consideration of action:

11. What are the pros and cons of Doug Rowe's action—chastising the section and walking out?
12. What is the situation now? What are his alternatives for following up?

The following questions now shift to generalization:

13. What questions does this case raise for you?
14. What can an instructor do to counter apathy and poor preparation when those problems first appear?

The Section Just Took Over: A Student's Reflections

TEACHING NOTE

This teaching note was prepared by James Moore as an aid to instructors in the classroom use of the case "The Section Just Took Over" No. 9-379-007.
(HBS No. 5-384-043)

Distributed by HBS Publishing Division, Harvard Business School, Boston, MA 02163.
Printed in U.S.A.

Introduction

This case centers on a discussion that turns into an angry session, undermining the tight control usually maintained by the instructor. The content of the outburst revolves around the ethics of a controversial marketing plan, and thus "The Section Just Took Over" is often read as a case about the challenges of discussing ethical questions in class. We believe, however, that the explanation of the explosion lies less in the particular content of the day than in the instructor's excessively controlling teaching style. This sort of style can prevent a section from developing the capacity for real dialogue, including the ability to consider truly conflicting points of view. Thus we try to use this case as an opportunity to explore the vital issue of guidance vs. control in case teaching.

Case Summary

"The Section Just Took Over" is brief, and thus lends itself to use in a variety of situations, including those—such as workshops—where participants have limited preparation time. It is an exciting, engaging case, described entirely through the eyes of a student who was present but relatively uninvolved in the incident. "The Section Just Took Over" includes little background information about the institutional context, the course, or the protagonists. The heart of the text is a characterization of the instructor's style of managing case discussions, as seen through the eyes of the student, and the account of the incident itself.

A Suggested Process Plan for the Case

In previous discussions, we have found that this case draws energy not only from the power of the text but from the ethical issues to which the protagonists allude. That is, several seminar participants often become exercised about the issues of birth control, multinationals in the third world, and religious authority—and whether or not these issues are directly discussed in the teaching seminar, they give added emotional charge to the case.

Our general plan is to play counterpoint against the natural focus of the text on ethics and ethical issues. We find that without direction, the group will gravitate toward a discussion of the appropriate role of ethics in the classroom and ways of handling ethical issues. While these are very valuable questions, we wish to take participants farther into the issue, so that they can see that the question of handling ethical issues is part of the broader question of developing a section's capacity for deep, emotionally involving, and diversity-respecting discussion.

We try to accomplish this with an intense focus on diagnosis in the case, and with a series of optional probes (Questions 2 through 4) that call attention to various features of the situation that help determine how the ethical issues are received. These features are the particular nature of Kay's comment, Professor Webster's style of discussion leadership, and the teacher-student relationship that is evolving in the section.

Once we have established the problems with Webster's style, we ask participants to consider what forces might push Webster or any young instructor to use such an approach. This question helps seminar members to empathize with Webster's difficult situation, and to realize the forces in their own practices that pull toward a similar style.

We continue the discussion with an extensive consideration of action alternatives. First, participants discuss how it might have been possible to respond to Kay and Bob more constructively. Second, participants consider alternatives to Webster's overall style of discussion leadership.

Finally, we ask participants to consider the more general issues of direction vs. control in case teaching.

Notes for the Discussion Questions

These notes parallel the suggested discussion questions presented in **Exhibit 2**. For each question a brief note is provided about the pedagogical intent and use of the question. In addition, for each question we have provided our best attempt at a reasoned response.

1. *What is your diagnosis of this situation? Why did the explosion occur?*

Usage Note

This broad opening question allows the seminar members to range widely in their diagnostic thinking. As the session proceeds, we use discussion management techniques, such as bridging and selective reinforcement of comments, to encourage participants to see the case not as an illustration of the explosiveness of ethical issues, but rather as an example of how such issues may become explosive when they arise in the context of a particular instructor-student dynamic.

Analysis

The immediate problem is why has this happened? Some participants may suggest that ethical issues of the type raised by Kay simply tend to be explosive. While this is in one sense true—birth control, exploitation of women, the activities of multinational corporations in third world countries are all questions of great current controversy—our experience is that, properly handled, each of these issues can be respectfully and profitably discussed in case classes.

The central problem, in our view, is that a number of factors have converged to create a class with almost no capacity for open, spirited, self-managed discussion of issues of great importance to the students.

The students—individually and as a group—appear to have developed little capacity for open exploration of differing perspectives. A very important part of the case method experience is that students learn that disagreement is all right—indeed, that it is through reasoned, trenchant dialogue that new insights can be created and learning can occur. Students learn to value differences of opinion, and increase their tolerance for healthy disagreement and even spirited conflict.

The members of Webster's class, or Webster himself, do not seem to have learned this lesson. Neither Kay nor Bob show tolerance for diverse views. On the contrary, they both react defensively, thus feeding the class's anxieties and triggering a free-for-all.

It is perhaps not surprising that the class does not have a capacity for disagreement. The students are relatively new to case discussions. Webster's class is apparently one of the few conducted in this manner at Southeastern, and the students are only halfway through their first semester. Thus they have had little experience with open discussions. Further, the cases examined so far in Webster's course have apparently concerned relatively circumscribed marketing questions, thus not affording great latitude for interpretation—or for differences of interpretation. Finally, Webster has not made his class a place where real disagreement is valued. The students must try to guess his view of the case—and any deviation from that view is apparently treated as evidence that the student has not grasped the point of the case.

Kay introduces her point in a provocative, challenging manner that increases the likelihood of a defensive reaction from other members of the class. Moreover, the class already appears to be chafing under Webster's close rein.

The following questions can be used to deepen the diagnostic discussion:

2. *What is there about the nature of Kay's comment that made it so difficult for others to handle?*

Usage Note

Focusing on the way in which Kay raised her objection helps seminar members understand that it is not necessarily ethical issues per se that are explosive, but rather the incendiary way in which they may be introduced. This insight suggests that there are more and less skillful ways to raise controversial issues in discussion—and that an important objective for students and instructors may be to learn how to introduce difficult concerns and questions in ways that maximize productive, respectful, and rational discussion.

Analysis

Kay does not simply raise ethical concerns about the marketing plan described in the case. Rather, she attacks the integrity of the class for not identifying these concerns earlier, accusing them of "avoiding" (rather than simply missing) these issues. She states that "this company's marketing plan should strike everyone's conscience as being highly unethical, even immoral"—in effect indicting those who did not find it so. Her language is emotionally charged and provocative—comparing the company to cases in *The Ugly American* and asserting that it is dedicated to immoral activities in the pursuit of "almighty profit."

Kay could have raised the same issues without accusing her classmates of immorality for not discussing them sooner. Had she done so, she might have found a good deal of support for at least some of her points. Further, had she simply avoided the use of highly charged, virtually taunting language, her comment would have had a better chance of drawing reasoned rather than defensive responses from those who did not agree.

3. *Could the explosion have been predicted? Why or why not?*

Usage Note

This question shifts the focus from Kay and the nature of her comment to other situational factors.

Analysis

Some cases raise issues that are more sensitive than others, and an instructor should be alert to the possibility that an emotional conflagration could develop in class. To some extent, what issues are hot depend upon what controversies are active in the world at large at any given time. Thus Webster should probably have realized the potential for deep differences of opinion in the class, for defensiveness and polarization, and therefore for comments like Kay's and Bob's.

On the other hand, it is in the nature of case discussions that one often cannot predict when an emotionally charged issue will surface. As one participant in the seminar wrote, "Emotions can run high over such unlikely subjects as monetarism versus Keynesianism, and market share versus cash flow." The case method instructor must be ready, to some extent, to deal with surprising outbursts whenever they occur.

In the case of Webster's section, certain other factors might have led an outside observer, if not to predict an explosion, at least not to be surprised that one occurred. Chief among these is Webster's tight control over the section, and the intimations of resistance seen in the passivity of the class on the day in question. This issue will be discussed in the analysis for the following question.

4. *What is it like to be a student in Kenneth Webster's class? What is his contract with the students? How has it been communicated?*

Usage Note

This question emphasizes Webster's role in creating a situation that invites an explosion. Further, it asks participants to examine in some detail the nature of his working relationship with the students, and how he maintains it. If much of this material has come out in previous discussion, there may be little need to ask this question.

Analysis

Webster's students spend most of their class session trying to guess his analysis of the case, while he alternates between prompting them to supply relevant details, and trying to lead them astray. In the final few minutes of the class Webster will dramatically point the students to a key insight, and then will summarize for them the important (for Webster) lessons of the case.

Webster communicates this contract in a variety of ways. He informs the class that his analysis is the "right" one by preparing a graphic summary before the session on a hidden chalkboard—and concluding the class with a dramatic unveiling and explication. He keeps a close rein on discussion, leading students toward the "discovery" of his analysis. When students go off track, he doesn't follow; rather, his and their comments simply become less connected—apparently until the students return to Webster's line of thinking. One seminar participant characterized Webster's approach as follows:

> Professor Webster believes there is an Easter egg buried in every case and that the students' job is to find it. He brings the egg with him to class wrapped in his class notes. Then, before the students arrive, he hides it behind the mechanical chalkboard, and

> draws a map of the garden it is hidden in for all to see. Whenever students get "warm" too soon, he shoos them into a "cold" corner. Then, when the class is almost over, he drops bigger and bigger hints until "Surprise!"—the most unlikely student finds the egg. Finally everyone oohs and aahs as he spends the last five minutes taking off the silver paper for all to view the fearful symmetry of the egg revealed.

Though the case contains little direct evidence of students' reactions to this game, one wonders if they weren't beginning to look for an opportunity to express their own sense of direction. The participant who wrote the Easter egg account of the case thought so:

> One day, instead of an egg, he brings a pill to hide. But, alas, the students are growing tired of the game. After looking in several different places, they begin to give up looking for so difficult a prize. Professor Webster doesn't give up though. When someone suggests one part of the map which is clearly not warm at all, he just tries another student, and then another. . . . Just as everybody is getting fed up with the guessing game, Kay Woodward says, "I don't think we should be playing hunt-the-pill at all! I think we should choose our own game."
>
> Pandemonium breaks out. Some students say, "No. We came here to play the teacher's game." Others begin talking all at once about the different games they would like to play—but no one can seem to agree. Finally the teacher tells them they have been very naughty. They can play any game they like after school, but in his class only hunt-the-pill is allowed. And so the class went unhappily ever after. . . .

5. *Why does Ken Webster behave so as to stay "on top of the class"? What situational or personal circumstances might encourage such an approach? What are its benefits and liabilities?*

Usage Note

This is a reflective question, and asks participants to mull over factors that can draw any instructor into the trap of trying to overcontrol a section. This question helps participants not only to understand others, but also to consider the pulls toward overcontrol in their own teaching.

Analysis

The case includes modest information about Webster. It is worth noting, however, that overcontrol is often a problem for new instructors. Many of them are used to thinking in terms of lectures—and thus preparing a sequence of ideas ("answers") they feel need to be transmitted to the students. If these ideas are not transmitted, the inexperienced instructor often feels the students are being cheated.

The remedy for this problem seems to involve thinking in terms of questions, issues, or themes that one wants one's students to examine rigorously. A body of knowledge consists of not only a set of standard techniques, but also a set of questions—often unappreciated by the novice—for which the standard techniques are working answers. From this perspective, each case becomes an opportunity to challenge students with a series of important questions—leaving primarily to them the task of working out responses to these questions.

A second reason instructors sometimes seek excessive control is insecurity about their role and authority in the classroom. This can be a particularly difficult problem for new instructors, who may be virtually the same age as their students—and who may feel slightly illegitimate in the new role of professor. With luck, a bit of successful teaching experience will remedy this sort of insecurity. In most universities, professors—even junior professors—are accorded respect and social power by the students. Once the new instructor experiences this, he or she can often loosen up and evolve a more open, interactive teaching style.

A third common reason for overcontrolling involves the instructor's insecurity about the subject matter. Open discussions sometimes move beyond the instructor's expertise, and this can be upsetting to new instructors, particularly those who are asked to teach courses outside their primary areas of competence. Fear of going beyond one's competence may also be an important reason why many instructors shy away from discussion of ethical issues: they do not know of any systematic way to consider such matters, and they feel out of their depth in attempting to do so.

6. *How might Webster have better handled Kay's comment? Bob Kinney's? What are their learning opportunities? For the class?*

Usage Note

Though the case text does not pose an action question, participants find it valuable to consider how one might respond constructively in a similar situation. The discussion may focus on either how to respond to Kay or Bob Kinney, or how to respond to Harry Jones and the entire class after the full explosion. In our judgment it is more useful to discuss how to respond to Kay and/or Bob, because the resulting discussion pertains to a relatively common and very important problem—particularly with students who are new to the case method: how does one respond to student comments that are emotionally driven, provocative, and (in Bob's case) insulting to another student?

Analysis

As soon as such an incident occurs, it becomes virtually impossible—at least for the moment—to continue with any prearranged teaching plan. Our first priority—perhaps paradoxically, given our contention that Webster has been overcontrolling—would be to maintain control of the discussion. This would probably require stepping in quickly and firmly to engage Bob and respond to his comment before the class can erupt. By figuratively positioning ourselves between Bob and Kay, we would hope to defuse the conflict and take command of the subsequent interchange.

Kay and Bob may be able to learn a great deal from this incident—both about the process of learning in a discussion class and about the content of their comments. On the process side, both students (as well as other members of the class) need to increase their ability to cope with differences of perspectives in their classmates. In our judgment Bob has violated a central norm of case discussions: that one must show respect for other persons in the classroom. The instructor should respond to this violation, sending a clear signal to Bob and the rest of the class that this is unacceptable behavior. Only in this way can we assure that the norms supporting open discussions are reinforced rather than weakened by this incident.

Kay's attack on the class is also counterproductive though, in the opinion of many participants, not as damaging as Bob's. Kay would probably benefit from being pressed to separate her core argument about the case from the fireworks of her presentation, and it would be good if she could realize how differently the two can be experienced. Probably the latter aim is too optimistic, but by asking her to clarify her position, the instructor can probably get her to disentangle the argument.

Once some decorum has been reestablished, we would strive to get both Kay and Bob to explore the assumptions and consequences of their positions. Their comments could then become the stimulus for further analysis of the case. Several approaches are possible. For example, Kenneth Goodpaster, formerly a professor of business ethics at Harvard Business School, made the following suggestions during one of our seminars, in response to this request:

> Instructor: Could you—as somebody who teaches students to discuss difficult ethical issues all the time—give us some sort of first steps? Because for most of us it is frightening. We know that we're waltzing on a minefield.
>
> Goodpaster: First I would try to elicit Bob's implicit ethical position—to peel back the onion for a while to see exactly what kind of value judgments are the premises of his remark. That in itself would demonstrate to Kinney that ethical issues are relevant, because there must be some ethical premises behind his conviction here.
>
> Then I'd shift ground back to Kay. There are two things that struck me about what she said. First, she was appealing to the potential harm and danger in marketing these drugs. Then she was appealing to religious authority. Those are two radically different kinds of ethical arguments. I would display that to her and ask her which one she thought was more crucial here.
>
> In this way the class would begin to see that ethical arguments are not just emotional explosions, but have some structure. They can be taken a lot farther than most people realize. But it would have to be part of your class preparation. Webster should have thought through these things.

In addition to this approach, there are a variety of other ways in which Kay's comment could be made the basis for further discussion of the case. For example, one could ask a member of the class, "Is Kay's query a useful one? Why or why not?" This would allow a discussion of the issues, of their appropriateness to the class, and perhaps of Kay's manner of raising them—but a discussion moderated by the instructor, not a free-for-all.

One could also turn the question into a corporate role-playing exercise, asking another student, "If you were the director of marketing for this corporation, how would you react to Kay's comment? Why?" This would demonstrate the relevance of at least considering Kay's type of concerns. Finally, one might work with the class's disagreement about the appropriate place for such concerns, and ask, "Where should we discuss ethical issues in business? Where do we now? Where should we do it at this school?"

7. Could such an incident have been prevented? How?

Usage Note

This question asks participants how they might handle a case course throughout the term in order to prepare the ground for the productive discussion of controversial issues. As such, it opens up a broad discussion of case method teaching, often (depending upon the seminar) focused on how to handle emotional issues and ethics, and more broadly how to direct but not overcontrol a section.

Analysis

In our experience, students sometimes have difficulties in respecting the opinions of their classmates. It is the job of the instructor to build that capacity, particularly during the first weeks of the term. Of many possible methods, three stand out for us as particularly important. First, the instructor needs to model respectful appreciation for student comments that reflect diverse perspectives. Particularly during the first sessions of a course, the instructor can help seminar participants to see the links between seemingly disparate contributions, and thus realize that consideration of a variety of opinions will build a richer view of the case. One small hint we have found helpful: in early sessions we tend to emphasize diagnosis rather than action planning, for the value of multiple perspectives is easier to appreciate during analysis of situations. In contrast, action planning often leads to conflict because many of the participants' suggestions will necessarily be mutually exclusive. Therefore, we tend to deemphasize action planning until the section has become respectful of its own richness.

Second, the instructor must insist that all student comments be treated with respect and given a fair hearing. Students may need to be reminded that comments that first seem naive or misdirected may later seem insightful. In any case, mutual respect must be an ironclad rule, and one that the instructor does not hesitate to enforce when necessary.

Third, students need to see that the way in which they make a comment influences how it is received. They need to be encouraged to avoid provocative, taunting language. Comments instead need to be made clearly and forcefully, but without the additional "spin" that communicates scorn or hostility. The possible exception is humorous banter between group members who are on good terms—but even this can be misunderstood and seems best avoided except on rare occasions.

As these norms and values are adopted, most sections develop an increasing capacity for genuine difference. Students test the water and, finding it safe, begin to join the discussion with their deepest insights and concerns. In talking about teaching, people often emphasize what one can control in a discussion. It is just as important to reflect on what one cannot control. An instructor cannot control the interests of the students, their true involvement in discussion, or their willingness to contribute their most precious insights. Individual students alone make their choices about how deeply they will become involved. In our experience, a major factor in this choice is the degree to which the students feel that their individuality—that is, the diversity of the section—is protected and valued by the instructor and other students.

8. What techniques can you use to encourage a section to achieve general discussion objectives without subjecting the students to the lockstep pattern Webster has chosen?

Usage Note

This question builds upon Question 7, asking participants to consider the more general issue of how to manage a case discussion effectively. Discussion may focus on philosophical considerations—centering on the need for both control and freedom in the discussion process—as well as to a concrete discussion of directorial techniques available to the case method instructor.

Analysis

Throughout this note and others, we have presented a variety of techniques for encouraging spontaneity in the discussion process—ranging from the design of question-based teaching plans to the use of bridging, selective reinforcement, and summaries to shape the content of discussion. A more concrete discussion of freedom and control might include the consideration of when and how to use these techniques. We will not provide such a review here, but will instead comment briefly on the overall stance of case method instructors.

Case instructors put a premium on student involvement and initiative, and accordingly try to maintain a great deal of classroom freedom to encourage a variety of contributions. But this freedom is most valuable when the students of the section are focused on a common set of questions. Only then can diverse comments be integrated, and a rich synergy emerge. Thus, in the service of productive freedom, the instructor exercises control over the questions, under consideration by the section.

Moreover, the constructed dialogue of a case discussion cannot continue without mutual respect and listening. Thus the successful instructor seeks to guide the process of the discussion—and the norms about communication in the group—in order to support its higher freedom. These matters bear underlining in a discussion of freedom and control in teaching.

However, these observations neglect another important dimension of case teaching: openness. Case teaching aims to involve the students deeply in the issues raised by the cases. It is often most successful:

> when students, on their own initiative, project themselves into the case situation. The classroom and business situation meld together, with the students vicariously acting as the firm's executive group, albeit a large executive group. Problems are not discussed as abstract topics, but as issues inextricably bound up in a manager's career circumstances. Student comments reflect a personal commitment to the arguments they advanced. This level of discussion comes as close to real life as can be achieved in an academic situation. Learning opportunities, and risk, are high for all involved.[1]

This sort of involvement, which requires so much openness on the part of the students, tends to require a corresponding openness on the part of the instructor. This openness is difficult to describe. It does not necessarily mean that instructors must share their views on the case, though they may wish to do so. Rather, it seems to involve an emotional openness, a certain willingness to care about the matters being discussed, a willingness—on the part of the instructor—to make this particular moment in this particular discussion the object of his or her total attention.

Student involvement requires that the participants take personal risks. It is often difficult for the instructor to appreciate the degree of jeopardy experienced by the students. Students are submerged in a powerful and often very judgmental peer culture; they have very little power except their social standing; and they are confronted in discussion with questions that are—by design—new and difficult for them. Under such conditions we believe an instructor's willingness to take a bit of emotional risk can go far toward building rapport and creating a safe climate for the genuinely hazardous activity of engaging important ideas.

---

[1] C. Roland Christensen, *Teaching and the Case Method* (Boston: Harvard Business School, 1981), pp. 15–16.

EXHIBIT 1 *The Section Just Took Over*

Study Questions

1. The case researcher comments, "I keep thinking about the class; it poses so many tough questions for me." What questions does this case raise for you?
2. Could the "explosion" have been predicted by Professor Webster?
3. How might he have responded to Kay's comment?
4. Should Professor Webster have presented his views on the ethical issues in the case to the class? Why didn't he?
5. From your teaching experience (or observation of instructors as a student), what philosophy, techniques, and/or methodology appear to be most useful in working out a balance between (a) *freedom* for the section to explore ideas of significance to them and (b) sufficient instructor *guidance* to prevent nonproductive discussion sessions?

EXHIBIT 2 *The Section Just Took Over*

Discussion Questions

1. What is your diagnosis of this situation? Why did the explosion occur?

The following questions can be used to deepen the diagnostic discussion:

2. What is there about the nature of Kay's comment that made it so difficult for others to handle?
3. Could the explosion have been predicted? Why or why not?
4. What is it like to be a student in Kenneth Webster's class? What is his contract with the students? How has it been communicated?
5. Why does Webster behave so as to stay "on top of the class"? What situational or personal circumstances might encourage such an approach? What are its benefits and liabilities?

These last three questions turn the discussion toward action planning and generalization:

6. How might Webster have handled Kay's comment? Bob Kinney's? What learning opportunities exist for them? For the class?
7. Could such an incident have been prevented? How?
8. What techniques can you use to encourage a section to achieve general discussion objectives without subjecting the students to the lockstep pattern Webster has chosen?

Kurt Jacobs

TEACHING NOTE

This teaching note was prepared by James Moore as an aid to instructors in the classroom use of the case "Kurt Jacobs" No. 9-376-094.
(HBS No. 5-384-094)

Introduction

This case describes an incident in the classroom of a senior faculty member and experienced case discussion leader. The key issue in "Kurt Jacobs" is the role of instructor response. In discussing this case, we focus on action planning—for while the problem facing Professor Brett is relatively clear-cut, he has many options for action and only moments to make a critical choice.

Compared with other cases in our syllabus, this case contains very little information about the institution, instructor, and substantive content of the course involved. Instead, readers simply share the experience of Professor Brett as he encounters Kurt Jacobs over the first eight weeks of the course, during the minutes leading up to the incident, and at the outburst itself.

A Note on Study and Discussion Questions

Typically we prepare at least two sets of questions for use with each case. The first set (**Exhibit 1**) comprises study questions and can be handed out for participants' use when preparing the case before class. The discussion questions (**Exhibit 2**) are used by the instructor of the seminar in preparing for class and in guiding the case discussion when appropriate.

A Suggested Process Plan for the Case

In our seminar, this case often heralds a shift in the construct of our teaching plans. In early modules we emphasize analysis of the case situation, limiting action planning. With "Kurt Jacobs," we emphasize action planning, with diagnostic analysis used primarily to argue for or against particular lines of action.

In the early modules we are encouraging participants to appreciate the complexity in the situations. Our experience is that the most common mistake made by participants early in the term is to assume the case situations are simple and the problems presented obvious. They have a strong tendency not to question their first interpretations. As instructors, we counter this tendency by emphasizing diagnosis and highlighting both the variety of initial interpretations made by participants, and the complexity of the situations when they are understood more fully. In this we feel a kinship with Louis Agassiz as he is described in "Louis Agassiz as a Teacher."

By the midpoint of the seminar, however, the participants may develop a tendency to focus exclusively on analysis, in isolation from action planning. At the extreme, this separation can lead to paralysis of action. That is, participants can learn to see complexity and implications everywhere, and be agonized over their inability to devise actions that are appropriate for every possible development. To counter this tendency, it seems necessary for participants to develop a kind of habitual courage (an optimistic fatalism?) that enables them to size up a situation, devise the best plan they can, and then take committed action.

To teach linking analysis to action, we often use a discussion plan that leads off with a call for action recommendations. This ensures that the participants will formulate action plans, and reminds the seminar that the goal is informed, effective action, and not simply analysis. Their analyses are discussed—with rigor and attention to detail—in the context of justifying and evaluating such plans.

We begin this discussion by briefly calling attention to Professor Brett's predicament: a crisis situation, involving an emotional and confrontational outburst from a socially isolated student. The student breaks the established norms of behavior in the classroom, and challenges the class's and Brett's moral integrity. We encourage the seminar to examine the implications of the situation and consider what Brett will need to accomplish in his response.

Next we ask the seminar to consider what response Brett should make. With this question we establish the central thrust for the discussion. We ask first for Brett's broad options which include calling the class off, responding directly to Kurt, or asking a class member to respond to Kurt. Then we ask seminar members to pick one of these main choices and explain in more detail how they would proceed, and why.

In this phase of the discussion we encourage participants to project themselves into Brett's situation and to spell out in detail how they would cope with Kurt's comments. At the same time we ask them to justify their plans. As the discussion proceeds, participants develop a deeper appreciation of the situation, while simultaneously linking this analysis to action planning.

Notes for the Discussion Questions

1. What makes this situation especially difficult? In managing this predicament, what might be some of Professor Brett's aims? Why?

Usage Note

This question asks participants to appraise the crisis and note how different it is from standard classroom situations. The question reinforces our central teaching emphasis that everything one does as an instructor needs to be grounded in an understanding of the specific situation.

Analysis

The conditions under which Professor Brett must act are very complicated. He must manage a student who has dramatically violated several classroom norms: Kurt has interrupted the flow of discussion, walked into the center of the arena, and chastised the section and—by implication—the instructor. Thus his stance becomes a major factor in determining Brett's response.

Kurt's clenched fists, flushed face, and dramatic speech show that he is intensely disturbed by what has been happening in the classroom. Brett probably cannot tell to what degree Kurt has control over himself at this time. Thus Kurt's emotional state is also a major factor in Brett's decisions about his response.

Finally, the substantive content of Kurt's comment is discontinuous with the preceding discussion. He appears not to realize that the class has been jesting and creating an impromptu parody of typical discussions. In addition, his comment runs counter to typical classroom remarks in several important ways. First, rather than commenting on the case, either in seriousness or in jest, Kurt comments on the behavior of the section. Second, his argument raises issues of morality rather than effectiveness. Third, his logic is built on the premise that in matters of morals the Bible is the final authority. Consequently it is less important for Professor Brett to deal with the substantive content of Kurt's outburst than to respond to his stance vis-à-vis section norms. In our judgment Brett's first priority must be to regain control of the section and reestablish classroom norms, while calming Kurt or at least avoiding antagonizing him further.

Beyond these immediate aims, Brett must get the section to return to the course agenda, without simply sweeping the incident under the rug. In addition, he will wish to protect Kurt from becoming a class pariah, while also signaling to both Kurt and the others that such outbursts, regardless of content, are not appropriate in class. Ideally, Brett will want to help Kurt become more constructively engaged in the learning activities of the course, if this is possible. And finally Brett will want to exploit the opportunities for teaching and learning opened up by this incident.

2. What general options for response does Professor Brett have now? Please hold off on detail at this time, and just sketch his broad choices.

Usage Note

This question asks the seminar to generate a simple decision tree, concentrating first on the major forks and branches.

Analysis

There appear to us to be three major immediate options, each of which leads to other choices that must be made. First, Professor Brett can respond to Kurt Jacobs directly. Second, he can ask members of the class to respond. Third, Brett can call off the class.

Responding directly to Kurt allows Brett more control over the situation than if he asks a class member to respond. In addition, with the enormous social power of an instructor, he might have a better chance of getting Kurt to comply with his wishes. But a direct response would be a further violation of the established classroom contract, substituting teacher-student interaction for the prevailing norm of student-to-student dialogue. And it has the further disadvantage of prolonging the confrontation between Brett and Kurt. It is possible that, instead of diminishing the conflict, a direct response could cause Kurt to harden and escalate his resistance.

If Brett decides to act directly, he must then choose whether to respond to the obvious manifest content of Kurt's speech (as he would to a normal contribution in class) or to the latent emotional content. There is a danger in responding to the substantive content. Not only is it discontinuous with the rest of the discussion, and based on premises not generally shared within the course, but in his present emotional state, Kurt is probably not able to respond coherently.

On the other hand, if Brett chooses to base his response on Kurt's emotional condition and stance, what should he do? How does one respond to a person in intense emotional disarray?

A second possibility is to ask a class member to respond to Kurt. This move would reestablish the classroom pattern of dialogue between students, with the faculty member moderating. It might also help to create dialogue between Kurt and the other students, thus reducing his isolation. A major risk of this strategy is that the instructor cannot determine the student's response. Thus there is some chance that a very unhelpful response will be made, perhaps a verbal attack on Kurt.

If Brett decides to ask a class member to respond, further choices ensue. He may ask a specific person to comment, or simply pose a general question to the class and pick a respondent from those who volunteer. He may ask the respondent to comment, or he may ask a specific question. In the latter case, he must choose a question from a wide range of possibilities.

A third major option is to call off the class. This has the advantage of taking Brett quickly off the spot, and gaining him some time to think. However, it has three major disadvantages, and we consider it a last resort. The first disadvantage is that it would break his contract with the other students to provide them with a full discussion session. Some might object and not wish to leave if the section is dismissed. Brett would then be faced with a double insurrection.

Moreover, dismissal might signal to the section members that the incident is more serious than it really is. Kurt's outburst might then become "the event that was SO wild it shut down the section." Finally, calling off the session would eliminate Brett's opportunity to manage the class's interpretation of the event by how he handles the situation. Instead the students would draw their own (perhaps angry, perhaps confused) conclusions and by the time Brett saw them again, their reading of the event would be well established.

If Brett calls off the class, his use of the time between this session and the next becomes crucial. He must decide when and how to talk with Kurt, and if, when, and how to talk with the rest of the class members.

3. *Which would you select? How would you proceed? Why?*

Usage Note

This question, which we regard as central to our discussion, moves the seminar from consideration of general options to designing specific lines of action. Participants must deepen their analysis of the situation as they evaluate the merits of various plans. We encourage this by mixing *how* and *why* questions—thus forcing a careful reexamination of the case in the context of action planning.

Analysis

Obviously, a wide range of responses could be made in this very complex situation, and none will be assuredly right or wrong. But because the better responses will be grounded in a sensitive appreciation of the situation, our analysis will examine in detail several features of the situation and their implications for action.

The case indicates that Kurt is socially isolated and does not seem to have the interpersonal ability to break out. He finds it uncomfortable to speak in any class and rarely does so, he sits alone, and he doesn't socialize before and after class. In his meeting with Brett, Kurt is abrupt and displays an unusual degree of condescension toward both his classmates and his professor.

Though schools like Metropolitan pride themselves on the diversity of their students, Kurt is farther from the norm than most. He is older, he is married, and rather than living in Metropolitan's dorms (which are the scene of much social activity), he lives in a married students' housing complex. Moreover he is German, with a technical background (in a school where many of the students have general business backgrounds); he is a Christian fundamentalist; and in classroom discussions he is apparently more engaged by issues of corporate and personal ethics than efficiency and effectiveness.

Overall, it seems safe to conclude that Kurt's view of the world differs profoundly from that of most of his peers. This in itself would not necessarily be a liability for Kurt or for the section. Students with unusual backgrounds and perspectives often enrich the life of the school and have a successful educational experience themselves. However, Kurt's social isolation and condescending attitude are likely to preclude the dialogue that is vital to such valuable learning opportunities. This problem is indicated in his brusque meeting with Brett and in his heated confrontation with Millicent Wyeth. Both interchanges seem to have been memorable but not enlightening.

On the basis of this diagnosis, we believe that a central teaching problem is how to help Kurt out of his isolation and into meaningful dialogue in the classroom situation. Kurt probably needs both help and some encouragement or pressure to genuinely listen to the views of others. He also probably needs assistance in finding appropriate and effective ways to make himself heard in the Metropolitan environment. This help might come from Professor Brett and/or other students, and might occur either in or out of class. It might also be valuable for Kurt to work on communication issues with a counselor or religious leader.

For many readers, Kurt's problem is obscured by the more dramatic issue of classroom control. Kurt has usurped the instructor's position and challenged his ethical legitimacy. In a sense he has hijacked the classroom to get attention for his concerns. The hijacking itself requires immediate attention.

In addition, concern for Kurt as an individual must be balanced against other competing demands, including responsibilities to the whole section. Until the moment of the incident, Kurt's isolation was more of a problem for him than for the section as a whole, and it is easy to see why this problem stayed on Brett's back burner during the early weeks of the term. Even now that the problem has erupted in the classroom, priority must be given to staying with the educational agenda of the course as a whole.

Finally, it is uncertain how much headway can be made with Kurt, given his demonstrated inflexibility and the effect of the incident itself. His relationship with the section is in danger of becoming irreversibly polarized.

And yet, if real in-class dialogue can be achieved, it is likely to benefit both Kurt and the other section members. Encouraging such communication is one of our most central aims as case method instructors. In case discussions we foster multiple points of view and work to strengthen the section's capacity for respectful consideration of differences of perspective and judgment. In responding to Kurt Jacobs, we believe it is crucial to keep this goal in mind. While it is important to reestablish control over the situation, and to signal clearly the inappropriateness of Kurt's manner of expression, it would be very detrimental to Kurt and the section to take action that diminishes the possibility of future dialogue. Kurt's outburst has certainly violated the classroom norms of respectful discussion moderated by the instructor. But to silence him forcefully, for example, or to allow other students to attack him, would also violate these norms. Ideally, a way will be found to use this incident to increase, rather than decrease, constructive communication between Kurt and other students.

A second important feature of the situation is the conflicting interpretations of the section's "game playing." To the professor it was a harmless way of letting off steam, as well as a welcome relief during a tedious discussion. With the exception of Kurt, most of the students seem to have agreed. However, there is no information in the case text about what the nonparticipating students thought of the banter, and it is possible that some of them found it objectionable but simply decided not to intervene. Kurt—much to the surprise of the instructor—not only found the situation objectionable but saw it as a symptom of deep ethical and spiritual irresponsibility, and felt compelled to interrupt the game and chastise the section and instructor.

Kurt does not seem to understand that the section has been jesting. As a socially isolated foreign student, he may find it difficult to pick up subtle verbal and nonverbal cues in conversation. He would find parody—such as that which has occurred in the classroom—particularly hard to identify, since much of the humor arises from the very narrowness of the line that separates the parody from its "straight" original. Even if Kurt understands that the section has been joking, he may still find the comments objectionable—especially given his beliefs.

Kurt's reaction to the section's game playing underlines the degree to which his view of the world differs from that of other members in the class. Somehow Brett and/or the class members need to ensure that, at minimum, Kurt realizes that they were joking. Even so, the job of bridging between Kurt's view of reality and that held by most students is likely to be difficult. Such bridging will probably have to be done explicitly, by highlighting the misunderstanding and talking directly with Kurt about the differences between the two views.

An additional problem is that Kurt is extremely upset. In his present emotional state he is unlikely to be able to participate in a rational discussion of his beliefs and values. It is wise to deal with him carefully to avoid provoking him further.

The reactions of the other students also need to be anticipated. The major threat to classroom control may lie in their reaction to Kurt, rather than in his outburst itself. Kurt is an unpopular classmate who has spoiled their game, attacked their moral integrity, disrupted the class, and violated section and school norms. In addition he holds minority religious views and is attempting to force them on the section. Though some students will probably see his vulnerability, and others may be embarrassed for him, there will probably be students who are quite angry at Kurt. In our opinion it is very important to protect Kurt from verbal assault by these students. Such an attack could be damaging to Kurt, and might signal to other class members that Brett cannot protect students with unpopular views. Further, there is much wisdom in the adage that after the hanging, the scoundrel becomes a martyr. A verbal assault on Kurt could raise sympathy for him and polarize the class into camps supporting and opposing him.

How then might Professor Brett respond? For clarity we break the problem down into three parts: what Brett should do in the moments immediately following the outburst; in the minutes following; and before the next class. We emphasize that the following remarks are merely suggestions.

Immediately after the outburst, Brett needs to reemphasize and reestablish classroom norms, while not further upsetting Kurt. One possibility is for Brett simply to remain silent, turning his gaze away from Kurt and/or physically moving over to the side of the room. In this way Brett diminishes his psychological contact with Kurt, thus reducing the possibility of further confrontation between them. The hope is that the silence will become too much for Kurt to bear, and that he will decide to resume his seat. Brett can then return to his normal discussion leadership stance, having regained immediate control of the class.

One seminar participant suggested that Brett acknowledge Kurt's feelings, his courage, and the importance of his point of view for the discussion. It often helps a person regain control of himself if a person he is confronting neither agrees nor disagrees with him, but instead communicates respect and understanding by acknowledging the person's strong feelings.

For example, Brett might say, "You seem to be extremely upset by this discussion, Kurt. I also imagine it took a great deal of courage for you to confront the entire class in this way. Though I don't agree with your point of view, I do value hearing from you and would like to make it more possible for you to be heard." The expectation here is that Kurt will feel relieved and affirmed by having his experience recognized and acknowledged by the instructor, and will relax. Building upon the rapport established in this way, Brett can then ask Kurt to go back to his seat so that the discussion can continue in a more orderly fashion.

If Brett is unable to regain control of the classroom through such measures, he might more forcefully ask Kurt please to take his seat. In the extreme situation that Kurt maintains the confrontation and refuses to sit down, it might be necessary to dismiss the class and give full attention to managing Kurt.

Assuming Brett can regain control of the classroom within the first few moments, he must then decide how to carry on. One option is simply to reopen the preceding case discussion, implicitly asking the class to disregard the incident. This has the risk of isolating Kurt further. In addition, it means that the class's first direct responses to Kurt will occur after the session—at a time when Brett cannot influence or even observe them.

Asking someone from the section to address Kurt has the risk of allowing a verbal attack. However, this approach has the advantage of reinforcing the section norm of dialogue between members and of connecting Kurt with another student and thus beginning to reduce his isolation. Brett can influence the interchange both through his choice of a respondent and by the particular task he sets for this person. Because of the possibility of an angry reaction toward Kurt, we believe it is crucial to keep control of the situation by asking a specific question of a specific student.

We would call on someone we believe has the capacity to address Kurt directly and humanely—someone who could sense Kurt's vulnerability and isolation, and who could perhaps appreciate Kurt's courage as well as his foolhardiness. This person might be another foreign student who could empathize with Kurt's cultural isolation. Another possibility is calling on Kurt's friend, Bob Anderson, who can be expected to understand Kurt's position and has his confidence. We also assume that Bob has been able to understand the perspective of the "game players" in the incident, and can thus act as a translator and bridge. Calling on Bob also involves some risk, however, since he might feel intense pressure to side publicly with Kurt, and could thus become isolated with him, further polarizing the class.

Perhaps the worst choice would be to call on the game players. They are the section members most directly attacked by Kurt, and are likely to be angered. In addition, Kurt may view them as ringleaders of just the movement and values he deplores, and may see talking with them as an opportunity for further crusading.

No matter who is chosen to respond to Kurt, the question posed and the manner in which it is delivered are very important. It is important to signal to the respondent, and to the class as a whole, that their help is needed to resolve the difficult situation facing the section. Thus we might ask if the student could "help us out here" by responding to Kurt. Our hope would be that he or she could somehow communicate respect for Kurt, while at the same time helping him see that the class had been playing a game and meant no harm by it. Assuming some sort of rapprochement is achieved—even if only a slight movement in that direction—we would be satisfied. At least a positive direction would have been established, and instructor support for it clearly communicated.

4. What would you do before the next class?

Usage Note

This question directs the seminar's attention to the possibilities of responding outside of class. A great advantage of talking with students out of class is that they often feel less formal and less anxious to protect their public image, and thus sometimes are willing to be much more candid with the instructor. In addition, one can meet students in a variety of locations, including neutral places not "owned" by the professor—e.g., a student lounge. This can put the student on a more equal footing with the instructor—again sometimes promoting more candor and less defensiveness.

Analysis

In our judgment it is important to contact both Kurt and the section's informal leadership. We want, first of all, to assess Kurt's emotional state—in order to know how to respond to him in the future—and to refer him for professional help if he appears unstable. In addition, we want to begin the process of linking him back into the section. This will involve explaining to him the game-playing circumstances from the perspective of the other section members, letting him know that the students were jesting and the suggestions were certainly not meant seriously.

We would offer Kurt an opportunity to make his views known in a forum where they could be heard and would not disrupt the class. In this way we would support a presentation of diverse views—one of our fundamental aims in case teaching. For example, Kurt could write a memo to the section, which would be duplicated and distributed (this is something that is done with some frequency in sections, and thus it would not seem abnormal); or he could call an out-of-class meeting to explain his position; or we might let him lead off the next class to explain his position. After supporting Kurt's right to express his views, we would remind him (rather gently) that his outburst was disruptive, and indicate that we hope it won't happen again.

In addition to talking with Kurt, we would approach the section's informal leadership—e.g., Mike Healey. Our primary purpose would be to enlist these students' support in keeping the class going: helping case discussions run strongly, and avoiding any section actions that would further isolate or offend Kurt. It would be helpful to try to get them to see Kurt's vulnerability rather than his disruptiveness, and to take it upon themselves to help the community renew itself, and perhaps even incorporate Kurt and his views into its range of acceptable experience.

5. What wider questions are raised by this case?

Usage Note

This question asks participants to generalize from this case, thus encouraging connections to their own experience as well as to the other cases used in the seminar. When a seminar member raises one of these questions, we usually ask him or her to try to answer it—and then ask if others would like to respond to that question or jump in with one of their own.

Analysis

Participants often mention a variety of questions raised by this case. To stimulate thinking and demonstrate just a bit of the range, four such questions are listed here, along with very brief sample reactions. It should be noted that any of these questions can also be used by the instructor as probes—if probes are needed to stimulate or broaden the range of discussion.

a) Has anyone in the seminar had a similar experience? How did you manage it? On the

basis of your experience, do you have any lessons you could share with us?

This question draws a variety of interesting responses. It can be helpful if the instructor asks the participant who shares an experience to say explicitly how his or her experience is similar to Brett's. In this way the general theme is articulated and emphasized.

b) We urge instructors to be sensitive to the students and to their points of view. Why didn't Brett pick up on Kurt's signals? Should he have? What might Brett have done to prevent the incident, anyway?

To use managerial terms, the instructor's span of control is terribly large. Brett probably had responsibility that term for two sections of 80 to 100 students each. Though he did notice Kurt's signals to some extent, he did not devote a great deal of time to following through. There is no reason to assume either malice or negligence on the part of Professor Brett; it was simply that he had little time available and other students seemed to have more pressing needs.

In our experience, instructors seem to spend most of their out-of-class time with two sets of students: those who are failing the course or doing very poorly—and thus need help simply staying afloat—and the very talented and involved students who can benefit from extra tutelage. The students in the middle who, like Kurt, are clearly capable of managing the course material but do not shine with interest are—rightly or wrongly—left more to their own devices. This raises another question: how should instructors allocate their scarce out-of-class time?

It is unclear whether Professor Brett could have prevented the incident, but he might have taken more initiative in reducing Kurt's isolation. Several possibilities come to mind. He could perhaps have responded to Kurt's visible interest in the ethical questions raised by cases by asking Kurt to comment on them in class, or to write supplemental reports on these issues in lieu of class participation. This might have made Kurt feel more listened to, and less alone and isolated in his concerns. Brett might also have talked with Kurt's friend, Bob Anderson—who appears to be more integrated into the section—about ways to involve Kurt. This might have led to some suggestions, and at the same time would have sent an indirect message back to Kurt about his participation.

c) Kurt seems to have wanted a special contract with Brett. Should he have one? Should instructors make special arrangements with students? If so, in what situations?

Kurt seems to have wanted a special contract that would absolve him of the need to participate with the rest of the students, except when he felt it important to instruct them as a superior. By not directly challenging Kurt—either in class, after class informally, or during the abrupt meeting in his office—Brett gave his tacit consent, if not exactly approval, to a special contract with Kurt.

This contract unfortunately increased Kurt's isolation from the class and decreased his opportunities for learning. Such a contract does not seem to be in his long-term interest, and as instructors we would probably not make one were we aware of it. In general our policy is to make special contracts only if they will increase a student's involvement and opportunities for learning. For example, some students find it virtually impossible to speak in class. Forcing them to do so simply makes no sense. In these cases we allow them to remain silent, but ask that they write supplemental analyses of the cases. In this way their involvement is increased.

d) What about humor? Should you keep the students' noses constantly to the grindstone, or allow humor to emerge? Should an instructor allow game playing in class? How much, and at what points? When and how should he or she step in to stop such gaming?

In our experience sections need a bit of relief from time to time, and humor and gaming definitely have their place. Usually humor emerges from the section and need not be artificially promoted by the instructor! In addition to relieving tension, humor can enhance creativity by expanding the range of thinkable options—and can sometimes lead to new and unique solutions to problems.

EXHIBIT 1 *Kurt Jacobs*

Study Questions

1. What response options are open to Professor Brett as of the end of the case? Which would you believe most appropriate? Why?
2. What should Professor Brett do in the next minute? The next few minutes? Before class meets again?

EXHIBIT 2 *Kurt Jacobs*

Discussion Questions

1. What makes this situation especially difficult? In managing this predicament, what might be some of Professor Brett's aims? Why?
2. What general options for action does Professor Brett have now? Please hold off on detail at this time, and just sketch his broad choices.
3. Which would you select? How would you proceed? Why?
4. What would you do before the next class?
5. What wider questions are raised by this case?

[The following probes can be used if desired]:

a) Has anyone in the seminar had a similar experience? How did you manage it? On the basis of your experience, do you have any lessons you could share with us?

b) We urge instructors to be sensitive to the students and to their points of view. Why didn't Brett pick up on Kurt's signals? Should he have? What might Brett have done to prevent the incident, anyway?

c) Kurt seems to have wanted a special contract with Brett. Should he have one? Should instructors make special arrangements with students? If so, in what situations?

d) What about humor? Should you keep the students' noses constantly to the grindstone, or allow humor to emerge? Should an instructor allow game playing in class? How much, and at what points? When and how should he or she step in to stop such gaming?

Trevor Jones

TEACHING NOTE

This teaching note was written by James Moore as an aid to instructors in the classroom use of the case "Trevor Jones" No. 9-380-016.
(HBS No. 5-384-045)

Introduction

Without announcing his intentions, an instructor engages this class in a role-playing exercise that he hopes will give them a feel for the pain of losing a job and/or causing others to lose their jobs. The role playing has an extremely powerful effect—more than the instructor intends, and more than the students find valuable or humane. The students become extremely hostile toward the instructor.

The case raises concerns about both the technical and the ethical aspects of using role playing and other involvement-increasing techniques in the classroom. It calls attention to the great power of the instructor's position—a power that can be abused, even when the instructor has the best of intentions.

"Trevor Jones" also calls attention to the problem of dealing with students who are unwilling to speak in class, particularly when the general instructor-student learning contract calls for a great deal of verbal exchange. And the case reemphasizes the importance of being sure that both instructors and students know clearly what their contract is, and respect it.

Further, the case asks participants to consider when it is constructive for an instructor to use his or her power to force students to confront difficult issues, and under what conditions such force is humiliating and constitutes an abuse of power. In "Trevor Jones," the instructor accidentally crosses this line and loses the trust and respect of his students. Seminar members are asked to consider how the instructor can make amends in such a situation and regain students' trust. The more general question is how instructors can recover from their mistakes.

In our own class students sometimes have asked if the incident described in the case could by any chance have been a "set-up" between Vinceberg and Trevor Jones. The answer is no, but this point is not made in the text. You may wish to share this information with your students.

A Suggested Process Plan for the Case

Because it deals with the volatile issues of rejection, manipulation, and abuse of power, this case can stimulate polarized discussions. Thus we do not use it until the seminar has become a coherent group of mutually respectful, trusting colleagues.

On the surface this is a case about the use, and misuse, of role playing and other involvement-stimulating techniques in the classroom. Though the case provides no direct information about Vinceberg's intent, it seems clear to most readers that he was pursuing a pedagogical strategy of showing rather than telling—that he hoped to demonstrate dramatically the pain experienced by all parties when a member of a close working group is fired. Vinceberg's attempt goes seriously wrong, raising a series of questions about how (and how not) to use role playing and how to recover from teaching disasters, particularly when one has lost the trust of the students.

"Trevor Jones" can also stimulate discussion of an even more fundamental issue in teaching. Many instructors feel that learning is best promoted when students perceive their teacher as a trusted, caring, and generally predictable guide who does not subject students to unnecessarily painful experiences. On the other hand, good teachers often sense a need to shake students out of their complacency and to force them to confront difficult issues of professional practice, which may mean putting them in uncomfortable positions. It can be difficult to promote this kind of learning while still maintaining the students' trust. The issue, then, is how to balance and integrate these two dimensions of teaching.

It sometimes seems that these dimensions require fundamentally different approaches to students—one calling for care and nurturance, the other for confrontation and "tough love." In the heat of face-to-face teaching practice, instructors often find these two stances contradictory and even mutually exclusive. Educational philosophies also seem to polarize around this question, with some advocating caring, accepting relationships with students, and others arguing for confrontation and challenge. While our judgment is that these two approaches are best blended, such an integration will not come easily, but requires—for most of us—conscious awareness and deliberate effort.

"Trevor Jones" tends to firm up responses along the dimension of care versus confrontation, and thus can provide an excellent opportunity for participants to develop a more sophisticated understanding and integration of the two approaches. Many seminar members initially see these two approaches as polar opposites rather than elements to be balanced. To the extent that they believe a teacher's fundamental role is to be a trustworthy guide, seminar members often react angrily to Vinceberg's actions. From this perspective, he has violated his contract to provide the section with a predictable range of classroom experiences; he has betrayed both Trevor and the other students.

Other participants may emphasize the instructor's responsibility to challenge students: to help them confront their own assumptions and behavior, and to grow through responding to experiences that simulate the complexities—and even the emotional agonies—of real-world decision making and action. This second conception emphasizes the need for "tough love" in teaching, to force students to confront the difficult issues involved in managing other people. As a participant in the seminar wrote:

> When I first read the Trevor Jones case, I agreed with Bob Smith's diagnosis. Professor Vinceberg was an SOB, no doubt about it. What he had done to Trevor Jones was sadistic and humiliating. There was, and is, no defense for that kind of behavior by anyone dedicated to teaching.
>
> I still believe that, but [another seminar member's] insightful comments opened up a new perspective for me on Vinceberg's behavior. Vinceberg discovered a very effective and emotionally riveting way of teaching this particular case. He made a group of relatively conservative, middle-class business school students really understand "the gritty realities of every day, blue-collar work life." For a few minutes, the students in his section felt the same powerful anger and resentment that the workers in the paternalistic Southern factory experienced after one of their number was fired.
>
> While I concede that Vinceberg's techniques were wrong—especially not informing Jones of his plan—the success of the role playing was extraordinary. If it had been done properly, Bob Smith—Mr. Middle America—could have come away with a much deeper insight into one of the realities of blue-collar life: namely, the rage and feeling of helplessness that follows a violation of trust, even if that violation was in the "best interests" of the rest of the workers. For a few moments Vinceberg had cut away from his students their complacency and detachment, and made them vulnerable to real learning.

Discussion of this case is often characterized by great sweeps of shifting emotion, as participants wrestle with their feelings about Al Vinceberg, Trevor Jones, Bob Smith, and the overall situation. Anger toward Al Vinceberg is especially prominent. Passion and condemnation of Vinceberg are not problems in themselves, but they can swamp discussion if not tempered by thoughtful reflection. Thus, while for many cases we choose discussion questions designed to stimulate involvement and emotional commitment, here we pose questions that we hope will encourage reflection.

Early in the session, moreover, we use questions that encourage empathy and identification with Al Vinceberg, in order to enrich the consideration of his actions and to balance the tendency for some participants to condemn him out of hand.

We begin with the broad diagnostic question of

what happened and why, inviting seminar members to take a reflective, analytic approach to the case, while allowing them freedom to express (and if necessary vent) their feelings toward the protagonists. The next two questions ask participants to speculate about Vinceberg's motivations for initiating the role playing and for choosing Trevor Jones. The hope is that, by putting themselves in Vinceberg's place, seminar members will develop empathy and understanding for his position.

Questions 4 through 7 move the seminar from analysis to action planning, but do so very gradually. Moreover, the questions emphasize analysis and evaluation of action, rather than involvement and commitment. To maintain an external perspective, we ask, "What do you think of Vinceberg's response—asking for process evaluation by the members of the section?" (not "If you had been Vinceberg, how would you have responded to the tension after the coffee break?"). Thus we hope to maintain a reflective attitude toward the case.

The high involvement typically stimulated by the case tends to pull discussion toward the specifics of the situation and away from generalization. But since we believe that we learn most by moving back and forth between the general and the specific, we try to call the seminar's attention to the broader questions raised by their deliberations. To this end we often use six probes, which are included as Questions 8 through 12 in the list of discussion questions. Those that ask seminar members to generate guidelines for role playing (Questions 11 and 12) often provide a particularly effective conclusion.

Notes for Discussion Questions

These notes parallel the suggested discussion questions presented in **Exhibit 2**. We have briefly indicated the pedagogical intent and use of each question, and provided our best attempt at a reasoned response. These analytical responses represent our current thoughts on the matters raised, and are provided primarily to aid instructors in preparing for discussions of the case by sensitizing them to key issues. We do not regard these responses as the definitive solutions to the questions raised by the case. "Trevor Jones," like other cases, can be profitably analyzed from a variety of viewpoints, and a variety of actions could be usefully taken in situations like that confronting Al Vinceberg. We hope each new discussion of the case will provide new insights of value to both the discussion participants and the discussion leader—and we can say with gratitude that this has been our experience in leading discussions of this case and others in the seminar.

1. What happened? Why? What key factors contributed to the problem?

Usage Note

This broad diagnostic question encourages the section to identify the variety of factors that contributed to the "mess" described in the case. The openness of this question allows participants to vent some of the strong feelings that may have been aroused by the case. But we avoid phrasing the question in a provocative manner (e.g., "We've heard from Bob Smith in the case; now what do you think about this situation?"). The somewhat abstract, evaluative stance encouraged by the question helps participants put a counterbalancing measure of reflective distance between themselves and the case.

Analysis

By calling on the usually silent Trevor, and then without warning leading the section into evaluating one of its own members and "firing" him, Vinceberg has violated his implicit contract with both Trevor and the other students. It seems likely that Trevor concluded after his meeting with Vinceberg that the two of them had agreed that he need not speak in class. This understanding was probably not shared by Vinceberg.

Moreover, since the expected range of course experiences clearly does not include expelling students from the classroom for mediocre performance, the firing constitutes a further violation of the implicit contract between Trevor and Vinceberg—and will probably make Trevor feel further betrayed and abused.

Whatever their feelings about Trevor's being able to avoid speaking in class, the other students appear to know that this is his pattern, and assume that he has made a contract with Vinceberg to maintain it. When Vinceberg calls on Trevor, they no doubt also feel confused at the apparent contract violation, in addition to feeling sympathetic to Trevor in his vulnerability.

Subsequently, Vinceberg gets them to publicly condemn their peer—something they are not normally asked to do and that runs against the norm in virtually all student cultures. They probably then feel guilty because they have violated their own standard and joined in the humiliation of their sectionmate. Their anger naturally builds as they quickly realize Vinceberg has manipulated them into this action.

In summary, the students are likely to perceive that Vinceberg has violated his implicit contract with the students, encouraged them to do something beneath their ethical standards, and publicly humiliated one of them. Since the section members have little experience with Vinceberg and do not find him particularly personable, they are not likely to trust his good intentions and give him the benefit of the doubt on this mistake. Instead, they will probably conclude that Vinceberg cannot be trusted, and that if he is willing to pick on poor Trevor Jones, then any of them could be his next victim.

An additional factor is Trevor's possible status as a class maverick. Many sections (and indeed most groups and organizations) include one or more members who deviate in some visible way from the general norms of conduct. These individuals often come to symbolize for others a certain independence of spirit which is admired. Perhaps the more conforming students derive a small vicarious pleasure from seeing someone act out contrary impulses. In any case, an instructor who humiliates or attacks such a person may be perceived as attacking the spirit of independence in the section. Such an action can quickly alienate the other students, and Vinceberg's firing of Trevor may have had this effect.

Vinceberg is difficult to confront, because of his imposing presence and his power (70% of students' grades will depend on his subjective rating of their in-class performance). Moreover, by initially ignoring the situation, Vinceberg signals that he does not wish to discuss it. The pot boils until finally—at Vinceberg's invitation—it explodes.

2. *What do you think might have been Vinceberg's reasons for using role playing? What was he trying to accomplish?*

Analysis

Vinceberg may well have been trying to stimulate the high level of student involvement that marks successful case discussions. Discussion dialogue can proceed on various levels. At the first level, students are purely observers, commenting on someone else's problem in a strictly classroom-academic mode. A second level of discussion may be stimulated by assigning students roles in the case situation under discussion. Their comments then tend to reflect their sense of the circumstances of the company managers whose robes they wear. When students step back into their own normal classroom mode of operation after a successful role-playing exercise, their perspective has moved a little closer to that of an involved corporate officer.

The third discussion level is reached when students, on their own initiative, project themselves into the case situation. The classroom and business situation meld together. Problems are not discussed as abstract topics, but as issues inextricably bound up in a manager's career circumstances. Student comments reflect a personal commitment to the arguments they advance. This level of discussion comes as close to real life as can be achieved in an academic situation. Learning opportunities, and risk, are high for all involved.

Al Vinceberg may have been trying to achieve Level 3 involvement in his case discussion. The case requires students to consider the task of evaluating employees for possible dismissal—an emotionally arduous experience for most managers. Vinceberg may have felt that a Level 1 discussion could not give the flavor of the central human dilemmas involved in such situations. Thus he may have chosen an intervention that would bring the situation to life in the classroom—not realizing the possible harm that could be done by a poorly planned and executed attempt.

3. *Why might he have chosen to call on Trevor Jones?*

Usage Note

This question too is intended to help make participants consider the possibility that Al Vinceberg had good intentions in what he was doing.

Analysis

Participants tend to mention two possible reasons for selecting Trevor. First, Vinceberg may have realized that Trevor—unprepared to speak and caught off guard—would do poorly in the recitation and thus be a good candidate for the role of the fired worker. We think it unlikely that Vinceberg would be so insensitive to Trevor's needs as to act on this perception. But the other students, whose trust in Vinceberg has been destroyed, may well put this interpretation on events.

We believe that, in Vinceberg's original plan for the class, the decision to call on Trevor may well have been unconnected to the decision to use a role-playing exercise. Al may have thought that this case would provide a good opportunity for Trevor to make a contribution to the class. Although we do not know what actually happened in the meeting between Vinceberg and Trevor, Vinceberg may have assumed that Trevor would eventually participate but merely hoped to wait until he was comfortable. In view of their conversation about Trevor's father's experiences in the declining British steel industry, Al may have thought that Trevor would be especially well prepared for this case and that his contributions might help the class understand the painful realities being described. Thus

Al may have decided to call upon Trevor for his potentially positive contribution.

Even taking this charitable view, it is difficult to justify Vinceberg's calling upon Trevor to lead off. Opening the class is a particularly stressful task, even for those who are more experienced at contributing in case discussions. It would have been more appropriate, in our judgment, to wait until the discussion had developed, and then to ask Trevor to comment upon the substance of the contributions so far. Nevertheless, participants should recognize that Al may have had a basically positive reason for calling on Trevor.

Whatever his thinking about Trevor, Vinceberg may have independently planned to introduce the role-playing exercise at whatever point in the discussion seemed most appropriate. After Trevor's dismal performance Vinceberg may have made a quick and ill-considered decision to use it then—perhaps out of irritation at Trevor's rambling contribution, or perhaps simply because it struck him that he had been presented with an example of poor performance that would enable the role play to "work" if introduced immediately.

Instructor errors of this type seldom spring from a conscious desire to hurt a student. Rather, they generally result from quick moves made during the heat of teaching without considering crucial features of the situation. An intervention as risky as this one, which raises feelings most people find very difficult to deal with, should not have been undertaken without very thorough advance planning. In our judgment Vinceberg should have (1) selected his "victim" very carefully, picking someone with a good deal of personal resiliency and a strong standing in the section, (2) asked his or her cooperation in advance, (3) made contingency plans to abort the role play if it seemed to be getting out of hand, and (4) debriefed the section immediately after the incident, letting students understand his educational intent and giving them a chance to share and sort out their feelings.

4. *At the end of Bob Smith's outburst, what are the critical tasks facing Al Vinceberg?*

Usage Note

This question begins the shift to action planning, while continuing to counterbalance strong feelings in the seminar by encouraging reflective distance.

Analysis

First, Al needs to keep the class from blowing up. If dialogue breaks down now, Vinceberg will lose an important opportunity to begin to reestablish a working relationship with the section, and will probably have a much harder time later on.

Second, Trevor Jones needs to be protected from further humiliation.

Third, and very important, Al must work to reestablish mutual trust between himself and the section members.

5. *What do you think of his response—asking for process evaluation by the members of the section?*

Usage Note

This question continues the gradual movement toward action planning, while maintaining a somewhat detached perspective.

Analysis

In our judgment Al Vinceberg's most difficult and crucial task is to regain the trust of the section. Students trust instructors who are open and fair, and who avoid humiliating them. Al's approach, which is to admit his failure and ask for student reaction and assistance, has the advantage of being open, of admitting culpability (and thus being fair), and of helping to undo the humiliation of Trevor and the other students by losing face himself.

However, Al's response comes much too late. Immediately after the firing and even before Trevor left the room, Vinceberg could have opened up and allowed the class to see his intentions. By trying instead to conduct classroom business as usual, Al has created two problems. First, he has reinforced the impression that he is insensitive to the feelings of the students and thus given them more reason to be angry at him. Second, he has put them in the position of stewing in these feelings without being able to confront him. Now the risk is much greater that, when he does open up and cede control to the section, there will be a complete blowup—a shouting session of the type inaugurated by Bob Smith.

6. *After Bob Smith's outburst, what are the alternatives open to Al Vinceberg?*

Usage Note

This question asks participants to suggest alternative ways to handle the difficult problem of a hostile blowup when a student's ire is justified.

Analysis

Al Vinceberg has several options. He could attempt to return to the case discussion, although that could probably not be sustained. Or, he could call off the class, either immediately or after apologizing once again. If he takes this tack, the crucial questions are: What should he do before the next class session, and how should he begin the next class?

Most likely he will try to continue the discussion of the incident itself, since he has asked for feedback; adjourning the class might, in this context, look like a further attempt to squelch the expression of student feelings. He can respond to Bob, or he can ask for other comments. If he chooses to respond to Bob, he must decide how to do so. If Al asks for other comments, he can do so with a general query, or he can call on specific students. Over the course of the ensuing discussion, Al will need to develop a process plan, if he can, to guide his attempt to regain authority while at the same time beginning to restore trust.

7. What would you do now, and why? [Optional probes: What would you suggest Al do before the next class? What might he do at the beginning of the next class?]

Usage Note

Finally, this question asks directly for action recommendations. Rather than asking what Vinceberg should have done, we take what has happened as an unfortunate given, and ask participants how they could make the best of the situation. The intent of this question is once again to encourage identification with Al Vinceberg and his predicament, rather than simple condemnation.

Analysis

Now that the discussion of the intervention and of Vinceberg's performance has been opened, it seems unlikely that it can be closed. Thus we would probably proceed with it, hoping to rebuild credibility and a working relationship with the section. Though it is difficult to plan such a discussion, the following points seem important. First, we would not want to get into a shouting match with Bob Smith, and thus would try hard to remain calm and poised during his blast. After he finishes, we would probably respond directly to him, in order to gain some control over the situation.

If other students now start in, we might handle them similarly. However, it seems more likely that the room would fall silent for a moment after Bob finishes, as the students collect their thoughts. We might then call on another student, asking for his or her thoughts. Calling on a specific student has two advantages. First, we can choose the student. We would probably try to find one who is clearly angry (we don't wish it to appear that we are trying to suppress dialogue) but with whom we have established trust, and who is known to be able to keep a clear head under pressure. This would increase the chances that his or her comments would be constructive. Second, by calling on a student—even one who is so agitated it seems he or she will jump in momentarily anyway—we begin to reestablish our control over the process of the discussion.

During the ensuing discussion we would keep several aims in mind. We would want to remain open, in order to reestablish communication and trust. We would want to regain control over the process of the discussion. At the very least, we would want to determine who speaks, and if possible we would begin to ask specific questions in order to establish control over the substantive direction as well.

Over the course of the discussion we would continually emphasize the overarching goal of developing a constructive working relationship that can make the rest of the semester's work a success. This is a goal the students will subscribe to, and focusing on it should lead the dialogue into more constructive channels.

Students can learn a great deal from the incident itself. If possible, we would point out that the feelings generated by the role playing and subsequent events are like those that arise in real life when retrenchment and dismissals are necessary. But it could be important not to raise this interpretation too early, lest it appear that we have not fully appreciated the ill effects of the incident and are merely hastening to return to the point of the original role-playing exercise. The students are unlikely to agree that the cloud has a silver lining until they are sure we have experienced the darkness everywhere else. Ideally, this interpretation might be made by a student and/or noted by the instructor at the beginning of the following session as a way to bridge between these events and the case content of the course.

The following probes highlight some wider issues raised by the case, and can be interspersed in the discussion wherever they seem appropriate. Each question moves the discussion toward greater generality, but also focuses consideration on a particular issue, creating opportunities both to consider general guidelines and philosophy and to examine similar situations in the participants' experience. Since increasing generality usually has the effect of cooling emotional involvement, these questions can be used to manage the level of involvement when desired.

8. How can an instructor deal with section members who contribute little or nothing verbally?

Analysis

There are probably as many ways to help students who do not participate verbally as there are instructors. One approach we favor is to give them more structured support for their contributions.

For example, we would avoid asking low contributors very wide, general questions—at least initially. Rather, we may try to use more specific questions, perhaps asking for help with a particular point, and/or a response to a previous contribution. In addition, we often assign special roles to low contributors, perhaps asking them (probably privately, before class) to monitor the first part of the day's discussion, and give a summary to the class at the halfway point, or to be part of a panel of contributors.

We also find it helpful to ask students to exercise the subskills of participation. For example, during the early weeks we often ask all members of the section to attend not only to the content of their sectionmates' contributions, but also to the way in which each contributor thinks—his or her style, biases, strengths, and so forth—and to consider how to respond to the person, as well as to the point, when addressing the question being discussed. This is a particularly good practice for low contributors, for it helps them to think of their prospective comments as rejoinders in a dialogue rather than a performance. In general, such students find participation easier when they feel less on stage, and when their comments can be directed toward a specific person or viewpoint.

To strengthen analytical skills, we may allow participants to submit written analyses of cases for reading and comment, without grade, by the instructor. Such work, completed before a given case discussion, warms up the students and often increases verbal contributions in class.

Learning from cases requires in-class engagement, including actively synthesizing ideas and testing them in dialogue with other students. As case method instructors we believe all should share in the benefits of this experience. For those who cannot make their contribution verbally, we may substitute written forms of communication, but we still try to design an experience that will come as close as possible to that of the other students.

For students with bona fide problems that seem beyond our corrective intervention, we will sometimes allow written papers to substitute for in-class participation. These papers are to be short, but of high quality, and submitted at regular intervals. Sometimes their substance may be a reaction to the in-class discussion, and in such instances we may ask that the student allow us to distribute the paper to the section.

9. Al Vinceberg used class participation to determine a large part—70%—of each student's grade. Do you think this was wise? Why or why not?

Analysis

In case-based courses it is common to award 30% to 50% of the grade on the basis of class contribution. In our experience this system puts great pressure on students to perform in class, and helps to ensure preparation. Assigning a weight of less than 30% to participation can lead students to conclude that the case discussions are unimportant, and to put their energies elsewhere.

Basing 70% of the grade on participation seems to us extreme, and probably unwise for several reasons in any but a public speaking or debating course. Assigning participation grades is ultimately a very subjective process; the instructor has a great deal of power, while students who feel unjustly evaluated have little opportunity for appeal. Weighting participation so heavily gives Vinceberg so much power that fearful students may adopt classroom strategies designed to satisfy him rather than maximize their learning. The casewriter, for example, notes that Vinceberg "tended to shape and guide the discussion to the point where . . . you know what he wanted you to say and you went right along."

Too much emphasis on classroom participation can have several sorts of negative consequences. Since grades are based on subjective evaluations by the instructor, an impression of arbitrariness and unfairness can easily develop, undermining trust between students and teacher. Students typically become resentful of the instructor's authority and/or begin playing games in order to conform to the instructor's position (as they perceive it).

This latter response causes communication between students and instructor to break down, with the result that the instructor cannot determine the students' genuine interests and concerns or track their progress in learning the material. Students become much less willing to risk being wrong or to become personally involved in their responses to the case. So while participation, as measured by number and length of comments, may remain high, involvement is likely to decline to practically nothing.

10. What is the place of confrontation and challenge in teaching?

Analysis

This question can be valuable in focusing attention on the need to manage the level and manner of confronting students. Helping students to see the limits of their present understanding is a central task in all teaching. The question is who should do this, and how such confrontations can be managed so that they result in student learning rather than humiliation.

We believe it is essential to create a learning situation in which (1) the instructor confronts the students by asking them to respond to difficult questions that, at least occasionally, raise profound issues not easily resolved; (2) student responses are examined carefully and critically—by the students themselves whenever possible; and (3) better responses are rewarded, while incomplete or even clearly mistaken responses (assuming they are the result of sincere engagement with the case material) are understood to provide valuable contributions to the section's learning process.

A great deal of the power of case method teaching lies in the questions posed to the students. Ideally, students are forced to confront difficult issues of professional practice—issues that cannot be resolved in any simple or final way. Students usually have not asked themselves these questions, at least not in a clearly articulated way. Formulating responses is a genuine challenge, and confronts each student with his or her limits of knowledge and experience.

We see the creation of such confrontation as a primary responsibility of the case method instructor. It is his or her job to raise central questions, and to insist that the students attempt to deal with them. Sometimes students resist a question—perhaps imagining they are answering it while actually skittering off on a tangent. In such instances the instructor restates the question, driving it home and insisting that it be considered. Rather than objecting to such pressure, students usually appreciate the challenges of difficult questions, and rise to meet them.

Beginning case method instructors are often concerned about how to handle poor student contributions. They may assume that if they don't catch a problem, no one will. Quite the contrary. If section members are encouraged to talk with each other, and not simply respond to the instructor, they will usually demonstrate considerable skill in sniffing out the weaknesses in each other's arguments.

As instructors we will usually correct factual errors made during the early laying out of the case—for otherwise these have a way of skewing the later discussion—but we try to do so as unobtrusively as possible. Once the basic facts of the case are on the table, and the key questions have been introduced and apparently understood, we seldom comment directly on the content of the discussion. Indeed, a key reason for using the case method is to teach critical thinking in a group context. Thus the development of the section's ability to examine the arguments presented is one of our primary tasks as instructors.

This process of critical thinking can be encouraged in a variety of ways. One can simply ask for students' comments about an argument just made, or a particular line of reasoning. Generally the section members will find it stimulating to be given responsibility for critical appraisal of contributions. The instructor's primary task is then to help them learn to disagree with tact and sensitivity as well as clarity. The instructor may sometimes feel like a boxing referee, insisting that the fight be fair—though most sections require no more than an occasional buffering of sharp-edged comments and the encouragement to maintain a certain lightness and a caring sense of humor in the rough-and-tumble of discussion.

We find that the process of discussion is profoundly affected by the section's overall attitude toward "mistakes" and apparently weak comments. We promote the attitude that all sincere comments (and even many of the humorous asides) are potentially grist for the mill, and may be refined by the section into more complex, sensitive, and powerful insights into the case material. Comments that at first seem weak often reveal facets of the case not yet taken into account by the section; they may provoke a better articulated presentation of opposing points of view and frequently contain seed ideas that will be developed later into effective responses. At the very least such contributions illustrate common traps and pitfalls presented by the material under consideration.

When such an attitude toward contributions prevails, students are more apt to work for effective comments without feeling crushed when the section points out weaknesses in their analyses. Though an instructor cannot always succeed in creating this sort of section process, there is much that can be done to foster its development. The instructor can demonstrate an appreciation of diversity, making it clear that any view—if soundly argued and supported—will be well received. He or she can show special interest in contributions that buck the tide in discussion—comments that counter premature consensus. When a student becomes isolated—apparently the only one holding an unpopular but defensible view—the instructor can step in to support it.

In these ways the instructor fosters dialogue—or more properly, perhaps, dialectic—in the classroom. The discussion becomes less a guessing game (with the instructor judging the responses) and more a genuine working conversation. At best, the level of confrontation is very high, while the level of hurt feelings is quite low.

11. *What ethical principles should govern role playing?*

Analysis

Role playing creates an extraordinary situation in the classroom, one that can powerfully enhance student learning. But the use of this technique should be guided by ethical principles. Though we do not wish to lay down the ten commandments of role playing, the following suggestions, derived from our experience and that of past seminar participants, seem to make sense.

In general, the well-being of one individual should not be intentionally sacrificed for the learning of the group. Humiliating a student (or, for that matter, an entire section) is not an acceptable price to pay for section learning—and in the long run will destroy the trust necessary to continued discussion teaching.

Role playing creates a situation of potentially high emotional stress. Since each individual responds differently to such conditions, the instructor should think carefully about who should be chosen as protagonists in the play. Those who seem emotionally or socially vulnerable should be avoided.

Special care should be taken with any role-playing situation that might arouse feelings of rejection—either the experience of being rejected, or the experience of rejecting someone. Such feelings are particularly difficult and painful for most people to handle.

Finally, in many role-playing situations it may be necessary to gain informed consent. One of the central problems in the present case is that Trevor was a totally involuntary victim. This issue is complex, however. Many of our finest discussions shade almost imperceptibly into Level 3 involvement, and much of the potency of the learning situations comes from the participants' initial lack of self-consciousness that they are responding in any other than a "real-life" situation. Stopping to get informed consent as involvement rises would break the flow of experience and introduce an element of self-consciousness that in our judgment would significantly reduce learning.

12. *What process issues are relevant in using role playing?*

Analysis

We have found it useful to keep several points in mind when using role playing and similar sorts of interventions. First, instructors often underestimate the impact role playing can have in the classroom. Though the instructor is often concerned that the students will not get into the roles, the more common problem is that they cannot get out of them when the simulation is over.

One should plan ways to abort or cool down the role playing during the process if it becomes necessary. For example, one can identify points at which the exercise can be stopped early—working out alternative ways to discuss the experience if it must be terminated before the originally intended completion point.

Role playing is not an effective learning tool unless the students reflect upon their experiences. Simply having an experience is not generally helpful; they also need to take in-class time to think about it. The instructor should devote as much effort to planning the reflective portion of the exercise as to designing the simulation itself. This "debriefing" can be structured very much like the flow of a case discussion. One can ask students to think about what happened, what problems came up, and how they were handled and might have been handled. Suggestions for alternative actions can sometimes be played out, thus extending the role playing and allowing students to experiment with new behaviors.

The simulation should normally be discussed as soon as it is completed. A prompt debriefing enables participants to separate themselves from the roles they have played; otherwise they may feel stuck in the role and overwhelmed by the emotions evoked by the situation. Prompt debriefing also allows participants to express feelings stimulated by the exercise, which might otherwise boil up at less helpful times in the following discussion—as seems to have happened in Al Vinceberg's class. Expressing these feelings in the context of the debriefing also serves an important pedagogical purpose, because it helps participants to become conscious of and learn from their emotional responses. And an early debriefing ensures relatively accurate memory of what went on, and promotes more detailed analysis.

Debriefing generally works best when the central protagonists are first asked to share the thoughts and feelings evoked by the simulation. They are the ones who have taken the risk of exposing themselves to their classmates, and it is they who have potentially the most to learn from reflecting on their actions and feelings. Thus we almost always start with them, listening carefully to what they are experiencing and focusing our instructional effort on helping them benefit from the experience.

A Suggestion for Closure

An interesting way to end the discussion of this case is to ask participants to comment on how the session felt to them, and perhaps to compare it with the previous meeting. This works well if the seminar session has been particularly lively, and provides an opportunity for the section members to reflect on their responses to a highly emotional discussion. The seminar leader may also call attention to his or her use of questions to manage the intensity. This raises the important topic of how to manage involvement, and can lead to an interesting discussion in its own right. Allowing the seminar to focus on the leader's actions may also stimulate participants to learn by reflecting more generally on how the instructor has conducted discussions throughout the seminar.

EXHIBIT 1 *Trevor Jones*

Study Questions

1. What is your diagnosis of the situation? What happened? When? Why?
2. What does Professor Vinceberg do immediately? Later?
3. More generally, under what circumstances is role playing an effective involvement technique? What are the key decisions an instructor has to make when deciding to use role playing?

EXHIBIT 2 *Trevor Jones*

Discussion Questions

1. What happened? Why? What key factors contributed to the problem?
2. What do you think might have been Vinceberg's reasons for using role playing? What was he trying to accomplish?
3. Why might he have chosen to call on Trevor Jones?
4. At the end of Bob Smith's outburst, what are the critical tasks facing Al Vinceberg?
5. What do you think of his response—asking for process evaluation by the members of the section?
6. After Bob Smith's outburst, what are the alternatives open to Al Vinceberg?
7. What would you do now? Why?

The following probes highlight the wider issues raised by the case, and can be interspersed in the discussion wherever they seem appropriate. We often use them when they help make explicit an issue already raised in a seminar member's comment.

8. How can an instructor deal with section members who contribute little or nothing verbally?
9. Al Vinceberg used class participation to determine a large part—70% of each student's grade. Do you think this was wise? Why or why not?
10. What is the place of confrontation and challenge in teaching?
11. What are the ethical principles that guide role playing?
12. What process issues are relevant in using role playing?

The Puzzling Student (A) and (B)

TEACHING NOTE

Introduction

"The Puzzling Student" (TPS) is a case, we believe, with which many instructors will identify. Mark Costello, a new faculty member at Kensington University, is concerned about a student whose intentions to complete her work seem honorable but whose follow-through is less than ideal. The case has two major themes and many other teaching issues:

A) When and how does an instructor intervene when a student's performance begins to deteriorate?
B) Should an instructor ever "give up" on a student?

Other issues include:

- grading and evaluation
- rights and responsibilities of students and teachers
- the inevitable (conscious or unconscious) comparison of one student to another
- teaching a compulsory versus elective course

"The Puzzling Student" is written from the perspective of Mark Costello, the instructor in the case. The appeal of this case, we believe, is in the universality of Mark Costello's experience: the student who is pleasant, seemingly cooperative, yet whose academic performance slowly deteriorates.

A second appeal is the "subplot" of a new faculty member arriving in a department with a different philosophy and orientation to teaching. Does he adjust and compromise or persist with his own style of teaching?

Process Planning

TPS is divided into an (A) and (B) case. We suggest that discussion time be distributed as follows:

Introduction	10 minutes
(A) Case	65 minutes
(B) Case	15 minutes
	90 minutes

Alternatively, the entire session could be spent on (A), and participants could be given (B) at the end, to be read later.

Study Questions

1. What is your diagnosis of Mark Costello's dilemma?
2. What are his current options?
3. What should he do?

This teaching note was prepared by Marina McCarthy as an aid to instructors in the classroom use of the case series "The Puzzling Student" (A) 9-387-207 and (B) 9-387-208.
(HBS No. 5-389-009)

Questions for the Seminar Discussion (A) Case

1. To the opening speakers:

Please summarize the situation for us. What's going on here? Or, what is Mark Costello's dilemma?

2. What is your diagnosis of the situation?

"The Puzzling Student" illustrates the complexity of when (and how) to intervene when a student's performance is slipping. When is too late? Mid-term? When is too soon? After her first missing paper? What are appropriate interventions? With whom, if anyone, should one consult beside the student? A friend (theirs? yours?)? A department head? The student's former teacher? A dormitory advisor? A dean? A parent? Finally, is there a time when one needs to just give up on a student? (See Mark's comments in Researcher's Note below.)

Some participants may argue that Cecelia pulled the wool over Mark's eyes. Others may feel he was too hard on her. Some will sympathize with Cecelia's personal and medical problems, while others will feel they are "a line." There may be more "hard-liners" and "soft-touchers" than "fence sitters" on this issue.

Expect some debate over the appropriateness of a college instructor's "calling home." Some may feel that this goes beyond one's duty.

Mark Costello's situation is compounded by his being new to the Rhetoric department; further, his teaching style differs from the mainstream department philosophy. Perhaps someone who was not a newcomer would have approached colleagues for advice. Mark didn't even ask who was Cecelia's instructor of the previous year. Did she fail the course? Not complete it? What type of instructor did she have—one of the "killers" of the department? Beyond calling Cecelia's dormitory advisor, he never approached the department head whom he had known before. There must have been another new instructor with whom he could have discussed Cecelia's situation. Is teaching for Mark so isolating that he feels, consciously or unconsciously, he must tend to everything himself? Was there a climate in the department that inhibited Mark from looking for a sounding board, asking for advice? Do some departments frown on faculty with problems?

Mark has set up a "time-eating" course. He is also a doctoral student and teaches at another university. Rhetoric is also a required course. These constraints may have a bearing on the outcome of the case.

Mark's efforts to solve the situation are not working, which may, in part, be due to his failure to ask the right questions. Maybe he needs to "get personal" despite his uneasiness in discussing medical matters. Some in the seminar, however, may feel this is overstepping boundaries.

3. Cecelia is out of her cohort/peer group; repeating a class. How might things have looked from her point of view?

a) Is it possible that she disagrees with Mark's way of running the class, despite her apparent agreeable demeanor in conferences?
b) Is it possible she is trying to send a message to her family? To the university?
c) Do you think Cecelia wants to fail?

"The Puzzling Student" is written only from the perspective of Mark Costello; we do not hear directly from Cecelia Lawrence. The discussion leader may want to question or push the group to identify with Cecelia. For example, Cecelia might have been more uncomfortable repeating the course than one might initially think. Further, Mark's teaching style—using peer editing and peer critiquing—might have been embarrassing or even humiliating for Cecelia—a sophomore in a class of freshmen. She is perhaps an uncertain member of the group. On the other hand, Cecelia may have also had a real hard-liner for an instructor the previous year and may simply see Mark Costello as a pushover. As an adolescent with both the privilege and burden of being from an illustrious family, she may have been using her poor academic performance to attract attention or even "get back" at her family. Part of her agenda may be wanting to fail, and there is nothing in Mark or the university's powers to stop her. Although Cecelia may be proud of her family, she may also resent the ceremonial and command performances she must attend and the image she probably feels she needs to project and maintain. Freshman Rhetoric may not be the issue at all.

Teaching students from special families can be a challenge from a variety of perspectives. While one doesn't want to give preferential treatment, one also must be wary of negative discrimination. In one's zeal to be fair, one might (consciously or otherwise) be tougher on such a student. The same can be said of students from "different backgrounds," broadly defined.

Finally, is Cecelia "going overboard" in not taking responsibility for her behavior? Is Mark aiding and abetting her?

4. What is your assessment of how Mark handled the situation?

Some participants may say Mark is handling the situation as best as can be expected. Others may be impatient with his apparently laid-back manner.

Mark does make a number of attempts; he touches base with Cecelia often. Perhaps he should be less permissive: If she misses an appointment, he should not rush to accommodate her with another time at the end of the day. He may need to be more "cruel to be kind" to help her become more responsible for her work and appointments.

One of the "carrots" Mark uses to encourage Cecelia to be more punctual and responsible is mentioning grades. This may have a negative effect: She might not care about grades. She might not even care whether she takes the course again—for a third time.

Mark appears to be unsuccessful in discovering what Cecelia does care about—and using that as a motivating tool.

5. Under what constraints does Mark work? What are the risks?

Mark has several constraints. In addition to being new to the department, he is still teaching at Baxter. Mark is the department head's former student as well as a doctoral candidate in another department. It is possible that he doesn't feel as "legitimate" a faculty member as the rest of his colleagues.

The course Mark designed was very time consuming. Perhaps he wanted to prove himself—he may have needed to overachieve to be as good as the rest. But the course didn't leave much time in his schedule for emergencies such as Cecelia's. He might have called the dorm advisor so late simply because he had so little time!

6. Why was Mark so surprised at Jim Roberts' assessment of the situation?

Mark did not expect Jim to be so permissive. At orientation, Mark was led to believe that the department philosophy included high student expectations; he began to see a gap between the party line and reality. Mark could have used this moment to inquire about Cecelia's teacher from last year, for Jim Roberts would probably have known all the details. But Mark chose not to probe.

7. How do you interpret Cecelia's "Federal Express" story?

Cecelia's Federal Express story may or may not be true. Some in the seminar may feel Mark should call Federal Express to verify Cecelia's story. Others may feel it is immaterial whether or not the truck caught fire.

Cecelia's story may be a last cry for help. On the other hand, she may have just been desperate for another story to cover her tardiness.

8. What do you think Mark will do next?

a) He could call Federal Express and determine if the story is true and give her an extension if in fact there was a fire.
b) Mark could give Cecelia another extension without calling Federal Express—taking her story at face value.
c) He could calculate Cecelia's grade and send it in to the registrar based on the work she had completed thus far.

9. What effect do you think being new in the department had on Mark and his decision-making process?

Mark had heard the department's philosophy of grading at orientation and perhaps didn't allow enough room for exceptions. In addition, he assumed what he heard in September was written in granite. Perhaps Mark needed another semester to learn that not all organizations adhere to their "promotional materials." In many ways, his decision making reflected a desire to save Cecelia from the system. Had Mark had a healthy sense of skepticism about the system, however, he might have approached others for help.

10. What fundamental issues does this case pose for you?

a) When should one intervene with a student when his or her performance is deteriorating? How?
b) What is the nature of the instructor's responsibility in such a situation? To what extent should he or she intervene? Should instructors contact students, work with them, or simply let them take responsibility for their actions?
c) What stigma is attached to a student repeating a course?
d) Have any of you had experience teaching children from prominent families? Students with "special" backgrounds?

Responses may vary. We believe all schools have influential families—whether on a local or wider level. In Mark's case, he admired the Lawrence family; he showed no apparent resentment. Mark was surprised, however, when Jim Roberts appeared to waive the "flunk 'em" approach when they discussed Cecelia's situation.

e) Should one ever give up on a student?
f) How does one resolve a philosophical and pedagogical difference of opinion with one's department and/or department head?

(B) Case

1. What is your assessment of Mark's decision? His handling of the overall situation?

2. How might Robbie's situation have influenced Mark's thinking about working with Cecelia?

Robbie's situation may easily have affected Mark's decision making. He may have seen a person with clear physical challenges make a valiant effort to get his work done. Mark may have held Robbie's perseverance up to Cecelia and felt she was lax by comparison. Although comparing students is not wise, it is often hard to avoid. Mark may have decided not to give Cecelia one more chance in part because Robbie had been so diligent.

3. How do you think Cecelia will react to Mark's decision?

Cecelia may be relieved to get a passing grade and at last be done with Rhetoric. On the other hand, she may think she legitimately deserved another extension. Cecelia may also have been frustrated by Mark's continuous extensions and not being held to a deadline; she may now be relieved that he finally stuck to his ultimatum. Finally, Cecelia may be disappointed that their seemingly pleasant association ended on an off-beat note.

Researcher's Note

In many ways, one can look at Mark as "Everyteacher." In trying to accommodate the various needs of individual students, teachers often wonder if they are being taken advantage of. "Is the Federal Express story for real?" "Am I being taken for a fool?" "Is another extension unfair to the other students?" Although teachers inevitably dwell on these questions, some are more concerned about them than others.

In a conversation with the researcher, it did not appear that Mark was particularly concerned that Cecelia was taking advantage of him. Although the situation admittedly gnawed at him, Mark seemed personally and professionally secure about the challenge, commenting:

> I guess it has much to do with already having taught for twelve years. As a rookie I used to believe the adage that "there are no student failures, only teacher failures." Now I realize that we [teachers] aren't miracle workers. We try our best, give students as many opportunities as possible . . . But we should not beat our breasts when we are not as successful as we would like . . . But it is important to realize that if you want to stay in this business [teaching] you can't always save the world, even your corner of it. You can surely try, but you must learn not to become discouraged. Too many people leave the profession because they think of themselves as failures . . . over such little things! I really believe teachers need to be less harsh on themselves. Our egos are too fragile at times.

An Earthquake Had Started (A), (B), and (C)

TEACHING NOTE

Introduction

"An Earthquake Had Started" is a case for modern times. It describes an incident in which the members of a tutorial seminar, like each one of us, brings his/her background interests and baggage into class. Given a volatile combination of these, the results can sometimes be explosive and memorable. For Brad Park, the teacher in this situation, they were. Brad was a Southerner from Georgia who served as a course tutor for six sophomores in an introductory Political Science class. He prided himself on being a nonstereotypical Southerner. In Brad's eyes, stereotypical Southerners were either (a) stupid or (b) racist. Brad thought of himself as being reasonably liberal and nonracist, although more conservative than most at Wellhaven. He disliked, but consciously used to advantage, the stereotypes that his southern background provided, mostly by acting in a nonstereotypical fashion.

The formula worked well until Brad encountered a student, Tracy Hall, who combined and transgressed stereotypes in ways that even Brad found hard to handle. What does that mean? Like most of us, Brad tended to categorize others in terms of age, education, gender, ethnicity, race, and other background attributes. Like other administrators and faculty at Wellhaven, Brad also wanted to respect the differences epitomized by women, foreign nationals, and people of color. As a teacher, however, Brad also struggled "to treat them the same as everyone else." He met his match in Tracy Hall, who was:

- Black (a person of color)
- A woman (gender)
- A fundamentalist Christian (religion)
- A Southerner (Louisiana)
- An outspoken critic of some faculty on racial issues

The earthquake began when Tracy implied that she had no sympathy for the Holocaust victims of World War II. With somewhat more than 15 minutes of class to go, she commented:

> . . . I'm not sure it happened like they [the Jews?] say it did, and . . . I'm sure they [the Germans?] had their reasons.

Then, as she noted during the last few minutes of class:

> Well, blacks have been persecuted over here for hundreds of years, so why should we go fight because they were persecuting Jews?

Louis B. Barnes prepared this teaching note as an aid to instructors in classroom use of the case series "An Earthquake Had Started" (A) DBC 1, (B) DBC 3, and (C) DBC 4.
(DBC No. 2)

The immediate teaching question for Brad Park was how should he deal with an apparently outrageous statement? Or was the statement not as outrageous as it originally sounded, given Tracy's own frame of reference and background? Should Brad and the rest of the class have made special allowances for Tracy's minority background and religious beliefs? But, on the other hand, what is the price of diversity? When and how should one make these allowances? Or does that simply lead to avoidance in the name of tolerance? If so, does one then also run the risk of seeming too "politically correct," and where is the line between political correctness and respect for diversity?

Discussion Suggestions

Tracy's Comment

We suggest a case discussion might first take Tracy Hall's statement by itself, and then include the various background ingredients to discuss how they further complicated the classroom into a potential earthquake for Brad Park. For example, how would one deal with Tracy's remark itself in any context? Then, what about the context, given the course background and class setting? Most people would consider the comment insensitive at best—repulsive at worst—although this kind of insensitivity also seemed widespread enough in world responses to the Bosnian-Serbian-Croatian disputes.

Beyond that issue, what difference, if any, did it make that Tracy was black? Of a fundamentalist religious persuasion? What if she were not black? An agnostic? What if Brad were not from the South, teaching in an upper Northwest university? Did it make a difference that David Eisenmann was Jewish or that there was another relatively uninvolved black student, William Taylor, in the class? And what were the dangers (or advantages) of stereotyping in each of these categories?

Conversely, what if the remark had come from the opposite direction and had been a racist remark from a white or foreign student who said, "I'm not sure that slavery was all that bad, and if it was, maybe the blacks deserved it." Would Tracy, or we, react the same way or do the same thing as the class did in this case, or would the outcry have been greater? Each dimension adds a new side to the picture of what was going on. Each also raises new questions about how we imagine teaching in areas where our own attitudes and assumptions enter. We can't help but bump up against our own confusions and fears about how to work effectively with students from other background groups than our own.

Problems of Stereotyping

Another realm involves the role of stereotyping in this case. Here are some places where stereotyping appeared:

- Tracy apparently stereotyped Jews. How might this affect our view of her and our feelings about how we would treat her in the classroom?
- Brad disliked the way Southerners were stereotyped. Did this seem to affect his attitude toward Tracy and her remarks?
- Given that Brad was from the South, do *we* read the case differently, knowing that? Do we stereotype him, or if not, why not? (Brad was apparently sensitive to that possibility and didn't tell the case writer where he was from or had gone to college until asked toward the end of his interviews.)
- Are readers and discussants also tempted to stereotype Tracy? How different is our emotional reaction to her comments when we learn that she is black, a religious fundamentalist, and is highly critical of some teachers on racist grounds?

These issues of stereotyping can provide a fruitful area for discussion. It is easy enough to criticize others like Brad who may stereotype when threatened. But when we examine the possibility that *we* may even do the same to him or to Tracy, the case becomes even more complex. Most of us fall into stereotyping at least some of the time—e.g., Congress, business, public education. As teachers, how can we avoid that? Can we? And should we? How can we help our students to avoid detrimental stereotyping? And where is the line between stereotyping and prejudice? Does the second require the first?

At still another level, how much should a teacher try to learn about the students' different backgrounds and cultural norms? Should a teacher struggle to understand the subtleties of an African American's experience? Do we need to know a student's various Hispanic histories, the different country backgrounds of Asian Americans, or the cultural mores of students from other countries? What about those from different geographical areas and class levels within the United States?

Once having learned all these details, how do we then go on, as Brad desired, "to treat them all alike" as individuals without stereotyping, according to some apparent cultural, ethnic, or background clichés? Must we thus forget or *unlearn* the background characteristics so as not to risk stereotyping? How do we respect the individual and not the generalizations?

The Guarded Teacher

Brad tells us that he felt he had to be careful about his comments around certain students for fear of being reported. Will this kind of caution lead to so-called "politically correct" behavior? Brad seemed fearful of negative comments from students even though he consistently received high evaluations from students for his teaching. One can only wonder how these feelings affected his behavior in this case. Brad said in the (C) case that he would have dealt differently with Tracy if she had been Sam. He would have felt freer to attack Sam. But how does the cautious teacher (Brad) find ways to talk to the outspoken student (Tracy)? Should Brad have tried to recover the relationship with Tracy when he met her after the course was over?

In a larger sense, what happens when a teacher becomes afraid of a student's power? How would we work with that issue in this case, either during or after the earthquake incident?

Who Failed Whom?

Did Brad fail Tracy as a teacher? If so, at what point did he fail her, and just what was the failure? One could argue that Brad might have talked with Tracy earlier in the semester either in or out of class when he began to sense her disapproval and intolerance of his teaching. One might also ask whether Brad was reading those signals correctly, and if so why he *didn't* do something about them. Or was his more serious deficiency failing himself in terms of moral and emotional honesty?

In the same vein, how might Tracy have felt when Brad said, "Ohhh Kayyy" and then went on to ask Sam what he thought, without examining or pushing Tracy to explain her comments, as she did to some extent later in the class (described in the B case)? Did his own embarrassment fail her? She remained silent until the very end of the class when she blurted out the comment about blacks being persecuted. We also know that she apparently gave him the most negative rating he'd ever received at the end of the semester. Conversely, did Tracy fail Brad in not speaking up to him sooner?

Did Brad fail the other students? How do we think the other students felt when Tracy made her original remarks, when those comments were seemingly ignored by Brad as she remained silent? Could Brad have done anything to clear what might have been uncomfortable feelings among the students in the room? Could he have protected other students who might have been affronted by her remarks about the Jews? Should he have done so?

Such questions ask us to reflect on what success or failure means in a classroom. It also can move us to articulate what is most important in our own teaching strategies. Is it covering the material or being sure that everyone gets the point? In that case, Brad probably did not fail anyone. Is it ensuring that the classroom is a safe place, so all points of view can be articulated? In this case, did Brad fail Tracy? Was it safe for her to make her point and to explore its implications? Was it safe for others when she made her point, saying that maybe the Jews deserved the Holocaust? Is the most important thing encouraging and working with each student individually, so that each can learn as much as possible?

These last questions cause us to reflect on what our relationships with students ought to be. Why might it be important for Brad to try to recover the relationship with Tracy after the fact? What would trying to recover it say about one's perception of the teacher's role?

What Should Brad Have Done?

The answers to this question are sure to range widely, from not doing anything at all to exploring specific and general issues of stereotyping and prejudice. It will be important in a discussion to examine the philosophies of education that seemingly lie behind each response. In a discussion of this case, one participant strongly believed that it was the instructor's task to deal directly with outright prejudicial remarks and to model correct behavior and ways of thinking. Another thought the teacher should say, "That's news to me. I've never heard that theory. Why do you think that?" He thought that he thereby let the class know that he considered her remarks inappropriate, but would also give Tracy a chance to respond and argue her case. His educational philosophy seemed to be to let each person argue his or her point in an open debate. Others sought ways in which Brad might have turned this incident into a teaching opportunity.

One way of trying to do this might have been to hang on to Tracy's late impulsive comment, "We have persecuted blacks in this country for hundreds of years, so why should we go to war because they were persecuting the Jews?" If that comment had come into the discussion sooner, it might have provided a better way of understanding her original statement about not going to war over the Holocaust. The comment gives some clues to what was behind her sentiments and brings out her most serious issue—shouldn't we put our own house in order before taking on crusades elsewhere? Or do we have a moral responsibility to address critical issues throughout the world regardless of the state of affairs at home? It is a pertinent question today, and one without easy answers. Another question that flows from Tracy's last remark would be, Why or when should members of one group struggling for survival go to war to defend another group in the same position?

Thus, one way to use the teaching opportunities inherent in this incident would have been for Brad to return to the discussion in the next class in order to: (a) explore Tracy's later remarks on the similarities and differences in the Holocaust and black suffering, (b) raise questions about moral responsibilities and obligations elsewhere when one's own house is not in order, and (c) debate whether assumptions like Tracy's have other implications (e.g., do two wrongs make a right? What is "fair" in this case?).

What Should We Do?

At a more general level, what do we do when a student makes what appears to be an outrageous racist, sexist, or, in this case, antisemitic remark?

- Do we stop it at once, making it absolutely clear that remarks of this sort are unacceptable in this classroom?
- Do we ask the student to give evidence and substantiate his or her point of view, thus lending it intellectual credence?
- Do we look for the music beneath the words and approach the emotional subtext? Why does the student feel this way? What's going on that would make him or her react with these sentiments? What can be found in the situation to promote a discussion that would enrich the entire class?

A subset of this question is, How do we handle emotionally loaded topics or incidents? Very often, when emotions are high, intense learning can take place. However, this requires that the teacher see through the emotions (his or her own included) to a strategy for dealing with them. Many teachers and students feel uncomfortable with strong emotions, fearing loss of control, chaos, hurt feelings, their own vulnerability, or incompetence. Many feel unskilled dealing with issues where feelings are strong and consequently shun them.

We find that bringing up *this* topic of what to do is often a good way to generate suggestions in a group. It may be useful to ask people to relate instances when they have seen emotions or emotional issues handled well, when they have seen controversial topics dealt with directly and effectively. Here are some examples of how some teachers made such discussions safe for both themselves and students, and useful too.

- One teacher we know loves intellectual conflict and actively stirs it up. His strategy for accomplishing this and making it safe for everyone to voice his or her view is to protect the weakest. Thus, if he accepts as worthy of consideration a weak position, everyone in the room knows that it is alright to speak up. He also never lets one person be scapegoated by other students.
- Another teacher begins a discussion of the civil rights movement by asking each student to write down who in the movement he or she most identifies with—whites, blacks, women, activist groups, or individuals. Students then tell what they have written down. By then, everyone knows that multiple perspectives are on the table, and that each one, no matter how much you might disagree with it, has its place on the table.
- After a particularly emotional exchange has begun to spin its wheels, a teacher asks students to step back and see how they can make something positive of this exchange, what they can learn from it. This moves the discussion to a broader, more general level that helps everyone see what issues are at stake and what the clash itself means.
- A teacher asks students to think about how their reactions mirror the subject at hand, and what they can learn about the subject from their own behavior.
- A student makes a blatantly racist assertion. The teacher stops the class and gives all the students an assignment to research the statement and write a short essay about their findings.
- Another teacher stops a charged discussion and goes around the room, asking each student who has spoken (and others if they wish) to state their views and explain their reasoning. Every student is heard and the class is enriched by the range of perceptions.

And If the Moment for Learning Is Lost?

This is not an easy question, but one response is to look for another moment. More often than not, it will appear, particularly if some of the issues can be predicted to recur. Brad probably could have come back to the issues Tracy raised in the next class, after he had had time to think and reflect on what had happened, or even after he had sought clarification from Tracy after class. In the same manner, Brad knew (and was avoiding) Tracy's growing disapproval of the way that he was dealing with the class. How might he have tried to face this problem either inside or outside class? In the interests of avoiding some of the unpleasantness and pain referred to in the section above, Brad made possibly the biggest mistake by not confronting Tracy at all.

Consequently, the best assumption, we suspect, is that the moments for learning are rarely lost, only postponed. The creativity of good teaching often lies in finding, bending, and recreating them in a future that may include time out of class, as well as in class, moments.

The Class Teaching Plan

With "An Earthquake Had Started," we suggest following the sequences above, using the (A) case for about the first half hour of the class, before students know that Tracy Hall had made a connection between the Holocaust and black persecution in this country. It might be noted that earlier Brad had asked if students would go to war over the issue of slavery, and some had said yes and some no. We don't know how Tracy interpreted those sentiments, and there is no evidence that she participated in that part of the discussion.

The bulk of the class would include the (A) and (B) cases, with some of Sam Beatty's comments added to those of Brad Park. During this part of the discussion, we would try to cover some of the larger questions described above. Finally, in the last ten minutes of class, we would hand out the (C) case for discussion and wrap-up.

Bob Lunt (A), (B), and (C)

TEACHING NOTE

Louis B. Barnes prepared this teaching note as an aid to instructors in classroom use of the case series "Bob Lunt" (A) 9-382-054, (B) 9-382-055, and (C) 9-382-056.
(HBS No. 5-394-160)

Introduction

The "Bob Lunt" (A) and (B) cases describe a tale of two people who could have been allies but wound up as apparent antagonists. Martha Elliot was 29 years old and a new assistant professor of financial management in the Graduate School of Social Policy and Research at San Francisco Bay University. The Financial Management 202 course was Martha's first full-time teaching assignment and is described as posing a "formidable challenge" to many first-semester students at Bay. Bob Lunt, one of Martha's students that semester, had an unusual background. He was in his late thirties (older than Martha), was a former associate professor of English at San Francisco State College (a less prestigious institution than Bay), and had academically outranked his new teacher, Martha.

Bob Lunt decided to change careers, apparently when his own promotion to full professor at S.F. State College was postponed for a year. Martha Elliot heard that Bob had left his college "in a huff," suggesting that Bob could be sensitive to perceived slights or failures to recognize his status or merits. If that were the case, he was in for a great shock when he moved back into the ranks of being a student at Bay.

The (A) and (B) cases describe Bob Lunt's failure to follow instructions on the final exam of the Financial Management 202 course. Rather than "crunch the numbers" required for an adequate case analysis, Lunt gave an opinionated view of what he felt the resolution should be to accomplish the goals that he favored. The (A) case states the problem, as Martha Elliot encounters it when she reads Bob's exam paper. The (B) case shows the somewhat angry letter and less negative course grade (Satisfactory) that Martha gave Bob Lunt. In her grade comments, Martha notes:

> Bob's final exam was superficial guesswork, rehashings of the most obvious management accounting generalizations, and hostile justifications for his flat denials to think about quantitative data. . . . I have suggested to Bob that he resolve the conflict or choose another field.

The (B) case ends by noting that Martha heard six months later that Bob Lunt had been asked to leave the graduate program in Social Policy.

The Bob Lunt (C) case presents Martha Elliot's reflections on the (A) and (B) case incidents a year later. These year-later thoughts contain a number of questions that Martha is now raising, and that many teachers might have raised earlier. Martha has apparently had some serious second thoughts and even made some follow-up inquiries on Bob Lunt. The case writer quotes Martha Elliot as commenting:

> Bob had more problems in the course than Martha realized, but his difficulties weren't really substantive. . . . Martha didn't realize his desperation.

Bob Lunt's—and Martha Elliot's—Problems

Indeed, on the surface, Lunt was a bright, courtly, articulate ex-academician who could well have gotten fed up with the bureaucratization of academic promotions. One can even admire him. On the other hand, Bob Lunt became an angry, confused man approaching middle age, who threw over an established career as an English professor at a time when liberal arts teaching positions were hard to find, academic budgets were tight, and any sensible person would have held on to any academic position he or she had—all in order to go back to school and start at the bottom. Such reasoning would ask if the pains of a new start-up career in another bureaucracy were worth losing what one had already achieved?

In addition to changing careers, other things were going on in Bob Lunt's life, a few of which we know and probably a number of which we are unaware. But even the ones we know about could have served as warning flags. For example:

- Looking at the cases from a slightly wider perspective, who was around to help Bob Lunt? Did he get any help from others as he began this life stage and career transition? We don't know the answer to this for sure, though Martha, for example, showed little sympathy. She tended to ignore and personalize the issue, stepping back only later, as described in the (C) case, after Bob had left. It seems likely that others abandoned Bob Lunt too. At least one can ask if the School of Social Policy and Research was set up to handle the Bob Lunt's of the world—mid-life career changers.
- Lunt was entering classes in which his peers were, on the average, some ten years younger than he was. Some were young enough to have been his own students, and even the teacher was younger than he was.
- Some of the students were clearly more comfortable with the quantitative course materials than Lunt was. This was a tough numbers-crunching course. Other students seemed to have a stronger management orientation. A third group seemed to be less active members scattered throughout the classroom. "And then there was Bob Lunt," as Martha said, "a different type of person from the rest of the students." Bob was an outsider in a number of ways.
- Martha Elliot was teaching a numbers course, reputed to be tough for students, for the first time. There is no evidence that she was getting much coaching or mentoring along the way.
- Lunt neither attended Martha's review sessions nor signed up for an appointment during Martha's office hours. He also seemed to become less and less involved with other students as the semester went on. "He began slumping low in his seat, cynically or disdainfully observing procedures from the sidelines, and participating only very occasionally."
- Bob's actions became more and more aggressive and argumentative. Nevertheless, Martha tended to ignore these and "not challenge Bob about his worsening attitude." Why?

Clearly something was going wrong for Bob Lunt. Martha had one meeting with him in the cafeteria in which Bob tried to give her his perspective on life in the academic world, especially in the confines of a state-funded school. Martha responded by asking him "pointed questions . . . about the pressures and problems of teaching in a public university." Bob seemed to want to discuss these issues but ended by putting Martha down with the comment that she was "insulated" from reality. However, Martha derived from that conversation only that Bob wasn't out to make trouble for her. That may have been true: he was more bent on making trouble for himself, but Martha would be caught up in his turmoil as she soon discovered when she received Bob Lunt's final exam. And yet, the final exam incident was only the delayed tip of the iceberg.

The Teaching Issues

Martha Elliot seemed to be on her way to becoming an excellent teacher. The dean of the school mentioned having heard "rave reviews" of her teaching. Before class, she was surrounded by students asking questions and making comments, and she received a number of complimentary notes and personal comments. She saw the class, separate factions early in the course, reach a "general class camaraderie." And she began to feel "proud of her performance in the first undertaking of her professional academic career." But what went wrong?

An initial question for participants to consider is, Should Martha Elliot have done anything beyond what she did do? As a first-time teacher, she had more than enough to do, made herself available to students at their initiative, and seemed to be doing an excellent job teaching a difficult subject area. So what more did she owe Bob Lunt, the person, over and above what she owed Bob Lunt, the student? The answer is debatable, but the fact is that Martha's own thinking on the question apparently changed from the time of the (A) and (B) cases to the (C) case a year later. Her concerns over what both she and Lunt had done wouldn't go away. Participants may argue that they should have disappeared, but apparently they didn't. Martha was bothered by her own handling of the case a year after the incident was evidently over.

Another dilemma that arises from this case involves the extent to which a teacher can, or wants to, attend to fringe members of a class *outside of class* as well as inside. And if so, how? Bob Lunt was a fringe member. He was different from other students to begin with. He sat in his own space in class and seemed to be a loner outside. He was apparently withdrawn and alone, almost from the beginning, but Martha never tried to engage him in conversation or draw out his views or experiences until *he* took the initiative in the cafeteria meeting. Nevertheless, he was always early to class and seemed to accept Martha until the exam incident. Lunt's previous action of leaving S.F. State College "in a huff" suggests that he was a person who wanted respect and recognition, but Martha's course was one in which he could apparently find neither—and it got worse as the semester went on.

A third major issue is the question of timing. When should Martha have taken action, if at all? Some might argue that she might have made some initial overtures early in the course and treated Bob Lunt more like a special colleague than a student. Others will balk at such special treatment, but still maintain that Martha might have at least touched base with Bob during one of those many times when he came to class early. In addition, there is the question of whether Martha might have done more at the end of the (A) and (B) cases—either before she saw Bob's exam when she met him in the hallway, or just after the grades went in with her frustrated comments. Bob Lunt was apparently in trouble by then, and not just in Martha's course, but what could she have done at these times, if anything? Martha did get another warning flag when she met Bob in the hall after he had not picked up his exam and he said that, "I just wanted to live my life differently."

Finally, as the (C) case notes, there is a larger philosophical question here—one that Bob Lunt tries to address in his exam. What should a student do when he or she perceives the exam assignment to be a game-playing exercise that fails to consider most aspects of reality? When is the point of absurdity reached? And even if it does seem absurd from the student's perspective, is it not still the assignment? One person's folly may be another person's metaphor for reality. Bob Lunt, the previous designer of many exams, may have been choking on the irrelevance of his own past efforts as well as Martha's F.M. 202 exam in this case. But does that forgive him for not following the assignment? Most participants will argue that it does not; that he must still fulfill the assignment. Lunt, the English professor, might still be inclined to maintain that there are qualitative logics as well as quantitative logics, and that he used these in his one-page exam paper. Indeed he did, for he had obviously read the exam and argued some of his points with passion and conviction.

Nevertheless, even this misses a still larger point—that it wasn't just Martha Elliot's course that was a problem for Bob Lunt. Being forced out of the program at the end of the year suggests a wider and deeper range of problems that no one addressed effectively.

A Teaching Plan

The (A) case sets the stage for this tragedy without giving any indication that Martha Elliot will have second thoughts a year later. By the time she receives Bob Lunt's exam paper, she is hurt and exasperated. She is also full of self-pity, and most teachers can identify with her—everything seems to have gone so well up until now. Then, at the end, *this* had to happen. The only recourse seems to be revenge, but that's what part of the (A) case discussion can be about. Consequently, our first question would be "What Happened?" Other questions would include:

- Could Martha have seen any handwriting on the wall in this case? If so, what were the early signals?
- How would you have felt if you were Martha Elliot going into your first course as a teacher of the F.M. 202 course?
- On the other hand, how would you have felt if you were Bob Lunt going into the F.M. 202 course? What about going into the entire program in Social Policy and Research?
- In your opinion, what, if anything, did Martha do wrong during the early weeks of her course? During the later weeks? At the cafeteria meeting with Bob Lunt?

Assuming a 90-minute class, we would spend about the first 45 minutes discussing the (A) case, and then hand out the (B) case for a 30–35 minute discussion. In the (B) case are Martha's responses to Bob, and it is worth examining in some detail her letter to Bob and her Instructor's Comments. Both tend to be loaded with what are, to some, overstatements—e.g., "The most pressing problem . . . *all along* has been attitudinal. . . . Whatever your hostility is . . . *I expect you will find, at most, it will interest only yourself.*" Is that the way Martha really wants it to be? Later, in the Instructor's Comments, Martha talks of Bob's "blind opposition to the content of management accounting." Martha again throws the burden onto Bob's shoulders by suggesting that he "resolve the conflict or choose another field." So much for either instructor or institutional support.

Possible questions are:

- How would you have dealt with Bob Lunt's exam paper?
- Did Martha do enough in her written comments? If not, what else might she have done at the end of the (B) case?
- In your judgment, is there more that she should do at this time?
- What do we learn about either Bob or Martha from the last sentence in the case with regard to Bob Lunt's being asked to leave the program?

The (C) case can be handed out at the end of the class, simply because it serves as a mini-teaching note and raises questions that the class probably will have raised during the discussion, even though Martha Elliot didn't do so earlier. Our inclination, though, is to hand out the (C) case with 10 or 15 minutes to go, simply because it provides the opportunity to discuss how teachers often relive and intensify earlier problems involving their own students. Martha, who gave no sense of remorse in the (A) and (B) cases, almost goes overboard in the (C) case, but with no evidence that she has much more data to go on than she had in the earlier cases. What happened here? We'll never know the answer in Martha's case, but those last few minutes may provide some time to raise questions of delayed recollections, remorse, and rebuke. Many of us tend to do it, sometimes too harshly. But the underlying message is one of trying to get beyond our own concerns long enough to focus on the student's—both with the course being taught and the life being lived.

The Blank Page (A) and (B)

TEACHING NOTE

This note was designed and written by Abby Hansen for use with the case series "The Blank Page" (A) HSPH 2 and (B) HSPH 8 to help instructors prepare to lead case discussions. It is meant to stimulate discussion, not present a definitive analysis. The School of Public Health is grateful to President Derek Bok of Harvard University for a grant in support of case development.
(HSPH No. 5)

The following remarks include ideas that arose for me during the research, design, and writing phases of this case project. I offer them in a spirit of helpfulness to all readers, and urge instructors to formulate their own lists of important issues and design their own teaching approaches. I will introduce the case by attempting to convey its uniqueness, then offer some suggestions about usage, survey two high-profile issues and a subset of other issues, and mention some further readings.

Special Features: Double Focus

Like the drawings of M. C. Escher (Does the stairway go up or down? Are those dark birds on a light background or light birds on a dark background?), this case can look different from different angles of vision. To me, the narrative suggests two major operational problems: how to deal with a disruptive student and how to evaluate such a student in writing. Both call for action, and action springs from assumptions about what one *ought* to do. (In this case, some of the major assumptions relate to how a teacher should lead a discussion group, observe the students in action, interpret those observations, describe the interpretation in a formal, written document, and manage his or her own emotional reactions throughout the whole process.) Because of its inherent richness, "The Blank Page" can stimulate discussions on a wide range of topics. There is ample data here to support considerations about the roles, responsibilities, and skills of discussion leaders.

An important distinction: Martin's challenge is not how to *grade* Kenneth Holmes, but how to evaluate him. Even in institutions that do not require formal evaluations, the act of evaluation can play a role in assigning course grades, and it is surely central to the preparation of recommendations.

Some Considerations on Usage

Each of the two major issues—handling disruption, preparing written student evaluations—could easily sustain a separate class discussion. Schedule permitting, seminar leaders might find it advisable to set aside two class meetings to discuss this case. If only one session is available, it is likely that both issues will surface. I would suggest airing both without worrying too much about striking a balance. Both are meaty issues that may well elicit anecdotes and firmly held convictions from seminar participants.

The preceding comments should make it apparent that I would not schedule this case early in a seminar—before participants have learned to read the implications of a story as well as its surface details—unless I planned to return to it at a later date. None of its issues is simple. Discussing this case in a one-shot session early in a seminar may frustrate the instructor (if not the participants) by leaving many of its rich implications untapped. Scheduling it later can provide an opportunity for complex, even profound reflection and learning.

At the end of the seminar, the instructor might want to revisit the issues of this case and ask seminar members if their views on its issues have changed or deepened.

The Two Major Issues: Dealing with and Evaluating a Difficult Student

Martin Davis's heavy responsibility to submit a formal, written evaluation to Kenneth Holmes's official academic record is the reason that I call this case "The Blank Page" and end the (A) segment with Martin about to fill in the official form. It may be interesting to know that the early working title of this case, "The Square Peg," emphasized a different aspect: Martin's challenge to help Kenneth adapt to group discussion learning (and to help the group adapt to Kenneth). In working with the material, I chose to shift its emphasis because I saw the written document as the culmination of the whole proceeding and Martin's ultimate challenge.

Dealing with Kenneth Holmes is the more accessible issue. Throughout a month-long discussion course in endocrine pathophysiology (the origins of diseases of the endocrine glands), instructor Martin Davis faces a string of unpleasant surprises that all spring from Kenneth's behavior and the way in which the other students in the discussion group react to it. Like all discussion teachers—and many professionals in other fields—Martin has a "numerator and denominator" problem: he must balance his responsibilities to Kenneth, who is one-eighth of the student body of this particular group, with his duty to the others. This problem requires him to think about helping not only Kenneth, who is the squeaky wheel, but also the other seven students, who appear to get along pretty well without much intervention from Martin. (An interesting question emerges from this consideration: What responsibility do the others in the section bear for reconciling the split between them and Kenneth?)

The evaluation form asks Martin to judge Kenneth in several domains: problem-solving, intellectual style, contributions to the learning of the group, and personal development. Four weeks is a short time in which to get to know any human being in so many contexts, but the prospect of committing one's impressions to writing (knowing that the resulting document may irrevocably alter the course of the student's career), puts extra pressure on the instructor.

A Subset of Related Teaching Issues and How They May Come up in Discussion

1. *Universality*

Stripped of their medical school setting and (to some) obscure course material, Martin Davis's operational challenges should strike familiar chords with most teachers. As a committed, reflective, moral, and sensitive person, Martin realizes the gravity of his responsibility when he discovers that the discussion group has found Kenneth irritating enough to ostracize. This situation violates all of Martin's assumptions about the ethics of the enterprise of discussion teaching, and Martin feels obliged to act. But how? (Note that his task is made even more difficult by his being, as he puts it, "the new kid on the block." This element may also jibe with the experience of many teachers who inherit groups that have established behavioral norms before meeting their new instructor. What are the special challenges of setting a teaching and learning contract with a group that has already forged one of its own?)

A second widely applicable challenge relates to the necessity of evaluating a process while participating in it. All teachers who prepare evaluations and recommendations—or who factor "participation" into students' course grades—face this problem.

2. *How Martin Describes Kenneth and the Other Students*

As readers, we see through Martin's eyes. It may be useful to read Martin's descriptions of Kenneth and the other students and note the details that he selects as significant and the words in which he conveys them. What do these passages in the text suggest about Martin's evaluation criteria? What broader issues do they raise for all teachers as they observe, categorize, and describe students? (Virtually all description rests on a substratum of evaluation; even the apparently simple matter of what one does and does not mention implies an implicit hierarchy of importance.) The seminar group may find it useful to reflect on common ways in which teachers describe students. What do these descriptions communicate? Seminar participants may well have anecdotes to tell about how they have described students, or about descriptions that they have read.

3. *How to Begin to Prepare for a Written Evaluation*

The seminar leader might introduce a question about what Martin could have done right after the first class to begin the evaluation process. Should he have taken notes? In what form? Are there any specific categories that can guide one's observation? Even at this early date, should Martin have sought some background information about Kenneth and his dealings with other students? If so, what information, and where?

(One operational suggestion for teachers facing the necessity of writing student evaluations might be to consider constructing student profiles and using these as memory aids. The act of recording one's impressions—privately, in whatever shorthand one finds comfortable—can save time and imprecision later, when evaluation becomes a necessity. The notation of separate comments about each student's command of content, participation in process, frequency of participation, and the like can be extremely helpful.

C. R. Christensen has summarized a practice that he developed and maintained over years of "filling out, for each student and my own use—not for the system—a 4x6 index card profile of strengths and weaknesses. I noted where, in working in a large-group, problem-solving self-educative system, a student had seemed to show effective practice skills. The shorthand notes I made for my own use said things like, 'good questioner, good listener, good summarizer,' and the like. I also talked about the student's mastery of the content and practices of the course. I would jot down phrases like 'consistent weakness in not seeing the strategic implication of an operational decision' and mention the discussion in which I had noted this. These cards were extremely helpful for me both in conferences with the student during the course as well as in writing recommendations years later—as well as for the students. I told them that these cards existed and invited them to come and discuss them with me if they chose. There were risks in writing down these evaluations, but they paid off for me. They forced me to think in greater depth about the students in at least two dimensions, command of material and command of processes and practices of the course. I found a 4x6 card is less formidable than a whole page—and conducive to brevity."

When students came to discuss their cards, Christensen would "debrief them over a cup of coffee in the office. I would test the student's reaction, look at the eyes, and, if I read pain, back off and approach these issues at a more constructive moment.")

4. *Context: Preparation vs. Current Challenges*

Many of Martin's difficulties spring from a pedagogical shift that his institution has undertaken in switching from a lecture-based to a discussion-based curriculum. Many instructors are now functioning in similar settings, or in institutions where the two instructional approaches coexist (sometimes uncomfortably). Is Martin's task complicated by his students' arriving in his discussion class directly from lecture? What does it mean that all of these students (one assumes) came from traditional transfer-of-information backgrounds and took batteries of objective (often multiple-choice) tests to win their acceptances to Farwestern Medical School?

The special case of Kenneth Holmes seems to crystallize some of these difficulties. Martin mentions that, late in the story, he learned through the grapevine that Kenneth's application had made the committee "gasp" with admiration. What does this mean? (Probably that Kenneth had the knack of "acing" objective tests—a knack that he also ends up displaying in Martin's course.) But this knack ill serves him in a discussion setting. Seminar discussion might focus on practical steps, in class and in office hours, that Martin might take to try to narrow the gap between Kenneth's accustomed learning style and the skills that the current situation called for. Is there any way in which Martin might enlist the help of the other students? What other resources might he invoke in the larger context of the Medical School? This challenge has broad applicability for instructors in many settings.

5. *Some Key Decision Points for Martin Davis*

This researcher discerned a series of decision points in Martin Davis's dealings with Kenneth Holmes. Others will doubtless see different key moments, but these may serve as a preliminary list to help instructors devise their teaching plans.

- Sometime before the first day of class, Martin must have decided how he wanted to lead this group. This decision is embedded in the one-sided teaching contract that he reports having offered the group. Martin stated ground rules for their work together. He unilaterally offered "a chit . . . for trivial facts," reserved the right to define what "trivial" meant, and declared that he would only provide a missing fact if (again, in his opinion) discussion seemed "stalled" without it.

Discussion participants might profit from exploring the implications of the elements of this teaching/learning contract [and compare Hansen, cited below]. Martin seems to claim some areas of power and relinquish others. But is he really free to make these claims? And do his actions bear them out? In the realm of content, he seems to be willing to play the role of expert, but only under certain conditions, which his statement implies that he alone has the power to recognize. By declaring that he will supply trivial facts when discussions stall, he implies responsibility not only for distinguishing a truly stalled discussion from one that is merely pausing for breath, but also—more generally—for keeping the process on course. Seminar leaders might ask participants to take the students' point of view: What might they expect from a leader who sets such a contract? Does Martin's willingness to jump-start a stalled discussion mean that the students needn't do so? (Astute participants will probably point out that, when the discussion really *does* break down—when Beth and the other students completely ignore Kenneth's "outburst"—Martin does not directly intervene. This is one of several points in the narrative at which a teacher with a more involved style might have halted the discussion and asked the students to diagnose and remedy the problems with their own discussion process.)

- During and immediately after the first discussion, Martin makes a second important decision. When it becomes obvious to him that, while the other students are joining the discussion in a lively, natural way, Kenneth is sitting rigid, expressionless, and silent, Martin notes, "I wasn't about to single him out in public by asking him a direct question. But I was concerned." What principles seem to condition Martin's impulse not to single out Kenneth in public? Like most teachers, Martin "assumed that [Kenneth's] silence meant that he was either unprepared or confused and embarrassed to ask the group for help." Discussion participants may want to take up the question of other possible interpretations and other possible reactions that Martin could have had to Kenneth's behavior. Was there some way in which he could have introduced the subject of Kenneth's silence helpfully? Are there perhaps some circumstances under which a teacher should single out a silent student in public? Are there some rules or techniques that might help a teacher do so with beneficial results? What are some ways to promote participation?

(C. R. Christensen notes that any discussion leader can make it an objective for the early part of a course getting students to listen to one another by asking them to link their comments, restate one another's contributions, question one another, and summarize. Another task that one can assign—one that carries clear implications that the students are now teachers—is a request that a student assume the instructor's role temporarily and pose the next question.)

Martin's section has already developed a measure of these skills. The culture and new pedagogy at Farwestern Med have encouraged them to do so. But the group has not succeeded in finding a productive role for Kenneth. On the contrary, Kenneth's oddly worded harangue set off alarm bells in Martin's head and so annoyed Beth and the other students that they just ignored it. What (if anything) might Martin have done, then and there, to teach them better teaching skills? What could any teacher do in a similar situation?

The culture of Farwestern Medical School, as Martin represents it in this case, seemed to place a high value on self-determination for students. Accordingly, Martin seems to have kept hoping ("ever more faintly") that the group would find a way to heal its own ailing discussion process. In a different culture, what might he have done to intervene? (The seminar might spin hypothetical scenarios: How might the discussion have turned out if Martin had asked Beth to respond to Kenneth's "off-the-wall" contribution? What would asking one of the other students have accomplished? What if he had asked Kenneth to rephrase his statement? What if Martin had "translated" the content into something more palatable to the rest of the group and checked his accuracy with Kenneth?)

- Martin's rather reserved reaction to Kenneth's bombshell after the first class ("The group asked me not to talk in class") is only one of many possible responses. Participants may wish to consider how they might have reacted in Martin's place. Martin "waited, hoping for more information." What questions might he have asked, instead of waiting? Martin "didn't want to press [Kenneth]." Why not? What might "pressing" him have done? Would *any* further questioning inevitably mean pressure? Martin chose to exercise self-restraint, err on the side of discretion, and deliver a formal statement about academic citizenship. Participants may wish to comment on the model of academic participation that this speech presents. What about the possible effect of the way Martin delivered the speech? (Note that Martin offered his statement as an opinion, "I consider you to be a citizen." What would have been the effect if he had instead said, "You *are* a citizen"? Also note the implications of mutual responsibility in the word "shortchanging." What assumptions underlie this statement?)

Even in this early stage of the case, the second issue—how to formulate, design, and present a written evaluation—may come up in discussion, because this episode is the first in a chain of uncomfortable surprises for Martin, and surprise is one of the elements in Martin's judgment that this student is unusual (conventional students don't present surprises). This interaction jolts Martin unpleasantly from the assumption that instructors would make—that Kenneth's silence in class indicated lack of preparation—to the worried realization that things are not what they seem in this group. In a school whose curriculum emphasizes student cooperation, Kenneth's peers have explicitly ostracized him. Nothing in Martin's teaching career at the institution has directly prepared him for this. What role does the shock of this discovery play in Martin's overall evaluation of Kenneth? Martin seems to have been highly aware of his own subjectivity and the inadequacy of his data for evaluating Kenneth. Discussion participants may wish to explore ways in which teachers may also acknowledge the impossibility of perfect objectivity and yet behave fairly.

- When Kenneth delivered his first speech in class, the effect on Martin and the other students was dramatic. Not only did the speech begin with a rude interruption of one of the weaker students in the group—a clear and, to Martin, unheard-of breach of Farwestern discussion class etiquette—but it also consisted of a rapid-fire, "off-the wall" string of initials and quotations from the text. Martin considered it shocking and unanswerable; not a contribution but a harangue. But instead of taking action, he responded only with "amazement." In this instance, it seems that a certain reticence on Martin's part (perhaps a personal distaste for public confrontation) precluded open intervention. But other instructors might have reacted differently.

Another aspect of this moment in the story might attract comment: Beth Kovell, the "no-nonsense Berkeley type," takes control of the discussion—something she seems to have done with considerable regularity. What are the implications of this? Is Beth the *de facto* discussion leader of this group? If so, was this a usurpation of Martin's prerogative or a natural and desirable state of affairs? Were there any other participants in the group who might have fulfilled the leadership role more productively? Was there some way in which Martin might have influenced this process? Martin presents himself at this point as reflective, eager to act fairly, and judicious enough to wait for a pattern to emerge before venturing a diagnosis of what's really going on. Even as he wonders how to "deal with the monster I had called out of the cave," he decides to "temporize and see how the group handled the problem." What principles of leadership does Martin seem to be applying at this point? Could other teachers, with equally benevolent intentions, apply different principles? What might a more interventionist instructor have done, and what might the consequence have been?

Underlying much of this discussion is a basic question of ethics: To whom is Martin Davis most responsible in this situation? Since this case deals with medical education, the undesirability of producing a dysfunctional doctor is readily apparent. But seminar participants may want to consider whether the game changes in other settings. Do teachers of other subjects have different responsibilities from Martin's?

- Another decision point for Martin occurred in class, when Kenneth addressed an outburst—"Come on! . . . I can't learn this way and I don't think anybody can!"—directly at Martin. Martin reports that he "felt attacked" as a teacher and outraged by Kenneth's violation of "just about every rule, stated and unstated, of the group." What *were* the stated and unstated rules of this group? Who was responsible for seeing that they were followed? What Martin did in this situation was pause, reflect, control his anger and his urge to react defensively, and deliver a controlled reprise of his implicit contract: "I have two obligations to you . . . not to tell you garbage . . . [and] to try to help you to understand some things that are inherently complicated."

Participants may want to examine this statement: Does it summarize the real situation? Is it adequate? Would they endorse it, amend it, replace it? How viable is it? Finally, what else, besides delivering this speech, might Martin have done to react to Kenneth's "attack"?

- Martin's next action was to telephone a colleague who had taught this group during the previous semester. Note that in this reported dialogue, Martin mentions no names. Instead he alludes indirectly to a student with certain problems and asks his colleague, "Can you tell me . . ." if such a thing has occurred before? This circumlocution and delicacy seem to imply that Martin is leaving the colleague free to answer, "No, I can't tell you." In the Farwestern culture, it seems that discretion rules; professors refrain from back-fence gossip about their students, even the infuriating ones. What is the effect of such discretion? What other sources of information might Martin tap to educate himself more broadly about Kenneth's behavior? Would it be appropriate to speak to some of the other students? If so, to whom? And what should Martin ask?
- Martin next considered interventions of a more decisive sort, including "removing Kenneth from the group" and continuing their one-to-one office conferences. What effect would this course of action have had (on Kenneth, the group, the culture, and Martin's own schedule)? What do participants think of Martin's decision to let the discussion process work itself out and hope "ever more faintly" that the group will fix its own relationship with Kenneth?
- Martin's biggest challenge comes at the end of the (A) case. I would suggest that seminar participants be encouraged to identify with him at this point. Having graded Kenneth's final exam, Martin now knows that—despite his anguished proclamations of despair—Kenneth possesses the classic "crammer's" talent of acquiring factual information and technical concepts efficiently under pressure. Confronted with an exam that rehashed familiar problem sets and took the same approach (possibly in the same words) as the text, Kenneth has produced a solid "High Pass" final exam. (This puts him in the top quarter of the class.) How does this complicate Martin's task? What does Kenneth's test-taking ability mean in the context of what the new curriculum is meant to accomplish?

6. The End of the (A) Case—Martin's Goals and Strategy

Throughout the narrative of these events, Martin presents himself as a thoughtful, moral, and responsible medical educator. In his eyes, Kenneth's behavior has deeply troubling implications. The option of letting such a student sail by on a high grade doesn't seem to take up much of Martin's time. He sets himself the uncomfortable task of writing a fair-minded evaluation that will make the academic "higher ups" examine Kenneth's record to see if a pattern of difficulties emerges that will require remedial action.

Martin appears to find this task—triggering a formal review of Kenneth's record—as unpleasant, but morally necessary. (He describes his reasoning, and it may be useful to read his words in class as a springboard to analyzing it and discussing other approaches that he might have taken.) I find it intriguing that written words are the tools that Martin uses to accomplish his goal. He knows how to write an intentionally controversial evaluation. Note that he presents samples of noncontroversial descriptions as comparisons. Seminar participants may wish to contribute similar samples from their own institutions—for the practice of using "code" or formulaic descriptions is widespread and deserving of examination.

The seminar leader might ask, "In your institution, what words would you use to single out a student? How do you convey excellence? How do you communicate trouble? What are the potential consequences of a negative evaluation? What goes through your mind as you write one?" (The same questions, of course, would apply to recommendations.)

The (B) Case

1. Goals and Strategy of the Evaluation

Martin makes his position clear: he considers it his duty (to Kenneth, the rest of the students, the school, the profession, and Kenneth's potential future patients) to bring this student to the attention of authorities, even though his action may ultimately trigger a request that Kenneth withdraw from medical school, at least temporarily. What other points of view might be possible? Do Martin's training and experience as a physician give a special cast to this evaluation? Would practitioners of other professions write something different?

(The discussion leader may wish to broaden the topic from evaluations to other documents, like recommendations, that can affect students' careers. What are the rules, stated and unstated, for writing these? What guidelines do institutions provide, and how readily may these be applied?)

2. *Objectivity (The Impossible Dream)*

What are Martin's challenges in managing his personal reactions to Kenneth? (Most teachers feel some tug between the impulse to defend themselves against implied attacks on their instructional effectiveness and professional concern for a student with problems.) On the one hand, Martin seems to find Kenneth's behavior personally unsettling. This student has "thrown cold water" on an otherwise lively discussion process, behaved rudely in class, and even "attacked" Martin's teaching in public. On the other hand, Martin seems to want to help Kenneth, whom he considers unusually pressured and vulnerable.

To what extent do teachers' feelings affect their judgments of students? And how can they manage those feelings when dealing with students and writing evaluations or recommendations? (Martin's wording of the evaluation shows a serious effort to achieve detachment and place Kenneth's behavior in context.) Participants may profit from a very practical-minded discussion of how to achieve such a goal. Self-management is an important subissue in this case.

3. *How Evaluations Communicate*

Teachers who consider evaluations routine will do well to give them a closer look. Most institutions have informal codes; in many cases, the messages of these documents lie between the lines, in things implied, but not said. Because students often read their own evaluations and recommendations—and teachers are reluctant to commit unflattering descriptions to paper—a sort of "evaluation inflation" (analogous to grade inflation) has crept into the practice. What happens when instructors attempt to couch negative assessments in ambiguous terms? What do common evaluative adjectives—like "intelligent," "competent," or "commendable," for example—really mean? What are the real risks of evaluation?

4. *What Martin Wrote*

After distributing the (B) case, the instructor might wish to ask a participant to read the evaluation out loud. This will give participants time to begin to digest Martin's words and ponder their implications. Note that the headings (prescribed by the institution) call for several different areas of evaluation. How has Martin reacted to each challenge? What overtones do his words carry? How has he communicated his intention to behave responsibly and fair-mindedly? What has he chosen not to say?

Students should compare Kenneth's evaluation to the more typical samples in the (A) case. What is unusual about this evaluation? What is the effect of quoting a student's words and describing his behavior, instead of just assigning evaluative adjectives?

What might the effect be of words like "urge" and phrases like "offer help if that is appropriate"?

5. *Outcomes*

This case does not give the results of Martin's evaluation. Seminar participants are left free to speculate. What, in their estimate, *should* happen to this student? On what do they base their opinions?

Having written and delivered his evaluation, what should Martin Davis do now? Where does his responsibility to this student and this discussion group end? And, finally, what wider issues does this rich, complex case suggest?

Further Readings

Julie H. Hertenstein, "Patterns of Participation," in *Education for Judgment,* Christensen, Garvin, and Sweet, eds., Harvard Business School Press, 1991, pp. 175–191, offers the suggestion that teachers take steps to help students "develop their skills in speaking and listening." Among other suggestions, Hertenstein suggests that teachers take some class time to give feedback on process and point out ways in which it might be improved.

For further considerations of the teaching contract, see Abby J. Hansen, "Establishing a Teaching/Learning Contract," in Christensen, Garvin, and Sweet, eds., 1991, pp. 123–136.

In "Every Student Teaches and Every Teacher Learns: The Reciprocal Gift of Discussion Teaching," in Christensen, Garvin, and Sweet, eds., 1991, pp. 99–122, Christensen argues that, in order to teach, students must learn how to listen, reformulate one another's comments, build group arguments, expose fallacies, and draw conclusions—all in a spirit of positive cooperation. How can Martin (or any discussion leader) teach these skills?

On observation, see the "Note on Process Observation," Harlan and Gabarro, found in the *Instructor's Guide* for this edition, which presents seven aspects of group discussion process (participation, influence, group climate, membership, task functions, maintenance functions, and feedback) that instructors can observe and assess.

H. B. Leonard, "With Open Ears: Listening and the Art of Discussion Leading," in Christensen, Garvin, and Sweet, eds., 1991, pp. 137–151, defines "good listening," lists "listening pathologies" typical of students and teachers, and makes suggestions for eradicating them and building up listening skills.

"Herr Faber's New Course" (A), (B), and (C)

TEACHING NOTE

This teaching note was developed, researched, and written by Abby Hansen for use with the case series "Herr Faber's New Course" (A) HGSE 4, (B) HGSE 19, and (C) HGSE 20 to help instructors prepare to lead case discussions. It is meant to stimulate discussion, not present a definitive analysis. (HGSE No. 9)

Aims and Methods of This Note

I intend this note primarily to help new instructors prepare to lead discussions about "Herr Faber's New Course" (note that the title focuses on course development, but there are many other facets to this case). Throughout the case, Walter Faber concentrates on his self-criticism on the central error of having let a variety of perceived pressures force him to bend admissions requirements and allow an ill-prepared student into an upper-level course. In Walter's words, "I should never have let this student into the course." This note will attempt to expand on Walter's observations and include other teaching issues as well.

In the "Teaching Challenges" section, I shall suggest a few aspects of the case that may give discussion participants trouble and propose ways to overcome those difficulties. And the final section on "Basic Issues" will trace five themes common to many teachers' experience:

1. The "marketing" aspect of academe—how it felt for Walter Faber to design German 204 under distinct, explicit pressure to boost departmental enrollments.
2. The difficulties of designing a course alone—how Walter followed the wrong model and the least appropriate promptings of his own inclination and ended up developing a course that was too complicated, diffuse, and eclectic in its pedagogical approach to serve the students' needs.
3. The problem of the admissions mistake—what happened when Walter let an unqualified student take an advanced course.
4. The familiar problem of deteriorating performance—Walter's growing frustration and intermittently promising (but ultimately only partially successful) efforts to keep German 204 from rocketing downhill.
5. The rebellious student—how Walter reacted to Elaine's (to him) unnerving defiance.

This teaching note will survey these issues, but present neither a detailed teaching plan nor an exhaustive analysis of the case. On the contrary, I feel confident that discussion will tease out meanings far beyond those that I perceive in these events. One of the most invigorating qualities of case teaching—and case learning, for the two are inseparable for student and teacher alike—is the power of each new group to generate a unique blend of perspicacity and experience and produce new insights. As I present my own tentative analyses, I will include questions that teachers preparing to lead discussions on this case may use as guides or indicators of potentially fruitful lines of inquiry.

Teaching Challenges

Like any teaching case, "Herr Faber's New Course" springs from a particular culture. In this instance, Lindhurst College and its German Department. Lindhurst, as Walter describes it, combines contemporary social values with somewhat outdated forms. At other institutions, students often call teachers by their first names, but at Lindhurst, Mr., Mrs., and Ms. are the rule—"Herr" and "Frau" in the German Department. Many seminar participants may find these Lindhurst customs hierarchical. This perception may point to revealing paths of inquiry. What is in a name? What effect does it have on the classroom atmosphere when American students call their teacher not "Walter," nor even "Mr. Faber," but "Herr Faber," while the teacher calls them "Jim" or "Susan"? How might this disparity of address affect the teaching/learning contract? What implicit message(s) does this sort of contract carry?

I would suggest that discussion leaders steer clear, if possible, of overly focused analysis of Walter Faber and his "problem student," whatever quirks each may or may not have. In a pedagogical discussion, analyzing particular personalities may be absorbing (it's certainly entertaining), and even useful (for participants who happen to share these traits or deal with colleagues or students who do), but the group as a whole will derive far more benefit from identifying structural elements in the situation that contribute to particular outcomes.

Finally, it is my opinion that the discussion should not linger overly long on the subject matter of Walter's course. Twentieth-century German history holds undeniable fascination, and German 204 was an attempt to exploit that fascination in multiple media. But the discussion leader who wishes to shed light on pedagogy will be better advised to focus on questions like, "How do you go about designing a course from scratch?" and "How well did Walter's opening meet the group's needs?" than "How do you feel about the German national anthem?"

Basic Issues

1. Marketing a Course

From the beginning to the end of the design process for German 204, Walter Faber served two masters: his own sense of intellectual quality and the painful constraints of academic politics. In the section of the case that describes the institution, Walter reveals, with some bitterness of tone, that he perceives a direct threat to the job satisfaction of professors of small liberal arts departments like his: "[I]f your enrollments decline too far, the administration takes your teaching positions away and awards them to the bigger departments. . . . [W]hen a senior colleague retires, the remaining instructors have to absorb that colleague's workload . . . spend less time teaching what they like, and more time on administrative duties." Walter then reports that his senior colleague is near retirement. This means that if enrollments in the German Department decline, Walter's job definition may very well enlarge in a way that he will find unpleasant.

Discussion participants may very well have similar tales of woe, or fear, to relate. If so, it will probably be useful to welcome their "stories" into the discussion, but give them breadth and depth by introducing elements of analysis and problem solving. First of all, it may be helpful to look at how Walter went about designing his intended "crowd pleaser." What did he do to seek advice? (We hear nothing but that he looked at an attractive course offering from the University of Munich, got excited about the course, and used it as a model.) Did he consult with other liberal arts professors who had managed to design popular upper-level courses in difficult disciplines? (He makes no mention of having done so.) Did he conduct any sort of informal canvas of students to find out their interests? (Again, we have no evidence that suggests that he did.)

Given that Walter seems to have guessed about students' interests—perhaps projecting his own interests or desire to "remedy my own lack of familiarity with East Germany"—one may find it not too surprising that the course he designed turned out to be too difficult for virtually all of the students who did enroll. (Walter himself suspects that the student who dropped the course found it too easy after he diluted the course content for the rest of the class.)

If the need to "market" or "sell" a course is a fact of academic life (as Walter certainly seems to think), how might other instructors in similar situations improve their ability to perform this task without compromising their intellectual standards? Some ideas: get feedback; survey your potential "market" of students; consult with colleagues who have had success in comparable situations; seek the opinions of students during the process of course design (as a corrective to your own singleness of perception).

2. *Course Design*

First, I would have the participants review the steps that Walter actually took to design German 204. Note that he had a major purpose (to increase departmental enrollments), as well as an awareness of a major obstacle (as he puts it in the "Institution" section, "Most Lindhurst students find German more difficult than, say, French or Spanish. So, beyond the first- and second-year courses, our enrollments really thin out"). Walter seemed to believe that the difficulty of advanced German courses made them less popular than advanced French or Spanish courses. Why then did he charge ahead and design a course of unusual linguistic and intellectual difficulty, even by Lindhurst standards? (Look at the steps he recalls in his design process.) How might he have avoided this damaging error? (Again, by consulting with students or talking through the design process with an observant colleague who might have pointed out the discrepancy between what Walter knew and what Walter did.)

The general rubric under which I would categorize Walter's mistakes in course design would be miscalculation, based on projection. Walter mentions in his opening statement that he had spent the previous sabbatical year in German archives and in "the world of ideas"—two places perfectly suited to putting him out of touch with undergraduates in an American liberal arts college. I detect a great deal of projection in Walter's assumptions about 204 and its potential student constituency. Is projection always the wrong way to approach course design? Probably not. An acculturated teacher may make a pretty good guess about students' tastes and abilities. But a teacher who has lived in another country *and* another intellectual realm (the abstract) for a year before designing a new course will probably need to do a good deal of "reality testing."

But Walter didn't. And as a result, he miscalculated the level of difficulty that Lindhurst students could handle (and enjoy). A second area in which he made mistakes (again, by projecting his own work habits onto the students) was in the integration of readings and classwork. In the "Course" section of the case, Walter notes that he put eight books on reserve as background reading, but didn't integrate these books into his lectures, quizzes, or classroom assignments. In the section called "To Mid-Semester," we see the result of this lack of integration: the students' performance became so dull that Walter initiated a "gripe session," in which they *asked* for more quizzes and exercises using the library materials. Had Walter known his students better, he might have designed these elements into the course in the first place.

Having constructed a dysfunctional course (it certainly wasn't working the way he had hoped it would), Walter realized his mistake and began to take corrective steps. Note his "mid-course correction," begun in the first month of the semester. What elements did he invite the students to help him redesign? (Assignments, integration of readings and lectures, even testing policy—they wanted more feedback on how they were doing with this challenging material.) Why might students actually ask for more, not less, evaluation in a course? (Perhaps it is less anxiety-provoking to gauge one's progress along the way. Perhaps it's relatively easy to swallow a poor grade on a small assignment because there will be many other opportunities for better grades.)

Discussion leaders should direct participants to look at the details of Walter's design process and question each step: Why did he proceed this way? How did this element influence the result? How might he have done it better? What does this suggest about course design in general?

3. *The Admissions Mistake*

When Walter Faber wrote his overall reflections on German 204 in his gradebook (see the "C" case), he concentrated on a mistake he made in admitting Elaine Rogers into the course: "This has been one of the most difficult and disheartening teaching experiences I can imagine. I should never have let this student into the course." What was his mistake with Elaine? I would imagine that discussion participants will point to many more than just one. Is it just that Walter should never have let her into the course? Should he have stuck "to the letter of the law"?—as he says he now does? Perhaps there may be value in exploring ways in which Walter might have done something to help boost her participation. He makes no mention of having offered her any particular remedial work, either during his own office hours or through tutoring. Nor does he mention having attempted to integrate her socially into the course. Perhaps a more advanced student might have functioned as a mentor and encourager, if not a tutor?

In the "Students" section, Walter describes departmental gossip about Elaine. His colleagues seem to have complained about her among themselves, but there is no reference to anyone having suggested academic remediation in any form. What does it mean when a student "just doesn't perform"? (Probably, it means as many things as there are nonperforming students. But the department in this case, one gathers, didn't try to find out what made Elaine tick, or fail to tick.) Perhaps this had always been the case in other German courses.

Discussion participants may discern a deeper issue in Walter's various confrontations with Elaine: the issue of "ownership." Who is the ultimate authority in education? As Elaine came to articulate very clearly (and repeatedly) to Walter, she measured her performance by *her* standards, not his, and not those of her fellow students. It appears that she considered herself to be the highest authority in this situation: Who could know more about *her* education, if she set her own goals and evaluated her own progress? By contrast, Walter seems to have assumed that authority lay elsewhere—in standards that he considered objective and institutional.

Walter seems to have prized the ability to discern and discuss abstractions. (See "The First Day" on which he announced his goals for the course, the note, *passim* his disappointment with the way the students grappled with abstractions in class discussions.) But what if Elaine had less respect for this particular brand of intellectual activity, or valued it more in other academic contexts? And what if she placed lower value on acquiring fluent conversational German than Walter did? After all, she was already bilingual in English and Spanish. Perhaps the idea of perfecting her German grammar held limited allure for her. Walter mentions that she "wasn't a German major . . . she was planning to go into business or banking." This suggests that her father—"a business executive" may have been an influential role model for Elaine. Perhaps he had managed to climb the corporate ladder with only modest proficiency in foreign languages. Perhaps Elaine was content with just enough German to read things that interested her. The point is not to second-guess Elaine, but to note that Walter does not seem to have thought about these issues or to have discussed them with her. Should he have? How might things have been different if he had?

Having admitted Elaine—certainly the "odd man out" in this group of advanced students—Walter discovered a whole range of problems that stemmed from her off-and-on, "lackadaisical" participation. Most of the problems surface in the section called "To Mid-Semester." Her attendance is sporadic, and that can damage morale in a small class. When she does show up, she cannot join the discussion on the other students' level, and that slows the momentum, ruins the pace, and gets on everybody's nerves (except, apparently, Elaine's). What happens when the teacher and seven students in an eight-student course feel disrupted? (One hint is obviously contained in the departure, at month's end, of one of the best-prepared students in the group.)

It seems interesting there was no classroom protest (other than the one that Walter himself initiated). No student complained, except the young woman who simply departed with (we assume) no comment. (Note that Walter, typically, speculates on what she might have felt—projecting again without actually asking the student for her impressions.) Why? I think there's a clue in the "Institution" section. Despite its heterogeneous student body, Lindhurst retains distinct traces of straitlaced, old-fashioned traditionalism. In how many other institutions of higher learning do students address instructors (*all* instructors, even the most junior) by Mr., Mrs., or Ms., while the instructors call the students by their given names? (If a discussion group is really "clicking," and people know one another well, perhaps some role-playing of this situation may stimulate lively, involved comment on this issue.)

4. Deteriorating Class Performance

"My frustrated efforts to give them a forum in which to show what they were learning began to suggest that maybe they weren't learning, despite their efforts and mine." "My frustration grew as the weeks wore on." " . . . a semicircle of stony faces."

Is there any experienced instructor who has completely escaped Walter's fate in this course? What might these students' halting contributions and "stony" faces have meant? That the material was too hard, that they felt "at sea," that Walter's outstanding German accent (they thought he *was* German), compared to their own less perfect commands of the language, intimidated them? That they were annoyed that Elaine waltzed in and out of class and messed up the discussions when she did bother to come, and Herr Faber did nothing to fix the problem? Were they baffled about his true expectations—why did he put eight books on reserve in the library and then never mention them?

Walter makes no reference in this case to what might have been happening in the rest of these students' lives, either academically or personally. There may have been many reasons for lackluster performance and stony faces, but his probing intellectual questions, assumptions about their study techniques (note how he questions "Lee" in class) and—one guesses—clear exasperation with the whole enterprise were probably no help in boosting their morale.

What contract had Walter set with these students?

On the first day, he seems to have dictated terms (announced "goals") and then launched into a highly prepared, intellectually rich (and potentially overwhelming) presentation that took so much time that students had no opportunity to respond to it during that class meeting. Is this a clue to how he taught? Was his contract always one-sided (just do what I say)—until four weeks of misery brought him up short, and he finally let the students have some say in the governance of their course?

What are some possible reasons for deteriorating performance in this course? Why might students have started with enthusiasm, but lost it with depressing swiftness? Is Elaine the major problem (for the class as well as Walter)? What is the effect on the class when an uncooperative student damages a professor's morale? What can the professor do about it? (What should the professor keep in mind when thinking about remedies—where should his or her primary loyalties lie?)

It seems significant that Walter's "gripe session" had some beneficial effect on the other students. At least Walter reports that "it paid off" because "the core group seemed to like the course better and their participation got livelier." How can an instructor tell when students like a course? What is the relationship between lively participation and educational quality?

5. *The Rebellious Student*

Perhaps a brief rehearsal of Walter Faber's academic-administrative options with respect to Elaine Rogers may help here. Walter had full authority to prevent her from taking the course in the first place; she was clearly unqualified. Having admitted her, he could have dropped her, unilaterally, at any time. Or he could have flunked her. Clearly, he also had the options of trying to cajole her into improving her performance or, failing that, dropping the course. But Elaine's repeated insistence that Walter *can't* flunk her or drop her from the course was mere bluster: he had full authority to do either one.

Why didn't he? Walter attributes his failure to face her to the Lindhurst culture (which, as we have seen, embodied rather old-fashioned values of formality and hierarchy). Then, too, students cycle through their colleges in four years, while instructors spend decades there. I think it may be safe to assume that Walter was more acculturated to reticence and formality than Elaine was. Her willingness to face *him* down must have taken him aback; at Lindhurst, most students who were asked to drop out of a course would slink away quietly.

I think the issue of academic contract also lies at the heart of the deteriorating relationship between "Herr Faber" and Elaine. Walter seems to have assumed that his first-day rehearsal of rather lofty intellectual goals (plus his hasty "gripe session" a month later) amounted to a working contract. I disagree. By its nature, the academic contract (the complex bilateral understandings between an instructor and a group of students about how to deal with one another throughout the course) has two components: one is explicit (Walter paid attention to this one), but the other is implicit (Walter seems to have been oblivious to this aspect). The implicit aspect of a contract involves modes of behavior. By allowing Elaine to steamroll him consistently (from their first encounter before the beginning of 204), he set (and never really varied from) a contract that gave her freedom to break the rules without negative consequences.

All contracts develop over time. Walter's with Elaine became, if anything, more lopsided as the course wore on. As she flouted the rules more and more blatantly, he would write her a note "suggesting" that she go away and stop being a problem. She would react by coming to his office, browbeating him, promising to "do more" than the others (in lieu of doing as much), and then reverting to her former behavior (or worse). I can imagine Elaine's friends saying, "Do you think he'll throw you out?" and Elaine saying, "Never—his bark is always worse than his bite." I think it will be helpful for discussion leaders to ask procedural, "action" questions that focus on this dynamic—focusing on the details of Walter's conversations and correspondence with Elaine. What is the tone of Walter's dialogue? How do his "curt" notes sound? What other actions might he have taken? What are his obligations to Elaine—and what to his other students?

Summary

"Herr Faber's New Course" traces an experience that frustrated and discouraged a teacher who had approached a new course with enthusiasm. Like most teachers, Walter had to function in a world of multiple, often contradictory pressures. Out of loyalty to his department (and to himself, as a tenured member of that department), Walter felt a sharp need to enlarge the potential market for upper-level German courses. To accomplish his purpose of boosting student enrollments, he set about designing a new, stimulating course by projecting his own tastes, enthusiasms, and values. German 204 would have attracted Walter Faber irresistibly. But it proved too abstract and difficult for the Lindhurst undergraduates.

Then, too, fate handed Walter an extra helping of

anguish in this course in the form of Elaine, the subject of much head-shaking among German Department faculty. Being naturally inclined to avoid confrontation and accede to students' requests—and also feeling the pressure to keep course enrollments as high as possible—Walter had understandable reasons for letting her into the course.

Not surprisingly, the course went downhill almost from the beginning. The best student left, and those remaining became listless. Elaine attended sporadically, rarely turned in work, and lowered the overall conversational level when she did attend and join discussions. Finally—the icing on the cake—she not only ignored the explicit requirements for the course, she openly defied Walter. It is rare, in any academic setting, for a student to say, "I may not be meeting your standards, but I'm meeting my own, so I should pass this course." Many teachers might reply, "I'm glad you're happy with yourself, but since I'm not happy with you, you flunk. In your own mind, feel free to award yourself an A+." But Walter behaved differently; he let Elaine's standards obliterate his. Was this a mistake?

A final note, on usage: Walter Faber's mishaps with course design, admissions standards, class morale, and a rebellious student all are worth attention. I would try to help a discussion group focus attention not only on the case, but also on the interplay between the case events and the institutional context, and on the potentially profound issue of academic grading: Who is the final judge of a student's performance? Who has the right to set and enforce standards, and how will they be applied to students?

The Thin Grey Line (A), (B), and (C)

TEACHING NOTE

This teaching note was prepared by Marina McCarthy as an aid to instructors in classroom use of the case series "The Thin Grey Line" (A) 9-387-201, (B) 9-387-202, and (C) 9-387-203. (HBS No. 5-387-211)

Introduction

"The Thin Grey Line" (TTGL) revolves around the dilemma of a Mid West College (MWC) Communication Seminar course head, Walt Holland. Walt must assess whether or not several Mid West College students have been sexually harassed by a member of his department. The case is not written from the perspective of a direct participant, but rather from the vantage point of a department head recollecting incidents that occurred over a several-year period.

The case embodies two recurring themes or questions. First, what is the nature of the student-faculty relationship; what are the boundaries of such a relationship? Second, what is the distinction, if any, between "sexual hasslement," "sexual harassment," and "sexual discrimination"?

Part (A) involves a female student at MWC who claims to have been harassed by Mr. Bob Spilletti, an instructor in Walt Holland's department. Part (B) details the action taken by Walt Holland. Part (C) takes place several years later. Walt Holland comes across an article written by an alumna who reflects on her four years at MWC. Although she does not name names, she notes that she still harbors resentment toward her freshman Communication Seminar (CS) instructor. Walt goes to his records and discovers it was none other than Bob Spilletti.

Process Planning (Starting Out)

Teaching TTGL may require more preparation than most cases given the sensitive nature of the subject matter—sexual harassment.

- The seminar leader should decide carefully whether his or her opening remarks should be relatively brief or more expansive. Does one want to encourage participants to be more personal or more cerebral? One's tone (intentional or not) can convey such a preference. One should be prepared if participants want to share personal experiences.
- The leader should give considerable thought as to who should open the case and who should serve as backup: one male, one female? two males? two females? Who should go first? second? Should you speak with the selected participants before class begins?

Process Planning (Other Considerations)

- Although TTGL is divided into three sections, (A) and (B) could be taught together. We feel, however, that the "triptych" effect is more challenging.

- We predict it will be difficult for the group to ignore the larger issue of gender discrimination. One should anticipate an interest in other types of discrimination (i.e., against racial, ethnic or linguistic minorities, as well as against handicapped, gay, and even international visitors). Does one want to expand the discussion to consider these other types of discrimination?
- The outcome of the discussion will be affected by the composition of the group. If the group is mixed, the male/female ratio is an important consideration, as is the gender of the discussion leader. Female participants may be reluctant to participate if the leader is a man, especially if the class is predominantly male. Male participants may take a back seat in the discussion if the leader is a woman.
- The involvement of some participants may differ from their pattern in previous class meetings. Those who could be counted on to contribute in previous weeks may be hesitant to get involved with TTGL. Reactions in the group may range from a prudish reluctance to join in the discussion to an overly graphic enthusiasm. The leader may need to enforce the bounds of good taste and propriety while encouraging reticent members of the group to participate.
- A suggested time allotment follows:
  (A) 55 minutes
  (B) 15 minutes
  (C) 20 minutes

Other Uses

TTGL may be used as a part of a series of cases in a module or workshop, or as a single session—say, for women. Accompanying cases could include "The Day the Heat Went On" and "The Introduction."

Questions for Discussion
Suggested Study Questions for (A)

1. What is your diagnosis of the situation?
2. What are Walt's options?

The (A) Case

1. To the opening speaker:
   Please summarize the situation for us. What's going on here? What is Walt's dilemma?
2. To the backstop:
   Please evaluate Walt's options. What are they? Which is more advisable?
3. What are the risks attached to Walt's options?
4. What is your assessment of Walt and Nancy Dienstag's analysis of Sandra's situation? Should Bob have been reprimanded?
5. What is your assessment of Walt's preliminary analysis of Tina's situation?
6. Why do you think Walt is so perplexed about Tina's situation?
7. Do you think that the problem in Bob's class was content (curriculum, short stories, etc.) or his presentation?
8. What are the unwritten (or written) rules—taboos—about faculty-student interaction? in the classroom? in one-to-one conferences? in the hallway? in social settings?
9. What is your appraisal of Walt's handling of Sandra's situation? How do you predict he will handle Tina's situation? Will he again seek the counsel of Nancy Dienstag?
10. How does one distinguish between someone lodging a complaint and complaining? Between a policy and a procedure?

The (B) Case

11. What is your assessment of Walt's handling of Tina's situation? Would you have acted differently?

The (C) Case

12. Given the alumna article, what is your diagnosis of Walt's previous decisions concerning Sandra, Tina, and George?
13. What do you think of Walt's long-term handling of the situation?

Other Questions for Discussion

14. What is your assessment of the title of the case?
15. How do you think everything would have turned out if the department head had been a woman? (Because Walt did consult with a woman, particularly one in charge of women's affairs on campus—seminar participants may not envision any difference in outcome. Some, however, may feel that a woman department head would have acted sooner regarding Bob's termination.)

A Night School Episode (A) and (B)

TEACHING NOTE

This teaching note was prepared by Abby Hansen as an aid to instructors in classroom use of the case series "A Night School Episode" (A) 9-384-085 and (B) 9-384-086.

(HBS No. 5-384-123)

This note will concentrate heavily on the discussion process, loosely following the suggested study questions for the (A) case and the discussion questions for the (B) case. The instructor may wish to forgo the study questions and simply distribute the minicase in class for "instant" discussion. The brevity and relative simplicity of minicases tend to generate discussions in which the rehearsal of case content plays a very minor role and the management of the discussion process itself becomes the primary challenge. The advantage of this primacy of process is that the discussion leader has an excellent opportunity to get to know the group and begin to encourage teamwork. Minicases may inspire some off-the-cuff, even ill-considered, remarks, but the loss of premeditation is balanced by a gain in momentum, which the discussion leader can use to steer the group fairly quickly beyond the rather accessible primary materials to a discussion of basic teaching issues.

The discussion leader should try to guide the group to cover the basic areas of analysis by relating various participants' points to those of their colleagues. The whole discussion will begin to approach completion when the basic questions—What *is* this situation? How did it come to be? What should one do about it?—have been explored and the class has begun to take a look at general issues. Success in teaching any case resides in the richness of the discussion. The instructor should always bear in mind that the primary task is to stimulate the group to consider the material from a variety of perspectives. The atmosphere should be friendly and courteous enough to permit participants to disagree with each other's points in a spirit of cooperation. Most important, the teacher should strive to listen to the participants and get them to listen to each other. Although a discussion leader need not assume the opacity of a classical Freudian psychoanalyst, a certain reticence about one's private opinions is often useful to help create an encouraging climate for discussion. The role of leader confers status in itself: many participants, perhaps unconsciously, defer to the instructor and hesitate to espouse contradictory opinions. Instead of agreeing or disagreeing with a comment, the discussion leader can adopt one of several genial but noncommittal modes of response. One mode is simply to repeat or rephrase a participant's contribution, inviting further comment. Another is to avoid words altogether. Body language—an encouraging nod or smile or a positive hand gesture—can convey the message that the comment is welcome and worthwhile.

Preparation

One effective method of preparation for teaching a case includes (1) careful reading of the case to extract its basic issues, (2) thought about teaching goals, and (3) some effort of imagination to project oneself forward to the discussion and anticipate the sorts of comments participants are likely to make. The third element is especially good preparation for teaching minicases, where, as we have noted, the discussion process is apt to be lively, spontaneous, and tied less to the case facts than to their implications.

One of the first questions the discussion leader should ponder during preparation is: Whom should I ask to open the case by offering the first comment for subsequent discussion? In this particular minicase the protagonist, Sylvia Nevins, is a female facing challenges on a matter connected, however tenuously, with her gender. Should you invite a woman to open this minicase? What would the implications be—for the particular group you are leading—if you were to do so? Would these implications change if you were to select a woman from an age group very different from that of the protagonist? By the same token, what might it imply if you were to ask a man to open this discussion? Might it be desirable to pick a man and a woman and ask them to form an impromptu team of two—one to open and the other to "backstop" (i.e., provide the group with clues to areas the initial speaker may have overlooked)? The discussion leaders' decision on these matters will have considerable impact on the first few minutes of the discussion.

The "Blocks" of Analysis

This writer has found it helpful to break case analyses into "blocks"—general topics that the material seems to suggest. In this instance, several arise. For example:

1. Leadership. Sylvia Nevins is a young woman leading a coeducational group including men and women old enough to be her parents, and the course includes material that some of these students might find embarrassing. Issues that arise from these circumstances might include (a) leadership in general, (b) special challenges for a woman leading a coeducational group, and (c) special challenges for a young instructor with much older students.

2. Preparation. Sylvia is caught unaware by her student's criticism, partly because she has not anticipated how widely his point of view might diverge from her own. Her personal convictions are so strong they have made it difficult for her to put herself in her participants' shoes. Sylvia is comfortable thinking about issues like abortion, divorce, and contraception, for example, but before this incident, it has not really occurred to her that these are highly explosive topics for many people. Accordingly, Sylvia's preparation to teach these materials ignored the crucial exercise of planning to deal with potential prejudices among her students. What place has Sylvia's personal conviction in her classroom? How could she have made herself more sensitive to the different convictions of her students?

3. Insecurity. Challenged by one student's objection to her terminology, Sylvia feels threatened. Her reaction is to become defensive, because she perceives her authority to be in jeopardy. The whole issues surrounding the teacher's right to lead the group and the group's right—or likelihood—to challenge that authority are almost inescapable in any teaching situation. To what extent do such issues manifest themselves in this minicase?

4. Contract. Sylvia describes herself as having invited the students to present their honest reactions in class, even to interrupt her lectures. Why, then, is she so upset when a student takes her up on this offer and presents an honest, negative reaction to her teaching? What are the implications for all teachers and their contracts—stated or implicit—with their students?

These are some "blocks" that occur to this writer. Other instructors will, doubtless, create their own systems, but the technique of writing these out on a single sheet and keeping that sheet in view during the class can give the discussion leader a sense of the structure of the proceedings and a quick reference point to show what areas of the case may have been insufficiently explored or, perhaps, entirely untapped.

Study Questions

For students' use when reading the (A) case:

1. What has triggered this particular episode?

Two extremes of the range of possible response to this question might take the forms of a defense or condemnation of Sylvia. One participant might reply, "Sylvia triggered the episode herself. She asked for honest criticism and then broke a cultural taboo: many older people—men, especially—feel uncomfortable hearing a younger woman talk about matters related to sex. This embarrassment was Sylvia's own fault." The opposite pole might be represented by an opinion like: "Sylvia could not have anticipated this challenge because her previous experience with the course material gave no inkling of possible trouble of this sort. The class included adults; she was an adult; the course description must have made the material clear. The man who took exception to her terminology was way out of line."

With these two opposed analytical positions stated, the discussion leader is in an ideal position to ask the other participants to help explore the reasoning and assumptions behind each position. Several "blocks" will doubtless be broached in the ensuing discussion. Sylvia was caught unprepared by the discussion process; how might the members of this group (the one discussing the minicase) have advised her the day before her class so as to prevent this incident? How serious was the man's challenge to her authority? What motivated him to object? To what extent did Sylvia create this situation herself? What really is at stake in this incident—for Sylvia, for the man who objected, and for the class as a whole? The discussion can move among several blocks as the students toss out variations on their analyses of the causes of Sylvia's embarrassment. Is this a case of hypersensitivity? If so, whose? Is this a case of cultural disparity? If so, what should Sylvia have done to take this into account? Is Sylvia really being challenged? If so, why, and what should she do about it?

2. *What should Sylvia do, immediately, in class, to respond?*

The group's answers to this question will, of course, be colored by the general trends of the earlier discussion of causes. One's ideas about what Sylvia should do will depend on one's views of her and her students. Some might say, "She should thank the man for his honesty, but state clearly that her terminology was perfectly appropriate for the material and that she intends to continue to use frank expressions. If the man feels uncomfortable under these circumstances, he may withdraw from the class." Others might say, "She should apologize and change her style of presenting the material to this particular group. This man was brought up in a far more conservative era than Sylvia. He might even be old enough to be her grandfather. She has probably offended him quite deeply. Surely there are ways to discuss issues of family life without trampling an older gentlemen's refined sensibilities." These two opposed points of view should both be explored. What does Sylvia owe this man? What does he owe her? The usual considerations of risk and reward should be broached. What does she lose or gain by apologizing? What does she lose or gain by standing firm? What does she lose or gain by reprimanding the man for prissiness? What are the consequences of each course for the group as a whole? Some of the blocks covered in this section of the discussion will include leadership, insecurity, and contract. (The reader may have noticed by this time that almost all of the blocks pertain in some fashion to every point of discussion; that is why it is a good idea to note them on a sheet of paper and let the discussion float naturally among them. There is no need to overstructure a discussion or try to direct a group methodically through the various topics of analysis in the order that happens to have occurred to the discussion leader. The various points of entry into a discussion can be connected naturally in a free discussion with no great loss either of coherence or content, so long as the discussion leader remains alert.)

Sylvia's response to the man's challenge will do much to condition the group's future response to her. After all, she is the one in the spotlight; that is the teacher's natural habitat. Her response can either antagonize the man, create a confrontation between him and her, or somehow broaden his challenge to involve the group as a whole in some educationally fruitful line of inquiry. It might be useful to try to have the class explore some of the consequences of each course. What are the risks/rewards of confrontation? How might Sylvia profitably include other members of the group—or *should* she? (What might she lose by widening the confrontation?) What is the "worst case" scenario? Where might Sylvia most effectively seek support in this group? How can she best turn this moment to advantage? In what sense does this challenge present her with an opportunity for teaching—or for learning?

3. *What are some "gut issues" in this situation?*

Certainly Sylvia's gender and relative youth present two "gut issues" that might lead to consideration of several others. Power—the tenuous reciprocity of rights and responsibilities in a classroom—is always, in this writer's estimation, an issue that lurks beneath the surface of almost any interchange. In this case, Sylvia has several obstacles to surmount: the material is intrinsically sensitive, and its potential for offending some segment of the student population has to do with issues of sex. Sylvia is a woman leading a group that includes men; this itself is another situation in which the issue of sex plays an unavoidable role. Finally, Sylvia's age presents another potential handicap. It is difficult for a younger person to assume unchallenged leadership of a group that includes older people. The group might very profitably explore shades of opinion on these topics and begin to evolve some strategies for dealing with them.

A popular way to end the discussion of an (A) case is to ask participants for predictions. With Sylvia's options all "on the table," and the risks and potential rewards of each having been explored, participants might like to speculate about which option they think she actually did take.

Discussion Questions

For use after the (B) case has been read:

1. Sylvia seems to have regretted her first response almost immediately. What is your appraisal of the first thing she did to "minimize the personal aspect" of the confrontation?

As usual, there may be a range of responses to this question. Some participants may think that Sylvia's first response was perfectly natural and exactly what they might have done in her place. Others might say (especially since the case shows this response backfiring) that Sylvia's urge to appeal to the rest of the class was disastrous from the outset, as it simply offered them a chance to align themselves against her *as a group,* thus maximizing the "personal aspect" of the confrontation by placing Sylvia, alone, on the spot. Other participants might remark that Sylvia's instinct included a strongly negative aspect: instead of seeking to remedy the situation she perceived as deleterious to her leadership, she exacerbated it by inquiring after further bad reactions to her teaching. She might have done better to ask a positive question: "Who agrees that this terminology is appropriate to our course material?" or "Who would like to reply to Mr. A's objection?"

As it turned out, when Sylvia asked who else had been offended, she got a sexually polarized response, thus turning the initial challenge into a potential male-female confrontation. This seems to fulfill Sylvia's own "worst case" scenario. Why? It might, at this point, be valuable to have the class spend some time discussing what a woman teacher has to lose when the class becomes polarized in this fashion on an issue involving sex. It might also be useful to ask the class to turn its attention to ways in which women teachers might avoid such confrontations, or respond to them if they should happen to occur despite their best efforts.

2. What is your opinion of her second response?

Sylvia's second response was to turn from the class to the material. Her purpose was, presumably, as before, to lessen the tension she perceived in the room by diffusing the source of anxiety. Her method was to inject a personal opinion, placing herself, as it were, on a par with the student who had objected. Sylvia tells the whole class that she, personally, finds the Victorian ideology offensive. This is a political statement, on an emotional level. It is, possibly, an irritant to some members of the class, and certainly—if they should wish to take it up as such—an invitation to further argument. Some students may praise Sylvia for her honesty—for having dropped the professorial mask for a moment to participate in her own class as a person rather than a symbol. Others may fault her for this very behavior: it wasn't her place, just then, to descend to the student's level and inject personal opinion into the class material. She should have shored up her right to lead the group by maintaining the discussion on an intellectual level. As a tactic for "minimizing the personal aspect" of a challenge, inserting a personal opinion into the class discussion is surely very peculiar.

But Sylvia's expression of dislike for the Victorian ideology seems to have mollified the man. Some explanations of the reason for this might include (a) her injection of personal emotion into the discussion, thus creating a sort of camaraderie between herself and the man; (b) simple lapse of time without any painful pauses in the flow of talk; and (c) Sylvia's continuation of control in this potentially dodgy situation: no matter what was said, she did not relinquish the right to redirect the flow of discussion, nor did she (apparently) appear rattled or upset by the (to her) unpredictable course of that particular class.

3. What do you think of Sylvia's long-term handling of this incident?

This question takes up Sylvia's unexpected and certainly unplanned "private" chat with the man, whom she happened to notice sitting alone during a class break in the very next session of the course. Sylvia "gathered her courage" to go over to the man. The discussion might spend some time in probing what *his* feelings might have been at that moment, as well. This might even be an opportunity for some role playing: What is the man thinking as he sits alone? (Why is he alone, not chatting with other students?) What is Sylvia thinking? What might other class members be thinking if they happen to be watching this little drama? In any case, Sylvia reports that, having had time to consider some implications of the man's challenge to her in the light of her own policies, she forced herself to thank him for his "honest, forthright comments." The man's surprise and his comments might tell us something about him: perhaps his own school days, decades ago, led him to expect retribution (rather than thanks) from a challenged teacher. (It is useful to remember that in the role of student, all of us, whatever our calendar age, regress at least a little.) Sylvia describes her "urge to placate" (a social urge) dominating her "instinct to tell him how annoyed" she really had been (a human, but less adaptive, instinct in this situation).

Sylvia herself ended by being glad that she had "trusted the urge to make peace" (the social urge). One of the least comfortable facts of teaching is the frequent necessity of the instructor to favor the socially adaptive response over the one that the ego might prefer. In terms of the class dynamic, Sylvia succeeded in several ways. She signaled acceptance to a potential isolate; she behaved graciously in sight and hearing of other members of the class, thus offering them the assurance that they too might expect gracious treatment from her; and she created peace where further confrontation might have erupted. Sylvia's payoff was that "the man became a more cheerful, friendly, and active member of the class." Surely this had a good effect on the whole group; cheerful, friendly, and active participants usually help create a good class atmosphere for the other participants.

Sylvia gives her own overall assessment of the incident, and this writer happens to agree with her. Perhaps some class participants may not. There may be hard-liners who say that Sylvia should have thrown the dissident out. Others may fault her for having taken two tries to arrive at the successful formula for reacting to the man. Some of the lessons to be derived from reviewing this incident surely cluster around the always paradoxical means by which discussion teachers best maintain their authority. They wield power through empathy, openness, and accessibility to legitimate challenge. In Sylvia's case, the best ultimate response to challenge was to welcome and absorb it in a spirit of cooperation. Sylvia's initial contract statements did ultimately condition her dealings with the student, and her own long-term evaluation of these contract terms was positive.

4. What basic issues does this case pose for you?

To this writer, the blocks of analysis contain the basic issues. Leadership, gender, insecurity, preparation, contract, the reciprocal rights and responsibilities of the teacher, the individual student, and the class as a whole comprise a loosely related system of issues that may be interrelated in as many ways as the class chooses. This section of the class discussion is both the most important and the most difficult to second-guess. In this section, the participants' personal experiences may with greatest appropriateness be described, analyzed, and compared with those of their colleagues. As I have mentioned, a schematic chart of topics (or blocks) may prove useful at this point in helping the discussion leader maintain coherence in the discussion and suggest new directions for the group to consider.

EXHIBIT 1 *A Night School Episode*

Study Questions

To be used with the (A) case:

1. What has triggered this particular episode?
2. What should Sylvia do, immediately, in class, to respond?
3. What are some of the "gut issues" in this situation?

EXHIBIT 2 *A Night School Episode*

Discussion Questions

After the (A) case has been read:

1. What do you think caused this incident?
2. If you were Sylvia Nevin's friend, sitting in that classroom, what would you hope to see her do to respond to the student's criticism?

After the (B) case has been read:

1. Sylvia seems to have regretted her first response almost immediately. What is your appraisal of the first thing she did to "minimize the personal aspect" of the confrontation?
2. What is your opinion of her second response? How do you account for its effect?
3. What do you think of Sylvia's long-term handling of this incident?
4. What basic issues does this minicase pose for you?

A Night School Episode (A) and (B)

RESEARCHER'S PERSPECTIVE

This commentary on "A Night School Episode" was prepared by Abby Hansen. Its objective is to help instructors in the development of their own teaching plans for this case. (HBS No. 5-384-124)

[Note: This brief essay will address itself to the study questions for the (A) case and the discussion questions for the (B) case.]

The (A) Case

The researcher's unique perspective—a privileged view that includes knowing not only the episode but also its protagonist and aftermath in the context of the principles and assumptions of the seminar—leads this writer to the opinion that Sylvia would have served both herself and her students best by paying greater attention to her own explicit learning contract in the first place. The (A) case mentions that Sylvia began the course by inviting students to contribute their own "family histories," behave spontaneously, and even interrupt her lectures if their inner voices so prompted. These instructions must have given a clear signal to the students: "This is *your* class, not mine. Even when I'm 'performing,' you should feel free to upstage me." Like most teachers, however, Sylvia seems to have cherished a few private, probably unconscious, reservations to her own policy of free speech. Few teachers *really* welcome interruptions, especially if they contain (or seem to contain) a kernel of challenge to the teacher's authority. This case shows Sylvia facing one direct consequence of her own open invitation to the students. Fortunately, although she falters, she also manages to show a certain graciousness. She does, ultimately, ratify her own contract.

Part of the problem seems rooted in Sylvia's unfamiliarity with this group of students. She has taught this material before, but to a considerably different audience: undergraduate liberal arts students nearly a continent away. Her students in the night school in New York must be culturally quite different from the late adolescents she teaches at Farwestern. The particular student who unsettles Sylvia with a public criticism of her teaching is *a generation or two older* than her typical students. In fact, he is probably old enough to be Sylvia's father, and this is likely to account for some of his discomfort. One can well imagine a man in his sixties (seventies?) blushing to hear a young woman making public references to matters that his background has conditioned him to consider supremely private. A great cultural divide separates Sylvia from this particular student. But she has failed to anticipate problems arising from this disparity. This minicase shows Sylvia learning something about judging her audiences.

Given the explicit contract Sylvia has set with her students—openness in the classroom—her best response to the man's objection would have been the one most consistent with her own policies: she should have thanked him for his frank contribution and turned the remark into the basis for further class discussion. How might she have done this? By tossing the ball right back to the class with some abstract, analytical questions to cool any rising blushes (including hers). Abstractions are always useful to defuse potentially tense situations. She might have asked some young student (likely to hold opinions like her own) to present the class with an assessment of the cultural content of the term *offensive,* both for Victorians (the subject of the class discussion) and contemporary college students. The man who objected had taken a step in the direction of confrontation, saying, "*I* find such and such offensive." Sylvia had reacted to this, and immediately felt personally defensive. She might have taken up the challenge with a calculated risk (assuming she had been able to think fast enough to plan a few analytical "fallback" questions), asked the man to analyze his own objection, and then offered the analysis to the class for discussion.

This writer thinks Sylvia overreacted. The man's challenge was there, but mild. He did not demand an apology; he merely expressed a personal opinion. She reacted a bit touchily, but this is understandable in a young woman in an unfamiliar setting teaching a group of people whose backgrounds are rather foreign to her. All women in coeducational institutions face the challenge, explicit or covert, of establishing and maintaining their authority in the classroom. When challenged by a male—especially an older male—they may well overreact a bit. Perhaps, knowing this, they should be doubly vigilant against overreacting.

Sylvia hasn't as much to lose as she fears. She seems to have been leading the class satisfactorily up to this point, and she has, apparently, conducted her lecture impeccably—surrounding the "offensive term" with bibliography on the chalkboard that should make it clear that the term is not her own coinage, but one of established scholarly currency. What she can gain, in this researcher's opinion, is enhanced authority. Any challenge, if well and gracefully met, bolsters a teacher's position as a leader. Furthermore, the man may well be speaking for a significant segment of the class in voicing his discomfort with the term. The material of the course does, in fact, contain issues that raise many people's temperatures: womanhood, manliness, contraception, abortion, child labor, and so on. If Sylvia has taught the course previously *without* encountering contentiousness among the students, she has been unusually lucky. These issues are all potential grenades. Wise preparation for teaching such a course might well include some speculation on emotional outbursts that may occur, and what course the teacher might take to contain them or turn them to use.

What can the students lose? If she falters badly, they can lose respect for her and also the opportunity to explore some of the unexamined prejudices many of them have brought to the course. What can they gain? If Sylvia skillfully turns the man's objection into an opportunity for class discussion, they may gain insight into themselves—individually, and as a group.

Some of the larger issues that this writer sees implied by this minicase are the dynamics of power in the classroom, the advisability of a teacher's psychological preparation for possible challenges, the necessity of abiding by one's own contract, and the inevitability of finding cracks and seams in the social structure of any extremely heterogeneous discussion group. It seems fair to say that women teachers, especially younger women teachers, might do well to prepare themselves for meeting challenges *gracefully.* Such challenges will probably occur, and serenity in meeting them will make its mark.

The "gut issue" is sex—in this case expressed indirectly through the Victorian ideology. But without poaching in the psychiatrists' preserve one may guess that a young woman discussing matters of sexuality with a coeducational group of various ages has enmeshed herself in symbolic conflicts on several levels. First, she is a woman leading men (many men find this uncomfortable; some, intolerable). Second, she is a young woman (daughter figure) speaking about sexual matters, however dryly, to older men. Symbolically, and very subtly, she may even be treading near some sort of cultural incest taboo. All these unconscious issues and resonances "float around" in any situation where women and men work together. It is this writer's opinion that, having recognized these resonances, one should give them a silent nod and simply attend to the business at hand courteously but without hypersensitivity or undue self-consciousness.

The (B) Case

Sylvia's first response backfired to produce exactly what she least wanted: controversy between the men and women in the class. Why should this be particularly undesirable? In this writer's estimation, the reason lies in many women professionals' fear of stereotypical situations. If a woman presides over a discussion that degenerates into a battle between the sexes, this means she has failed to guide the class to a truly intellectual consideration of the unique problem at hand. Worse, an observer might infer that the women in her class are "sticking together" to oppose the men out of camaraderie, not conviction, and that the situation is the same with the men. Not an ideal academic environment! Sylvia's question to the class—asking who else felt offended by her terminology—was fairly certain to spread bad feelings around the room. She would have done far better to shift the grounds of discussion from emotion (*feeling* offended) to abstraction—analyzing the intellectual content of the man's objection or looking more closely at the other scholars' uses of the objectionable term.

Sylvia's second response seems to have been just as unfortunate as her first. Instead of intellectualizing the situation, she herself reacts on the emotional level. She finds Victorian stereotypes personally offensive. Fine. But *why?* The appropriate discussion topic isn't who feels offended by what: education will be better served by analysis of these feelings and their cultural assumptions.

Lest we be too hard on Sylvia, let us remember that she found the man's challenge upsetting. Much of what she did in the classroom was instinctive. Caught off-guard, she tried to protect her dignity. Finding the best method took her a bit of time, but she did ultimately solve her problem. Her most successful gesture toward the man was to approach him during a class break and force herself to thank him for his honest comment. This was the best teaching tactic and the most consistent with her own stated policy. Her graciousness gratified the man, reassured him, showed him Sylvia's generous side, and ultimately integrated him better into the group. This researcher agrees with Sylvia's considered analysis of her own reactions, by and large. The man who objected to her terminology was, in fact, following Sylvia's contract better than she was. When he voiced an honest reaction, as the class had been invited to do, he had a right to expect Sylvia to welcome his contribution. In a free discussion, all opinions—if courteously expressed—are admissible and worthy of analytical consideration by the whole group, teacher included.

The Blooper of the Week (A) and (B)

TEACHING NOTE

Introduction

"The Blooper of the Week" is an unusual case because it describes an instructor's encounter with her class even before her classes had begun. It raises intriguing questions of where and when teaching and learning begin and end. Do they begin with the subject matter? With one's own beliefs and values? Beyond even those? It also presents a dilemma whose rough outlines will be distressingly familiar to many women instructors and students. A male-dominated class encourages sexual harassment in the name of sport and fun but at the expense of a woman classmate. Specifically, when a woman student is honored with "The Blooper of the Week" award, the "humorous" presentation contains sexual overtones. Nancy O'Donnell, the instructor, is an offended observer of the whole scene. Many readers of the case agree with one male participant who wrote before reading the (B) case:

> Why do I squirm in my seat over this case? The most obvious reason is sympathy. Jen appears to be extremely uncomfortable. I cannot help but feel uncomfortable with her. Beyond her immediate discomfort, however, I am also concerned about the longer-term effects this experience may have on her. . . . In addition to my concerns about Jen, I also worry about what this event will do to the section. Will it set a precedent? Will other women be subjected to similar humiliation? Will they be more inhibited in their classroom performance as a result? Will the section fall into a pattern of behavior that many of the students in the section will regret, but few, if any, have the courage to challenge? I worry about the norms being established. Perhaps most importantly, I am disturbed by the explicitly sexual aspects of this teasing, particularly when the target is a woman in a male-dominated situation, institution, and society. The society has a history of sexual discrimination, harassment, and abuse against women. This element would bother me even if Jen showed no signs of discomfort and was strong enough to take it without lasting damage. I see this as a verbal form of sexual harassment, morally objectionable in its own right. Jen was not the only victim.

Nancy O'Donnell was in her second year of teaching the Organizational Behavior (O.B.) course to first-year MBA students at Heritage University. Her first year had left her with feelings of mixed success as a teacher. First-year classes at Heritage were divided into nine sections. One of Nancy's sections had given her good feedback at the end of the course; the other had not.

Louis B. Barnes prepared this teaching note as an aid to instructors in classroom use of the case series "The Blooper of the Week" (A) 9-390-143 and (B) 9-390-144.
(HBS No. 5-394-165)

Distributed by HBS Publishing Division, Harvard Business School, Boston, MA 02163. Printed in U.S.A.

The Blooper case describes a student section meeting that was called at the end of the section's second week at Heritage. Section C met with its teaching faculty following Friday afternoon's final class. Section faculty chair and marketing professor Peter Koslowski wanted to formally introduce the rest of the section faculty, some of whose courses wouldn't begin until much later in the year. Nancy O'Donnell's course, however, was scheduled to begin the following week. Also scheduled was the awarding of several humorous tributes to section members. The case notes that:

> Most of Heritage's faculty considered humor an important element in the classroom. Sometimes a "blooper" could imprint a lesson indelibly on students' minds. Sometimes it could derail an important discussion. Sometimes it simply served as "comic relief"—an outlet for the nervous energy in the room.

The blooper award at the section meeting went to student Jen Jacobsen for what the presenter described as:

> ". . . Jen Jacobsen's *extremely* personal marketing strategy. 'I would bend over *backwards* to satisfy a customer. . . .'" As if to exaggerate the innuendo, he leaned back until he was nearly lying on the instructor's table, grinning at Jen the whole time.

Nor was the presenter alone in considering his accolade humorous.

> Sheer bedlam engulfed Section C. Students were pounding on their tables, stamping their feet, whistling and chanting, "Jen! Jen! Jen!" There was clearly no real contest for this week's blooper award.

Nancy O'Donnell felt embarrassed for Jen and offended for herself and the other women in the room, including the two other women faculty members. However, no one took action then or later. The Blooper (B) case goes on to note that Section C developed a reputation for being one of the "most blatantly sexist first-year sections that year at Heritage."

Background

First and foremost is the "heritage" of Heritage. The school had a reputation as "a male bastion," slowly giving way as more women students and faculty joined its programs. Another feature of Heritage was its student sections, which became "home" for its members for the entire year. Each section had its own classroom, developed its own norms, created its own history, and implicitly competed with all other sections, albeit with a misery-loves-company connotation. Faculty members came to the section's classroom to teach and were, in a sense, the visitors. Faculty were treated with some ambivalence. They had the power to grade, and fail, students. They also had the power to reward, not only with grades, but with recognition and attention. However, faculty typically went by their first names, taught informally, had frequent office hours for students, attended student social functions, and often lunched once or twice a week with student groups.

Nancy O'Donnell had newly come to all this the year before the blooper incident. From the Midwest, she was the oldest of six children and came from a traditional educational background interrupted by a two-year Peace Corps stint in Afghanistan, before she went on for her master's and doctoral degrees. In a sentence possibly portending her approach to Heritage, the case notes that O'Donnell's Peace Corps years were:

> perhaps the strongest of her experiences in learning to respect another culture while also sensing its need to adapt to modern realities.

There seems little doubt that Nancy, among others, thought that Heritage needed to adapt to modern realities. With reference to Heritage, Nancy reasons that:

> it was a good place for a faculty member to make a difference in the way people thought about and behaved in their relationships to work. Nancy aspired to be that sort of faculty member—synthesizing what was valuable in Heritage's established culture with new facets that would produce the more flexible, adaptive managers that she felt the future required.

Nancy was also somewhat shaken, at the end of her first year's teaching, by the "significantly lower" student ratings she received from what seemed to be the academically stronger of her two sections. Some students apparently thought she did not push them hard enough, some women students thought she favored male students, and a senior colleague speculated that she had unknowingly committed a blooper of her own and offended the class.

All in all, Nancy O'Donnell entered the second year of teaching at Heritage with somewhat less than total assurance. She was probably not alone, but she had no way of knowing that at the time.

The Blooper Incident

A discussion of the Blooper case brings forth a range of opinions on how serious the offense is and what, if anything, to do about it. Although Nancy O'Donnell was the central character, the case was told from her viewpoint, and presumably she *could* have done something, there were a number of other actors worth focusing on, but none of whom appear to have taken the event seriously or as cause for anguish.

But why didn't they? For example, as one thinks about both the incident and about those who might have usefully responded to it (but didn't), consider:

- Professor Peter Koslowski. Koslowski taught one of the mainstream courses—Marketing—and was the section chairperson, theoretically concerned about the section's ongoing evolution and development. Jen Jacobsen's class comment was apparently made in Koslowski's Marketing class where her "extremely personal *marketing strategy*" drew all of the laughter and attention. Koslowski apparently said and did nothing during that earlier class, during the blooper discussion itself, or at any time later. Why?
- The other two women faculty members in Section C. One was new, the other a recently promoted associate professor. They too kept low profiles during and after the incident. Why?
- The other male faculty members for Section C. There was no evidence of any concern on their part at any time. Why?
- Jen Jacobsen, the student. New to the school, to the section, and to her own social standing in the class, she played the good-natured accomplice. Why?
- The other women and men students. They were clearly setting their norms that Friday afternoon for gender and humor relationships. No one seemed to question the pattern that began to evolve with the blooper award. Why?
- The entire first-year teaching faculty. Though not explicitly mentioned in the case, we can assume that similar incidents would occur, and had occurred, in other sections. Had any agreed-on procedures been developed that could serve as guidelines for all first-year sections? There is no evidence that such attention had been given. Why?

The Aftermath

The (B) case suggests that nothing happened afterwards, except that Section C's sexist behavior continued to increase. Neither Nancy O'Donnell, her faculty colleagues, Jen Jacobsen, nor the other students acted as though this was an afternoon to remember or review. Yet women participants, in our discussions of this case, become incensed for that very reason. Such incidents have happened too often to many of them with too little follow-up. Some simply remain angry. Some take it out on the offenders or lash out more broadly. Some forget it, while others feel powerless to respond with anything but humor, feeling that nobody else will notice their dismay.

Teaching the Case

There are enough potential complications in this case for everyone. Almost all parties seemed immobilized during and after the blooper award incident, so the discussion bears fruit on at least two levels. One is the level of the case itself. The other, and potentially richer, level pertains to the experiences and questions raised among class participants themselves. Our discussions typically move back and forth between these two levels beginning with questions about the case itself. Some of these might include:

1. What is going on here, and how did it get that way?
   (See above comments.)
2. Is Nancy O'Donnell *caring* too much about the plight of a single student in her concerns for Jen Jacobsen?
   (No. Some participants will raise the opposite question. Did she care enough to learn, or do, anything about the incident afterwards for Jen as well as for others? Others will ask, Could she have realistically done anything, given Section C's reward and punishment norms?)
3. What are the differences, if any, between Nancy O'Donnell's desires to influence and adapt to Afghanistan and her desires to influence and adapt to Heritage? To Section C? Some thoughts might include suggesting that she was:
   a. A guest-visitor in Afghanistan vs. a potential architect-builder at Heritage?
   b. To Section C students, she was part of the "establishment," although a relative newcomer to the faculty.
   c. Each setting represented and challenged different levels of understanding, familiarity, and responsibility.
   d. Nancy seemed to have a greater missionary zeal in the Heritage situation than in Afghanistan, but equally few action tools.
4. Whose "class" was it on that Friday afternoon? The faculty's? The students'? A vociferous student subgroup's?
   (It was "officially" turned over to the students for announcements and awards, but a small subgroup of

self-appointed leaders was clearly running that session.)

5. When does it become "necessary" for a faculty member to interfere with, or try to reshape, a class's norms? When some people are hurting? What if those people don't "want" help, or at least say that they don't?

   (At worst, sections and classes turn deaf ears to the pain of others in order to protect themselves—e.g., the Kitty Genovese incident in which a whole neighborhood ignored the cries of a woman being murdered on the street below.)

6. If the "real world" is a jungle, as some Heritage faculty claimed it to be, why not train for that world—as exemplified by Professor Kingsfield in "The Paper Chase"? Why not that world rather than the idealized world that Nancy O'Donnell sought?

7. Where does a teacher draw the line on humorous "teasing" by self or students when it comes to:
   a. Women?
   b. Minority ethnic groups?
   c. Gays and lesbians?
   d. White males?
   e. Lawyers, engineers, doctors, company CEOs?
   f. Others?

During the first half hour, if no personal stories have already entered the discussion, we would ask if anyone in the class had seen or experienced events similar to the one Nancy O'Donnell described. Usually at least one or more women will report such incidents.

Two other questions also become relevant. Are these "real" problems? There are occasionally male—and some female—skeptics who argue that these are only minor events and disturbances. Some others are surprised to learn that these issues "really" offend women colleagues. The second question relates to action taking in those incidents. Aside from the protagonist, *who else* might take useful action? Or does the entire responsibility lie with the offended person? In the blooper case, many participants strongly believe that Peter Koslowski was remiss in not blowing the whistle at some point and was in a better position than Nancy O'Donnell to take immediate action. Others blame any and all members of the section faculty—and the students. As one participant wrote in commenting on this case:

> My initial reaction is that Nancy should not directly intervene. She can attempt to exert some dampening influence on the proceedings by giving nonverbal signals of sympathy for Jen and of general discomfort, but I cannot think of a way for her to actively intervene that is constructive and does not have serious downside risks. . . .
>
> . . . My hope was that Peter Koslowski would intervene. He could do that more effectively than Nancy and in a nonscolding manner. . . . His interruption of the section's announcements might appear rude, but he is more familiar with the students than Nancy and has the official role of faculty chair. Perhaps Nancy could encourage such an intervention by catching Peter's eye. If he does not act, she still faces a tough decision. . . .
>
> . . . At a minimum, Nancy should take action later on to address the issues raised by the event.

About 20 minutes before the end of class we hand out the (B) case. Most participants are discouraged, but not surprised, to learn that no further actions were taken by anyone. Skeptics are usually sobered by the fact that Section C apparently went on to intensify its sexist behavior and gained a reputation for such deeds.

The final 10 minutes of discussion are often centered around what an institution should be doing to cope with or avoid incidents like that described in the case. Though the answers don't come easy, the discussions on this question have been rich and provocative.

Postscript

Throughout her two years at Heritage, Jen Jacobsen never accepted Nancy O'Donnell's invitation to discuss the incident. It was only after she had graduated, when Nancy accidentally saw Jen a year or so later, that Jen described her feelings of embarrassment and fear at the time—embarrassment at the blooper award being given in the way that it was, and fear of challenging the chauvinistic norms that prevailed in Section C. As the case suggests, she was not alone in those concerns.

Peter Morgan (A) and (B)

TEACHING NOTE

There are three central teaching themes in "Peter Morgan": instructor style, responding to a student concern, and the issue of gender. Also related are the use of humor in the classroom; the integrity of course curriculum and materials; and methods of class planning, with an emphasis on summaries for the conclusion of a case discussion. "Peter Morgan" brings to the surface the challenges of a discipline-trained instructor, whose interests tend to be more theoretical, in a practice-oriented school. It also raises the dilemma of teaching a required versus an elective course.

Questions for Discussion
Peter Morgan (A)

1. What is going on? How did Peter Morgan get into this predicament?
2. How might the situation appear to Cindy and her colleagues? (The case is written from Peter Morgan's point of view.)
3. What is your appraisal of Peter's comment? Was it sexist? Appropriate or inappropriate? What difference might it have made if Peter had said "man" or "guy" instead of "person"? Can jokes about sex be gender neutral?
4. Was it appropriate for Peter to defend the style and construction of the *Werner Apparel* case? Should the case be updated to meet current circumstances?
5. What and why are there major differences between Cindy's and Peter's interpretations of their meeting in Peter's office?
6. What should Peter do after Cindy's comment?

Peter Morgan (B)

1. What, if anything, should Peter do now? Immediately? Before the next class? At the beginning of the next class?

General Questions

1. What are the challenges of an instructor summary in a discussion class? Should one prepare a summary before class? Should the summary be extemporaneous—based on the discussion of that day? When does an instructor summarize during a class?
2. At what level should an instructor be aware of a student's personal problems—e.g., health, etc.?

Marina McCarthy prepared this teaching note as an aid to instructors in the classroom use of the case series "Peter Morgan" (A) 9-389-080 and (B) 9-389-030.
(HBS No. 5-389-091)

Distributed by HBS Publishing Division, Harvard Business School, Boston, MA 02163. Printed in U.S.A.

"Am I Going to Have to Do This by Myself?": Diversity and the Discussion Teacher (A) and (B)

TEACHING NOTE A

This teaching note was developed by Abby Hansen as an aid to instructors in their classroom use of the case series, "'Am I Going to Have to Do This by Myself?': Diversity and the Discussion Teacher" (A) HGSE 5 and (B) HGSE 21.
(HGSE No. 10)

Distributed by HBS Publishing Division, Harvard Business School, Boston, MA 02163.
Printed in U.S.A.

As I developed this case, I was struck by the way in which diversity characterizes every aspect of it—and also by the very practical implications of such diversity. This student group is so intensely heterogeneous that even the linguistic subgroups—speakers of Spanish, Portuguese, Chinese, and English, for example—come from places as diverse as New York City, Spain, Mexico, Brazil, Portugal, mainland China, Taiwan, the United States, Canada, Kenya, and Liberia. How can one design a single course to meet the needs and goals of such a group? Although the language of instruction in this case is American English and the students seem able to read the instructor's assignments (although at different paces), about half of the class feels more comfortable with a language other than English, and only the U.S.-trained participants have had a lot of experience with group discussions.

At least eleven native tongues and dialects are represented in this classroom. In professional terms, the group includes teachers, public servants, educational administrators, nonprofessionals seeking education for personal intellectual enrichment, and academics preparing for careers in research. The students' ages range from twenty years younger than the professor to twenty years older.

Even the setting embodies diversity. The Farwestern Graduate School of Education is a collection of departments, degree programs, and centers. And so does the material of this course, whose very title, "Sociolinguistics and Education," includes three distinct and complex subjects of study: Sociology, Linguistics, and Education. And Marian's inclusiveness reflected the same attraction to diversity: she tried to make the readings reflect the languages and backgrounds of all the students and called the course "a banquet of theories and approaches."

The instructor's task—to lead this group in an American-style group discussion—would be complex enough if she only needed to cope with the students' different levels of proficiency with the language of instruction. But she set herself an even more difficult problem: to try to accommodate all of their backgrounds and goals with a single course. Her group included students planning to teach English and Japanese as second languages; professors of sociology, linguistics, and psychology; academic administrators of a range of levels; and educational policymakers in systems from all over the world. The prospect is dizzying.

But that does not exhaust the diversity in this situation. The students come from at least eleven different educational systems. In some of these systems—the American, Canadian, and, to a lesser extent, the European—discussion teaching and learning are familiar experiences. Students often speak, and even argue, in class. In other systems represented in this class, no such experience exists: students attend lectures; professors never hear their voices. What can a discussion teacher in an American institution do to "level the playing field" for free discussions when more than half of the class has no preparation for speaking in front of a large group of peers and a professor?

To continue the theme of diversity, consider Marian Blanchard's mixed teaching format. She began some classes with minilectures to help those students who were having difficulty in reading English improve their grasp of the previous night's reading assignment. But then she turned the class into a public forum (and sometimes a public argument among the U.S. and some of the European-trained students)—virtually excluding the non-U.S. trained students from participation.

The diversity of all of these elements put an immense burden on Marian. She meant to include the whole group, but the public discussion seems to have erected barriers to the participation of many of the students in the class. How else might she have worked to achieve universal participation? How else might she have introduced discussion-learning? What are the practical implications of mixing complex material, a complex student body, a complex syllabus, and complex academic disciplines in a complex academic institution? Could Marian have done anything to reduce the complexity to a more manageable level? (What?)

In analyzing the implications of this case, I think it is fair to ask whether a class *this* diverse tests the limits of discussion teaching. What are the implications of the speed with which different people and different linguistic subgroups can understand the spoken language of instruction and formulate their own contributions? What are the implications of the level of sophistication that different people's command of the language will impose on their ability to express themselves extemporaneously? How will those differences—in pace and sophistication, for example—affect the overall quality of the discussion? And how might various groups in the class react to this issue?

I wonder if the resistance of these Japanese students might not be interpreted as a signal that they would make better progress with a different teaching format—perhaps one that presented them with readings, writing assignments, and lectures.

Failing that option—to design different courses for students with different levels of fluency with spoken English and different cultural assumptions about public speaking—might Marian have made separate teaching and learning contracts with subgroups of students in this course—contracts that reflected both their specific goals and their linguistic and cultural backgrounds? Should Marian have made separate contracts with educators, administrators, and public servants? Should she have made separate contracts with those studying just for personal enrichment and those studying for a professionally indispensable certificate? Should she have made separate arrangements with students who absolutely did not wish to speak in class and those who absolutely *did?* Might this enterprise have been better conducted as two or three small-group classes rather than one large one?

Japanese Students' Participation in American Classrooms: A Sociolinguistic Perspective

TEACHING NOTE B

This note was prepared by Lowry Hemphill and Masahiko Minami for use in the case series "'Am I Going to Have to Do This All by Myself?' Diversity and the Discussion Teacher". (HGSE No. 11)

Distributed by HBS Publishing Division, Harvard Business School, Boston, MA 02163. Printed in U.S.A.

In a classroom exchange in a graduate course on language and culture, an American professor attempted to draw out student contributions about women's language patterns in different societies. With examples from Europe and the Americas already recorded on the blackboard, she asked general questions of the class about patterns of women's language use in Japan. Neither her Japanese advisee nor his four somewhat younger Japanese classmates answered. Instead a young American woman who had lived in Japan offered a halting, vague comment. The professor asked more specific follow-up questions of the class, attempting to make eye contact with her advisee and the other Japanese students, but they remained silent. Finally, in frustration, she called on her advisee by name, but elicited only an embarrassed, almost inaudible comment.

Why do Japanese students hold back from participating in classroom contexts like this, and what can instructors do to support these students' participation in discussion? We offer an interpretation of Japanese students' "reticence" that is based on our own experience teaching and learning in United States and Japanese classrooms, and that is informed by the discipline of sociolinguistics. We also offer suggestions for supporting classroom participation by students who may hold back from active engagement because of sociocultural differences.

Japanese students' reluctance to speak in U.S. classrooms reflects in part their very different experience of classroom discourse in Japan. In Japanese universities, large lecture classes are the norm, and even in seminars, students are rarely expected to offer opinions or describe personal experiences. When student participation is invited in Japanese university classrooms, typically only the "top" students speak. The top students in a sense represent the student voice, speaking on behalf of their classmates, a cultural pattern that is typical of Japanese society (Yamada, 1992).

Thus Japanese students bring to U.S. university classes specific sets of expectations about appropriate student participation in classroom discourse and a lack of experience with discussion classes. In addition, they bring Japanese notions of "outsider" and "insider" status, and cultural notions of the relative privileges of in- and out-group members. Regardless of their intellectual abilities, Japanese students may not think of themselves as "top" students in a U.S. context because of their less than native command of English and because of their outsider status as foreign students. Since insider/outsider distinctions play such an important role within Japanese society, Japanese students abroad may feel their outsider status more acutely than other groups of international students. As outsiders, they may feel they are not really expected to participate actively and, in fact, are not privileged to do so. In addition, Japanese students may also be particularly cautious about publicly displaying less than perfect command of spoken English because of Japanese sensitivity about issues of self-presentation.

These cultural factors may explain why Japanese students deferred in classroom discussion to an American student who had lived in Japan. Although the young American woman lacked native knowledge of Japanese language patterns (and thus was unable to make a completely adequate contribution to a discussion of women's language use in Japan), her Japanese classmates may have cast her in the insider's role of "top student." She, in a sense, represented their voices, however inadequately, and was able to do so in flawless English. Once the professor had specifically solicited contributions from Japanese students, the students may have waited for the most senior Japanese student present, the professor's advisee, to speak on their behalf. Although the professor clearly indicated that she was looking for more than this student was able to contribute, his less senior classmates may have been reluctant to appear to challenge his precedence by speaking themselves. Relatively small distinctions in status, for example, several years' age difference among adults, are attended to keenly in Japanese society in determining speaking rights and other kinds of social precedence (Usami, 1993; Yamada). Adult Japanese students will assess these kinds of distinctions carefully and will consider these in planning the timing of their contributions even to an informal conversation.

Japanese students' participation may also be hindered by a range of sociolinguistic differences. Japanese conversational style, particularly in semiformal contexts like classroom discussion is marked by longer within- and between-turn pauses than are typical for U.S. conversations. These pauses among other things serve as opportunities for co-participants to plan their conversational contributions. In a faster-paced U.S. discussion, Japanese participants, even those with highly developed English abilities, may have trouble simply keeping up with the rapid flow of talk.

A major task for participants in any kind of conversation is to keep track of the shifting conversational topic and to assess the topic relevance of any contribution they might potentially offer. Japanese and local norms for topic structure vary considerably, both in general and in semi-formal contexts like classroom discussion (Hinds, 1984). Topic boundaries are quite explicitly marked in Japanese, through use of topicalization devices which signal the introduction of a new topic (Maynard, 1989). Although English has topicalization devices as well, these are less explicit and are frequently omitted in relatively informal interaction. Once a topic has been introduced in Japanese discourse, subsequent mention of key entities related to the topic are often omitted. Shared knowledge between speaker and listener is used to specify these, rather than direct mention (Clancy, 1980; Hinds, 1982). Two Japanese students discussing their proposed coursework might say this:

STUDENT A: Ah so, so, kono jurasu no koto to yu to paper nani suru ka mo kimeta?

TRANSLATION: Well, **as for this class**, what kind of paper have (you) decided to write?

STUDENT B: Mada kimete na in da kedo itido sensei ni atta ho ga i ka na?

TRANSLATION: (I) have not decided yet but (do you think it would be) better to see (the course instructor)?

The example above shows the very explicit marking of conversational topic (as for this class) in Japanese and the deletion of references to people (you, the instructor, and I) and whole clauses (do you think it would be), which are left for the conversational partner to infer, using what has already been said and using shared knowledge of the situation being discussed. These features of Japanese conversational style contrast rather dramatically with English, where topic-initiation can be done much more indirectly, but where there are generally more constraints on the deletion of direct mention of topic-related entities.

The following excerpt from high school students' discussion of summer jobs illustrates characteristics of topic behavior in American English:

SANDY: I worked at the First Federal Bank.
CONNIE: How much did you get paid?
SANDY: Six-ten an hour.
CONNIE: No way!
SANDY: Yeah. But the thing is, they took out like forty bucks for taxes. So . . .
CONNIE: Still, you were at least making that kind of money.
SANDY: Yeah.
CONNIE: Are you gonna do that again next summer?
SANDY: Yeah.
CONNIE: I like that watch. Oh I **love** that watch.

Connie's first turn here, "How much did you get paid?" presents a kind of topic **shading** from the previous version of the topic that the young women were discussing, which was summer jobs in general. A

Japanese speaker making this kind of shading move would use a very explicit topic marker, which would translate in English as "as for salary." The American teenager, however, having made her indirect shift in topical emphasis to "salaries," then uses explicit mention of salary-related entities ("bucks," "taxes"), as does her conversational partner ("that kind of money"). All of these topic-related entities would be omitted by Japanese conversationalists making the same kinds of points, as part of a strategy for showing that they were in agreement about what they were talking about. Interestingly, the American teenager goes on to make a **very** abrupt topic shift, "I like that watch," which is completely unmarked for any kind of disjuncture with the preceding line of talk. A Japanese speaker who wanted to make this kind of topic leap would have to mark it with a topic signal like the English, "Speaking of something completely different."

Although these differences in topical behavior are somewhat attended to in Japanese students' instruction in English as a second language, in actual fast-paced interaction with native English speakers, these differences may pose serious comprehension problems for Japanese students. Keeping track of the shifting topic of conversation may be almost impossible in the absence of very explicit topic markers, and lacking the Japanese use of ellipsis (deletion of topic-related entities) to mark topic continuity.

In Japan, to a much greater extent than in the United States, it is the higher-status participants in a conversation or discussion who have the right to change the topic at hand and, in a context where they assess their status as subordinate, may be reluctant to offer any kind of contribution that could be perceived as "off-topic."

Japanese and American English discourse also varies in relation to norms for conversational relevance, in particular what kinds of topics or subtopics can appropriately follow each other. In informal contexts in the United States (for example, family meal-time conversations or the peer conversation we report above), almost anything a participant chooses to offer can be viewed as relevant. In a sense, topic relevance derives from the fact of shared group membership in the family or peer unit, since the speech events, meal-time conversation or informal talk, take as a defining characteristic the active participation of all members (Blum-Kulka & Snow, 1993). Discussion classes in U.S. universities have a similar free-wheeling character, where often almost anything a student might offer can be constructed as relevant by virtue of shared class membership and the common goal of hearing from all participants. In Japanese informal and formal interaction, however, narrower and stricter notions of topic relevance may apply. Japanese mothers, for example, will cut off their children's reporting of personal experiences when these go beyond the specific intent of a parent's question (Minami & McCabe, 1992). As our examples illustrate, topic shading, the conversational phenomenon where one topic is gradually shifted into another through a chain of associated subtopics, is more typical of U.S. than Japanese conversational interaction. Japanese students in U.S. university classrooms may therefore be baffled by the seemingly chaotic topic structure of group discussion, may be unclear about what counts as a relevant (and hence acceptable) contribution, and may be hesitant to offer anything that might go beyond the bounds of the topic defined by the instructor.

These factors taken together, lack of experience with discussion format classes, concern about appearing incompetent in front of an audience of foreigners, hesitance to violate cultural notions of precedence, and problems with planning, timing and assessing the relevance of potential contributions, can account for considerable reluctance to speak. What, however, can U.S. instructors do to support greater participation by their students from Japan?

First of all, faculty can slow down the pace of discussion by talking more slowly themselves, modeling through their own use of longer within-turn and between-turn pauses a more relaxed pace of interaction. These pauses provide space where listeners can "catch up" with the flow of talk and possibly plan relevant contributions. These pauses are particularly important for participants who are not native speakers of English, but they may also support better comprehension and fuller participating by other groups of reticent students. Without monopolizing the floor unduly, instructors can also periodically restate the topic on the floor and recap the various directions the discussion has been taking. These more overt topic "flags" can serve to confirm student assessments of what is now under discussion, and what might count as an appropriate contribution. This oral summing-up can be usefully augmented by board notes as the discussion progresses, which signal important themes as they emerge in the discussion. Board notes provide an additional source of information about topical entities for students whose comprehension of written English is more accurate than fast-moving spoken English.

In our own teaching, we have also found that a direct approach can make a difference in reluctant students' participation. Speaking to a student privately outside of class, we have said something like, "Next Tuesday we'll be talking about patterns for women's language cross-nationally. Because of your firsthand knowledge of this topic, and because I know you have some insights that would be important for other students to hear, I'd like to call on you during that discussion. Would that be okay with you?" This direct approach signals our desire to have students participate, allows them advance planning time to think through their contribution, and gives a convincing rationale for their participation. By saying something like this, we have opened a continuing conversation in which the student may eventually volunteer specific factors that have inhibited his or her previous participation. We have also used occasions like our written comments on student essays to encourage greater participation in discussion, writing something like this: **"Great example! Can I call on you in lecture next week to report on this for the rest of the class?"**

We also support the use of varied classroom formats, for example, frequently breaking into small groups or even pairs or trios, which can provide less daunting settings for reticent students to develop their own styles of participation. These small group settings also change the normal power relationships that govern large-group classroom discussions. The instructor isn't present, and typically the "top" students aren't either. Reluctant participants can use these more egalitarian settings to become more skilled at a range of types of response. We have also constructed tasks for small groups that require some reporting back to the whole class, and we have asked reticent students to volunteer for this reporter role.

We feel that the particular case of Japanese students in U.S. classrooms has relevance for other groups of students as well. Even in an exclusively U.S. cultural context, there are fairly profound differences in students' willingness to self-disclose, to appear authoritative, and to publicly take on knowledgeable roles. Although these differences obviously reflect individual styles and temperaments, they also reflect some of the major divisions in U.S. society, those of gender, race, and social class (Hemphill, 1989). If Japanese students do not feel privileged to take the insider, high-status role in a class discussion and are frequently confused by the rules governing topic development, these problems are also experienced by many other members of a typical large discussion class. The approaches that we advocate for increasing the participation of Japanese students are likely to be of positive benefit for these other students as well.

References

Blum-Kulka, S. & Snow, C. (1992). Developing autonomy for tellers, tales, and telling in family narrative events. *Journal of Narrative and Life History,* 2, pp. 187–218.

Clancy, P. (1980). Referential choice in English and Japanese narrative discourse. In W. Chafe (ed.), *The pear stories: Cognitive, cultural, and linguistic aspects of narrative production* (pp. 127–201). Norwood, NJ: Ablex.

Hemphill, L. (1989). Topic development, syntax, and social class. *Discourse Processes,* 12, pp. 267–286.

Hinds, J. (1982). Japanese conversational structures. *Lingua,* 57, pp. 301–322.

Hinds, J. (1984). Topic maintenance in Japanese narratives and Japanese conversational interaction. *Discourse Processes,* 7, pp. 465–482.

Maynard, S. (1989). *Japanese conversation: Self-contextualization through structure and interactional management.* Norwood, NJ: Ablex.

Minami, M. & McCabe, A. (1991, October). *Rice balls versus bear hunts: Japanese and Caucasian family narrative patters.* Paper presented at the Boston University Conference on Language Development, Boston, MA.

Usami, M. (1993). *Politeness and Japanese conversational strategies.* Unpublished Special Qualifying Paper, Harvard Graduate School of Education, Cambridge, MA.

Yamada, H. (1992). *American and Japanese business discourse: A comparison of interactional styles.* Norwood, NJ: Ablex.

Diversity Unfulfilled: Foreign Students in Discussion Classrooms

TEACHING NOTE C

Louis B. Barnes prepared this note for use in the case series "'Am I Going to Have to Do This All by Myself?': Diversity and the Discussion Teacher".
(HGSE No. 22)

Distributed by HBS Publishing Division, Harvard Business School, Boston, MA 02163. Printed in U.S.A.

Diversity as an Intervening Variable

Two pedagogical themes recur throughout *Teaching and the Case Method.* The first entails recognizing and addressing students as *individual persons* with distinct learning paths and patterns. The second involves creating *integrative processes* that encourage and move productive classroom interactions toward what is today sometimes called a learning community. For us, neither individualism nor community is sufficient by itself. The first theme emphasizes individual understanding and differences. The second focuses upon interactive communities. The art we espouse tries to implement both themes as major keys to learning.

Enter now a third theme, one that can be either disruptive or constructive and that, at its extreme, can represent either obsessive special needs or pluralistic power. It falls somewhere inbetween the first two as the theme of *participant diversity.*

Participant diversity has implications for both individualism and community. It assumes that while people are different, they also want to identify with others they perceive to be like themselves. For an instructor, a practical question arises: how can a classroom benefit from participant diversity and aid the instructor's overall classroom goal of building a discussion community whose members will contribute the best ideas they have to offer while listening openly to the best, and the worst, that others will present?

When diverse subgroups obstruct this goal, they seem to do so because individuals, feeling separated and alienated from the dominant society, band together primarily to advocate their own interests. The diversity of individualism then becomes a medley of subgroup causes. In higher education, these causes cry out for appreciation and recognition from those in power—be they power figures, teachers, administrators, or students.

The logical extension of these efforts to recognize diversity leads neither to healthy individualism nor to a productive community but rather to fragmentation. The outspoken subgroups divide against each other as well as against those in power. Repeatedly in recent years those cries of despair, or sometimes anger, have come from many sources—women, racial minorities, gays and lesbians, nontraditional students, religious coalitions, and political activists. In a climate of such unrest, individualism collapses into special interest, and disunity supercedes either individualism or community.

There is one surprise in all this. Few of the louder cries come from those vast numbers of foreign students who populate American higher education. These students come from a wide assortment of educational systems, cultures, language backgrounds, traditions, values, and upbringings. The foreign students with the greatest problems in U.S. discussion sessions are those who feel uncomfortable with *their* English and *our* traditions. Poor spoken English is the usual reason for noninvolvement in class, particularly among the many visitors from the Pacific Rim countries, Latin America, the Middle East, and Africa.

Sadly, the potential benefits of the diversity they could bring to wider learning are often lost as the foreign students become alienated and embarrassed, then withdraw in silence. For some, hesitant speaking means losing face. After all, many were the social and academic elite in their own countries. Now as newcomers in America's "exalted" education system, they often feel out of the mainstream, ignored, and unappreciated by teachers and students alike—their accomplishments and talents are hard to display in an unfamiliar language where others exhibit more obvious fluency.

To be sure, the same phenomena can be found with American students in overseas schools. They too can feel lost, alienated, and undervalued. However, foreign students coming into an American-style discussion classroom are experiencing not only a new country but, for the most part, an entirely new form of pedagogy. Discussion-method classes are still relatively few in universities overseas. Lecturing, in settings that give professors high status, prevails.

In this vein, many of these visitors do have something in common—their upbringing and early education were hierarchical in nature. Parents and teachers were the authority figures. In both home and school, children and students were to be seen and not heard. When these same students come into our discussion classrooms, they are all too often at a loss. The world is playing tricks on them. Their upbringing and educational training virtually ensure that they will *not* be among the most outspoken students in class, even when class participation is graded. Instead, they are among the most *un*spoken, there to listen and to soak up professorial knowledge. In these cases, diversity serves neither individualism nor the learning community. Instead of becoming a raucous underclass, as some diverse subgroups do, these hierarchically trained students become almost a non-presence. For an instructor who values class involvement, these students represent diversity unfulfilled.

Helping Foreign Students—and the Rest of Us—Get Beyond Unfulfilled Diversity

What guidelines can we suggest for moving these quiet foreign students from withdrawal and retreat toward recognized individualism and community involvement in class? Guideline number one would be don't give up. Our own experience shows that the transition is well worth the time and considerable effort it may take once reticent students muster courage and build not only discussion bridges but self-confidence and group enthusiasm as well.[1] Timidity and subservience are often more cultural than linguistic—even though professed language weakness often provides the excuse that disguises a general reluctance to speak in class. But this form of sound barrier can be broken with patience, persistence, and the students' own pride.

Diversity guideline number two probably applies to all subgroups: an instructor must help the entire class, *including* all subgroup members, to appreciate themselves and their own points of view in *this* classroom context. Scaring the insecure students by letting everyone know how demanding the work will be is not effective. Ironically, a teacher's over-attention to subgroup values and needs may actually reduce subgroup egocentricity and encourage individuality. While guideline number two applies to all subgroups, it may benefit most the quieter foreign students who are less likely to step forward.

Guideline number three is don't respond to shyness and withdrawal with shyness and withdrawal. Many quieter foreign students are used to the initiative coming from people with higher status, and instructors have that position in class. While a case method instructor will not initiate in the command-and-control fashion that such students may expect, he or she can still initiate support and attention. Not surprisingly, there are better and worse ways of doing this. For example, some instructors try to increase foreign-student involvement in discussion classes by emphasizing the importance of class participation as part of the course grade. Even that aspect of a class contract can strike terror into the hearts of students who already feel deficient in English language or discussion skills, unless the potential threat is accompanied—possibly out of class—by the instructor's frequent supportive comments encouraging involvement.

Some teachers go further to urge non-native English speakers to recognize that learning by listening is

[1]A related question is raised in the previous teaching note for this case, which suggests that too much diversity accompanied by poor English language skills might force the instructor to fall back on individual student contracts of not speaking in class and "readings, writing assignments, and lectures." My own feeling is that before taking that path, the instructor might warn prospective students that their English language proficiency, at least, should be adequate for *discussion* tasks ahead. Cultural hesitancy is another matter, but that can be addressed during the course.

only a *small* part of what they can master in this classroom. Thoughtful dialogue is what the instructor wants to develop. Sometimes modeling such conversations on a one-to-one basis, even outside of class, can help the process. This third guideline includes providing ongoing support of the student's English involvement.

Instructors can also help by suggesting outside study groups. Often, students with poor English skills meet only with their same-language colleagues. This can mean longer-term disaster for both their English language and their academic course learning, worsened when the course topic is centered on local or North American issues. Far better that the groups be more heterogeneous. Although an instructor cannot mandate study group membership, this topic of membership in such groups is worth discussion in and after class.

One teacher held a meeting early in the course for all foreign students who thought that their English skills might be a problem. Follow-up meetings were also held. The teacher's main agenda was to get the students talking among themselves about how they could get the most out of a discussion-learning experience. A list of objectives became part of that meeting. In other classes, international foodfests or country days were held to help American students understand the menus and habits of the various countries represented in the classroom—another opportunity for a dialogue in English. All of these gestures were designed to recognize and appreciate the class's foreign students.

Still another guideline involves host-student to foreign-student bridge building. Some classes do this informally by taking early personal introductions in class well beyond name, rank, and serial number cosmetics. One class of 90 students met together after class over a period of several weeks just to ensure that members could describe themselves and ask questions of others in enough depth and detail so that each person became three-dimensional and real in the eyes of peers.

Finally, alliances can be established between teacher and foreign students when the course material draws upon the students' own background and expertise. This clearly requires more international material than many courses have, but not necessarily more than they should have. An advance appeal for help by the teacher, mixed-group assignments, casewriting exercises, and even in-class questions (possibly with notice beforehand) can all help foreign students feel more comfortable with a discussion environment.

All of these gestures require extra effort from instructors, and all can honor foreign students' identities. Still, the larger purpose remains most important. We want to develop the thinking and wisdom of the individual by placing him and her in a supportive learning environment where ideas, not special interests or backgrounds, can prevail and build upon each other.

Kho Tanaka

TEACHING NOTE

This note was designed and written by Abby Hansen for use with the case "Kho Tanaka" No. 9-381-127 to help instructors prepare to lead seminar discussions, not to present a definitive interpretation or illustrate either effective or ineffective handling of any instructional situation.
(HBS No. 5-394-163)

Special Features

Many teaching cases present instructional situations from the teacher's point of view, but this case gives student-readers a rare glimpse into the life and thoughts of a student—in his own words. In this instance, the student is a young Japanese executive whose challenges arise from his having, unwittingly, enrolled in a North American business school where most instruction takes place by the case discussion method. Obviously of high intelligence, Kho Tanaka has met with little but success in his life to date, but now almost everything in his situation conspires to frustrate him. His previous educational experience has not included what we would now call interactive learning; he has excelled primarily by listening attentively, memorizing, and reproducing material—not very useful preparation for the impromptu rough and tumble of a U.S.-style open discussion class. Although Kho has studied English, both in its written and spoken forms, he finds both the reading assignments and discussion environment overwhelming. Faced, probably for the first time, with a setting for which his training has not adequately prepared him, Kho becomes discouraged and unsettled. As teachers, we can read the details of Kho's frustration with sympathy, develop ideas about how to understand and help students with challenges like his, and come to see the advantages that his participation can present to all concerned.

Kho Tanaka's story has increasing relevance to education at virtually all levels, as more and more students, from both the U.S. and other countries, spend time studying in countries and cultures other than their own, and as all classrooms become more culturally diverse. When seen as a source of insight, the perspective of the "foreign student" can bring rich benefits to the educational environment. Students whose backgrounds differ from the culture in which they are studying will observe and interpret their new situations with a freshness and perspective that can be extremely illuminating and helpful to those who have grown up in that culture. And the necessity of speaking slowly and clearly, and eliminating some of the more opaque idioms and slang expressions, can increase clarity of thought and expression for the "native speakers" who, out of courtesy, adapt their spoken contributions to make them more readily understandable to fellow-students with a more halting command of the language of instruction.

Because the student in this case is a young Japanese executive in a U.S. discussion-based educational setting, it makes a useful contrast with "Am I Going to Have to Do This by Myself?" which presents the perspective and reactions of an instructor in a U.S. discussion-based classroom (although not in a business school), as she tries to coax participation from a group of Japanese students in the class. (Another difference between these two cases lies in the number of Japanese students involved. In "Am I Going to Have to Do This . . . ," the teacher tries to work with a small but cohesive subgroup of Japanese students. Kho Tanaka, by contrast, functions *solo,* and reveals the intensity of the emotional discomfort that this brings, in a very personal way.)

Both cases provide opportunities for seminar participants to explore the subtle implications of how teachers versed in discussion teaching can help students from linguistic, cultural, and educational backgrounds alien (or even antithetical) to this teaching methodology function in this sort of setting. What sorts of teaching and learning contracts can one forge with such students? To what signals should teachers be alert, and how might they be interpreted? When foreign students constitute a small minority of the class, how can instructors balance their responsibilities to these students with their responsibilities to the others in the group, the institution, and the course material? What challenges and opportunities do students like Kho Tanaka present? What do U.S.-trained instructors need to learn in order to help students like him? And, finally, what, and how, can teachers learn from students like Kho?

One caveat. I would strongly advise that the seminar instructor try to prevent the group from interpreting Kho Tanaka's narrative as the story of "every Japanese student." Not every student from Japan encounters exactly this difficulty, or in this measure. Kho's story is just that: Kho's story. His difficulties in absorbing English-language material swiftly, devising analyses and hypotheses in English, and coming to a large group discussion prepared to articulate his points in English presented upsetting obstacles. And the business writing course, in which the instructor (or grader) seems to have adopted a blunt, informal, conversational tone in written comments, and in which the expectations for performance do not appear to have been tailored to Kho's needs, presents another important issue: that of evaluating students like Kho, and giving them useful feedback.

Kho mentions a number of elements in his Japanese background that do not help him to function well in this U.S. business school. His cultural background has emphasized a sense of hierarchy, and polite silence in the presence of authority figures. Neither of these values prepare him well for the informality and assertiveness of public debate—especially in a setting in which the instructor, the highest authority in the classroom setting, often intentionally relinquishes the metaphorical reins of control to students. To top the situation off, Kho's language preparation has not included the necessary vocabulary or (one gathers) a great deal of training in impromptu conversation (at least not in the kind of conversation appropriate to a business classroom).

It would be useful for a group to discuss ways in which an instructor (and a grader) might get to know more about Kho. What are his strengths, expectations, and challenges in this situation? In what areas can the instructor be helpful? For example, one might ask the other students to make an effort to speak more clearly and understandable until Kho's spoken English improves. And one might simply keep in touch with Kho—invite him for frequent, brief, office conferences, to get some idea of how his English is coming along. And it would be interesting to know how Kho had previously been graded, and what his own expectations are for his written work. Kho's situation is not his alone. His presence in the classroom and the school affect the teacher and the other students. They also constitute an opportunity for the instructor who would like to include him in discussion, and for the other students in the class, who can teach themselves by teaching him. The question is not whether to help Kho, but how. Given the combination of high intelligence and expectations, and significant stumbling blocks, how can an instructor capitalize on the implicit benefits in this situation, and turn minuses into pluses for all?

Appreciating students from other countries and cultures as unique individuals is essential. Some may learn English quickly; others, not. Some may read better than they speak; with others, the reverse may be true. Some may find it helpful to write, rather than speak, their comments and analyses—perhaps even throughout a whole course. Some may find the challenge of a new environment, educational style, and language invigorating. Others may find it terrifying, and daunting. It would be simplistic to assume that, having gained some insight into the predicament of Kho Tanaka, one has understood the predicament of all young Japanese executives new to American business classrooms.

Usage

The most obvious place in which to use this case is, as we have, in a section in "Diversity in the Discussion Classroom," paired with "Am I Going to Have to Do This By Myself?" But the student's point of view that this represents links it to other cases (for example, see "The Puzzling Student," "The Earthquake Had Just Started" in the Teacher Student Relationship Section), and it could also be usefully placed in the section on "Evaluation and Discipline," because the triggering event is a distressing written comment on a paper.

Some Major Issues

Action

As the number of international students increases, worldwide, more and more instructors will find themselves faced with challenges that arise from teaching linguistically and culturally diverse groups. This challenge will require them to think through new ground rules, assumptions, principles, values, and actions (which flow from and harmonize with values). Action issues may not be the major focus of discussion in this case, but it can present a good opportunity for the seminar group to discuss objectives. For example, one objective that the instructor might have in dealing with Kho is to obtain appropriate and helpful information about him. How might an instructor do this? In a formal meeting, by asking other Japanese students how he is doing, from other instructors, from a dean who works with foreign students? Perhaps there might be some considerations about the services that exist to support foreign students' adjustments, their effectiveness, and when and how instructors should invoke them.

Implications: Some Wider Issues

The important issue of grading and evaluation should not be overlooked in this case. One technique that might emerge is to make sure, before grading a foreign student, that one has a face-to-face conference with this student, in order to get an impression of his or her facility with the language of instruction, goals, and sensitivities. Such a meeting would help the grader develop a sense of the student's initial level of linguistic competence—which can help the grader read the student's work sympathetically, suggest specific areas for improvement, and also provide a way to gauge the student's progress.

The effect of cultural background on assumptions and behavior is inescapable in this case. Kho tells the reader about his own training and the skills that it had promoted in him: collaboration, teamwork, concentration, loyalty. Public speaking or spontaneous debating in public do not feature in his list of accomplishments based on his previous training in Japan.

The instructor might wish to ask a seminar group to spend some time on developing strategies for working with a student with a background like this, whether in class or outside of class. How can instructors make considerate, effective requests about public speaking to students with decades of practice in *refraining* from speaking in public?

Grading and Evaluation

This case raises the question of what Kho found so discouraging in his paper grade. How could the grader have delivered a similar message more effectively? (Perhaps in person.) Is this the most helpful message for Kho? What could the grader (or the instructor, if this is a different person) have done to prepare Kho for this grading system, or to modify it?

Kho provides the reader with a snippet of the grader's actual comments. In this instance, they seem to be particularly blunt, and aimed at a more robust recipient than Kho, whom they plunge into "hell." Perhaps a participant might read the grader's comment and make observations about its wording. What does it mean to hail a student with an exclamation point? What does it mean to raise emotional issues in a written comment ("I'm reacting strongly . . .)? How do phrases like "too wordy, too long, awfully wishy-washy" resonate? What does it mean to confront a foreign student with the inadequacy of his language without being specific? ("I can't understand some of your sentences.") Above all, what does it mean to tell a Japanese student, "your logic is cowardly." How can a grader examine his or her assumptions and take thought for how these may, or may not, match with those of the student being graded?

To this reader, the grader's comment seems to assume exactly the sort of hail-fellow-well-met culture that Kho finds unsettling. The comment seems provocative, with a sort of slap on the back energy that expects the student to argue with it mentally, or at least to find it stimulating. It is conversational, casual in tone, and breezy. None of these qualities strike me as helpful or very appropriate as conversational gambits to approach a traditionally educated Japanese student new to an American campus.

Cultural Background

The details of Kho's life—his marital status, position in the company, attitude toward its culture (in particular)—have great importance to his feelings about Metropolitan. What does it mean to teach a student who is capable of seeing nobility in a metal manufacturing company and who can say, quite seriously, "I love this company"? Students might wish to comment on Kho's inclination to love Metropolitan (his new "company," at least for a while), and the effect of his reception (and particularly his writing grade and its "disgrace") on his initial inclination to devote himself to the institution. What is lost by clumsy handling of a student like Kho? How might this situation have been prevented from deteriorating to this level of misery for Kho?

Also important is the detail that Kho was a sponsored student. He came to Metropolitan as part of an executive training program, at the expense of his company. What should the sponsoring institution have known about the "fit" between Kho and Metropolitan? How could Kho's application process and preparation have been improved? What should Kho have known before he came to Metropolitan?

It would be useful to spend some time talking about the particular details of Metropolitan instructional life that cause difficulty for Kho. In the section labelled "Kho's Campus Life," a contrast is drawn. Before coming to Metropolitan, Kho did well at another U.S. university, just studying English. But at Metropolitan, he was expected to use his English to do more than converse and socialize. He was expected to read daily case assignments, full of specialized, unfamiliar words, and analyze them. He was also expected to participate in fast-paced public discussions, and we gather, evaluated by a single standard, which measured all students regardless of linguistic background. The question arises, should Kho be at Metropolitan? (The case hints at a concatenation of accidents that brought him there. Kho had no idea that Metropolitan was a case-based school, nor did he have a particular reason for applying to this place. His company seems to have given him no specific advice, and his purpose in acquiring an MBA is far from clear. He states, "it would be no problem . . . if I failed," but then contradicts this in broad terms: "As a Japanese, I feel pressed to complete the MBA program successfully. No one from my company has failed in an American graduate school." It might be useful for a student to read this passage in class, and for the group to discuss the implications for this particular Japanese student, of failure and disgrace.)

Other issues that might come up include the stresses of Kho's daily routine at Metropolitan. As he describes his life there, he has just enough time to study, worry, and drink a bit too much. Perhaps one useful tack would be to discuss which instructors came into contact with Kho, and what opportunities each might have to talk with him, learn about his situation, develop rapport with him, and find others to form some kind of support network.

Given that Metropolitan did accept Kho, despite his poor preparation for this particular *milieu*, and that Kho's cultural background predisposed him to avoid failure (particularly in the academic realm) and to prize institutional loyalty, one might conclude that Metropolitan has a responsibility to do something to help Kho. What might that be? What kind of teaching and learning contract should the institution forge with Kho and others who might share his situation? What standards should be applied? To what end? And who in the institution should apply them?

From a teacher's point of view, some questions might include:

- how to grade and evaluate Kho
- how to comment on his work helpfully
- how to build a useful network for him
- how to devise a realistic and useful set of standards for him and others like him
- how to (whether to) integrate him into the oral culture of the class

Some Possible Approaches

Attention to the specifics of the text seems particularly helpful with this case. Kho Tanaka has provided the reader with many details that give substantial clues to his world. Teaching questions might, accordingly, encourage participants to read from the text, and cite examples that stimulate their specific observations.

Some Possible Questions

1. What strike you as the most important contributing factors to Kho's predicament at Metropolitan?
2. What details of Kho's path to the school seem to be causing difficulties now?
3. What strike you as the most significant cultural factors in Kho's difficulties at the school?
4. If you were Kho's instructor, how would you "read" this student?
5. What challenges and opportunities would Kho present to you as an instructor and grader?
6. Would you make special arrangement with Kho?
7. If so, what would they be?
8. How would you balance these against your responsibilities to the other students? What would be the costs and benefits of having a unique contract with Kho?
9. What wider issues does this case pose for you? What does it suggest about students who are "different," whether from foreign countries or not? What about students with unusual learning styles? What about students from

cultures other than Kho Tanaka's? What about their concepts of proper public behavior, approaches to education, facility with reading and writing English?

10. Every student is unique, with a personality, a family background, and an emotional life. But teachers with large groups to lead haven't got the time to forge unique contracts and relationships with each and every student. To what extent must teachers standardize their contracts, even with members of challenging subgroups, as Kho seems to be? Most institutions have study councils, extra classes for non-native speakers of the language of instruction, counselling centers. What can an instructor realistically do to help students like Kho and encourage them to give the institution and their fellow students the benefit of their unique perspectives?

Message Intended and Message Received

TEACHING NOTE

Louis B. Barnes prepared this teaching note as an aid to instructors in classroom use of the case series "Message Intended and Message Received" No. 9-390-143. (HBS No. 5-394-161)

Distributed by HBS Publishing Division, Harvard Business School, Boston, MA 02163. Printed in U.S.A.

Introduction

Catherine Webb had taught for many years in urban high schools. However, as a 47-year-old, second-year doctoral student, she was a first-time discussion group leader in a graduate course called "Images as Text in the History of Christianity" at Pacific Memorial Graduate School of Divinity. The course explored the power of images in religious history. Its title was abstract enough, but now Catherine suddenly found that she had "broken her own rule" and inadvertently represented herself as a controversial image to her students. She had come to class unintentionally wearing a large Pro Choice button, used during a rally earlier that afternoon. She now represented something she believed in but didn't want to portray in class. In her judgment, this was inappropriate instructor imagery. As the case notes:

> She had long considered it important to refrain from imposing (or even stating) her political opinions while teaching, so that students could develop their own ideas without fear of evaluation from the powerful instructor's role.

Catherine's Pro Choice button apparently attracted particular attention from Charles Campbell, one of four Jesuit priests from a nearby Catholic seminary who had cross registered for the class. Catherine also worried about how "this" message and image would be received by her other students who included several undergraduates, an ardent feminist lesbian, Maria Fierro—a Maryknoll nun, and Sarah Jacobs and her husband who came from a conservative protestant parish in Nova Scotia. How would each of these receive Catherine's unintended message as well as the intended one meant for the outside world?

A Case of Multiple Messages

"Message Intended and Message Received" raises the problems that all instructors face when it comes to both intended and unintended messages they send to—and receive from—students or even from other teachers. Two fundamental questions arise:

1. How can a teacher discover when an intended message has gone awry and is received in very different, and possibly distorted, ways from those intended?
2. How can a teacher learn what unintended messages he or she may have conveyed, particularly those that get distorted or misinterpreted?

An instructor is often unaware of the dramatic differences between intended and perceived messages as they appear to students. Unintended messages are particularly apt to be distorted. Students all too often perceive messages that are very different from anything an instructor intends, *or would want to intend*. Worse yet, our unintended messages often speak louder than the ones we try to convey. Think of some of the combinations:

		Messages Received by Other	
		Teachers	Students
Messages Sent by	Teacher	Intended Unintended	Intended Unintended
	Student	Intended Unintended	Intended Unintended

In "Message Intended and Message Received," there is another subtle difference. Catherine *does* intend to convey her Pro Choice values and beliefs to the world, but not to her students in a particular setting—the classroom—at a particular time, during class. Thus, the whole issue of setting and time appropriateness arises. Catherine Webb did not intend to wear the button to class nor impose her beliefs on her students. But she did do the first and is now worried about the second. A whole series of interesting discussion questions come out of the dilemma that Catherine has created for herself.

1. To what extent should a teacher reveal or conceal his/her political opinions in class? Do you agree with Catherine Webb that students will feel obligated to conform to the more powerful teacher's perspective? At what level can students be expected to be more autonomous in forming or expressing their opinions?
2. What does Catherine Webb's inadvertent Pro Choice emblem have to do with the course she is part of—Images as Text in the History of Christianity? Should it be treated as unrelated to the course by Catherine? By the students?
3. Many teachers believe that they should be a "whole person" in their classrooms—that is, they should clearly state their beliefs, thus providing a role model for their students to become "whole persons" too. Is it possible in such a situation, for students to disagree with a teacher? If so, are they merely reacting to the teacher's stance rather than developing their own independent thought? How do you react to a student who expresses opinions that are abhorrent to you?
4. What kind of opinions, if any, are important enough to assert in the classroom, and which, if any, should be kept out of the classroom?
5. How does the setting (e.g., Divinity School vs. Arts and Sciences or another professional graduate school) affect your decisions about self-expression in the classroom?
6. To what extent is it important, in general, for a teacher to understand the differences between his or her messages intended and the messages that are received by students? How would you go about doing that? Would you do that in this particular case? Why?
   a. Most instructors will probably agree with the general notion that it is important to discover the differences. However, some will argue that it is neither useful nor helpful in *this* case. After all, Catherine did not *intend* a particular message to be sent to her class on this issue, and she may not wish to magnify the issue by seeking feedback on their messages received.
   b. Others will see this as an opportunity for Catherine to further implement another of her strongly held values.

      She cared deeply about students as individuals and worked hard to create an atmosphere that was open, sensitive, and respectful of all views and opinions they wanted to voice in her classroom.
7. To what extent should a teacher conceal or disclose her/his political opinions? Where? In class? Outside? On buttons or bumper stickers? In public forum meetings?
8. If not, should you ask a student to do the same? What about personal opinions on such issues as birth control, environmental disputes, crimes, corruption, pacifism, religious intolerance, marital fidelity, taxes, government policies, or political candidates? Only when it seems PC (politically correct) in the setting? Should a teacher encourage students to express *their* opinions on these issues if the issues are brought up during a discussion? What if, as the instructor, you know that your own views are unpopular with the class? Do you still express them even at the cost of popularity and course ratings?
9. On the other hand, how much does an instructor want to encourage and tolerate *other* viewpoints in class? Does a science teacher encourage a fervent student to present arguments for creationism, racism, or animal rights? How do

you react to a student whose views are personally offensive to you? Where and how do such lines get drawn?

10. At what point do you as the teacher sacrifice your "whole person" image to the stated course agenda and its purposes? What if you are trying to serve as a "whole person" role model for your students, teaching "life" and not just a course? Or should you not have that aspiration?

11. Assuming that Catherine's Pro Choice button will arouse different reactions from different students—they will perceive the message differently—how would you respond as Catherine in this class? Apologize? Quietly remove the button? Try to link it's meanings to the course content? Ignore it? Who, if anyone, would you speak to in particular in delivering this newest message?

Teaching the Case

Many questions involving assumptions and perceptions abound in this case, but most of them are hard to interpret so far, because the messages haven't been discussed. Catherine's class went on for 15 minutes before she realized that Charles Campbell had been unduly quiet and seemed focused upon her Pro Choice button. Other students, including Maria Fierro, the Maryknoll nun, seemed unfazed and were participating as actively as usual. The other three Jesuit brothers, who might possibly be most offended, had sent neither verbal nor nonverbal messages that Catherine had discerned, except that "Catherine took the whispering as a sign of dismay from the Jesuits."

However, that might not be the case. Even though Charles Campbell generally seemed to be the most outspoken of the four, he seemed to be the least worldly. The other three had served in Latin America where the Catholic clergy, in some countries, were known to be both radical and anti-establishment. Possibly the whispering meant something far different than what Catherine had interpreted.

In addition, the case provides an intriguing picture of both Charles and Catherine as people in transition. They have both moved into their current lives with some uncertainty. Both seem to have strong needs for approval. Both worked in "lower" education, Catherine as a high school teacher and Charles as "just an eighth grade teacher." Neither may feel very much at home in this course, Catherine because "she would be unable to meet the needs of students seeking a religious point of view," and Charles because his presence and comments were possibly "somewhat marginal" to both the class and its discussions.

Consequently, it is probably useful to begin the class in a conventional way by asking several students for their perceptions of what is happening in this case. And how "should" Catherine construe events so far? Opinions will typically include:

- Catherine is making a mountain out of a mole hill. She needs to forget the Pro Choice button—after all some of the students wear them—and get on with the class.
- Catherine has not only broken "her rule." She has overstepped the bounds of instructor etiquette and should apologize. Such personal politicizing has no place in a classroom, particularly in a divinity school classroom where religious opinions on abortion may be particularly heartfelt and meaningful.
- Catherine has a golden teaching opportunity on the topic of images in life and in religion. She can bring the topic of "images as text" out of history and into the modern world of her own classroom. She couldn't have designed a better teaching opportunity if she had tried, and she should take advantage of it.
- Catherine doesn't have the data yet to know just what is going on. She has clearly disrupted her teaching plan—if only in her own mind—and needs to quickly adopt a new one. She might lean in the direction of trying to ignore, down play, or make amends for her mistake. Or she might figure out ways to take advantage of it for teaching and learning purposes. But before doing either, can she get more data on where the class's thoughts are? Does she want those data?

About this time, it also might be worth discussing experiences that participants themselves might have had with regard to:

a) what happens, and how do we deal with situations, when our intended messages get received in distorted ways, and
b) how can we discover the unintended interpretations of our messages that other people make?

These are not simple questions in and around the classroom, as Catherine Webb recognizes. The power imbalance favors the teacher, but for just that reason, students may react negatively to their own dependency on the teacher-authority figure. Catherine has tried to rebalance the power-dependency equation by encouraging classroom openness and dialogue. But the teacher with grading power always has that slight advantage.

About a half hour into the diagnostic discussion, there should already have been a series of proposals as to what Catherine Webb should do. If those have not appeared, ask for some of them. If they have, summarize them and arrange them across the spectrum of avoidance of the issues raised by the Pro Choice button to efforts to fold it into Catherine's class discussion as part of the learning experience. What are the pros and cons of each approach, and what are the delicate issues that need to be addressed. Furthermore, what would one do as Catherine if, having decided that the issue was more of a classroom embarrassment than an enhancement, either Charles Campbell, an undergraduate, or the outspoken feminist raised the issue and wanted to discuss it? Would you handle it the same, or differently, in each case?

It might also be useful during the last 20 minutes or so of the class to explore some of the wider issues raised by this case. Some of these are referred to above and should relate to issues experienced or anticipated by participants. Several others might include:

- When does the teacher sacrifice his or her own control of the classroom in order to pick up a "hot" topic—at least as perceived by some students? Would direction and control have been mutually exclusive in this case? If not, when are they?
- If we really feel embarrassed or trapped by our own behavior in the classroom, when do we: a) apologize, b) try to fold the behavior into the teaching plan as though it had all been intentional, c) change the teaching agenda, d) deny any mistakes in judgment or behavior in order to maintain status, or e) adopt the strategy that the best defense is a good offense?
- When does course content become less important than class process? And when should concern for an individual student (e.g., Charles Campbell) and his or her concerns replace the instructor's concerns for course content *and* the other students?
- Finally, on the "whole person" theme, what responsibilities does an instructor have outside of class to teach the "whole student" about life as opposed to teaching about knowledge restricted to the course?

"When the Cat's Away" (A), (B), and (C)

TEACHING NOTE

This note was designed and written by Abby Hansen for use with the case series "When the Cat's Away" (A) HSPH 3, (B) HSPH 9, and (C) HSPH 10 to help instructors prepare to lead case discussions. It is meant to stimulate discussion, not present a definitive analysis. The School of Public Health is grateful to President Derek Bok of Harvard University for a grant in support of case development.
(HSPH No. 6)

Distributed by HBS Publishing Division, Harvard Business School, Boston, MA 02163.
Printed in U.S.A.

Usage

"When the Cat's Away" is a multifaceted case that could fit well in several teaching contexts. A few might be:

1. unit on operational problems;
2. series of two or three cases dealing with diversity;
3. unit on instructors' teaching styles;
4. section on the teaching/learning contract;
5. unit on ethics.

Case Organization

The (A) case focuses on questions of responsibility and the necessity for action that become more complex as one probes the complexity of the situation.

On returning to campus from a brief business trip, Professor Gregory Lewis learns that, during his absence, a student in his course not only interrupted a distinguished guest lecturer but also labeled her contemptuously as "a white South African" and walked out of the classroom before she had finished speaking. Greg finds the incident personally and morally repugnant. In his mind, there is no doubt that the responsibility for doing *something* is his. But his path to action is muddied somewhat by his not having personally witnessed the disturbing events and the fact that he had to approach students—they did not seek him out. The (A) case delineates the situation from Greg's point of view and places the student-reader in his shoes (as one removed from the trigger events, but poised to take action).

The (B) case details what Greg did: he delivered a brief, formal speech to the whole class, recapitulating the rules of proper classroom behavior among adults (rules which he had expected these people to know and observe, whether the professor was in the classroom or not).

The (C) case then presents Greg's considered view, after the fact, of the implications of these events and the seriousness of the issues.

The overall progression of this case (A through C) is from action to analysis—in other words, from the concrete to the abstract. The discussion might follow the same pattern, with the final portion challenging discussion participants to enunciate, compare, and evaluate their own philosophies of proper behavior in academe.

Some Teaching Approaches

Overview

Discussion of this case can take place on many levels. If the case is taught early in a seminar, the group may leave some of its deeper implications unexplored and spend more time discussing action issues. Instructors may direct attention to the details of action and dialogue reported in this case, and ask participants to interpret these details. How did Greg behave in the classroom? What did he say? What effects might his actions and words have had on the students? The answers to questions of this sort must be grounded in the case details; an instructor might ask the group to begin the discussion simply by picking out significant details.

A deceptively simple question—"What's the situation? What is Greg facing here?"—will open the discussion territory to analysis and evaluation. Participants may take sides here—some championing Greg's views of propriety, while others defend Jay's right to express himself. To promote balance in this section of the discussion, the instructor might wish to draw attention to details in the case that participants have not mentioned. Does introducing these details change the interpretation in any way?

Finally, the (C) case is a personal credo, which the instructor may use in many ways to shed light on the case and the discussion that it has inspired. One way to introduce the (C) case might be to ask students to use it as an overlay to compare what Greg did and said with his stated beliefs. Another way might be to ask students to think about the assumptions that Greg's students might have brought to the classroom and how these might have tallied with Greg's. A third might be to ask participants to compare Greg's beliefs with their own. If the case discussion has included conflicts, students may find themselves questioning their own assumptions—and this would be a useful place to leave participants mulling over questions about courtesy, freedom of speech, proper treatment of guests, behavioral contracts in academe, and any other questions of principle that the discussion has raised, but not settled.

The (A) Case Discussion

Although advanced seminar groups may profitably begin with questions of analysis ("What's the problem here?" "What went wrong while Greg was away?"), the easiest way to open this territory might be to confine opening questions to the most accessible realm: action. Given Greg's situation, what would participants do? If they were Greg's friend, what advice would they give him? How would they personally react if they were in his shoes?

Some possible teaching questions: "What action do you think Greg should take?" "What can he gain? What risks might he be running?" "What *shouldn't* he do?" "To whom is Greg responsible?" "What might help him deal with this dilemma?" It might be fruitful to focus at least a portion of the (A) section of this discussion on behavior in and out of class. Greg Lewis has furnished the reader with a good deal of detail on this subject. How does Greg get his information? What does he know about his students? How does he set his teaching contract? How does he prepare the students for the visit from the guest lecturer? Greg provides a description of how he started this class and how he ran it. Students might profit from reviewing these sections of the case in class and selecting details that they consider significant. Does Greg seem to behave differently in and out of class? (The answer would probably have to be "yes." We all tend to behave differently in front of groups and "one on one" in our offices and around campus. But what does this imply? What can teachers accomplish by becoming more aware of these differences? What tactical and ethical questions does this awareness raise?)

A discussion of the (A) section could end with invitations to predict what Greg actually did, and speculations on the risks and benefits of various possible courses of action.

The (B) Case Discussion

A teacher may begin to probe additional levels of meaning by asking some "why" questions in this section of the discussion. "Why did this happen?" "What elements in the setting contributed to this outburst?" "In retrospect, do you see anything that Greg might have done differently to prevent this?" "What is your rationale for X or Y course of action for Greg?" Since the (B) case describes what Greg did and said, questions could begin with selection of significant details, analysis of those details, and assessment of the worth of various analyses, and progress to suggestions of alternatives. Hypothetical questions might be useful here: "What might he have done differently?" "What might he have done besides deliver a speech?" "What else might he have said?"

The (C) Case Discussion

In wrapping up a session, seminar leaders might ask participants to go beyond Greg's handling of the situation and to reflect on how their views about what was at stake may have changed or become more complex during the discussion. Among the many topics the (C) case raises are academic freedom (as embodied in stated and unstated behavioral norms); assumptions about courtesy, respect, the treatment of guests, mutual respect, the responsibility of a group for one of its members; and the enormously complex (and potentially explosive issue) of prejudice. Instructors may suggest further private reflection and outside discussion, encourage students to capture their thoughts in written form, or designate a future date for further class discussion of these vitally important topics.

Special Features

This case has the potential to trigger emotional fireworks and conflict in the classroom. The words "white South African" may be a lit fuse to some participants. And Greg's opinion (in the "C" case) that stereotyping Sylvia as a white South African leads to the conclusion that "only women can teach women, only blacks can teach blacks, only suburbanites can teach suburbanites" may irritate people who find some germ of truth in the statements to which Greg takes exception. Seminar leaders would do well to plan for the possibility that this case might reenact itself in the seminar. If some of its details should touch raw nerves—the way Sylvia Hall's *persona* infuriated Jay Narayan—what will the seminar leader do?

Planning some possible responses to potential classroom dynamics can, at the very least, provide instructors with a feeling of security as they enter the seminar room. Some issues to consider: How much time will you let elapse after an outburst before you make some response? With whom will you make eye contact? Will you, as the discussion leader, respond directly to the outburst, or will you leave it up to the group? (And how will you make these wishes known?) Are there particular participants in the group to whom you might turn in moments of general distress—people who are perhaps likelier than others to soothe injured feelings? Also, if there is an outburst, should it be treated as a violation of decorum or a signal of high interest in a topic that, while painful, ought to be aired?

A suggestion about questions to pose in difficult moments: the more abstract the topic, as a rule, the cooler the discussion becomes. It is less upsetting to consider the merits of two contrasting models of courteous discourse than to discuss the pros and cons of walking out on a lecturer.

Case Overview

Returning to campus after a brief business trip, Greg Lewis (an epidemiologist and Professor of Public Health) learns "secondhand"—first from his administrative assistant and then from students whom he encounters in the halls—that a student in one of his courses interrupted a distinguished guest speaker so relentlessly that she couldn't finish her presentation. Even worse, the student insulted the speaker in a way that Greg considers prejudiced and unacceptable in a culture that values freedom of speech and debate. An additional factor that adds to Greg's outrage at these events is the passivity of the rest of the group. In a course of nearly fifty people—all adults (median age 31) and many with years of challenging professional experience—no one intervened, it seems, either to halt the interruptions or to apologize to the speaker. An additional factor that complicates this case is the diversity (in almost every aspect—nationality, home language, educational background, professional experience, age, gender, future career plans, etc.) of the student group. How can one set and maintain behavioral norms in a group so heterogeneous?

Greg describes how he set his teaching contract with this group. Having announced certain rules in his introductory remarks to the course, he seems to have assumed that his teaching contract was solid enough to govern the students' actions in his absence. Part of his challenge upon discovering that he was wrong was to manage his anger, communicate his displeasure constructively, and lead the participants back to the path of appropriate, proper, courteous, respectful behavior. The (A) case ends with Greg Lewis angry, but determined to take responsible action to confront an issue of great seriousness: academic courtesy and the unwritten rules of respectful debate. One slight quirk of this case is that Greg did not actually witness the trigger events.

In some ways, this is a case of teaching outside the classroom, an activity that instructors undertake routinely, often without realizing that they are doing so. Some fruitful discussion questions might be: "What should the relation be between teachers' behavior in and out of class?" "What is the difference between our relationships with students in office hours, around the campus, in lecture, and in discussion classes?" "How do these fit together?" "How can teachers influence the culture of a discussion group even in their absence?" "What roles do other members of the staff—like Cathy St. Claire—play in teaching?"

The (B) and (C) cases follow naturally: Greg delivers a general lecture on proper academic conduct, focusing on modes of appropriate behavior, and then sets forth his own interpretation of the deeper meaning of the events that he has described. The progression of this case is from problem to prescription to principle.

Some Basic Issues to Consider

The following survey is not meant to be exhaustive, but rather to amplify the thoughtful analysis that Greg Lewis presents, suggest places in the text that may require particular attention, and suggest questions that a seminar leader might wish to pose in class.

1. *The Teaching/Learning Contract*[1]

a. How Greg set the contract. Human relationships rest on rules, stated and implied, of conduct. The teaching/learning relationship is a special category of relationship, and the particular culture of this school, this course, and this group of students is yet another subcategory. In a lecture course, the instructor usually exercises the right to set a largely one-sided contract. In a discussion course, the rules are different. What exactly are the responsibilities of a discussion leader? Certainly, they are less easy to state than those of a lecturer. In this case, Greg Lewis provides the reader with several glimpses of the way in which he set and applied his teaching contract with this group. Seminar leaders may wish to direct participants' attention to the dialogue that Greg reports. "I said, 'This is a lecture and discussion course. We're here to discuss . . . we're not looking for right answers; we're here to explore various approaches to problems.'" What might the students take this statement to mean, in terms of the behavior he expected from them? (Note his use of the word "we," which implies a shared task, and his emphasis on exploration and "various approaches.") What implications might such words carry about students' rights and responsibilities in this course? How would the following statement—"I would call on people even if they hadn't asked to participate if I really wanted to hear from them"—further affect the implied contract?

b. How Greg implemented the contract. Greg describes how he led discussions, "I called on [people] by name or by nodding at them. I made sure that they addressed each other's points. I'm very good at running a class, moving discussion around, making sure everybody contributes and no one dominates . . . I don't let anyone overrun the class." What kind of dynamic is he describing? Certainly, all dialogue seems to involve him. He solicits each comment personally by calling a student's name or nodding, and makes a personal response to each contribution that often combines a brief judgment ("interesting idea," for example) with a direction. (By reacting to a comment with, "Maria, how does this fit with what you said earlier today?" Greg is calling on Maria. The primary responsibility for the shape of the discussion—who speaks when—appears to reside with Greg.) In the examples he gives, Greg does not describe student-to-student dialogue. Every exchange in this case focuses on him. The net effect of this pattern may be to suggest that he is the central (perhaps the only) authority in the room. Given this mode of interaction—with the teacher as arbiter of the whole discussion process—should one surmise that, in this class, the students had little opportunity to practice self-management? From the evidence in this case, it seems that Greg expected them to look to him at every juncture of the discussion. Since their discussions immediately followed lectures from Greg (and took place in a large, formal lecture hall), it may have been difficult for them to switch gears from the passive to the active mode. Greg seems to have accepted the responsibility for making sure that the students followed his rules—attended to one another's points and gave one another time to finish speaking. At the risk of exaggeration (and fully acknowledging that this case presents only snippets of reported class interaction; other sorts of interchanges may have occurred), may one surmise that the dynamic encouraged a certain dependence on Greg? Could the students have come to assume, implicitly, that the responsibility for the quality of the discussion rested with him (not them)? If so, then their failure to seize control of the process (censure Jay for rudeness or publicly apologize to Ms. Hall) might not be overly surprising.

Discussion teachers might wish to ask the seminar

---

[1] I have provided fuller comments on this topic in "Establishing the Teaching/Learning Contract," in *Education for Judgment: The Artistry of Discussion Leadership*, Christensen, Garvin, and Sweet, eds. (Boston, Mass.: Harvard Business School Press, 1991), pp. 123–136.

groups to speculate on different ways in which Greg might have led his class. How might he have solicited comments and responded when students spoke? What might he have done to disperse responsibility for the quality of discussion? What might he have said, and how might he have behaved, to communicate to this group that the active maintenance of a productive group dynamic was their responsibility?

2. *Classroom Culture and Community*

In a diverse society like the one depicted in this case, what basic assumptions of shared culture may one make? May one, for example, assume that students from extremely different academic cultures share a common core of assumptions about how to conduct discussion? Some cultures prize consensus over controversy; in others, the reverse is true. Some cultures value polite silence; others reward public eloquence. What consequences might these basic cultural differences have for Greg Lewis and instructors in similar institutions? How does one both announce and enforce a culture in which students address one another's points, refrain from personal attack, permit each other to express thoughts freely, and treat guests with respect? In the absence of universally accepted standards, how may a group create and maintain communal standards?

In the (B) and (C) cases, Greg explicitly states rules of classroom behavior that he considers absolutely basic. The values that he invokes are "decorum and order," focus on "the issue, not the individual," "give and take," "respect," "politeness," and avoidance of disruption. Greg describes himself as "old-fashioned" for believing that, "When I invite someone to speak in my class, . . . they are like a guest in my house—and guests should be treated with respect." Compare his physical description (casual in dress, given to playing jazz tapes in the background during office hours) to the adjective "old-fashioned"? How do these aspects of his self-presentation fit to convey a total picture of this instructor? This aspect of the discussion could lead to general speculation about the effect of instructors' personal styles—including hairstyle, dress, office decor, and choice of words in class and in extracurricular contexts with students.

There seems to be a failure of community in this group.[2] In a setting in which students have formed a strong mutual academic bond and learned how to help one another learn, disruptions of the sort that Jay produced will either not occur or be taken care of by the group. What can an instructor do, in class and elsewhere in the academic context, to promote community? (Practical suggestions might be welcome in a discussion of this point, such as encouraging student-to-student dialogue; stepping off the podium or stage and asking students to take over sections of the class; asking the group to elect student representatives; and introducing elements of peer grading.)

3. *Classroom Architecture*

This crucial aspect of teaching is also one of the most commonly ignored. Greg describes the room in which this episode occurred—"the crypt"—as "the worst lecture hall at the school." Greg doesn't mention whether he attempted to secure a different classroom assignment, but assuming that he did, unsuccessfully, what might he have done to overcome some of the worst obstacles of this particular lecture hall? Other instructors may take warning from the alienating effect that this environment had on the students in this course and make energetic attempts to avoid leading discussions in such hostile environments.

Dealing with this question will require identifying the worst features of the room. Surely size is one. Built to hold 200, it now held 45. Atmosphere would probably be another negative element: it is "windowless," and its lighting gives it an eerie feel. The seats all face the stage. What effect does this rigid alignment have on the discussion process? Confronted by such an uncongenial space, students in this course "sat in little clusters," rather than in a group. What does this geographical grouping convey? Might these aspects of setting also have contributed to the social collapse that occurred when Greg left town for a couple of days?

What effect might it have had if—instead of letting students sit in clusters all around the room (even in the last rows)—Greg had asked them to sit in a group at the front? Perhaps he could have suggested that students take every other seat, leaving room for stowing books and coats and for turning around (however awkwardly) to look at one another during discussion. Seminar participants may come up with other creative suggestions for warming up a large, cold teaching space and making it more conducive to the creation of community.

4. *Review: Some Teaching Questions*

A genial way to open this potentially explosive case might be to introduce Greg Lewis's predicament by stressing its positive aspects. Before asking "what

[2] For further comments on the issue of community, compare "Premises and Practices of Discussion Teaching," in *Education for Judgment: The Artistry of Discussion Leadership*, Christensen, Garvin, and Sweet, eds. (Boston, Mass.: Harvard Business School Press, 1991), pp. 19–24.

went wrong?" the seminar leader may wish to emphasize how much seemed to be going right. Greg had an outstanding reputation and undisputed command of the material. The students were adults—interested, experienced, and well-prepared. The guest speaker had an enormous amount to offer them and decades of experience in the very setting in which she was now a visitor. And Greg had not only informed the students that they would have a guest lecturer, but also told them who she was, and what a distinguished practitioner and educator she was. Introducing the material in this fashion might start the class off on a positive note and help the group appreciate Greg's shock at having his expectations reversed. One may assume that he left town expecting a good report from the students and Sylvia—and that his piecemeal discovery of how badly his guest had been treated (and how passive the class had been during this discourtesy) had caused him a great deal of pain and embarrassment.

A very basic (and by no means simple) question that emerges from these considerations is: To what extent is the discussion teacher responsible (even *in absentia*) for the conduct of his or her students? (An operational question that follows is: What can a discussion leader do to foster the development of a community that will function on its own?) To ground this discussion in the text, one might ask, "What details do you think are important in helping us understand why this class didn't intervene to silence the disruptive student and support the guest lecturer?"

Broader questions might include real "mind-benders" like "What is proper decorum in a discussion class?" "Can one make universal generalizations in this matter?" "What is the intellectual price of disrupting polite discourse?" "What is the appropriate way to treat a guest?" "Is it ever proper to interrupt and walk out?" "Is there a difference between identifying or categorizing and labeling?" "What values does Jay's denouncement of Sylvia Hall imply, and what is the proper way to respond to these values in a healthy academic environment?"

As I have noted, this case may arouse powerful feelings, but it also has the potential to stimulate discussion ranging from nuts-and-bolts operational issues (how to set and maintain a teaching contract that will remain in force "when the cat's away" and how to call on students, phrase questions, respond to contributions, choose or adapt rooms for discussion-teaching, set an erring class back on the right track, and so forth) to issues of the uttermost profundity, like prejudice and academic freedom.

Bob Thompson (A), (B), and (C)

TEACHING NOTE

Louis B. Barnes prepared this teaching note as an aid to instructors in classroom use of the case series "Bob Thompson" (A) 9-379-004, (B) 9-379-005, and (C) 9-379-006.
(HBS No. 5-394-164)

Introduction

Leo Durocher, the legendary manager of the old Brooklyn Dodgers, once noted that "nice guys finish last." And so it would seem with Bob Thompson whose situation moved from magnificence to mess in very short order. After trying to help Toby Bona, with the best of intentions, Thompson seems to have fallen into increasingly deep and hot water with little appreciation from anyone. At the heart of the cases is the question, when should an instructor change a grade for a student? And to what extent does a teacher bend to a student's needs and wishes?

The three Bob Thompson cases present a set of cascading difficulties that descend upon this new lecturer at Urban University after his first seemingly successful venture into the classroom. In the Bob Thompson (A) case, we learn that Bob has just completed teaching a fall, second year MBA course in International Finance. By all apparent measures, the course went very well. There is a further possibility that Bob will be invited to join the faculty full time the following year, a possibility which materializes in the "B" case. Bob has just returned from a two-week skiing trip during the holidays and is basking in reflective satisfaction.

The satisfaction is disturbed by "a loud knock on the door" and the appearance of Toby Bona, a tall, muscular, Nigerian student who needed a B+ in Bob's course in order to graduate from Urban. Instead, Bob had given him a B−. Toby Bona was supposed to have graduated *the previous* spring semester, but his grades were so poor (including one F) that he had been suspended by the school's Academic Performance Board.

Rather than taking the suspension seriously, Toby reappeared the next fall to register for courses. The Academic Performance Board was apparently persuaded to hear, and eventually grant, his appeal at that time, but would not let him attend classes until the matter was settled. When Toby Bona was allowed to begin attending the classes he had already registered for that fall; Bob Thompson's course on International Finance was one of these.

Bob, however, put Toby on an excruciatingly tight deadline and a tough schedule. Toby showed up in Bob's class "midweek" (Tuesday or Wednesday?) in the fifth week of classes—nearly a third of the way through Bob's course. Bob did not allow Toby into the class until he had checked the story out with the registrar, presumably on Wednesday or Thursday. He then decided to resolve the issue "by giving Toby the exam that the class had taken the previous week, apparently covering the first five weeks of the course," even though Toby was probably woefully unprepared. Then followed an interesting series of events.

> He called Toby, gave him all the assignments, and told him to be in his office at 3:30 P.M. *that* Friday (the next day?) to take an exam. After that Bob would decide about admitting him into the course.
>
> On Friday morning, Bob received a call from Toby who said that he had come down with pneumonia and couldn't take the exam that day. Bob rescheduled the exam for the following Tuesday.
>
> Toby missed class on Monday, but did arrive to take the exam in Bob's office on Tuesday afternoon. Bob told Toby he had an hour and a half to complete the exam. After 45 minutes, Toby handed in the exam and said he would be in class the following day.

We never do learn how well Toby did on that entrance exam. All we know is that he *did* show up in class for the rest of the semester, apparently with Bob Thompson's approval.

Despite Toby's apparent accomplishments, writing skills that were "better than some of the other foreign students," and being "very active in classroom discussion work," Toby wrote a final exam that was in the bottom third of the class and a final paper that "showed some thought and a great deal of effort," but also showed "immature reasoning." He received a B− in the course where "class performance was so excellent that I felt a B+ median was appropriate," notes Bob Thompson. Toby's B− grade led to his appeal for a grade change to a B+. The (A) case ends with a rueful Bob Thompson commenting that:

> With the benefit of doubt, I might change a grade one level—but two?

The (B) case shows that Thompson did change the grade one level up to a B. When Toby calls a week later, as Thompson had requested, he is distraught:

> You can't do that. That's not enough. I need at least a B+ to graduate. Please, Please.

Toby asks for another meeting which Bob (surprisingly?) agrees to and pursues his cause with further pleas, but makes no headway until later that week. Then, the plot thickens as two things happen. First, the dean of the business school informs Bob Thompson that he is the unanimous choice of his colleagues to join them as a full-time assistant professor the following year. Second, a senior international business colleague, in effect, tells Thompson to change Toby's grade from a B to a B+. According to Bob's senior colleague:

> Toby has had a lot of problems here, but now he is so close to completion that we should let him graduate. . . . Toby has been counting on you to change his grade.

In the very short (C) case, Bob Thompson gives Toby Bona one more chance. Toby is allowed to make up the first five grading units (weeks) of the course that he had missed. Toby picked up the assignments on Tuesday morning and turned them in 48 hours later "typed and neatly presented." Bob Thompson concludes that:

> Toby had obviously put a great deal of effort into the presentation. The quality of the work was better than Toby's past efforts.

He finally gave Toby the B+ grade, but still felt "uneasy about the whole business" as well he might.

The Teaching Issues

The Bob Thompson cases present a real tangletown of ethical dilemmas due to its cross currents of data and inferences that we might make. At one point in the case, Bob notes that "Toby had probably put less into the course than any of the other students." Yet earlier he comments that Toby was very active in class, and "his comments were usually relevant," though "Toby sure wasn't a business type." In addition, "Toby did work hard, and his writing skills were better than some of the other foreign students." Though Toby's final exam was in the bottom third of the class, he covered five weeks of assignments in 48 hours when Bob Thompson gave him one more chance. Furthermore, Thompson comments that "Toby had obviously put a great deal of effort into the presentation. The quality of work was better than Toby's past efforts."

Furthermore, who are we to blame (if anyone) for Toby's late start in the semester? The Academic Review Board would not let him attend classes for the first five weeks, and Bob Thompson disregarded that period when he made up his final grade of B-. But shouldn't Toby get *some* credit for catching up with the class after that five-week absence? And a whole series of other questions add to our ethical uncertainties. For example:

1. There are always possibilities of racial/ethnic tensions in a case like this. We know that Toby Bona is Nigerian, delayed going home in order to plead his case with Bob Thompson, and had possible speaking and writing problems as do many foreign students in American universities.

Should these be taken into account by faculty and given extra tolerance?

2. In addition, when do academic standards give way to human compassion? Were Toby Bona's problems worth Bob Thompson or others bending their standards? If so, why should Bob Thompson be the one to bend? Why should not one of his more experienced colleagues (who also had Toby in a course that term) be the one to compromise? It might have been useful if Bob Thompson (and not just Toby) had contacted *them too* for advice and reasoning.
3. In that vein, is there such a thing as student harassment (of instructors)? When *should* Bob Thompson have told Toby Bona to simply stop harassing him? How much pressure should an instructor take from a badgering student?
4. What responsibility does the Academic Review Board bear for this whole situation? After all, if they hadn't either a) agreed to review Toby's case in the fall or b) prevented him from attending class while they considered his future, he might have either been out of school altogether as they had judged appropriate earlier, or he would have been able to take a normal course load in regular scheduled hours. Looking ahead, couldn't they have seen the trouble they were causing for either Toby or the faculty?
5. On the other hand, is Toby Bona just a sophisticated con artist? The registrar notes that:

   That fellow has had more change-of-grade forms than anyone I've ever seen. He's been playing this game ever since he's been here, and I'm tired of it. It was a real mistake to admit him in the first place.

   In addition, Bob Thompson knows that Toby had some problems with other students. But why? Thompson never tries to find out whether Toby's negative reputation with his own colleagues preceded him into Bob's class or was because of his behavior within the course. It might have been useful to know.
6. The real villain, for many discussants, will be Bob Thompson's senior colleague in international business—or is he simply the (so far) absent good Samaritan? There seems to be no question but that he is trying to influence Bob's grading practices. That in itself will be enough to anger many. But if there are overtones of racial prejudice in the school (as some may be tempted to argue), is this person simply trying to give Toby more even handed treatment? If so, he seems to be doing it in a curious way (with arms folded and intense looks at Bob Thompson).
7. Some discussants will also wonder whether Toby Bona really did the five credits of remedial work *himself* at the end of the (C) case when Bob gave him that final chance. After all, the results turned out to be "better than his past efforts." But does that make one suspicious or encouraged? There are bound to be skeptics in class who will doubt Toby's integrity at this point given the strains he was under and the mixed reputation he has with people like the registrar and some of his student colleagues.
8. When does a new—or even an experienced—instructor seek advice, and when do we go it alone on difficult moral dilemmas like this one?

A Teaching Plan

The (A) case is an excellent vehicle for starting in an open-ended fashion. Some discussants will leap immediately into the ethical issues that permeate the case. Others will identify with one of the central characters. Some will identify with Toby Bona, the beleaguered student, others with Bob Thompson's wounded perspective. Many will attack the high pressure tactics of the senior colleague, though at times, even he may find some defenders. Many will feel that Bob Thompson didn't lean upon other senior colleagues for guidance, but others will argue that this is a time when one's own moral fortitude has to meet its own tests. It is a time for Bob Thompson to stand up for what he himself stands for.

Timing wise, all three cases offer rich material and separate topic opportunities for discussion. Consequently, one possible teaching plan calls for spending about half of the class time on the (A) case, and divide the rest of the class equally into times for the (B) and (C) cases. Each picks up its own set of moral dilemmas.

The (A) Case—Some Teaching Questions

In the (A) case, some of the questions that might interest an instructor and provide bases for discussion could include:

- What is your diagnosis of this situation? How did Bob Thompson get into this predicament?
- What is Toby Bona asking for? Does this issue mean a grade or graduation and future career success to Toby? In his own Nigerian culture, what are the relative meanings of *graduation from* as compared to *attendance at*?

- Should he even have let Toby Bona into the International Finance course after five weeks of the course had gone by?
- How reasonable was Bob being in giving Toby an exam on all of the assignments given so far for five weeks? Rather than showing up for the exam on Friday, was Toby just stalling for time until Tuesday when he took the test?
- What else might Bob have done before taking Toby into the course?

  He might have checked with the Academic Review Board to learn of their intentions and perspective. Did they really say that Toby could not attend class for the first five weeks, and if so why, knowing his academic problems as they did?

  Bob might have talked with the professor who gave Toby an F grade the previous semester. What were the circumstances from *his* point of view?
- What is your evaluation of Bob's grading standards and effort?

  Is the B− grade simply a catchall grade for Bob's poorer students, and is a B+ median grade simply a reflection of grade inflation at Urban University? Given Bob's mixed bag of comments about Toby Bona, was he *that far* below the median of B+?
- Why would Bob Thompson even consider a grade change?

  He was young and inexperienced. Most of the grades were petty high.

  Bob might have seen the cruel irony of Toby's graduation (and possibly his short-term future) depending upon him, Bob—a young teacher who had never graded students before in his life.

The (B) Case—Some Teaching Questions

An initial question for discussants who have just read the (B) case is, should Bob Thompson have raised Toby's B− grade to a B? If so, why, and if not, why not? And there are other questions:

- If yes to the question of raising Toby's grade to a B, then why not go all the way to a B+? After all, some will argue, a B grade can still condemn Toby to a career of failure back home. And, after all, this is a larger issue of graduation, isn't it, not grading?
- Should Bob then review *all* of his B− grades?
- Are there other steps that Bob Thompson might have taken before changing or not changing Toby's grad to a B?

In addition, as we go over the (B) case, we note other influences. What do we make of the roles taken not only by Bob, Toby, and the other students but by the registrar, the senior faculty colleague, and even the dean? In a sense, the dean has given Bob a vote of confidence. Bob has a job offer for next year and could have a) asked the dean's advice on his dilemma or b) used the dean's offer as a reason for *not* listening to the entreaties of his senior colleague.

The (C) Case—Some Teaching Questions

The obvious startup question for the (C) case is similar to the one used in the (B) case—should Bob Thompson have raised Toby Bona's B grade to a B+? And why? How will this kind of "emotional blackmail" by Toby affect Bob in the future?

Some of the (C) case discussion might also focus upon the implications of all this for Bob Thompson's future at Urban University. Does he now become the instructor who is known to buckle under pressure, or as one of the "good guys"? Has he burned all bridges with the registrar, and how much does it matter if he has?

The Wider Issues

Finally, the Bob Thompson cases, like so many others, provide a springboard for classroom participants to describe their own reactions to similar dilemmas and actions beyond the case. The action choices in these cases seem to offer no simple escape clauses as is so often true outside as well. Toby Bona may be no better than a charming scoundrel, but the issues and pressures he presents are familiar territory for almost all instructors. At the end of the case, Bob Thompson still did not know whether Toby represented villainy or virtue. Thompson seems to have remained skeptical throughout the case, and yet there is always the chance that Toby suffered from problems that many foreign and minority students face once they become entangled in academic jungles. These lead to a few other questions:

- Should student grades be influenced by factors *other than* the academic criteria established by formal course protocol?

  For example, what about such a benchmark as progress? In Toby's case, if he started five weeks behind the rest of the class through no fault of his own (not clear in the case), do we give any credit for any catch-up improvement?

  Should effort, as well as accomplishment, be rewarded? What if the student is disadvantaged and struggling against physical or mental obstacles?

In a discussion class, should a student be rewarded (as part of a grade) for contributions to the *process* of the discussion as well as to its *content* as shown by qualities of listening, questions, syntheses and summaries?

- Is a single grade enough feedback for a student? How does one make a single letter/number grade *not* seem simplistically unfair to the recipient?
- What do grades have to do with meaningful feedback to students? How should they fit into other forms and patterns of evaluation?
- Finally, what do discussants see as the benefits and drawbacks of unidimensional grading of multidimensional behaviors?

I Felt as If My World Had Just Collapsed! (A), (B), and (C)

TEACHING NOTE

Special Features

A three-part case, "I Felt as If My World Had Just Collapsed!" contains some of the protagonist's general reflections based on an upsetting incident, but deals mainly with a classroom crisis and its possible implications. All three parts should be read, for the long-term outcome is not clear until the (C) case. The setting is "a typical New England women's college" (a phrase that would irk the protagonist, Sue Roper, intensely). The teacher is a woman, and so are all her students. The subject is advanced Spanish Conversation. Special care should be taken to prevent these particulars from limiting the discussion because the underlying issues of this case include racism, trust, control of the classroom, the effectiveness of modeling ethical values, and crisis-management—all issues with universal applicability.

The case is particularly rich in description of the teacher's feelings. Sue Roper speaks of her intense misery and sense of failure when she found herself stymied in "her" classroom by a remark she considered racist. Her honesty and commitment make it easy to empathize with her. This openness and the issue of racism itself allow participants to get involved with this case quite readily.

Mood

Sue "still shakes" when she recalls these events. A long-time social activist, she recoils at the possibility that racism could have cropped up in a class she was leading. Like-minded discussion participants will share her agony. Others of a more skeptical vent may accuse her of hypersensitivity. If both opinions (and the spectrum in between) appear in the discussion, controversy may accompany them. As with most episodes of human interaction, the true significance of what really occurred will retain its essential mystery. Did Carrie, a white student, balk at working with Sarah, a black student, out of blatant, reckless racism? The teacher assumed so, and still feels certain she was right. But Carrie denied it, and we will never know. The discussion leader should prepare to explore the ambiguities, exploiting the participants' involvement to first encourage close attention to the case details, and then a lasting appreciation of the limits of any teacher's perceptions and power (particularly under conditions of stress).

Suggested Uses

In this researcher's opinion, this is a reasonably advanced case whose details bring out important ques-

This teaching note was prepared by Abby Hansen as an aid to instructors in the classroom use of the case series "I Felt as If My World Had Just Collapsed!" (A) 9-383-171, (B) 9-383-172, and (C) 9-383-173.
(HBS No. 5-384-276)

tions of methodology and philosophy. Sue Roper is an experienced teacher with a clear idea of her multiple purposes and sufficient expertise to know how to arrange things to serve her ends. Neither a beginner nor a jaded old-timer, she blends innocence and experience in a way that can stimulate wide-ranging discussion, partly because Sue's behavior seems contradictory at times. A committed liberal, she behaves autocratically in the classroom and feels almost violently betrayed when a student seems to differ from the values she labors so hard to impart.

Sue's challenges are those of the experienced teacher. Having done many things "right" for a long time (even winning several teaching awards), she finds herself completely derailed by a student who breaks from the norm of unquestioning, polite compliance with the teacher's directions. Sue assumes that the teacher can create the classroom's emotional climate almost singlehandedly, and that modeling moral qualities is a virtual guarantee that the students will pick them up. If a student violates Sue's moral code, that must mean either that Sue has made some obscure but fatal error or that the student is willfully refusing to cooperate. The challenge to the discussion leader is not only to elicit these poles of interpretation but to get the group to color in the gray area between them.

Conflicts, Sensitivities

The first word of the (A) case is "Racism!" This, of course, poses an obvious challenge. How can the discussion leader protect any "minority" participants from embarrassment during the discussion of this case? One obvious answer is not to single them out for "expert" testimony unless they clearly signal their desire to present a specialized viewpoint. Another way to cushion the issue—appropriately, in this researcher's opinion—is to lay early stress upon the wider issues like perception, challenge to authority, and morality in classroom process. Some participants have tended to shrug off as minor the central incident in this case because they have experienced or witnessed far less ambiguous incidents of prejudice. The discussion leader should be prepared to handle potentially disturbing anecdotal material if the participants present it.

The "Blocks" of Analysis

The following rubrics occur to the researcher as convenient segments into which to divide the topics of discussion—simply for purposes of providing a rough map of the terrain by which the discussion leader may remain oriented during the free give-and-take of the actual conversation.

1. Setting. Note the school, its popular reputation, what we know of its actuality, and the classroom itself.

2. Characters. What information do we have about the teacher, the two key students, the rest of the class?

3. The course. First of all, does a language class involve special teaching problems? What about the composition of the class? How does Sue Roper seem to approach the course?

4. Operational issues. What sorts of tasks does Sue assign her students? How does she lead the group? In other words, how does the class operate (perform the assigned tasks)?

5. Contract. Sue sets a one-sided contract with her students. In her case, it seems to be a highly personal, emotionally charged one. What does she offer the students, and what does she expect in return?

6. Control. How does Sue lead the group? Where do you place her on a spectrum from authoritarian to laissez-faire?

7. Establishing a good classroom atmosphere. What does Sue seem to be doing to encourage her students to feel comfortable with her and with each other? How does she try to promote the "right atmosphere" and what does she think that atmosphere should be?

8. Modeling. Sue seems to place a great deal of faith in modeling values (openness, acceptance) as a means of imparting them. To what extent does she succeed? How reliable is this technique?

9. Questions. Several of Sue's quoted questions are really disguised commands. What are some of the subtle functions of questions—and how do these vary by phrasing, tone of voice?

10. Responses. Note that Sue's greatest problem in this crisis is how to respond. When Carrie refuses to work with Sarah, Sue feels all eyes are on her, waiting for her to do something. What options does she have? What are some of the ways teachers can respond in the classroom, and what are their implications?

11. Limits of influence. How much control does a teacher really exert over students? What are some of the limits of that control?

12. Protection. The issue of protecting the weak is always embedded somewhere in the teaching situation. The question of who, exactly, needs protection and how best to protect them is often far from simple to answer.

13. Interpretation. This dovetails with response. Sue Roper interprets Carrie's remark as racist. Is this the only possible interpretation?

14. Responsibility. Closely allied with the issue of protection is the question of responsibility. Who is accountable for what happens in the classroom? What are the reciprocal rights and responsibilities of teacher and students?

15. Timing. This relates to the issue of response. How much time can a teacher allow to pass before making some sort of response to a situation that he or she considers unacceptable? Is swiftness of response a virtue or a mistake? What about delay as a tactic?

These topics neither exhaust all the possibilities in this case, nor segment it with perfect neatness. It will be noted that some of them overlap. Nonetheless, the discussion leader who uses these—or some logical breakdown of the issues in this case—will ease the burden of staying oriented during the sometimes associative ebb and flow of discussion.

Preparing for the Discussion Opening Speaker; Backstop

This case presents no particularly knotty problems in the choice of a first speaker. Sue Roper is a woman, rather liberal in her social views, and a teacher of Spanish at a New England women's college. The usual considerations apply: to start "from strength," one might call on a participant with a similar profile, at the risk of beginning the case on too limited a note and allowing teachers from other disciplines to assume at first that the problems of teaching Spanish are unique and not transferable to their disciplines. To avoid this, one could select an opening speaker with a very different profile from Sue Roper—perhaps a male teacher of science—and ask him to concentrate on those elements of Sue's predicament that are human and universal. Balance is a reasonable criterion for selecting the backstop. If one has asked a woman somewhat like Sue Roper to open, one might choose a male backstop—and vice versa.

The Discussion Questions

Foreword. This case can be taught with emphasis on either the operational (action-oriented) or the theoretical (principle-oriented) aspects of teaching. The discussion leader must decide whether to stress and amplify questions related to what Sue Roper did (or might have done) to create the atmosphere she wanted and inculcate morality as well as good Spanish conversational skills in her students, or to stress questions that probe the situation and raise basic issues such as control, influence, modeling of values, and teaching style. This note will provide both sorts of questions and consider possible answers. Varying our frequent practice, we will begin with an action question and then broaden the discussion to include analysis and theoretical considerations.

After the (A) case has been read, the following questions can be addressed:

1. [To the opening speaker]: Could you start us off with a recommendation to Sue? Speaking as a friend of hers, what would you advise her to do at the end of the (A) case?

Responses to this action-oriented question will vary according to one's approach to the whole situation. The discussion leader should be alert for clues to the speaker's basic orientation in order to assure that other points of view also emerge. One's reply will tally with one's attitude toward the inculcation of morality in the classroom. What is Sue Roper's real mission in this Spanish class? What is her most basic, most inescapable responsibility—to teach Spanish conversation skills or to teach ethical values?

If one agrees with Sue that morality is key to true education and its teaching is the instructor's most abiding, most important responsibility, one may very well recommend forcing the issue of racism. Sue has two extreme choices: she could stop the class, confront Carrie's racism, declare this behavior unacceptable, and demand that Carrie work with Sarah. Or—on the other end of the spectrum—she could "roll with the punch," pretend nothing had happened, assign Carrie a different partner, and swallow her own fury. The discussion group should mention as many middle courses as possible.

While many find the classroom the ideal arena for moral education—and the teacher's responsibility an essentially moral trust—others may differ violently. Not everyone equates teaching with preaching. Why should a superior grasp of Spanish language and literature certify Sue as an ethical model? Some might assert that the teacher's highest duty in the classroom is to avoid partisanship and refrain from abusing the intrinsic influence of the teacher's position.

On the side of moral modeling, participants will recommend a variety of responses that may include delivering a speech on racism to Carrie, giving a general speech to the whole class, demanding a personal apology to Sarah, and buying time—if only to formulate a more effective strategy for confronting the issue of racism in class at some future date.

On the other side, some participants may express lack of sympathy for Sue Roper's whole approach to teaching. She deliberately introduces personal details of family life, embraces "openness" and "honesty," and expects her students to reciprocate in kind. Some teachers espouse objectivity, neutrality, purely intellectual (rather than emotional) content, and a certain mystery about their private lives.

2. *[To the backstop]: What would you select as the most important factors in the whole situation?*

This extremely broad, open-ended question could lend itself to considerations of the setting (women's school, conventional classroom with movable desk-chairs), the racial composition of the class, Sue Roper's personality, approach, and reputation, or the material of the course. The discussion leader should be prepared to work with whatever the participants select as paramount—suggesting the remaining elements for consideration during the rest of the discussion.

Let us begin with the personalities of the principal characters as they are given in the (A) case. Sue Roper dominates the description, partly because she is the case informant and partly because she is an eloquent, lively, intense person. Her self-description is extremely apposite: a civil rights activist, who "consciously" models moral values in the classroom in line with her "conviction" that "teachers shouldn't shy away from moral issues," she asserts that she "doesn't hesitate to reveal" herself and that, to her, there is nothing more personally offensive than racism. Added to this, we have a description of Sue's office (to which the discussion leader might refer in class if no participant mentions it): the room is cluttered with colorful objects (sombreros, toys, posters, shawls), notes for several projects, and many people. What attracts these people to Sue? Is her warmth unusual at Greenwood College? Despite Sue's emotional intensity, she does not seem to function purely on instinct in the classroom; she plans, theorizes, and works out tactics to achieve her pedagogical purposes.

Our data on the involved students are a great deal thinner. The offending student, Carrie Draper, is "a rather quiet white girl from Ohio, a sophomore interested in European art history." The "insulted" student, Sarah Hawley, is "a black girl from Washington, D.C.," a junior majoring in economics. We know that both girls have "shown strong language skills," and that Sue, who encourages social mingling in her classes, has not previously seen them speaking together.

What can we guess from these few details? Possibly, the white student comes from a wealthier background: art history is a less practical major than economics. We have no way of knowing what previous experience either student has had with members of other races. In any case, we may gather that the two students have different interests, and they are not members of the same graduating class. Also they are clearly not friends. It is even possible that there may be some sort of grudge between them. This is a conversation class, but Sue has not seen them in conversation: are they intentionally avoiding each other? Proponents of the "live and let live" school of teaching may point out this possibility. Sue Roper has an interventionist teaching style. People of a more self-contained inclination might say that, having noticed that these two students had not spoken together, Sue should have refrained from pairing them (at least until she had privately raised the possibility with them to see if it provoked painful grimaces).

Another significant factor in the situation is certainly the school itself. Greenwood College for Women is suburban, almost a hundred years old, and generally considered "predominantly white and middle class." The case notes the college's "significant efforts to recruit minority students." Is this a sign that minority students would not expect Greenwood to be hospitable without special prompting? At the time of this incident, 75 out of 800 Greenwood students were "officially classified as 'minorities.'" That's less than 10%, and we should bear in mind that the term *minorities* includes several racial and ethnic groups besides American blacks like Sarah. It seems reasonable to assume that students like Sarah felt conspicuous and outnumbered on this campus.

In the opinion of this researcher, the single most important factor in this situation is the teacher's highly personal style. Sue mentions that she deliberately introduces opinions into the classroom, creates assignments to break up cliques she perceives, and tries to get students of different backgrounds to befriend each other. In her extracurricular time she is something of a crusader for racial equality. Sue is not a woman to accept the world as she finds it, and her forthright nature expresses itself in an interventionist teaching style. As a teacher Sue seems to fall closer to the "controlling" than the "directing" end of the spectrum—the difference being one of subtlety. She is friendly, warm, and cordial, but she gives orders. Her description of the exercise that provided the background for this upsetting incident shows her assuming most of the responsibility for what occurred in the classroom. She had "begun to prepare some students for their next task," in which she would "pair" them according to her own priorities (although her system may have seemed arbitrary to the students).

At this point in the (A) case, Sue shows a certain dissociation from the process. Having directed this exercise for several years, she can fly on automatic pilot. Instead of observing the students' responses to her orders, she delivers a "standard speech" and does not look intently at their reactions. One important element of the situation might be Sue's momentary inattention. This was, after all, a routine classroom assignment that had never triggered any particularly unpleasant scenes before. Why should she have scanned the students for danger signs? We gather that Carrie had never given any warning of unusual recalcitrance or deviation from the social norms of the college. But there does seem to be some irony in comparing Sue Roper's extremely accepting social philosophy with her directive method of leading the class and anger at Carrie for resisting.

When this issue—Sue's classroom style—is raised, it might be useful to brainstorm a bit. What other techniques might she have tried to accomplish her purpose? For example, she might have invited the students to choose their own partners for classroom dialogues with the stipulation that she—or some recording secretary chosen by the class—would be responsible for making sure that every student had spoken with every other member of the class by the end of the semester. Such an approach would have given at least the illusion of free choice, within a clear framework. In this system, Carrie might have postponed working with Sarah, but not avoided it, and the postponement might have given her time to perform her task more graciously.

3. *What is at stake at the end of the (A) case?*

This question is a lead-in for the (B) case, which reveals what Sue Roper did in response to Carrie's shocking refusal to work with Sarah. There are, of course, several viewpoints from which to answer this question. At the end of the case, we find Sue Roper feeling shell-shocked by what she is certain was a racist remark. She describes herself as "positively sick." But she is trapped in front of a class of fifteen Greenwood students; five of them are black, and one of them—Sarah Hawley—is the victim of what Sue calls "a stunning slap in the face." Sue has to maintain her dignity. The other students have not "dared look at Sarah"; we do not know if they are looking at Carrie. But the teacher remembers "feeling them watch me to see what I'd do." What is at stake for Sarah Hawley, whom Carrie has just rejected as a partner because "we're . . . we're not in the same dormitory"? (One's reaction to this will depend on one's interpretation of Carrie's remark. Is she hastily wallpapering a rabidly racist remark? Might she have some other reason for balking at working with Carrie—whose language skills, we have been told, were as good as hers?) Also very important is the question of what is at stake for Carrie. If her remark *was* racist, what consequences can she expect? If the remark was innocent, what price will she pay for having been misunderstood?

The most striking character in this configuration is, of course, the teacher, to whose intense misery we have extensive testimony. Having carefully constructed a socially healthy microcosm in her Spanish Conversation class, Sue feels personally betrayed, sick, and shocked when Carrie refuses to get up and sit beside Sarah and begin to plan a small class presentation with her. To Sue, her authority as a teacher and moral model is clearly on the line; her orders have been defied. But in her opinion, there is also much more at stake: her whole world. The discussion leader should ask some probing questions on this point. In what sense is the classroom a "world"? And who rules it? How does the teacher control this little planet? In what way (if at all) does Carrie's uncooperative reaction reflect upon Sue's leadership?

Finally, we must consider the other students. How might the other minority students in the room have felt? What about the "non-blacks"? At the very least one would expect embarrassment on every side, and a great deal of sympathy for Sarah. We can also probably count on feelings of intense discomfort. Any breach of social norms will produce a general squirm. Racism aside, Carrie's refusal to cooperate with Sue's polite request was quite enough to produce an undercurrent of tension in the class. One wonders, however, whether the other students in the room immediately and unequivocally interpreted Carrie's words as racist, and whether they—like Sue—felt that their tacit contract to accept and trust each other had been brutally violated.

After the (B) case has been read:

1. *Sue seems to have acted on instinct—most of us do under fire. What do you think of her response?*

The participants should take a close look at Sue's movements—"I turned back *to Sarah,*" she says, adding these words: "Please take out your minidrama so you can see which one you and Carrie will perform." In a sense, Sue has symbolically rejected Carrie by turning away from her. She has made her physical gesture (of solidarity) in the direction of the injured party—Sarah—and seems simply to be ignoring Carrie's refusal as if it were so ludicrous that it could not possibly be taken seriously. Sue's actual words are a repeated command. In the mouths of teachers, polite questions beginning with "Would you please" are generally orders—as students learn, almost as early as they learn to brush their teeth. (To demonstrate this subtext of command we have Sue's report of her accompanying thoughts: "Damn it, there's no way I'm going to let Carrie get away with this sort of behavior in my class!" One could hardly ask for a clearer statement of determination.) Participants will react to Sue's actions and words in ways that tally with their sympathy for her and her point of view. If they, too, consider Carrie's refusal to work with Sarah as racist, and find Sue's social mission in the classroom appropriate (or even noble), they will either applaud her for standing firm or suggest that she might have gone much further in the direction of confrontation. Perhaps she could have turned toward *Carrie*—with a stinging rebuke. On the other side, participants who think Sue has overreacted, or who differ with her directive style of managing the undergraduates, will say that she should have backed off, bought time, and let the situation cool off.

In discussing the (B) case, the leader should note that Sue's response took a while to develop. Only after repeating her words to Sarah did she turn back to Carrie and begin to argue: "It doesn't matter if you aren't in the same dorm. . . . There's absolutely no reason you can't work together." What is the effect of this direct refutation of Carrie's stated reasons for refusing to work with Sarah? Participants may applaud its comprehensiveness or disapprove of it because it brings the teacher down to Carrie's level, exposing her to charges of "protesting too much." Sue seems to be overwhelming Carrie with advice, and her statement that there is "absolutely no reason you can't work together" is a risk. Perhaps there *is* some reason, something that should be aired only in private. How can Sue know? Is she treading on thin ice by insisting that these two students work together? (At this point in the case, there's no way to tell.)

2. *What about Sue's concern with "the larger sense" of the problem?*

As the class hour progressed, Sue intentionally tried to dissociate her boiling feelings from her public behavior. Carrie did get up and walk across the room to sit beside Sarah, and Sarah permitted her to do so without demanding an apology or creating any sort of public stir, but Sue continued to stew over the larger implications of the incident. It is interesting to note that Sue's self-control seems to have paid off, for she got through the rest of the class without incident (despite her private agonizing), and the two girls did perform their minidrama in class a week later.

The discussion leader should draw attention to their performance. Is there, perhaps, something suspicious about its "innocuousness"? What significance is there in the fact that the two students chose Sarah's script, and that the content of that script was conventional, to say the least? And what about the grade (B+) Sue awarded both students for this bland performance?

The central issues to discuss in this section of the case are those of responsibility, public versus private confrontation (what would have happened if Sue had stopped the class to accuse Carrie of blatant racism?), and, finally, the overarching question of the larger implications of this incident.

3. *Should Sue have let the matter drop after the girls performed their minidrama in class?*

Again, there will be a spectrum of response. Answers will range from "certainly" to "certainly not," depending upon how pernicious people consider the initial incident. Those who share Sue's orientation—or who have become more sympathetic during the discussion—may argue that the classroom is truly a microcosm, and the teacher's duty included publicly labeling and rejecting clearly unacceptable behavior. Some will say that a flimsy excuse like Carrie's so obviously masked pure prejudice that only a cowardly teacher would have let her get away with it (and Sue did not). On the other hand, some participants may cling to their skeptical view of the prospects for success of Sue's social mission. A classroom is just another room, they may say. Students do not surrender their free will or their prejudices at the door. Whatever sort of modeling a teacher may choose to do still leaves them room to demur and disagree. Furthermore, some might argue, the responsibility for protecting Sarah should really rest with Sarah herself. Shouldn't Sue have allowed her the privilege of seeking Carrie out privately and demanding an apology? Some may also argue that Sue's passing thought of alerting a black dean (Cynthia Wilson) was an excellent idea.

4. *Given that Sue felt obliged to pursue the matter, how would you have advised her to do this?*

There are several courses of action Sue might have taken. She might have called each student to her office for a private rehash of the incident and, in Carrie's case, an explanation. She might have called them in together to make it clear that she expected them to learn to work together—as a lesson in cooperation as well as Spanish conversation. She might have taken the weekend to plan a cool-headed, well-reasoned speech on racism for the whole class. She might have telephoned Dean Wilson to ask what similar incidents had occurred on campus and how these had been treated. Or she might have lodged some sort of formal complaint with Carrie's dean and asked for an official reprimand.

Certainly, whatever course of action Sue decided upon, the prime ingredients to improve this situation had to include time and information (they usually do).

It would be valuable to call for discussion of Sue's compulsion to take some long-term action. The students had complied with her initial request and performed their assignment together. Wasn't that enough? Did Sue feel unsatisfied because of her personal sensitivity to racism? Or is there possibly some broad issue of institutional responsibility at stake? Can one extrapolate from a teacher's permitting a hint of racism to drop in class unremarked and unchallenged to an institutional personality? If black students are permitted to be insulted in class, what does this mean for the institution? And what does it mean for the larger society that holds such an institution in generally high esteem? Putting yourself in Sarah's shoes, how might you have felt when Carrie balked at having you as a working partner, and then only grudgingly agreed to team up with you?

The discussion leader should take care to assure that participants do not brush Sue off as a knee-jerk liberal, just as they should not leap to brand Carrie as a racist.

After the (C) case has been read:

1. *How do you appraise Sue's report of her conferences with the two students?*

Carrie, it seems, stubbornly denied any racist content to her remark even though it had struck Sue (and, apparently, many other students in the class) as patently prejudiced. Is it possible that Sue lost an opportunity to educate Carrie, letting her animosity show and inspiring feelings of defensiveness? Accusations usually breed denials and rationalizations (often quite creative ones). What tactics might Sue have adopted to relax Carrie, find out what she really meant by her refusal to work with Sarah, and ascertain whether actually going through with the assignment had done anything to change her views?

Sarah, on the other hand, seems to have relaxed with Sue—not surprisingly, given Sue's reputation for friendliness and helpfulness to black students. In fact, Sarah's attitude, as Sue reports it, confirms Sue's assumptions about the implications of Carrie's remark in class. Her words might be stressed and offered for consideration to participants who have been espousing the "tempest in a teapot" approach. Sarah applies the microcosm/macrocosm model here and associates the incident with larger structures: There *is* racism at Greenwood, she says. Everybody knows it; nobody really fights against it; and some teachers actively promote it. In this interview, we note that Sue truly assumes an advisory position and offers Sarah some responsibility for improving her own situation: "Sit with Carrie . . . make conversation . . . you can't always expect other people to assume the burden of friendship," she says.

The discussion leader should try to emphasize this passage, citing it if no participant does. For this is a true nugget of instruction. In this part of the case we see Sue focusing on the larger implications of the incident and trying to help her student learn to solve her own problems. Carrie has objected to the black students' cliquishness (which is, no doubt, the result of their fear of rejection). Sue tells Sarah to break away from her black friends and make a few overtures to people like Carrie. Multiply this several hundredfold and more interracial friendships might indeed take root at Greenwood. Sue seems finally (in this case, at least) to have grasped the sad truth that she cannot protect her students all the time. They have to learn to protect themselves and, further, help lay the groundwork of structures (wider friendships, for example) that will extend the protection throughout society.

2. *What about Sue Roper's feelings that Carrie had "duped" her and that she, the teacher, had "somehow failed the group"?*

This question carries deep implications in the realms of contract, more modeling, and responsibility—all of which should have been touched upon in the discussion. But these are enduring problems; they should be reconsidered often. Sue learned a bitter lesson of the limitations of her power to create atmosphere and control the classroom dynamic. Some teachers try to stuff information into students' heads and feel frustrated when they absorb it incorrectly (or not at all). In Sue's case, the lessons she wanted to inculcate were emotional and ethical, and her technique was double-barreled: she both instructed her students openly, and created assignments to force them out of their social ruts. She also assumed that modeling a system of values and practicing emotional honesty would inspire exactly those qualities in her students. The questions are: *Has* she failed? What is success? Can one look for instantaneous results in teaching? How can one measure students' moral progress?

Needless to say, these questions have no simple answers, but they are, in the opinion of the researcher, essential.

EXHIBIT 1 *I Felt as If My World Had Just Collapsed! (A)*

Study Questions

1. What is most significant about the principal characters of this situation?
2. How does the school's atmosphere affect the main incidents?
3. How do Sue Roper's assumptions affect her teaching?
4. What is the greatest challenge Sue faces at the end of the (A) case?
5. What should she do?

EXHIBIT 2 *I Felt as If My World Had Just Collapsed! (A)*

Discussion Questions

After the (A) case has been read:

1. [To the opening speaker]: Could you start us off with a recommendation to Sue Roper? Speaking as her friend, what would you advise her to do at the end of the (A) case?
2. [To the backstop]: What would you select as the most important factors in the whole situation?
3. What is at stake at the end of the (A) case?

After the (B) case has been read:

1. What do you think of Sue's response to Carrie's unexpected refusal to cooperate?
2. What about Sue's concern with "the larger sense" of the problem?
3. Should Sue have let the matter drop after the two girls performed their minidrama in class?
4. Given that Sue felt obliged to pursue the matter, how would you have advised her to do so?

After the (C) case has been read:

1. How do you appraise Sue's report of her conferences with the two students?
2. What about Sue's feelings that Carrie had "duped" her and that she, the teacher, had "somehow failed the group"?

I Felt as If My World Had Just Collapsed! (A), (B), and (C)

RESEARCHER'S PERSPECTIVE

This commentary was written by Abby Hansen for the Developing Discussion Leadership Skills and the Teaching by the Case Method seminars. Its objective is to help instructors in the development of their own teaching plans for this case. (HBS No. 5-384-277)

Among the usual "who, what, where, when, how" of the typical analysis, I consider two factors—the *where* and the *who*—by far the most important in this particular set of incidents. Despite its official policy to recruit minority students, Greenwood College for Women comes across as a conservative, upscale institution, preppy, Ivy League, and exclusive. Such an environment, with its traditional social homogeneity, would seem somewhat uneasy for at least two of the important characters in this case—Sue Roper and Sarah Hawley. Sue's emotional forthrightness and outgoing approach to teaching seem out of step with the generally muted, reticent sort of style one associates with places like Greenwood (at least traditionally). Sarah Hawley, Sue's student, is a black girl from Washington, D.C. The (C) case tells us that Sarah's background is working-class, and she, herself, thought of leaving Greenwood until her parents persuaded her to stay.

Sue Roper portrays herself as an activist for racial equality, unusually sensitive to the feelings of minorities, and extremely zealous in protecting their interests. In any case, Sue has other characteristics that mark her as unusual, perhaps *sui generis*, in a "New England women's college." Her personal warmth and outgoing, honest, almost confessional style of teaching set her apart, and the case shows us her effusive, expressive gestures (she "pushes" the very word *racism* away from her physically, for example). Her office is another clue to her personality. It is friendly in its clutter, full of inviting, almost childlike objects (sombreros, posters, toys) that she uses as audiovisual aids. Even more important, her office is full of people—students, fellow teachers, and friends. This copiousness seems almost an objective correlative for some aspects of Sue's personality: she surrounds herself with bright, playful objects and a variety of people (while many college teachers opt for neat bookshelves and as few people as possible to interrupt their private thoughts).

We also note Sue tapping a pencil nervously as she speaks to the researcher. She is a volatile woman, we gather—used to expressing powerful emotions physically and verbally, and also used to having people like and respect her for this quality. (Her office would not have been so full of colleagues, students, and friends if her style had not attracted them.)

Let us turn to the other important characters in this case—Sue's students. We know a good deal less about them because Sue is the case informant; we must be content with her impressions of them. Carrie Draper, a sophomore, is a white girl from Ohio, and a student of European art history. What does this tell us? Perhaps we may infer a degree of affluence in her Midwestern background from her declared major in European art history, which is not a subject that one takes in preparation for a lucrative career. We also know that she has "strong language skills," but not any stronger than Sarah Hawley's (her black colleague). Not until the (C) case do we learn a few more things about Carrie. Confronted with a direct accusation of racism, she flatly denies it. But Sue Roper follows this information with some behind-the-scenes gossip she has heard about Carrie: apparently Carrie had been assigned a black roommate at the beginning of the semester but had arranged to have the assignment changed. Why? On this point we have no information. Carrie herself makes two negative statements about blacks at Greenwood College: they are cliquish and they play loud music in the dorms.

About Sarah we have only a bit more information. She is a junior from Washington, D.C., proficient in Spanish, and an economics major. Her purpose in remaining at Greenwood despite some misgivings about the place (where she thinks racism is so embedded that nobody notices it except those who suffer from it) is to become "upwardly mobile," and enter the job market with a prestigious degree in economics. In other words, Sarah is doing her best to improve her socioeconomic status. To Sarah, Carrie's instinctive and rude public rejection was obviously racist. "I know Carrie didn't want to work with me because I'm black," she says, and goes on to tally Carrie's feelings with the whole background of Greenwood culture: "There's plenty of racism at Greenwood." "One teacher assigns a textbook that describes blacks as inferior. If the teachers are racist, what can you expect of the students?" Sarah thus comes off as a sensitive person under family pressure to endure the sometimes bruising rejections implicit in the culture of a basically alien environment.

Interestingly, each of these girls feels that the other wants nothing to do with her. Carrie finds the black girls cliquish (which implies hostility to non-blacks like herself) and alien in their musical tastes. Sarah, on the other hand, finds the dominant culture at the school shot full of racism and includes at least one teacher in her assessment. Such mutual distrust cannot fail to have its effect in the classroom.

The issue of trust (or its opposite) brings us back to Sue Roper again—for trust is one of her most cherished values. In the (C) case, Sue cites trust when she explains why she continued to "feel distant from Carrie," who, she thinks, had "deceived" her. What form had this deceit taken? "A betrayal of trust." To Sue, the fact that Carrie had "openly rejected Sarah" in class (even though she did later rescind that rejection and publicly accept Sarah as a working partner) constituted a violation of faith. "I still feel that Carrie duped me," says Sue. To dupe someone is to fool them, to conceal the truth from them, to lie. Sue seems to think that Carrie sneaked her intrinsic racism into the classroom and sat in silent cynicism as Sue openly proclaimed her liberal views and confided her deepest feelings about the necessity for social equality. Then Carrie took the first opportunity in class to reveal her true colors. ("Wham!" says Sue. "She openly rejected Sarah.") This seems overstated.

In my opinion, the private content of Carrie's rejection, "I'm not going to work with Sarah," will forever remain a mystery to us. Only Carrie can know what really motivated it, if her subsequent rationalizations have not clouded the truth, even for her. We do know that the reason she gave ("We aren't in the same dorm") might or might not have had something to do with race (the black students chose to live apart). It might have had more to do with accessibility.

It seems surprising that the initial incident with all its potential for true, lasting hurt, blew over with relative gentleness. Sue stood her ground, and—without stopping the class for a passionate address on the subject of social acceptance or the utter perniciousness of racism—made it clear that "there was no way" Carrie was going to get out of working with Sarah. Sue stuck to practical details as she argued her point with Carrie: the girls could meet in the student union, or they could talk on the phone. (This seems considerate.) Leaving the volatile and potentially devastating issue of racism aside in a class that is 30% black seems to embody the better part of diplomacy. Had Sue stopped the class for an impromptu speech on racism, I believe the black students would have felt not only rejected and singled out for special treatment, but also condescended to by their non-black protectress. These feelings would have been not only extremely painful (rejection always hurts) but also "infantilizing."

In sum, I find the actual course of action that Sue Roper took to deal with this situation to have been the best, given the circumstances. In this, I disagree with Sue, herself, who "still feels I failed the whole group and I failed myself" for not confronting the issue instantly.

In any teaching case, the question of long-term success or failure is always complex. What lesson did Sue's action teach her students? Perhaps one could say that her self-control under pressure was educational. Certainly, the students must have known Sue well enough to realize that Carrie's initial rejection of Sarah had shocked and upset her deeply. Second, she decided to postpone any confrontation of the issue until after the two girls had worked together in class and completely fulfilled the original terms of her assignment. In other words, Sue insisted on exercising her classroom prerogative of making assignments as she thought best and requiring that the students perform them. In this we see another side of Sue's personality that I think extremely apposite, for a certain directive quality distinguishes her teaching style. Her personal intensity seems to be powerful enough to envelop the students in a charged emotional force field—one that they enter either because they agree with her values and inclinations or because they are drawn into her vortex by sheer energy.

Sue seems aware of her ability to create a unique emotional climate in the classroom. Her fifteen years of teaching experience have certainly not been lost on her. On the contrary, she has learned a great deal of sophistication in controlling the class. She knows how to speak to students. She knows what kind of body language to use to involve and include them in the classroom process. She also knows how to create assignments that will give the illusion of turning the classroom over to them—pairing them in teams, for example. But she really continues to hold all the cards. Her overarching purpose is indisputably benevolent: she wants to break up cliques in order to widen students' social horizons and, at the very least, expose them to a variety of conversational styles. But her assumptions about the true power of any teacher to impart basic values seem to be inflated. Can one always transmit social values by modeling them? What about students' private right to disagree, to find the teacher's values untenable, even to consider the teacher ridiculous? Does a teacher who notices disagreement on a student's part have the right to feel duped, cheated, thwarted, betrayed? To what extent can a teacher monitor the impression he or she makes on a student's mind and heart?

A further caveat I would add to these considerations is the possibility that Carrie did learn a lesson about racism. She performed the team assignment successfully with a black partner, and it can hardly have escaped her attention that her partner's command of Spanish was equal, if not superior, to her own. Also the girls chose Sarah's, not Carrie's, dialogue to memorize and present. I wouldn't put too much emphasis on Carrie's evasiveness in conference with Sue, because Sue's hostility must have been apparent to Carrie, and defensiveness is not a favorable soil in which to nurture honesty.

It is possible that Carrie did, in fact, blurt out her initial remark from racist motivations, but the ensuing emotional turmoil—Sarah's hurt feelings and the teacher's obvious shock—may have horrified her sufficiently to prevent her from making a similar remark again. Unless we assume that Carrie was some sort of monster (she seems to have been quite an ordinary student), she can hardly have failed to regret her own remark. Perhaps having made it and then realizing she would have to live it down was lesson enough for her.

To my way of thinking, this case provides a lesson in humility for teachers. Sue Roper came to this Spanish class with fifteen years of teaching experience, solid credentials as a crusader for social equality, and an extremely engaging teaching style. But all of these positive factors did not prevent disaster. Sue faced the limits of her power to create the sort of classroom atmosphere she valued. And she faced the ineradicable recalcitrance of human nature. Despite Sue's heroic efforts to model certain values, Carrie let slip an unfortunate remark of the very sort Sue most detested. But Sue's self-control and instinctive realization that direct confrontation would only exacerbate the painful situation seem to have been laudably tactful reactions. They pointed the way to a long-term solution to the problem in which Sue's initial requests were successfully met. In the long run, she finally took her opportunity to discuss the event privately, calmly, and in some depth with its two protagonists. The art of teaching can never be sufficiently mastered to prevent all unsettling reversals, but the realization that tact, above all, must be invoked to contain them can help teachers through the initial few moments after a shock, when the temptation for hasty, emotional reaction is almost overwhelming. Her actual classroom behavior was protective in the best sense and avoided hurting either Carrie or Sarah. As Sue herself puts it in the (B) case, "When a teacher humiliates a student, it shows the teacher's weakness, not the student's."

Who Should Teach? (A), (B), and (C)

TEACHING NOTE

Marina McCarthy prepared this teaching note as an aid to instructors in the classroom use of the case series "Who Should Teach" (A) 9-387-139, (B) 9-387-140, and (C) 9-387-141. (HBS No. 5-387-029)

Introduction

"Who Should Teach?" is a complex case, recommended for use toward the end of the seminar. The case addresses two major (as well as several minor) concerns. The two major blocks of analysis (discussed in more detail below) are professional gatekeeping and recommending counseling to a student.

Whereas many seminar cases focus in depth on a single classroom incident, "Who Should Teach?" revolves around the summer experience of a Kensington University graduate student, Paul Warburton. Admitted to a professional training program, he is on the verge of being "thrown out," to use the words of his supervisors, who face a difficult policy decision. The case reminds us that not all teaching (teacher/student interactions) takes place within the confines of a classroom.

Usage

The case addresses two major (as well as several minor) concerns:

1. *Professional Gatekeeping*

- What criteria are (or should be) used to grant entrance to a professional school, and ultimately to the profession itself? What qualitative and quantitative data, objective and subjective information does one use to determine entry?
- Who determines the content/curriculum of preprofessional training? How do these gatekeepers receive their credentials? Who in turn evaluates them?
- How does one handle a student who does not conform to the philosophic norms of a preprofessional training program?
- How valuable are preprofessional apprenticeships? Do they really provide an accurate gauge of how a student will perform in his/her chosen profession, or is the experience more like "learning to cook in your mother-in-law's kitchen"?

2. *Recommending Counseling to a Student*

- How should one handle a difficult student?
- What are the appropriate boundaries between a faculty member and a student's nonacademic life?
- To what extent should a faculty member become involved with and evaluate the nonintellectual dimensions of a student?
- What ethical and legal considerations are involved in a decision to require a student to go to counseling?

- What rights or recourse does a student have who disagrees with such a requirement?

Other Issues

- How does one constructively critique another person's teaching?
- Do certain physical attributes enhance or detract from effective teaching: in other words, is it an asset to be beautiful or handsome? (One of the key actors in "Who Should Teach?" is under four feet tall.)
- How much should an instructor know about a student? How much is too much? (We do not necessarily mean here a student's "romantic" life, although seminar participants may argue that this information is helpful, even vital at certain times.)

Case Summary

Part (A) describes Kensington University and its program for teacher training, and introduces three key individuals: Christine Smith, director of the Master of Arts Program for beginning teachers; Ellen Bailey, one of the three master teachers supervising the entering MA group; and Paul Warburton, a newly enrolled MA student. (A) details a particular dilemma from the perspective of Ellen and Christine; (B) and (C) from Paul's point of view.

"Who Should Teach?" revolves around the summer experience of Paul Warburton, a recent college graduate who wants to be a teacher more than anything else. Because of a series of circumstances, Ellen Bailey, the master teacher, feels Paul is not fit for the classroom. Christine Smith, the new director of the MA Program is ambivalent at first, but ultimately concludes that Paul must see a counselor before he is allowed to student teach during the academic year. Paul admits having some adjustment difficulties but resents the ultimatum to go to counseling.

Part (B) ends with Paul feeling uncertain of his options. He resents the decision that he must go to counseling, and one does not know what will happen next.

After discussing parts (A) and (B) of the case, participants receive (C), which takes place in the middle of the fall term. We learn that Paul has decided to go to counseling. He reflects on his counseling experience thus far and expresses his ambivalence about its value. He questions whether going through the process will really make him more fit to teach come second semester. Even so, Paul appears to have found some value in his counseling sessions.

Study Questions

Questions to accompany parts (A) and (B):

1. What is the situation from Christine's point of view? From Ellen's? From Paul's?
2. What is your appraisal of Christine and Ellen's handling of the situation?
3. As a friend of Paul, what advice would you give him?

Preparing to Teach "Who Should Teach?"

Seminar leaders may wish to have the group briefly discuss each part of the case individually, but it is our advice to treat (A) and (B) as one unit.

We predict a wide range of responses from seminar participants. Individuals may identify more with Christine or Paul than with Ellen—who serves as the bearer of bad news, not really the decision maker or the student. But some participants may have had to play the heavy, may have felt the need to come forward about a colleague or co-worker, or may have been involved in some other way in proceedings to let someone go. They may identify more closely with Ellen Bailey.

"Who Should Teach?" can be used as a "prediction" case (that is, to let seminar participants test their ability to predict the outcome of the events described in (A) and (B)). But we believe its primary potential is to prompt a discussion of broader questions related to preprofessional training and faculty-student relationships.

We recommend that the first half of the class be devoted to discussion of parts (A) and (B). This leaves the second half of the class for (C) and larger issues presented by the case as a whole. Handing out (C) too early might limit the initial discussion.

The sequencing of the following discussion questions reflects our sense that it is a useful way to focus first on Ellen and Christine, then on Paul.

Discussion Questions

What follows is a list of questions that should help get the discussion moving. Of course, these questions serve only as a guide and should not substitute for questions that naturally arise from the discussion itself.

Christine and Ellen (A)

1. ***Please outline the situation for us. Let's review the what, when, where, and who to get our discussion going.***

2. ***What is your diagnosis of the situation from Ellen and Christine's point of view? What are the pressures on them?***

Ellen finds Paul resistant to criticism of his teaching. He balks at suggestions for changing his teaching style or experimenting with alternative methods. Paul persists in lecturing and planning only teacher-centered activities, whereas Ellen prefers a student-centered classroom with the teacher as facilitator. Ellen's real concern, however, is Paul's inability to get along with his colleagues. He is abrupt and impatient and has been antagonizing the two other students in his small group. Ellen becomes particularly concerned about Paul the Friday evening they walk to his dormitory. He seems distraught, and she begins to question whether he can emotionally handle the teaching profession. She makes an appointment to speak with Christine. Ellen is particularly troubled by a comment Paul made earlier in the summer: "I like teaching because I like to be the center of attention."

Like Ellen, Christine is concerned about Paul's difficulty getting along with others. He is having organizational as well as interpersonal troubles in her class. Christine asks Dick, another master teacher, to work with Paul, hoping that Paul will respond differently to Dick. By the end of the week, however, Dick concurs with Ellen's assessment.

Christine perceives her decision about Paul's future as both a professional and a moral dilemma. She feels Paul would be a good role model in a classroom, yet she is concerned that teaching could be detrimental to both Paul and the profession. Her decision is further complicated by the difficulty she is having in finding someone willing to be Paul's supervising teacher in the academic year. Christine seems less pessimistic about Paul than Ellen is, yet her concern is very strong. She doesn't want to kick Paul out of the program, but feels he needs to work on his interpersonal skills. "He needs help getting along with other people."

While Ellen feels Paul might be able to finish the program, she maintains that he is unfit to teach. Christine, on the other hand, feels that requiring Paul to go to counseling might solve the problem.

3. ***What options does Christine think she has? Are there others? Which makes sense to you?***

According to the case, Christine thinks she has three options: (1) requiring counseling, (2) referring Paul to the doctoral program in history, (3) letting Paul go. But there are other possibilities. Christine could work with Paul herself during the fall term, helping him to iron out his problems. (She could seek advice from the counseling center on how best to intervene. Many universities have such services.) Alternatively, someone else in the department might be asked to meet with him on a regular basis. Or Christine could suggest that Paul transfer to a teacher training program at another university, or take a year's leave of absence.

4. ***What is your appraisal of Christine and Ellen's handling of the situation? What other options did Christine and Ellen have regarding the format, agenda, timing, and locale of the meeting?***

Some participants may argue that there was no need for Christine and Ellen to treat Paul's situation as a crisis. Others may criticize Ellen's resistance to regrouping Paul. (According to the case, the purpose of the small groups was to provide a "support system and to provide an opportunity to exchange ideas.") Ellen seemed irritated by Paul ("It's 7:30 p.m. . . . how far does my obligation to you last?"), and perhaps this influenced her thinking. Yet she was sensitive about Paul's feelings.

Participants may criticize Christine for relying so heavily on Ellen's assessment. They may further feel uncomfortable with the fact that they both had relatively few years (three) of full-time classroom teaching experience. On the other hand, they may applaud Ellen and Christine for their handling of Paul's situation, for taking the initiative and for following through.

Some may point to the location of the meeting (Christine's office) as too authoritarian; others may feel it was a necessary setting to connote the seriousness and gravity of the situation. Participants may disagree with the time initially allotted for the meeting—30 minutes. Some may feel the meeting went on too long and should have been cut short; others may feel that because Paul was upset by the decision to require him to go to counseling, it was important to allow the meeting to go on as long as it did.

5. Christine is new to Kensington and relatively new to teaching. (The case says she entered the MA Program in teaching at 29/30 years of age, after working for some years in government. She spent the year following her MA working part-time. She then began a doctoral program, where she substitute-taught and coordinated a teacher training program at her university.) How has Christine managed her new position and its inherent power and responsibilities?

Some participants may argue that she lacks credibility, since her classroom experience is limited, while others will feel she has risen to the occasion.

Paul (B)

1. How does Paul see the situation? In what way(s) does his assessment differ from or complement Christine's and Ellen's?

Paul seems aware that he has some problems, but also notes that most MAs were experiencing anxiety during the summer. He felt a terrific time constraint: too much to do and too little time to do it.

Paul acknowledges that his own manner was interpreted as defensive and stubborn. We learn that Paul thought Greg and Joanne were quiet and perhaps passive-aggressive. He acknowledges that when there is silence, he tends to fill it, and that perhaps he misread their silence as indicating that they had nothing to say.

Yet Paul feels Ellen didn't adequately respond to his plea to change sections. He seems to feel things could have been different had she made a switch early on as he suggested. Further, he points out, his difficulties were not classroom ones. Although Ellen had concerns about his teaching techniques, her real concern was his inability to get along with others in the program.

He resents the ultimatum to go to counseling. He wants to teach yet is unsure what to do now.

2. How would you explain Paul's performance in the summer program?

Paul, like many of us, appears to have trouble with procrastination. He also seems to adjust relatively slowly to new settings. There also appeared to be a group chemistry problem: Greg, Joanne, and Paul did not work well together. Further, there was a philosophical rift between Paul and Ellen. Paul did not feel that Ellen was right to urge pedagogical experimentation; he thought it was best for beginning teachers to teach to their strengths.

3. Imagine that you are an official at Kensington and have been asked by Paul to arbitrate between him and Christine. How would you approach this task? What would you say and do?

4. Given what you know about Christine and Ellen, do you think Paul will be allowed to teach? What are the consequences if Paul is not permitted to student teach?

Participants' predictions are likely to vary. As for the consequences, Paul could protest a decision to deny him a student teaching placement (in particular, he could challenge the credentials of those evaluating him, file a discrimination complaint, transfer to another school, or reassess his career options).

Most prospective teachers need a 12-week practicum or internship in order to get their certification. Without completing a student teaching assignment, one has little or no chance of getting a job teaching in a public school, and a poor chance in a private school. Student teaching is the most critical gatekeeping element in the preprofessional program.

The state establishes the minimum standard for certification, but there is much discretion within individual university programs as to who completes the program and how well they do it. A decision to bar Paul from Kensington's student teaching component could mean that he will never have the opportunity to teach.

5. What would you have said to Paul in response to his final words at the end of the meeting?

6. What should he do? If you were Paul's friend, what would your advice be?

Paul (C)

1. Why did Paul decide to go to counseling?

It appears he felt he had no alternative. He characterizes the situation as "Catch-22." By arguing with the authorities, he thought, he would only dig himself in deeper, adding fuel to their argument.

2. What is Paul's attitude about going to counseling?

Paul appears cynical. Although he says he has made a commitment to counseling in order to satisfy the department's request, he finds it curious that by spring term he should be "fit to teach." He does not know what the criteria for a successful term of counseling are: "Is it the number of times I see the counselor? How does one measure progress?"

3. *How does Paul feel about Christine and her decision?*

Paul doesn't criticize Christine for her decision. Although angry at first, he empathizes with her position as director of the program. In fact, he remarks that he "wouldn't want to trade places with her." Paul finds Christine "a dedicated person, not at all vindictive." He feels she and Ellen "were only doing what they thought was best." He still suspects that their assumptions were a "quantum leap from reality," but concedes that "a different crisis might have brought everything out as well."

At the same time Paul feels trapped by the ultimatum. Although Kensington prides itself on a tradition of strong teacher-student interaction, Paul sees it as a one-sided top-down power relationship. He even regards the practice of encouraging students to call instructors by their first names as hypocritical "false advertising." (Participants, however, may see this as Paul's misreading of the department climate.)

Paul seems to respect Christine as a person and as a decision maker, yet he is still angry with the decision—cynical about both going to counseling and about Kensington in general.

4. *Was counseling useful for Paul?*

In some respects, Paul appears to have benefited from counseling, although he resents being compelled to go. His attitude, though resistant, is also somewhat open. He looks at counseling as an experience, and he appears to be learning from it. "It is interesting to have repeated back to me something I said . . . but didn't hear."

5. *What, in your judgment, should Christine do now? How should she appraise the success or failure of her plan? Should she speak to the psychologist? Should she approve Paul for a student teaching slot? What evaluative tools will guide her thinking?*

6. *Is Paul someone you would like to have as a teacher (or to teach your child)? How about Christine? Ellen?*

Other Questions for Discussion

At this point, the discussion leader might shift to a more reflective mood.

1. What basic issues does this case raise for you?
2. "Who Should Teach?" brings to the fore the issue of gatekeeping. By gatekeeping we mean the manner in which academics determine students' entry into the professions—education, medicine, law, architecture, and so on. Some aspects of gatekeeping are very obvious (e.g., certification boards), but others are more subtle. Preprofessional training programs include many unspoken rules. In addition to formalized expectations, there are informal norms, and much ambiguity in the process of guarding the gates. This ambiguity permits flexibility, but risks arbitrariness. The case presents several dilemmas related to gatekeeping. For example:
   - What criteria does one use to grant entrance to a profession?
   - What qualitative and quantitative data, objective and subjective information, does one use to determine "entry"?
   - Who determines the content and curriculum of preprofessional training? Must gatekeepers be senior and experienced persons? Tenured? Ellen and Christine had approximately three years of full-time teaching experience between them. Is this "enough"? At what point is an individual competent and credible enough to take on gatekeeping responsibilities?
   - Should a single individual be allowed to block a student from entering a profession?
   - How does one handle a student who does not conform to the philosophic norms of the preprofessional training program?
   - What are a student's rights in this process? What is implicit in a letter of acceptance from a professional school admissions office? Is it a guarantee to be allowed to complete the program barring academic deficiencies?
   - Finally, what are the ethics of gatekeeping? What is just?
3. Another major issue raised by the case is how to decide whether to recommend/require that a student go to counseling.
   - What ethical (and legal) considerations are involved in requiring a student to go to counseling?
   - An implicit issue is the student's recourse when he or she has been required to go to counseling. What rights does a student like Paul Warburton have?
4. The case also raises the issue of teacher evaluation.
   - How does one constructively evaluate another person's teaching?
   - Is it a balance of the positive (validating what he or she has done right) and the negative?

(Evaluating someone's teaching—particularly someone as new to the profession as Kensington student teachers—requires tact and sensitivity. Teaching is an extension of a person's ego. It is not just your teaching that is being evaluated, it seems, but your self.)

- How does an evaluator adequately—and firmly, if necessary—convey "tips" or suggestions for improvement? Is there any evidence in the case that Paul received any positive feedback for what he did well?
- Finally, should behavioral characteristics be part of the process of evaluating a student? What about physical characteristics? Several studies have shown that instructors give lower grades to students who are obese or less physically attractive, or who have relatively unappealing surnames. What implications does this have for race, gender, ethnic groups, handicap, general state of health?

5. The case raises questions about the usefulness of preprofessional apprenticeships.
   - What is the purpose and value of student teaching? or a medical internship? or a public policy placement?
   - Does performance in such settings provide an accurate gauge of how a student will perform in his/her chosen profession?
   - Are student teachers really on their own with an opportunity to prove themselves? Or is the experience rather like "learning to cook in your mother-in-law's kitchen"?
6. What implications does the case hold for other preprofessional programs (e.g., in medicine, law, or business)? Who are the gatekeepers, how did they get their authority, and can it (should it) be challenged?
7. Finally, if you were writing a letter of recommendation for Paul, what would you say?

Winter Oak

TEACHING NOTE

This note was prepared by Abby Hansen for use with the case "Winter Oak" No. 2-394-220.
(HBS No. 5-394-162)

Distributed by HBS Publishing Division, Harvard Business School, Boston, MA 02163. Printed in U.S.A.

Usage and Special Characteristics

The most obvious characteristic of Yuri Nagibin's lovely "Winter Oak" is that it is not a case, but a short story. While traditional teaching cases—designed and produced to support group discussions about pedagogy—present carefully labelled details of institution, curriculum, and key characters' backgrounds, "Winter Oak" works by image and poetic suggestion. As readers, we do not learn the sort of specifics about Anna Vasileyvna's educational background ("college") or her subject ("Russian") that a teaching case would provide. Nor does Nagibin tell us how many grades were in Uvarovka School, or what its curriculum was. "Winter Oak" enchants by bringing even simple nouns to life, almost as if they were animals. The "caps, kerchiefs, hats, hoods, and bonnets" at Uvarovka School do not sit on students' heads, or on hat racks, they "flock" to school. And when Anna meets the parent of a student on the path, the man's whip, "thin" and "snakelike," "smacks" against his boots as he inquires about his son's behavior. Instead of describing this man's respect for the Uvarovka schoolteacher, Nagibin portrays it by showing the reader how the man steps off the narrow path into knee-deep snow to let her pass.

In the most poignant way, "Winter Oak" takes readers on a winter walk with Anna and her student Savushkin—the poorly dressed son of a widowed "withered, tired-looking woman who worked at the sanatorium's hydrotherapy section." The Winter Oak of the title was the reason for Savushkin's lateness: he stopped to visit the majestic, protective oak, which the narrative invests with preciousness, "as if inlaid with silver," and maternal power, with its "store of vital warmth" for the "poor creatures" of the forest. By contrast to Anna, a stranger to the forest, little, awkward Savushkin treated the tree "with the familiarity of a long-standing friendship." Walking with him literally on his turf, the teacher realizes that this seemingly inept learner actually knows a great deal about the forest and its creatures, including the numinous elk.

Reading the story, the reader is awed and touched by Savushkin's friendship with the Winter Oak, an icon of life in harsh, frozen circumstances (metaphorically, like his own, and those of many of this poor region's children). When Anna realized Savushkin's deep understanding of the lore of a "hidden forest life, so little known to her," Anna is humbled. She sees that her student has become her teacher, and she accepts her new wisdom with grace and gratitude. The vividness of Nagibin's prose style gives the reader a chance to have the same experience.

For these reasons, "Winter Oak" works well at the

end of a teaching seminar. The power of its imagery and its profoundly humane and embracing ethic help frame the seminar and link its fundamental concerns to the everyday concerns of students' lives outside of class. Assigned as the material for their last discussion, "Winter Oak" can trigger vivid and thoughtful reflections—not only about the course that the students have just taken together, but also about other teaching and learning experiences in their lives. Like Anna Vasilyevna, in whose boots they have walked the winding path to the Winter Oak, they can see the teacher in the student and the student in the teacher, and recognize personal moments in which this insight has lived for them, too.

Because this isn't a case, it doesn't lend itself to a formal teaching plan in a pedagogical seminar. Rather than construct lessons from this story, seminar instructors should try to help their groups find their own appropriate forms of closure, invigorated by the insights that the story has stimulated. After this, it is useful for instructors to present a summary that links the day's spur of the moment discussion about "Winter Oak" and participants' personal moments of illumination to a brief overview of the path that this group has taken, including any mystical clearings that it has discovered. After this, instructors may find it useful to present a more formal overview of the course from their own perspectives, as closure for the entire seminar.

Teaching Questions

In teaching "Winter Oak" like a case, instructors can help discussion groups get started by beginning with general questions that implicitly invite participants to link the story to their own experiences. Opening questions of a broad and fairly abstract nature can encourage general participation and freewheeling associations. Then the seminar group can narrow (and deepen) focus to concentrate on more personal, experiential aspects of teaching and learning. Because of the vividness of its metaphors and the power of its prose, "Winter Oak" often helps students tap memories and present them to the class. Such personal contributions can stimulate a flow of recollections of moments in which individual participants have, like Anna, experienced the oneness of teaching and learning.

The following are five broad teaching questions that can help discussion leaders encourage a group to examine the dynamic between Anna Vasilyevna and Savushkin and apply it to the group and then to individuals in the group. In past seminars, discussion has at times been so lively as to require little intervention from the instructor.

1. *What questions does Anna's experience with Savushkin pose for you as a student of the teaching/learning process?*

This open-ended question often triggers a discussion of issues as fundamental as one's philosophy of teaching. It opens the door to reflections upon one's own experience in the current teaching seminar, and the way in which the seminar fits into the greater context of one's previous teaching and learning experiences. The concrete particulars of the language of "Winter Oak" often help students link abstractions and practical considerations. The story's unique combination of down-to-earth (literally; it is full of references to dirt, dead leaves, and even animal droppings) and mystical elements often inspires participants to link these two ways of thinking.

Participants who begin by reflecting on general questions about "Winter Oak" often find ways in which they might expect to bring the insights of the teaching seminar to bear on their own classroom practice.

2. *What happened in that hour and a quarter walk? What did Savushkin teach Anna? How?*

Savushkin was in his world of knowledge in the forest. Anna was a novice. Savushkin was eager and enthusiastic. He wanted to reveal his knowledge and teach Anna. He made no negative judgments about Anna, in contrast to her first judgments of him. He allowed her to see the Winter Oak, and then to learn about it in depth. In seeing the tree in Savushkin's "secret" clearing, Anna could, if she wished, see the real, inner Savushkin, and he allowed her this private vision of himself.

It might be said that Savushkin taught Anna to observe—to look beneath surfaces, to brush away the clump of snow and dead leaves that hide a tiny and see the tiny, hibernating life that these seemingly worthless things serve to protect.

3. *What was Anna's style of teaching? What assumptions did she make? What assumptions has this teaching seminar suggested for you?*

Anna's training appears to have been traditional. She takes pride in her competence and in her ability to pose rote questions interestingly. In rural Russia, soon after "the war" (The Second World War), a young, college-trained educated teacher would have had little reason to think of her job as requiring her to craft questions and exercises to help students to think creatively and work as active partners in their own teaching. Implicit in this line of discussion is the notion that the teaching seminar has, at various points and in various cases, opened the way to different assumptions. How have these been put into practice? What are the implications of what participants have experienced, thought about, and learned in this seminar, for future practice?

A further question relating to Anna's teaching style might be, "Why didn't Anna remember that Savushkin's mother was a widow?" Her traditional approach—in which the teacher dispenses knowledge and students then demonstrate that they have received it—did not require that she learn about her students' personalities or private circumstances. In this model of teaching, all the instructor need learn about any students is how well she or he listens, understands, memorizes, applies, and reports.

The author shows the reader how Anna taught by depicting the way in which she gave the students a lesson on "subjects in grammar." Anna prided herself on being competent and knowing how to "hold the interest" of her pupils. The story shows her holding their interest by a fast-paced question-and-answer exchange in which, after explaining what a noun is, she asks them to show her that they have understood by naming some nouns. The seminar instructor might ask what strengths this style of teaching might have—in Anna's, or any other setting. Are there some subjects that this style suits particularly well? Are there some for which other styles might be more effective?

What were the risks of Anna's customary style of teaching? The story suggests one possible answer. Before taking her epiphanic walk with Savushkin, Anna considered the phrase "winter oak" as nothing more than a noun and another part of speech that "we have not studied yet." And when Anna hears Savushkin insist that "an oak is nothing, but a winter oak, there's a noun for you," her reaction is merely: "difficult boy." Later, after her moving experience of seeing, really *seeing* the Winter Oak, Anna has gained both knowledge and insight. Perhaps one risk of her accustomed style of teaching was that, pursued unswervingly, it would have prevented her from doing anything so unconventional as letting Savushkin lead her into the forest. Adhering to her style of instruction would have made it unlikely that she would have learned of the boy's generosity, perception, and dignity. Anna's great lesson in this story is that "the most wonderful being in that forest was not the winter oak but this small boy in battered felt boots and patched clothes, the son of a 'shower nurse' and a soldier killed in the war." Surely it would have been a loss to miss such an opportunity.

Some other aspects of Anna's style might include the possibility of forgetting, or overlooking:

- that students start from where they are, not where the teacher wants them to be.
- that they often are often more knowledgeable about the topic under consideration than the instructor thinks—sometimes even more knowledgeable than the instructor.
- that no group is the same on Tuesday as it was on Monday, or will be on Wednesday.
- that the rebellious, those who don't want grades, are often the most interesting students to work with—the teacher's best teachers.

What did Savushkin teach Anna?

- that we need to know something about students as people—their itches and ouches, what their victories are, what the instructor might learn from them, and what their classmates might learn.
- to accept, as she learned, that even superficially "difficult" students can teach their teachers valuable, even brilliant, lessons, as Charles Gragg's "Teachers Also Must Learn" reminds us.
- Perhaps he taught her to re-experience being a "learner" again.

4. *Every student, we believe, has his or her Winter Oak—an experience, a place, a relationship, which energizes learning, stimulates questions, a place where he or she feels safe in taking risks, a still point in a rapidly changing world. How do you, the teacher, learn about these Winter Oaks? Should you? How do you approach the tree, enter the place where risk-taking is safe, find the clearing, see and sense the Winter Oak, and learn from it?*

The intrinsic imbalance of power in the teacher-student relationship often includes many implicit barriers to learning about students' special strengths, whether of wisdom, experience, talent, or character. By defining a value system that honors students, and designing questions that invite them to talk to one another in class, summarize one another's remarks, respond to one another's objections and elaborations—in a courteous manner—instructors can open a learning space in the classroom.

5. *Can one create a classroom that is a Winter Oak for a group? How?*

Instructors may wish to ask the group as a whole if anyone there has worked with an instructor whose skill and values converted his or her own classroom into a grove of Winter Oaks, where all students taught as well as learned. What went on in these classrooms? How did those teachers behave? What did they say?

What did they do? What did students say and do? What greater lessons might one draw from their practices?

When instructors embrace, and apply, fundamental values of respect, understanding, partnership, community, and communication, the physical classroom can be converted into a joyous, exploding learning space.

Perhaps the full magnificence of the clearing in which the Winter Oak majestically held court will not appear in every classroom. But when teachers listen respectfully to students, encourage them to listen and respond to one another, pose open-ended questions, and freely admit the limits of their own knowledge and join students in a common pursuit of further illumination, the chances for creating at least a small clearing grow higher.

One way to end a seminar that concludes with a discussion of this magical tale might be to wish that all of the participants might turn their classrooms or labs into clearings "flooded with sunlight" and graced by Winter Oaks like Savushkin's—"tall and majestic like a cathedral," its branches spreading "far out over the clearing," and its trunk brushed with sunlit snow that shone "as if inlaid with silver." No wonder Anna Vasilyevna gasped at the sight and approached the gigantic tree "reverently." How wonderful it would be if all classrooms inspired the same response.

PART IV

Synopses of Additional Teaching Cases

This section prepared by Joyce Wadsworth includes abstracts of additional teaching cases, which you may want to insert in your seminar program. These cases are available from the Harvard Business School Publishing Corporation, Soldiers Field, Boston, Massachusetts 02163. Identifying case numbers are included at the end of each abstract.

Assistant Professor Brian Duncan

This case series is seven pages long and divided into three units. It would be particularly useful for teachers who find themselves in situations where both faculty and students seem to have low self-esteem, or where they try to motivate—while grading fairly—students with a low self-image.
HBS Case Nos. (A) 9-381-121; (B) 9-381-122; (C) 9-381-123

Case Overview

(A) Case

In August Brian Duncan, 33, resigned as assistant to the vice president of operations of a Pittsburgh, Pennsylvania, firm and accepted an assistant professorship in the Business Department at Mountain State College (MSC). In the first case in the series we learn why Brian Duncan made the move, what he encountered at MSC, and how he attempted to solve what he considered a serious problem: the fact that the majority of his students not only had little grasp of material fundamental to his courses but that they lacked "personal standards."

The case gives background information on MSC, a branch of the state's university system—located in an eastern U.S. mountain resort area—with an enrollment of 3,000 full-time students. In brief, it was founded as a teachers' college but expanded in the sixties under the direction of a president who developed undergraduate degree programs in the liberal arts and degree programs in the liberal arts and business administration. The student body is predominantly white, with in-state students coming largely from working-class families, and out-of-state students tending to be affluent and—according to Brian—a "breed of fun-loving, academically underachieving recreational athletes." MSC has an open admissions policy for in-state students and while this policy has helped the college to grow, Brian feels that it contributes to the sense of inferiority pervading the institution.

We learn how Brian introduced himself to his students as a professional manager, not a professional teacher; how Managerial Control (MC) would be like a math course with each step built on preceding steps; and that managerial control was "the use of managerial accounting information in decision making." We then read about early student feedback and Brian's reactions to it. His students, although willing, had real trouble with the problems presented, and their efforts indicated weak preparation in accounting. They considered many of the problems unfair because they were distracted by irrelevant data. Brian reminded them that in the working world neat problems are rare, and that choosing relevant from irrelevant data was essential. Students expressed anxiety about the upcoming exam; Brian told them what sorts of problems to anticipate and scheduled optional review sessions. He then asked a colleague how his section of MC was going—expecting similar sorts of difficulties—and was surprised to hear that all was going smoothly. A student told him later that the colleague had "mostly just been lecturing so far."

(B) Case

Brian grades his Labor Relations midterms and expresses his exasperation to his wife. He shows her, for example, one exam where the student attempts to answer a question with one sentence. He gives the exam an *F*. By the time he has finished grading Managerial Control and Labor Relations, he has given over 70 *F*'s.

(C) Case

Four years later, we see the results of Brian's steady attempts to improve students' personal standards as well as faculty grading standards at MSC. First we read Brian's critique of a grade monitoring report submitted by the Academic Standards Committee (ASC). He comments on the almost total absence of *D*'s and *F*'s and the extremely high percentage of *A*'s for education majors. Making his feelings known to the faculty, he is elected to the ASC and becomes its chairperson. Brian has prepared a new type of grade monitoring report which holds each teacher accountable for his or her grades.

Case Issues

This case series focuses on the efforts made by a professor to improve the motivation, standards, and ultimately the self-image of students at a little-known state college. We read his initial reactions of dismay and exasperation, and then see how, over a period of four years, he is able to make significant and fundamental changes, while remaining a well-respected teacher and colleague. What were the secrets of his success? How was he able to avoid being thought of by students as condescending, punitive, or destructive? How was he able to persuade certain faculty members that they were not meeting their responsibilities to students, and how was he able to do this without alienating them? What sorts of values sustain him? How was he able to communicate those values to his students in a way that motivated them to change?

Assistant Professor Donna Oscura and Ms. Sarah Summers

This case is approximately eight pages long and divided into three units.
HBS Case Nos. (A) 9-380-213; (B) 9-380-219; (C) 9-380-220

Case Overview

This case series describes a teacher's handling of what she perceives to be a suicide threat from one of her students. First we read the student's emotional and ambiguous comments, after which we are given background on the academic institution.

(A) Case

Assistant Professor Donna Oscura teaches in the Humanities Department at Central State University. She feels out of place at Central, alone in her commitment to excellent teaching. Even though she publishes, Donna feels that in the eyes of her colleagues the time she spends with her students [instead of devoting to research] reflects negatively on her impending tenure decision. She feels a victim of sexist discrimination at Central, and to make matters worse, her marriage is currently unstable.

Sarah Summers is a student who seems different from the others, but it takes Donna many weeks to realize that Sarah has emotional problems. In the meantime her response to Sarah differs from her response to other students. For example, she reacts with sympathy to Sarah's complaints and sets no limits on the length of time or number of Sarah's visits. One week after telling Donna that she is going to stop seeing her counselor, Sarah says, "I've been thinking that I really ought to listen to those voices inside me that tell me to give it all up." Stunned, Donna wonders what to do.

(B) Case

After consulting with another teacher, Donna locates Sarah and asks her to come to her office. She asks Sarah directly whether or not she means to hurt herself. Sarah shrugs off the concern and says she was only speaking metaphorically. Later Donna is able to talk to Sarah's counselor who tells her that in his opinion, Sarah will not attempt suicide.

(C) Case

Several years later, Donna reviews the incident. She realizes that Sarah's behavior was a kind of emotional blackmail and that her suicide threat was a bid for attention, yet she is glad that she did not rely on her own judgment and that she sought professional counsel.

Case Issues

This case describes a teacher's response to a student's apparent suicide threat. It also describes the relationship between the teacher and student, and we watch as the teacher unwittingly encourages the student's disturbed behavior. She finally takes steps to remedy the situation. Among the issues for the reader to consider are the sense of alienation teachers can experience at institutions that do not share their values, how such feelings of alienation can influence their behavior, and how an unhappy situation can also influence their behavior—often without their knowing. The readers also consider the symptoms of disturbed behavior and what might be done in response to those symptoms.

Assistant Professor Patrick Grady

Case Overview

(A) Case

Patrick Grady, a hard-working assistant professor of history in his second year at Brown University, is faced with making a decision that might have profound consequences for one of his students. He has just turned in a failing grade for Tom Morrow—a student who failed to hand in his term paper despite two phone calls from Grady and two clearly defined extensions. Four hours later, Tom calls the weary Professor Grady, saying his paper will be ready by the next morning. He pleads with his instructor to tell the registrar that the failing grade was a clerical error. And he informs Grady that he (Tom) is on probation and will be dropped if he fails the course.

(B) Case

After some discussion, and though he wavers fleetingly, Professor Grady tells his student that he would benefit from taking time off from school—and sticks with the failing grade.

Case Issues

This case series takes on the subject of when to make exceptions for students. How does one deal with rule infractions? What are conditions for leniency, for clemency, for finality? How much effort should a professor put into these problems, before or after the fact? Should an evaluation or grade be influenced by the professor's knowledge of the student's personal situation? Are there factors regarding a professor's personal life that can influence a student's evaluation? Does a teacher's responsibility end with giving a grade?

This case series is two and one-half pages long and divided into two units of unequal length (the second case consists of one paragraph). It could be used most effectively in a liberal arts seminar.

HBS Case Nos. (A) 9-380-221; (B) 9-380-222

Distributed by HBS Publishing Division, Harvard Business School, Boston, MA 02163. Printed in U.S.A.

Bob Peters

Case Overview

In this case series we watch how a teacher's condescending remark in class toward one of his students backfires dramatically. It is his first teaching experience, and we anticipate trouble as we catch glimpses of his in-class behavior. His remark humiliates a student in front of her classmates, and though he later offers an apology and hopes that the incident will be forgotten, the student threatens retaliation, gangster-style, the night of the final exam.

(A) Case

Bob Peters teaches introduction to Economics I, a course offered in the Evening Division of Newtown Community College (NCC). We learn that the Extension Division attracts students who work full time, that for many of these students tuition is reimbursed by their employers, and that some of the employers stipulate that their employees earn at least a *C* in order to be reimbursed.

Bob Peters received his MBA from Wharton and felt, five years later, that his marketing management career had reached a plateau. He responds eagerly to an advertisement for part-time teachers at NCC, hoping to explore teaching as a second career. Bob determines that in his class of fifteen there are a few bright students, but also a sizable minority weak in simple arithmetic. He compromises and puts together a course that he considers the bare minimum level of attainment.

On the night of the review class from the final exam, Donna Gardella, a student who received a *D* on the midterm, asks a question. Bob proceeds to try to drill the answer out of her. As she finally falters, he provides the answer, only to see Donna walk out of the room.

(B) Case

Bob looks for ways to convince himself that the episode is minor. He telephones Donna to apologize. When she does not sound angry he is relieved and offers her any special help she may need.

(C) Case

In the two weeks before the final exam Bob has convinced himself that Donna, in fact, has apologized for blowing out of proportion his remark in class. He is shocked, therefore, on the evening of the exam when she tells him she needs a *C* in the course to get reimbursed by her employer; if she doesn't get the *C*, Peters will be in trouble, as she "has friends" and she knows where he lives.

The case series is seven pages long and divided into three units.
HBS Case Nos. (A) 9-381-015; (B) 9-381-016; (C) 9-381-017

Distributed by HBS Publishing Division, Harvard Business School, Boston, MA 02163. Printed in U.S.A.

Case Issues

In this case a teacher is threatened with "retaliation" for a humiliating remark he made to a student in his class. The teacher does not always seem aware of his "superior" attitude, but it quietly pervades his opinion of Newtown and his approach to teaching. A key teaching question is, How could Bob Peters have handled this situation differently, will he be able to learn from the experience, and what *should* he learn from the experience?

The Case of the Disgruntled Student

This case is one unit, nine pages long, and would be useful to any seminar wishing to discuss the topic of how to handle an angry, disruptive student. The topic is enriched by its setting—that of complicated relationships within a minority group.

HBS Case No. 9-380-017

Case Overview

In this case we witness a series of encounters at DuBois College between an angry black Vietnam veteran and a highly educated young black instructor. The instructor is teaching for the first time and has introduced the case method to his Business Policy class—the capstone integrative course in the business administration program. The veteran feels that his teacher and classmates are naive, and that he is wasting his time listening to case method "speculation." He purposely disrupts class. The instructor seems at a loss when faced with the student's provocations. The tension escalates and erupts into an explosion in class.

The instructor, Larry Young, 29, a graduate of the MBA program at Charles River Graduate School of Business, plans to enter the doctoral program at Charles River but hopes to obtain college-level teaching experience first. We learn that many students in Business Policy are perceived to have less than adequate skills in communication and mathematics.

The "disgruntled student," Johnny Davis, 27, is one of the oldest students at DuBois. We learn that he had been suspended from State University during his freshman year and had subsequently spent four years in the Navy. He returned to college at 24 to obtain a B.A. in business administration. In addition to interrupting Larry, Johnny constantly arrives late to class, takes no notes, and stares out the window. Larry tries to speak with him after class, but Johnny's manner is offensive, and he insists on being called "Mr. Davis."

We watch as Larry develops the case method successfully in Business Policy. As the class becomes more sophisticated in working with cases, Johnny's dissatisfaction grows. Larry still does not know how to handle his disruptive comments. We then read about "the explosion," a shouting match that erupts in the classroom. Once again, Johnny arrives late but he is more disruptive than usual. He listens impatiently as the class tries to analyze a case and come up with strategic recommendations. He shouts out his recommendation—a market research study. At this point another student, Hank Nelson, without waiting to be recognized, lambastes Johnny's suggestion, and ends with barbed personal comments. Johnny jumps to his feet and shouts at the class, saying he spent four years in the Navy defending the likes of them and that he "didn't come back to school to speculate. . . ." Then he leaves the room.

Case Issues

This case touches on an exceedingly complex situation—the feelings that developed between an angry black Vietnam veteran and his black instructor during a course. The instructor is able to take risks when it comes to teaching (introducing the case method to students who were comfortable only with lectures) but he is unable to take risks over personal confrontations. The student *seems* to enjoy confrontations. When the instructor consistently ignores the student's provocative remarks in class, everyone's tension escalates (class, instructor, student) until the student responds with an enraged outburst. The case ends with the outburst and the instructor knows he must take the situation in hand—but how?

The Case of the Frustrated Feminist

The (A) case is three pages long; each (B) case is about two pages. "The Case of the Frustrated Feminist" is particularly appropriate for a single session of discussion, or it could be used in an early session of a series of discussions.
HBS Case Nos. (A) 9-387-002; (B1) 9-387-003; (B2) 9-387-004

Case Overview

(A) Case

Penny Steers is a 39-year-old mid-level administrator in personnel at Midwestern University. In the course of interviewing faculty women about their benefits, she has heard from many of them disquieting news about male/female faculty relations: to wit, that in some departments the atmosphere is still unpleasantly chilly toward women, who are still a tiny percentage of all faculty at Midwestern. She has written up a report of her interview findings, and at the suggestion of her male boss (the director of personnel), has presented it to *his* boss (the provost), Gloria Barnes. Gloria, one of the highest-placed women in the university, has been cordial to Penny, and is known to be an advocate for women.

We meet Penny coming out of Gloria's office in a shocked and agitated state. In the hall outside she fortunately meets her friend, Shirley Napier (professor of economics). Through their conversation, we learn that Gloria Barnes has reacted in a hostile way to the report, suggesting that its conclusions are unrepresentative of the atmosphere at Midwestern and going so far as to question the accuracy of Penny's reporting.

In the rest of the case we learn more about Penny (a divorced mother of two), her feminist convictions, and the situation women face at a large co-ed university in the Middle West. Penny and Shirley discuss some of Penny's options: the question is, What should she do now? Shirley advises her to "bury" the report ("*You* don't have tenure, kid!"); Penny, while admitting that she is loathe to "fight," feels it would be wrong to suppress the stories that women faculty were so eager to tell her.

Two (B) Cases

"The Frustrated Feminist" is unusual in having two (B) cases. In one, despite Penny's efforts, the report remains suppressed. In the other, it is incorporated into a larger, more general report on the status of women at the university. As a discussion leader, you might choose to use the one that runs counter to the expectations of your group about the outcome: e.g., if most group members would expect the report to be suppressed, use the (B) case in which the institution goes far beyond what Penny expected it to do in reporting on the condition of women at all levels.

The (B) cases begin similarly. In both, after anxious deliberation, Penny sends the report to all the faculty women she interviewed, along with a form asking each to (1) assess how accurately her comments were reported; (2) suggest whether the report should be sent to all female faculty, all faculty, or to no one; (3) comment on whether the report would discourage female faculty from coming to Midwestern. The responses are the same in both (B) cases: favorable to Penny and to dissemination. Gloria Barnes, given the responses, answers in a memo: "Okay to go to women faculty, but not yet." It is at this point that the two (B) cases diverge.

(B1) Case. A few months later, Gloria Barnes announces she wants to do her own study of female faculty. Penny's boss—Danny Morris, an amiable and adroit administrator (who happens to be black, sympathetic to feminism, and respectful of Penny's work)—sees this as an opportunity to get support from both the president and from Gloria for a complete study of the climate for women. The study is carried through under Penny's supervision and (after much debate) made public.

(B2) Case. Over the course of a year, Penny quietly manages to bring her report to the attention of two committees entrusted with oversight of the status of women at the university—one composed entirely of women faculty and the other composed jointly of men and women trustees. No action ensues. The efforts of a few female faculty members to persuade Gloria Barnes that the time is ripe for tackling the problems mentioned in Penny's report are also of no avail.

In both cases Penny Steers leaves Midwestern to take a job in a smaller college as dean of students.

Case Issues

"The Case of the Frustrated Feminist" focuses on a crucial moment in the life of an individual woman with a modest amount of power and influence when she feels she has an opportunity to help other women, and is stymied—and personally wounded—by the initial institutional reaction to her endeavor. The fact that the institution's reaction is expressed by another woman—and a woman whom she has known and liked and respected—is another complicating factor of the case. In trying to bring about change in such circumstances, how does a woman handle her feelings—particularly when there is some tension between her career ambitions and her idealistic goals? In a complex institutional setting, what are her strategic choices at various points? How does she decide where her responsibilities end?

Cathy Ross

Case Overview

Tim Walsh, one year out of business school, teaches Control, a required course in the first year of an MBA program. The course deals with issues in accounting and behavioral science that would be relevant to a corporate controller. Tim thinks back over the completed course and wonders what part he played in losing the active involvement of one of his stronger students. Despite two appointments and one telephone conversation with the student, he does not fully grasp the changes in her performance and attitude, nor what message she may have been trying to convey to him.

The student was Cathy Ross, an engineer from Texas with solid work experience, enthusiastic and popular, adept at the case method, and an active participant in class. She had worked for Hightech Limited for three years immediately prior to coming to business school. In mid-October the section was assigned a case on Hightech Limited. Tim entered the classroom fifteen minutes early and listened to Cathy as she talked to a large cluster of students about her former company, commenting on its management control system and its evolution in the ten years since the case was written. Tim was impressed by her comments and by the signs of respect from the students and asked her to recap her analysis for the benefit of the entire class. The presentation turned out to be impressive, eliciting questions from usually reticent students, and she received a standing ovation. Tim made closing comments and openly acknowledged Cathy's expertise.

Cathy's presentation on Hightech became a model for other student contributions. The continual comparisons to her earlier presentation, however, finally elicited quiet hissing from disenchanted students. Cathy's class participation began to drop off. Tim saw no reason to intervene formally but looked for an opportunity to broach the topic indirectly; Cathy avoided such opportunities. When Cathy finally scheduled an appointment (after doing well on the midterm), they had a conversation in which her approach was indirect. Whatever points she was trying to make did not get across.

Three weeks after Christmas Cathy made another appointment and said she became engaged over Christmas, that she couldn't "get excited" about cases in his course, but that she would get by. Subsequently, Cathy remained quiet in class with some increased participation toward the end of the course. Her final exam was in the middle range and her final grade was a Satisfactory. Cathy called Tim to register surprise over her grade. After the conversation he wondered

---

This case is one unit, four pages long, and could be used in either a liberal arts or a professional school.
HBS Case No. 9-381-223

if his handling of the Hightech case had been a factor in losing Cathy's active class participation.

Case Issues

This case concerns the challenge of getting the most out of gifted students without damaging their image in the eyes of the class. It also points up subtle issues in teacher-student dynamics. How does a teacher follow up on a student's exceptional performance without setting the student up for a fall? If there is a significant decrease in an active student's class participation, under what circumstances is it the teacher's responsibility to find out the reason? In teacher-student meetings, what are effective methods of asking questions? Similarly, what are effective listening techniques? In these meetings what sorts of considerations inhibit students from being direct? What are some inherent difficulties when the teacher and students are approximately the same age or when the teacher has only recently been a student?

Dick Johnson

Case Overview

Dick Johnson, an idealistic young professor of Marketing Strategy, is facing a perplexing teaching situation. Two weeks into his course with undergraduates at Inner City University he asks for guidance on how to handle a student who works hard to prepare for class but who consistently presents superficial in-class comments and seems unable to "hear" opposing arguments. Professor Johnson describes a similarly frustrating earlier teaching situation with an evening MBA course. He describes that class in detail—its composition, the mixed mode of teaching with both lectures and case discussion, the marketing case under discussion and how it was approached by students and professor, the particular student involved, and finally the professor's teaching style. Not wanting to experience failure again in front of his students or in his own eyes, he asks for help.

Case Issues

This case hinges on the age-old issue of how to balance the needs of regular and slow learners. In addition, it raises the issue of how to develop one's own effective teaching style. Keeping these two themes in mind, the following questions would be useful: How does an instructor develop techniques for asking effective questions? How does one build section support and get students to help teach other students? How does one balance support and criticism of students? How does one get a student who talks glibly to give a more reasoned, logical explanation? If a variety of strategies fail to get a particular student to modify his class preparation and contribution, what does the instructor do?

This case is one unit, five pages long. Because it presents a marketing strategy case in detail, it would be used to best effect in a seminar or where business administration students are in the majority.
HBS Case No. 9-379-024

Distributed by HBS Publishing Division, Harvard Business School, Boston, MA 02163.
Printed in U.S.A.

The Final Exam

Case Overview

Ted Brown, an assistant professor in the MBA program at Far Western State, needs help in thinking through a problem. One of his good students, Paul Clark, has refused to complete the final exam and instead has articulately written up his reasons for taking this action. Ted asks his grader, a Ph.D. candidate, to help him resolve the problem.

First, we read Paul Clark's written statement entitled "Business Policy II—Second Term Final Exam." It is clear that he has read the case carefully but that he has many principled objections to going through with a tedious exercise that he considers an affront to the class's intelligence and irrelevant to what the class has been learning. In brief, he feels that the Business Policy department (and thus the exam case) is preoccupied with the role of a consultant who appears, makes suggestions, and disappears—whereas the class, many of whom are prospective middle managers, need to wrestle with issues in which they themselves make critical decisions. He ends his remarks saying that if Professor Brown would like him to write on a more relevant problem he would be happy to do so.

The case outlines information on the background of the course, including Ted Brown's statement of course organization and objectives. We are also given personal data on professor and student. Finally we are given information about the exam case.

Professor Brown acknowledges that the section's reactions to this particular exam are overwhelmingly negative, yet Paul Clark is the only student who refused to take it. He tells his grader that the situation is a "hornet's nest of questions and uncertainties" for him and that he needs help in assessing Paul Clark's statement in order to come up with his final grade.

Case Issues

This case looks at a thorny issue: how to give a final grade to a student who—on principle—refuses to complete an exam but whose argument, articulately stated, resonates with the instructor. How does the teacher sort out his decision? Where lies fairness: is it fair to other students if he makes a principled exception? Is it fair to the student in question to let him sacrifice his grade, yet later improve the course and the exam? How does the teacher (in this case a relatively inexperienced assistant professor) balance his ethical responsibilities to himself and to school bureaucracy?

This case is one unit, five pages long. Because of its focus on the Business Policy course, it would be used to best advantage in a seminar where business administration students are in the majority, although it raises issues about grading that would be useful in other seminars as well.

HBS Case No. 9-377-120

HB I

Case Overview

(A) Case

The class of second-quarter MBAs at City University's evening MBA program waits for the new instructor of Human Behavior (HB) to arrive and for the first class of the quarter to begin. They speculate as to what the teacher will be like—they know only that his name is Calvin Banks and that he has been hired as a part-time instructor. Most of the students expect the class to follow the pattern of other courses in the MBA program in which they receive a syllabus and hear introductory remarks about the subjects to be covered. This pattern generally fits well with their busy schedules, as most of them hold full-time jobs.

Five minutes after class is to have begun, not one, but two instructors enter the room—Calvin Banks who is black, and Ed Jones, who is white. Contrary to the class's expectations, they ask all class members to say something about themselves. The instructors discuss their own backgrounds and how they have taught career development seminars together (rather than Human Behavior). Then Calvin Banks asks the class to suggest "course objectives" in order to establish "a contract." It becomes apparent that the instructors know little about the material previously covered in the first quarter of HB.

Gradually the students offer various course objectives but the discussion lags. One student, a white woman who is vice president of an advertising firm, states her lack of respect for this teaching method and leaves the room. Another student, a black man who is an architect, angrily tells the class that they are prejudiced because their instructor is black.

Neither the class nor the two instructors know how to proceed. Calvin Banks looks mystified, trying to comprehend what has gone wrong.

(B) Case

Calvin Banks attempts to salvage the class and continues in the manner in which he feels comfortable, asking the class their thoughts rather than stating his. We follow the rest of the semester in which discussions go poorly and the instructor comes to interpret the students' poor performance as personal hostility. In his last class he tries a new technique and the class explodes in anger. One week later the dean of the College of Business schedules a meeting with Calvin Banks and presents him with students' negative interpretations of each of his teaching techniques. Calvin is astonished at their interpretations but is given no chance to defend his approach.

This case series is five pages long, divided into two units. It is of special interest to instructors who teach in the evening or in work/study programs.

HBS Case Nos. (A) 9-380-018; (B) 9-380-019

Case Issues

This case series concerns several interesting issues, such as the critical decisions an instructor makes on his first day of class, the resistance of students to new or different methods of teaching, the hidden agenda of racial prejudice, and how to regroup when a class gets out of control. What are the basic responsibilities of instructors to their classes on the first day (knowledge of previous semester course, arriving on time, and so on)? What opportunities do they grasp if they meet these responsibilities, and conversely, what traps do they fall into if they do not? Do these decisions vary if a teacher is experienced (as opposed to being a doctoral student)? When students are comfortable with one method of teaching? And finally, what can instructors do when their first class goes badly? What changes can one make if resistance continues throughout the semester?

Janice Posner

This case is short—one unit, three pages long. It would be useful in a seminar where teachers wish to analyze and respond to provocative class behavior. (If the focus is to include the development of a "section personality," this case might be discussed in conjunction with another short case, "The Mechanical Hand.")

HBS Case No. 9-379-205

Case Overview

Three weeks into the semester, Janice Posner, a marketing professor at Far Western State University Business School, wonders who or what is responsible for the negative and provocative dynamics in one of her marketing sections. Could it just be a "bad section"? Is something about her teaching style at fault? Is it a bit of both, or something else altogether? She reviews the background of the course, her impressions of Section Q, and the progression of the first five classes.

Janice reviews her introduction to Section Q and tells us how, after the first class, she feels distinctly uncomfortable with the section. The students seem caustic and cliquish, as if they don't like each other. She concludes she would not really like most of them as individuals either. After the second class, she continues to feel uncomfortable. During the third class, as she writes on the chalkboard, she hears a student leave the class. She feels there is a "message" in this exit, but makes no comment. Later in the day, she happens to meet a member of Section Q and asks him the name of the student who left class. She is told that the student is Brian Thomas (an Afrikaner, 28 years old, with impressive work experience in the field of mining), and that he has challenged authority in various ways in other classes as well. During this conversation Janice is also told that she may be "too nice" to this particular section. Janice defends herself to us, however, saying that she likes to run a "free and open" style of discussion and that she doesn't "saw students' heads off."

The fourth class brings no problems; Brian Thomas is present, though silent. Soon after, Janice reviews the section with Tom Harris, a junior faculty member who was Section Q's first-quarter production instructor. Tom tells Janice that he had to "sit on" the section several times and that he once called Brian Thomas into his office. Janice decides to invite a senior course professor to sit in on her fifth class. We learn that the discussion gets off to a slow start, that after forty-five minutes Brian Thomas makes another exit, and that the entire section seems to be waiting for her reaction.

Case Issues

This case focuses on the elusive phenomenon of negative "class vibes," of provocative group behavior. How does a section develop a personality? What difference do a few student personalities make? What contributes to the evolution of a section that does not seem to like each other? What are effective ways for a teacher to analyze negative class dynamics—for example, what response is class behavior trying to elicit?

When the behavior seems purposeful, what are effective responses and when should they be made? How are the issues further complicated when the professor is female (or, as in this case, a woman who is not assertive)? How can one help a section become more likable?

The Mechanical Hand

Case Overview

With the help of the section's education representative, Professor Simons reviews an incident that happened in his class. The section educational representative feels that Professor Simons was justified in reprimanding the class "clown" for his antics; the professor, however, feels that he would not have been so angry had he not been embarrassed over two gaffes he had just made in class.

The case details the cause of his embarrassment. That week Professor Simons had been particularly overextended and he is tired. He listens to a student in Section J lead off the class with a mediocre presentation. The class discussion in turn is slow. After thirty minutes it becomes more animated, and Professor Simons feels some relief. He refers to his "call list" and calls on one of the quiet foreign students; he addresses him by the wrong name, however, and calls him "Christian"—the name of another quiet foreign student. The class laughs good-naturedly, Professor Simons apologizes, and the discussion continues. Shortly thereafter Professor Simons calls on a third foreign student but makes the same mistake—he addresses him as "Christian" also, and the class roars with laughter. The professor apologizes but feels "like sinking through the floor." Mitch Menron the class "clown" decides to perform one of his pranks. He has constructed a "mechanical hand" from erector set pieces and he cranks it up, making a loud mechanical whirring sound. Professor Simons is furious and interrupts the class laugher by shouting at Mitch. The class is startled into silence and a chagrined Mitch Menron slouches into his seat. All eyes are on the professor.

Case Issues

This case concerns the issue of how to deal with problem behavior in class. What are appropriate responses from the teacher to a student prankster? In what ways can section dynamics be expected to solve the problem of student misbehavior? How can the teacher steer section dynamics toward solving the problem? In what ways can a teacher's personal reactions interfere with appropriate responses to provocative behavior?

This case is very short—one unit, approximately two and one-half pages long. It would be useful to a seminar group wishing to discuss the development of section "personality" or appropriate responses from a teacher to student antics. (It might well be discussed along with another short case, "Janice Posner.")

HBS Case No. 9-381-021

Michelle Grinald

Case Overview

Michelle (Mickey) Grinald is faced with a vaguely troubling political issue. What is the right thing to do and how should she go about it? Before we learn the issue, we learn about Mickey and her environment. She is a part-time faculty member at a small private college, the University of Cranston, in Cranston, New York. It is her first year of teaching and she is into her second semester. She is a 24-year-old CPA with a B.A. degree in accounting. In addition to teaching two sections of Cost Accounting at U.C., she works full time as controller of a local, non-profit organization. After three years of work experience, Mickey has become concerned about ethical issues in accounting. She thinks that by entering the academic world she will have the best leverage to affect problems in the field. Before committing herself to graduate school, however, she is trying out teaching to see if she likes it—hence her double load of teaching while working full time.

We go back to the beginning of Mickey's first semester and learn that her department is headed by a dynamic young man, that two sections of Cost Accounting are taught by another young woman (Linda) with whom Mickey feels an instant rapport, and that one section is taught by an older man (Mr. Wilson), a senior financial administrator of the school. It is Linda who helps Mickey at the start of the first semester, giving her the course outline, course requirements, and the textbook that has been used for years. Mickey describes the tension in her early classes where she faces thirty students (most of whom are older than she) with more work experience, and how she gradually relaxes as the semester progresses—receiving positive feedback.

As a second-semester teacher and beginning to feel like an "old hand" she takes over Mr. Wilson's evening section, although she has heard many negative rumors about his teaching. During the second meeting of Mickey's new evening section, a bright student makes comments to her during class break—not only about his wasted semester with Mr. Wilson but also about the poor textbook that Mr. Wilson used and the one Mickey continues using. He asks if Mickey has considered changing the textbook. Not wanting to comment negatively about a colleague or her department, Mickey uncomfortably mumbles a reply about it being too late to change the textbook but she hoped to improve the course. Later Mickey wonders what her position should be and how she should deal with it: Should she report student criticism or should she pass it by because she will be at Cranston for only a

---

This case is one unit, three pages long. It may be of special interest to instructors who are teaching for the first time.
HBS Case No. 9-379-015

year? How can she present negative feedback for students without appearing critical of her department?

Case Issues

This case deals with being caught between student criticism and department politics. How does a new, inexperienced teacher deal with student criticism of departmental decisions? How does one decide which issues are important enough to report? How does one balance an allegiance to students with sensitivity to departmental politics (what if the teacher needs a recommendation for graduate school)?

ORG-10

Case Overview

"ORG-10" presents a class situation seen first from the perspective of two graduate students, and second from the perspective of two professors. In the first account we share the students' frustrations and incredulity; in the second we try to understand a theoretical perspective that hardly seems to describe the same experience.

(A) Case

Organizational Theory and Practice (ORG-10) at the Bay Area Graduate School of Public Health was a required course for first-year doctoral students, though other students could elect to take it as well. All students in ORG-10 were required to participate in a small group project on the application of organizational theory to analyze and improve group process within ORG-10 itself.

Doctoral student Louise Bray described events from the first day of class which she perceived as contrived and confusing. For example, Professors Barton and Ford pointed out how students might get a "yes" from one and a "no" from the other, and, after saying that they didn't want master's degree students to feel like "second-class citizens," dismissed them early in order to serve wine to the doctoral students. Louise recounted that despite criticism from the class, the course did not improve.

The case history also notes the point of view of doctoral student Hank Grivers who described his Project Intervention Group. In brief, he was enthusiastic about his group and about the relevance of their task—a class survey designed ultimately to improve group process within ORG-10. Hank then described an event that greatly angered him. At the end of a class, his survey results were distributed and discussed by the professors. When he and another group member tried to raise objections, their comments were cut short by the professors.

(B) Case

Barton and Ford presented their viewpoints to the school's curriculum committee in a report entitled, "Some Explanations for Why ORG-10 Unfolded as It Did." They acknowledge that student dissatisfaction was higher this year than last. They stated that, due to their interest in organizations, they were interested in learning the explanation for the dissatisfaction.

ORG-10 is a long case series—ten pages—and is divided into two units. It would be especially stimulating in a seminar where students have some background in Organizational Behavior, though such background is not a necessity.
HBS Case Nos. (A) 9-381-008; (B) 9-381-084

Case Issues

ORG-10 depicts a situation in which two graduate students on the one hand, and two professors on the other, present dramatically different perspectives on a shared experience. What inferences can be drawn from the different *types* of reports (direct and emotional reporting from the students, vague and theoretical reporting from the professors)? How is it that two professors with good credentials and good reputations taught a course that was inferior to the one they taught the previous year, alienated a sizable portion of the students, and seemed impervious to criticism? ORG-10 raises questions about professor credibility, student credibility, trust, teacher-student communication, teacher-student contracts, and the ability to use feedback constructively.

Sheila Lund

Case Overview

Sara Andrews has just had an unpleasant and unsettling confrontation with Sheila Lund, one of her graduate students. The conversation left her perplexed. Even though she instinctively feels that the department chairperson will support her position, she wonders if Sheila, with nothing left to lose, will sabotage the remaining weeks of class. Sara looks back on the semester and tries to figure out how she let the situation slip out of her control.

Sara is 31 and a first-year assistant professor of English at Eastern, a small, illustrious private university. She recently completed her Ph.D. at Metropolitan—another excellent university. One of her first teaching assigments at Eastern was a graduate seminar entitled Methods of Literary Analysis. The purpose of the course was to introduce doctoral students to research techniques and skills of analysis and critical argument. The grade depended heavily on one long paper and its defense in class.

We meet Sara as she enters her classroom on the day that the long papers are due. After the students hand in their papers, Sheila Lund informs Sara that she was ill over the weekend, could not complete her paper, and will "have to take an incomplete." Sara says she will see Sheila during office hours, and class continues (as students begin the process of presenting and defending their papers). During their appointment Sheila once again asks for an incomplete. Sara denies the request. Condescendingly, Sheila says she will speak to "Fred," the department chairperson, about Sara's decision, and calmly walks out of the room.

At a subsequent appointment Sara denies Sheila's request to do the long report along the lines of a feminist analysis. During the conversation Sara thinks fleetingly that some of Sheila's comments have truth to them, but she insists that Sheila's paper be less "polemical." Sheila leaves the office without a word.

After this episode Sheila changes her behavior in class. She vehemently and angrily argues against "male perspectives," "objective standards," or books written by males that were "degrading to women" (such as *Daisy Miller* by Henry James). She accuses a female student of having "male eyes." She is sometimes quiet and sullen, but whenever she participates the class seems to get out of control.

Case Issues

This case describes how a teacher's handling of a potentially valuable discussion topic—a feminist analysis of literature—turns the topic into a political battleground. The focus of the case is not the political

This case is one unit, eight pages long. It raises extremely important issues about personal reactions to students who seem threatening, as well as the handling of topics which seem threatening to the teacher or to the class.
HBS Case No. (A) 9-381-216

content; instead it is how and for what reasons a teacher misses important cues and opportunities, lets her anxieties and politics interfere with her judgment, and alienates the student in question. What are some behavior patterns we fall into when we feel threatened? In this case, how might the teacher have handled the situation differently (such as further conversations with the student in order to know her better or understand her point of view, attempts to understand her term paper proposal, attempts to help her make it more "professional" and less "polemical")? How might she have enlisted the support of the class? What kept her from trying to help the student? What kept her from realizing she might need advice on how to handle the situation? Once the student had her first outburst in class, what sorts of interventions would have been effective? And as the teacher predicts disaster for the last two weeks of class, what should she do now?

Student Boycott/Teacher Strike for Divestiture of South African Holdings

Case Overview

(A) Case

This case series focuses on the circumstances confronting Assistant Professor Neil Larson in deciding whether or not to participate in a strike/boycott organized by the Coalition for Awareness and Action at Harvard University. The purpose of the strike was twofold: divestiture of Harvard's South African holdings and support for its Afro-American Studies Department.

Neil Larson is one of three junior faculty members teaching Biology 124—a "slightly revolutionary new introductory biology course"—which received glowing student evaluations. Neil is 31, described by a former student as an excellent teacher—disciplined, demanding, and accessible. We learn from Neil that he was politically active in high school but at college turned his energies toward educational reform. By 1979 he had been teaching biology and doing research for about five years. He expects to be appointed to an associate professorship in July.

The (A) case describes how Neil came to his decision about the boycott. He felt that he had to choose between holding class and not holding class but that neither choice was a politically neutral action. Holding class was a political statement. Canceling class would impose his views on students. Postponing class would deprive certain students of their right to make a political statement. Letting students vote on the matter would mean an abdication of his responsibility for the decision.

(B) Case

This section of the case series details Neil Larson's account of his handling of the lecture period immediately preceding the proposed boycott/strike. At the start of class he handed out a statement concerning his views on the upcoming boycott. He announced that we would leave time at the end of class for discussion. We read his policy statement which made three general points (including one which stated his belief that in all but the most extreme cases it was wrong to champion political beliefs in the classroom). He presented the options of holding class as usual, canceling class, and postponing class, and followed with his reasons for rejecting those options. Instead he suggested that he hold two classes—one during the day of the boycott at the regularly scheduled time, and one the following morning. He would not lose valuable teaching time and would provide a class for those who had opposing views on the boycott. At the end of his prepared lecture, Neil discussed the reasons for his decision with the class.

This case series is fifteen pages long and divided into three units.

HBS Case Nos. (A) 9-381-018; (B) 9-381-019; (C) 9-381-020

Distributed by HBS Publishing Division, Harvard Business School, Boston, MA 02163. Printed in U.S.A.

(C) Case

The final case in the series details the outcome of Neil's decision. On Monday, April 23, approximately 75% of his class attended the regularly scheduled lecture, and the other 25% came to the alternate lecture the following day. Neil reported that there was no further discussion of the boycott, either in class or in confidential course evaluations. A teaching fellow for Biology 124, interviewed about the class's reaction to Neil's statement preceding the boycott, said that Neil had "Stopped apathy dead in its tracks. He forced everyone's actions to be seen as political."

Case Issues

This case focuses on the relationship between politics and academia and raises questions of the following sort: Is it possible to separate politics and academia? Is there a place for politics in the classroom? Is it possible to teach anything completely objectively without personal opinions and politics influencing the presentation of facts? Is there such a thing as a politically neutral action? Would teachers' responses to these questions vary according to the academic institutions in which they teach or their particular status in those institutions? Why?

Timothy D'Olivier, Jr.

Case Overview

(A) Case

Professor Hamid Morabak of the Bengali Institute of Management (BIM) has assigned a discussion topic concerning bribery and corruption to his class in Environmental and Social Analysis. He is slightly uneasy, as only a few students volunteer to participate, and those who do participate speak only in lofty generalizations. For reasons we learn later, he hesitates before choosing Tim D'Olivier, an American and the only non-Bengali student eager to participate. When finally called on, Tim launches into a condescending critique of corruption in the host country. As classmates become angry and Professor Morabak contemplates how best to intervene, Tim is interrupted by a Bengali student who challenges him about a well-known American scandal.

The case gives detailed information about the Bengali Institute of Management and the composition of faculty and student body. We learn that BIM is an excellent institution with high standards, modeled on Western business schools. Scholarships are provided for highly qualified international applicants, most of whom are from Asia and the Middle East. We learn about the current class (in particular how the high-pressure atmosphere inevitably increases the competition among students, especially in classes where the case method is used), how students from Asian countries learn to coexist in school, how the Westerners find the adjustment process difficult, and what contributes to the students' sense of polarization. We are then given a detailed description of Tim D'Olivier, the contentious American student, and Professor Hamid Morabak's background.

(B) Case

In this section of the series we come back to the incident of Tim's original condescending outburst. Professor Morabak walks to the center of class amid cries of "Yankee, go home" and the class hushes. As he assembles his thoughts and is about to comment, Malik—a thoughtful, well-respected student from Indonesia—raises his hand. Professor Morabak calls on him. Malik gives a sensitive quasi-lecture, first on corruption's place in social-cultural history, and second on business situations in which the students may one day find themselves—faced with having to make difficult moral decisions. There is a round of applause, the class seems calmed, and Professor Morabak gives a closing statement.

This case series is seven pages long and is divided into three sections. It would be particularly useful for an international seminar or a graduate seminar dealing with cultural differences in a discussion class.

HBS Case Nos. (A) 9-379-008; (B) 9-379-009; (C) 9-379-010

(C) Case

This third section follows up on the eventful class. We learn that Tim is effectively isolated from most of the students who expect him to make a gesture of reconciliation. Tim, however, sees no need for any such gesture and associates only with international students. He was described sympathetically by his dorm-room neighbor. We learn that contributing to Tim's low spirits is his worry as to whether or not he had passed his bar exam back home.

Case Issues

What is an effective way to organize a discussion around a threatening topic (graft, corruption) or one that bears on personal morals and values? Where do the professor's responsibilities lie when a student has adjustment or personal problems, when students are polarized in and out of class? Where do those responsibilities end? How do racial or cultural differences affect a competitive situation? How does one build a supportive atmosphere in a highly competitive environment?

PART V

Readings

Different Worlds in the Same Classroom: Students' Evolution in Their Vision of Knowledge and Their Expectations of Teachers

William A. Perry
Former Director
Bureau of Study Counsel
Harvard University

Distributed by HBS Publishing Division, Harvard Business School, Boston, MA 02163. Printed in U.S.A.

I want to describe an orderly variety in the ways students in your classroom make sense—including their sense of what you should be doing to be a good teacher. We labor among our students' individual differences daily, and yet the way these differences are categorized tends to mislabel the variables I have in mind. In the parlance of college pedagogy, the phrase "individual differences" usually refers to relatively stable characteristics of persons, such as academic ability, special talents or disabilities, or the more esoteric dispositions called "learning styles." We are, of course, expected to accommodate all such differences in our teaching, perhaps by broadening our teaching styles, and you may anticipate that I am about to add to our burden.

My hope, rather, is to lighten our burden, or at least to enlighten it. The variations I wish to describe are less static; they have a logical order, and most students tend to advance from one to another in response to teachings or readings that impinge on the boundaries of their intelligible universe of the moment. These variables are therefore more fun to address, and in my opinion often more determinant of what goes out of our classrooms than all the other individual differences put together. At the very least, an understanding of them makes intelligible many of those aberrations of the pedagogical relation that we must otherwise ascribe to a student's stupidity or, more generously, to a clash of "personalities."

Let's start with one of the ordinary enigmas—students' persistent misreading of examination questions. Perhaps "unreading" would be a better term. We commonly struggle in staff meetings for nearly an hour over the wording of an essay question for the midterm. The choice of topic takes only five minutes. It is the wording of the intellectual issue we wish the students to address that takes the labor. At last the issue is stated clearly, concisely, and *unambiguously.* Yet, if the class contains a large contingent of freshmen, the blue books will reveal that a third of the students looked at the question to locate the *topic* and ignored all the rest of the words, so carefully crafted. It will seem as if these students read the question as saying, "Tell all you know about . . . ," and then did so, sometimes with remarkable feats of irrelevant memory.

Such evidence of misplaced diligence can be marvelously depressing, but we realize we should not be surprised. In their years of schooling what else have these students learned to suppose an examination question intends? Clearly we have an educational job ahead of us, and we undertake it with spirit in class and in office hours, student by student. We explain with patient clarity. The students assure us that they understand and thank us profusely.

At midyears, however, most of our grateful beneficiaries dismay us by doing just what they did before. Our instructions were quite simple, and when intelligent students cannot keep a simple idea in mind, we can suspect them of being diverted by more pressing considerations. I choose here an example, extreme for this community, in the hope that stark simplicity may lay a foundation for more general observations.

A top student from a good rural school came to Harvard at a young age, possibly a year too young. Since he had won a regional prize in history, he enrolled in a section of Expository Writing that focused on writing about history. He consulted me in a state of some agitation, having failed in three attempts to write a satisfactory response to the assignment: "Consider the theory of monarchy implied in Queen Elizabeth I's Address to Members of the House of Commons in 1601." "Look," he said, "I can tell what she said—all her main points. I've done it three times, longer each time. But he says he doesn't want that. What is this 'theory of monarchy implied' stuff anyway? He says to read between the lines. So I try to read between the lines and—huh—there's nothing there."

The intellectual problem is not too obscure. The student cannot see *a* theory of monarchy because he has never been confronted with *two*. Until he sees at least two, a monarch is a monarch and who needs a theory? I was aware, of course, that his writing instructor had tried hard, but I decided to try once more. We devised alternative theories together, but the more he seemed to understand, the more agitated he became. Then he complained that his mind had gone blank. I shall return later to this student's shock to help us understand the courage required of more advanced students if they are to hear what we are saying about the world. After all, why should two theories of monarchy be so terrifying?

Such curious reactions are not limited to exceptional students. In Freshman Week over the years the staff of the Bureau of Study Counsel has asked entering students to grade two answers to an essay question. Again, fully a quarter of the class gives higher grades to the essay crowded with facts utterly devoid of relevance to the question. In response, we have tried to help these students see that college instructors consider relevance the sole justification for memorizing a fact. Accordingly, we try to teach them simple reading strategies, such as surveying for a sense of the author's purpose before starting to collect detail. Half the students catch on with enthusiasm; the other half accuse us of urging them to "cheat."

This brings me to the last enigma we need to share: the range of perception in students' evaluations of their teachers. Most evaluations are invited by rating scales. The computer will give the mean and the standard deviation. As a teacher I have never found the figures very informative, and on occasion I have ventured to inquire beyond them, inviting my students to write me anonymous "free comments." I expect a range of opinion; I would not want to please everybody. But nothing ever prepares me for the range I get. How can I possibly be the one who has "opened the world to me. Now I know what learning is about; and the rest is up to me!"—and at the same moment "the most dishonest, hypocritical and careless teacher I've had the misfortune to meet—and Harvard *pays* you!"

Can differences in "personality" explain all this? Every student who came to us for counseling seemed, if we listened long enough, to be attending a different college; each student enrolled in a given course was in a different course; and the instructor was an angel, a dud, and a devil. Was this variety common only among the fifteen percent of undergraduates whose distress brought them to us? We thought not, and we set out to inquire of some students who had expressed no need of our wisdom.

We asked half the freshman class to submit to tests measuring aspects of personality we thought relevant, and in May we invited representatives of all dispositions to come to tell us about their year. They responded enthusiastically. We soon learned not to ask them questions that imposed frameworks of sense-making on a conversation that we intended to be an opportunity for the students to inform us of theirs. The individual variety then exceeded our expectations, the students enjoyed it, and we parted in agreement to meet again next spring, and also in junior and senior year.

It was in this setting that the students rewarded us. As we first listened to them as freshmen, they interpreted their experience in ways that seemed harmonious with those traits of "personality" our measures had ascribed to them. But then, in sophomore year, to our astonishment, most of these students changed their "personalities"—and did so again as juniors and as seniors. Each year they interpreted their educational experience through frameworks of assumptions and expectations that placed knowledge and learning, hope, initiative, responsibility, and their teachers, in new relations. Perhaps our original tests in freshman year had reflected not so much enduring bents of personality as temporary constellations of perceived relations. Gradually we came to see that these constellations through which the students made sense of their worlds followed one another in an orderly sequence. Finding that their current ways of making sense failed to comprehend the increasing complexities and uncertainties in their intellectual and social lives, the students "realized" (as they phrased it) that the world was other than they had thought; that only a new way of seeing and thinking could encompass the new set of discrepancies, anomalies, or contradictions. Each of these new realizations comprehended the old as the old could not encompass the new. This was development, a visible, even explicit broadening of the mind—not simply change, but evolution.

We sensed that each step in this evolution involved a challenge. We had yet to realize the depth of these challenges, but we could see that some students refused, at one point or another, to take the next step. We went so far as to dub the sequence a Pilgrim's Progress and made a map of it. Slough of Despond and all. Every student, as we saw it, spoke from some place or "position" on this journey.

But it is now time to enter your classroom. You, however, are late—unavoidably, but conveniently for our purpose. The last thing you said, on Friday, was, "Next week we'll consider three theories of the economic cycle" (or the equivalent in your particular field). As restlessness sets in this Monday morning a conversation begins, and I am going to cast it in the mold of our Pilgrim's Progress. That is, I shall label the dramatis personae First Student, Two, Three, etc., letting each express in sequence the outlook from the several positions of our map.

By this device I hope not only to convey a sense of the order in the varied perceptions and expectations that await your arrival, but also to make it possible for you to imagine that each of the speakers might be one and the same student speaking from outlooks attained sequentially over a number of years—perhaps in just the four years of college.

I have already mentioned the First Student—he of the history prize. He saw me on Saturday. He sits near the door watching for you. He is too anxious to speak or even to think well. His despair about theories of monarchy has probably left him so mute that if he heard you mention "three theories of the economic cycle" at all, it only added boundlessness to his terror. His inability to understand the nature of knowledge as Harvard sees it has become less an epistemological problem than an ontological horror. If there are several theories of monarchy, why shouldn't there be infinite theories of monarchy? So is there such a thing as a monarch? Is the same true of all authority and so of all obedience? Of parents and sons? Of all meaning?

The camaraderie of the dorm might have carried him through this existential crisis, but this lad seems to lack the humor to become one of the boys. His is primitive shock, but we shall find in the class other, more sophisticated approaches to the abyss.

Several low-key conversations are now going on in the room. The voice of the second student—I shall call him Two—rises above the rest as he talks to his neighbor. "What's this rigmarole about three theories of the cycle anyway? Why doesn't he give us the right one and forget the bullshit?"

Someone laughs. "You're not in high school anymore, Joe."

"Yeah, I know. Here they give you problems, not answers, I see that. That's supposed to help us learn independent thought, to find the answer on our own. That's what he said when I asked him—or I guess it's what he said, along with the rigmarole. OK, but enough is enough. We gotta know what to learn for the exam." Two's voice has become plaintive, almost desperate; there is silence as he pauses. "My roommate's in the eleven o'clock. He says his instructor really knows and really answers your questions. Maybe I should go ask her."

It is hard to portray Two's thinking without seeming to caricature it. Do I need to assure you that he exists? He has brought with him from years of schooling a clear epistemology. Knowledge, he learned early, consists of right answers, and there is a right answer for every question: e.g., spelling words, arithmetic problems, dates. These truths are discrete items and can be collected by memorization; so some people know more, others know less. ("Better" or "worse" are not applicable.) Teachers know these answers in their own fields. The answers seem to exist up there somewhere, and the teacher is privy to them.

In the stage setting of this epistemology the roles of the actors are clearly prescribed. The teacher's duty is to "give" the student the truth, the right answers, in assimilable, graduated doses. Two's duty is to "absorb" them by honest hard work known as "study." Then the teacher will "ask for them back" in the same form in which they were originally given. Two's responsibility is then to re-present them unmodified and unabridged for the teacher's inspection.

The morals of this world are equally coherent. The teacher must not ask questions in a strange form—"trick questions." That teachers often give problems to solve, withholding the answers which they already know, can at first seem an anomaly in this world, something to make sense of. As the First Student might say, "I think they're hiding things." Two has made sense of it, acknowledging that beneficent Authority should help us learn "independent thought": i.e., to find the answer for ourselves. Assigning problems therefore falls within the bounds of the moral contract so long as the teacher makes the problems clear and the procedures for solving them memorizable.

As student, then, Two's reciprocal moral duty requires him to collect truth through honest hard work, never by guessing. Right answers hit by guesswork (including "thought") are false currency, and when he accepts credit for them he feels guilty.

Freshman Adviser Perry (after November hour exams): How'd it go?

Freshman: Four 'A's.

Adviser (swallowing praise): How do you feel about that?

Freshman: Terrible. I didn't deserve any of them.

Two's logical corollary, of course, is that if he's worked hard he should get some credit even when he comes up with the wrong answer. The gods and similar authorities have always been bound by the rituals they have established for their appeasement. This myth, to the extent that Authority shares it, provides safety to the weak. The vital requirement of ritual is that nothing be omitted—that it be *complete.* Since neglect of the smallest detail invalidates the whole, every detail is of equal import.

It is therefore of fundamental urgency for Two that you stipulate the nature of the ritual, particularly its *length.* He has been stopping you in the door at the end of class.

"You said three to five pages, sir. Does that mean four?"

Can Authority refuse to answer? "Well, whatever you need."

"Oh, then, four will be satisfactory?"

"OK, sure, if they make your point."

"Thanks, sir—oh, will that be double-spaced or single?"

I have more than once found myself pressed to the wall and settling, to my chagrin, for "1200 words." And I have received them, tallied in the margin, the final entry a smug "1204."

Quantity and "coverage" are visible entities, making obedience palpable. "Organization and coherence"—meaning the logical subordination and sequencing of relationships in the service of an overarching theme—these are not yet visible to Two. A recent study has revealed that the students who think as Two thinks use "coverage" as their criterion for "coherence" as they write, sometimes going so far as to "organize" by putting "similar" details together. If you ask Two to rewrite his paper to improve its organization, he will therefore submit more of the same.

Two knows that there are Rights and Wrongs and a cold world outside of Eden. In Eden the only role is obedience; the only sin is arrogating to oneself the knowledge of good and evil (the power to make judgments). In the Bureau's class in strategies of learning, when we urge students to find the main theme of an article or chapter first (perhaps by starting at the end) so that they can judge the function of details, those who think like Two cry out, "Do you want us to be thrown out of here?" Two recognizes the college instructor who asks him to exercise his judgment as Serpent.

Two, then, construes the world (and teachers) dualistically. Along with right and wrong, he has come to see that some teachers know, and some do not. The truth is One and Invariable, yet teachers disagree about it. There is only one possible sense to make of this without disaster to Truth: just as there are right answers and wrong answers, so there are good teachers and frauds, beneficent teachers and those who are mean. ("My roommate says *his* instructor *really* knows.")

Two thinks in a noble tradition. A study of examination questions given to freshmen at Harvard at the turn of the century reveals them all to be just the kind that Two expects questions to be. They ask for memorized facts and operations in a single assumed framework of Absolute Truth. It wasn't until midcentury that half the questions would require consideration of data from two or more perspectives. And surely today there are still many ways in which we confirm Two's vision.

Indeed, the meanings Two attributes to the educational world are so sensible—and he has such ready categories for dismissing incongruities—that his system seems almost closed. And if this system were as perfect as Locke portrayed it, then all knowledge, judgment and agency would reside out there in Authority, and the student's sole duty would be to absorb. Some Twos do indeed stay closed. Our Two, however, has unknowingly opened a door by conceding legitimacy to Authority's assigning problems instead of giving answers. Solving problems, he has found, is kind of fun, and he derives more satisfaction from *doing* than from memorizing. In arithmetic one can even check an answer for oneself to see if it's right or wrong. This temptation to agency and judgment is the first step in a path that will lead Two away from the safety he presumes to lie in obedience in Eden toward ultimate questions about the very nature of truth itself.

What is required next is for Authority to be allowed

just a bit of legitimate uncertainty. Student Three supplies it: "Well, there may have to be some different theories for a while," she ventures; "after all, Ec. is sort of a new science and there's lots they don't know the answers to yet—like some things in Physics even." By using the word "yet" she has legitimized present uncertainty without disturbing her vision of an orderly Laplacean universe out there waiting to be known, bit by bit. Three's assimilation of temporary uncertainty makes the system even more vulnerable. A little temporary uncertainty legitimizes a little difference of opinion. "Temporary" can now reveal itself to extend longer and longer, and uncertainties can appear in wider domains. The mind is then likely to be overwhelmed by the sheer quantity of possibilities.

There are two Fours in the class, one a bit of a fighter, the other more trusting. I shall call them Four A (Adam) and Four B (Barbara). Four A makes sense out of the impending chaos by exploiting it. He "realizes" that the world, instead of being divided between right and wrong, is divided between those things about which right/wrong can be determined and those about which not even Authority knows. In this new domain of indeterminacy, where "Everyone has a right to his own opinion," he feels a new freedom. In this domain no one can be called wrong because the right is unknown. By implication all opinions are equally valid. This broad tolerance provides for peace in the dormitory before dawn. At the same time it means that Four A will feel outraged when you question his opinion, especially if you asked for it.

He says to Three: "Yeah, that's right. There's so much they won't know for a hundred years, so why only three theories? Anyone can have a theory, and if it's neat for them it's neat for them."

This ultimate individualism, when applied to the moral sphere, is of course absolute license, and since it is often spoken of as "relativism" it has given actual disciplined relativism a bad name. There is of course no relationship in sight, only solipsism: "My opinion is right because I have it." We called this view multiplicity, an awkward word we stole from Henry Adams. In any case, the view is not relative but absolute, just as absolute as the right/wrong dichotomy. What Four A has done is to save the dual character of the world by doubling it, leaving right/wrong on one side and if-I-can't-be-called-wrong-I'm-right on the other. He feels no need as yet to relate opinions to their supporting data and limiting contexts.

Three's interest in how to solve problems and her realization of temporary uncertainty are leading her to a curiosity about "how" we know, or if we can't know yet, how we develop an opinion tenable on grounds other than "It's my opinion." Four B (Barbara) has taken a course in literary analysis in which she has discovered that "What they wanted wasn't just an answer but a *'way,'* a *'how'*. I came to see that what a poem means isn't just anybody's guess after all. The way they wanted us to think was maybe special to that course, but you had to put all kinds of evidence together to build an interpretation and then try it out against others. So we'd end up with a few good interpretations to choose from, like three theories maybe, but a lot of others turned out to be nonsense—at least that's how it was in that course. Maybe . . ."

Four B is on the brink. She has allowed a special case into the world of "right answers for credit." With this "way" she can be an agent in using relationships among data and contexts to generate interpretations. She realizes then that these interpretations may be compared to one another. Some few may appear most valid; others less so; others unacceptable. In the special case of this one course, Authority itself has introduced knowledge as qualitative. But a special case can be a Trojan horse. Its contents can burst forth to take over the whole fortress.

Four A (Adam) is entrenched in his efforts to expand the realm of indeterminacy at Authority's expense. If he is to discover a contextual qualitative world, he may do so more readily when the prodding comes from peers. In the bull sessions in the dorm a colleague more advanced than he may ask him, "Well, how do you substantiate that?" again and again until he discovers that things relate and that he can relate them.

Five: "Hell, *everything's* like that—like Barbie says, not just in one course. There isn't a thing on earth sensible people don't disagree about—and if they don't today they will tomorrow! Even the hard scientists: look what Gödel did to math! It's not like Adam says, 'When no one knows anything goes.' Just because there's no single certainty in the end and individuals will have to choose—that's no reason to give up thinking. Maybe it's the reason to begin. I mean, you've gotta use all the analysis and critical thinking and stuff as advertised. Theories—they aren't the Whole Truth anyway, they're just models like they say, some of them pretty good. So you've got to know how each one works, inside with its logic and outside with the world. It's like different geometries . . . like games really."

Two interrupts. "I can't follow all this bull you're all talking. Isn't anyone going to help pin him down? How can you study for an exam with all that crap you're talking about?" Everyone looks at Two, but no one responds. "Well, maybe it's me. I mean I can learn things, but I can't seem to do what people do around here, whatever it is—interpret or something." He hangs his head.

Three attempts a rescue. "Well, I kind of agree. I mean he ought to tell us sooner or later. After all, there are right answers, right ways."

"Sure, there's rights and wrongs if you know the context," resumes Five. "It's all set by the context and the assumptions and all. Sure it gets complicated and some contexts are looser than others. Like in History and in Lit., there may be more different, defensible things to say. But still, idiot opinions, they're infinite. I thought everybody knew that."

Five "realized" all this only eighteen months ago, but he has so completely reorganized his view of the world, and in the process perhaps recatalogued his memory, that he has forgotten that the world ever seemed different from the way he now sees it to be. We wouldn't forget—or might we?

We should pause here. A rift has been revealed in the class, and the rest of the conversation will further our understanding of it. Five has taken us over a watershed, a critical traverse in our Pilgrim's Progress. On the first side of the watershed the students were preoccupied with the frightening failure of most college teachers to fulfill their assigned role as dispensers of knowledge. Even Barbara, who has mastered the initial process of analytical, contextual, relativistic thought, has assimilated this form of thought by assigning it the status of an exception in the old context of What They Want. Five, in crossing the ridge of the divide, has seen before him a perspective in which the relation of learner to knowledge is radically transformed. In this new context, Authority, formerly source and dispenser of all knowing, is suddenly authority, ideally a resource, a mentor, a model, and potentially a colleague in consensual estimation of interpretations of reality. What-They-Want is now a special case within this context. As for the students, they are now no longer receptacles but the primary agents responsible for their own learning.

Not all teachers will fulfill these expectations, of course, but to Five, Six, Seven, and Eight their failures will not be so demoralizing—or preoccupying. Most students will turn their attention to the implications of the new perspective: choosing among interpretations in their studies, making decisions in a relativistic world, and deciding how to make commitments to career, persons, values and to what they "know" in a world in which even Physics changes its mind. Some, perhaps lacking support or stuck in old resentments, will opt out by shrugging off responsibility.

As students speak from this new perspective, they speak more reflectively. And yet the underlying theme continues: the learners' evolution of what it means to them to know.

Another student now speaks to Five. "Well, I've just come to see what you're talking about and it helps. I've begun to be able to stand back and look at my thinking—what metaphors and stuff I'm using. Not just in my studies, I mean I find the same goes for people. I've begun to get the feel too of where the other guy is coming from and what's important to him—huh, this sounds corny, but I get along better with most people."

There's a silence, then Five speaks more tentatively in a lower voice: "Yeah, I can do this all in my head. I like learning the games and seeing what model fits best where and all. But I can't see how to make any big decisions—there's always so many other possibilities. That's been a real downer. I list all the reasons for doing *this* and for doing *that* and all the reasons against and then I get depressed [laughs], so I go back to playing the games, 'cause that's something I can do well. I mean I get 'fine critical thinking' and jazz like that all over the margins of my papers and it keeps me going, but where to? I know it's I'm still trying to be too sure, but I can't let go, I don't want to just plunge."

A student is sprawled in the back of the room. "Games is right! So who cares? If they want independent thought, just give it to them. Always have an opinion. I say—but don't forget to be 'balanced' and all that crap."

"Yeah," replies Six, "and then when you get to General Motors, what's good for them will be good for you. I was lost a whole year, felt like copping out like that plenty—then thought what'll *that* be like when I'm forty? Now I've got it narrowed down some. I don't see how some guys seem to know from age two—always knowing they'll be doctors. Did they ever have a doubt? Or will it hit 'em later? Like midlife crisis, huh? Anyway, guys like me—you gotta plunge, I think. I'm not quite there yet, but I can see there's different ways of plunging. You can jump in just to get away from the agony—or you can do your thinking, and when your guts tell you 'this is it,' you listen. They're *your* guts. I mean you gotta plunge, in a way, because you know you can't be sure—you're risking it—but it'll be sort of a positive plunge. And once I'm in, I think everything else will fall in line."

"I did that last spring," says Seven, "and now that I'm getting deeper into things—I'm in Bio—it helps, feeds on itself I guess and I see it isn't narrowing down like I thought it would but spreading out bigger than I can handle. But I wouldn't say—I wouldn't say . . ."

"That it straightens everything else out?" The prompting comes from Eight. She laughs ruefully, "I got everything straightened out last spring. I'd gone round and round. There was premed I've been in forever, I'd got more and more into Linguistics, and here was this guy I'd been going with who wanted to get married. So I thought all my thoughts and everyone else's and then one day told my parents, 'Sorry, Linguistics is it. I've really listened, but this has to be mine.' And then I let the guy go to the Amazon to study birds without me. Did everything straighten out? Like hell it did, and then it *did,* in a funny way. I mean there was the thesis in Linguistics; I still love that guy and don't want to marry him; I'm all wound up in this day care thing; my father's sick in San Francisco, and I met this intern who's taking care of him, and and and. Before, it seemed there was just premed or Linguistics, marriage or no marriage, so now I ought to feel worse, all divided up, but it's *better.* I find I even believe in some things, like they're really true." She pauses; no one says anything. "It's like with the thesis, somehow. Seems I hit on something new—well, not new, just joining a couple of old procedures to tackle an old problem they'd never been used on before. My tutor says I'm really on to something—we can't find anything wrong about it or too far out. I've never known something new to be mine like this before. And the feeling goes over into all the rest in a way, only I don't have my tutor to check me out. It's all bits and pieces with cracks in it, but I'm the center of something, a place from where I see things as I see them and all that jazz. Get things together—that's it I guess, not getting everything I want but getting things together. Oh hell, maybe all that holds me together is irony."

After a moment, somebody laughs, "Nice try, nice try, but these verities seem a long way from those three theories of the economic cycle, whatever they are. Anybody done the reading?"

"Sure the reading's important," says Six, "but what we've all been saying *does* connect. What I want to know is what *he* does with those three theories. As a person, I mean, an economist-type person. I mean he seems to care about Ec.—he's kind of zestful about it really. I want to know what he does with all this. Not just *which* he thinks is right but *does* he, or if all three are valid, then what? I don't think he's kidding himself, so what does he do? Let's some of us ask him for lunch someday [laughs]. See if he's for real."

At this point you hurriedly enter the room. Under your arm you carry a sheaf of forms from University Hall. They are questionnaires for students' evaluation of teaching—an experimental form, it says, for trial at midterm. You have been assured that giving them out is purely voluntary.

You—and I—are at "Nine" (so we hope), the farthest reach of our map. At Nine we have had time to realize that growth is not linear as the metaphor of our map implies, but recursive. We turn and turn again, and when we come across our own footsteps we hope it will be with the perspective of some altitude and humor. We have also seen that in the several areas of their lives, such as their work, politics, social relationships, family, or religion, people (including ourselves) often employ somewhat different levels of thought. As teachers, we often use these variations by finding the areas of students' most sophisticated thought and helping them to move by analogy into areas in which they are less advanced. Indeed, students, will often do so spontaneously.

But first, you may ask, "Am I supposed to *do* something about all this development?" I must state my premise. I do believe that the purpose of liberal education is to assist students to learn to think the way Eight is thinking. The goals are stated in the catalogues of all liberal arts colleges. In these terms the development the students reveal is a Good, and we are enjoined to promote it. You may disagree, sensing that I am loading on you a trip into personality development; your responsibility, you may say, is to teach History. I hope you have sensed that this makes no difference. Students who have not progressed beyond the outlook of Three will be unable to understand what you as a modern historian want them to understand about History. To the extent that you wish your subject to become accessible to as many students as reasonably possible, the development we have been tracing remains a Good, and you have already been promoting it.

After all, the students who told us of this adventure were not taking a course in cognitive development complete with maps. They came to "realize" through the necessities of the intellectual disciplines as you taught them. This is not to say, however, that as teachers we have nothing to gain from a more explicit awareness of the steps in the students' progression. At the very least, an understanding of Two's expectations somewhat reduces the personal abrasion of his anger. Similarly, we can feel less assaulted by the outrage of Four when he feels we do not accept his "opinion." Beyond saving our energies, this awareness extends the possibility of our staying in communication long enough for seeds to take root.

Our outline of the successive ways in which students make sense throws some light on the potentials and constraints of this communication. It has been observed for two millennia that in any learning situation the learner requires the support of *some* elements that are recognizable and familiar. Then, if the experience is to be anything more than drill, the second requirement is a degree of challenge. In the decade since the publication of our scheme, a younger generation of teacher-researchers has spelled out the characteristics of learners at each position and traced the sequential changes in the conditions students experience as support and challenge as they progress. Two, for instance, feels supported by explicit directions—supported enough to tolerate the challenge of being directed to read contradictory authorities. Looking back at the First Student we see him overwhelmed by challenge; he may make it through, but only with the community's support—and time. Looking ahead, Five feels supported in being turned loose on the reserve shelf to find and write up an interesting problem, and can be challenged afterward by such a question as "And what did doing all that mean to *you*?"

This question of personal meaning leads toward the concerns voiced by Six, Seven, or Eight, who are searching to orient themselves in the profusion of legitimate possibilities they discovered in the relativism of position Five. They seek a way to make commitments to career, companions, values, and to make them wholeheartedly in a world in which knowledge and meaning are tentative. In the midst of this challenge they seek support in models, especially in their teachers. In providing this support, the best we can do is to let them see that we share with them the risks that inhere in all commitments. Then their sense of ultimate aloneness in their affirmations becomes itself a bond of community.

It is revealing to observe what happens when the teacher's and the students' ways of making sense are uncompromisingly disparate by two or more levels. If students Five through Eight are taught in the manner expected by Two, they may be bored or frustrated, but they understand what the teacher is doing. In the reverse of this mismatch, however, when students at the level of Two are taught in a manner that is good teaching only for Five and above, they panic and retreat. Over the past twenty-five years the position of the *modal* entering freshman at Harvard has advanced from around Three to nearly Five. Yet many Twos and Threes and Fours are among us. Since we tend as teachers to address the more responsive students at and above the mode, we can be concerned about the remainder, who feel they are outsiders to the enterprise. I hope, if only for their learning, that they are fortunate in their advisers and their friends, and that their instructors, if opportunity permits, confirm the legitimacy of their bewilderment.

This concern has brought me to my last observation. What powers do we *not* have? Clearly (if we remember), we cannot push anyone to develop, or "get them to see" or "impact" them. The causal metaphors hidden in English verbs give us a distracting vocabulary for pedagogy. The tone is Lockean and provocative of resistance. We *can* provide, we *can* design opportunities. We can create settings in which students who are ready will be more likely to make new kinds of sense.

But what happens to the old kinds of sense? Where do yesterday's certainties go? Are Two and Three and Four the only ones in need of support? Five and Six and Seven and Eight (and you and I) have dared at each step to approach the abyss where the First student has stumbled into meaninglessness. For the advancing students a new world has opened from each new perspective, to be sure, but the mind is quicker than the guts. The students had invested hope and aspiration and trust and confidence in the simpler design of their world of yesterday. How long will it take them to dig out their vitality and reinvest it in the new, problematical vision? And all the while they are told that these are the happiest days of their lives.

The students do find their gains expansive and fulfilling, but does no one see the losses? If no one else does, can they? They can but wonder: "What is this cloud, this reluctance?" It can't be grief, can it? I believe that students will not be able to take a next step until they have come to terms with the losses that inhere in the step just taken.

In ordinary daily work, our understanding of how students see, whether we agree or not, legitimizes their being as makers of sense. If they make overly simple sense, we must ask them to look further. But by acknowledging that making sense as they used to do was legitimate in its own time, and even a necessary step, we empower them to learn new and better sense. Our recognition is most encouraging in moments when the student is moving from one level of sense-making to another. When the transition happens right in front of us, we will see the eager realization and then, perhaps very shortly, the shadow of the cloud. We say something like, "Yes, you've got the point all right . . . but we do wish it made things simpler." The most heartening leaven for the mind can come from just such a brief acknowledgment as this.

References

Copes, Larry (compiler). *Bibiliography and Copy Service Catalog: Perry Development Scheme.* St. Paul, MN (10429 Barnes Way, 55075), ISEM, Oct. 1984.

Knefelkemp, L. Lee, and Janet L. Cornfeld. "Combining Stages and Style in the Design of Learning Environments." Address to American College Personnel Association, 1979. Reprints obtainable from author at College of Education, University of Maryland, College Park, MD 20742.

Perry, William G. (and associates). *Forms of Intellectual and Ethical Development in the College Years.* NY: Holt, Rinehart and Winston, 1970.

Perry, William G. "Cognitive and Ethical Growth: The Making of Meaning" in Chickering, Arthur (editor). *The Modern American College.* San Francisco: Jossey-Bass, 1981.

Perry, William G. "Examsmanship in the Liberal Arts: A Study in Educational Epistemology." Harvard College, 1963. Reprints available at the Harvard-Danforth Center. Also reprinted in Zeender, Karl and Linda Morris (editors), *Persuasive Writing: A College Reader* (NY: Harcourt Brace Jovanovich, 1981).

How I Taught Myself How to Teach

Selma Wassermann
School of Education
Simon Fraser University

I. Allegro Vivace: Learning to Teach

Mary Dare Hitchcock taught Human Growth and Development, 3 credits, to sophomore students in the teacher education program at my undergraduate university. I remember her very well; she was a southern lady who spoke in the soft, drawn-out vowel tones of eastern Geo-ja. Her distinguishing characteristic was that she always managed to look cool and unperturbed on those beastly hot and humid days that slip too early into the New York spring, while we lot, scraped from the New York sidewalks, were always sweating and grubby. Her presence alone made us feel less dignified. From the raised teacher's platform where she sat, distant from us in metre and in measure, she told us that children were different—physically, intellectually, emotionally, and socially different from each other. (If we could only remember P-I-E-S, that would surely help us to pass the final exam. We copied pies into our notebooks.) And because children are different in pies ways, our teaching methods should emphasize INDIVIDUALIZATION OF INSTRUCTION. She spoke the words in capital letters—it was the *only* sensible way to teach.

Individualization of instruction was a foreign idea to all of us who had spent twelve or so years in the nailed-down desks of the New York City Board of Education standard classroom issue. But in our willingness to please—and pass—we embraced it. It was *the* current motto of the faculty of education—the new panacea and holy grail of methodology. We learned that the amount of emphasis we gave to the slogan in writing essays and final exams directly correlated with higher grades. We mouthed the slogan, as we had the rule, "invert the divisor and multiply," in Grade 5. Naturally, in our understanding of and in our ability to apply theory, we were as ignorant of the how as we had been unable in Grade 5 to figure out which fraction was the divisor. Mary Dare wasn't much of a virtuoso on the how, either. As she sat on her platform, day after blah-blahing day, we sat, too, in straight rows of tablet armchairs, listening, taking notes, and collecting our 3 credits' worth of human growth and development.

In my teacher education program, we were required to collect 36 hours of credits in course work theoretically designed to teach us to become "good" teachers. With the exception of my practice teaching (which deserves a story of its own), the style and manner of the courses we took were the same: distinguished professors of education, lecturing to students, with an occasional counterpoint of question and answer. That is how we were taught to teach. Needless to say, what I learned best was how to listen, how to take notes, how to read quickly, and most important, how to take and pass exams with high marks.

I remember my first day of teaching as clearly as I would recall sinking with the Titanic. A small detail had been left out of my preparation: I had no teaching skills. I fumbled and bumbled and limped through five interminable hours of the school day, frequently wishing to die. Kenny Henderson didn't help either. He kept tagging along behind me telling me that his last year's teacher never did it *that* way. At the end of the day, I was very close to leaving that room, that school, that city, that world. Who the heck wanted to be a teacher, anyway? I could always earn my living making cabbage rolls—a profession in which I had at least some minimal competence.

In the years to come, I found to my astonishment and consternation that what I had endured during my first days of teaching was not unique. It is the same for very many of us entering the classroom for the first time—a universally shared trauma. The ordeal of those first 60 days are the beginning teacher's initiation rites into the profession, the time during which we face up to the bankruptcy of what little we know about teaching. It is the time during which we begin to teach ourselves how to survive in the classroom. Some of us teach ourselves to teach in the process. It's either that, or making cabbage rolls—in the kitchen, or in the classroom.

What is it, exactly, that is missing from our training programs? Why do beginning teachers feel disabled, rather than enabled, during those first, critical days of teaching? Imagine, for a moment, a scenario in which a student wished to learn to play the harpsichord. Imagine her attending university classes for four years, during which she engaged primarily in listening to her teachers play *their* harpsichords, and which culminated in a practicum experience of actual harpsichord playing lasting only five months. It would be silly to expect this student to perform as a competent professional. We are content that she has learned to play "The Happy Farmer." Her technical skills are understandably weak, and her artistry nonexistent. We would not dream of awarding her a certificate so that she might now teach others. Yet, this is the route by which students are expected to learn how to become classroom teachers. It is no wonder that so many graduate lacking both the technical skills and the artistry.

A pair of seemingly incompatible ideas are being presented in this paper—and as a closing note to this section, it may be of value to look at each, and their relationship to each other. Theme A, carrying the melody, takes the position that a teacher ought to leave his professional training program with at least a set of skills which will enable him to function with some degree of competence in the classroom. In the development of this very familiar theme, it is suggested that such an idea is subscribed to more in theory than in practice.

Theme B, in a somewhat discordant tone, suggests that the artistry found in excellent teaching comes about largely as a result of the process of self-teaching. There is no contradiction here. As the contrapuntal melody does not exist outside of the main theme, so can artistry not evolve in the absence of skill mastery. It is on both themes—how a training program may help a student to move from technical competence toward the evolving of personal artistry—that the following three movements play.

II. Adante Cantabile: What Is Teaching?

> I have come to feel that the only learning which significantly influences behavior is self-discovered, self-appropriated learning.[1]

It may well be that the most important process learnings of life are actually self-taught. How else do we learn about loving, about parenting, about artistry? Who taught Beethoven to compose the Eroica? Where did Einstein learn about the theory of relativity? (His Ph.D. thesis was rejected by his examining committee.) How did Michelangelo learn to sculpt David?

I want to go off, for a moment, to play a small cadenza on the act of teaching—a word which seems to be at the heart of this report. I believe that there is *teaching*, and there is *Teaching*. Almost any damn fool may think he knows all there is to know about teaching—and given half the chance, without benefit of consultant's fee, will gladly tell a teacher *exactly* what that teacher *ought* to be doing. A six-year-old shows his five-year-old brother how to tie his shoelace. He is teaching. Your mother explains why your rye bread did not rise. She is teaching. The tax consultant tells you what deductions are allowed on your tax form.

---

[1] Carl Rogers, *On Becoming a Person* (Boston: Houghton Mifflin Co., 1961), p. 276.

She is teaching. In all of these acts, teaching is occurring and it doesn't take a lot of teacher training to do it. Almost anyone with knowledge and skill in a particular content area might teach that skill to another with relative ease. The common thread which runs through all of these "anyone can teach" examples is that teaching is telling—informing, explaining, demonstrating, showing how. This kind of teaching goes on much of the time and most of us interchange learner and teacher roles many times a day. Yet, in spite of what we can and do learn as a result of teaching by telling, I have come to call this "small 't' teaching."

> It seems to me that anything that can be taught to another is relatively inconsequential, and has little or no significant influence on behavior.[2]

But there is also Teaching—what I call "capital 'T' Teaching"—the Teacher as Artist. While content, knowledge and skills are also learned as part of the process of capital "T" Teaching, it goes much, much further than the mere act of informing, explaining and showing how. It is different in style, in the strategies employed and the attitudes conveyed. Its end result is that the learner is *enabled* by the process. The outcome of capital "T" Teaching is that the learner becomes more free to engage in a process of self-teaching. (To call it self-learning is redundant. There is no other kind of learning.) Capital "T" Teaching is liberating; the learner increases his autonomy, his self-initiative, his confidence in himself and consequently his ability to take risks. He therefore grows in his ability to teach himself. (On the other hand, the end result of small "t" teaching is that the learner is informed. Frequently, the act of informing by itself results in the learner's decrease in autonomy. He learns dependence upon the teacher, since it is the teacher who sets himself up as the one who "knows.")

How does the capital "T" Teacher achieve these awe-inspiring goals? It is difficult to describe with precision, but if you've been lucky enough to have studied with such a Teacher, you will have shared some of these observations.

Goldhammer[3] has said, "It is the relationship that teaches, rather than the text." And that is the starting point—the quality of the relationship which the capital "T" Teacher is able to achieve with the learner, and what is communicated to the learner via that relationship.

In his teaching, the capital "T" Teacher communicates a genuine prizing and valuing of the student. He listens deeply—and this communicates that he is attentive, caring, interested in what the student has to say. The student does not have to be concerned about defending himself against ridicule, belittlement or rejection. There is a deep respect for the dignity of the learner—for his individuality, for his capacity, for his gifts, for his right to make choices—and there is also a sensitivity to the needs, problems and feelings of the student.

This Teacher reveals an openness to growing and learning; and the student comes to see that self-teaching is a continuous process for him. He has sufficient self-regard that he does not become defensive when his beliefs are under question. He communicates a joy—almost a passion—about his work, and it is clear that he loves what he is doing.[4] The student experiences this teacher not as an "all-knowing sage" but as a resource person who has faith and trust in the learner's ability. While in almost every sense the capital "T" Teacher is a model to the learner, the message communicated to the learner is that he is free to develop his own unique style.

There is, of course, more. The Artist Teacher has the skill which enables him to make accurate assessments of student performance and initiate teaching strategies which help the student grow in autonomy. All of this is done in a way which does not undermine the learner's confidence in himself, and does not diminish his self-esteem. A student's mistakes are seen as opportunities for understanding how the learner perceives the learning task, rather than as misdemeanors with penalties owing.

Recapitulation. In small "t" teaching, we can and do teach by informing, explaining and showing how. This can be done stylishly, or it can be done in a dull and boring manner. Either way, it is an act which requires a high degree of teacher control over learner behavior.

In capital "T" Teaching, the Teacher not only provides for the development of knowledge and skill, but he does this in such a way that *enables* the learner to move to higher positions on the continuum of personal autonomy.

While it is true that skill mastery will never guarantee the quantum leap to artistry, there can be no artistry without the skills and the development of personal autonomy.

---

[2] Ibid., p. 176.

[3] Robert Goldhammer, *Clinical Supervision* (New York: Holt, Rinehart and Winston, 1969).

[4] Gerald Pine and Angelo Boy, *Learner Centered Teaching* (Denver: Love Publishing Co., 1977).

III. Menuetto. Allegretto: Promoting Artistry in Teaching via the Harpsichord Theory of Teaching Education

What does it take to produce a Landowska? A Segovia? A Rostropovich? A Menuhin? A musician of incomparable artistry and skill, who will thrill you with his/her performance, as the capital "T" Teacher thrills you with his/her teaching?

In the beginning, there is the *Passion*—the all-consuming desire that makes it possible to give your life to the art. Without the passion, there cannot be the commitment to endless hours of *Practice;* without the practice, there can be no mastery of technique, no musical understanding, no development of style, of performance skill, musicianship. Finally, there is the intervention of the *Master Teacher,* who enables in a variety of ways. The Master Teacher enters into a relationship with the student that is consistently enabling. He provides practice tasks which will help you to advance your technical know-how. He knows just how to identify your specific performance difficulties and, what's more, introduce procedures which help to alleviate the difficulty. Wrong notes are not matters for ridicule; they are important keys to understanding how the process of learning has been impeded. The sum of all the strategies used by the Master Teacher is that you become more and more enabled, more skilled, more confident. You are able to take more risks. And as you gain in skill and in personal autonomy, you increase your self-teaching capabilities.

There are some clear parallels for the training of Teachers. Because of these parallels, I have come to call this training model the Harpsichord Theory of Teacher Education. The theory attempts to do the following:

a. It attempts to show that current teacher education requires students to learn the wrong skills. (In effect, students engage in practicing the wrong tasks.)
b. It attempts to identify those practice tasks which are related to developing skill in classroom teaching.
c. It attempts to show that these skills can be taught effectively and in enabling ways.
d. It attempts to establish a relationship between skill mastery, personal autonomy and the process of self-teaching required of the Artist Teacher.

It has been said that there is nothing new under the sun, and I would like to admit straight away that the Harpsichord Theory is only a new name for what we already know and for what many of us deeply believe about teaching and learning. It rests primarily on the "theory of engaged time" which is in current vogue in some educational research circles. In laymen's terms, this means that the more time a person spends on a particular task, the more competent he is apt to become at that task. Not only is the idea not new, but it is at least as ancient as my old grandmother, who, while thoroughly unschooled, used to tell me that "practice makes perfect." Even John Dewey was known to have written, "We learn what we do."[5]

If we examine current practices in most teacher education programs, we can see pretty clearly what students are spending most of their time practicing. It is listening, note-taking, reading, exchanging ideas, writing and passing exams. It should, therefore, come as no surprise that this is what they learn to do, and to do very well. These types of learning experiences are found in courses in theory, in courses in "foundations" and curiously enough, in courses in methodology. If an observer were to follow a randomly selected teacher-trainee around from class to class during the course of a university day, he would find that students are engaged more than 80% of the time in practicing listening, talking, and note-taking, while the professor is actively engaged in teaching (telling). If the theory of engaged time has any validity, it is little wonder that students emerge from these programs without the competence in the highly sophisticated and complex skills required of the Teacher.

Playing on the harpsichord metaphor a little more, we can also say with some confidence that if practice tasks are to be introduced into the existing course work structure, these tasks ought to have some relevance to those professional skills that are required of the classroom teacher. In other words, in order to perform more competently on the harpsichord, it is essential that the student engage in practicing scales and arpeggios, fingering, sight reading, phrasing. Seeing a film about Chopin and making a harpsichord out of papier-mâché are quite nice to do, but largely irrelevant to the development of technical keyboard know-how.

Teacher trainees may engage in reviewing children's books, making phonics games and learning about the difference between reliability and validity. But such practice tasks do little to increase skill in the teaching of reading, or in the development of class-

[5] John Dewey, *The Child and the Curriculum* (Chicago: University of Chicago Press, 1906).

room tests. Segovia once told an aspiring musician, "I never practice my scales more than five hours a day." And that was when the maestro was 75 years old. There is a vast difference between *learning about* teaching, and practicing the tasks of teaching.

There is little in the whole of the educational process that is actually enabling. Moreover, it is pretty clear that many students leave school at the end of Grade 12 as less autonomous learners than they were when they started. In what other institutions, after all, do we have so much emphasis on controlling and directing the behavior of others—with very little opportunity for exercising personal options? A Grade 3 class in Salmon Arm participates in "organized peeing"—an activity which may only occur at half-past ten in the morning.

Teacher trainees come into university programs needing very much to be more enabled—and this process ought to be the primary outcome of what we do in our courses. It is not enough to help our students to practice the right tasks. It is vitally important that we teach them in enabling ways—so that they may embark in a direction of self-teaching. Without the enabling, their teaching may never be more than mechanical and deadly dull. It is through the enabling that the self-teaching required to become the Artist Teacher is made possible.

What follows now is the articulation of three categories of experiences which I believe to be essential in the education of self-teachers. These, of course, are not the *only* experiences in which teacher-trainees need to engage. However, I believe each of these to be not only vitally important to competent teaching—but *the* key practice tasks, providing the skills as well as the enabling, and without which the self-teaching required at the capital "T" level of performance cannot occur.

A. The Development of a Clear Set of Educational Beliefs from Which Teaching Practices May Flow

In almost every teacher education program, there is at least one course devoted to the "foundations" of education, dealing with the analysis and articulation of educational issues and ideas. The focus of such courses, however, is usually upon the examination of the ideas and beliefs of others; and/or the presentation of ideas by the teacher—hopefully to be examined, but in any event, embraced by the students. Exhortations to the students to "feel free to disagree" are quickly seen as phony. What the teacher really wants is for the students to accept his/her point of view and, what's more, to trade it in on the final exam for a good grade. The practice tasks in which the student engages are primarily those of listening, note-taking, reading, and group discussions.

Most of the current literature dealing with the preparation of teachers emphasizes the need for the student's development and articulation of his own beliefs, since it is the student's own beliefs about teaching and learning which will guide his/her actions in the institutional press of the classroom. If a student's beliefs are unclear, unformed, uncritically derivative, confused, the resulting teaching behavior is likely to be erratic, confused, inconsistent, chaotic.

Unfortunately, we cannot *give* students beliefs. Beliefs do not come about from reading or listening or group discussion. A belief one truly owns comes about as a result of having had an opportunity to reflect on that belief, over a period of time, having had many opportunities to turn it over in the mind, this way and that way, examining it from many angles, and finally, by testing it in the marketplace of life. All this has to take place before a belief can be truly owned, and it is generally a long-term process.

A teacher helps a student to reflect upon his beliefs through the use of clarifying questions. Can you give me an example of what you mean?, What data support that point of view?, What might be some assumptions you are making? are the types of questions that allow the student to examine his belief from a variety of angles. Moreover, these clarifying questions are raised without verbal or nonverbal cues which in any way undermine the student's confidence in deciding the issue for himself. Clarifying a student's idea is not to be confused with manipulating the student around to the teacher's point of view. If the student is not permitted the freedom to choose for himself, the process of enabling is greatly impeded.[6]

In the absence of sufficient practice in reflecting upon and working through their own educational beliefs, students will most likely revert to using those classroom practices through which they themselves have been heavily programmed, perpetuating the small "t" teaching cycle.

How much practice does a teacher-trainee need in the task of reflecting on educational beliefs? If Segovia can be believed, certainly not more than five hours a day, for about 75 years. Like learning to play the harpsichord, the practice of a skill is a life-long activity. But more, much more, of this kind of practice experience needs to find its place in the teacher-education curriculum.

[6] Louis E. Raths, et al., *Teaching for Thinking: Theory, Strategies and Activities for the Classroom* (New York: Teachers College Press, 1986).

B. Practicing the Skills of Teaching

Toward the end of almost every teacher-education program is an experience called practice teaching. It *is* there—but, in most programs, there is too little of it, and it occurs only at the culmination of the program. Five months of limited harpsichord practice may help the budding artist to become proficient at "The Happy Farmer" stage of musical performance, but it is hardly a sufficient practice experience for the Goldberg Variations. Not only that; we do expect the student, in his practicum, to perform at the level of the Goldberg Variations, playing the correct notes, the correct fingering, the correct phrasing, with much attention to the crescendoes and decrescendoes, if you please.

There is very little opportunity in teacher education courses for the student to begin practicing at "The Happy Farmer" stage and proceed through increasingly difficult stages of performance. Our programs only create the illusion that this is happening, but in actual fact, few courses allow for the student to engage in those practice tasks that have direct relevance to classroom teaching skill. A glance into any methods course will reveal that it is the professor who is practicing the methods, while the student is primarily practicing the listening, the note-taking and the group discussions.

What is proposed then, is not only the addition of more practice teaching time in actual classrooms, but also the inclusion in methods courses of opportunities for students to engage in those professional practice tasks which will help them to acquire skill in a variety of teaching strategies.

For example, in a course dealing with the teaching of reading, instead of learning *about* the teaching of reading, students ought to be engaged in practicing tasks such as conducting reading conferences; making diagnoses of weaknesses in reading performance; using remedial intervention strategies; using a variety of different reading programs in practice sessions; providing instruction in word analysis skills; providing instruction in comprehension/thinking skills. What's more, students should be required to practice these tasks until the professor has seen a demonstration of the student's ability to perform the task competently.

In a course in evaluation, instead of learning *about* evaluation, students should be practicing at the professional tasks of providing informed, nonpunitive feedback to pupils; developing good evaluative procedures; conducting parent-teacher conferences; writing thoughtful and accurate descriptions of pupil performance.

Where the practice tasks may be continually interfaced with actual classroom teaching performance, under the rigorous scrutiny of a videotape feedback system, the student's opportunities to strengthen his skills grow enormously. This is due to the added dimensions of practice, combined with actual performance and focused self-scrutiny, which require the student to undertake the self-teaching necessary for improved performance levels. Without the advantages of the practice task/classroom teaching interface, students may have to practice primarily in role-playing contexts, which, like dummy pianos, can also help to sharpen technique, facility and overall skill in quite adequate ways.

C. The Intervention of the Master Teacher

I have said in an earlier section that the critical dimension in Master Teaching is that of *enabling*. Students who have undertaken studies with a Master Teacher find themselves more enabled in a variety of ways—more skilled, more knowledgeable, more self-confident, and most certainly, more autonomous. The Master Teacher employs strategies which, in the end result, enable the student to move forward on the self-teaching continuum.

There are hundreds of statistical studies which attempt to zero in on what it is a teacher actually does in the classroom to bring about certain learning outcomes, and the results are, at best, ambiguous and inconsistent. Yet, if we have been lucky enough to have been a student in the class of a Master Teacher, we *know* it—and we come away from the experience deeply affected in profound and intense ways.

The Master Teacher functions in at least three domains. First of all, he functions as a *person*—and in doing so, he reveals much about himself via his very presence. What's more, the qualities which are being revealed about his person are the very qualities which we admire, value, prize and respect. To merely possess information about his subject is not sufficient. A Master Teacher who has acquired knowledge, but behaves in ways that are churlish, hostile, or morally repugnant does not earn our esteem. What he does, what he says, and who he is speaks loudly to us, and on that basis, we make our assessments of him. He is, of course, eminently knowledgeable in his field; he is open and nondogmatic about ideas; his behavior may be characterized as "thoughtful" in that his actions seem reasoned and reasonable. He is a person who is able to take risks, to take and defend an unpopular stand, to take initiatives. There is a consistency about him that is clearly observable—not only is there consistency about his beliefs, but between what he says and what he does. Some call this *congruence*—the quality of authenticity. He is no phony. The admired Master Teacher functions much of the time as a "problem solver"—as one who is unafraid of the challenges of new problems and undertakes to solve them in imaginative and highly skillful ways. There are qualities of creativeness attached to his Teaching and to his thinking that are both refreshing and stimulating. Moreover, as a person, he is reliable and dependable with respect to his obligations to students, to colleagues and to his own scholarly activities.

Another domain in which we assess the Master Teacher is through his interactions with his students and the quality of the relationship that occurs as a direct consequence of those interactions. In the very first order of priority, there is communicated in this Teacher's interactions a deep and genuine prizing and caring about the learner. He reveals this through his ability to be undogmatic and nonjudgmental in the face of students' ideas, opinions, beliefs. He is considerate of the feelings of students and communicates genuine warmth and regard for them.

A second type of interactive skill has to do with this Teacher's ability to make astute observations of individual pupil performance, diagnose specific weaknesses and suggest plans of action that are truly helpful. Casals listened intently to the young cellist perform and said, "You are playing the trill with the third and fourth fingers. I think if you use the fourth and fifth fingers instead, you will get a better, fuller tone." An English teacher writes on a student's essay, "You seem to be having difficulty with your syntax. Please come to me for some help with it." In each of these instances, the student is not made to feel stupid as a consequence of his inability; evaluative judgments are not demeaning nor punitive. They are specifically diagnostic to the individual learner's difficulty. As a consequence of these specific diagnostic interventions, the learner is enabled to understand a little more about his performance and he is enabled to do the self-teaching required to move himself to the next level of mastery. The teacher who attempts to help a student learn by writing "tighten your style" on his paper, is not only nonspecific in pinpointing weakness, but also nonhelpful in directing remediative procedures. The consequence for the student is increased confusion and frustration.

I have heard students say about a Master Teacher, "He makes me think"—at first said grudgingly, and then with admiration. The teacher who, through his questions and responses, expands and extends the thought processes of his students puts into operation a process of enabling which may serve the students throughout their lives.

There is a third domain in which the Master Teacher outperforms the rest and that is in the area of curriculum. In his classroom, whether at the music school, or in the kindergarten, or at the university, there is a quality about what is happening in the class that might be called "dynamic." The Master Teacher may achieve this through a combination of his own enthusiasm, his choices of curriculum materials, the content and purposefulness of the subject matter, and the way he organizes and orchestrates the learning experiences. His class is never boring or routine; it is alive and zestful and rich. The student comes away from it inspired, knowing more, being more interested, and feeling good—and all of these contribute richly to his movement along the self-teaching continuum.

In all of what the Master Teacher does, he is continually a model for us, to which we frequently aspire. Yet, we are free to develop in our own unique ways, our own talents and our own capabilities.

If you have had the good fortune of studying with such a Teacher, you will know the feeling of being liberated instead of being controlled, of being invited instead of being dismissed, of being enabled instead of being disabled. The Master Teacher thus plants the seeds by which the student, in turn, may grow to teach himself to become a Master Teacher.

IV. Allegro Molto: How I Taught Myself How to Teach

Marshall McLuhan told us: "The medium is the message."

Postman and Weingartner also told us: "The critical content is the process through which learning occurs."

Teachers teach not as they are taught *how* to teach, but as they themselves are taught.

It was perfectly natural then, that one day, early in my teaching career, in a blinding recognition scene, I should find myself teaching as a cloned version of Mary Dare Hitchcock. There were my students—sitting in their tablet armchairs. There was I, elevated, not in wisdom, alas, but on the teacher's platform, telling them about pies, day after blah-blahing day. There is a lot of safety in doing things in the same old way. There are no risks, no personal involvement, no putting your tenure on the line, no making waves in your faculty boat which might rock that solid ship of state. But then, Beethoven did not write the Rasoumowsky Quartets by following mechanically in the footsteps of Haydn.

I guess all significant learning comes about as a consequence of the need for resolution of cognitive dissonance. One cannot endure for long a period of such disharmony as is encountered in a clash between a conflict of personal beliefs and discrepant personal behavior. Once you have identified such a conflict, something has to give if you are to restore homeostasis. It is as uncomfortable as hearing the last movement of a symphony, without the concluding tonic chord.

After that first awareness, some change must inevitably follow.

> I find that another way of learning for me is to state my own uncertainties, to try to clarify my own puzzlements, and then get closer to the meaning that my experience has for me.[7]

Alas, there is no magical transformation, no chemical potion that allows you to awaken in the morning as THE NEW YOU, no telephone booth scene in which you shed the garments of the ordinary teacher and leap out as Superteacher! There is, instead, after the initial insight, the beginning of a growth process which is as slow, and as painful, as teething.

Once your teaching performance has become unacceptable to you, you begin a self-teaching program to change, so that what you do in the classroom may be more congruent with your personal beliefs. First, there is the undertaking of "field trials"—the setting up of your classroom as a laboratory in which the testing of new ideas, the examination and interpretation of results, the learning to live with failure, the recreating, retesting, reshaping of methodology, materials, interactive strategies, may all occur. There is the continued seeking of additional information, the identification and selection of specific new teaching skills, of sharpening old ones and discarding others which are no longer appropriate. There is the continuous and painful process of self-assessment, in which you learn to depend more and more upon your own internal evaluation system. In the process of self-teaching, the locus of evaluation rests heavily within the learner.

None of this is very easy. Most colleagues and friends don't seem to understand what all the fuss is about and why you can't be content with what you are doing. Some students, like Kenny Henderson, find the difference in your classroom expectations extremely unsettling. ("Why can't you just *tell* us what to do?") Support systems fail all around you when you travel uncharted territory, and the open hostility can be very punishing.

What, then, have I taught myself about teaching? That I am discontent to follow in the footsteps of Mary Dare Hitchcock; that I must learn to do it better. I am deep in the process of teaching myself how, and there is only one thing left for me to learn. Everything.

---

[7] Rogers, *On Becoming a Person*, p. 277.

Hybrids Are Successful Adaptations

Jeffrey Zax
Department of Economics
University of Colorado

I've always been very uncomfortable in the multifaceted role of the section person. The satisfactions you get from each of the roles are by no means complementary, and for a long time it seemed to me that successfully performing one role meant that the others were sacrificed.

In particular, it's very hard to establish satisfactory relationships with both the professor and the students. What you really want from the professor is patronage. You want him to help you get where he is now. You want him to like you and you want him to support you. On the other hand, what you want from the students is fear and respect. You want to cash in on all the agony you've gone through to master the material by making sure they suffer. You want them to be in awe of the searing brilliance of your intellect. You want to dominate them, exploit them, pure and simple.

Getting both the professor and the class to see you as you'd like them to is hard. You want to impress the professor with the clarity of your perception, which means you agree with him. But you need to distinguish yourself to the class, which means you don't. Professors in my experience get very nervous when you steal their students. But students get really snotty when they realize you're a lapdog.

So what do you do? The root of the problem is that the teaching fellow [TF] is no longer an undergraduate and not yet a professor. The answer is to remember that he once was an undergraduate and soon will be a professor. This is a subtle distinction. But the point is that the teaching fellow stands somewhere between the class and the professor. In the course of the semester the two of them are going to have to come together—and that means they're headed in the teaching fellow's direction.

A successful course is one in which students get out of it something like what the professor puts in. This doesn't happen often. The professors I've worked with spend hours, literally, on a single lecture. No student puts in that kind of time understanding it. And they come at the material with much less background. So it is clear that students never manage to pump all the depth out of the material.

For a professor, a good lecture is one in which the subtlest relationships are revealed with wit of the most refined, penetrating sort; where all the points of view are caressed and molded into a unity that hits with a little pop of clarity and he goes away feeling smug.

Students generally have notes on this kind of lecture which wander off the page or don't stay within the lines or go both ways on the same page. They look like zombies when they leave. And there's a reason for this. Professors, really, can't be any less abstruse. Most of them want or need to get a book out of their lecture notes, and that immediately means that the tone is going to be less than conversational. Those who don't are at least mildly interested in the abstract beauty of the whole thing, which means again that the tone will be anything but conversational.

In any event, it's common for a professor to spend lecture after lecture on nuances which resolve contractions which students never perceived as a problem in the first place. Students have three other courses, they have social lives (that's something teaching fellows find very hard to relate to), they are majoring in something else. The big difference is that all this is new to them, each lecture unfolds a new chapter, and they really don't know where it's all heading until it gets there.

Until then, they don't understand why what they're doing right now is important. They have trouble identifying the main thread. The professor knows the whole story already; he's been anticipating the punch line since the first lecture. The way he retraces his path is by no means the way you would go exploring it for the first time. The students and the professor are by necessity operating at completely different intellectual levels and neither has the freedom to move closer to the other.

That's where teaching fellows come in. Luckily, teaching fellows combine the worst characteristics of both student and professor. Teaching fellows think they like the nuances, but they're not sure they follow them. They like to worry about the subtle problems, but they'd like their degree and tenure first. They know the punch line, but they don't think it's funny (but they will). They can follow the flow, but they don't know how to contribute to it. This is their strength, and it is when they exercise it that they are most appreciated. There are imbalances in any course which only the teaching fellow is sufficiently detached to observe.

What, specifically, can the teaching fellow do? An example: Suppose the reading list in the undergraduate course is more demanding than in the graduate course. The professor thinks it's all very necessary, and the teaching fellow knows that. The students are never going to read more than a quarter of it, and the teaching fellow knows that too. Now, the teaching fellow could keep quiet. Each student would guess at the 20 articles which will be most important, so that no two students will have read more than five articles in common. They'll all be petrified at the exam because they'll each be prepared to answer at best a third of each question and they'll do miserably. There will be no pattern to the ignorance and grading will be difficult. The professor will be horror-struck and his response will be to assign more readings. A situation like this can often be foreseen by the second week of the term.

The teaching fellow's strategy is obvious. He organizes a conspiracy. In sections he makes it clear that a quarter of the readings are absolutely critical, double and triple asterisks, and he talks about which these are. At first this may feel subversive, but it's really a completely positive step. He is giving nothing away to the students, since whatever he says, they are only going to read a quarter of the readings.

He certainly has not undermined the professor, since now at least the class will be homogeneous in its ignorance. And the thing works itself out so much more nicely. When the test comes the whole class is well prepared for two out of five questions. The answers to the other three will be uniformly gibberish. So the two questions will be the basis of the grading, which is fair. Furthermore, any professor will immediately notice that there is this collective myopia and reconsider the sections the class seems to have ignored and either cut or improve them.

There are many other opportunities to pull the same kind of maneuver. It's very popular, for instance, for professors (especially in survey courses) to deal with an issue by taking two lectures and presenting all sides of the debate, all the strengths and weaknesses, and the names associated with each position. In order to impress students with the solemnity of the whole thing, he speaks of the interchanges with the kind of reverential awe that makes you feel the discussion has taken place at a very stately pace since the Middle Ages.

And that's exactly what it sounds like to the students. The proof of this is that the instant they're asked a question, they ascribe opposing views to the same person, or they talk about the opinions and names they remember in such vague terms that they'll never positively associate one with the other. They hope you'll just impute the correct relationships and give them full credit. Here again, without hurting anyone you can make everyone happier by simply having an opinion.

The professor will probably have summed up the discussion by indicating what he believes to be the truth of the matter, the academic truth, which amounts to saying that the question requires more study. That is not the same as the undergraduate truth. In sections, the TF picks a likely opinion and states that while it has not been conclusively proven, for the purposes of the class it is correct. This may seem overassertive, but it's not. It gives the students a chance to bring focus into a subject that they would have ignored altogether otherwise. And when the professor sees on all the exams these cogent arguments all in favor of the same viewpoint, he is going to rethink his own presentation. He'll be surprised that his lectures were so conclusive; he didn't realize he felt so strongly, but next year he'll be more explicit. Again, everyone profits.

One last example. Even when everything about the course is right, it is easy for the motivation to be missing. It's easy for the professor to spend hours on material that doesn't suffer from ambiguity or multiple viewpoints, where the reading list is manageable and helpful, and where the students simply don't care. Unfortunately, there are occasions when, fundamentally, there's no reason why they should. But there are times when the professor just doesn't get around to addressing the relevance directly. Such comments just don't fit into the flow of what he's trying to do. Anyhow, relevance for him means something he can write an article on. Relevance for the students means something they can talk about at parties. There may be no relation.

Sections on current events are an obvious ploy, but students do not demand anything that bald. I once had a very successful section in which I discussed a research idea that the professor and I had developed in casual conversation earlier that day. Anything which breathes life into the litany of constructs and generalizations is going to be well-appreciated, whether it sheds light on the process of real life—or just academic life. The students will follow the lectures with renewed enthusiasm, and the professor will be very grateful for a class that stops sleeping.

I think the lesson to be learned from these examples is that the most precious thing the teaching fellow possesses is his independence. That's a commodity which is easy to forgo. If he finds himself spending all his section time working problem sets step-for-step, he's become another button on the students' calculators. If he finds himself being asked to spend sections re-delivering the professor's last lecture, he has become a phonograph.

His perspective is unique; it is all the more valuable the more acutely he feels within him the contradictions of being a teacher while simultaneously being a student.

Professors and students are often unsatisfied, but they have to talk to each other to resolve anything. A teaching fellow is both, so he only has to talk to himself—and there it's much easier to get an answer. Changes that would make the teaching fellow feel more comfortable with the course are changes which will make everyone feel more comfortable. In the end, making the course better is the only role for the teaching fellow.

Writing Cases: Tips and Pointers

Jane Linder
Harvard Graduate School of Business Administration

(HBS No. 9-391-026)

Case writing is a creative process. In the simple outline that follows, I will describe my approach. It is certainly not the only approach and may well be unsuitable for some people. This process has worked well for me, has produced some very interesting teaching materials, and has been enjoyable for those who participated.

Before I describe the process, let me say a few words about overall timing. Writing a case can take as little time as four weeks, and as long as six months, from beginning to end. An aggressive schedule might be as follows:

Preparation	1 week
Interviewing	2–4 weeks
Draft	2 weeks
Quote approval	2 weeks
Case review and sign-off	2–4 weeks

The description that follows assumes the case site has been chosen and the company is willing to participate. It is well worth discussing how one selects case sites and how one "sees" the story that is there, but that conversation is for another day. I divide the case-writing process into four simple stages: preparation, interviews, writing, and closure. Each of these is described below.

1. Preparation

The first step in writing a case is to make a plan for the course of the interviews. You have to decide whom to see and what to talk about. It helps to know something about the company and industry you will be discussing.

To prepare an industry and company overview, review the annual reports of the firm for the past three to five years. Conduct a library search of articles in the business press about the firm for this period. Compile a view of the industry from public sources. This work serves two purposes. It is the foundation for one section of the case document. It also prepares the casewriter for informed discussions with executives.

Develop a case theme and interview list. Discuss the case with the key contact. Identify the central theme of the case. Three favorite themes are a particular player in an interesting situation, a key decision, or a specific organizational problem or issue. It is enormously helpful to have a theoretical framework that relates to the issues you will be discussing. The framework helps guide the interview without turning it into a rigid, spoken questionnaire.

With the theme in mind, work with the contact person to compose a list of interviewees. If possible, have company personnel set up the meeting times and places. Allow one hour for each interview and at least 15 minutes between them, not including travel time. For most people, six interviews in a day is intensive, but feasible. I like to interview the most senior people in the case at the very beginning, and again at the end of the roster. Scheduling at least two visits with critical interviewees results in much better information. During the second conversation, they often ask you what you are hearing. They know you. The follow-up conversation can get beyond the party line or superficial explanations that often characterize first meetings.

Develop an interview guide. This can be very rough or extremely detailed. I prefer a general outline for the hour that I can describe in one sentence. For example, in a recent case experience, I opened each interview by stating that the agenda was to talk about where the company was with information technology, how it got there, where it needed to go in the future, and what that would require. This is a simple chronological flow that most people can follow easily.

2. Interviews

I have found that interviews are best conducted two-on-one. Two casewriters interview one respondent. One casewriter is the chief questioner and the other is responsible for taking copious notes. While you can rotate roles, I have found it is best not to. In this way, you build a complete set of notes that at least one of you can read.

You should write down as much as you possibly can. I try to capture every word. It is impossible, especially when you have to stop to think of or ask a question, but it is still an appropriate goal. Great notes make the job of writing much easier.

Tape recorded interviews are an alternative to written notes. The advantages are that every word is faithfully recorded and that your mind is free to focus on questioning. The disadvantages are that some people are wary of recorded conversations, even those who trust you otherwise, I have found. Also, transcription is expensive and takes time. You end up with an enormous amount of data that you have to boil down into meaningful information.

You should be prepared to introduce yourself and your project in a very clear and concise way. In most cases, the people you are interviewing will have some understanding of what you are doing, but they will want to hear it from you.

You will also want to prepare a wrap-up statement with which to close the interview. This should tell people what to expect after you have left. I try to tell them what they will next see from me and when and what our overall schedule looks like. For example, I say something like this:

> I will be interviewing over the next two weeks. Then I will prepare a draft of the case. If I want to quote you by name in the case, I will send your quotes to you for your approval before the draft is circulated to the company. After everyone has agreed to their quotes, I will send the case to [the prime contact] who will circulate it for review. [An officer of the company] must sign off before we can release the case for publication.

The substance of the interview itself is art. For me, it is a mixture of very specific questions like the annual budget for Information Systems and very open-ended questions like "How did you decide to centralize your operations?" I am most likely to abandon my interview guide when the person to whom I am talking seems bored by the questions. I test this by asking something like, "How big a deal are these issues for you?" If the answer is "Not big," I ask what kinds of issues are a big deal, then follow that thread. By letting your interview subject set the agenda, you do not fill in the blanks on your interview guide, but you can get a much richer and more interesting story.

I listen carefully for the turns of phrase that people share. In one company, the word they all used most often to describe their management process was "debate." In another company, consultants' words like "empowerment" and "time-based management" were on everyone's lips. This shared language tells a great deal about what is going on in the organization, and you can often ask people about it directly to get interesting perspectives.

At a more mundane level, it is important to bring lots of paper and pens. I take one tablet for every two interviews. The object is to capture each interview on consecutive pages of one tablet so the notes can be easily compiled later.

Back at the Ranch

Within 24 hours of the interview, I suggest going over the notes to fill in the phrases that were left out and correct the words that are unreadable. Add notes that explain more about the context or how the person looked or acted as they spoke. Did they get up and close the door before they made the comment? I try to do this in a pen of another color so I can distinguish it from the "true" interview notes. Do not underestimate the amount of time this takes. I often spend three hours reviewing six interviews.

The most unpleasant kind of interview is the dinner meeting where it is unfeasible or inappropriate to take notes. In this case, someone must sit down after the meal, no matter how late, and regurgitate as much of the conversation as possible. [Sorry for the unappealing image.]

3. Writing

To me, the key point about *writing* the case is that one person is in charge of getting the job done. If I am responsible for writing the case, I own it. I get feedback from others, but I drive the process.

When the interviews are completed and materials collected, I sit down to write the first draft. I like to leave two whole days to get started. These big blocks of time are important to me to internalize the story and get most of it down on paper. The refinements can be made in smaller increments. It is very important to draft the case as quickly as possible after the interviews are done. I have found that, if I delay, the real story fades and everyone loses interest. Timing is everything in keeping the momentum alive. Additionally, people in companies can change positions. Losing a sponsor can imperil the entire effort, and dragging the project out increases the likelihood that this will happen.

The first step in producing the draft is reading all of the materials and interview notes in one sitting, with a highlighter in hand. I look for three things when I do this—interesting themes and issues, exhibits, and an opening. The interesting themes are threads that you will want to develop in the case. Exhibits are usually company documents that summarize important data.[1] The opening is the quote or statement that introduces the case and sets its entire tone. (*Exhibit 1* shows two case openings and why they were chosen.)

After I have my list of issues and openings, I choose a general flow for the case. Cases almost always start with a description of the setting—the problem or situation at hand—then go to company and industry background. With these two sections, I almost always include at least three years of financials and a current organization chart. Beyond this formula, we have little guidance about how the rest of the material plays out. Three general frameworks are used frequently:

A. Chronology—Where we were; where we are now; where we need to go.
B. Organizational Structure—Describe the situation by moving through the key blocks in the organization chart. This works best when the chart is reasonably clear and clean.
C. Problem Structure—Lay out the problem as the company sees it, then work through the alternatives or different positions on what should be done.

When the story is told, I write my closing paragraph. It recapitulates the central issues and focuses the students' attention on the decision makers' situation. In some cases, I save a particularly meaty quote for this capping role.

At this point, I go back to my theme list and the interview notes again to identify threads that have not been woven into the fabric and good quotes that can add spice to what is usually dry prose. I then set the case aside for a day.

Finally, I reread the case to edit it for clarity, content, and length. Cases are often too long. Several techniques can help. First, eliminate everything that is not related to the story. Second, check the line inches of various sections of the case. The length of the section should be commensurate with its importance. If you need to shorten a piece, try to summarize a paragraph by using only its topic sentence. Alternatively, convert text into exhibits.

I circulate the draft among my colleagues for review. The document is marked "Confidential" so readers understand that the material is sensitive. I do not normally wait for their feedback, however, before I proceed to clear the quotes.

A Few Comments About Style

The only legitimate way to include editorial comments in the case is through quotes. A statement like "Bromfelder was justifiably proud of his accomplishments" is a point of view that should be attributable to someone other than the casewriter.

We use a person's first name, last name, and title when they are first mentioned in the case. Afterwards, only last names are used. Titles, by the way, are not capitalized.

Cases are written in the past tense. This way, they can be taught for years without seeming outdated. We run into trouble occasionally with this practice. For example, the case may state that the corporation's headquarters *was* in Piscataway, New Jersey, when it still *is* there. One common approach to this particular issue is the following sentence construction: "ABC Company, headquartered in Piscataway, . . ."

We try to use no sexist language, even in quotes,

[1] In unusual cases, I develop my own exhibits from company or alternative sources. For example, in a snack food company case, I listed the new product introductions for the past twenty years from their annual reports. They said they were great at product innovation, but the list showed the majority of their successes were new flavors of their old-line products.

unless it contributes in some way to readers' understanding of the case content.

4. Closure

Clearing the Quotes

Before a case draft can be sent to the company for review, each person quoted in the case is sent a personal letter that asks him or her to approve the exact wording of the quote. It makes no difference whether the quote has captured their exact words or not. The idea is to make them comfortable with the way it will be presented in the case before their colleagues see it.

I compose a letter that goes to every participant. Attached to each letter is a listing of that person's quotes with a few words of description about the context in which each is used. (*Exhibit 2* shows a sample letter.)

If I haven't heard from everyone within two weeks, I begin calling. I have found this follow-up to be especially important with overseas cases because the communications links are sometimes tenuous. When time is short, I clear quotes by fax or, as a last resort, on the phone.

As I receive the edited quotes, I update the document. I always keep the hard copy of the quotes in case questions arise later. In some situations, you will lose quotes you think are exciting and important. Remember, you can always make the statement anonymous: "A senior executive remarked, ..." If I plan to do this, I try to find out whether the individual will be recognized even if his or her name is not attached. For example, one individual called his supervisor "the lead goat." At the time, he told me everyone would recognize that phrase as his, so I didn't use it, even though it certainly would have made the case more exciting.

Circulating the Draft

When the draft is completed and the quotes are approved, I send a copy to the contact person. I ask this individual to make sure "the company" is happy with the document. The purpose of this review process is to get the facts right and to make sure the company is comfortable with the case. There is some room for negotiation on sensitive issues—especially if they are documented in public sources. For example, the case can quote an industry analyst or an article in the trade press that is not complimentary. The firms I have worked with have not complained about including such material as long as their own points of view were well represented.

I try to establish a time frame for the review process with the key contact. Again, if it drags on too long, people lose interest. I keep in touch to move things along.

The easiest firms to work with are those that compile their comments in some way. I have sent diskettes to firms for them to make their own changes. More often, companies return marked up copies of the original document. I transfer these changes to my diskette, then send the completed draft to our word processing group for final typing.

If a case is to be disguised—a common practice when the company is likely to look bad—it is at this point that the disguise is added. It could be done earlier, I suppose, but I find it very difficult to keep track of the content if the names have been changed. The most limited disguise is to change the names of the company and individuals in the case. A slightly more complex exercise is to alter the numbers so that the relationships between figures remain constant, but scale is hidden. A third level of disguise is to change the industry in which the firm competes. This entails researching the contrived industry so that students are not misled, and using casewriter's license to map the real situation onto it.

A disguised case must go through a second company review, although only with the individual who must approve the document.

The Sign-Off

An officer of the company must formally sign off for a case to be published. The simplest version of this procedure is when the executives of the firm have been involved in the interviews and have reviewed the case draft. I either send a "green card" (a case release form) or hand-carry one with a finished copy of the document. They sign, and the case is entered into our case distribution system.

Occasionally, we run into trouble at this point. The company may decide for a variety of reasons that it doesn't want the case released. You know you are in trouble when they send it to their lawyers for review. Cases can be signed off for limited distribution—this is a specific, one-time or one-place use that is acceptable to the firm. They can be disguised, as described above. They may also be held for a stipulated period before being taught. At times, they may also be completely lost.

EXHIBIT 1 *Case Openings*

The following quote opens Frito-Lay case No. 9-187-065. Its purpose is to focus the case on the competitive advantage of information technology infrastructure. The central issue in the case is the introduction of the hand-held computer to the sales force, and this opening encourages students to interpret the project in the broadest way. The quote also happens to be from the most senior executive interviewed for the case. His name was removed—he left the company before the case was released, and his successors felt more comfortable with his being anonymous—but some of his style and charisma were captured in these few words. They help set the tone.

In July 1986, a senior executive of Frito-Lay, Inc., explained the company's competitive picture:

> In the food industry, the retailers are slowly becoming more powerful than the manufacturers. As this plays out, it won't be enough just to know our business. We have to know theirs as well. We'll have to own the big brands and the key real estate in the store and generate the most profit for the store owners. The manufacturers who are important to the store will win.
>
> There is no single sustainable competitive advantage in this business. I can't think of a single thing that can't be duplicated. What we try to do is compete with class. We put a good mix of product on the shelves; we out-execute our competition; and we try to be "blue chip" in every aspect of our business. There's a whole book to be written on the strategic advantage of execution. It's not a few big ideas; it's a whole series of little things that add up to superiority.

The following quote opens Hercules Incorporated, case No. 9-186-305. The quote was drawn from a speech that Al Giacco, President and CEO, delivered to an industry conference. He describes the technology as "forcing" change which is the linchpin of the case. He claimed he wanted to use I/T to drive organizational change. His view of organizational structure is also fairly clear in this statement. Again, he sets the tone for the case right here.

> Computer technology is allowing us as managers—I should say forcing us—to move to new and different organization types so that we can better meet competitive needs. And the people who can best harness these new technologies in the future will be the most successful. Information becomes the key to success only with a management and information system that causes information to flow up to top management where we can make decisions . . . and where we can effectively communicate back down so our decisions can quickly be put into action.

EXHIBIT 2 *Quote Clearing Letter*

Dear [whoever]:

I have completed a first draft of the ABC case, and you are one of the featured speakers. I have attached a list of quotes I have attributed directly to you for you to look over before the draft is distributed for review. I will not proceed until I have heard from you. Please feel free to mark up the quotes and send them back to me at the above address, or call me at (phone number).

Thank you for your help with the case. I believe it is going to be a very exciting piece of teaching material.

Sincerely,
(Case Author)

Teaching Notes: Communicating the Teacher's Wisdom

James E. Austin
Harvard Graduate School of Business Administration

Teaching notes are an essential companion on an instructor's journey toward excellence in case method teaching. There is nothing automatic about case teaching; it requires careful planning and thorough preparation. Teaching notes capture and communicate the wisdom inherent in that process and constitute high-value intellectual capital for the teaching community.

Teaching notes play five important roles that justify the time and effort required to produce them:

Increase Teaching Effectiveness—By making the why, what, and how of our teaching more explicit, teaching notes enhance our capacity to lead more productive learning discussions. The guidance provided by teaching notes increases the probability of classroom success, thereby enhancing the return on the investment made in developing the case study and preparing to teach it.

Save Time—Teaching notes are not a surrogate for preparation, but they greatly enhance the efficiency of the preparation process. They provide the instructor with a running start. As one professor put it: "I spend 6 hours preparing; without teaching notes, another 3 hours would be required."

Build Confidence—By reducing the unknown and providing a map, the risk of venturing into the untried waters of a new case is lowered. The resultant increased confidence is particularly helpful to teachers new to the case method or to a particular case course. One new instructor stated: "I would have died without teaching notes. The teaching group discussions were helpful, but the teaching notes were essential."

Guide Casewriting—Case studies are prepared to serve "as the basis of discussion." They are crafted as discussion vehicles, which is what creates their special literary genre. To fulfill this educational mission, they need to be prepared with the probable discussion dynamics in mind, both process and content. These dynamics are at the heart of teaching notes and therefore interact with case writing in an iterative fashion. One experienced case teacher put it plainly: "A case ought not be written without having its educational objectives and general teaching plan clear."

Contribute Intellectual Capital—Teaching notes are carriers of ideas and communicators of insights about both the subject matter and the pedagogy for disseminating it. As such they constitute another instrument to stimulate

---

(HBS No. 9-793-105)

> intellectual dialogue. Teaching notes are significant academic endeavors and should be viewed as an important part of a professor's publication portfolio. The notes, even more than case studies, reveal quality of mind, pedagogical creativity, and communication skills. They can demonstrate conceptual ability, an administrative point of view, clarity in thinking, and skill in organizing material in a user-friendly way. Teaching notes are a valuable part of the individual's and institution's intellectual capital and should be duly recognized and reviewed in promotion assessments.

Given the importance of teaching notes, there is a surprising and disturbing absence of guidance on what teaching notes should consist of. Yet there is a wealth of cumulative wisdom in the minds of case teachers who have been preparing notes throughout their careers. This paper is an attempt to tap some of that wisdom with the hope that it will provide helpful guidance and encouragement. What follows is based on interviews with a variety of my Harvard Business School colleagues, who have collectively almost 300 years of cumulative experience with the case method and who have demonstrated superior talent as course developers and teachers. I am merely the gatherer and quilter of this community's collective knowledge about teaching notes, and my intellectual stitching will only do partial justice to the richness of their wisdom. There was considerable diversity of perspectives on teaching notes, yet there was a striking convergence on the importance of teaching notes and the central elements in them.

What Should a Good Teaching Note Contain?

A standard structure or format for teaching notes can facilitate preparation and usage but is not essential. The goal is to create a user-friendly document that will be helpful to other teachers and there are many forms to achieve that. Nonetheless, there are five main components critical to a teaching note's utility: synopsis, positioning, learning objectives, substantive analysis, and teaching process. In effect, a teaching note explains:

- what the case is about
- where it fits in a course
- why we are teaching it
- what we are going to teach
- how we can teach it.

Synopsis

This is a half-page summary of the case and its major issues. Its purpose is to provide the instructor with a brief overview of the case. Although it is generally preferable to have read the case before examining the teaching note, some find perusing the note first facilitates their study of the case. It is also useful to instructors who are "shopping" for cases that might fit their course needs and go to the teaching notes first to ascertain the relevancy.

Positioning

Teaching notes are generally written to guide the teaching of a case at a certain place in a specific course with a particular type of student. Pedagogical positioning fundamentally affects what goes into the note, so it is important that the reader understand this perspective. Such usage transparency will allow the instructor to make any necessary adjustments in the note's teaching suggestions to fit his or her educational setting and needs.

Objectives

The educational objectives of the case are the cornerstone of the teaching note. Everything else should build off these. Clarity about the learning agenda creates focus for the teaching exercise. Too often objectives are vaguely stated or left implicit. Such vagueness creates ambiguity and confuses teaching direction. We must be clear why we are teaching the case and what we expect the students to learn.

Clarity is enhanced by specifying the type of learning sought. Three general categories are useful: skill building, knowledge enhancement, and attitudinal development. There are a multitude of critical managerial skills case teaching aims to build, such as problem or opportunity identification, strategy formulation and implementation, function-specific analytical techniques, and more generic analytical capabilities. Knowledge enhancement encompasses theory, frameworks, concepts, and information. Attitudinal development involves dealing, for example, with values, beliefs, self-awareness, intellectual openness, and receptivity to change. The overarching educational goal of a management education program is to develop the capability to analyze problems, make decisions, implement them, and lead organizations. The teaching note's objectives should specify with precision the skill, knowledge, or attitude development that is sought and that will contribute to the overall educational mission.

Clarity of objectives is often hindered by a failure to distinguish case issues from learning objectives. Issues represent the topics around which a discussion can focus; the educational objectives specify the type and nature of learning to be gleaned from that examination. For example, in one case the central issue concerned "the strategic and organizational responses to globalizing consumer, economic, technological, and competitive forces." Simply preceding this with the phrase "To examine" would not create a useful learning objective. This particular teaching note went on to provide the needed specificity of objectives in terms of conceptual knowledge enhancement and skill building ". . . to reinforce the concept of a company's 'administrative heritage' as an asset that must be captured and used rather than denied" . . . "to illustrate the concept of worldwide learning as an important source of competitive advantage for MNCs" . . . "to sharpen skills in analyzing the diverse environmental forces driving globalizations, *and* their limits." For each of these objectives the note briefly elaborated the substantive nature of the expected learning.

Objectives can also be clouded by confusing what the students will **do** in the discussion with what they will **learn** from it. For example, one note specified as an objective "Review issues in. . . ." The reader is left not knowing what is supposed to be accomplished educationally by reviewing the specified issues. The phrasing of objectives often begins with similar action adverbs: explore, examine, identify. This is okay if they are followed by the "why" that explains the learning target. For example, one note stated that the students "will identify two very different approaches to quality . . ." It went on to explain "by comparing these two approaches, students should develop a greater sensitivity to the different meanings of the term quality, as well as an improved understanding of their relationship to firms' manufacturing strategies." This elaboration makes the learning agenda clear. Another example: "Introduce students to the different kinds of work marketing managers do in order to aid students in making career choices." Information was being disseminated to improve students' decision-making capability.

A final cautionary note on learning objectives: don't overload the session with too many objectives. More than four probably places you in the overly ambitious zone. It may also be useful to prioritize the objectives, if some merit more emphasis than others. Another type of pedagogical objective is worth mentioning, even though it might not always be incorporated into a written teaching note. Whereas the above mentioned objectives deal with substantive learning, the case teacher is also managing an on-going *learning process.* To optimize this, the instructor may have process objectives having to do with, for example, student participation, classroom dynamics, or discussion norms. Early on in a course he or she may be striving to ensure that all students will have participated in class discussion. Or students may not have been relating adequately their remarks to their classmates' comments made previously. Such concerns lead to process objectives that affect the way the instructor should conduct the class. Because they are so situation specific, these objectives seldom appear in written teaching notes but should always be in the instructor's personal teaching plan. They are helpful to put in teaching notes prepared for use by various instructors teaching multiple sections of the same course and possibly facing similar process challenges.

Substantive Analysis

The note needs to lay out the analysis of the case's key issues that are tied into the learning objectives. There is a divergence in preferred presentation style for this component. Some prefer to have separate sections for analysis and teaching process, while others like to integrate the two. In the classroom, the two ultimately fuse together, and so even if presented in separate sections, it is helpful to give adequate guidance on their integration.

The substantive analysis should be thorough, clear, and tailored to the note's mission. One is not writing a journal article but rather giving analytical guidance about material specific to the case and its use. Two considerations are useful to keep in mind in developing the analytical section: what kinds of analyses will contribute to the specified learning objectives and what analytical processes will the students likely go through as they prepare and discuss the case. Putting yourself in the shoes of the student is particularly important so that you can pinpoint the areas where greatest difficulty or confusion might arise and where the richest discovery opportunities are. Empathy with the intellectual challenges and learning process is central to presenting a thorough and relevant analysis in the note.

Pointing out alternative paths of analysis that might be followed and the pros and cons surrounding issues is helpful. This broadens the reader's awareness to possibilities that might arise. Similarly, flagging discussion danger areas due to confusing facts, intricate numbers, or conceptual complexity is always appreciated. Forewarned is forearmed; better still, give advice on how to handle the possible problems. Cases with considerable quantitative data require exceptionally thorough data analysis in the teaching note. Calculations should be clearly laid out in terms of where the numbers come from in the case and how they have been manipulated. Again, pointing out likely tripping points for students is helpful.

Case exhibits often contain information central to the analyses. It is often useful to include the exhibits in the teaching notes and annotate them such that the relevant data are flagged and their meaning interpreted in hand notations on the exhibits. The note's textual analysis can elaborate further on how to use the data from the exhibits, but annotating the exhibits themselves will make the reader's examination of them much more focused and efficient.

Either within each analytical subsection (often corresponding to a key issue) or as a separate subsection, it is helpful to distill out the potential main lessons or "intellectual take-aways" from the analysis. These generally will be elaborations of and responses to the learning objectives. These should not be seen as *the* answers or solution to the case. There is never a single set of "right" answers; the organic and dynamic nature of the discussion process produces its unique set of insights and conclusions. Nonetheless, having some of the possible lessons in mind facilitates focus, which is critical to an effective discussion. The cautionary note is simply to remain intellectually open and inclusive to the additional insights that the discussion can generate.

Users of teaching notes may have varying degrees of knowledge of the particular technical material or contextual setting of the case. As an assist to those lacking such background, it may be useful to include as an appendix to the note optional readings (or at least their bibliographical references) to provide supplemental information.

Teaching Process

Teaching notes without process guidelines are only half-finished. The importance of process was highlighted by one colleague's comment: "We're smart enough to do the analysis; I want to know the teaching plan, and this is often missing." As another put it: "We use the *how* to get more out of the *what*." Substantive expertise is no guarantee of teaching effectiveness. Case discussions are guided inquiries with purpose and structure. Classroom execution can be enhanced by providing guidance on eight aspects of the teaching process: teaching strategy and discussion structure, question plan, special techniques, opening, transitions, closing, board plan, and audio-visuals.

(1) Teaching Strategy and Discussion Structure

Providing an initial overview of the teaching approach and structure of the discussion gives the reader a useful map for the class session. This lays out the sequence in which major topic areas will be discussed and explains the pedagogical logic for following this path. It is helpful to indicate the nature of the discussion dynamic and process in each topic area and how this shifts during the class, e.g., from problem identification and causality analysis to option specification and debate over action recommendations. One can indicate the required degree of instructor directiveness and how this might change throughout the class. It is important to recognize that a planned structure should not be viewed as rigid. The learning map has many possible routes and the class discussion may turn in directions quite different than the path originally planned in the note. The instructor should be willing to explore spontaneously these alternative directions to see if they lead to collective progress. Teachers must share with students the task of guiding the direction of the discussion. To the extent that the teaching note can flag such alternative routes (perhaps based on classroom experience with the case), the instructor will be better prepared to go with the flow intelligently and willingly.

Some colleagues refer to the discussion areas as "pastures" in which the class is intellectually "grazing." The students play a central role in deciding where to graze. The teaching note can indicate whether the sequence in which pastures are grazed is pedagogically significant or whether the order is flexible. The note should also indicate where the "gates" between the pastures are and what words or topics might signal the desirability of moving from one pasture to another under the watchful eye and gentle prodding of the "shepherd." (See subsequent section on Transitions.)

The discussion "map" should indicate where the greatest tensions and puzzles are likely to be and how this will affect the students' behavior in terms of degree of engagement. Just as it is important to highlight substantive "traps," so too is it helpful to point out the process pitfalls . . . the areas where discussion problems might occur, e.g., sinking into a swamp of conflicting or confusing number crunching or emotional explosions due to sensitive topics being touched. The warning signs are important, but suggestions on how to deal with these pedagogical challenges should also be given. A final dimension of the map should be a time line. Class time is the inescapable finite resource, so managing it carefully is wise. The teaching strategy should estimate how much time should be allocated to the different discussion areas. It is also useful to flag particular areas that classroom experience with the case indicates as time-problematic, in that discussions can get stuck there and absorb much time. It can also be helpful to suggest which topic areas can be dropped or added if the instructor runs short or long on time in the class.

(2) Question Plan

The primary instrument of the discussion leader is questions. These drive the collective discovery process and so merit major attention. As James Thurber wisely observed: "Better to know some of the questions than all of the answers," which stands in contrast to the admonition to lawyers, "Don't ask a question to which you don't know an answer." The discussion leader's task is not to know all the answers but to trigger productive exploration by the students.

Teaching notes generally include two sets of questions. The first are Assignment Questions distributed to the students in advance to help focus their analysis of the case. The second are Discussion Questions to be posed by the instructor in class. The first are sometimes, but not necessarily, a subset of the second. Posing relevant questions that the students have neither seen nor thought of is a way to evoke in class greater interest and real time thinking.

It is important to think carefully about the type and wording of questions because these can lead to very different types of discussions. One is not running a question and answer session; we are generally seeking questions that can be discussed rather than simply or definitively answered. A typology of questions used by various colleagues includes the following:[1]

Information-seeking: These are the "who, what, when, where" questions that elicit factual responses, which can highlight certain particularly relevant pieces of information and ensure a common data base. However, they also can result in unproductive regurgitation of already known case facts. This almost inevitably triggers boredom. Students tune out and their listening acuity plummets.

Analytical: These "why and how" type questions provoke diagnostic, causal, and interpretive thinking, which is often central to achieving mental skill-building objectives.

Challenge: These are "why" questions to force students to extend and deepen their analyses by giving supporting statements or by responding to counter arguments. When a student is pushed intellectually that individual's level of involvement and the class's collective attention and tension heightens.

Action: These "what would you do when, how, and why" questions press the students into making decisions and dealing with implementation processes. Students almost always have a high interest in action recommendations, so these questions are useful if you want to recapture and focus a wandering discussion.

Hypothetical: These "what if" questions allow you to create new situations that force the students to extend their thinking under different assumptions; this is a way to go beyond certain factual constraints or information gaps in a case.

Predictive: These "what will happen" questions force students to plunge into uncertainty and to substantiate their forecasts. These may be useful when the instructor knows what actually happened and wishes to reveal that after the students have given their predictions, thereby enabling a comparative discussion.

Generalization: These "what general lessons" questions push the student into a more abstract level of cognitive reasoning, which is often particularly helpful to achieve knowledge-enhancement objectives dealing with conceptualization. These are generally very open-ended questions; narrower, more restrictive questions, in contrast, might be appropriate for highly technical parts of a class discussion. Abstract questions generally require the students to reflect, so they will cause a pause in the discussion while the students cogitate. Thus, they affect the pace of the class.

The type of questions chosen will shape the nature of the discussion and learning process in each topic area. In formulating your questions, you should ask what type of thought processes and substantive analysis will this wording elicit. Additionally, how will the question affect the pace, tone, and attentive-

---

[1] For a more extensive examination of discussion questions see C. Roland Christensen, "The Discussion Teacher in Action: Questioning, Listening, and Response," in C. Roland Christensen, David A. Garvin, and Ann Sweet, eds., *Education for Judgment: The Artistry of Discussion Leadership,* Boston: Harvard Business School Press, 1991, pp. 156–63.

ness of the class. For example, do you want to accelerate pace with an action question or slow it down with a reflective generalization question? Or intensify debate and attentiveness via a series of challenge questions?

Generally each discussion block or "pasture" will be initiated by a primary question, with a series of follow-on questions. These should be laid out sequentially with the expected type of student responses indicated. This might mean cross-referencing back to or distilling from the Analysis Section of the teaching note, unless the analysis was integrated with the Process section. It can also be useful to include as a separate annex to the teaching note a sequential list of the questions indicated and explained in the text. Some instructors use variants of this question plan as a visual summarizing vehicle for the teaching note. For example, on a single page they would place the key discussion questions for each pasture, the corresponding time allocation, and the discussion linkages or sequence among the pastures. This "snapshot" serves as a review sheet or an in-class reminder sheet. It is also helpful to add to the main discussion questions some "reserve questions" that could be used by the instructor in case the discussion unexpectedly covered the planned areas rapidly, thereby confronting the instructor with dreaded dead time. Even if not used in the discussion, these reserve questions might be posed to the students at the end of class as areas meriting further contemplation.

Most colleagues incorporate their classroom experiences with the case into the teaching note, which is particularly useful in suggesting how students tend to react to certain lines of questioning. Even though each group of students is unique and classroom dynamics are never identical, including these experiences in a teaching note does alert the instructor to possible reactions and patterns that otherwise might not have been contemplated. This experiential information can spark ideas for different types or sequencing of questions.

(3) Special Techniques

In addition to questions, the note might suggest other techniques for managing the discussion. For example, role playing can be used to foster greater empathy with a case protagonist or to set up an interchange between different case actors, such as a business manager negotiating with a government official. Such role plays can be assigned to individual or groups of students spontaneously during class or prior to the session. This technique almost always increases class attentiveness.

Examples of other in-class techniques are (a) taking votes on a decision or issue in order to create polarity or identify consensus; (b) breaking into dyads or triads to get everybody to focus on and discuss a particular issue and then regroup to debrief; (c) having one group of students present their collective analysis and then defend it against the rest of the class. Special techniques are used as mechanisms to foster certain learning process dynamics that will enhance teaching effectiveness. The nature and form of these special discussion enrichers are limited only by our own creativity.

(4) Opening

Every class has a beginning, and that moment is perhaps the only one that is entirely in the hands of the instructor. So we better make the most of it! And we should, because how a class starts off can significantly affect the tone, interest, and focus of the entire session.

Although the nature of openings should always be subject to adjustments called for by the on-going dynamics and situation peculiar to each instructor's class, the teaching note should provide suggested ways for starting class, for which there are many options. Referring back to previous cases might be desirable where the case is part of a linked series of cases building up related techniques or concepts. Laying out the session's agenda might be useful where the material is dense and greater structure is demanded. Providing a quote or reading a relevant literary reference are ways to capture interest or add some new perspective on the case issues. Starting by directly asking the first discussion question signals immediate substantive engagement. As mentioned above, the type of question you choose to open with will affect the nature of the class's initial engagement. Great beginnings don't guarantee great classes, but they sure help. And the better you plan them, the better they will be.

(5) Transitions

Thinking through how to move the discussion along from one topic area to the next helps smooth the flow and ensure progression. Sometimes the transition will occur organically in the discussion process by a student moving into the next topic area with little direction from the instructor. The note might flag certain cues or discussion points that would signal the transition point. Sometimes the nature of the material or the discussion plan calls for more explicit transition planning. For example, for a complex or technical discussion area a helpful transition might be a brief summary of the salient points followed by the primary question for the next topic area. Another transition form that the note might indicate is a linking comment relating the exiting and entering topics. If the discussion topic areas are tightly related and the logic of the questioning sequence readily apparent, the instructor can make a transition simply by asking the next primary question. Finally, if the discussion plan requires a major shift, the note might indicate that one should be explicitly directive and state that we will now turn to the next topic.

(6) Closing

As with beginnings there are always endings. Although these are less controllable, being the caboose trailing the discussion train, they should be planned and indicated in the teaching note. What form the closing ultimately takes should always be subject to on-the-spot adjustment depending on what happened in the class discussion. Still, various types of closings can be designed to serve a variety of purposes.

A summary of the salient points or lessons might be presented by the instructor, either verbally or from prepared transparencies. There is a risk that such "precanned" lessons will vary from what actually emerged in the discussion, thereby discounting the merit of the discussion. The instructor should be advised to expand the prepared points through references to insights generated by the discussion. An alternative mechanism is to have a student or several students do the summarizing and lesson-generating. The instructor might make linking comments tying this case to previous ones, which might be a particularly appropriate way of getting closure at the end of a module of cases. The linking might be prospective to alert students to the following set of cases and issues. In some instances an update about what happened subsequently to the company in the case can be of interest to the students and provide additional insights. A mini-lecture relating the case to larger bodies of literature or theories might be appropriate. To leave the students thinking, you might pose additional questions that broach issues not covered in the discussion.

The impact of a session is disproportionately affected by how it ends. Ending without finishing fosters frustration. Planning the closing pays good learning dividends. A teaching note that gives no guidance on how to close, remains incomplete. It should, at a minimum, suggest optional ways to close. Even better, it should offer a very detailed closure. Not all users of the note will utilize this specifically, but for many it will be a treasured time-saver.

(7) Board Plan

Recording discussion points on the chalkboard serves multiple functions. It serves as the class's collective memory, thereby facilitating linkages, cohesion, and a sense of progress. It is a control mechanism for the instructor by creating and communicating order, structure, and importance. The medium becomes the message.

It is never possible to predict precisely how a discussion will unfold and therefore what specific points will be raised and recorded. It is, however, generally possible to predict the main categories of discussion and therefore create a layout of the topics headings under which specific points discussed in class can be recorded. The importance of this is captured by a colleague's comment: "When not planned, the boardwork can really constrain quality. If you haven't thought it through and fill up the board too soon, you're screwed." It is useful to think through what should go on which boards when and which should be visible at what time as boards are moved or flipcharts flipped. Some colleagues caution against creating too detailed board plans because of the risk of becoming a prisoner to them or leading the class to conclude that the discussion is "preprogrammed," thereby stifling creativity. The board plan is a means not an end.

(8) Audio-Visuals

There are a multitude of other audio visual teaching aids that can be used to enrich or supplement the discussion process. Transparencies can be used for information transmittal and hard copies should be included. Video and audio tapes can be shown to capture the dynamics not transmitable via paper cases. Computer models can be used with projection equipment to facilitate in-class data analysis, scenario-building, and discussion. The teaching note needs to describe these aids thoroughly and explain how, when, and why they are to be used. Duration and any special equipment operating instructions should also be provided.

The foregoing section described what ought to go into a teaching note, and the paper's opening section explained why we should prepare notes. The final section provides some brief thoughts on the process of preparing them.

How to Prepare Teaching Notes

Preparing teaching notes should be conceived as an integral part of writing cases. The note's conception and construction evolves in conjunction with the development of the case. The formulation of the learning objectives may even guide the search for case leads. The issues and managerial problems uncovered in the initial case research process should be reviewed in terms of both their substantive content and how they might be discussed: what the important issue areas are and what the discussion questions might be. These preliminary notes for the teaching note are tentative. They interact with the emerging case material and case writing; the iterative process shapes each other. For example, the learning objectives guide what goes in the case and what to leave out; case construction involves "deanalyzing," removing some information or analyses so as to avoid robbing the students of their own discovery opportunities. The case research often uncovers new issues that cause the instructor to broaden or reformulate the initial learning and discussion topic agenda. Having discussion questions in mind helps the case writer think through what type of information the student will need or not need in the case to respond adequately. This helps discover holes and fat in the case draft. A case writer should be able to explain why each piece of the case is needed in terms of contributing to the discussion and learning process. It should be noted that teaching notes can also be prepared for existing cases. The task and the process is different and more difficult in that the case information and structure is a given that the note must work with rather than shape.

Even though the preparation of the case and the teaching note march forward together, the note should not be finalized until after the case is finished and taught. The teaching plan embodied in a new note is an untried set of ideas; like a new product, it must be tested in the market place. Trying it out in the classroom yields valuable insights that invariably lead to alterations in the note. Multiple classroom trials produce richer data on what works, what doesn't, what's possible, what isn't. This fact highlights a distinctive characteristic of teaching notes as a literary form: a note is an organic document subject to continual revitalization through the new insights gained from the teaching experiences of the original author of the teaching note or other instructors who teach the corresponding case with the benefit of the note's guidance.

Teaching notes are living, ever-evolving creatures. They should be subject to continual revision and updating to incorporate the new insights gleaned from the classroom experiences. After class most effective teachers jot down notes on the discussion experience: new substantive or process aspects or ideas that emerged, the results of trying some new pedagogical twist, special problems that arose etc. These generally have to be recorded soon after class because their half-life is shortened by the imperative of the next day's preparation. For multi-instructor courses, allocating time in teaching group meetings for a collective debriefing of the group's classroom experiences with the case can provide a rich offering of improvement possibilities. These insights too often, however, remain as handwritten notes stored away in the instructor's personal teaching file. These "shadow notes" too seldom make their way back into the formal teaching notes that reside in the public domain, accessible to the larger community of teachers. Unlike journal articles, teaching notes can and should be revised subsequent to their initial publication. If a note remains unrevised two years after its publication date and the case is still being taught, then it is almost certain that accumulated teaching wisdom is not being adequately tapped. It is hidden away in the informal shadow notes.

The challenge is to create the incentives for ongoing revitalization of teaching notes. Giving significant credit in the promotion process and recognition in the institutional culture for preparing and revitalizing teaching notes will encourage such investments. This should also include encouraging instructors to revise or develop new versions of teaching notes prepared by other colleagues. It often takes greater pedagogical creativity to develop an innovative way to teach a classic case than to devise a note for a new case. Teaching notes are individuals' creative products, but they become part of the community's intellectual capital. They are used by many, and those users, in turn, need to enrich the notes further. They are part of our "educational commons" and we all have a shared responsibility for the upkeep.

We end with a final comment on the use of teaching notes. They are not substitutes for preparation or surrogates for creative reflection. Rather, they are preparation accelerators and pedagogical stimulators. They are reference maps, not drama scripts. They provide valuable guidance that should expand rather than constrain the user's teaching frontiers. Teaching notes are our communicators of pedagogical wisdom and are essential to achieving individual and institutional excellence in teaching.

Note on Process Observation

John J. Gabarro and Anne Harlan
Harvard Graduate School
of Business Administration

"A camel is a horse put together by a committee" is a saying frequently applied to group decision making. What is it that makes so many groups inefficient, slow, and frustrating, instead of effectively combining the insights and expertise of its members? To some extent the answer may be found in the formal group design. Perhaps the people chosen were not the ones who should have been included in such a group, or perhaps the group's goal was simply unattainable. More often, however, the difficulties encountered have less to do with content of task issues than with the *group process,* or how the group is going about achieving its formal task.

Each group member is a unique individual, bringing certain expectations, assumptions, and feelings to the group, not only about his or her own role but also about the roles of other members in the group. As a result of these expectations certain interrelationships develop. These patterns may become either beneficial or detrimental to the group's purpose. Spotting detrimental patterns is the first key to understanding and improving the functioning of any group; but often these patterns are hard to identify because you cannot read each person's mind. For instance, how do you know that everyone understands what the agenda is, or that person X understands it but is likely to deviate from it if possible, or whether person X has the leverage to change the agenda if he or she wants to? While you cannot see inside others' minds, you can develop a greater awareness of what is and what is not likely to happen in a group, and of what the group is or is not capable of doing at a given meeting by being attentive to what is happening among group members.

Being able to observe and understand a group's process is important for two reasons. First, it enables you to understand what is taking place covertly as well as overtly in the group's behavior. Second, it can provide you with insights into what you and others can do to make the group's interactions more productive.

Listed below are seven aspects of group behavior that can furnish valuable clues on how effectively a group functions. It is unlikely that all of these will be relevant to your concerns at a given point in time, or that you can attend to them all simultaneously. The more adept you are at observing and assessing them, however, the more likely it is that you will spot potential difficulties early and act on them to improve the group's effectiveness.

Participation

Participation—who participates, how often, when, and to what effect—is the easiest aspect of group

(HBS No. 9-477-029)

process to observe. Typically, people who are higher in status, more knowledgeable, or simply more talkative by nature, tend to participate more actively. Those who are newer, lower in status, uninformed, or who are not inclined to express their feelings and ideas verbally, generally speak less frequently. Even in groups composed of people of equal status and competence, some people will speak more than others; this variation is to be expected and is not necessarily a sign of an ineffective group. When large disparities exist among the contributions of individual members, however, it is usually a clue that the process is not effective—particularly when individuals or coalitions dominate the group's discussion.

There are many reasons why unequal participation can reduce a group's effectiveness. Low participators often have good ideas to offer but are reluctant to do so, or they cannot contribute their ideas because they are squeezed out by high participators who dominate the meeting. This imbalance can be a potential problem when we consider that those ideas receiving the most attention inevitably become the ones that are most seriously considered when it is time to make a decision. Considerable research shows that the most frequently stated ideas tend to be adopted by the group, regardless of their quality. Maier calls this the *valence effect*[1] and it is one of the reasons why groups often make poor decisions. Thus, large imbalances in participation can result in potentially good ideas being underrepresented in the discussion, or perhaps not even expressed.

Another negative consequence of uneven participation, understood through common sense as well as research, is that low participators are likely to tune out, lose commitment to the task, or become frustrated and angry—especially if they have tried to get into the discussion but have been ignored or cut off by high participators. These negative attitudes result not only in poorer quality decisions but also in less commitment to implementing the group's decision.

Several factors contribute to uneven participation. One is that people who have the most at stake in a given issue (and may therefore be the least objective) are more motivated to participate than others who may have better ideas to offer. Another is that different people have different internal standards on which they judge whether or not an idea they have is worth offering to the group. Thus, people with higher internal standards may be less likely to contribute than those with lower internal standards, with negative consequences for the quality of the group's discussion.

A marked change in a person's participation during a meeting is also a clue that something important may be going on. If a person suddenly becomes silent or withdraws during part of a meeting, it could suggest a number of possibilities (depending on the person's nonverbal behavior). For example, it might simply mean that the person has temporarily withdrawn to mull over the comments of a prior speaker. It may also be that the person has tuned out, or it may be a sign of hostility or frustration. Whatever the case, it could be a sign that something is not right.

Some questions to consider in observing participation include the following:

1. Who are the high participators? Why? To what effect?
2. Who are the low participators? Why? To what effect?
3. Are there any shifts in participators, such as an active participator suddenly becoming silent? Do you see any reason for this in the group's interaction, such as a criticism from a higher-status person or a shift in topic? Is it a sign of withdrawal?
4. How are silent people treated? Is their silence taken by others to mean consent? Disagreement? Disinterest? Why do you think they are silent?
5. Who talks to whom? Who responds to whom? Do participation patterns reflect coalitions that are impeding or controlling the discussion? Are the interaction patterns consistently excluding certain people who need to be supported or brought into the discussion?
6. Who keeps the discussion going? How is this accomplished? Why does the group leader want the discussion to continue in such a vein?

Interventions. There are a number of simple and unobtrusive process interventions that you can make, either as a group leader or group member, to bring about a better balance in participation. These interventions are particularly important if you think that potentially valuable minority views are not getting their share of time, that certain people have not had a chance to develop their ideas fully, or that some group members seem out of the discussion. One intervention is to try to *clarify* a point that someone had made earlier which seemed to fall through the cracks—going back to that person's point by saying something like "Tom, let me see if I understood what you said a moment ago." A related technique is simply to *rein-*

[1] Norman R. F. Maier, "Assets and Liabilities in Group Problem Solving: The Need for an Integrative Function," *Psychological Review*, vol. 74, no. 4 (July 1967), pp. 239–248.

force a prior point by asking the person to elaborate on it—"Sue, I was interested in what you were saying earlier; can you elaborate on it?" Similarly, a very direct technique for bringing out silent people is to simply *query* them—"Mary, you haven't said a word during this discussion; what are your ideas on it?" or to make a comment as direct as "We've heard a lot from the marketing people, but very little from production scheduling. What do you guys think about the problem?"

Influence

Influence and participation are not the same thing. Some people may speak very little, yet capture the attention of the whole group when they do speak. Others may talk frequently but go unheard. Influence, like participation, is often a function of status, experience, competence, and to some degree personality. It is normal for some people to have more influence on a group's process than others, and this fact is not necessarily a sign that a group is ineffective. However, when one individual or subgroup has so much influence on a discussion that others' ideas are rejected out of hand, it is usually a clue that the group's effectiveness will suffer and that the discussion will fail to probe alternatives. This imbalance is particularly dangerous when minority views are systematically squelched without adequate exploration.

An asymmetry in influence can have a number of negative consequences on a group's effectiveness. As we have already noted, it can result in the suppression of potentially valuable minority views, it can contribute to imbalanced participation, and it will inevitably result in hostility and lack of commitment by group members who feel that they have been left out. As with participation, considerable research on group behavior and alienation shows that the more influence people feel they have had on a group's discussion, the more committed they are likely to be to its decisions, regardless of whether their own point of view has been adopted by the group.

One way of checking relative influence is to watch the reactions of the other group members. Someone who has influence is not only likely to have others listening attentively but is also less likely to be interrupted or challenged by the others. He or she may also be physically seated at or near the head of the table or near the center of a subgroup.

Struggles for influence and leadership often characterize the early stages of a group's life, especially in temporary groups such as task forces, project teams, or committees. To some extent these struggles occur in most groups, although usually in a mild, covert fashion. Vying for leadership can become a problem, however, when it disrupts the group's ability to deal with the task at hand. The disruption occurs when being dominant is an important need for those who are vying for leadership. Under these circumstances, the competition gets played out in a sub-rosa fashion with one person disagreeing with the other because of his or her need to establish dominance, regardless of the relative merits of the other's arguments. The hidden agenda then becomes scoring points rather than working on the problem. Often two people engaged in such a power struggle are not even aware of their hidden motives and genuinely think that they are arguing about the problem at hand.

In assessing influence patterns within a group, you may find the following questions useful:

1. Which members are listened to when they speak? What ideas are they expressing?
2. Which members are ignored when they speak? Why? What are their ideas? Is the group losing valuable inputs simply because some are not being heard?
3. Are there any shifts in influence? Who shifts? Why?
4. Is there any rivalry within the group? Are there struggles among individuals or subgroups for leadership?
5. Who interrupts whom? Does this reflect relative power within the group?
6. Are minority views consistently ignored regardless of possible merit?

Interventions. If you observe that the opinions of an individual or subgroup of people appear to be unduly influencing a group's progress, there are several brief interventions that can be made to open up the discussion. One strategy is simply to *support or reinforce* the views of minority members—"I think there is some merit to what Jane was saying earlier and I'd like to elaborate on it," or "I think that we're not giving enough thought to Jane and Sam's position and I think we should explore it further before dropping it." Another intervention is to actually *point out* that the opinions of certain people are dominating the discussion—"Mary, you've made your point quite forcefully and clearly, but I'd also like to hear the other side of the question before we go further." Similarly, another technique is to ask the group to *open up* the discussion—"So far we've spent a lot of time talking about Jane and Bill's proposal, but I'd like to hear some differing opinions," or "The managers seem to agree strongly on what needs to be done, but I'd like to hear more about what the customer representatives think are the problems."

Group Climate

Members bring with them many assumptions of how groups ought to function generally and how their particular group should function. Frequently, these expectations of assumptions will be quite different from one member to another. One person may feel that the way for a group to work effectively is to be strictly business—no socializing and with tight leader control over the group. Others may feel that the only way a group can work creatively is to give each person equal time for suggestions, get together informally, and use relatively loose leadership. After group members have tested each others' assumptions early on in the group, a climate or atmosphere becomes established that may or may not facilitate effective group functioning. Different group climates are effective in different situations; what is good for one situation is not necessarily good for another.

For example, if the problem to be solved is one that demands a creative, new solution and the collaboration of a number of different experts (such as on a task force problem), then a climate of openness in which everyone has an equal opportunity to participate will be most effective. In other situations, however, a more competitive or structured group climate might encourage a higher quality solution, especially if expertise is not distributed equally among all group members. To gauge a group's climate you should observe:

1. Do people prefer to keep the discussion on a friendly, congenial basis? Do people prefer conflict and disagreement?
2. Do people seem involved and interested? Is the atmosphere one of work? Play? Competition? Avoidance?
3. Is there any attempt to suppress conflict or unpleasant feelings by avoiding tough issues?

For most task groups an unstructured, laissez-faire, or conflict-free climate is not effective: Important issues and conflicts are not explored sufficiently, and the quality of the group's work is sacrificed for the maintenance of friendly and smooth relations. Conversely, a highly structured climate can impede effective problem solving because members do not allow each other enough freedom to explore alternatives or consider creative solutions. A highly competitive climate can also be dysfunctional; competition can get in the way of thoughtful deliberation and exchange, resulting in failure to build on other people's ideas.

Interventions. Intervening to alter a group's climate is more difficult than the previous interventions described. It can be done, however, by reinforcing and supporting desirable behavior, as well as by raising the issue directly. Where a group is smoothing over and avoiding important problems, for example, a useful intervention would be, "We seem to have a lot of agreement, but I wonder if we have really tackled some of the tougher underlying issues." When a group seems to be tied up by its own structure, often a comment as simple as the following will suffice: "I think that maybe we're looking at the problem too narrowly, and it might be useful to discuss whether we should also consider X which isn't on the agenda but seems to have relevance to what we're talking about."

Membership

A major concern for group members is their degree of acceptance or inclusion in the group. Different patterns of interaction may develop in the group, providing clues to the degree and kind of membership:

1. Is there any subgrouping? Sometimes two or three members may consistently agree and support each other or consistently disagree and oppose one another.
2. Do some people seem to be outside the group? Do other members seem to be insiders? How are outsiders treated?
3. Do some members move physically in and out of the group—for example, lean forward or backward in their chairs, or move their chairs in and out? Under what conditions do they come in or move out?

The problem of in-groups and out-groups is closely related to the earlier discussion of influence within the group. The interventions described earlier are also useful for bringing in marginal members—for example, supporting, querying, and opening up the discussion.

Feelings

During any group discussion, feelings are frequently generated by interactions among members. These feelings, however, are seldom talked about. Observers may have to make guesses based on tone of voice, facial expressions, gestures, and other nonverbal cues.

1. What signs of feelings (anger, irritation, frustration, warmth, affection, excitement, boredom,

defensiveness, competitiveness, etc.) do you observe in group members?

2. Are group members overly nice or polite to each other? Are only positive feelings expressed? Do members agree with each other too readily? What happens when members disagree?

3. Do you see norms operating about participation or the kinds of questions that are allowed (e.g., "If I talk, you must talk")? Do members feel free to probe each other about their feelings? Do questions tend to be restricted to intellectual topics or events outside of the group?

Most groups in business develop norms that only allow for the expression of positive feelings or feelings of disagreement, but not for anger. The problem with suppressing strong negative feelings is that they usually resurface later. For example, a person who is angry about what someone said earlier in the meeting gets back at that person later in the discussion by disagreeing or by criticizing his or her idea regardless of the idea's merit. The person's hidden motive becomes getting even and he or she will do so by resisting ideas, being stubborn, or derailing the discussion. This retaliation is usually disguised in terms of substantive issues and often has an element of irrationality to it. It is often more effective to bring out the person's anger in the first place and deal with it then.

Task Functions

In order for any group to function adequately and make maximum progress on the task at hand, certain task functions must be carried out. First of all, there must be *initiation*—the problem or goals must be stated, time limits laid out, and some agenda agreed upon. This function most frequently falls to the leader, but may be taken on by other group members. Next, there must be both *opinion* and *information* seeking and giving on various issues related to the task. One of the major problems affecting group decisions and commitments is that groups tend to spend insufficient time on these phases. *Clarifying* and *elaborating* are vital not only for effective communication but also for creative solutions. *Summarizing* includes a review of ideas to be followed by *consensus testing*—making sure all the ideas are on the table and that the group is ready to enter into an evaluation of the various ideas produced. The most effective groups follow this order rather than the more common procedure of evaluating each idea or alternative as it is discussed. Different group members may take on these task functions, but each must be covered.

1. Are suggestions made as to the best way to proceed or tackle the problem?
2. Is there a summary of what has been covered? How effectively is this done? Who does it?
3. Is there any giving or asking for information, opinions, feelings, feedback, or searching for alternatives?
4. Is the group kept on target? Are topic jumping and going off on tangents prevented or discouraged?
5. Are all the ideas out before evaluation begins? What happens if someone begins to evaluate an idea as soon as it is produced?

Maintenance Functions

Groups cannot function effectively if cohesion is low or if relationships among group members become strained. In the life of any group, there will be periods of conflict, dissenting views, and misunderstandings. It is the purpose of maintenance functions to rebuild damaged relations and bring harmony back to the group. Without these processes occurring, group members can become alienated, resulting in the group's losing valuable resources.

Two maintenance activities that can serve to prevent these kinds of problems are *gate keeping*, which insures that members wanting to make a contribution are given the opportunity to do so; and *encouraging*, which helps create a climate of acceptance.

Compromising and *harmonizing* are two other activities that have limited usefulness in the actual task accomplishment, but they are sometimes useful in repairing strained relations.

When the level of conflict in a group is so high that effective communication is impaired, it is often useful for the group to suspend the task discussion and examine its own processes in order to define and attempt to solve the conflicts. The following questions will focus attention on a group's maintenance functions:

1. Are group members encouraged to enter into the discussion?
2. How well do members get their ideas across? Are some members preoccupied and not listening? Are there any attempts by group members to help others clarify their ideas?
3. How are ideas rejected? How do members react when their ideas are rejected?
4. Are conflicts among group members ignored or dealt with in some way?

Process Observation and Feedback

This note has covered seven important aspects of group process that can influence a group's effectiveness. The interventions suggested are relatively simple and can be made naturally and unobtrusively during the normal progress of a meeting. The more people in a group skilled at making process observations, the greater the likelihood that the group will not bog down, waste valuable time, or make poor decisions. For this reason an increasing number of U.S. and foreign firms have developed norms that encourage open discussions of group process. In many companies, meetings are ended with a brief feedback session on the group's process, during which the meeting's effectiveness is critiqued by the group members.

It is not necessary, however, to be in such a firm or to use terms such as *process feedback* to contribute to a group's effectiveness. Most of the ideas presented in this note are based on common sense; practicing them does not require using the terms described here. The underlying ideas described here are more important than the specific labels, such as task and maintenance functions, applied to them.

Foreign Students: Opportunities and Challenges for the Discussion Leader

Harvard Graduate School of Business Administration

(HBS No. 9-382-150)

The challenge which discussion pedagogy presents to North American students and instructors is well documented in many of the cases taught in this seminar. Those complexities, and opportunities, become increasingly evident when some members of a section come from overseas universities where teacher-student relationships are bounded by a very formal protocol and lecturing is the almost universal educational mode.

This note summarizes observations made by two Asian students about their experiences with discussion pedagogy. Student "A," currently twenty-eight years of age, had military and business experience before coming to this country. His undergraduate degree was from his nation's foremost university. He also had achieved an MBA from a leading American university; that school used cases only infrequently. He commented that he was "firmly determined to dedicate his life to the progress of human welfare through teaching and research in management."

His friend, Student "B," twenty-five years of age, was a citizen of the same Asian country. Student B had lived in five countries achieving his B-Comm and MBA at leading North American universities. "My career goals," he stated, "are to return home, after obtaining my doctorate, to pursue a life of learning, teaching and contributing to the field of business management."

Both students were aware of the instructional complexities created by the addition of foreign students to the typical seminar setting. But, they also stress the learning opportunities created for both American and foreign students, as well as for the instructor, in such a situation. Both commentaries stress two themes: first, that there is a need for greater sensitivity by instructors toward the foreign students' difficulties with language and culture and, secondly, that learning, given these circumstances, must be a collaborative effort among instructor, foreign students and American students.

Student A describes the difficulties confronting a foreign student both inside and outside the classroom. It is a very personal exploration of this problem. Student B's observations focus on the classroom process only and conclude with several normative suggestions to help instructors maximize the foreign students' personal learning and his or her contribution to the section's discussion process.

Student "A" Observations

To any foreign student, studying in the United States is one of the most memorable experiences in his or her life. This experience can be either rewarding or frustrating depending upon how he or she handles this unique opportunity. Suppose a typical foreign student in a developing country decides to go to the United States to study. Let's track the path he is going to take during the first several months.

Going to the U.S.A. to study is a culmination of his academic preparation in his country. Many people who love him see off him in the airport. Now, the long path of academic trial has begun. It will continue several years, involve a lot of money, and the sacrifice of many things he wanted to do but decided not to do in favor of study abroad. The goal is challenging, but potentially very rewarding: to become a leading scholar in his field who would enhance his and his country's prestige and leave an indelible mark on the history of his field.

Upon arriving in the U.S., he soon finds that his English is far from adequate and the linguistic handicap is more serious than he expected. Totally different culture, people, way of life buffet him day and night. Telephone ring often frightens him. He is afraid of speaking over the phone. Understandable! The guy phoning him has no idea of his listening and speaking ability, and speaks quite fast. Our poor student is so shy that he is reluctant to say "pardon." Oh, poor guy! At any rate, the first few weeks of tough adjustment pass by and school begins.

On the way to school, he recollects how the foreigners used to be treated by his compatriots in his country. They are curious to know something foreign, and very kind to foreigners. As a result, most foreigners visiting his country unanimously praise the people, the country, and say they will definitely visit this lovely land again. Now, he enters the classroom, and soon finds that he is the only foreigner in the class. What happens then? It doesn't take long time for him to find that nobody in the class is interested in him, nobody is curious to know something foreign, let alone his country. The contrast with his country cannot be sharper. Class after class, his sense of isolation deepens. Nobody speaks to him. He has nobody to talk to. The assignments for each class are literally pouring. But his classmates seem to master them quite easily. Everybody seems more brilliant than he. To get an A in any course seems almost impossible. His lofty goal of becoming a leading scholar seems so unrealistic. The time goes by so fast, and one day he finds that already several months have passed since he left home. On that day, the mid-term exam papers are returned. When the papers are being distributed, he becomes very nervous. He says to himself, "Anyway, I did my best despite formidable disadvantages. And given my well-recognized academic ability and best efforts, the result can't be bad." Finally, he receives his paper back. Oh, poor grade. It's "D." It's the first time that he gets D in any exam in his life. Moreover, the instructor wrote on the paper that he should see him sooner or later. On the way home, he compares himself to a defeated soldier.

When he arrives home, he finds a letter from his father. He hastily opens the envelope. The letter reads; "I'm very proud of you. Everybody who knows me envies me because I have such a bright son as you. They ask me how I taught you at home. My dear son, don't worry about anything except studying. We are sure that you will succeed." How would he react if he knows that I got D? Imagining his father's reaction, he becomes deeply depressed. He feels himself miserable. That night, he reflects on what has been wrong with the way he has been studying. He finally concludes that he was not making enough efforts to catch up with the class. Given his serious disadvantages as a foreign student, he should study much more, sleep less, than his classmates. With firm determination, he promises himself: "I will overcome." Suddenly, he finds himself recovering from pessimism and depression. The atmosphere of optimism and hope fills his room. He writes a reply to his father to the effect that he is doing quite well and he'll do his best to be a nice student whom his country can be proud of. The next day, he meets the professor who gave him "D." The professor's attitude is unexpectedly warm and encouraging. He says he understands the foreign student's predicament but there's nothing which cannot be overcome by honest efforts and strong will. Any foreign student who is bright enough to get into the university can meet all the academic requirements the School imposes. It sounds like a gospel to him. The professor looks like a Saint to him. He realizes how strong the power of a few words of consolation and encouragement can be. His resolution is further strengthened by his godsent stimulus. The professor is the first man who has shown sincere willingness to help him since he came to the U.S.

What really pleases him, however, is the realization of the fact that not everybody is indifferent to him and he need not feel so lonely. He is told that he can make friends with his classmates, provided he becomes open-minded enough to understand other people's differences. One of the most valuable lessons he should learn during his study abroad is that people are different but difference is not an obstacle to friendship and cooperation. Open your mind. Adopt a more positive attitude to your classmates. There's a common language between you and them which is called "understanding." World is more beautiful because it is so diverse and civilization rests on diversity of opinion and variety of thought, not on uniformity or standardization. He comes home with refreshed mind. It is not difficult to imagine how he did during the rest of the semester. He studied much harder, made several American friends, and enjoyed his life in the U.S. The final grades were not bad.

The reason I'm telling this story is to call the attention to the problems that are peculiar to foreign students. Studying in the U.S. has a very special meaning to every foreign student. To many of them, America is the academic paradise. They were told so many times about the prominent scholars, advanced facilities, the earnest atmosphere of the academic community dedicated to the cause of scholarly progress, in all of which America is No. 1 by any standard. In their mind, America is the Mecca of academia which any scholar committed to academic life should visit at some point in his life. They have spent many years to learn English. They have been highly regarded by their teachers, peers, and family. They expect something of those going abroad to study. This invisible expectation functions both as a positive stimulus and as pressure. The pressure sometimes is so overwhelming that some foreign students have committed suicide when they prematurely concluded that they were not meeting their country's expectation of them. When they decided that they are not doing well enough or their intellectual ability is short of the required level, the devil called "frustration" creeps in on them and obsesses them. This feeling of frustration can shatter the whole base of their self-confidence. They may even feel a sense of guilt toward their country, family, and former teachers. Also, their own expectation of study abroad is usually high. This is a very delicate problem. On the one hand, if the campus life and learning experience meet their expectation, they are sure to be strongly motivated to devote themselves to studying. On the other hand, the higher their expectation, the deeper their disappointment will be if, for one reason or another, the experience in a foreign university doesn't meet their expectation. In this case, the result can be serious. Unless they are mature enough to overcome such a deep feeling of disappointment, they are likely to feel a sense of regret, which they probably would not have felt had they stayed in their country.

In short, there are many occasions that are peculiar to them which can lead to catastrophic results. But the barriers—emotional, psychological, cultural, etc.—are far from insurmountable. Often it turns out that some barriers really do not exist, but *seem* to exist. The last thing they should develop is an inferiority complex. What is tricky with inferiority complex is that it tends to be self-fulfilling, i.e., when one senses a sense of inferiority, he is likely to be really inferior. Persistent and determined efforts to understand America and Americans, adjust to American life, and firm commitment to scholarly life is all that is required of them. Admittedly it's easier said than done, but it's a must.

I have no clear idea of what foreign students mean to their American counterparts and professors. One thing should be made clear. Foreign students add diversity to the campus life and their potential to contribute to academic progress is enormous. Think of the many current outstanding scholars who came to the U.S. as students and stayed here to become the stars in their field. Of course, they also have potential to disturb the campus life. It is not uncommon to find foreign students who have become troublemakers. Anything I have discussed—maladjustment, frustration, inferiority complex, regret, disappointment—can cause misbehavior. It is tempting to say that all depends upon who the individual in question is. Might be? It should be noted, however, that there are roles the American students and professors can play to help maximize the positive potential and minimize negative potential of foreign students. As the above story shows, a few words of encouragement is one way of doing that. The starting point should be the realization that they have been the invaluable reservoir of the innumerable brilliant figures in every field of science and their presence here is a boon to the U.S. Therefore, they are to be treated decently as welcome guests. A few kind acts, words, and warm attitude would do a great deal to boost their morale which is an easy prey to melancholy. Conversely, a few contemptuous acts, or a diatribe may produce more negative results than is thought.

If you are kind enough to listen to them carefully, and show your willingness to understand and help them, they will greatly appreciate your kindness and you will find that they have much to offer to you. It pays off to be their friends. You will find that they are eager to be friends of America and Americans. It's not too late to begin to listen to them. You will learn a lot from them. You will know how powerful the mutual trust can be, how fragile the nationality barrier is.

In conclusion, we can help each other, learn from each other, cooperate with each other. We are all families of the academic community. All those differences, nationality, custom, temperaments, etc., are concepts of low dimension that should be subordinated to the lofty and common goal that unites us all together; DEVOTION TO THE PROGRESS OF MANKIND THROUGH ACADEMIC ACHIEVEMENTS.

Student "B" Observations

A well-established pedagogical principle is that instructors should be sensitive to the particular needs of their students. This task is undoubtedly the most difficult in the case of the foreign student for here we are dealing not only with language difficulties but something much more fundamental—culture. While most instructors realize these problems exist, not all address them in an effective manner and some ignore them altogether. And yet, as foreign students increase at North American institutions, the instructor's ability to attend to the needs of this segment of the class will become more important. This being so, what then are the specific challenges and opportunities of having students from abroad in your class?

Language and culture seem to be the two most frequent issues mentioned regarding the difficulties of the foreign student. If instructors know what the key dimensions are, why can't they tackle the problem? The answer to that is that some, all too often, take simplistic approaches toward language and culture. For instance, some instructors assume that if a foreign student can speak and write English in a fairly understandable manner (to the instructor), the student will not have problems understanding the language. Of course, to be able to communicate at a reasonable level of English requires a certain amount of proficiency in the language.

The reality is, however, that most foreign students encounter difficulties with English in much more subtle ways. For instance, students in some Asian countries mockingly refer to their English as "Dictionary-English": in high school, we build up our English vocabulary by literally memorizing a dictionary. It is a small wonder then that we are mystified when a word is used with a different shade of meaning—there are only so many (meanings) one can memorize per word when the objective is vocabulary breadth! Also, a sentence can take on a different interpretation depending on the intonation, stress, or syntax. The foreign student has limited sensitivity to differentiate between such nuances. Finally, foreign students have trouble dealing with the colloquial expressions. That is something which is not emphasized enough abroad where greater stress is placed on formal usage of English. This might explain why the tone (such as in written reports) used by foreign students often appears to be unnecessarily formal.

A simplistic attitude toward culture also prevails often in the classroom. During college, this writer was always called upon in certain classes to be the "expert on Asia" ignoring the fact that he knew more about Chile and Spain than about this area. This tendency seems to be symptomatic nowadays in most business schools regarding Japanese students. People automatically assume Japanese students will talk about robots and quality control circles. Of course, foreigners often do conform to certain known cultural traits. However, instructors should treat foreign students on an individual level before boxing them into any cultural stereotypes.

The importance of understanding culture cannot be overstated. It permeates almost every facet of our lives, and consequently it is a major determinant of our behavior including that of the classroom. The foreign student's difficulties with cultural differences inside the classroom are usually manifested in two ways: (1) by his attitude toward the teacher-student learning contract, and (2) by his attitude toward class discussion process. The two are necessarily highly interdependent.

The teacher-student relationship is a very special institution in some cultures, particularly in the oriental countries. In those cultures obtaining an education is one of the primary goals in life. Because of the importance of the task (the students' learning), a teacher bears a tremendous responsibility toward not only his students but also to their parents and even in a remote sense to society in general. Because authority usually follows responsibility, teachers come to assume almost absolute control in the classroom. The teacher-student contract therefore is very explicitly clear: the teacher will set the premises in which learning will take place, it is his responsibility to determine how learning will be accomplished, and the student's role is to comply with the teacher's rules.

In one Asian country, two reasons are usually given as to why students are willing to accept this arrangement. One is that there is a strong cultural tradition that learned people should be regarded with the utmost respect and therefore students must obey them. A more cynical view espoused by some is that students abdicate control because they are lazy and find it easier to let others think for them. Regardless of which rationale is correct, the results appear to be virtually the same; students become highly dependent on their instructors. Some instructors who have had their academic training in the United States have returned to their native land and have tried to encourage more class participation from the students. They are, however, the exception rather than the rule.

The superior-subordinate relationship that exists between the instructor and the students in countries like the one described above also affects both their attitudes toward individualism. In most cases, instructors tend to treat their students as a single entity. This is a logical consequence of overcentralization of control especially when the class is large. The result is that there is little room for differences among individuals. This lack of individualism in the classroom is also reinforced by the type of examinations administered: standardized (nonessays), specific (nonopen-ended), and generally of the multiple-choice variety. In a sense, there is no ambiguity regarding the "right" answer. This also tends to encourage conformity, a factor which many Asian students attribute as causing them to appear to have limited creativity. While it is true that not all levels of education in Asia follow this system (e.g., in the last year of college instructors place more emphasis on individual work, but students often react perfunctorily rather than with enthusiasm to the new conditions), it is deeply ingrained in the formative years of schooling such that it influences future behavior.

Coming from a background such as the ones described above, many foreigners who come to the United States are often perplexed with their newly found "freedom" (or responsibility) in the classroom. This is especially true of the case method of instruction where the discussion by fellow students is one of the key modes of learning. Some foreigners believe the case method is too informal, aimless and without guidance. They are used to seeing much more discipline and structure in their classes.

They also have a hard time coming to grips with the fact that they and the instructor are "equals" (i.e., the terms of the teacher-student contract have changed), a difficulty often reflected in their persistence in calling instructors "Professor" and not by the first names, even when allowed. While maintaining their respect for the instructor they, in turn, sometimes decry the contribution of their fellow classmates especially when it is incongruent to their own beliefs. This also leads them to complain that the instructor tolerates too much "irrelevant" discussion without getting to the "right" answer. Of course, these students may be missing the essence of the case method which is predicated upon an open discussion of alternate viewpoints. In fact, divergence of opinion is encouraged so that students can help each other look at a particular issue from different standpoints. Although this idea runs counter to their deeply rooted beliefs, many foreign students come to adopt and enjoy this new style of learning. Hence, it is improper to assume all foreign students will resist change. Still, instructors must bear in mind that it is not easy for foreign students to bridge the cultural gaps which have taken years to form.

The opportunities of having foreign students participate in class discussions are great. First, it allows American students to learn about different cultural perspectives on any particular issue; this would be especially useful if the discussion is international in context. Second, the foreign students may be able to look at domestic issues in a more objective fashion; everyone is guilty of falling prey to ethnocentrism now and then, and hence foreigners can help American students be more even-handed in their approach. Finally, because of foreign students' difficulty of understanding different cultural viewpoints, American students are forced to be more articulate in class. Of course, all these benefits can be said conversely about the foreign student, i.e., he or she will also learn about American perspectives or other foreign cultures. In sum, class participation is meant to be a mutual learning process and therefore American students as well as the instructor have as much to learn from the foreign students as the foreign students do from them.

Given the challenges or difficulties of foreign students in adapting to the cultural and language differences, and also as we have seen the potential opportunities, what can an instructor do to encourage their participation?

Obviously, the first step an instructor should take is to recognize that foreign students do have a "handicap." But, many instructors stop right there. One possible reason for this is that it makes life less complicated (for the instructor). A more plausible argument is that even when instructors are sympathetic to the foreign student's difficulties, they feel they cannot help because it would be inequitable to the American students who represent the majority ("we cannot slow down the class just for them, besides, they are not the only students who have difficulties understanding . . ."). Another possible explanation for their inaction is that some instructors feel that by "helping," the "learning value" for the foreign students will be diminished; the so-called "learning-by-doing" school of thought. These latter two considerations are certainly valid concerns that any instructor should always have.

Nevertheless, instructors do not have to go too far out of their way to make life a little bit easier for the foreign students without violating equity and learning value. For example, some instructors speak more deliberately and less idiomatically when addressing foreign students. This certainly does not create inequity nor does it diminish learning value. One point that should be made here is that when instructors do help they should do so without appearing to be patronizing; foreign students despite their difficulties also have their dignity and it is possible that they might misunderstand the instructor's help as a subtle "putdown" of their contribution.

The second step instructors might take is to increase

their sensitivity toward possible difficulties encountered by foreign students. In our seminar, we talk often of the need to "read" signals being sent by students in difficulty. This is extremely difficult with the foreign student because the instructor is dealing with a different cultural base. There are, however, certain caveats that instructors should be aware of. First, do not confuse silence with apathy or lack of ability. The causes for the silence could be language problems or difficulties with the class process. Second, do not assume foreign students understand the material being discussed if they do not ask question; many cultures consider it improper to ask the instructor questions. Finally, do not assume students have no problems if they fail to come to talk about them in your office. Admittedly, these are very general, but given the fact that so many cultures may be involved in a classroom, it can be dangerous to be too specific.

The final step is to encourage everyone's participation. Professor Christensen's principle of giving students "small victories" seems to be ideally suited for this purpose. Instructors should relax (that is, if they have these rules) the process rule of not evaluating on students' contributions by saying simply, "good point" if it is a good point. We must remember that feedback to the students should be constructive in terms of learning value and also equitable to the other students. On the other hand, instructors should also pay particular attention to avoid sending the wrong signals. It is possible foreign students will misunderstand feedback which is too honest because they will interpret it using their own cultural frame of reference. If instructors are more sensitive to cultural differences, such misunderstandings might be avoided.

There is no denying that the steps outlined above demand a certain amount of effort on the part of the instructor. His or her task, however, will be appreciably facilitated if foreign students make a conscious effort to meet them halfway. With this mutual effort, the rewards to be realized will be tremendous. Without it, the costs will be equally great.

Talk and Chalk: The Blackboard as an Intellectual Tool

Michael O'Hare
University of California, Berkeley

How are we to explain the persistence of the classroom chalkboard in an electronic world? If it's still good enough for the twenty-first century, why is it rare in teaching spaces like hotel conference rooms, where mid-career training occurs?

These questions occurred to me as I spent several hours outside my own classroom in the space of a month, teaching a group of third graders how an airplane flies, watching some high school history and English classes, and being trained in media and press skills by experienced staff of a large public affairs firm. Forced to cope with alternatives at conferences and invited presentations, I have long realized how much variation existed among the information carrying capacities of the blackboard (I include wipe-off markerboards in this category) and its competition, the newsprint tablet on an easel, the slide projector, and the overhead projector.

I had not until recently realized how differently a blackboard functions in different institutions that all use it, or even among individuals similarly situated. Since I recall little conversation about this among colleagues, it seems worth recording some reflections on this venerable technology and its alternatives. The following is much in debt to the kind of exploration Erving Goffman demonstrated in *Forms of Talk* (1983) and elsewhere.

Aids to Talk

We may begin with Archimedes in the agora at Syracuse. Explaining to disciples what he had learned in his bathtub, it's hard to think he didn't scratch in the sand, and not "ευρεκα," either. Although the standup oral lecture can transmit a lot of information, sometimes you just have to show a picture of some sort. From this necessity arise such lecture aids as blackboard notes, the buildings in a walking tour, the slides an art historian shows, and the constructions in high school geometry class.

At the start, I want to exclude the category of props suggested by the buildings on the tour, or the slides of paintings in the art course, or an experimental setup in chemistry class. These are *exhibits:* they are the subject of the lecture, not part of it. Of such exhibits, we don't ask whether they are "true" or try to guess them as correct answers. If Archimedes had brought a curved mirror to class to explain his idea for burning attacking ships, it would have been an exhibit. What I'm concerned with is non-verbal elements of a class itself, what we say in ways other than speech *about* the subject of the class.

Did Archimedes draw the picture as he went along, starting out with an empty tub and then adding his body and changing the water level as he described his experiment, or did he start his lesson after preparing a complete diagram? Did his best student feel authorized to poke his own stick in and sketch a rubber ducky and a bronze one, saying "... what if the object is heavier than water?"

Slides and Notes

The answers to these questions are important, for they extend the idea of unspoken aids to talk in directions that have no standard names, but deserve them. The first version I will call *slides*. These may be sometimes the polished and colorful images prepared by presentation software, sometimes a professor's handwritten stack of lecture notes on acetate, sometimes photos from your cousin's summer vacation (but *not* from the fine arts library; see above). Slides appear on a blackboard when the teacher puts up notes, diagrams, or whatever before class starts. The critical quality is that they are prepared complete by the speaker before the event. (A degenerate form of such slides is the homework assignment or announcements of exam dates that find their way onto a corner of the board in many classrooms.)

Another way to use a blackboard and, sometimes, an overhead projector is to accumulate notes of a lecture as it unfolds. I will call these *lecture notes,* and they indeed often appear verbatim in the manuscripts students call by that name. These can be a few key vocabulary words or names to show spelling, key concepts, or the geometric proof itself as it progresses, or a full outline of the talk. Such aids are importantly different from slides, even though many teachers feel tempted to turn the one into the other, by means such as covering part of a prepared overhead with cardboard and then revealing it during the talk.

The difference is in the constant reminder transmitted by slides that nothing the listeners might do can change the discourse under way—indeed, that it would be presumptuous to even think about it. A stack of slides embodies the idea of one-way fact transmission. A stack of professionally prepared slides is probably its apotheosis. To alter the former would be presumptuous for a member of the audience; to amend the latter with the tools at hand during a meeting would be vandalism. Questions in such discourse are for the anticlimactic ten minutes at the end; help is neither sought nor welcome.

Conversely, if the pictures or notes really take form as the talk proceeds, the idea of interaction between audience and speaker is much more legitimate. If one were to interrupt with a question or a remark, the next notes would be different. One still might not do so, but one knows one could, so making slides as one talks engages an audience rather like a rhetorical question or a phrase like ". . . probably many of you noticed this driving here today. . . ."

If Archimedes allows his students to bring their own sticks to class, or even hands his to one of them and says, "here, show us, Harpides; why a duck?" his lecture becomes to some degree a collaborative exercise. It still has a leader and a hierarchy, but a lot of responsibility has suddenly been delegated (or shown to be delegated). The classroom analogue of this third model, which I will call *discussion notes,* is what might collect on a blackboard during a specific type of teaching, namely case-method discussion or a seminar. What is diagnostic here is not, incidentally, whether the students can actually write on the board but (i) the degree to which they can cause things to be written, and (ii) the creation of a single record visible to all at all times. Partly for reasons of arm length and avoiding distracting running back and forth, most discussions have a designated secretary recording the discussion—usually the teacher—but the model is unchanged; my colleague Robert Leone recommends that one not write anything on the board, except students' remarks, and in their own words.

Aids to Thought

Such teaching is organized so as to induce students to think through a real problem in a self-conscious and critical way. What we're concerned with is the process of thinking, not the answer; if the problem has a single right answer, like "22.3%", such that if someone blurted it out in the first five minutes the class would be ruined, it was the wrong sort of assignment. And the self-consciousness of the process is sought by doing the thinking in class, out loud, together; contrast this with having students present completed work in class, which is another sort of thing entirely, really a group of mini-lectures. Indeed, to the degree that students start lecturing each other in a discussion class, the class is in trouble and needs fixing.

A blackboard record of this kind is thus the physical symbol and embodiment of intellectual work of a certain kind. Since there is one of it, that everyone can see, it focuses attention on the task. Since everyone contributes to it, it is collaborative. Since it is constructed in real time, it has a history and sequence. Since it is extensive in two dimensions, it allows a more complicated structure than linear logical evolution or chronological or causal sequence.

Used for discussion notes, recording a group's intellectual work as it is performed, a blackboard has technical advantages that no other medium provides, despite efforts to update or adapt it and despite its subtle and significant defects. (Furthermore, this is the only visual aid function for which the blackboard is the best device; exhibits, slides and lecture notes are all better presented by other media.) Its particular virtues will be best revealed by considering the alternatives.

The overhead projector seems to be the coming thing. A colleague for whom I have great respect as a teacher and a thinker pulled a bunch of handwritten slides out of his briefcase on an airplane flight once, and remarked to me, "I love this technology; all I have to do is go over these slides from my files and I'm prepared for class." What he liked, I think, was that with transparencies instead of paper notes, he could look at what the students would be looking at, a sort of prewritten blackboard. There is more to an overhead projector, however; not only does it separate the writing of notes from their display like a 35mm projector, but it also allows these events to coincide, by writing directly on the slide currently in view. Furthermore, the optical path of an overhead allows a unique arrangement: the speaker can face the audience and the "canvas" which is being shown to it.[1]

The fact that the audience isn't quite looking at the work, but only at an image of it, is probably a minor disadvantage, though most people have trouble knowing where to point (at the screen, adopting the audience's point of view, or at the slide) for emphasis. The disjunction between the speaker's gaze as he highlights something and says "here," and the audience's appropriate response, which is to look somewhere else entirely, still makes me uncomfortable but I expect the awkwardness can be overcome with practice on both sides.

The great defect of the overhead projector for discussion notes, however, is that only one screen is visible at a time, and given the constraint that everything be legible from the back row, this simply does not allow enough of a record for a whole class. This defect is fatal. It's extremely important that everyone can see the whole history of the discussion at once; no courteous person will interrupt a class to ask for the sheet two slides back so he can confirm a recollection or find the third item in a list. For exactly the same reason that a painter stands in front of her canvas looking at it while she works,[2] the "artist" of the conversation, which is the whole group, must keep a single, consensual, summary of the work to date in view.

I have seen repeated efforts to duplicate a blackboard's function with newsprint pads on an easel, but they are only a little more successful than the overhead projector process. In the first place, the pad itself is even smaller than a projection screen, so one can only fit a few legible words on each sheet. In the second place, the endless running around taping or pinning sheets on the wall is distracting, and in any case no overall relationship among entries can be preserved, whereas one can write anywhere on a blackboard at any time ("lets put that over here at the side under 'tentative conclusions' and get to it later . . .").

Equally important, the blackboard is ephemeral, word by word or by larger units, and obviously so. Changing something on a newsprint pad just makes a mess of carats and strikeouts or scribbles or loses everything on the sheet; changing something on the blackboard requires only an effortless swipe. This has two important consequences: first, people are more willing to speak because they know that the group won't be stuck with what they say; second, people are willing to disagree and correct or sharpen insights ("shouldn't we have used the word *influence* back there instead of *power*?"). In this sense, a blackboard has a position in between informal speech and a written record, and there is not really any medium like it.

(In my dreams, I envision a classroom with a very large computer input pad at each desk. If recognized to "speak," a student can not only say something but can amend the screen before him—and before everyone else—with a stylus. At the end of class, everyone gets a paper printout of the screen to take home. I'm pretty sure I'm describing a minimal standard for the "new" blackboard, and not an ideal; anything less

[1] Well, theoretically "shown." Most meeting rooms and classrooms are provided with beaded screens whose reflectivity is restricted to a narrow cone that excludes many seats. People on the sides not only suffer the cosine error of obliquely viewing a flat object, but also cope with an extremely dim image. As the axis of the screen is usually higher than the projector's lens, keystoning throws the top and bottom thirds of the screen out of focus.

Further separating potential from actuality is the extreme difficulty most presenters have realizing how large they have to write, or what large type is necessary, to make a slide legible to the back rows. There is no mystery about this; but since the formula is not well known, I will provide it here:

If you take ordinary printed material in 10 pt. type at normal reading distance as a minimum, your characters on the screen should be about a hundredth as high as the distance from the viewer to the screen, which is about 1/8" per foot, or 3/8" per row of seats plus 1/2" for the space between the screen and the first row. In most rooms, the largest screen visible above heads is about five feet high, so a full vertical page of typed 10 pt. material will be 50 pt. type on the screen, or about 5/7" tall, legible about *five* feet away. At ten feet it will be like reading a phone book, and beyond . . . well, the speaker had better have a good oral style. An 8 1/2 × 11 transparency will hold about *four lines* of text for presentation to a group of 75. Most people have less trouble writing large enough, if not neatly enough, on a blackboard than they do on slides.

[2] Wollheim, Richard, *Painting as an Art*, Princeton U. Press, 1987, pp. 39–43.

(text terminals and keyboards, for example) is much less, indeed, not enough.)

Not understanding what a blackboard is has given rise to some unfortunate outcomes. My favorite professional association is engaged in a constant war with the hotels that host its conferences to get meeting rooms with conversational (horseshoe or circle) seating and blackboards, and because the hotels usually win, our sessions keep degenerating into lectures with snoozing, passive audiences instead of the electric exchanges we keep hoping for. The blackboard that will display an adequate record of an hour's work by twenty or more adults is not one of the flimsy wooden wheelabout things hotels keep in the basement, but something more like seventy-five square feet, firmly fixed to a wall.

I had the chance recently to teach in a "high-tech" classroom whose architects had been carefully protected from the faculty they were designing for. It had three enormous blackboards that slid up and down, with controls that were easy to understand at a glance. It had a powerful overhead projector with a tremendous reflective screen that went up and down quickly and quietly. And it had a truly priceless asset; a rear-projection video setup that could display a computer screen large enough for everyone to read right to the back of the room. Of course it had equipment for slides and movies; there was probably a virtual-reality setup that I never discovered.

However, the screens and the blackboards were one in front of the other, so only one could be seen at a time! This simplified sightlines, but it crippled the room for teaching purposes other than lectures, because the design failed to recognize the difference between an exhibit and discussion notes. If you're going to use a computer in a discussion class, or show a slide, you're going to have a discussion *about* the slide, or about what is happening in the spreadsheet, and the discussion has to go on the blackboard, and be visible at the *same time* people are looking at what they are talking about. We wound up with a ten-cent kludge for this million-dollar setup; the standard setup for screen use was to raise one of the three blackboards over the lower third of the projection screen, and illuminate it with the overhead projector so as not to wash out the whole screen.

Implications for Practice

Since we provide them no training, it must be the case that university teachers are all adept at using a blackboard; it's one of those things, like making up a reading list or grading papers, that we know magically from the moment we receive a doctorate. However, people in government and industry seem to spend a lot of time thinking about how to make presentations to groups and to make meetings productive. Those who do not share professors' good fortune might find the following questions about this low-tech backdrop useful, as I must admit I still do:

1. How do I want the work of the class allocated between myself and the students? Should they listen quietly, speak lines from a script that I will hint at as we proceed, or say things new to each other and to me?
2. What should be written or drawn on a blackboard, and when?
3. What should be written somewhere else (handouts, overhead slides, nowhere, etc.)?
4. Who gets to put things on the board, literally or in effect?
5. What does "higher" and "toward the right" mean about things written in different places on the board?
6. How many colors of chalk can I keep track of? What does each color mean?
7. What will the foregoing decisions signal to an alert student about her obligations and opportunities? How does this match my intentions in question 1?

The Crisis of Professional Knowledge and the Pursuit of an Epistemology of Practice

Donald A. Schön
Massachusetts Institute of Technology

The Crisis of Confidence in Professional Knowledge

Although our society has become thoroughly dependent on professionals, so much so that the conduct of business, industry, government, education, and everyday life would be unthinkable without them, there are signs of a growing crisis of confidence in the professions. In many well-publicized scandals, professionals have been found willing to use their special positions for private gain. Professionally designed solutions to public problems have had unanticipated consequences, sometimes worse than the problem they were intended to solve. The public has shown an increasing readiness to call for external regulations of professional practice. Laymen have been increasingly disposed to turn to the courts for defense against professional incompetence or venality. The professional's traditional claims to privileged social position and autonomy of practice have come into question as the public has begun to have doubts about professional ethics and expertise.[1] And in recent years, professionals themselves have shown signs of a loss of confidence in professional knowledge.

Not very long ago, in 1963, the editors of *Daedalus* could introduce a special volume on the professions with the sentence, "Everywhere in American life the professions are triumphant."[2] They noted the apparently limitless demand for professional services, the "shortages" of teachers and physicians, the difficulty of coordinating the proliferating technical specializations, the problem of managing the burgeoning mass of technical data. In the further essays which made up the volume, doctors, lawyers, scientists, educators, military men, and politicians articulated variations on the themes of professional triumph, overload, and growth. There were only two discordant voices. The representative of the clergy complained of declining influence and the "problem of relevance,"[3] and the city planner commented ruefully on his profession's lagging understandings of the changing ills of urban areas.[4] Yet in less than a decade the discordant notes had become the dominant ones and the themes of professional triumph had virtually disappeared.

In 1972 a colloquium on professional education was held at the Massachusetts Institute of Technology.

[1] Everett Hughes, "The Study of Occupations," in Merton and Broom, eds., *Sociology Today* (New York: Basic Books, 1959).

[2] Kenneth Lynn, Introduction to "The Professions." *Daedalus* 92, no. 4 (Fall 1963): 649.

[3] James Gustafson, "The Clergy in the United States." *Daedalus* 92, no. 4 (Fall 1963): 743.

[4] William Alonso, "Cities and City Planners." *Daedalus* 92, no. 4 (Fall 1963): 838.

Participants included distinguished representatives of the fields of medicine, engineering, architecture, planning, psychiatry, law, divinity, education, and management. These individuals disagreed about many things, but they held one sentiment in common—a profound uneasiness about their own professions. They questioned whether professionals would effectively police themselves. They wondered whether professionals were instruments of individual well-being and social reform or were mainly interested in the preservation of their own status and privilege, caught up in the very problems they might have been expected to solve. They allowed themselves to express doubts about the relevance and remedial power of professional expertise.

It is perhaps not very difficult to account for this dramatic shift, over a single decade, in the tone of professional self-reflection. Between 1963 and 1972 there had been a disturbing sequence of events, painful for professionals and lay public alike. A professionally instrumented war had been disastrous. Social movements for peace and civil rights had begun to see the professions as elitist servants of established interests. The much-proclaimed shortages of scientists, teachers, and physicians seemed to have evaporated. Professionals seemed powerless to relieve the rapidly shifting "crises" of the cities—poverty, environmental pollution, and energy. There were scandals of Medicare and, at the end of the decade, Watergate. Cumulatively, these events created doubts about professionally conceived strategies of diagnosis and cure. They pointed to the overwhelming complexity of the phenomena with which professionals were trying to cope. They led to skepticism about the adequacy of professional knowledge, with its theories and techniques, to cure the deeper causes of societal distress.

Sharing, in greater or lesser degree, these sentiments of doubt and unease, the participants in the MIT colloquium tried to analyze their predicament.

Some of them believed that social change had created problems ill-suited to the traditional division of labor. A noted engineer observed that "education no longer fits the niche, or the niche no longer fits education." The dean of a medical school spoke of the complexity of a huge health care system only marginally susceptible to the interventions of the medical profession. The dean of a school of management referred to the puzzle of educating managers for judgment and action under conditions of uncertainty.

Some were troubled by the existence of an irreducible residue of art in professional practice. The art deemed indispensable even to scientific research and engineering design seemed resistant to codification. As one participant observed, "If it's invariant and known, it can be taught; but it isn't invariant."

Professional education emphasized problem solving, but the most urgent and intractable issues of professional practice were those of problem finding. "Our interest," as one participant put it, "is not only how to pour the concrete for the highway, but what highway to build? When it comes to designing a ship, the question we have to ask is, which ship makes sense in terms of the problem of transportation?"

And representatives of architecture, planning, social work, and psychiatry spoke of the pluralism of their schools. Different schools held different and conflicting views of the competences to be acquired, [of] the problem to be solved, even of the nature of the professions themselves. A leading professor of psychiatry described his field as a "babble of voices."

Finally, there was a call for the liberation of the professions from the tyranny of the university-based professional schools. Everett Hughes, one of the founders of the sociology of the professions, declared that "American universities are products of the late nineteenth and early twentieth centuries. The question is, how do you break them up in some way—at least get some group of young people who are free of them? How do you make them free to do something new and different?"

The years that have passed since the 1972 colloquium have tended to reinforce its conclusions. In the early 1980s, no profession could celebrate itself in triumphant tones. In spite of the continuing eagerness of the young to embark on apparently secure and remunerative professional careers, professionals were still criticized, and criticized themselves, for failing both to adapt to a changing social reality and to live up to their own standards of practice. There was widespread recognition of the absence or loss of a stable institutional framework of purpose and knowledge within which professions can live out their roles and confidently exercise their skills.

In retrospect, then, it is not difficult to see why participants in the 1972 colloquium should have puzzled over the troubles of their professions. They were beginning to become aware of the indeterminate zones of practice—the situations of complexity and uncertainty, the unique cases that require artistry, the elusive task of problem setting, the multiplicity of professional identities—that have since become increasingly visible and problematic. Nevertheless, there is something strange about their disquiet. For professionals in many different fields do sometimes find ways of coping effectively, even wisely, with situations of complexity and uncertainty. If the element of art in professional practice is not invariant, known, and teachable, it does appear occasionally to be learnable. Problem setting is an activity in which some professionals engage with recognizable skill. And students and practitioners do occasionally make thoughtful choices from among the multiple views of professional identity.

Why, then, should a group of eminent professionals have been so troubled by the evidence of indeterminacy in professional practice?

It is not, I think, that they were unaware of the ways in which some practitioners cope reasonably well with situations of indeterminacy. Indeed, they might easily have counted themselves among those who do so. Rather, I suspect, they were troubled because they could not readily account for the coping process. Complexity and uncertainty are sometimes dissolved, but not by applying specialized knowledge to well-defined tasks. Artistry is not reducible to the exercise of describable routines. Problem finding has no place in a body of knowledge concerned exclusively with problem solving. In order to choose among competing paradigms of professional practice, one cannot rely on professional expertise. The eminent professionals were disturbed, I think, to discover that the competences they were beginning to see as central to professional practice had no place in their underlying model of professional knowledge.

In the following pages, I shall describe this underlying model—this implicit epistemology of practice—and I shall outline a fundamental dilemma of practice and teaching to which it leads. I shall propose that we seek an alternative epistemology of practice grounded in observation and analysis of the artistry competent practitioners sometimes bring to the indeterminate zones of their practice. I shall attempt a preliminary description and illustration of the "reflection-in-action" essential to professional artistry, and I shall suggest some of its implications for professional education.

The Dominant Model of Professional Knowledge

The epistemology of professional practice which dominates most thinking and writing about the professions, and which is built into the very structure of professional schools and research institutions, has been clearly set forth in two recent essays on professional education. Both of these treat rigorous professional practice as an exercise of technical rationality, that is, as an application of research-based knowledge to the solution of problems of instrumental choice.

Edgar Schein, in his *Professional Education,*[5] proposes a threefold division of professional knowledge:

1. An *underlying discipline* or *basic science* component upon which the practice rests or from which it is developed.
2. An *applied science* or *"engineering"* component from which many of the day-to-day diagnostic procedures and problem-solutions are derived.
3. A *skills and attitudinal* component that concerns the actual performance of services to the client, using the underlying basic and applied knowledge.

In Schein's view, these components constitute a hierarchy which may be read in terms of application, justification, and status. The application of basic science yields engineering, which in turn provides models, rules, and techniques applicable to the instrumental choices of everyday practice. The actual performance of services "rests on" applied science, which rests, in turn, on the foundation of basic science. In the epistemological pecking order, basic science is highest in methodological rigor and purity, its practitioners superior in status to those who practice applied science, problem solving, or service delivery.

Nathan Glazer, in a much-quoted article, argues that the schools of such professions as social work, education, divinity, and town planning are caught in a hopeless predicament.[6] These "minor" professions, beguiled by the success of the "major" professions of law, medicine, and business, have tried to substitute a basis in scientific knowledge for their traditional reliance on experienced practice. In this spirit, they have placed their schools within universities. Glazer believes, however, that their aspirations are doomed to failure. The "minor" professions lack the essential conditions of the "major" ones. They lack stable institutional contexts of practice, fixed and unambiguous ends which "settle men's minds,"[7] and a basis in systematic scientific knowledge. They cannot apply scientific knowledge to the solving of instrumental problems, and they are, therefore, unable to produce a rigorous curriculum of professional education.

> Can these fields (education, city planning, social work, and divinity) settle on a fixed form of train-

[5] Edgar Schein, *Professional Education* (New York: McGraw-Hill) p. 43.

[6] Nathan Glazer, "The Schools of the Minor Professions," in *Minerva* 12, no. 3 (1974): 362.

[7] Ibid., p. 363.

ing, a fixed content of professional knowledge, and follow the models of medicine, law, and business? I suspect not because the discipline of a fixed and unambiguous end in a fixed institutional setting is not given to them. And *thus* [my emphasis] the base of knowledge which is unambiguously indicated as relevant for professional education is also not given.[8]

Glazer and Schein share an epistemology of professional practice rooted historically in the positivist philosophy which so powerfully shaped both the modern university and the modern conception of the proper relationship of theory and practice.[9] Rigorous professional practice is conceived as essentially technical. Its rigor depends on the use of describable, testable, replicable techniques derived from scientific research, based on knowledge that is objective, consensual, cumulative, and convergent. On this view, for example, engineering is an application of engineering science; rigorous management depends on the use of management science; and policymaking can become rigorous when it is based on policy science.

Practice can be construed as technical, in this sense, only when certain things are kept clearly separate from one another. Deciding must be kept separate from doing. The rigorous practitioner uses his professional knowledge to *decide* on the means best-suited to his ends, his *action* serving to "implement" technically sound decisions. Means must be clearly separated from ends. Technical means are variable, appropriate, or inappropriate, according to the situation. But the ends of practice must be "fixed and unambiguous," like Glazer's examples of profit, health, and success in litigation; how is it possible, otherwise, to evolve a base of applicable professional knowledge? And finally research must be kept separate from practice. For research can yield new knowledge only in the protected setting of the scholar's study or in the carefully controlled environment of a scientific laboratory, whereas the world of practice is notoriously unprotected and uncontrollable.

These tenets of the positivist epistemology of practice are still built into our institutions, even when their inhabitants no longer espouse them. Just as Thorstein Veblen propounded some seventy years ago,[10] the university and the research institute are sheltered from the troublesome world of practice. Research and practice are presumed to be linked by an exchange in which researchers offer theories and techniques applicable to practice problems, and practitioners, in return, give researchers new problems to work on and practical tests of the utility of research results. The normative curriculum of professional education, as Schein describes it, still follows the hierarchy of professional knowledge. First, students are exposed to the relevant basic science, then to the relevant applied science, and finally to a practicum in which they are presumed to learn to apply classroom knowledge to the problems of practice. Medical education offers the prototype for such a curriculum, and its language of "diagnosis," "cure," "laboratory," and "clinic" have long since diffused to other professions.

From the perspective of this model of professional knowledge, it is not difficult to understand why practitioners should be puzzled by their own performance in the indeterminate zones of practice. Their performance does not fit the criteria of technical rationality; it cuts across the dichotomies built into the positivist epistemology of practice. Artistry, for example, is not only in the deciding but also in the doing. When planners or managers convert an uncertain situation into a solvable problem, they construct—as John Dewey pointed out long ago—not only the means to be deployed but the ends-in-view to be achieved. In such problem setting, ends and means are reciprocally determined. And often, in the unstable world of practice—where methods and theories developed in one context are unsuited to another—practitioners function as researchers, inventing the techniques and models appropriate to the situation at hand.

The Dilemma of Rigor and Relevance

For practitioners, educators, and students of the professions, the positivist epistemology of practice contributes to an urgent dilemma of rigor or relevance.

Given the dominant view of professional rigor—the view which prevails in the intellectual climate of the universities and is embedded in the institutional arrangements of professional education and research—rigorous practice depends on well-formed problems[11] of instrumental choice to whose solutions

[8] Ibid., p. 363.

[9] For a discussion of positivism and its influence on prevailing epistemological views, see Jergen Habermas, *Knowledge and Human Interests* (Boston, Mass.: Beacon Press, 1968). And for a discussion of the influence of positivist doctrines on the shaping of the modern university, see Edward Shils, "The Order of Learning in the United States from 1865 to 1920: The Ascendancy of the Universities," *Minerva* 16, no. 2 (1978).

[10] See Thorstein Veblen, *The Higher Learning in America,* reprint of the 1918 edition. (New York City: August M. Kelley, 1965).

[11] I have taken this term from Herbert Simon, who gives a particularly useful example of a well-formed problem in *The Science of the Artificial* (Cambridge, Mass.: MIT Press, 1972).

research-based theory and technique are applicable. But real-world problems do not come well formed. They tend to present themselves, in the contrary, as messy, indeterminate, problematic situations. When a civil engineer worries about what road to build, for example, he does not have a problem he can solve by an application of locational techniques or decision theory. He confronts a complex and ill-defined situation in which geographic, financial, economic, and political factors are usually mixed up together. If he is to arrive at a well-formed problem, he must construct it from the materials of the problematic situation. And the problem of problem setting is not a well-formed problem.[12]

When a practitioner sets a problem, he chooses what he will treat as the "things" of the situation. He decides what he will attend to and what he will ignore. He names the objects of his attention and frames them in an appreciative context which sets a direction for action. A vague worry about hunger or malnourishment may be framed, for example, as a problem of selecting an optimal diet. But situations of malnourishment may also be framed in many different ways.[13] Economists, environmental scientists, nutrition scientists, agronomists, planners, engineers, and political scientists debate over the nature of the malnourishment problem, and their discussions have given rise to a multiplicity of problem settings worthy of *Rashomon.* Indeed, the practice of malnourishment planning is largely taken up with the task of constructing the problem to be solved.

When practitioners succeed in converting a problematic situation to a well-formed problem, or in resolving a conflict over the proper framing of a practitioner's role in a situation, they engage in a kind of inquiry which cannot be subsumed under a model of technical problem solving. Rather, it is through the work of naming and framing that the exercise of technical rationality becomes possible.

Similarly, the artistic processes by which practitioners sometimes make sense of unique cases, and the art they sometimes bring to everyday practice, do not meet the prevailing criteria of rigorous practice. Often, when a competent practitioner recognizes in a maze of symptoms the pattern of a disease, constructs a basis for coherent design in the peculiarities of a building site, or discerns an understandable structure in a jumble of materials, he does something for which he cannot give a complete or even a reasonably accurate description. Practitioners make judgments of quality for which they cannot state adequate criteria, display skills for which they cannot describe procedures or rules.

By defining rigor only in terms of technical rationality, we exclude as nonrigorous much of what competent practitioners actually do, including the skillful performance of problem setting and judgment on which technical problem solving depends. Indeed, we exclude the most important components of competent practice.

In the varied topography of professional practice, there is a high, hard ground which overlooks a swamp. On the high ground, manageable problems lend themselves to solution through the use of research-based theory and technique. In the swampy lowlands, problems are messy and confusing and incapable of technical solution. The irony of this situation is that the problems of the high ground tend to be relatively unimportant to individuals or to society at large—however great their technical interest may be—while in the swamp lie the problems of greatest human concern. The practitioner is confronted with a choice. Shall he remain on the high ground where he can solve relatively unimportant problems according to his standards of rigor, or shall he descend to the swamp of important problems and nonrigorous inquiry?

Consider medicine, engineering, and agronomy—three of Glazer's major or near-major professions. In these fields, there are areas in which problems are clearly defined, goals are relatively fixed, and phenomena lend themselves to the categories of available theory and technique. Here, practitioners can function effectively as technical experts. But when one or more of these conditions is lacking, competent performance is no longer a matter of exclusively technical expertise. Medical technologies like kidney dialysis or tomography have created demands which stretch the nation's willingness to invest in medical care. How should physicians behave? How should they try to influence or accommodate to health policy? Engineering solutions which seem powerful and elegant when judged from a relatively narrow perspective may have a wider range of consequences which degrade the environment, generate unacceptable risk, or put excessive demands on scarce resources. How should engineers take these factors into account in their actual designing? When agronomists recommend efficient methods of soil cultivation that favor the use of large landholdings, they may undermine the viability of the small family farms on which peasant economies

---

12 Martin Rein and I have written about problem setting in "Problem Setting in Policy Research," in Carol Weiss, ed., *Using Social Research in Public Making* (Lexington, Mass.: D. C. Heath, 1977).

13 For an example of multiple views of the malnourishment problem, see Berg, Scrimshaw and Call, eds., *Nutrition, National Development, and Planning* (Cambridge, Mass.: MIT Press, 1973).

depend. How should the practice of agronomy take such considerations into account? These are not problems, properly speaking, but problematic situations from which problems must be constructed. If practitioners choose not to ignore them they must approach them through kinds of inquiry which are, according to the dominant model of technical rationality, unrigorous.

The doctrine of technical rationality, promulgated and maintained in the universities and especially in the professional schools, infects the young professional-in-training with a hunger for technique. Many students of urban planning, for example, are impatient with anything other than "hard skills." In schools of management, students often chafe under the discipline of endless case analysis; they want to learn the techniques and algorithms which are, as they see it, the key to high starting salaries. Yet a professional who really tried to confine his practice to the rigorous applications of research-based technique would find not only that he could not work on the most important problems but that he could not practice in the real world at all.

Nearly all professional practitioners experience a version of the dilemma of rigor or relevance, and they respond to it in one of several ways. Some of them choose the swampy lowland, deliberately immersing themselves in confusing but crucially important situations. When they are asked to describe their methods of inquiry, they speak of experience, trial and error, intuition or muddling through. When teachers, social workers, or planners operate in this vein, they tend to be afflicted with a nagging sense of inferiority in relation to those who present themselves as models of technical rigor. When physicians or engineers do so, they tend to be troubled by the discrepancy between the technical rigor of the "hard" zones of their practice and the apparent sloppiness of the "soft" ones.

Practitioners who opt for the high ground confine themselves to a narrowly technical practice and pay a price for doing so. Operations research, systems analysis, policy analysis, and some management science are examples of practices built around the use of formal, analytical models. In the early years of the development of these professions, following World War II, there was a climate of optimism about the power of formal models to solve real-world problems. In subsequent decades, however, there was increasing recognition of the limited applicability of formal models, especially in situations of high complexity and uncertainty.[14] Some practitioners have responded by confining themselves to a narrow class of well-formed problems—in inventory control for example. Some researchers have continued to develop formal models for use in problems of high complexity and uncertainty, quite undeterred by the troubles incurred whenever a serious attempt is made to put such models into practice. They pursue an agenda driven by evolving questions of modeling theory and techniques, increasingly divergent from the contexts of actual practice.

Practitioners may try, on the other hand, to cut the situations of practice to fit their models, employing for this purpose one of several procrustean strategies. They may become selectively inattentive to data incongruent with their theories,[15] as some educators preserve their confidence in "competency testing" by ignoring the kinds of competence that competency testing fails to detect. Physicians or therapists may use junk categories like "patient resistance" to explain away the cases in which an indicated treatment fails to lead to cure.[16] And social workers may try to make their technical expertise effective by exerting unilateral control over the practice situation—for example, by removing "unworthy" clients from the case rolls.

Those who confine themselves to a limited range of technical problems on the high ground, or cut the situations of practice to fit available techniques, seek a world in which technical rationality works. Even those who choose the swamp tend to pay homage to prevailing models of rigor. What they know how to do, they have no way of describing as rigorous.

Writers about the professions tend to follow similar paths. Both Glazer and Schein, for example, recognize the indeterminate zones of professional practice. But Glazer relegates them to the "minor" professions, of which he despairs. And Schein locates what he calls "divergent" phenomena of uncertainty, complexity, and uniqueness in concrete practice situations, while at the same time regarding professional knowledge as increasingly "convergent." He thinks convergent knowledge may be applied to divergent practice through the exercise of "divergent skills"[17]—about which, however, he is able to say very little. For if divergent skills were treated in terms of theory or technique, they would belong to convergent professional knowledge; and if they are neither theory nor technique, they cannot be described as knowledge at all. Rather, they function as a kind of junk category

[14] See Russell Ackoff, "The Future of Operational Research is Past," *Journal of Operational Research Soc.* 30 (1979): 93–104.

[15] I have taken this phrase from the work of the psychiatrist, Harry Stack Sullivan.

[16] The term is Clifford Geertz's. See *The Interpretation of Cultures: Selected Essays* by Clifford Geertz (New York: Basic Books, 1973).

[17] Schein, *Professional Education*, p. 44.

which serves to protect an underlying model of technical rationality.

Yet the epistemology of practice embedded in our universities and research institutions—ingrained in our habits of thought about professional knowledge, and at the root of the dilemma of rigor or relevance—has lost its hold on the field that nurtured it. Among philosophers of science, no one wants any longer to be called a positivist.[18] There is a rebirth of interest in the ancient topics of craft, artistry, and myth—topics whose fate positivism seemed once to have finally sealed. Positivism and the positivist epistemology of practice now seem to rest on a particular *view* of science, one now largely discredited.

It is timely, then, to reconsider the question of professional knowledge. Perhaps there is an epistemology of practice which takes full account of the competence practitioners sometimes display in situations of uncertainty, complexity, and uniqueness. Perhaps there is a way of looking at problem setting and intuitive artistry which presents these activities as describable and susceptible to a kind of rigor that falls outside the boundaries of technical rationality.

Reflection-in-Action

When we go about the spontaneous, intuitive performance of the actions of everyday life, we show ourselves to be knowledgeable in a special way. Often, we cannot say what we know. When we try to describe it, we find ourselves at a loss, or we produce descriptions that are obviously inappropriate. Our knowing is ordinarily tacit, implicit in our patterns of action and in our feel for the stuff with which we are dealing. It seems right to say that our knowing is *in* our action. And similarly, the workaday life of the professional practitioner reveals, in its recognitions, judgments and skills—a pattern of tacit knowing-in-action.

Once we put technical rationality aside, thereby giving up our view of competent practice as an *application* of knowledge to instrumental decisions, there is nothing strange about the idea that a kind of knowing is inherent in intelligent action. Common sense admits the category of know-how, and it does not stretch common sense very much to say that the know-how is *in* the action—that a tightrope walker's know-how, for example, lies in, and is revealed by, the way he takes his trip across the wire; or that a big-league pitcher's know-how is in his way of pitching to a batter's weakness, changing his pace, or distributing his energies over the course of a game. There is nothing in common sense to make us say that know-how consists in rules or plans which we entertain in the mind prior to action. Although we sometimes think before acting, it is also true that in much of the spontaneous behavior of skillful practice we reveal a kind of knowing which does not stem from a prior intellectual operation.

As Gilbert Ryle puts it:

> What distinguishes sensible from silly operations is not their parentage but their procedure, and this holds no less for intellectual than for practical performances. "Intelligent" cannot be defined in terms of "intellectual" or "knowing-*how*" in terms of "knowing *that*"; "thinking what I am doing" does not connote "both thinking what to do and doing it." When I do something intelligently . . . I am doing one thing and not two. My performance has a special procedure or manner, not special antecedents.[19]

Andrew Harrison has expressed a similar thought by saying that when someone acts intellectually, he "acts his mind."[20]

Examples of intelligence in action include acts of recognition and judgment, as well as the exercise of ordinary physical skills.

Michael Polanyi has written about our ability to recognize a face in a crowd.[21] The experience of recognition can be immediate and holistic. We simply see, all of a sudden, the face of someone we know. We are aware of no antecedent reasoning and we are often unable to list the features that distinguish this face from the hundreds of others present in the crowd.

When the thing we recognize is "something wrong" or "something right," then recognition takes the form of judgment. Chris Alexander has called attention to

---

[18] As Richard Bernstein has written in *The Restructuring of Social and Political Theory* (New York: Harcourt, Brace, Jovanovich, 1976), "There is not a single major thesis advanced by either nineteenth century Positivists or the Vienna Circle that has not been devastatingly criticized when measured by the Positivists' own standards for philosophical argument. The original formulations of the analytic-synthetic dichotomy and the verifiability criterion on meaning have been abandoned. It has been effectively shown that the Positivists' understanding of the natural sciences and the formal disciplines is grossly oversimplified. Whatever one's final judgment about the current disputes in the post-empiricist philosophy and history of science . . . there is rational agreement about the inadequacy of the original Positivist understanding of science, knowledge, and meaning."

[19] Gilbert Ryle, "On Knowing How and Knowing That," in *The Concept of Mind* (London: Hutchinson, 1949), p. 32.

[20] Andrew Harrison, *Making and Thinking* (Indianapolis: Hacket, 1978).

[21] Michael Polanyi, *The Tacit Dimension* (New York: Doubleday Publishing Co., 1967), p. 12.

the innumerable judgments of "mismatch"—deviations from a tacit norm—that are involved in the making of a design.[22] And Geoffrey Vickers has gone on to note that not only in artistic judgment but in all our ordinary judgments of quality, we "can recognize and describe deviations from a norm very much more clearly than we can describe the norm itself."[23] A young friend of mine who teaches tennis observes that his students have to be able to feel when they're hitting the ball right, and they have to like that feeling, as compared to the feeling of hitting it wrong; but they need not, and usually cannot, describe either the feeling of hitting it right or what they do to get that feeling. A skilled physician can sometimes recognize "a case of . . ." the moment a person walks into his office. The act of recognition comes immediately and as a whole; the physician may not be able to say, subsequently, just what led to his initial judgment.

Polanyi has described our ordinary tactile appreciation of the surface of materials. If you ask a person what he feels when he explores the surface of a table with his hand, he is apt to say that the table feels rough or smooth, sticky or slippery, but he is unlikely to say that he feels a certain compression and abrasion of his fingertips—though it must be from this kind of feeling that he gets to his appreciation of the table's surface. Polanyi speaks of perceiving *from* these fingertip sensations *to* the qualities of the surface. Similarly, when we use a stick to probe a hidden place, we focus not on the impressions of the stick on our hand but on the qualities of the place which we apprehend through these tacit impressions. To become skillful in the use of a tool is to learn to appreciate, as it were, directly, the qualities of materials that we apprehend *through* the tacit sensations of the tool in our hand.

Chester Barnard has written of "non-logical processes" that we cannot express in words as a process of reasoning, but evince only by a judgment, decision, or action.[24] A child who has learned to throw a ball makes immediate judgments of distance, which he coordinates, tacitly, with the feeling of bodily movement involved in the act of throwing. A high-school boy, solving quadratic equations, has learned spontaneously to carry out a program of operations that he cannot describe. A practiced accountant of Barnard's acquaintance could take a balance sheet of considerable complexity and within minutes or even seconds get a significant set of facts from it, though he could not describe in words the recognitions and calculations that entered into his performance. Similarly, we are able to execute spontaneously such complex activities as crawling, walking, riding a bicycle, or juggling, without having to think, in any conscious way, what we are doing, and often without being able to give a verbal description even approximately faithful to our performance.

In spite of their tacit complexity and virtuosity, however, our spontaneous responses to the phenomena of everyday life do not always work. Sometimes our knowing-in-action yields surprises. And we often react to the unexpected by a kind of on-the-spot inquiry which I shall call *reflection-in-action.*

Sometimes this process takes the form of ordinary, on-line problem solving. It need not even be associated with a high degree of skill but may consist in an amateur's effort to acquire skill. Recently, for example, I built a wooden gate. The gate was made of wooden pickets and strapping. I had made a drawing of it, and figured out the dimensions I wanted, but I had not reckoned with the problem of keeping the structure square. I noticed, as I began to nail the strapping to the pickets, that the whole thing wobbled. I knew that when I nailed in a diagonal piece, the structure would become rigid. But how would I be sure that, at that moment, the structure would be square? I stopped to think. There came to mind a vague memory about diagonals—that in a square, the diagonals are equal. I took a yardstick, intending to measure the diagonals, but I found it difficult to make these measurements without disturbing the structure. It occurred to me to use a piece of string. Then it became apparent that I needed precise locations from which to measure the diagonal from corner to corner. After several frustrating trials, I decided to locate the center point at each of the corners (by crossing diagonals at each corner), hammered in a nail at each of the four center points, and used the nails as anchors for the measurement string. It took several moments to figure out how to adjust the structure so as to correct the errors I found by measuring; and when I had the diagonals equal, I nailed in a piece of strapping that made the structure rigid.

Here—in an example that must have its analogues in the experience of amateur carpenters the world over—my intuitive way of going about the task led me to a surprise (the discovery of the wobble) which I interpreted as a problem. Stopping to think, I invented procedures to solve the problem, discovered further unpleasant surprises, and made further corrective inventions, including the several minor in-

[22] Chris Alexander, *Notes Toward the Synthesis of Forum* (Cambridge, Mass.: Harvard University Press, 1964).

[23] Geoffrey Vickers, unpublished memorandum, MIT, 1978.

[24] Chester Barnard, *The Functions of the Executive* (Cambridge, Mass.: Harvard University Press, 1968), p. 306; first published in 1938.

ventions necessary to make the idea of string-measurement of diagonals work.

Ordinarily, we might call such a process "trial and error." But it is not a series of random trials continued until a desired result has been produced. The process has a form—an inner logic according to which reflection on the unexpected consequences of one action influences the design of the next one. The "moments" of such a process may be described as follows:

- In the context of the performance of some task, the performer spontaneously initiates a routine of action that produces an unexpected outcome.
- The performer notices the unexpected result which he construes as a surprise—an error to be corrected, an anomaly to be made sense of, an opportunity to be exploited.
- Surprise triggers reflection, directed both to the surprising outcome and to the knowing-in-action that led to it. It is as though the performer asked himself, "What *is* this?" and at the same time, "What understandings and strategies of mine have led me to produce this?"
- The performer restructures his understanding of the situation—his framing of the problem he has been trying to solve, his picture of what is going on, or the strategy of action he has been employing.
- On the basis of the restructuring, he invents a new strategy of action.
- He tries out the new action he has invented, running an on-the-spot experiment whose results he interprets, in turn, as a "solution"—an outcome on the whole satisfactory—or else as a new surprise that calls for a new round of reflection and experiment.

In the course of such a process, the performer *reflects,* not only in the sense of thinking about the action he has undertaken and the result he has achieved, but in the more precise sense of turning his thought back on the knowing-in-action implicit in his action. He reflects *in action,* in the sense that his thinking occurs within the boundaries of what I call an action-present—a stretch of time within which it is still possible to make a difference to the outcomes of action.

Examples: These are examples of reflection-in-action drawn from some of the familiar contexts of professional practice:

- A designer, hard at work on the design of a school, has been exploring the possible configurations of small, classroom units. Having tried a number of these, dissatisfied with the formal results, she decides that these units are "too small to do much with." She tries combining the classrooms in L-shaped pairs and discovers that these are "formally much more significant" and that they have the additional, unexpected educational advantage of putting grade one next to grade two and grade three next to grade four.
- A teacher has a young student, Joey, who disturbs her by insisting that an eclipse of the sun did not take place because "it was snowing and we didn't see it." It occurs to the teacher that Joey does not know that the sun is there, even if he can't see it, and she asks him, "Where was the sun yesterday?" Joey answers, "I don't know; I didn't see it." Later, it occurs to her that his answer may have reflected not his ignorance of the sun remaining in the sky but his interpretation of her question. She thinks that he may have read her as asking, "*Where* in the sky was the sun?" With this in mind, she tries a new question: "What happened to the sun yesterday?"—to which Joey answers, "It was in the sky."

In such examples as these, reflection-in-action involves a "stop-and-think." It is close to conscious awareness and is easily put into words. Often, however, reflection-in-action is smoothly embedded in performance; there is no stop-and-think, no conscious attention to the process, and no verbalization. In this way, for example, a baseball pitcher adapts his pitching style to the peculiarities of a batter; a tennis player executes split-second variations in play in order to counter the strategies of his opponent. In such cases, we are close to processes we might recognize as examples of artistry.

When good jazz musicians improvise together, they display a feel for the performance. Listening to one another and to themselves, they feel where the music is going and adjust their playing accordingly. They are inventing on-line, and they are also responding to surprises provided by the inventions of the others. A figure announced by one performer will be taken up by another, elaborated, and perhaps integrated with a new melody. The collective process of musical invention is not usually undertaken at random, however. It is organized around an underlying structure—a shared scheme of meter, melody, and harmony that gives the piece a predictable order. In addition, each of the musicians has ready a repertoire of musical figures that he can play, weaving variations of them as the opportunity arises. Improvisation consists in varying, combining, and recombining a set of figures within the scheme that gives coherence to the whole performance. As the musicians feel the direction in which the music is developing out of their interwoven contributions, they make new sense of it and adjust their performances to the sense they make. They are reflecting-in-action on the music they are collectively making, though not, of course, in the medium of words.

Their process is not unlike the familiar improvisation of everyday conversation, which does occur in the medium of words. A good conversation is both predictable and, in some respects, unpredictable. The participants may pick up themes suggested by others, developing them through the associations they provoke. Each participant seems to have a readily available repertoire of kinds of things to say, around which we can develop variations suited to the present occasion. Conversation is collective verbal improvisation which tends to fall into conventional routines—for example, the anecdote (with appropriate side comments and reactions) or the debate—and it develops according to a pace and rhythm of interaction that the participants seem, without conscious attention, to work out in common. At the same time, there are surprises—in the form of unexpected turns of phrase or directions of development. Participants make on-the-spot responses to surprise, often in conformity to the kind of conversational role they have adopted. Central to the other forms of improvisation, there is a conversational division of labor that gradually establishes itself, often without conscious awareness on the part of those who work it out.

In the on-the-spot improvisation of a musical piece or a conversation, spontaneous reflection-in-action takes the form of a kind of production. The participants are involved in a collective *making* process. Out of the "stuff" of this musical performance, or this talk, they make a piece of music, or a conversation—in either case, an artifact that has, in some degree, order, meaning, development, coherence. Their reflection-in-action becomes a reflective conversation—this time, in a metaphorical sense—with the materials of the situation in which they are engaged. Each person, carrying out his own evolving role in the collective performance, *listens* to the things that happen—including the surprises that result from earlier moves—and responds, on-line, through new moves that give new directions to the development of the artifact. The process is reminiscent of Carpenter's description of the Eskimo sculptor who, patiently carving a reindeer bone and examining the gradually changing shape, finally exclaims "Ah, seal!"

That one can engage in spontaneous reflection-in-action without being able to give a good description of it is evident from experience. Typically, when a performer is asked to talk about the reflection and on-the-spot experimenting that he has just carried out, he gives at first a description which is obviously incomplete or inaccurate. And by comparing what he says to what he has just done, he can often discover this for himself.

Clearly, it is one thing to engage spontaneously in a performance that involves reflection-in-action, and quite another thing to reflect on that reflection-in-action through an act of description. Indeed, these several, distinct kinds of reflection can play important roles in the process by which an individual learns a new kind of performance. A tennis coach (Galloway) reports his use of an exercise in which he repeatedly asks his students to say where their racket was when they hit the ball; he intends to help them get more precisely in touch with what they are doing when they hit the ball, so that they will *know* what they are doing when they try to correct their errors. Seymour Papert used to teach juggling by informing would-be jugglers that they are susceptible to a variety of kinds of *bugs*—that is, to typical mistakes ("bugs" by analogy with computer programming) such as "throwing too far forward" or "overcorrecting" an error. He would ask them from time to time to describe the "bug" they had just enacted.

Professional practitioners, such as physicians, managers, and teachers, also reflect-in-action—but their reflection is of a kind particular to the special features of professional practice. *Practice* has a double meaning. A lawyer's practice includes the kinds of activities he carries out, the clients he serves, the cases he is called upon to handle. When we speak of practicing the performance, on the other hand, we refer to the repetitive yet experimental process by which one learns, for example, to play a musical instrument. The two senses of *practice,* although quite distinct, relate to one another in an interesting way. Professional practice also includes repetition. A professional is, at least in some measure, a specialist. He deals with certain types of situations, examples, images, and techniques. Working his way through many variations of a limited number of cases, he "practices" his practice. His know-how tends to become increasingly rich, efficient, tacit, and automatic, thereby conferring on him and his clients the benefits of specialization. On the other hand, specialization can make him narrow and parochial, inducing a kind of overlearning which takes the form of a tacit pattern of error to which he becomes selectively inattentive.

Reflection *on* spontaneous reflection-in-action can serve as a corrective to overlearning. As a practitioner surfaces the tacit understandings that have grown up around the repetitive experiences of a specialized practice, he may allow himself to notice and make new sense of confusing and unique phenomena.

A skillful physician, lawyer, manager, or architect continually engages in a process of appreciating, probing, modeling, experimenting, diagnosing, psyching out, evaluating—which he can describe imperfectly if at all. His knowing-in-action is revealed and presented by his feel for the stuff with which he deals. When he tries, on rare occasions, to say what he knows—when he tries to put his know*ing* into the form of know*ledge*—his formulations of principles, theories, maxims, and rules of thumb are often incongruent with the understanding and know-how implicit in his pattern of practice.

On the other hand—contrary to Hannah Arendt's observation that reflection is out of place in action—skillful practitioners sometimes respond to a situation that is puzzling, unique, or conflicted, by reflecting at one and the same time on the situation before them and on the reflection-in-action they spontaneously bring to it. In the midst of action, they are able to turn thought back upon itself—surfacing, criticizing, and restructuring the thinking by which they have spontaneously tried to make the situation intelligible to themselves. There are, for example:

- managers who respond to turbulent situations by constructing and testing a model of the situation and experimenting with alternative strategies for dealing with it;
- physicians who, finding that "80% of the cases seen in the office are not found in the book," treat each patient as a unique case—constructing and testing diagnoses, inventing and evaluating lines of treatment through processes of on-the-spot experiment;
- engineers who discover that they cannot apply their rules of thumb to a situation because it is anomalous or peculiarly constrained (like the shattering of windows on the John Hancock building in Boston), and proceed to devise and test theories and procedures unique to the situation at hand;
- lawyers who construct new ways to assimilate a puzzling case to a body of judicial precedent;
- bankers who feel uneasy about a prospective credit risk—even though his "operating numbers" are all in order—and try to discover and test the implicit judgments underlying their uneasiness;
- planners who treat their plans as tentative programs for inquiry, alert to discovering the unanticipated meanings their interventions turn out to have for those affected by them.

Kinds and Levels of Reflection

Many such examples of reflection on reflection-in-action occur in the indeterminate zones of practice—uncertain, unique, or value-conflicted. Depending on the context and the practitioner, such inquiry may take the form of on-the-spot problem solving, or it may take the form of theory building, or reappreciation of the problem of the situation. When the problem at hand proves resistant to readily accessible solutions, the practitioner may rethink the approach he has been taking and invent new strategies of action. When he encounters a situation that falls outside his usual range of descriptive categories, he may surface and criticize his initial understandings and proceed to construct a new, situation-specific theory of the phenomena before him. (The best theories, Kevin Lynch observed, are those we make up in the situation.) When he finds himself stuck, he may decide that he has been working on the wrong problem, and evolve a new way of setting the problem.

The objects of reflection may lie anywhere in the system of understanding and know-how that a practitioner brings to his practice. Depending on the centrality of the elements he chooses to surface and rethink, more or less of that system may become vulnerable to change. But, systems of intuitive knowing are dynamically conservative, actively defended, highly resistant to change. They tend not to go quietly to their demise, and reflection-in-action often takes on a quality of struggle. In the early minutes and hours of the "accident" at the Three Mile Island nuclear power plant, for example, operators and managers found themselves confronted with combinations of signals they could only regard as "weird"—unprecedented, unlike anything they had ever seen before.[25] Yet they persisted in attempting to assimilate these strange and perplexing signals to a situation of normalcy—"not wanting to believe," as one manager put it, that the nuclear core had been uncovered and damaged. Only after twelve hours of fruitless attempts to construe the situation as a minor problem—a breach in a steam line, a buildup of steam in the primary circulatory system—did one anonymous key manager insist, against the wishes of others in the plant, that "future actions be based on the assumption that the core has been uncovered, the fuel severely damaged."

Many practitioners, locked into a view of themselves as technical experts, find little in the world of practice to occasion reflection. For them, uncertainty is a threat; its admission, a sign of weakness. They have become proficient at techniques of selective

[25] Transcript of *Nova*, March 29, 1983: "60 Minutes to Meltdown."

inattention—the use of junk categories to dismiss anomalous data, procrustean treatment of troublesome situations—all aimed at preserving the constancy of their knowing-in-action. Yet reflection-in-action is not a rare event. There are teachers, managers, engineers, and artists for whom reflection-in-action is the "prose" they speak as they display and develop the ordinary artistry of their everyday lives. Such individuals are willing to embrace error, accept confusion, and reflect critically on their previously unexamined assumptions. Nevertheless, in a world where professionalism is still mainly identified with technical expertise, even such practitioners as these may feel profoundly uneasy because they cannot describe what they know how to do, cannot justify it as a legitimate form of professional knowledge, cannot increase its scope or depth or quality, cannot with confidence help others to learn it.

For all of these reasons, the study of professional artistry is of critical importance. We should be turning the puzzle of professional knowledge on its head, not seeking to build up a science applicable to practice but also to reflect on the reflection-in-action already embedded in competent practice.

We should be exploring, for example, how the on-the-spot experimentation carried out by practicing architects, physicians, engineers, and managers is like—and unlike—the controlled experimentation of laboratory scientists. We should be analyzing the ways in which skilled practitioners build up repertoires of exemplars, images, and strategies of description in terms of which they learn to see novel, one-of-a-kind phenomena. We should be attentive to differences in the framing of problematic situations and to the rare episodes of frame-reflective discourse in which practitioners sometimes coordinate and transform their conflicting ways of making sense of confusing predicaments. We should investigate the conventions and notations through which practitioners create virtual worlds—as diverse as sketchpads, simulations, role-plays and rehearsals—in which they are able to slow down the pace of action, go back and try again, and reduce the cost and risk of experimentation. In such explorations as these, grounded in collaborative reflection on everyday artistry, we will be pursuing the description of a new epistemology of practice.

We should also investigate how it is that some people learn the kinds and levels of reflection-in-action essential to professional artistry. In apprenticeships and clinical experiences, how are textbook descriptions of symptoms and procedures translated into the acts of recognition and judgment and the readiness for action characteristic of professional competence? Under what conditions do aspiring practitioners learn to see, in the unfamiliar phenomena of practice, similarities to the canonical problems they may have learned in the classroom? What are the processes by which some people learn to internalize, criticize, and reproduce the demonstrated competence of acknowledged masters? What, in short, is the nature of the complex process we are accustomed to dismiss with the term *imitation*? And what must practitioners know already—what kinds of competences, what features of stance toward practice must they already have acquired in order to learn to construe their practice as a continuing process of reflection-in-action?

Clearly, just as some people learn to reflect-in-action, so do others learn to help them do so. These rare individuals are not so much *teachers* as *coaches* of reflection-in-action. Their artistry consists in an ability to have on the tip of their tongue—or to invent on-the-spot—the method peculiarly suited to the difficulties experienced by the student before them. And, just as professional artistry demands a capacity for reflection-in-action, so does the coach's artistry demand a capacity for reflection-in-action on the student's intuitive understanding of the problem at hand, the intervention that might enable her to become fruitfully confused, the proposal that might enable her to take the next useful step.

The development of forms of professional education conducive to reflection-in-action requires reflection on the artistry of coaching—a kind of reflection very nicely illustrated by the studies of case teaching conducted over the past many years at the Harvard Business School. If educators hope to contribute to the development of reflective practitioners, they must become adept at such reflection on their own teaching practice.

In this way, perhaps, we will be heeding Everett Hughes's call for a way of undoing the bonds that have tied the professional schools to the traditions of the late nineteenth-century university. At least, and at last, we will be getting some group of young people who are free of those bonds, making them free to do something new and different.

The Fine Line between Persistence and Obstinacy

Judah Folkman, M.D.
Harvard Medical School

First, I'd like to tell a cautionary tale. In 1970 my colleagues and I published a hypothesis that argued that all solid tumors are angiogenesis dependent. In its simplest terms this hypothesis stated, "Every increase in tumor cell population must be preceded by an increase in new capillary blood vessels that converge upon the tumor."

The first grant we applied for on the basis of this idea was turned down with the following criticism: "It is common knowledge that the hypervascularity associated with tumors is due to dilation of host vessels and not new vessels and that this dilation is probably caused by the side effects of dying tumor cells. Therefore, tumor growth cannot be dependent upon blood vessel growth any more than infection is dependent upon pus."

I was crestfallen. John Ender's lab was on the floor below mine at Children's, and I sought his advice. "The experts don't think I should continue to work on this problem," I said. He perused the study section's comments and replied, "Keep on going. This just demonstrates that there are only experts of the past. There are no experts of the future."

It turned out to be good advice. But during these years of struggle, I began to ask myself: how does one know when to keep going and when to cut one's losses and start a new project? how does one make the decision to persist when the experts are insisting that the quest is futile?

In fact, there seems to be a fine line between persistence and obstinacy in research, and, when one thinks about it, in other aspects of life as well. Persistence is a quality much respected by our British ancestors. The English language has more synonyms for this character trait than does any other language. Just a few examples: perseverance, tenacity, doggedness, resoluteness; and slogans such as "don't give up the ship," and "stick to your guns."

If a long-term discovery or project succeeds, then the success itself is said by everyone to be based on this admirable trait of the investigator, his or her perseverance in the face of overwhelming obstacles.

The dilemma here is that if a long line of experiments fails or does not succeed in the lifetime of a grant (three years?) or the time period before the researcher comes up for tenure (11 years) or occasionally in the lifetime of the scientist, then the same trait, the exact same phenotype, so to speak, is now blamed for the failure. The researcher is now said to be obstinate, inflexible, stiff-necked, wedded to a theory and pigheaded—the worst opprobrium.

One can hear these words applied on occasion in an ad hoc committee for promotion. They say, "She stayed with this idea too long," or "He is no longer productive because he should have given up this line of experiments and switched to so and so's approach. He is inflexible."

In the course of creative or innovative work of any kind, but especially experimental work, how *does* one know when to persist and when to stop or change direction? In an effort to formulate an answer, a brief look at "outtakes" in the history of science may be in order.

A Romanian scientist in Bucharest, Nicolas Paulesco, almost discovered insulin three years before the report by Banting and Best. An extract he called "pancreine" lowered blood sugar in dogs, Paulesco found, but he was dissuaded by his colleagues from giving it to a diabetic patient.

Alexander Fleming himself gave up on the purification of penicillin from mold broth. Subsequently, he tried the crude material on a few patients and then discontinued this effort also. In 1932, in a report in the *Journal of Pathology* he writes, "We used it as a dressing on a few septic wounds with favorable results, but as in peace time, septic wounds are uncommon in hospital, and as the potency of penicillin rapidly disappears on keeping, the therapeutic aspect of this substance was dropped." It was not until ten years later that Sir Howard Walter Florey and Ernst Chain took up the problem, and because of their persistence in the face of one failure after another, penicillin became available as a therapeutic agent. In a recent biography of Florey, Lennard Bickel argues that Florey saved Fleming's reputation.

The list continues. Nevertheless, as part of my hobby of analyzing this matter, I wondered whether it might be possible to elaborate some general warning signs of persistence turning into obstinacy, so that such principles could then be taught to graduate and medical students?

Thus, over the years I've asked other scientists about this. Most of them are very familiar with the problem. However, no one has been able to explain just how he or she knew when to persist and when to desist. Most scientists with whom I've discussed the problem somehow just knew on the basis of a completely subjective feeling which was the best course to take at any given moment in time. One can certainly reflect on—and learn to trust in—one's own experiences, but this is not easily taught to others.

This feeling of "just knowing" was perhaps best articulated by the author P. D. James, famous for her mysteries, who in an interview with *The New York Times* said that before sitting down to start writing a book, she would spend considerable time, often years, going around with a notebook. She said, "The length of my research varies, but I always seem to know when the time comes to begin writing." So listening to one's inner voices—the gut instincts—may be one way to judge whether it's better to keep going or to quit and begin again.

The larger question of the difference between persistence and obstinacy remains unanswered. But perhaps we can find in the problem itself a take-home message. I think that what we have learned from all of this is that words like persistence and obstinacy have value only in retrospect—*after* the completion of some enterprise, some difficult effort. They are of little or no value when they are employed in the midst of the project, while the effort is underway and the outcome is unclear. The dilemma is that we trap ourselves when we use these terms prospectively. It is an illusion to think that one can tell at the time where the line is or which fork in the road should be taken.

In my own case, the problem of understanding the phenomenon of angiogenesis, of working out its biology, of connecting it to a large family of clinical diseases once thought to be totally separate entities, seems to have been tackled in somewhat the same way that the novelist E. L. Doctorow describes it is like to write a novel. "Writing is like driving at night," he said. "You cannot see beyond your headlights, but you can make the whole trip that way."